Communitarianism

A New Public Ethics

Communitarianism

A New Public Ethics

Edited by

Markate Daly
San Francisco State University

Wadsworth Publishing Company

Belmont, California
A Division of Wadsworth, Inc.

Philosophy Editor: Kenneth King
Editorial Assistant: Kristina Pappas
Production: Del Mar Associates
Print Buyer: Randy Hurst
Permissions Editor: Peggy Meehan
Designer: Vargas/Williams/Design
Copy Editor: Robin Witkin
Cover: John Odam
Compositor: Kachina Typesetting, Inc.
Printer: Arcata Graphics/Fairfield

 This book is printed on acid-free recycled paper.

International Thomson Publishing
The trademark ITP is used under
license

Printed in the United States of America

1 2 3 4 5 6 7 8 9 10—98 97 96 95 94

Library of Congress Cataloging-in-Publication Data

Communitarianism : a new public ethics / Markate Daly, editor
    p.   cm.
  ISBN 0-534-20088-5 :
  1. Individualism. 2. Liberalism. 3. Community. 4. Pluralism
(Social sciences) I. Daly, Markate.
JC571.C6418 1994
321.4—dc20   93-16006
                                     CIP
                                     Rev.

For my mother
Helen Boemer Wall
From whom I learned the value of community

Contents

Preface

In designing this anthology, I have tried to capture both the excitement of the communitarian challenge to traditional liberal theory and its importance for the future of our country. At the same time I wanted to represent the breadth of communitarian thinking, from conservative to progressive and across many disciplines. A unique political vision unites these many perspectives, that of a democratic community. The resulting collection concentrates on the ethics and politics that this new conception of public life would make possible.

Each chapter presents readings that raise a central issue in the debate between liberals and communitarians, assessing the advantages and disadvantages of each view or the possibility of integrating them. Proposals to place community values at the heart of political theory raise questions about the place of individual liberty, the structure of ethics, and the obligations of citizens. Because these issues are fundamental to change in our society, I believe this collection will be useful to anyone who is interested in political philosophy, ethics, or social theory. With this in mind, I chose readings that would be accessible to students from a wide range of interests and levels of philosophical training.

The Need for this Anthology

I was drawn to this task, because no existing anthology brings together the many diverse philosophers who have given a central place to the ideal of community and who have analyzed human life and action in terms of the social relationships among members of a community. The need for such an anthology is new. Until just recently, the fact that our dominant ethical and political theories were built upon the concept of a self-interested and solitary individual seemed unproblematic. That is no longer true. This model of a person

has been undermined by the recent communitarian critique of liberalism, evidence from the social sciences that supports a social conception of human nature, and the social consequences of an exaggerated individualism. It is now widely accepted that the social nature of human life structures individual consciousness and shapes action.

To what extent we will have to change our social theories, our ethics and political philosophy, to accommodate this insight, and what kinds of institutions can be built upon these changes, are the subject of intense debates. The readings in this volume give an extended, in-depth view of one alternative: communitarianism. Those thinkers who have been labeled communitarians believe that a social conception of human life gives rise to a distinctive set of concepts and values, and leads to a different vision of a good society. They believe that in order to do justice to the importance of social relationships, philosophy must be formulated in such terms as the common good, commitments to particular others, social practices, shared meanings, and public spiritedness, rather than in the terms of traditional liberalism. My goal in selecting these readings is to give voice to this philosophy.

The Authors and Readings

Communitarian philosophy is an amorphous and complex topic that has as yet no theoretical statement. Even among those who take community rather than the individual as their basic theoretical concept, some define the field so as to exclude others. The diversity seems to be as great as it is among liberals whose members span the spectrum from libertarian anarchists to welfare liberals. In choosing the readings for this anthology, I have tried to be inclusive and to present each major idea in the words of its most distinguished and eloquent advocate.

Inevitably, I could not include all of the important contributions to communitarian thought nor cover all of its practical applications. In particular, I was unable to include chapters on education, economics, work, and the environment. To compensate for this, I have presented a fuller treatment of a few central issues: the socially embedded self, community membership, citizenship, ethics, and women's ideals in family and public life.

The Debate

Criticism of liberalism has a venerable history. But the current communitarian critique was published in the 1980s, largely in response to John Rawls's revitalization of liberal theory a decade earlier. I have presented this criticism in the form of a debate between liberals and communitarians for two reasons. Most importantly, each author directly replies to the argument of the previous author; this involves the reader in the intellectual excitement of an actual debate. A second advantage of a debate format is that the text is to some extent self-guiding. The authors themselves provide the connections between the selections.

Two debates are reprinted in Chapters 2 and 3. The first focuses on the merits and limitations of Rawls's theory of justice. The second presents and critiques Michael Walzer's communitarian theory of justice and Alasdair MacIntyre's account of moral life within a tradition. These debates brought the communitarian perspective to serious consideration as an alternative to traditional liberal conceptions. They are preceded by a chapter giving their historical background, a good introduction for those who are unfamiliar with the history of philosophy.

Proposal for a Democratic Community

In traditional liberal theory, community has been relegated to the nonpolitical sector. There its virtues have been tainted by authoritarian structures and undemocratic practices. The modern communitarian proposal not only moves community into the center of political theory but weds it to the traditional liberal values of freedom and equality. I wanted to choose readings that reflect both the tension between these two ideals and the almost irresistible appeal of their union in the ideal of a democratic community. The authors in this part of the anthology struggle either to clarify this concept or resolve its tensions.

This project was well under way before the debates of the 1980s. As you might expect, the range of issues considered by many diverse thinkers over the past half century is much broader than those in the two debates I reprinted. Robert Nisbet, for instance, interprets community in terms of the function families and other intimate associations serve in their members' lives; John Dewey identifies community with an informed, public-spirited, and active citizenry engaged in self-government. In the three chapters on citizenship, ethics, and women's ideals in family and public life, I tried to present all of the major positions on each topic in order to give the broadest view of communitarian thinking. The liberal critics are not included in this part of the book, but each chapter ends with an author who questions the consensus that emerges from the previous selections.

Course Possibilities

This anthology was designed to be used as a supplementary text in courses on political and social theory, but it could also be used in any course dealing with the nature of the self, ethics, or social organization. Because the two halves, the debate part and the proposal part, do not depend on each other, one could choose to use only half of the book. For example, in a course on liberalism the readings on the debate would fit nicely. Or in an ethics course the second part of the book on the communitarian proposal could provide a fresh alternative to traditional approaches. The readings should be accessible to students new to the field, with the exception of the Rawls-Sandel-Gutmann debate and the Sunstein article.

Someone who wants to teach a course on communitarian philosophy could use this anthology as the central text and add other readings tailored to the interests and background of the students. For example, in a higher-level philosophy course some of the recent proposals for a "liberal community" could be considered. A more practically oriented course might need a section on economics and work. Or a course could be slanted toward the traditional sociological literature using Tonnies and Durkeim.

Acknowledgments

My first debt of gratitude is to the authors whose works are included in this anthology. They have labored against the prevailing intellectual winds to present an alternative political vision. I hope that my introductory interpretations and my juxtaposition of their ideas do justice to their intentions and to the importance of their contributions. A special thanks is due to Alasdair MacIntyre who allowed me to reprint his Lindley Lecture even though he denies that his philosophy is communitarian.

The impetus for this book came from Anatole Anton, San Francisco State University. I want to thank him for the initial idea and also for his suggestions as the book developed. I deeply appreciate the support of my editor, Ken King. He has been extraordinarily flexible in the development of this anthology. My original commission was for a slim volume of eight readings, but he allowed an expansion to the present size when reviewers called for a more extensive treatment of the topic. I want to thank these reviewers for their many helpful suggestions: John Ahrens, Hanover College; Jack Doody, Villanova University; Lawrence Haworth, University of Waterloo; Justin Schwartz, Ohio State University; Robert T. Sweet, University of Dayton; and Art Wolfe, Michigan State University.

I am indebted to Bill Verick and Ruth Elowitz for their assistance, especially their editorial suggestions. The Wadsworth team has been unfailingly helpful and understanding: Kristina Pappas, Peggy Meehan, Sarah Hubbard, Nancy Sjoberg, and Robin Witkin.

Markate Daly

Introduction

The Place of Community in American Political Thought

Communitarianism is a new philosophy, even though communal relationships form the fabric of all human societies and community-centered philosophy goes back at least to ancient Greece. Even the term is a contemporary neologism. As a political philosophy, its originality lies in its union of community values with the democratic values of personal freedom and equality; its ideal is a democratic community. Communitarianism is a postliberal philosophy in the sense that it could only have developed within a liberal tradition of established democratic practices, and in a liberal culture that had allowed community values to decline to the extent that a corrective seemed necessary. Communitarianism was proposed as just such a corrective; its purpose is to bring the welfare of communities into the center of political discourse by establishing in the public domain the values of communal associations.

Although liberalism has been the philosophy of our country since its founding, in practice it has never operated alone. When liberal institutions were established in Europe, the public morality of individual freedom was grafted onto an authoritarian social order in private life. The mixture of democratic institutions in the public sphere and authoritarian institutions in the private sphere of family, education, and religion was brought to America by European immigrants. In this country, those robust institutions, which had been refined over centuries of use, continue to provide stability under a liberal political order. Liberal society relies on the public spirit of involved citizens who learned community values in their families, schools, and religions. In his description of American culture in 1841, Alexis de Tocqueville observed that de-

votion to liberty was confined to the public spheres of politics and business. But in the private sphere, young people were trained in traditional values: loyalty to family, friends, and community; generosity to others; sacrifice for the common good; respect for elders, God, and national traditions. American women, Tocqueville noted, were the guardians of tradition and set the moral tone for their husbands and children and, taken together, for the community. Traditional American culture has had two sharply divided ethics, that of liberty in the public sphere of business and politics and of community in the private sphere of family and friends.

This division between the public sphere and the private sphere has often been gender based. As Robert Fowler put it, "De Tocqueville's model was highly gender specific, of course. For him, the second language of community was spoken by women, the first language of liberty by men. Women were essential, then, in the American story, for they measured the restraints, they built the communities. At the same time they were clearly the voice of the second language, second in the obvious senses of place and power."[1] The boundaries between these two spheres has eroded since Tocqueville's time. The language of liberty is now spoken in the home by both men and women, and women have entered public life. But, while the language of liberty has increased its scope, the language of community has not been similarly expanded into public policy debates and business decisions. Communitarians warn that the language of liberty threatens to take over the private sphere without any reciprocal commitment of individuals to the public good. The net effect is a decline in the practice of community values compounded by a decline in the moral education of young people. In remedy, they propose a reconstitution of our public ethics to

include those values that communities cultivate, but suitably purged of their authoritarian
and hierarchical bias.

By now, the defects of liberalism are available for all to assess. But a communitarian
political philosophy has yet to be tried or even
well formulated. To begin with, communitarians are interested not only in the development of strong and sustaining communities, but they are also concerned that an
effective democracy be established by the
citizens of these communities. As a positive
ideal then, communitarian theorists have proposed a union between the values of community and the liberal values of freedom and
equality in the conception of a democratic
community. This concept is reminiscent of the
old liberal rallying cry "liberty, equality, and
fraternity." Fraternity, the solidarity of social
bonds, has been lost in modern liberalism.
Communitarians argue that liberty and equality are not worth much without it. To assure all
three, social solidarity must either come first
or be guaranteed an equal standing.

One of the central issues communitarians
raise in their critique of the liberal tradition is
the role of individualism in its ethics, politics,
and institutions. Indeed, opposition to individualism is contained in the term communitarianism itself. When we call a philosophy
or perspective communitarian, we mean to
contrast it with an individualistic alternative.
Each term carries with it a denial of the opposing term, much as calling something large denies that it is small. The communitarian/
individualistic dichotomy implies a contrast
between two conceptions of the self: one
grounded in community membership and the
other in individual autonomy.

In American culture, the individualistic
conception has shaped the way we see ourselves and our place in society. As an individual, each person has a unique identity
defined by a subjective consciousness, forms
and carries out projects that unfold in a personal history, holds an inalienable right to pursue this life plan, and follows universal principles of morality in relationships with others.
But at the practical level of everyday life, a
communitarian conception can be felt. As a
member of a community, each person belongs
to a network of family and social relationships

and is defined by this membership, and each
person seeks personal fulfillment through
participation in the evolving social structures of this community, finds personal liberty
in an expanded self-development cultivated
through these activities, and honors a traditional complex of agreed-on commitments.
While these conceptions are contradictory,
most people adopt both views, either applying
them to separate spheres of life or holding
them in uneasy tension together.

The individualistic conception of the self
has long been the ideal in our culture, despite
the nearly universal experience of living as a
member of some kind of community. Communitarians argue that not only is the communitarian conception of the person a more
accurate description of human life, but if it
were the cultural ideal informing our policies
and institutions, community bonds would be
strengthened and the character of its members
reinforced. By developing a strong and
virtuous people within the bonds of a well-
functioning community, this program would
lead not only to greater personal satisfaction
but also to a superior public ethics and a more
effective democracy.

Many different perspectives can be gathered under the communitarian banner. Some
communitarians view community as the most
natural and highest form of life for human
beings; some argue that community is a basic
human need, that frustration of this need
leads to alienation, addictions, crime, and ineffective families; some identify true democracy with a community controlled by an active
citizenry; some look to the customary morality
of a community, winnowed and refined by
generations of intelligent members, for an
ethical standard. But all communitarians believe that under the influence of a revitalized
community we would be able to live more
fulfilling personal lives than is now possible
under the dominance of the individualistic
ideal. The communitarian program, then,
embraces a metaphysics of the person, an
ethics, a concept of community, and a political
philosophy.

The development of this philosophy is just
in its beginning stages. For the past 300 years,
the liberal project of establishing individual
liberty and democratic government on the

base of an individuated self has attracted the interest of most philosophers. The urgency of this project is not the only reason for the neglect of a community-centered philosophy. During the early part of liberalism's reign, strong local communities existed both in Europe and in America. As you might expect, what was old received scant attention. And when you consider that these communities were remnants of the defeated feudal order whose internal structure was incompatible with liberal values, their neglect is even more understandable. It wasn't until the current century that the decline of these traditional communities reached a point where a social vacuum was felt. The accelerated pace of social change in the past few decades has now moved the community with its problems to the center of political discourse.

What Is a Community?

Just as the first task of liberal philosophy was to articulate a theory of individual freedom, the first task of communitarian philosophy will be to develop a theory of community. But the concept of community is notoriously ambiguous; a sociologist, for instance, has distinguished 94 meanings for the term.[2] However, everyone agrees that a small town whose inhabitants build their whole lives within the framework of their relationships with each other, united both by necessity and by a sense of solidarity or "we-ness," is a paradigm case of a community. Communities of this kind used to be the norm in America. But as the towns grew and changed, their members no longer knew one another and they lost their sense of community. When new communities formed in neighborhoods, growth and diversity weakened the bonds among the inhabitants, and the much-lamented "decline of community" was under way.

But what is it that declined? Certainly not the local group of people; they may actually have increased in number and prosperity. What declined or was lost seems to be a distinctive quality of social relationship that members of a community form with one another. But other forms of association have been built upon relationships with the same functional interdependence and solidarity as a small town, even though the members are not residents of the same locality. Take, for instance, a network of professional associates: fishing boat owners who work the same coastal waters might bring their families together into an intimate group, or artists who work in the same medium often bring together and share their networks of friends. Another example from modern society is a group of extended families whose members have intermarried and perhaps set up businesses together.

Are these modern forms of community on a par with the small towns of the past? To answer this question, we need to know what criteria mark the quality of relationship we associate with community. There is fairly wide agreement on this: a community is composed of a limited set of people who are bound together in networks of relationships; the members share a set of beliefs and values; the relationships are personal and unmediated, usually face-to-face; friendship or a sense of obligation, rather than self-interest, holds the members together; the ties among members encompass the whole of their lives rather than only one or a few aspects; members feel a sense of belonging—a sense of "we-ness"; the interests and identity of each member intimately depends on and forms that of the whole; and members demonstrate solidarity with one another.

To the extent that all of these conditions are fulfilled, a group would clearly be a community, as in the paradigm case of a small town. When none of these conditions apply, a group is not a community. Consider a corporation or occupational group, a local PTA, an aerobics class, those who share a hobby or activity, the residents of Chicago, or sports fans. All of these have some communal elements. But how many are enough to constitute a community? Which ones are most important? Is any one crucial? Because these questions may be unanswerable, community will very likely remain a contested concept for the foreseeable future. But this should not deter the formation of a communitarian philosophy; after all, liberal philosophers have yet to agree on the concept of liberty.

When community is interpreted as a network of relationships among a limited group of people whose interactions bear communal qualities, communities can also be found in the public sphere and across both spheres. Not all of these communities are socially beneficial. For example, an intimate network of friends and families who possess great financial resources and political power constitute a ruling elite and pose a danger to democracy. At the other end of the social spectrum, we have gang development in the inner cities, a proliferation of religious cults, and a burgeoning crop of 12-step programs. So the problem is not that we don't have enough community in our country. The questions are, What form of community is best? What quality of relationships do we want in our communities? What is its proper place in our hierarchy of treasured goods?

The Liberal Tradition

Because communitarianism arose as a critique of liberalism, its rhetoric is often negative and its alternatives are cast in response to the dominant philosophy. To a large extent then, communitarianism takes its shape from liberalism's defects and excesses. Before exploring communitarian philosophy, we need to place it within the context of a robust and effective liberal tradition. Liberal philosophy has certainly not been static, but has adapted to changing political, social, and economic conditions as it evolved over the centuries. In the process, it has branched in many directions. Thus, any single characterization of liberalism will not encompass all of its major adherents. Having made this disclaimer, I will try to provide a core definition of the liberal tradition that will provide the context for the communitarian critique.

First in importance is the liberal claim of the priority of right.[3] This means that in a constitutional democracy, the guarantees of individual political and civil liberties take priority over any good that could be accomplished by rescinding those rights. Only the protection of a more basic human liberty can justify curtailing another. This inviolability of basic personal rights is grounded in the equal worth and dignity of each individual human being.

Once the priority of right is established, the second liberal claim of neutrality follows. Liberal neutrality requires that a government be neutral between competing conceptions of what is good in life or which way of life is morally preferable; that is, that it make no laws favoring one conception of the good over another. Imposing one conception of the good on all citizens would violate the most basic individual liberty: to live in accordance with one's own values. These two doctrines restrict the scope of government to the status of a referee; it must ensure each individual's freedom to form a conception of a good life and pursue it, provided that he or she does not infringe on the freedom of others to do likewise.

As a morality, liberalism retains many elements of this political theory: the moral value of an action is determined by a body of universally applicable principles and each individual is equally subject to their authority. When I interpret and apply these moral principles, I must treat you and myself and every other person equally. In the interest of fairness, liberal morality does not allow me to make exceptions; moral principles are universal. Both of our major ethical theories—deontology and utilitarianism—follow this legal model of ethics. In deontological ethics, a plurality of principles regulates human interactions roughly according to the importance of the good each protects. For example, "Do not take a life" outweighs "Do not break a promise." On the other hand, utilitarianism honors a single principle: "Choose whichever action would promote the greatest happiness for the greatest number of people." In both of these moralities, the moral agent deliberates and chooses according to his or her understanding of these principles and is, therefore, individually responsible for that choice.

In the moral and political theories of liberal philosophy then, the solitary individual bears both rights and obligations. Because the properties and capacities of this individual are of immense importance to the liberal program, they have been the prime focus of modern metaphysics. Until very recently, both the philosophy of mind and the theory of the person have been preoccupied with the solitary individual, and this individualism has served as a base for modern moral theories and liberal politics. The rational, coherent, and tightly fitting set of interlocking ideas that forms the liberal tradition has excluded the social dimension of human experience. When communitarians criticize liberalism, they refer to this complex of metaphysics (individualism), ethics (universalism), and politics (the priority of right and neutrality).

Individualism has been the target of much communitarian criticism, but it has also lost the support of many liberals. It no longer seems politically necessary or theoretically reasonable or even practical to exclude the social character of human life from our philosophy. Just as liberal theorists have adjusted their philosophy to social changes in the past, so too current liberals have begun work on a more social conception of the person to replace their individualistic metaphysics. Now the question for liberalism is, Can liberal philosophers graft a well-developed morality and politics onto a new conceptual base without losing the advances they have made or undermining the legitimacy of their institutions? Or to put the question another way: Can liberal philosophy and institutions be developed from a metaphysics assuming that a person is embedded in a community network? But the future development of liberalism is another topic for a different book.

The Communitarian Critique

In this anthology we will be exploring the kind of morality and political theory that directly follow from, and is cast in the terms of, a social metaphysics. Instead of such values as individual interests, autonomy, universality, natural rights, and neutrality, communitarian philosophy is framed in terms of the common good, social practices and traditions, character, solidarity, and social responsibility. The question for communitarian philosophy is, Can a philosophy whose aim is to strengthen the community that supports its members' fulfillment also conserve and deepen personal liberty? Can communitarian philosophy also legitimate democratic institutions as it cultivates a richer and fuller moral life?

We have already discussed the communitarian conception of a person. As a member of a community, each person forms an identity through personal attachments with others and finds a life purpose as a part of an established social practice. The members of a community express their values by directing the evolution of their institutions, adjusting them to meet changing social needs. To some extent this conception is an ideal, but at a minimal level it describes the life of any functioning person. Since liberal philosophers in the past could take for granted the existence of community in the private sphere, this aspect of life was not reflected in their theories and ideals. The communitarian attack on individualism commends this model of the self on both levels, as a description of ordinary human life and as an ideal any adequate social philosophy should attempt to realize. As we have noted, many liberals have recently acknowledged the need to incorporate some elements of this view into their own theories.

Because community morality is confined to a particular historical group, it is radically particularistic, in sharp contrast with liberalism's universalistic morality. This ethics honors the kind of commitments the members of a community have made to each other and encodes their combined wisdom in its norms and social practices. Such a customary morality exists in every functioning local group, including our own, even though the official morality may be based instead on rationally understood universal principles. The modern conception of a communitarian ethics is based on this customary morality, but tempered by the more universal rules of justice and kindness.

Some recent criticisms of a morality of universal principles have included the following:

- An ethics of universal principles ignores the special commitments a person makes to particular others in family relationships and friendships and to various groups. The practical effect is to undermine the importance of these obligations and weaken the core institutions that constitute a community.
- Universalistic ethics relies on intellectual judgment alone and therefore neglects the importance of feeling in an ethical response. For example, the extensive recent literature on women's distinctive morality stresses the importance of emotional sensitivity in a caring response to others.[4]

- Universalistic morality is arrogant, or it is at least undemocratic in that it supposes that an intellectually satisfying set of principles or ideals is a higher moral standard than the customs and practices developed by many intelligent people in the conduct of their daily lives.
- Principles are impotent unless a moral agent has a well-developed character. But character is developed within the customary moral systems of families and local groups. So the set of universal principles is a secondary morality, dependent on a well-functioning customary morality.

Against this barrage of criticism, liberal moral philosophers have argued that the particularistic ethics of a local group is most often limited to its own members. As a consequence, members of an in-group treat each other in accord with their ethical standards of conduct, whereas the members of an out-group are excluded. One of the most horrific examples of this contrasts the kind and honorable conduct of Nazi officials in their private lives with their murderous cruelty toward other groups—Jews, gypsies, and the handicapped. Some universal rules are necessary to protect nonmembers from abusive treatment. The force of this rejoinder highlights the contrast between these two views of morality.

Communitarians have launched a comparable attack on the liberal tradition. Criticism of liberal political philosophy has involved some variation on these themes:

- The liberal commitment to the priority of right and value neutrality in fact endorses one form of civil association, that based on the priority of one value: individual liberty. A form of social organization that treasures a value that is incompatible with liberty will not be able to develop under a liberal regime, even though citizens may prefer that way of life. So liberalism does not allow for the full diversity in the conceptions of the good that it claims to guarantee.
- The liberal concern with each individual's right to choose how to live accentuates the importance of private life at the expense of public life. Under the influence of this bias, citizens concentrate their energies on themselves, their work, their families, and their friends. Public affairs are turned over to hired officials whose leaders are reelected or replaced every few years. Lack of citizen involvement has led to a corrupt government that is by now virtually immune from citizen oversight. Without this accountability, government officials have neglected to provide necessary public goods. The model of community moves the emphasis from individual satisfactions to the sphere of public goods and in the process ensures citizen control.
- Even within a person's private life, liberalism devalues commitments to others because these commitments restrict an individual's ability to realize personal goals or find self-fulfillment. The most serious consequences have been felt in family life, but this lack of commitment has weakened all forms and levels of social organization. As a consequence, these associations are then less capable of serving their function: to support their members' well-being.
- A principle of liberty is unable to distinguish between those activities that should be protected and those activities that are harmful both to the citizens and to the social fabric. Some substantive conception of the good—such as a general notion of human flourishing, Aristotle's eudemonia—is needed to regulate its application. Without any restrictions the principle of liberty protects self-destructive activities that are easily curtailed in other forms of society.

What can liberals say in response? In a first kind of defense, they have argued that liberalism can be interpreted in a way that avoids the most serious of these problems or that liberal philosophy can be reformulated to satisfy their critics' demands. As a second defense, liberals acknowledge these problems in their theories but argue that the communitarian alternative has defects that are much worse. They fear that a philosophy in which community is the fundamental good would legitimate features of existing communities that are unacceptable in a democratic society—for example, authoritarian culture, entrenched social hierarchy, and male dominance. Liberals fear that a community-centered political philosophy could lead to government intrusion in private affairs and suffocating conformity in social life. Ties that bind give support and security, but they also can restrict and entrap. Probably everyone reading this page has chafed under pressure to conform in a family, friendship group, or work situation. When community is expanded into the public sphere, these dangers may also expand.

This danger has been acknowledged in communitarian writings. The possibility of a collectivist or majoritarian tyranny haunts even the most ardent proponents of a community-centered philosophy. Because no form of tyranny is acceptable, the model of a democratic community is probably the only workable ideal for modern America. When the conditions of equal respect for all members of the community and personal freedom are united with a concern for the common good, the danger of majority dominance is minimized. The second half of this anthology presents many theories that support different aspects of this ideal.

Communitarians argue that liberalism cannot be the guiding philosophy for a complete social order, because its language and ideals fail to cultivate community values. In practice, liberals have tolerated authoritarian social institutions to fill in this gap. But the continuing expansion of liberal philosophy into these institutions has undermined their ability to provide communal support to their members. This has provoked a crisis for the legitimacy of liberal philosophy because it has failed to cultivate liberal institutions that serve communal needs. Only a minority of social critics would want to stop expansion of liberal values and democratic practices. Most liberals and a good many communitarians would like the liberal ideals of equality and freedom to be integrated with community commitments in all aspects of American society: families, educational institutions, businesses, health care institutions, religions, and political institutions. Such an integration would realize the communitarian ideal of a democratic community. But communitarians believe that liberalism lacks the theoretical resources to form community at any level of organization. A new philosophy, framed in the terms central to community, must be constructed for this task.

With this background information in hand, let us turn now to the readings. The book is divided into two parts: the selections in the first part are arguments in favor of either the liberal or communitarian conception of the best social order; those in the second part propose an alternative philosophy in which community is the central value.

The Liberal-Communitarian Debate

This debate is not a conflict between the values of liberty and of community. None of the great philosophers disparaged either and some, such as John Stuart Mill, are cited by both liberals and communitarians in support of their points. Nor are the extreme positions—self-seeking individualism and unreflective collectivism—under consideration. The debate focuses on the theoretical and social consequences of stressing either liberty or community as the primary value in a society. Philosophical theories stress one or another ideal, because philosophers construct their theories in a particular historical circumstance to meet some need of their own society. A theory that successfully serves the needs of a society, as liberalism has, lives on to guide future generations, other people in other circumstances. The debate now turns on the question of whether circumstances still justify stressing the ideal of personal liberty, or whether the problems facing our society are sufficiently different to justify forming a new philosophy stressing a different ideal, that of community.

The historical background for the modern debate is laid out in Chapter 1, beginning with two liberal philosophers, John Locke and John Stuart Mill. The task of the early liberal philosophers was to justify replacing the old monarchies with a democratic political order. The first selection, by Locke, was written in the wake of the English Revolution of 1688. Locke's purpose was to deny that monarchs have a divine right to rule and to establish that all political authority derives from the consent of the governed. Citizens, then, must possess this authority independently of and prior to any existing government. To explain how this can be possible, Locke supposes that individuals existed in a state of nature prior to any social organization. Locke's state of nature is a philosophical device that allows him to establish a base for individual freedom that is independent of any government's claim to authority. For Locke, each person has a natural property right to his or her own person. From this basic right of self-ownership flow all other individual rights, including the right to enter into a contract with others whereby each may transfer a portion of personal rights to a government. Through the theoretical device of a contract among free and equal people in a state of nature, Locke establishes the legitimacy of democratic government.

By the time Mill wrote in the middle of the nineteenth century, the basic political liberties at issue in the previous centuries had already been won. He campaigns for liberty on a new front. Mill argues that promoting the personal development of each individual and increasing his or her happiness increases social utility for the whole. And further, true liberty is not limited to political rights, but includes the more personal freedoms of conscience, thought, sensibilities, expression, and taste. In this second selection, Mill discusses the social order that would best cultivate such liberties.

The roots of a community-based philosophy are explored in selections from Aristotle, Jean-Jacques Rousseau, and G. W. F. Hegel. These selections emphasize those parts of their authors' systems that have served as an inspiration for modern communitarian thinkers. The first selection, by Aristotle, gives an account of human nature and social organization in an ancient Greek city-state, or polis. In Aristotle's theory, humans are political by nature; that is, they live and find their fulfillment only in the polis. Human happiness is achieved by exercising the virtues learned in this social organization. The Greek democracy was limited; women, slaves, and foreign-born men were excluded from citizenship. Nevertheless, the male citizens formed a democracy that united freedom and equality in a strong community, and this served as the background for Aristotle's philosophy. Aristotle's theory of a life of virtue and his conception of citizenship in an ancient Greek polis have inspired nearly everyone who has since written on the democratic community.

The next selection by Rousseau was written shortly before the French Revolution. While he used the philosophical device of a social contract to justify citizens' rights to self-government, the nature of this contract in his version is more communal than was Locke's in the previous century. All parties to the social contract put themselves and all their powers under the direction of the whole community, and they then derive all of their rights from this association. When, by deliberating together, the citizens form a conception of their common good, they form a general will. In Rousseau's philosophy, the general will is the sovereign. Rousseau is a favorite precursor for communitarians who look to citizen participation in the formation of community because he denied that any intermediary could represent a citizen in this legislative office.

In the nineteenth century Hegel abandoned the fiction of a presocial, self-interested individual who voluntarily enters a contract with others to form a civil society. Instead, he proposed a well-developed alternative to social contract theory. He located the individual in a particular social network within a historical tradition and then sought to show how rational, self-reflective members of a community adjust their customs to meet current needs and to embody universal moral principles. In the excerpt from *Phenomenology of Spirit*, Hegel argues that individual freedom can only be attained in this kind of rational ethical community. Because he derives personal freedom from an existent community, Hegel is the most important progenitor of a modern communitarian philosophy. Philosophy derived from his work and from the similar perspective presented by Karl Marx have provided the most sustained dissent from liberal philosophy in modern times.

The last reading in this chapter is from *Democracy in America*, published in 1840 by Alexis de Tocqueville. As a French observer, he analyzed democracy's effects on the lives of American people and on the institutions they developed. Tocqueville was concerned that the leveling effect of democracy would produce isolated citizens, each pursuing a separate self-determined purpose. He called this "individualism" and predicted that such isolated citizens would be vulnerable to various forms of tyranny, either by a supremely powerful central state or by majoritarian sentiment. In the chapters reprinted here, Tocqueville discusses the nature of individualism and how the intermediate forms of association found in American communities strengthen the citizens to resist such tyrannies.

The next two chapters reproduce some of the philosophical debates of the 1980s between liberals and communitarians that brought community into the center of political discourse. The issues under contention in these two debates raise some of the more important communitarian criticisms of liberalism listed earlier. Chapter 2, "Individualism and the Socially Embedded Self," examines the individualism at the core of liberal philosophy. The first selection by Charles Taylor introduces the problem of individualism and community in the modern liberal state, an update on Tocqueville's project. Taylor's main concern is the quality of life experienced by its citizens, and in particular the self-concept that is shaped by the structure of a liberal state. He first describes a modern social malaise that he attributes to the overgrowth of individualism. By pursuing personal liberty as an ultimate good, he argues, we have undermined its very foundations in family and community.

The next three selections are a debate on the compatibility and relative importance of individual liberty and the common good. To put it in philosophical terms, the liberal philosophers argue that what is right—what justice requires for each individual in society— is prior in importance to what is good—what most improves the well-being of the community and its members. In the first selection, John Rawls presents his theory supporting the liberal position. He shows how self-interested individuals constructing their social order would choose principles of justice that establish the priority of individual liberty. In response, Michael Sandel claims that Rawls's theory of the moral person ignores the social commitments and community ties that in a large measure constitute a person. Justice for the individual, then, is not independent of what is good for the whole community. Amy Gutmann continues the debate by defending Rawls; she argues that his theory can be in-

terpreted in a way that avoids many of Sandel's criticisms.

The great diversity of the American people raises difficulties for any political philosophy that seeks both to accommodate the differing values, traditions, and needs of all groups and to guarantee freedom for all individuals. Both liberalism and communitarianism have had difficulties meeting these requirements. Chapter 3, "The Problems of Pluralism," presents some of the debate on this issue. Michael Walzer and Alasdair MacIntyre speak for the autonomy of a community in setting goals and endorsing values. Ronald Dworkin and Susan Moller Okin raise liberal objections to their proposals.

In the first selection, Michael Walzer presents a theory that preserves a plurality of goals, goods, and values. By confining the operation of justice to a particular sphere of life—business, family, religion, neighborhood, ethnic group—the good that is appropriate to that sphere will be the dominant standard of justice there. He calls this system of justice "complex equality," because no sphere would be able to dominate the others by making their own good the standard in those other spheres. In response, Ronald Dworkin charges that this "complex equality" leads to a radical relativism, uncritical of locally endorsed injustices. And further, when the members of a sphere of justice debate their ruling ethic, there is no guiding principle within that sphere to help resolve that dispute. Walzer's defense rests on the fact that all theories fail in some difficult cases, and he points to similar failures of liberal philosophy and argues that this does not invalidate the philosophical system.

The next selection by Alasdair MacIntyre provides another perspective on the goods and traditions internal to a social group. In this excerpt from *After Virtue*, MacIntyre explains what it means for a person to belong to a tradition. He explains how each person forms an identity and becomes a moral agent by living in intimate association with a particular group of people who are guided by a set of social practices. It is MacIntyre's examples of traditions that Susan Moller Okin attacks in her response. She charges that the Thomistic tradition that MacIntyre admires, together with his other examples of well-functioning historical traditions, assimilate women to the model of a male head of a household, thus ignoring their special contribution to society and excluding their voices from public policy formation. She includes Walzer's spheres of justice in this criticism. Neither philosopher adequately addresses the values and needs of women in traditions that have an established pattern of male dominance, Okin argues.

The Communitarian Proposal

The second part of this collection is primarily devoted to positive proposals for a community-based political philosophy, although they were written in response to the dominant liberal culture. Any philosophy based on community must provide an interpretation of its central concept. The interpretation of community that emerged from the debates of the 1980s grounded community on shared understandings and historical traditions. One of the sharpest criticisms of this communitarianism is that its concept of community is too vague or too insubstantial to bear the weight of a new political philosophy or to legitimate the institutions it would found. But community-centered philosophy from earlier decades provides fresh resources for the development of a communitarian philosophy. During the past half century, sociologist Robert Nisbet has analyzed the problem of American communities with persistence and eloquence. A few decades earlier, John Dewey's philosophy proposed the union of democracy and community. And, while John Mohawk's writing is contemporary, he presents the traditional philosophy of the Iroquois Nation. The rest of the readings in this part of the book are recently published, unless otherwise stated.

Three very different interpretations of community—overlapping intimate groups, a national public, and the web of life—are reprinted in Chapter 4, "The Scope of Community." In the first selection, Robert Nisbet locates community in the small, intimate associations of local culture: the family, the neighborhood, and religious institutions. These associations have lost many of their primary functions in people's lives, Nisbet says, as large governmental, medical, and educational bureaucracies have assumed responsibility

for individual security and well-being. As these intimate associations become functionally irrelevant, the interpersonal bonds on which everyone depends are disrupted. Distressed by their isolation, people turn to the central state and the cycle repeats. Nisbet sees a kind of totalitarianism, a loss of individual freedom, in the growth of the Western political state. Only by rebuilding fully functioning intimate associations, he argues, can we lead fully satisfying lives and preserve our freedom.

John Dewey agrees with Nisbet in lamenting the loss of local community in America, but he assumes that this loss is irreversible. In the selection reprinted here, Dewey looks toward the emergence of something like a national community, "the Great Community." He defines community in terms of an association of free and equal citizens who join together to form a common vision of their communal life and participate in the activities necessary to achieve this common good. For Dewey, community and participatory democracy are virtually synonymous. Most of this selection considers how a public can form, sustain, and carry out its conception of the communal good. An informed and well-organized public, Dewey claims, could function like the traditional communities of American towns and villages, if the media would provide accurate information and the public were able to respond effectively.

In the last selection, John Mohawk, drawing from the traditional philosophy of the Iroquois people, interprets community as a spiritual union of all beings. The central elements of such a spiritual community are a recognition of the equal worth of all its members—human beings, animals, plants, the waters, the earth, the forces of Life, and the Creators of Life—an acknowledgment of the interdependence among these members, and a respect and gratitude guiding human actions in this web of life. Mohawk argues that traditional Iroquois philosophy has been successful in preserving both ecological harmony and a politics of liberty, and that it could provide guidance for the future. The tradition of democracy on this land is as old as living memory, he writes, but the European settlers have neglected to incorporate its spiritual basis into their institutions. This spiritual philosophy was designed to create a strong society rather than a strong government.

Chapter 5, "Citizenship in a Democratic Community," gives several analyses of this central concept, each highlighting a different feature that is necessary for a citizen in a democratic community. The proposals range from a commitment to one's tradition, to civic virtue as a form of self-development, to political friendship, to the formation of a common vision and will in grassroots organizations. The common threads among all of the writings are that citizens of a democratic community rise above their own self-interest in public matters to seek the common good, that they join together with others to form public policy, and that they act to bring this vision to fruition. In brief, citizenship is virtuous and participatory.

In the first article, Sheldon Wolin discusses what it means to be political. He argues that the myth of the social contract encourages the model of economic relationships in the political sphere because its concept of a person is self-interested. Citizens who follow this model bring the model of self-interest into the political world where an ethical attitude is more appropriate. Wolin proposes an ethical mythology based on rights and obligations—the image of a birthright. Our American "birthright" was formed by all of the events in our country's history from the landing of the English Pilgrims up to the crises that now dominate the news. This long, complicated story is our tradition. Its main themes command our allegiance, shape what goals we should as a nation pursue, and order the distribution of our rights and responsibilities. A citizen, then, is an interpreting being who carries this tradition into the future.

William Sullivan speaks for the civic republican tradition in the next selection. Modern republicans look for inspiration to the ancient Greek polis with its tradition of mutual respect and equality among citizens, just as the founders of own country did 200 years ago. In this tradition, civic virtue motivates individual citizens to support laws that promote the common good, but each age interprets civic virtue in its own way. In Sullivan's contemporary interpretation, civic virtue is a form of self-development. A republican citizen has an ex-

panded sense of self that includes everyone in his or her community and responds with a sensitivity and care that acknowledges their mutual interdependence. Authentic citizenship looks first to the common good and finds that each citizen is more enriched than would be possible by acting on his or her self-interests.

In another interpretation of citizenship, Jane Mansbridge presents a model of a unitary democracy in which the relationship among citizens is a variety of friendship. Again, she presumes a rough equality of power and mutual respect. But the distinctive features of a unitary democracy are the direct participation of all citizens and a consensual model of decision making. Mansbridge claims that this is the oldest form of democracy and one still used by half of the world's democratically organized societies. Face-to-face interaction is crucial in forming a consensus because common courtesy when listening to another and a natural empathy in interpersonal relationships helps the listener identify with the speaker's position and adopt his or her interests. In the aggregate, this encourages an identification between individual interests and the common good. Mansbridge also notes some informal methods of dominance that can mar the democratic nature of a consensus.

Benjamin Barber argues for the third model of citizenship, a modern grassroots model of participatory self-government. His project is to show how we can build democratic communities in contemporary America and educate people in the art of citizenship through active participation in local problem solving. For Barber, this form of civic activity can make citizens out of self-interested individuals. In the selection reprinted here, he describes how this can be done: first, citizens talk with and really listen to each other; through this process, they form a common vision and a common will; and last, they act together to build that future. The most important part of Barber's theory is political communication among citizens.

Carole Pateman has long been an advocate of participatory democracy. In this article she examines liberalism's own justification for the authority of a representative government—the social contract. She finds that the social

contract can justify obligations between
citizens but cannot justify citizen obligations to
a government by elected representatives. She
gives an extended argument supporting Rousseau's contention that only direct, participatory democracy is legitimate. In the last selection, written by Robert Dahl, the practicality of
popular self-government in the modern world
is debated by fictional characters. They
represent the views of Jean-Jacques Rousseau
who supported direct democracy and of James
Madison who helped fashion our current political system of representative democracy.
This debate questions the feasibility of the participatory form of self-government that communitarians advocate.

All conceptions of citizenship rely on a system of moral education. Liberal citizens learn
to honor their contracts and obey the agreed-
on rules. When citizens of a liberal state fail in
these commitments, they can be forced to
comply. A democratic community depends
heavily on the moral performance of its
citizens. They must develop character, school
their sensibilities to respond to others, absorb
a tradition, and actively develop that tradition
to meet changing needs and circumstances. So
the heart of a communitarian political philosophy is an ethics. The ethics distinctive to communitarian philosophy is, as explained earlier,
highly particularistic. It arises out of the particular interactions of real people who form
and are formed by the historical tradition in
which they live.

Chapter 6, "Ethics and the Law," begins
with Michael Oakeshott whose essay sets up
the problem for this chapter. He explains in
great depth and with great eloquence the nature of customary morality and why it should
be supported in modern society. He calls this
morality an ethics of habit and affection and
contrasts it with a universalistic ethics of rational ideals. These two can coexist and support each other, he argues, if the morality of
habit and affection dominates. Then universal
principles can be used to correct habitual patterns. But under liberalism the mode of rational ideals dominates. Since habits and affections have no standing in a universalistic
morality, it has little effect in a combined system. And since it can lend no resilience to the
dominant form, the morality of universal prin-

ciples and ideals tends to fragment into an
incoherent and unstable moral system, a process he believed was well advanced when he
published this article in 1948.

Little philosophical work has been done on
the morality of habit and affection, since the
main strands of the Western moral tradition
are universalistic in character; the exceptions
are Hegel and his most prominant de-
cendents—Marxists and American pragmatists. The next two selections present competing theories of how actions within a customary
set of practices can gain moral legitimacy. In
the first, Andrew Oldenquist presents a theory
that he calls "group egoism." Oldenquist's
theory leans on the commonsense notion that
a person accepts responsibility for only that
limited portion of the world that belongs to
him or her. He is trying to capture the ethics
of a tribal society and to show how that tribalism is the essence of our customary morality.
His theory expands individual egoism to include other people; for example, I expand the
conception of myself to include "my" family,
"my" city, "my" country and then act on this
expanded "self-interest." An ethics of the common good, according to this view, is just an
enlightened and enlarged ethics of self-
interest. This ethics raises many questions
about what limits, if any, there are to actions
on behalf of what is "mine."

By contrast, psychologist Norma Haan next
presents a social theory of everyday morality
that locates ethics in the interactions and negotiations among people, rather than in an expanded egoism. Her studies of young adults
explore the social features of moral conduct in
small friendship groups. She observes that
adequate moral conduct is a product of
negotiation and sensitivity to others in interpersonal exchanges. The central concept in
Haan's ethics is the moral dialogue. By discussion and negotiation with one another, each
participant strives to achieve equity among the
competing interests of all parties. All moral
claims must be socially validated in a dialogue.
Through this procedure, many minds con-
sulting together can choose a wiser course
of action than the wisest single person, and
this is how moralities of habit and affection
can develop and change. Haan argues that
the structure of morality as it is practiced

on an everyday basis is social and practical, rather than the product of a solitary deliberation.

In the next selection Philip Selznick moves the discussion to the arena of public ethics and uses the model of common law adjudication to explain the function of customary ethics in modern American society. He first describes two foundations for a community's social order—piety and civility—and locates them in the tradition of American pragmatism. Piety is an almost religious attitude of reverence and affection for our intimate associates and for the world on which we depend. It is the source of our own being and the foundation of self-respect. Civility, on the other hand, is a commitment to respectful dialogue with others to resolve differences. The line between them blurs when such dialogue enlarges the circle of belonging and fellowship. This is the ideal of a communitarian ethics in Selznick's theory. He illustrates the dialectic that builds toward a resolution with case studies from constitutional law.

In the next article Cass Sunstein argues for a form of legal paternalism, even though he does not believe that a representative government should establish a conception of the good. First, he calls into question the current practice of seeking to satisfy the subjectively experienced and publicly expressed desires of its citizens as if they represented the citizens' true interests. Sunstein shows how subjective preferences can be distorted by unjust and restrictive circumstances or biased by physical conditions. When this happens, subjectively felt preferences neither serve the person's welfare nor express personal autonomy. Sunstein argues that these distortions are a form of coercion and that government regulation can remove this coercion. He concludes that sometimes a democratic society can legitimately override its citizens' preferences. Sunstein illustrates his thesis with many examples from American law and public policy debates.

In the last selection Alasdair MacIntyre raises the disturbing idea that an ethics of patriotism, of particular loyalties and tradition, cannot be reconciled with an ethics of universal principles. In a morality of particular loyalties, a commitment to another person or to one's group has at its core an un-conditional element. If this were not so, if there was always room for withdrawing one's allegiance, we would be inclined to say that no definite commitment was made. If so, as MacIntyre believes, then the conflict between a community morality based on particular commitments and any form of universal morality cannot be eliminated. They cannot be combined as Oakeshott, Haan, and Selznick believe. If we must choose between them, MacIntyre argues, we should choose the morality of patriotism, because a person is brought into being as a moral agent in a particular community with particular norms and traditions and to call these into question will undercut his or her hold on moral judgment.

We move next to Chapter 7, "Women in the Family and in Public Life." For many writers the family is a model for a community; or alternatively, a community is a family writ large. Much public concern over the decline of families, communities, and moral values has focused on the changing role of women in our society. Women strive to balance their needs for self-fulfillment and an adequate income with the needs of those who depend on their services. The main locus of the discussion has been among women, since they traditionally build families. Nearly all philosophers writing on these questions hold as an ideal a democratically organized family serving the traditional functions of providing care and security for its members and moral education for its young; that is, a family that functions as a small democratic community.

Until recently, an American family was a small authoritarian community composed of several generations and extended through marriage and sibling relations. Extended families are the norm in all parts of the world, although the forms a family can take vary widely from one cultural group to another. Our nuclear family is a very recent experiment. Unusual as it is in human history, however, a family composed only of a mother, a father, and their children has become the norm in American society. While this nuclear family may be too small to be called a community, it has continued to carry the responsibilities and perform the functions of a traditional extended family. In the last few decades, it has increasingly been influenced and restructured by liberal values: the right to divorce, the right to self-fulfillment, freedom from physical and sexual abuse, freedom from excessive burdens. Whether liberal values are compatible with a family's traditional functions is a hotly debated issue. In the first essay Christina Hoff Sommers blames the liberal philosophy of neutrality for legitimating only those obligations that would hold between any two nonrelated individuals. By ignoring the special obligations of family relationships, these obligations have been trivialized and made to seem optional. This, she charges, has led to the breakup of families and to the neglect of children and elderly parents.

Another debate among women is whether their traditional culture, geared to building family and community, can be brought into the public domain. Jean Bethke Elshtain in the next article presents the case for bringing a culture of "mothering" into public life. "Mothering" is not only an attitude of care and devotion; it also acknowledges the powerful ethic of family loyalties and traditions of honor. Women, she argues, could bring both of these ethics to a reform of the modern bureaucratic state. Currently, the bureaucratic state and corporate power structures are ruled by the male ethic of instrumental rationality. Rather than conform to this ethic. Elshtain urges women to embrace the ideals and values of the traditional feminine world as powerful alternatives that could humanize our public culture.

In the last article Carol Gould reviews the insights women could bring from their experiences in a liberal democratic state to the construction of a democratic community. She begins by defining a democracy in terms of an equal opportunity for self-development through each member's effective participation in the community's activities. Gould next considers how women's experience in the private sphere, both its lack of democracy and its well-developed community, can help shape a new public ethics in a democratic community. Although she considers women's experience of domination, Gould focuses on an ethics of care. She separates those features of a care ethic that could usefully be transferred to the public domain from those that are inappropriate. She concludes that too many dissimilarities exist between public life and family life for an ethic of care to be used as a foundation for building a democratic community. A philosophy based on the distinctive features of citizenship in a democratic community must be formulated.

Notes

1. Robert Booth Fowler, *The Dance with Community: The Contemporary Debate in American Political Thought* (Lawrence: University of Kansas Press, 1991), p. 36.

2. G. A. Hillery, "Definitions of Community: Areas of Agreement," *Rural Sociology 20* (1955).

3. See John Rawls, "The Priority of the Right and Ideas of the Good," *Philosophy and Public Affairs 17,* no. 4 (1988): 251–276.

4. Cf., for example, Carol Gould, *In a Different Voice* (Cambridge: Harvard University Press, 1982) and Nel Noddings, *Caring: A Feminine Approach to Ethics and Moral Education* (Berkeley: University of California Press, 1984).

Communitarianism

A New Public Ethics

1

History of the Debate

On the Extent and End of Civil Government

John Locke

The earliest forms of liberalism developed as a revolt against the authority of hereditary monarchs, landed aristocrats, and powerful clergy. The moral basis of any government's authority, liberal philosophers argued, must come from the citizens, because originally only they possess this authority. Their central moral claim was that God directly endowed each person with many natural rights, prior to and independently of any social order. This was "the state of nature." But to ensure private safety and the provision of public goods, people contracted with one another to give up some portion of their rights—provided that others did likewise—to the community as a whole in order to establish a government.

John Locke's version of "contract theory" was especially influential among the framers of the American Constitution. His theory justified the transfer of a citizen's legislative and executive rights to a representative, while reserving to the community the supreme authority over a government by those representatives. The selection reprinted here begins by denying the possibility of the divine right of a king. Locke then describes his "state of nature" and explains what rights, dispositions, and limitations each person experiences in this primitive state of freedom. He then describes how aggression in the state of nature leads to war, and how to prevent war each person contracts with all others to refrain from aggression. In the last section Locke shows how the social contract is formed when each individual, by consenting to form one body politic, agrees to submit to the will of the majority. The government's authority comes from the people, not from God.

Chapter I

1. It having been shown in the foregoing discourse:

Firstly. That Adam had not, either by natural right of fatherhood or by positive donation from God, any such authority over his children, nor dominion over the world, as is pretended.

Secondly. That if he had, his heirs yet had no right to it.

Thirdly. That if his heirs had, there being no law of Nature nor positive law of God that determines which is the right heir in all cases that may arise, the right of succession, and consequently of bearing rule, could not have been certainly determined.

Fourthly. That if even that had been determined, yet the knowledge of which is the eldest line of Adam's posterity being so long since utterly lost, that in the races of mankind and families of the world, there remains not to one above another the least pretence to be the eldest house and to have the right of inheritance.

All these promises having, as I think, been clearly made out, it is impossible that the rulers now on earth should make any benefit, or derive any the least shadow of authority from that which is held to be the fountain of all power, "Adam's private dominion and paternal jurisdiction"; so that he that will not give just occasion to think that all government in the world is the product only of force and violence, and that men live together by no other rules but that of beasts, where the

From John Locke, *An Essay Concerning the True and Original Extent and End of Civil Government*, book II of *Two Treatises of Government* (London: Guernsey Press Co. Ltd., 1924), pp. 117–132, 164–168. Footnotes omitted.

strongest carries it, and so lay a foundation for perpetual disorder and mischief, tumult, sedition, and rebellion (things that the followers of that hypothesis so loudly cry out against), must of necessity find out another rise of government, another original of political power, and another way of designing and knowing the persons that have it than what Sir Robert Filmer hath taught us.

2. To this purpose, I think it may not be amiss to set down what I take to be political power. That the power of a magistrate over a subject may be distinguished from that of a father over his children, a master over his servant, a husband over his wife, and a lord over his slave. All which distinct powers happening sometimes together in the same man, if he be considered under these different relations, it may help us to distinguish these powers one from another, and show the difference betwixt a ruler of a commonwealth, a father of a family, and a captain of a galley.

3. Political power, then, I take to be a right of making laws, with penalties of death, and consequently all less penalties for the regulating and preserving of property, and of employing the force of the community in the execution of such laws, and in the defence of the commonwealth from foreign injury, and all this only for the public good.

Chapter II
Of the State of Nature

---

4. To understand political power aright, and derive it from its original, we must consider what estate all men are naturally in, and that is, a state of perfect freedom to order their actions, and dispose of their possessions and persons as they think fit, within the bounds of the law of Nature, without asking leave or depending upon the will of any other man.

A state also of equality, wherein all the power and jurisdiction is reciprocal, no one having more than another, there being nothing more evident than that creatures of the same species and rank, promiscuously born to all the same advantages of Nature, and the use of the same faculties, should also be equal one amongst

another, without subordination or subjection, unless the lord and master of them all should, by any manifest declaration of his will, set one above another, and confer on him, by an evident and clear appointment, an undoubted right to dominion and sovereignty.

5. This equality of men by Nature, the judicious [Thomas] Hooker looks upon as so evident in itself, and beyond all question, that he makes it the foundation of that obligation to mutual love amongst men on which he builds the duties they owe one another, and from whence he derives the great maxims of justice and charity. His words are:

> The like natural inducement hath brought men to know that it is no less their duty to love others than themselves, for seeing those things which are equal, must needs all have one measure; if I cannot but wish to receive good, even as much at every man's hands, as any man can wish unto his own soul, how should I look to have any part of my desire herein satisfied, unless myself be careful to satisfy the like desire, which is undoubtedly in other men weak, being of one and the same nature: to have anything offered them repugnant to this desire must needs, in all respects, grieve them as much as me; so that if I do harm, I must look to suffer, there being no reason that others should show greater measure of love to me than they have by me showed unto them; my desire, therefore, to be loved of my equals in Nature, as much as possible may be, imposeth upon me a natural duty of bearing to themward fully the like affection. From which relation of equality between ourselves and them that are as ourselves, what several rules and canons natural reason hath drawn for direction of life no man is ignorant. (*Eccl. Pol.* i.)

6. But though this be a state of liberty, yet it is not a state of licence; though man in that state have an uncontrollable liberty to dispose of his person or possessions, yet he has not liberty to destroy himself, or so much as any creature in his possession, but where some nobler use than its bare preservation calls for it. The state of Nature has a law of Nature to govern it, which obliges every one, and reason, which is that law, teaches all mankind who will but consult it, that being all equal and independent, no one ought to harm another in his life, health, liberty or possessions; for men being all the workmanship of one omnipotent and infinitely wise Maker; all the servants of

one sovereign Master, sent into the world by His order and about His business; they are His property, whose workmanship they are made to last during His, not one another's pleasure. And, being furnished with like faculties, sharing all in one community of Nature, there cannot be supposed any such subordination among us that may authorise us to destroy one another, as if we were made for one another's uses, as the inferior ranks of creatures are for ours. Every one as he is bound to preserve himself, and not to quit his station wilfully, so by the like reason, when his own preservation comes not in competition, ought he as much as he can to preserve the rest of mankind, and not unless it be to do justice on an offender, take away or impair the life, or what tends to the preservation of the life, the liberty, health, limb, or goods of another.

7. And that all men may be restrained from invading others' rights, and from doing hurt to one another, and the law of Nature be observed, which willeth the peace and preservation of all mankind, the execution of the law of Nature is in that state put into every man's hands, whereby every one has a right to punish the transgressors of that law to such a degree as may hinder its violation. For the law of Nature would, as all other laws that concern men in this world, be in vain if there were nobody that in the state of Nature had a power to execute that law, and thereby preserve the innocent and restrain offenders; and if any one in the state of Nature may punish another for any evil he has done, every one may do so. For in that state of perfect equality, where naturally there is no superiority or jurisdiction of one over another, what any may do in prosecution of that law, every one must needs have a right to do.

8. And thus, in the state of Nature, one man comes by a power over another, but yet no absolute or arbitrary power to use a criminal, when he has got him in his hands, according to the passionate heats or boundless extravagancy of his own will, but only to retribute to him so far as calm reason and conscience dictate, what is proportionate to his transgression, which is so much as may serve for reparation and restraint. For these two are the only reasons why one man may lawfully do harm to another, which is that we call punish-

ment. In transgressing the law of Nature, the offender declares himself to live by another rule than that of reason and common equity, which is that measure God has set to the actions of men for their mutual security, and so he becomes dangerous to mankind; the tie which is to secure them from injury and violence being slighted and broken by him, which being a trespass against the whole species, and the peace and safety of it, provided for by the law of Nature, every man upon this score, by the right he hath to preserve mankind in general, may restrain, or where it is necessary, destroy things noxious to them, and so may bring such evil on any one who hath transgressed that law, as may make him repent the doing of it, and thereby deter him, and, by his example, others from doing the like mischief. And in this case, and upon this ground, every man hath a right to punish the offender, and be executioner of the law of Nature.

9. I doubt not but this will seem a very strange doctrine to some men; but before they condemn it, I desire them to resolve me by what right any prince or state can put to death or punish an alien for any crime he commits in their country? It is certain their laws, by virtue of any sanction they receive from the promulgated will of the legislature, reach not a stranger. They speak not to him, nor, if they did, is he bound to hearken to them. The legislative authority by which they are in force over the subjects of that commonwealth hath no power over him. Those who have the supreme power of making laws in England, France, or Holland are, to an Indian, but like the rest of the world—men without authority. And therefore, if by the law of Nature every man hath not a power to punish offences against it, as he soberly judges the case to require, I see not how the magistrates of any community can punish an alien of another country, since, in reference to him, they can have no more power than what every man naturally may have over another.

10. Besides the crime which consists in violating the laws, and varying from the right rule of reason, whereby a man so far becomes degenerate, and declares himself to quit the principles of human nature and to be a noxious creature, there is commonly injury done, and some person or other, some other

man, receives damage by his transgression; in which case, he who hath received any damage has (besides the right of punishment common to him, with other men) a particular right to seek reparation from him that hath done it. And any other person who finds it just may also join with him that is injured, and assist him in recovering from the offender so much as may make satisfaction for the harm he hath suffered.

11. From these two distinct rights (the one of punishing the crime, for restraint and preventing the like offence, which right of punishing is in everybody, the other of taking reparation, which belongs only to the injured party) comes it to pass that the magistrate, who by being magistrate hath the common right of punishing put into his hands, can often, where the public good demands not the execution of the law, remit the punishment of criminal offences by his own authority, but yet cannot remit the satisfaction due to any private man for the damage he has received. That he who hath suffered the damage has a right to demand in his own name, and he alone can remit. The damnified person has this power of appropriating to himself the goods or service of the offender by right of self-preservation, as every man has a power to punish the crime to prevent its being committed again, by the right he has of preserving all mankind, and doing all reasonable things he can in order to that end. And thus it is that every man in the state of Nature has a power to kill a murderer, both to deter others from doing the like injury (which no reparation can compensate) by the example of the punishment that attends it from everybody, and also to secure men from the attempts of a criminal who, having renounced reason, the common rule and measure God hath given to mankind, hath, by the unjust violence and slaughter he hath committed upon one, declared war against all mankind, and therefore may be destroyed as a lion or a tiger, one of those wild savage beasts with whom men can have no society nor security. And upon this is grounded that great law of Nature, "Whoso sheddeth man's blood, by man shall his blood be shed." And Cain was so fully convinced that every one had a right to destroy such a criminal, that, after the murder of his brother, he cries out, "Every one that findeth me shall slay me," so plain was it writ in the hearts of all mankind.

12. By the same reason may a man in the state of Nature punish the lesser breaches of that law, it will, perhaps, be demanded, with death? I answer: Each transgression may be punished to that degree, and with so much severity, as will suffice to make it an ill bargain to the offender, give him cause to repent, and terrify others from doing the like. Every offence that can be committed in the state of Nature may, in the state of Nature, be also punished equally, and as far forth, as it may, in a commonwealth. For though it would be beside my present purpose to enter here into the particulars of the law of Nature, or its measures of punishment, yet it is certain there is such a law, and that too as intelligible and plain to a rational creature and a studier of that law as the positive laws of commonwealths, nay, possibly plainer; as much as reason is easier to be understood than the fancies and intricate contrivances of men, following contrary and hidden interests put into words; for truly so are a great part of the municipal laws of countries, which are only so far right as they are founded on the law of Nature, by which they are to be regulated and interpreted.

13. To this strange doctrine—viz., That in the state of Nature every one has the executive power of the law of Nature—I doubt not but it will be objected that it is unreasonable for men to be judges in their own cases, that self-love will make men partial to themselves and their friends; and, on the other side, ill-nature, passion, and revenge will carry them too far in punishing others, and hence nothing but confusion and disorder will follow, and that therefore God hath certainly appointed government to restrain the partiality and violence of men. I easily grant that civil government is the proper remedy for the inconveniences of the state of Nature, which must certainly be great where men may be judges in their own case, since it is easy to be imagined that he who was so unjust as to do his brother an injury will scarce be so just as to condemn himself for it. But I shall desire those who make this objection to remember that absolute monarchs are but men; and if government is to be the remedy of those evils which necessarily follow from men being judges in their own cases, and

the state of Nature is therefore not to be endured, I desire to know what kind of government that is, and how much better it is than the state of Nature, where one man commanding a multitude has the liberty to be judge in his own case, and may do to all his subjects whatever he pleases without the least question or control of those who execute his pleasure? and in whatsoever he doth, whether led by reason, mistake, or passion, must be submitted to? which men in the state of Nature are not bound to do one to another. And if he that judges, judges amiss in his own or any other case, he is answerable for it to the rest of mankind.

14. It is often asked as a mighty objection, where are, or ever were, there any men in such a state of Nature? To which it may suffice as an answer at present, that since all princes and rulers of "independent" governments all through the world are in a state of Nature, it is plain the world never was, nor never will be, without numbers of men in that state. I have named all governors of "independent" communities, whether they are, or are not, in league with others; for it is not every compact that puts an end to the state of Nature between men, but only this one of agreeing together mutually to enter into one community, and make one body politic; other promises and compacts men may make one with another, and yet still be in the state of Nature. The promises and bargains for truck, etc., between the two men in Soldania, in or between a Swiss and an Indian, in the woods of America, are binding to them, though they are perfectly in a state of Nature in reference to one another for truth, and keeping of faith belongs to men as men, and not as members of society.

15. To those that say there were never any men in the state of Nature, I will not only oppose the authority of the judicious Hooker (*Eccl. Pol.* i. 10), where he says, "the laws which have been hitherto mentioned"—i.e., the laws of Nature—"do bind men absolutely, even as they are men, although they have never any settled fellowship, never any solemn agreement amongst themselves what to do or not to do; but for as much as we are not by ourselves sufficient to furnish ourselves with competent store of things needful for such a life as our Nature doth desire, a life fit for the dignity of

man, therefore to supply those defects and imperfections which are in us, as living single and solely by ourselves, we are naturally induced to seek communion and fellowship with others; this was the cause of men uniting themselves as first in politic societies." But I, moreover, affirm that all men are naturally in that state, and remain so till, by their own consents, they make themselves members of some politic society, and I doubt not, in the sequel of this discourse, to make it very clear.

Chapter III
Of the State of War

16. The state of war is a state of enmity and destruction; and therefore declaring by word or action, not a passionate and hasty, but sedate, settled design upon another man's life puts him in a state of war with him against whom he has declared such an intention, and so has exposed his life to the other's power to be taken away from him, or any one that joins with him in his defence, and espouses his quarrel; it being reasonable and just I should have a right to destroy that which threatens me with destruction; for by the fundamental law of Nature, man being to be preserved as much as possible, when all cannot be preserved, the safety of the innocent is to be preferred, and one may destroy a man who makes war upon him, or has discovered an enmity to his being, for the same reason that he may kill a wolf or a lion, because they are not under the ties of the common law of reason, have no other rule but that of force and violence, and so may be treated as a beast of prey, those dangerous and noxious creatures that will be sure to destroy him whenever he falls into their power.

17. And hence it is that he who attempts to get another man into his absolute power does thereby put himself into a state of war with him; it being to be understood as a declaration of a design upon his life. For I have reason to conclude that he who would get me into his power without my consent would use me as he pleased when he had got me there, and destroy me too when he had a fancy to it; for

nobody can desire to have me in his absolute power unless it be to compel me by force to that which is against the right of my freedom—i.e., make me a slave. To be free from such force is the only security of my preservation, and reason bids me look on him as an enemy to my preservation who would take away that freedom which is the fence to it; so that he who makes an attempt to enslave me thereby puts himself into a state of war with me. He that in the state of Nature would take away the freedom that belongs to any one in that state must necessarily be supposed to have a design to take away everything else, that freedom being the foundation of all the rest; as he that in the state of society would take away the freedom belonging to those of that society or commonwealth must be supposed to design to take away from them everything else, and so be looked on as in a state of war.

18. This makes it lawful for a man to kill a thief who has not in the least hurt him, nor declared any design upon his life, any farther than by the use of force, so to get him in his power as to take away his money, or what he pleases, from him; because using force, where he has no right to get me into his power, let his pretence be what it will, I have no reason to suppose that he who would take away my liberty would not, when he had me in his power, take away everything else. And, therefore, it is lawful for me to treat him as one who has put himself into a state of war with me—i.e., kill him if I can; for to that hazard does he justly expose himself whoever introduces a state of war, and is aggressor in it.

19. And here we have the plain difference between the state of Nature and the state of war, which however some men have confounded, are as far distant as a state of peace, goodwill, mutual assistance, and preservation; and a state of enmity, malice, violence, and mutual destruction are one from another. Men living together according to reason without a common superior on earth, with authority to judge between them, is properly the state of Nature. But force, or a declared design of force upon the person of another, where there is no common superior on earth to appeal to for relief, is the state of war; and it is the want of such an appeal gives a man the right of war even against an aggressor, though he be in

society and a fellow-subject. Thus, a thief whom I cannot harm, but by appeal to the law, for having stolen all that I am worth, I may kill when he sets on me to rob me but of my horse or coat, because the law, which was made for my preservation, where it cannot interpose to secure my life from present force, which if lost is capable of no reparation, permits me my own defence and the right of war, a liberty to kill the aggressor, because the aggressor allows not time to appeal to our common judge, nor the decision of the law, for remedy in a case where the mischief may be irreparable. Want of a common judge with authority puts all men in a state of Nature; force without right upon a man's person makes a state of war both where there is, and is not, a common judge.

20. But when the actual force is over, the state of war ceases between those that are in society and are equally on both sides subject to the judge; and, therefore, in such controversies, where the question is put, "Who shall be judge?" it cannot be meant who shall decide the controversy; every one knows what Jephtha here tells us, that "the Lord the Judge" shall judge. Where there is no judge on earth the appeal lies to God in Heaven. That question then cannot mean who shall judge, whether another hath put himself in a state of war with me, and whether I may, as Jephtha did, appeal to Heaven in it? Of that I myself can only judge in my own conscience, as I will answer it at the great day to the Supreme Judge of all men. . . . .

Chapter VIII
Of the Beginning of Political Societies

95. Men being, as has been said, by Nature all free, equal, and independent, no one can be put out of this estate and subjected to the political power of another without his own consent, which is done by agreeing with other men, to join and unite into a community for their comfortable, safe, and peaceable living, one amongst another, in a secure enjoyment of their properties, and a greater security against any that are not of it. This any number

of men may do, because it injures not the freedom of the rest; they are left, as they were, in the liberty of the state of Nature. When any number of men have so consented to make one community or government, they are thereby presently incorporated, and make one body politic, wherein the majority have a right to act and conclude the rest.

96. For, when any number of men have, by the consent of every individual, made a community, they have thereby made that community one body, with a power to act as one body, which is only by the will and determination of the majority. For that which acts any community, being only the consent of the individuals of it, and it being one body, must move one way, it is necessary the body should move that way whither the greater force carries it, which is the consent of the majority, or else it is impossible it should act or continue one body, one community, which the consent of every individual that united into it agreed that it should; and so every one is bound by that consent to be concluded by the majority. And therefore we see that in assemblies empowered to act by positive laws where no number is set by that positive law which empowers them, the act of the majority passes for the act of the whole, and of course determines as having, by the law of Nature and reason, the power of the whole.

97. And thus every man, by consenting with others to make one body politic under one government, puts himself under an obligation to every one of that society to submit to the determination of the majority, and to be concluded by it; or else this original compact, whereby he with others incorporates into one society, would signify nothing, and be no compact if he be left free and under no other ties than he was in before in the state of Nature. For what appearance would there be of any compact? What new engagement if he were no farther tied by any decrees of the society than he himself thought fit and did actually consent to? This would be still as great a liberty as he himself had before his compact, or any one else in the state of Nature, who may submit himself and consent to any acts of it if he thinks fit.

98. For if the consent of the majority shall not in reason be received as the act of the whole, and conclude every individual, nothing but the consent of every individual can make anything to be the act of the whole, which, considering the infirmities of health and avocations of business, which in a number though much less than that of a commonwealth, will necessarily keep many away from the public assembly; and the variety of opinions and contrariety of interests which unavoidably happen in all collections of men, it is next impossible ever to be had. And, therefore, if coming into society be upon such terms, it will be only like Cato's coming into the theatre, *tantum ut exiret*. Such a constitution as this would make the mighty leviathan of a shorter duration than the feeblest creatures, and not let it outlast the day it was born in, which cannot be supposed till we can think that rational creatures should desire and constitute societies only to be dissolved. For where the majority cannot conclude the rest, there they cannot act as one body, and consequently will be immediately dissolved again.

99. Whosoever, therefore, out of a state of Nature unite into a community, must be understood to give up all the power necessary to the ends for which they unite into society to the majority of the community, unless they expressly agreed in any number greater than the majority. And this is done by barely agreeing to unite into one political society, which is all the compact that is, or needs be, between the individuals that enter into or make up a commonwealth. And thus, that which begins and actually constitutes any political society is nothing but the consent of any number of freemen capable of majority, to unite and incorporate into such a society. And this is that, and that only, which did or could give beginning to any lawful government in the world.

100. To this I find two objections made: 1. That there are no instances to be found in story of a company of men, independent and equal one amongst another, that met together, and in this way began and set up a government. 2. It is impossible of right that men should do so, because all men, being born under government, they are to submit to that, and are not at liberty to begin a new one.

101. To the first there is this to answer: That it is not at all to be wondered that history gives us but a very little account of men that

lived together in the state of Nature. The inconveniencies of that condition, and the love and want of society, no sooner brought any number of them together, but they presently united and incorporated if they designed to continue together. And if we may not suppose men ever to have been in the state of Nature, because we hear not much of them in such a state, we may as well suppose the armies of Salmanasser or Xerxes were never children, because we hear little of them till they were men and embodied in armies. Government is everywhere antecedent to records, and letters seldom come in amongst a people till a long continuation of civil society has, by other more necessary arts, provided for their safety, ease, and plenty. And then they begin to look after the history of their founders, and search into their original when they have outlived the memory of it. For it is with commonwealths as with particular persons, they are commonly ignorant of their own births and infancies; and if they know anything of it, they are beholding for it to the accidental records that others have kept of it. And those that we have of the beginning of any polities in the world, excepting that of the Jews, where God Himself immediately interposed, and which favours not at all paternal dominion, are all either plain instances of such a beginning as I have mentioned, or at least have manifest footsteps of it.

102. He must show a strange inclination to deny evident matter of fact, when it agrees not with his hypothesis, who will not allow that the beginning of Rome and Venice were by the uniting together of several men, free and independent one of another, amongst whom there was no natural superiority or subjection. And if Josephus Acosta's word may be taken, he tells us that in many parts of America there was no government at all. "There are great and apparent conjectures," says he, "that these men (speaking of those of Peru) for a long time had neither kings nor commonwealths, but lived in troops, as they do this day in Florida—the Cheriquanas, those of Brazil, and many other nations, which have no certain kings, but, as occasion is offered in peace or war, they choose their captains as they please" (lib. i. cap. 25). If it be said, that every man there was born subject to his father, or the head of his family, that the subjection due from a child to a father took not away his freedom of uniting into what political society he thought fit, has been already proved; but be that as it will, these men, it is evident, were actually free; and whatever superiority some politicians now would place in any of them, they themselves claimed it not; but, by consent, were all equal, till, by the same consent, they set rulers over themselves. So that their politic societies all began from a voluntary union, and the mutual agreement of men freely acting in the choice of their governors and forms of government.

103. And I hope those who went away from Sparta, with Palantus, mentioned by Justin, will be allowed to have been freemen independent one of another, and to have set up a government over themselves by their own consent. Thus I have given several examples out of history of people, free and in the state of Nature, that, being met together, incorporated and began a commonwealth. And if the want of such instances be an argument to prove that government were not nor could not be so begun, I suppose the contenders for paternal empire were better let it alone than urge it against natural liberty; for if they can give so many instances out of history of governments began upon paternal right, I think (though at least an argument from what has been to what should of right be of no great force) one might, without any great danger, yield them the cause. But if I might advise them in the case, they would do well not to search too much into the original of governments as they have begun de facto, lest they should find at the foundation of most of them something very little favourable to the design they promote, and such a power as they contend for.

104. But, to conclude: reason being plain on our side that men are naturally free; and the examples of history showing that the governments of the world, that were begun in peace, had their beginning laid on that foundation, and were made by the consent of the people; there can be little room for doubt, either where the right is, or what has been the opinion or practice of mankind about the first erecting of governments.

On Liberty

John Stuart Mill

First published in 1859, John Stuart Mill's classic defense of liberty from the encroachments of governmental authority is still timely and relevant. Although earlier political theorists sought liberty from the tyranny of kings and petty princes, Mill was horrified by the "tyranny of the majority" that Tocqueville warned against in his study of democracy in America. This tyranny would be more completely repressive because under its authority the whole community would enforce conformity. The first and last chapters of Mill's essay are reprinted here. He begins by arguing that a democratic people have no need to limit their own freedom and would never seek to do so. But Mill notes that democratic governments tend to be controlled by one faction or another. The ruling faction, acting in the name of the majority, he believes, will try to impose their tastes and morals on everyone. Mill shows how this decreases social utility. He lists the liberties citizens must be able to exercise if they are to reach full development, both of their intellectual abilities and of their sensibilities and tastes. The good of society, as well as the happiness of each person, depends on these liberties. In the last chapter Mill considers the limits to society's authority over the individual and concludes that government interference in the lives of its citizens is justified only to ensure a citizen's self-protection and to prevent one person from harming others.

Chapter 1
Introductory

The subject of this Essay is not the so-called Liberty of the Will, so unfortunately opposed to the misnamed doctrine of Philosophical Necessity; but Civil, or Social Liberty: the nature and limits of the power which can be legitimately exercised by society over the individual. A question seldom stated, and hardly ever discussed, in general terms, but which profoundly influences the practical controversies of the age by its latent presence, and is likely soon to make itself recognised as the vital question of the future. It is so far from being new, that, in a certain sense, it has divided mankind, almost from the remotest ages; but in the stage of progress into which the more civilised portions of the species have now entered, it presents itself under new conditions, and requires a different and more fundamental treatment.

The struggle between Liberty and Authority is the most conspicuous feature in the portions of history with which we are earliest familiar, particularly in that of Greece, Rome, and England. But in old times this contest was between subjects, or some classes of subjects, and the Government. By liberty, was meant protection against the tyranny of the political rulers. The rulers were conceived (except in some of the popular governments of Greece) as in a necessarily antagonistic position to the people they ruled. They consisted of a governing One, or a governing tribe or caste, who derived their authority from inheritance or conquest, who, at all events, did not hold it at the pleasure of the governed, and whose supremacy men did not venture, perhaps did not desire, to contest, whatever precautions might be taken against its oppressive exercise. Their power was regarded as necessary, but also as highly dangerous; as a weapon which they would attempt to use against their subjects, no less than against external enemies. To prevent the weaker members of the community from being preyed upon by innumerable vultures, it was needful that there should be an animal of prey stronger than the rest, commissioned to keep them down. But as the king

From John Stuart Mill, *On Liberty* (Cleveland: World Publishing Company, 1969), pp. 126–140, 205–210.

of the vultures would be no less bent upon preying on the flock than any of the minor harpies, it was indispensable to be in a perpetual attitude of defence against his beak and claws. The aim, therefore, of patriots was to set limits to the power which the ruler should be suffered to exercise over the community; and this limitation was what they meant by liberty. It was attempted in two ways. First, by obtaining a recognition of certain immunities, called political liberties or rights, which it was to be regarded as a breach of duty in the ruler to infringe, and which if he did infringe, specific resistance, or general rebellion, was held to be justifiable. A second, and generally a later expedient, was the establishment of constitutional checks, by which the consent of the community, or of a body of some sort, supposed to represent its interests, was made a necessary condition to some of the more important acts of the governing power. To the first of these modes of limitation, the ruling power, in most European countries, was compelled, more or less, to submit. It was not so with the second; and, to attain this, or when already in some degree possessed, to attain it more completely, became everywhere the principal object of the lovers of liberty. And so long as mankind were content to combat one enemy by another, and to be ruled by a master, on condition of being guaranteed more or less efficaciously against his tyranny, they did not carry their aspirations beyond this point.

A time, however, came, in the progress of human affairs, when men ceased to think it a necessity of nature that their governors should be an independent power, opposed in interest to themselves. It appeared to them much better that the various magistrates of the State should be their tenants or delegates, revocable at their pleasure. In that way alone, it seemed, could they have complete security that the powers of government would never be abused to their disadvantage. By degrees this new demand for elective and temporary rulers became the prominent object of the exertions of the popular party, wherever any such party existed; and superseded, to a considerable extent, the previous efforts to limit the power of rulers. As the struggle proceeded for making the ruling power emanate from the periodical choice of the ruled, some persons began to think that too much importance had been attached to the limitation of the power itself. *That* (it might seem) was a resource against rulers whose interests were habitually opposed to those of the people. What was now wanted was, that the rulers should be identified with the people; that their interest and will should be the interest and will of the nation. The nation did not need to be protected against its own will. There was no fear of its tyrannising over itself. Let the rulers be effectually responsible to it, promptly removable by it, and it could afford to trust them with power of which it could itself dictate the use to be made. Their power was but the nation's own power, concentrated, and in a form convenient for exercise. This mode of thought, or rather perhaps of feeling, was common among the last generation of European liberalism, in the Continental section of which it still apparently predominates. Those who admit any limit to what a government may do, except in the case of such governments as they think ought not to exist, stand out as brilliant exceptions among the political thinkers of the Continent. A similar tone of sentiment might by this time have been prevalent in our own country, if the circumstances which for a time encouraged it, had continued unaltered.

But, in political and philosophical theories, as well as in persons, success discloses faults and infirmities which failure might have concealed from observation. The notion, that the people have no need to limit their power over themselves, might seem axiomatic, when popular government was a thing only dreamed about, or read of as having existed at some distant period of the past. Neither was that notion necessarily disturbed by such temporary aberrations as those of the French Revolution, the worst of which were the work of a usurping few, and which, in any case, belonged, not to the permanent working of popular institutions, but to a sudden and convulsive outbreak against monarchical and aristocratic despotism. In time, however, a democratic republic came to occupy a large portion of the earth's surface, and made itself felt as one of the most powerful members of the community of nations; and elective and responsible government became subject to the observations and criticism which wait upon a great existing act. It was now perceived that such phrases as "self-government," and "the power of the people over themselves," do not express the true state of the case. The "people" who exercise the power are not always the same people with those over whom it is exercised; and the "self-government" spoken of is not the government of each by himself, but of each by all the rest. The will of the people, moreover, practically means the will of the most numerous or the most active *part* of the people; the majority, or those who succeed in making themselves accepted as the majority; the people, consequently *may* desire to oppress a part of their number; and precautions are as much needed against this as against any other abuse of power. The limitation, therefore, of the power of government over individuals loses none of its importance when the holders of power are regularly accountable to the community, that is, to the strongest party therein. This view of things, recommending itself equally to the intelligence of thinkers and to the inclination of those important classes in European society to whose real or supposed interests democracy is adverse, has had no difficulty in establishing itself; and in political speculations "the tyranny of the majority" is now generally included among the evils against which society requires to be on its guard.

Like other tyrannies, the tyranny of the majority was at first, and is still vulgarly, held in dread, chiefly as operating through the acts of the public authorities. But reflecting persons perceived that when society is itself the tyrant—society collectively over the separate individuals who compose it—its means of tyrannising are not restricted to the acts which it may do by the hands of its political functionaries. Society can and does execute its own mandates: and if it issues wrong mandates instead of right, or any mandates at all in things with which it ought not to meddle, it practises a social tyranny more formidable than many kinds of political oppression, since, though not usually upheld by such extreme penalties, it leaves fewer means of escape, penetrating much more deeply into the details of life, and enslaving the soul itself. Protection, therefore, against the tyranny of the magis-

trate is not enough: there needs protection also against the tyranny of the prevailing opinion and feeling; against the tendency of society to impose, by other means than civil penalties, its own ideas and practices as rules of conduct on those who dissent from them; to fetter the development, and, if possible, prevent the formation, of any individuality not in harmony with its ways, and compels all characters to fashion themselves upon the model of its own. There is a limit to the legitimate interference of collective opinion with individual independence: and to find that limit, and maintain it against encroachment, is as indispensable to a good condition of human affairs, as protection against political despotism.

But though this proposition is not likely to be contested in general terms, the practical question, where to place the limit—how to make the fitting adjustment between individual independence and social control—is a subject on which nearly everything remains to be done. All that makes existence valuable to any one, depends on the enforcement of restraints upon the actions of other people. Some rules of conduct, therefore, must be imposed, by law in the first place, and by opinion on many things which are not fit subjects for the operation of law. What these rules should be is the principal question in human affairs; but if we except a few of the most obvious cases, it is one of those which least progress has been made in resolving. No two ages, and scarcely any two countries, have decided it alike; and the decision of one age or country is a wonder to another. Yet the people of any given age and country no more suspect any difficulty in it, than if it were a subject on which mankind had always been agreed. The rules which obtain among themselves appear to them self-evident and self-justifying. This all but universal illusion is one of the examples of the magical influence of custom, which is not only, as the proverb says, a second nature, but is continually mistaken for the first. The effect of custom, in preventing any misgivings respecting the rules of conduct which mankind impose on one another, is all the more complete because the subject is one on which it is not generally considered necessary that reasons should be given, either by one person to others or by each to himself. People are accustomed to believe, and have been encouraged in the belief by some who aspire to the character of philosophers, that their feelings, on subjects of this nature, are better than reasons, and render reasons unnecessary. The practical principle which guides them to their opinions on the regulation of human conduct, is the feeling in each person's mind that everybody should be required to act as he, and those with whom he sympathises, would like them to act. No one, indeed, acknowledges to himself that his standard of judgment is his own liking; but an opinion on a point of conduct, not supported by reasons, can only count as one person's preference; and if the reasons, when given, are a mere appeal to a similar preference felt by other people, it is still only many people's liking instead of one. To an ordinary man, however, his own preference, thus supported, is not only a perfectly satisfactory reason, but the only one he generally has for any of his notions of morality, taste, or propriety, which are not expressly written in his religious creed; and his chief guide in the interpretation even of that. Men's opinions, accordingly, on what is laudable or blamable, are affected by all the multifarious causes which influence their wishes in regard to the conduct of others, and which are as numerous as those which determine their wishes on any other subject. Sometimes their reason—at other times their prejudices or superstitions: often their social affections, not seldom their antisocial ones, their envy or jealousy, their arrogance or contemptuousness: but most commonly their desires or fears for themselves—their legitimate or illegitimate self-interest. Wherever there is an ascendant class, a large portion of the morality of the country emanates from its class interests, and its feelings of class superiority. The morality between Spartans and Helots, between planters and negroes, between princes and subjects, between nobles and roturiers, between men and women, has been for the most part the creation of these class interests and feelings: and the sentiments thus generated react in turn upon the moral feelings of the members of the ascendant class, in their relations among themselves. Where, on the other hand, a class, formerly ascendant, has lost its ascendancy, or where its ascendan-

cy is unpopular, the prevailing moral sentiments frequently bear the impress of an impatient dislike of superiority. Another grand determining principle of the rules of conduct, both in act and forbearance, which have been enforced by law or opinion, has been the servility of mankind towards the supposed preferences or aversions of their temporal masters or of their gods. This servility, though essentially selfish, is not hypocrisy; it gives rise to perfectly genuine sentiments of abhorrence; it made men burn magicians and heretics. Among so many baser influences, the general and obvious interests of society have of course had a share, and a large one, in the direction of the moral sentiments: less, however, as a matter of reason, and on their own account, than as a consequence of the sympathies and antipathies which grew out of them: and sympathies and antipathies which had little or nothing to do with the interests of society, have made themselves felt in the establishment of moralities with quite as great force.

The likings and dislikings of society, or of some powerful portion of it, are thus the main thing which has practically determined the rules laid down for general observance, under the penalties of law or opinion. And in general, those who have been in advance of society in thought and feeling, have left this condition of things unassailed in principle, however they may have come into conflict with it in some of its details. They have occupied themselves rather in inquiring what things society ought to like or dislike, than in questioning whether its likings or dislikings should be a law to individuals. They preferred endeavouring to alter the feelings of mankind on the particular points on which they were themselves heretical, rather than make common cause in defence of freedom, with heretics generally. The only case in which the higher ground has been taken on principle and maintained with consistency, by any but an individual here and there, is that of religious belief: a case instructive in many ways, and not least so as forming a most striking instance of the fallibility of what is called the moral sense: for the *odium theologicum*, in a sincere bigot, is one of the most unequivocal cases of moral feeling. Those who first broke the yoke of what called itself the Universal Church, were in general as little willing to permit difference of religious opinion as that church itself. But when the heat of the conflict was over, without giving a complete victory to any party, and each church or sect was reduced to limit its hopes to retaining possession of the ground it already occupied; minorities, seeing that they had no chance of becoming majorities, were under the necessity of pleading to those whom they could not convert, for permission to differ. It is accordingly on this battle field, almost solely, that the rights of the individual against society have been asserted on broad grounds of principle, and the claim of society to exercise authority over dissentients openly controverted. The great writers to whom the world owes what religious liberty it possesses have mostly asserted freedom of conscience as an indefeasible right, and denied absolutely that a human being is accountable to others for his religious belief. Yet so natural to mankind is intolerance in whatever they really care about, that religious freedom has hardly anywhere been practically realised, except where religious indifference, which dislikes to have its peace disturbed by theological quarrels, has added its weight to the scale. In the minds of almost all religious persons, even in the most tolerant countries, the duty of toleration is admitted with tacit reserves. One person will bear with dissent in matters of church government, but not of dogma; another can tolerate everybody, short of a Papist or a Unitarian; another every one who believes in revealed religion; a few extend their charity a little further, but stop at the belief in a God and in a future state. Wherever the sentiment of the majority is still genuine and intense, it is found to have abated little of its claim to be obeyed.

In England, from the peculiar circumstances of our political history, though the yoke of opinion is perhaps heavier, that of law is lighter, than in most other countries of Europe; and there is considerable jealousy of direct interference, by the legislative or the executive power, with private conduct; not so much from any just regard for the independence of the individual, as from the still subsisting habit of looking on the government as representing an opposite interest to the public. The majority have not yet learnt to feel the power of the government their power, or

its opinions their opinions. When they do so, individual liberty will probably be as much exposed to invasion from the government, as it already is from public opinion. But, as yet, there is a considerable amount of feeling ready to be called forth against any attempt of the law to control individuals in things in which they have not hitherto been accustomed to be controlled by it; and this with very little discrimination as to whether the matter is, or is not, within the legitimate sphere of legal control; insomuch that the feeling, highly salutary on the whole, is perhaps quite as often misplaced as well grounded in the particular instances of its application. There is, in fact, no recognised principle by which the propriety or impropriety of government interference is customarily tested. People decide according to their personal preferences. Some, whenever they see any good to be done, or evil to be remedied, would willingly instigate the government to undertake the business; while others prefer to bear almost any amount of social evil, rather than add one to the departments of human interests amenable to governmental control. And men range themselves on one or the other side in any particular case, according to this general direction of their sentiments; or according to the degree of interest which they feel in the particular thing which it is proposed that the government should do, or according to the belief they entertain that the government would, or would not, do it in the manner they prefer; but very rarely on account of any opinion to which they consistently adhere, as to what things are fit to be done by a government. And it seems to me that in consequence of this absence of rule or principle, one side is at present as often wrong as the other; the interference of government is, with about equal frequency, improperly invoked and improperly condemned.

The object of this Essay is to assert one very simple principle, as entitled to govern absolutely the dealings of society with the individual in the way of compulsion and control, whether the means used be physical force in the form of legal penalties, or the moral coercion of public opinion. That principle is, that the sole end for which mankind are warranted, individually or collectively, in interfering with the liberty of action of any of their number, is self-protection. That the only purpose for which power can be rightfully exercised over any member of a civilised community, against his will, is to prevent harm to others. His own good, either physical or moral, is not a sufficient warrant. He cannot rightfully be compelled to do or forbear because it will be better for him to do so, because it will make him happier, because, in the opinions of others, to do so would be wise, or even right. These are good reasons for remonstrating with him, or reasoning with him, or persuading him, or entreating him, but not for compelling him, or visiting him with any evil in case he do otherwise. To justify that, the conduct from which it is desired to deter him must be calculated to produce evil to some one else. The only part of the conduct of any one, for which he is amenable to society, is that which concerns others. In the part which merely concerns himself, his independence is, of right, absolute. Over himself, over his own body and mind, the individual is sovereign.

It is, perhaps, hardly necessary to say that this doctrine is meant to apply only to human beings in the maturity of their faculties. We are not speaking of children, or of young persons below the age which the law may fix as that of manhood or womanhood. Those who are still in a state to require being taken care of by others, must be protected against their own actions as well as against external injury. For the same reason, we may leave out of consideration those backward states of society in which the race itself may be considered as in its nonage. The early difficulties in the way of spontaneous progress are so great, that there is seldom any choice of means for overcoming them; and a ruler full of the spirit of improvement is warranted in the use of any expedients that will attain an end, perhaps otherwise unattainable. Despotism is a legitimate mode of government in dealing with barbarians, provided the end be their improvement, and the means justified by actually effecting that end. Liberty, as a principle, has no application to any state of things anterior to the time when mankind have become capable of being improved by free and equal discussion. Until then, there is nothing for them but implicit obedience to an Akbar or a Charlemagne, if they are so fortunate as to find one. But as soon as mankind have attained the capacity of being guided to their own improvement by conviction or persuasion (a period long since reached in all nations with whom we need here concern ourselves), compulsion, either in the direct form or in that of pains and penalties for non-compliance, is no longer admissible as a means to their own good, and justifiable only for the security of others.

It is proper to state that I forego any advantage which could be derived to my argument from the idea of abstract right, as a thing independent of utility. I regard utility as the ultimate appeal on all ethical questions; but it must be utility in the largest sense, grounded on the permanent interests of a man as a progressive being. Those interests, I contend, authorise the subjection of individual spontaneity to external control, only in respect to those actions of each, which concern the interest of other people. If any one does an act hurtful to others, there is a prima facie case for punishing him, by law, or, where legal penalties are not safely applicable, by general disapprobation. There are also many positive acts for the benefit of others, which he may rightfully be compelled to perform; such as to give evidence in a court of justice; to bear his fair share in the common defence, or in any other joint work necessary to the interest of the society of which he enjoys the protection; and to perform certain acts of individual beneficence, such as saving a fellow-creature's life, or interposing to protect the defenceless against ill-usage, things which whenever it is obviously a man's duty to do, he may rightfully be made responsible to society for not doing. A person may cause evil to others not only by his actions but by his inaction, and in either case he is justly accountable to them for the injury. The latter case, it is true, requires a much more cautious exercise of compulsion than the former. To make any one answerable for doing evil to others is the rule; to make him answerable for not preventing evil is, comparatively speaking, the exception. Yet there are many cases clear enough and grave enough to justify that exception. In all things which regard the external relations of the individual, he is de jure amenable to those whose interests are concerned, and, if need be, to society as their protector. There are often good reasons for not holding him to the responsibility; but these reasons must arise from the special expediencies of the case: either because it is a kind of case in which he is on the whole likely to act better, when left to his own discretion, than when controlled in any way in which society have it in their power to control him; or because the attempt to exercise control would produce other evils, greater than those which it would prevent. When such reasons as these preclude the enforcement of responsibility, the conscience of the agent himself should step into the vacant judgment seat, and protect those interests of others which have no external protection; judging himself all the more rigidly, because the case does not admit of his being made accountable to the judgment of his fellow-creatures.

But there is a sphere of action in which society, as distinguished from the individual, has, if any, only an indirect interest; comprehending all that portion of a person's life and conduct which affects only himself, or if it also affects others, only with their free, voluntary, and undeceived consent and participation. When I say only himself, I mean directly, and in the first instance; for whatever affects himself, may affect others through himself; and the objection which may be grounded on this contingency, will receive consideration in the sequel. This, then, is the appropriate region of human liberty. It compromises, first, the inward domain of consciousness; demanding liberty of conscience in the most comprehensive sense; liberty of thought and feeling; absolute freedom of opinion and sentiment on all subjects, practical or speculative, scientific, moral, or theological. The liberty of expressing and publishing opinions may seem to fall under a different principle, since it belongs to that part of the conduct of an individual which concerns other people; but, being almost of as much importance as the liberty of thought itself, and resting in great part on the same reasons, is practically inseparable from it. Secondly, the principle requires liberty of tastes and pursuits; of framing the plan of our life to suit our own character; of doing as we like, subject to such consequences as may follow: without impediment from our fellow-creatures, so long as what we do does not harm them, even though they

should think our conduct foolish, perverse, or wrong. Thirdly, from this liberty of each individual, follows the liberty, within the same limits, of combination among individuals; freedom to unite, for any purpose not involving harm to others: the persons combining being supposed to be of full age, and not forced or deceived.

No society in which these liberties are not, on the whole, respected, is free, whatever may be its form of government; and none is completely free in which they do not exist absolute and unqualified. The only freedom which deserves the name, is that of pursuing our own good in our own way, so long as we do not attempt to deprive others of theirs, or impede their efforts to obtain it. Each is the proper guardian of his own health, whether bodily, *or* mental and spiritual. Mankind are greater gainers by suffering each other to live as seems good to themselves, than by compelling each to live as seems good to the rest.

Though this doctrine is anything but new, and, to some persons, may have the air of a truism, there is no doctrine which stands more directly opposed to the general tendency of existing opinion and practice. Society has expended fully as much effort in the attempt (according to its lights) to compel people to conform to its notions of personal as of social excellence. The ancient commonwealths thought themselves entitled to practise, and the ancient philosophers countenanced, the regulation of every part of private conduct by public authority, on the ground that the State had a deep interest in the whole bodily and mental discipline of every one of its citizens; a mode of thinking which may have been admissible in small republics surrounded by powerful enemies, in constant peril of being subverted by foreign attack or internal commotion, and to which even a short interval of relaxed energy and self-command might so easily be fatal that they could not afford to wait for the salutary permanent effects of freedom. In the modern world, the greater size of political communities, and, above all, the separation between spiritual and temporal authority (which placed the direction of men's consciences in other hands than those which controlled their worldly affairs), prevented so great an interference by law in the details of private life; but the engines of moral repression have been wielded more strenuously against divergence from the reigning opinion in self-regarding, than even in social matters; religion, the most powerful of the elements which have entered into the formation of moral feeling, having almost always been governed either by the ambition of a hierarchy, seeking control over every department of human conduct, or by the spirit of Puritanism. And some of those modern reformers who have placed themselves in strongest opposition to the religions of the past, have been noway behind either churches or sects in their assertion of the right of spiritual domination: M. Comte, in particular, whose social system, as unfolded in this *Système de Politique Positive,* aims at establishing (though by moral more than by legal appliances) a despotism of society over the individual, surpassing anything contemplated in the political ideal of the most rigid disciplinarian among the ancient philosophers.

Apart from the peculiar tenets of individual thinkers, there is also in the world at large an increasing inclination to stretch unduly the powers of society over the individual, both by the force of opinion and even by that of legislation; and as the tendency of all the changes taking place in the world is to strengthen society, and diminish the power of the individual, this encroachment is not one of the evils which tend spontaneously to disappear, but, on the contrary, to grow more and more formidable. The disposition of mankind, whether as rulers or as fellow-citizens, to impose their own opinions and inclinations as a rule of conduct on others, is so energetically supported by some of the best and by some of the worst feelings incident to human nature, that it is hardly ever kept under restraint by anything but want of power; and as the power is not declining, but growing, unless a strong barrier of moral conviction can be raised against the mischief, we must expect, in the present circumstances of the world, to see it increase.

It will be convenient for the argument, if, instead of at once entering upon the general thesis, we confine ourselves in the first instance to a single branch of it, on which the principle here stated is, if not fully, yet to a certain point, recognised by the current opinions. This one branch is the Liberty of Thought: from which it is impossible to separate the cognate liberty of speaking and of writing. Although these liberties, to some considerable amount, form part of the political morality of all countries which profess religious toleration and free institutions, the grounds, both philosophical and practical, on which they rest, are perhaps not so familiar to the general mind, nor so thoroughly appreciated by many even of the leaders of opinion, as might have been expected. Those grounds, when rightly understood, are of much wider application than to only one division of the subject, and a thorough consideration of this part of the question will be found the best introduction to the remainder. Those to whom nothing which I am about to say will be new, may therefore, I hope, excuse me, if on a subject which for now three centuries has been so often discussed, I venture on one discussion more. . . .

Chapter IV
Of the Limits to the Authority of Society over the Individual

What, then, is the rightful limit to the sovereignty of the individual over himself? Where does the authority of society begin? How much of human life should be assigned to individuality, and how much to society?

Each will receive its proper share, if each has that which more particularly concerns it. To individuality should belong the part of life in which it is chiefly the individual that is interested; to society, the part which chiefly interests society.

Though society is not founded on a contract, and though no good purpose is answered by inventing a contract in order to deduce social obligations from it, every one who receives the protection of society owes a return for the benefit, and the fact of living in society renders it indispensable that each should be bound to observe a certain line of conduct towards the rest. This conduct consists, first, in not injuring the interests of one another; or rather certain interests, which, either by express legal provision or by tacit understanding, ought to be considered as rights;

and secondly, in each person's bearing his share (to be fixed on some equitable principle) of the labours and sacrifices incurred for defending the society or its members from injury and molestation. These conditions society is justified in enforcing, at all costs to those who endeavour to withhold fulfilment. Nor is this all that society may do. The acts of an individual may be hurtful to others, or wanting in due consideration for their welfare, without going to the length of violating any of their constituted rights. The offender may then be justly punished by opinion, though not by law. As soon as any part of a person's conduct affects prejudically the interests of others, society has jurisdiction over it, and the question whether the general welfare will or will not be promoted by interfering with it, becomes open to discussion. But there is no room for entertaining any such question when a person's conduct affects the interests of no persons besides himself, or needs not affect them unless they like (all the persons concerned being of full age, and the ordinary amount of understanding). In all such cases, there should be perfect freedom, legal and social, to do the action and stand the consequences.

It would be a great misunderstanding of this doctrine to suppose that it is one of selfish indifference, which pretends that human beings have no business with each other's conduct in life, and that they should not concern themselves about the well-doing or well-being of one another, unless their own interest is involved. Instead of any diminution, there is need of a great increase of disinterested exertion to promote the good of others. But disinterested benevolence can find other instruments to persuade people to their good than whips and scourges, either of the literal or the metaphorical sort. I am the last person to undervalue the self-regarding virtues; they are only second in importance, if even second, to the social. It is equally the business of education to cultivate both. But even education works by conviction and persuasion as well as by compulsion, and it is by the former only that, when the period of education is passed, the self-regarding virtues should be inculcated. Human beings owe to each other help to distinguish the better from the worse,

and encouragement to choose the former and avoid the latter. They should be for ever stimulating each other to increased exercise of their higher faculties, and increased direction of their feelings and aims towards wise instead of foolish, elevating instead of degrading, objects and contemplations. But neither one person, nor any number of persons, is warranted in saying to another human creature of ripe years, that he shall not do with his life for his own benefit what he chooses to do with it. He is the person most interested in his own well-being: the interest which any other person, except in cases of strong personal attachment, can have in it, is trifling, compared with that which he himself has; the interest which society has in him individually (except as to his conduct to others) is fractional, and altogether indirect; while with respect to his own feelings and circumstances, the most ordinary man or woman has means of knowledge immeasurably surpassing those that can be possessed by any one else. The interference of society to overrule his judgment and purposes in what only regards himself must be grounded on general presumptions; which may be altogether wrong, and even if right, are as likely as not to be misapplied to individual cases, by persons no better acquainted with the circumstances of such cases than those are who look at them merely from without. In this department, therefore, of human affairs, Individuality has its proper field of action. In the conduct of human beings towards one another it is necessary that general rules should for the most part be observed, in order that people may know what they have to expect: but in each person's own concerns his individual spontaneity is entitled to free exercise. Considerations to aid his judgment, exhortations to strengthen his will, may be offered to him, even obtruded on him, by others: but he himself is the final judge. All errors which he is likely to commit against advice and warning are far outweighed by the evil of allowing others to constrain him to what they deem his good.

I do not mean that the feelings with which a person is regarded by others ought not to be in any way affected by his self-regarding qualities or deficiencies. This is neither possible nor desirable. If he is eminent in any of the qualities which conduce to his own good, he is, so far, a proper object of admiration. He is so much the nearer to the ideal perfection of human nature. If he is grossly deficient in those qualities, a sentiment the opposite of admiration will follow. There is a degree of folly, and a degree of what may be called (though the phrase is not unobjectionable) lowness or depravation of taste, which, though it cannot justify doing harm to the person who manifests it, renders him necessarily and properly a subject of distaste, or, in extreme cases, even of contempt: a person could not have the opposite qualities in due strength without entertaining these feelings. Though doing no worse to any one, a person may so act as to compel us to judge him, and feel to him, as a fool, or as a being of an inferior order: and since this judgment and feeling are a fact which he would prefer to avoid, it is doing him a service to warn him of it beforehand, as of any other disagreeable consequence to which he exposes himself. It would be well, indeed, if this good office were much more freely rendered than the common notions of politeness at present permit, and if one person could honestly point out to another that he thinks him in fault, without being considered unmannerly or presuming. We have a right, also, in various ways, to act upon our unfavourable opinion of any one, not to the oppression of his individuality, but in the exercise of ours. We are not bound, for example, to seek his society; we have a right to avoid it (though not to parade the avoidance), for we have a right to choose the society most acceptable to us. We have a right, and it may be our duty, to caution others against him, if we think his example or conversation likely to have a pernicious effect on those with whom he associates. We may give others a preference over him in optional good offices, except those which tend to his improvement. In these various modes a person may suffer very severe penalties at the hands of others for faults which directly concern only himself; but he suffers these penalties only in so far as they are the natural and, as it were, the spontaneous consequences of the faults themselves, not because they are purposely inflicted on him for the sake of punishment. A person who shows rashness, obstinacy, self-conceit—who cannot live within moderate means—who cannot restrain himself from hurtful indulgences—who pursues animal pleasures at the expense of those of feeling and intellect—must expect to be lowered in the opinion of others, and to have a less share of their favourable sentiments; but of this he has no right to complain, unless he has merited their favour by special excellence in his social relations, and has thus established a title to their good offices, which is not affected by his demerits towards himself.

What I contend for is, that the inconveniences which are strictly inseparable from the unfavourable judgment of others, are the only ones to which a person should ever be subjected for that portion of his conduct and character which concerns his own good, but which does not affect the interest of others in their relations with him. Acts injurious to others require a totally different treatment. Encroachment on their rights; infliction on them of any loss or damage not justified by his own rights; falsehood or duplicity in dealing with them; unfair or ungenerous use of advantages over them; even selfish abstinence from defending them against injury—these are fit objects of moral reprobation, and, in grave cases, of moral retribution and punishment. And not only these acts, but the dispositions which lead to them, are properly immoral, and fit subjects of disapprobation which may rise to abhorrence. Cruelty of disposition; malice and ill-nature; that most anti-social and odious of all passions, envy; dissimulation and insincerity, irascibility on insufficient cause, and resentment disproportioned to the provocation; the love of domineering over others; the desire to engross more than one's share of advantages (the πλεονεξια of the Greeks); the pride which derives gratification from the abasement of others; the egotism which thinks self and its concerns more important than everything else, and decides all doubtful questions in its own favour;—these are moral vices, and constitute a bad and odious moral character: unlike the self-regarding faults previously mentioned, which are not properly immoralities, and to whatever pitch they may be carried, do not constitute wickedness. They may be proofs of any amount of folly, or want of personal dignity and self-respect; but they are only a subject of moral reprobation when they involve a breach of duty to others, for whose sake the individual is bound to have care for himself. What are called duties to ourselves are not socially obligatory, unless circumstances render them at the same time duties to others. The term duty to oneself, when it means anything more than prudence, means self-respect or self-development, and for none of these is any one accountable to his fellow-creatures, because for none of them is it for the good of mankind that he be held accountable to them.

The distinction between the loss of consideration which a person may rightly incur by defect of prudence or of personal dignity, and the reprobation which is due to him for an offence against the rights of others, is not a merely nominal distinction. It makes a vast difference both in our feelings and in our conduct towards him whether he displeases us in things in which we think we have a right to control him, or in things in which we know that we have not. If he displeases us, we may express our distaste, and we may stand aloof from a person as well as from a thing that displeases us; but we shall not therefore feel called on to make his life uncomfortable. We shall reflect that he already bears, or will bear, the whole penalty of his error; if he spoils his life by mismanagement, we shall not, for that reason, desire to spoil it still further: instead of wishing to punish him, we shall rather endeavour to alleviate his punishment, by showing him how he may avoid or cure the evils his conduct tends to bring upon him. He may be to us an object of pity, perhaps of dislike, but not of anger or resentment; we shall not treat him like an enemy of society: the worst we shall think ourselves justified in doing is leaving him to himself, if we do not interfere benevolently by showing interest or concern for him. It is far otherwise if he has infringed the rules necessary for the protection of his fellow-creatures, individually or collectively. The evil consequences of his acts do not then fall on himself, but on others; and society, as the protector of all its members, must retaliate on him; must inflict pain on him for the express purpose of punishment, and must take care that it be sufficiently severe. In the one case, he is an offender at our bar, and we are called on not only to sit in judgment on him, but, in one shape or another, to execute our own sentence: in the other case, it is not our part to inflict any suffering on him, except what may incidentally follow from our using the same liberty in the regulation of our own affairs, which we allow to him in his.

A Life of Virtue

Aristotle

Aristotle's ethical and political philosophy, based on the ancient Greek city-state, has inspired many communitarian writers. In the Greek polis the citizens lived together very closely: They had common meals, they conducted their business with one another, they formed marriage alliances with each other's families, and they met together as free and equal citizens to make the laws and judge cases. The ruling ideals in Aristotle's political philosophy are the good of the whole community and a life of virtue for its citizens. To the extent that a citizen's freedom would contribute to the well-being of the whole and increase personal virtue it would find support in Aristotle's work. But freedom holds the place of an instrumental good, a precondition for human dignity and effective participation in government. In the first part of this selection, taken from his Nichomachean Ethics, *Aristotle asks: What is the aim of political science? What is the good that all men seek? Clearly, he answers, it is happiness, not just of the moment, but of a whole life. That settled, he then asks: What is the content of this happiness that all men seek and that is universally the end of political life? His answer is less apparent: A man is happy to the extent that he fulfills his function as a man, and man's distinctive function as a political being is a life of virtue. In the second part of the selection, taken from the* Politics *Aristotle asks whether the virtue of a citizen is the same as the virtue of a good man. He develops his account of citizenship as the ability both to govern and to obey, arguing that the deliberations of an assembly of citizens, each of whom has a deficient vision, will be wiser than the wisest single man. In the last section he defines what is just as that which is equal, and what is right as that which promotes the common good of the citizens.*

Nichomachean Ethics

Let us . . . state, in view of the fact that all knowledge and every pursuit aims at some good, what it is that we say political science aims at and what is the highest of all goods achievable by action. Verbally there is very general agreement; for both the general run of men and people of superior refinement say that it is happiness, and identify living well and doing well with being happy; but with regard to what happiness is they differ, and the many do not give the same account as the wise. For the former think it is some plain and obvious thing, like pleasure, wealth, or honour;

they differ, however, from one another—and often even the same man identifies it with different things, with health when he is ill, with wealth when he is poor; but, conscious of their ignorance, they admire those who proclaim some great ideal that is above their comprehension. Now some thought that apart from these many goods there is another which is self-subsistent and causes the goodness of all these as well. To examine all the opinions that have been held were perhaps somewhat fruitless; enough to examine those that are most prevalent or that seem to be arguable.

Let us not fail to notice, however, that there is a difference between arguments from and those to the first principles. For Plato, too, was right in raising this question and asking, as he

From Aristotle, *Nichomachean Ethics*, W. D. Ross, trans., book 1, chaps. 4 and 5 (1095a, line 13–1096a, line 10), chap. 7 (1097a, line 15–1098a, line 23); *Politics*, Benjamin Jowett, trans., book 3, chap. 4 (1276b, line 17–1277b, line 15), chaps. 10 and 11 (1281a, line 10–1282a, line 41), chap. 13 (1283b, line 28–1284a, line 2). In *Works of Aristotle* (Oxford: The Clarendon Press, 1925). Footnotes omitted.

used to do, "are we on the way from or to the first principles?" There is a difference, as there is in a race-course between the course from the judges to the turning-point and the way back. For, while we must begin with what is known, things are objects of knowledge in two senses—some to us, some without qualification. Presumably, then, *we* must begin with things known to *us*. Hence any one who is to listen intelligently to lectures about what is noble and just and, generally, about the subjects of political science must have been brought up in good habits. For the fact is the starting-point, and if this is sufficiently plain to him, he will not at the start need the reason as well; and the man who has been well brought up has or can easily get starting-points. And as for him who neither has nor can get them, let him hear the words of Hesiod:

Far best is he who knows all things himself;
Good, he that hearkens when men counsel right;
But he who neither knows, nor lays to heart
Another's wisdom, is a useless wight.

Let us, however, resume our discussion from the point at which we digressed. To judge from the lives that men lead, most men, and men of the most vulgar type, seem (not without some ground) to identify the good, or happiness, with pleasure; which is the reason why they live the life of enjoyment. For there are, we may say, three prominent types of life—that just mentioned, the political, and thirdly the contemplative life. Now the mass of mankind are evidently quite slavish in their tastes, preferring a life suitable to beasts, but they get some ground for their view from the fact that many of those in high places share the states of Sardanapallus. A consideration of the prominent types of life shows that people of superior refinement and of active disposition identify happiness with honour; for this is, roughly speaking, the end of the political life. But it seems too superficial to be what we are looking for, since it is thought to depend on those who bestow honour rather than on him who receives it, but the good we divine to be something proper to a man and not easily taken from him. Further, men seem to pursue honour in order that they may be assured of their goodness; at least it is by men of practical wisdom that they seek to be honoured, and

among those who know them, and on the ground of their virtue; clearly, then, according to them, at any rate, virtue is better. And perhaps one might even suppose this to be, rather than honour, the end of the political life. But even this appears somewhat incomplete; for possession of virtue seems actually compatible with being asleep, or with lifelong inactivity, and, further, with the greatest sufferings and misfortunes; but a man who was living so no one would call happy, unless he were maintaining a thesis at all costs. But enough of this; for the subject has been sufficiently treated even in the current discussions. Third comes the contemplative life, which we shall consider later.

The life of money-making is one undertaken under compulsion, and wealth is evidently not the good we are seeking; for it is merely useful and for the sake of something else. And so one might rather take the aforenamed objects to be ends; for they are loved for themselves. But it is evident that not even these are ends; yet many arguments have been thrown away in support of them. . . .

Let us again return to the good we are seeking, and ask what it can be. It seems different in different actions and arts; it is different in medicine, in strategy, and in the other arts likewise. What then is the good of each? Surely that for whose sake everything else is done. In medicine this is health, in strategy victory, in architecture a house, in any other sphere something else, and in every action and pursuit the end; for it is for the sake of this that all men do whatever else they do. Therefore, if there is an end for all that we do, this will be the good achievable by action, and if there are more than one, these will be the goods achievable by action.

So the argument has by a different course reached the same point; but we must try to state this even more clearly. Since there are evidently more than one end, and we choose some of these (e.g. wealth, flutes, and in general instruments) for the sake of something else, clearly not all ends are final ends; but the chief good is evidently something final. Therefore, if there is only one final end, this will be what we are seeking, and if there are more than one, the most final of these will be what we are seeking. Now we call that which is in itself worthy of pursuit more final than that which is worthy of pursuit for the sake of something else, and that which is never desirable for the sake of something else more final than the things that are desirable both in themselves and for the sake of that other thing, and therefore we call final without qualification that which is always desirable in itself and never for the sake of something else.

Now such a thing happiness, above all else, is held to be; for this we choose always for itself and never for the sake of something else, but honour, pleasure, reason, and every virtue we choose indeed for themselves (for if nothing resulted from them we should still choose each of them), but we choose them also for the sake of happiness, judging that by means of them we shall be happy. Happiness, on the other hand, no one chooses for the sake of these, nor, in general, for anything other than itself.

From the point of view of self-sufficiency the same result seems to follow; for the final good is thought to be self-sufficient. Now by self-sufficient we do not mean that which is sufficient for a man by himself, for one who lives a solitary life, but also for parents, children, wife, and in general for his friends and fellow citizens, since man is born for citizenship. But some limit must be set to this; for if we extend our requirement to ancestors and descendants and friends' friends we are in for an infinite series. Let us examine this question, however, on another occasion; the self-sufficient we now define as that which when isolated makes life desirable and lacking in nothing; and such we think happiness to be; and further we think it most desirable of all things, without being counted as one good thing among others—if it were so counted it would clearly be made more desirable by the addition of even the least of goods; for that which is added becomes an excess of goods, and of goods the greater is always more desirable. Happiness, then, is something final and self-sufficient, and is the end of action.

Presumably, however, to say that happiness is the chief good seems a platitude, and a clearer account of what it is is still desired. This might perhaps be given, if we could first ascertain the function of man. For just as for a flute-player, a sculptor, or any artist, and, in general, for all things that have a function or activity, the good and the "well" is thought to reside in the function, so would it seem to be for man, if he has a function. Have the carpenter, then, and the tanner certain functions or activities, and has man none? Is he born without a function? Or as eye, hand, foot, and in general each of the parts evidently has a function, may one lay it down that man similarly has a function apart from all these? What then can this be? Life seems to be common even to plants, but we are seeking what is peculiar to man. Let us exclude, therefore, the life of nutrition and growth. Next there would be a life of perception, but *it* also seems to be common even to the horse, the ox, and every animal. There remains, then, an active life of the element that has a rational principle; of this, one part has such a principle in the sense of being obedient to one, the other in the sense of possessing one and exercising thought. And, as "life of the rational element" also has two meanings, we must state that life in the sense of activity is what we mean; for this seems to be the more proper sense of the term. Now if the function of man is an activity of soul which follows or implies a rational principle, and if we say "a so-and-so" and "a good so-and-so" have a function which is the same in kind, e.g. a lyre-player and a good lyre-player, and so without qualification in all cases, eminence in respect of goodness being added to the name of the function (for the function of a lyre-player is to play the lyre, and that of a good lyre-player is to do so well): if this is the case, [and we state the function of man to be a certain kind of life, and this to be an activity or actions of the soul implying a rational principle, and the function of a good man to be the good and noble performance of these, and if any action is well performed when it is performed in accordance with the appropriate excellence: if this is the case,] human good turns out to be activity of soul in accordance with virtue, and if there are more than one virtue, in accordance with the best and most complete.

But we must add "in a complete life." For one swallow does not make a summer, nor does one day; and so too one day, or a short time, does not make a man blessed and happy. Let this serve as an outline of the good. . . .

Politics

. . . There is a point nearly allied to the preceding: Whether the virtue of a good man and a good citizen is the same or not. But, before entering on this discussion, we must certainly first obtain some general notion of the virtue of the citizen. Like the sailor, the citizen is a member of a community. Now, sailors have different functions, for one of them is a rower, another a pilot, and a third a look-out man, a fourth is described by some similar term; and while the precise definition of each individual's virtue applies exclusively to him, there is, at the same time, a common definition applicable to them all. For they have all of them a common object, which is safety in navigation. Similarly, one citizen differs from another, but the salvation of the community is the common business of them all. This community is the constitution; the virtue of the citizen must therefore be relative to the constitution of which he is a member. If, then, there are many forms of government, it is evident that there is not one single virtue of the good citizen which is perfect virtue. But we say that the good man is he who has one single virtue which is perfect virtue. Hence it is evident that the good citizen need not of necessity possess the virtue which makes a good man.

The same question may also be approached by another road, from a consideration of the best constitution. If the state cannot be entirely composed of good men, and yet each citizen is expected to do his own business well, and must therefore have virtue, still, inasmuch as all the citizens cannot be alike, the virtue of the citizen and of the good man cannot coincide. All must have the virtue of the good citizen—thus, and thus only, can the state be perfect; but they will not have the virtue of a good man, unless we assume that in the good state all the citizens must be good.

Again, the state, as composed of unlikes, may be compared to the living being: as the first elements into which a living being is resolved are soul and body, as soul is made up of rational principle and appetite, the family of husband and wife, property of master and slave, so of all these, as well as other dissimilar elements, the state is composed; and, therefore, the virtue of all the citizens cannot possibly be the same, any more than the excellence of the leader of a chorus is the same as that of the performer who stands by his side. I have said enough to show why the two kinds of virtue cannot be absolutely and always the same.

But will there then be no case in which the virtue of the good citizen and the virtue of the good man coincide? To this we answer that the good *ruler* is a good and wise man, and that he who would be a statesman must be a wise man. And some persons say that even the education of the ruler should be of a special kind; for are not the children of kings instructed in riding and military exercises? As Euripides says: "No subtle arts for me, but what the state requires." As though there were a special education needed by a ruler. If then the virtue of a good ruler is the same as that of a good man, and we assume further that the subject is a citizen as well as the ruler, the virtue of the good citizen and the virtue of the good man cannot be absolutely the same, although in some cases they may; for the virtue of a ruler differs from that of a citizen. It was the sense of this difference which made Jason say that "he felt hungry when he was not a tyrant," meaning that he could not endure to live in a private station. But, on the other hand, it may be argued that men are praised for knowing both how to rule and how to obey, and he is said to be a citizen of approved virtue who is able to do both. Now if we suppose the virtue of a good man to be that which rules, and the virtue of the citizen to include ruling and obeying, it cannot be said that they are equally worthy of praise. Since, then, it is sometimes thought that the ruler and the ruled must learn different things and not the same, but that the citizen must know and share in them both, the inference is obvious. There is, indeed, the rule of a master, which is concerned with menial offices—the master need not know how to perform these, but may employ others in the execution of them: the other would be degrading; and by the other I mean the power actually to do menial duties, which vary much in character and are executed by various classes of slaves, such, for example, as handicraftsmen, who, as their name signifies, live by the labour of their hands:—under these the mechanic is included. Hence in ancient times, and among some nations, the working classes had no share in the government—a privilege which they only acquired under the extreme democracy. Certainly the good man and the statesman and the good citizen ought not to learn the crafts of inferiors except for their own occasional use; if they habitually practise them, there will cease to be a distinction between master and slave.

This is not the rule of which we are speaking; but there is a rule of another kind, which is exercised over freemen and equals by birth—a constitutional rule, which the ruler must learn by obeying, as he would learn the duties of a general of cavalry by being under the orders of a general of cavalry, or the duties of a general of infantry by being under the orders of a general of infantry, and by having had the command of a regiment and of a company. It has been well said that "he who has never learned to obey cannot be a good commander." The two are not the same, but the good citizen ought to be capable of both; he should know how to govern like a freeman, and how to obey like a freeman—these are the virtues of a citizen. . . .

There is also a doubt as to what is to be the supreme power in the state:—Is it the multitude? Or the wealthy? Or the good? Or the one best man? Or a tyrant? Any of these alternatives seems to involve disagreeable consequences. If the poor, for example, because they are more in number, divide among themselves the property of the rich—is not this unjust? No, by heaven (will be the reply), for the supreme authority justly willed it. But if this is not injustice, pray what is? Again, when in the first division all has been taken, and the majority divide anew the property of the minority, is it not evident, if this goes on, that they will ruin the state? Yet surely, virtue is not the ruin of those who possess her, nor is justice destructive of a state; and therefore this law of confiscation clearly cannot be just. If it were, all the acts of a tyrant must of necessity be just; for he only coerces other men by superior power, just as the multitude coerce the rich. But is it just then that the few and the wealthy should be the rulers? And what if they, in like manner, rob and plunder the people—is this

just? If so, the other case will likewise be just. But there can be no doubt that all these things are wrong and unjust.

Then ought the good to rule and have supreme power? But in that case everybody else, being excluded from power, will be dishonoured. For the offices of a state are posts of honour; and if one set of men always hold them, the rest must be deprived of them. Then will it be well that the one best man should rule? Nay, that is still more oligarchical, for the number of those who are dishonoured is thereby increased. Some one may say that it is bad in any case for a man, subject as he is to all the accidents of human passion, to have the supreme power, rather than the law. But what if the law itself be democratical or oligarchical, how will that help us out of our difficulties? Not at all; the same consequences will follow.

Most of these questions may be reserved for another occasion. The principle that the multitude ought to be supreme rather than the few best is one that is maintained, and, though not free from difficulty, yet seems to contain an element of truth. For the many, of whom each individual is but an ordinary person, when they meet together may very likely be better than the few good, if regarded not individually but collectively, just as a feast to which many contribute is better than a dinner provided out of a single purse. For each individual among the many has a share of virtue and prudence, and when they meet together, they become in a manner one man, who has many feet, and hands, and senses; that is a figure of their mind and disposition. Hence the many are better judges than a single man of music and poetry; for some understand one part, and some another, and among them they understand the whole. There is a similar combination of qualities in good men, who differ from any individual of the many, as the beautiful are said to differ from those who are not beautiful, and works of art from realities, because in them the scattered elements are combined, although, if taken separately, the eye of one person or some other feature in another person would be fairer than in the picture. Whether this principle can apply to every democracy, and to all bodies of men, is not clear. Or rather, by heaven, in some cases it is impossible of application; for the argument would equally hold about brutes; and wherein, it will be asked, do some men differ from brutes? But there may be bodies of men about whom our statement is nevertheless true. And if so, the difficulty which has been already raised, and also another which is akin to it— viz. what power should be assigned to the mass of freemen and citizens, who are not rich and have no personal merit—are both solved. There is still a danger in allowing them to share the great offices of state, for their folly will lead them into error, and their dishonesty into crime. But there is a danger also in not letting them share, for a state in which many poor men are excluded from office will necessarily be full of enemies. The only way of escape is to assign to them some deliberative and judicial functions. For this reason Solon and certain other legislators give them the power of electing to offices, and of calling the magistrates to account, but they do not allow them to hold office singly. When they meet together their perceptions are quite good enough, and combined with the better class they are useful to the state (just as impure food when mixed with what is pure sometimes makes the entire mass more wholesome than a small quantity of the pure would be), but each individual, left to himself, forms an imperfect judgement. On the other hand, the popular form of government involves certain difficulties. In the first place, it might be objected that he who can judge of the healing of a sick man would be one who could himself heal his disease, and make him whole—that is, in other words, the physician; and so in all professions and arts. As, then, the physician ought to be called to account by physicians, so ought men in general to be called to account by their peers. But physicians are of three kinds:—there is the ordinary practitioner, and there is the physician of the higher class, and thirdly the intelligent man who has studied the art: in all arts there is such a class; and we attribute the power of judging to them quite as much as to professors of the art. Secondly, does not the same principle apply to elections? For a right election can only be made by those who have knowledge; those who know geometry, for example, will choose a geometrician rightly, and those who know how to steer, a pilot; and, even if there be some occupations and arts in which private persons share in the ability to choose, they certainly cannot choose better than those who know. So that, according to this argument, neither the election of magistrates, nor the calling of them to account, should be entrusted to the many. Yet possibly these objections are to a great extent met by our old answer, that if the people are not utterly degraded, although individually they may be worse judges than those who have special knowledge—as a body they are as good or better. Moreover, there are some arts whose products are not judged of solely, or best, by the artists themselves, namely those arts whose products are recognized even by those who do not possess the art; for example, the knowledge of the house is not limited to the builder only; the user, or, in other words, the master, of the house will even be a better judge than the builder, just as the pilot will judge better of a rudder than the carpenter, and the guest will judge better of a feast than the cook.

This difficulty seems now to be sufficiently answered, but there is another akin to it. That inferior persons should have authority in greater matters than the good would appear to be a strange thing, yet the election and calling to account of the magistrates is the greatest of all. And these, as I was saying, are functions which in some states are assigned to the people, for the assembly is supreme in all such matters. Yet persons of any age, and having but a small property qualification, sit in the assembly and deliberate and judge, although for the great officers of state, such as treasurers and generals, a high qualification is required. This difficulty may be solved in the same manner as the preceding, and the present practice of democracies may be really defensible. For the power does not reside in the dicast, or senator, or ecclesiast, but in the court, and the senate, and the assembly, of which individual senators, or ecclesiasts, or dicasts, are only parts or members. And for this reason the many may claim to have a higher authority than the few; for the people, and the senate, and the courts consist of many persons, and their property collectively is greater than the property of one or of a few individuals holding great offices. But enough of this. . . .

All these considerations appear to show that none of the principles on which men claim to rule and to hold all other men in subjection to them are strictly right. To those who claim to be masters of the government on the ground of their virtue or their wealth, the many might fairly answer that they themselves are often better and richer than the few—I do not say individually, but collectively. And another ingenious objection which is sometimes put forward may be met in a similar manner. Some persons doubt whether the legislator who desires to make the justest laws ought to legislate with a view to the good of the higher classes or of the many, when the case which we have mentioned occurs. Now what is just or right is to be interpreted in the sense of "what is equal"; and that which is right in the sense of being equal is to be considered with reference to the advantage of the state, and the common good of the citizens. And a citizen is one who shares in governing and being governed. He differs under different forms of government, but in the best state he is one who is able and willing to be governed and to govern with a view to the life of virtue.

The General Will

Jean-Jacques Rousseau

Jean-Jacques Rousseau's treatise On the Social Contract, *published in 1762, was rescued from obscurity several decades later when it was used to justify the French Revolution. In this work Rousseau presents a social contract theory of civil society beginning with a state of nature in which solitary individuals possess both personal freedom and political authority, much as John Locke's theory in the previous century. Rousseau, however, conceived of the social contract in terms of a community rather than of individuals. When individuals enter into the social contract, they alienate all of their rights to the body politic, and then they derive their very identity and all of their rights from membership in the community. Rousseau sought a form of association through which the members could unite with a single purpose to support the common good, and yet one that guaranteed them a liberty equal to what they enjoyed in the state of nature. His conception of the general will served both of these theoretical requirements. The general will is formed through the collective deliberation of a community's citizens. The interests they seek are not their private interests, but rather the good of their whole community, so the general will is the collective embodiment of the moral will of the people, and as such, it is the sovereign. When the people form a general will and make a decree concerning only themselves, that decree is a law. Therefore, in obeying the law each person freely does what he or she has already agreed to do. Equality among the citizens and their direct participation in self-government are necessary features of Rousseau's republic. Many contemporary communitarians have used Rousseau's defense of participatory democracy and his portrait of public-spirited citizens as support for their own theories.*

Man was born free, and everywhere he is in chains. Many a one believes himself the master of others, and yet he is a greater slave than they. How has this change come about? I do not know. What can render it legitimate? I believe that I can settle this question.

If I considered only force and the results that proceed from it, I should say that so long as a people is compelled to obey and does obey, it does well; but that, so soon as it can shake off the yoke and does shake it off, it does better; for, if men recover their freedom

From Jean-Jacques Rousseau, *The Social Contract* (1762), Henry J. Tozer, trans. (New York: Charles Scribner's Sons, 1895), book 1, chaps. 1, 6–8, book 2, chaps. 1–4, 6. Footnotes omitted.

by virtue of the same right by which it was taken away, either they are justified in resuming it, or there was no justification for depriving them of it. But the social order is a sacred right which serves as a foundation for all others. This right, however, does not come from nature. It is therefore based on conventions. The question is to know what these conventions are. Before coming to that, I must establish what I have just laid down.

The Social Pact

. . . Now, as men cannot create any new forces, but only combine and direct those that exist, they have no other means of self-preservation than to form by aggregation a sum of forces which may overcome the resistance, to put them in action by a single motive power, and to make them work in concert.

This sum of forces can be produced only by the combination of many; but the strength and freedom of each man being the chief instruments of his preservation, how can he pledge them without injuring himself, and without neglecting the cares which he owes to himself? This difficulty, applied to my subject, may be expressed in these terms:—

"To find a form of association which may defend and protect with the whole force of the community the person and property of every associate, and by means of which each, coalescing with all, may nevertheless obey only himself, and remain as free as before." Such is the fundamental problem of which the social contract furnishes the solution.

The clauses of this contract are so determined by the nature of the act that the slightest modification would render them vain and ineffectual; so that, although they have never perhaps been formally enunciated, they are everywhere the same, everywhere tacitly admitted and recognized, until, the social pact being violated, each man regains his original rights and recovers his natural liberty, while losing the conventional liberty for which he renounced it.

These clauses, rightly understood, are reducible to one only, viz., the total alienation to the whole community of each associate with all his rights; for, in the first place, since each gives himself up entirely, the conditions are equal for all; and, the conditions being equal for all, no one has any interest in making them burdensome to others.

Further, the alienation being made without reserve, the union is as perfect as it can be, and an individual associate can no longer claim anything; for, if any rights were left to individuals, since there would be no common superior who could judge between them and the public, each, being on some point his own judge, would soon claim to be so on all; the state of nature would still subsist, and the association would necessarily become tyrannical or useless.

In short, each giving himself to all, gives himself to nobody; and as there is not one associate over whom we do not acquire the same rights which we concede to him over ourselves, we gain the equivalent of all that we lose, and more power to preserve what we have.

If, then, we set aside what is not of the essence of the social contract, we shall find that it is reducible to the following terms: "Each of us puts in common his person and his whole power under the supreme direction of the general will; and in return we receive every member as an indivisible part of the whole."

Forthwith, instead of the individual personalities of all the contracting parties, this act of association produces a moral and collective body, which is composed of as many members as the assembly has voices, and which receives from this same act its unity, its common self *(moi)*, its life, and its will. This public person, which is thus formed by the union of all the individual members, formerly took the name of *city*, and now takes that of *republic* or *body politic*, which is called by its members *State* when it is passive, *sovereign* when it is active, *power* when it is compared to similar bodies. With regard to the associates, they take collectively the name of *people*, and are called individually *citizens*, as participating in the sovereign power, and *subjects*, as subjected to the laws of the State. But these terms are often confused and are mistaken one for another; it is sufficient to know how to distinguish them when they are used with complete precision.

The Sovereign

We see from this formula that the act of association contains a reciprocal engagement between the public and individuals, and that every individual, contracting so to speak with himself, is engaged in a double relation, viz., as a member of the sovereign towards individuals, and as a member of the State towards the sovereign. But we cannot apply here the maxim of civil law that no one is bound by engagements made with himself; for there is a great difference between being bound to oneself and to a whole of which one forms part.

We must further observe that the public resolution which can bind all subjects to the sovereign in consequence of the two different relations under which each of them is regarded cannot, for a contrary reason, bind the sovereign to itself; and that accordingly it is contrary to the nature of the body politic for the sovereign to impose on itself a law which it cannot transgress. As it can only be considered under one and the same relation, it is in the position of an individual contracting with himself; whence we see that there is not, nor can be, any kind of fundamental law binding upon the body of the people, not even the social contract. This does not imply that such a body cannot perfectly well enter into engagements with others in what does not derogate from this contract; for, with regard to foreigners, it becomes a simple being, an individual.

But the body politic or sovereign, deriving its existence only from the sanctity of the contract, can never bind itself, even to others, in anything that derogates from the original act, such as alienation of some portion of itself, or submission to another sovereign. To violate the act by which it exists would be to annihilate itself; and what is nothing produces nothing.

So soon as the multitude is thus united in one body, it is impossible to injure one of the members without attacking the body, still less to injure the body without the members feeling the effects. Thus duty and interest alike oblige the two contracting parties to give mutual assistance; and the men themselves should seek to combine in this twofold relationship all the advantages which are attendant on it.

Now, the sovereign, being formed only of the individuals that compose it, neither has nor can have any interest contrary to theirs; consequently the sovereign power needs no guarantee towards its subjects, because it is impossible that the body should wish to injure all its members; and we shall see hereafter that it can injure no one as an individual. The sovereign, for the simple reason that it is so, is always everything that it ought to be.

But this is not the case as regards the relation of subjects to the sovereign, which, notwithstanding the common interest, would have no security for the performance of their engagements, unless it found means to ensure their fidelity.

Indeed, every individual may, as a man, have a particular will contrary to, or divergent from, the general will which he has as a citizen; his private interest may prompt him quite differently from the common interest; his absolute and naturally independent existence may make him regard what he owes to the common cause as a gratuitous contribution, the loss of which will be less harmful to others than the payment of it will be burdensome to him; and, regarding the moral person that constitutes the State as an imaginary being because it is not a man, he would be willing to enjoy the rights of a citizen without being willing to fulfil the duties of a subject. The progress of such injustice would bring about the ruin of the body politic.

In order, then, that the social pact may not be a vain formulary, it tacitly includes this engagement, which can alone give force to the others—that whoever refuses to obey the general will shall be constrained to do so by the whole body; which means nothing else than that he shall be forced to be free; for such is the condition which, uniting every citizen to his native land, guarantees him from all personal dependence, a condition that ensures the control and working of the political machine, and alone renders legitimate civil engagements, which, without it, would be absurd and tyrannical, and subject to the most enormous abuses.

The Civil State

The passage from the state of nature to the civil state produces in man a very remarkable change, by substituting in his conduct justice for instinct, and by giving his actions the moral quality that they previously lacked. It is only when the voice of duty succeeds physical impulse, and law succeeds appetite, that man, who till then had regarded only himself, sees that he is obliged to act on other principles, and to consult his reason before listening to his inclinations. Although, in this state, he is deprived of many advantages that he derives from nature, he acquires equally great ones in return; his faculties are exercised and developed; his ideas are expanded; his feelings are ennobled; his whole soul is exalted to such a degree that, if the abuses of this new condition did not often degrade him below that from which he has emerged, he ought to bless without ceasing the happy moment that released him from it for ever, and transformed him from a stupid and ignorant animal into an intelligent being and a man.

Let us reduce this whole balance to terms easy to compare. What man loses by the social contract is his natural liberty and an unlimited right to anything which tempts him and which he is able to attain; what he gains is civil liberty and property in all that he possesses. In order that we may not be mistaken about these compensations, we must clearly distinguish natural liberty, which is limited only by the powers of the individual, from civil liberty, which is limited by the general will; and possession, which is nothing but the result of force or the right of first occupancy, from property, which can be based only on a positive title.

Besides the preceding, we might add to the acquisitions of the civil state moral freedom, which alone renders man truly master of himself; for the impulse of mere appetite is slavery, while obedience to a self-prescribed law is liberty. But I have already said too much on this head, and the philosophical meaning of the term *liberty* does not belong to my present subject. . . .

That Sovereignty Is Inalienable

The first and most important consequence of the principles above established is that the general will alone can direct the forces of the State according to the object of its institution, which is the common good; for if the opposition of private interests has rendered necessary the establishment of societies, the agreement of these same interests has rendered it possible. That which is common to these different interests forms the social bond; and unless there were some point in which all interests agree, no society could exist. Now, it is solely with regard to this common interest that the society should be governed.

I say, then, that sovereignty, being nothing but the exercise of the general will, can never be alienated, and that the sovereign power, which is only a collective being, can be represented by itself alone; power indeed can be transmitted, but not will.

In fact, if it is not impossible that a particular will should agree on some point with the general will, it is at least impossible that this agreement should be lasting and constant; for the particular will naturally tends to preferences, and the general will to equality. It is still more impossible to have a security for this agreement; even though it should always exist, it would not be a result of art, but of chance. The sovereign may indeed say: "I will now what a certain man wills, or at least what he says that he wills"; but he cannot say: "What that man wills tomorrow, I shall also will," since it is absurd that the will should bind itself as regards the future, and since it is not incumbent on any will to consent to anything contrary to the welfare of the being that wills. If, then, the nation simply promises to obey, it dissolves itself by that act and loses its character as a people; the moment there is a master, there is no longer a sovereign, and forthwith the body politic is destroyed.

This does not imply that the orders of the chiefs cannot pass for decisions of the general will, so long as the sovereign, free to oppose them, refrains from doing so. In such a case the consent of the people should be inferred from the universal silence. This will be explained at greater length.

That Sovereignty Is Indivisible

For the same reason that sovereignty is inalienable it is indivisible; for the will is either general, or it is not; it is either that of the body of the people, or that of only a portion. In the first case, this declared will is an act of sovereignty and constitutes law; in the second case, it is only a particular will, or an act of magistracy—it is at most a decree.

But our publicists, being unable to divide sovereignty in its principle, divide it in its object. They divide it into force and will, into legislative power and executive power; into rights of taxation, of justice, and of war; into internal administration and power of treating with foreigners—sometimes confounding all these departments, and sometimes separating them. They make the sovereign a fantastic being, formed of connected parts; it is as if they composed a man of several bodies, one with eyes, another with arms, another with feet, and nothing else. The Japanese conjurers, it is said, cut up a child before the eyes of the spectators; then, throwing all its limbs into the air, they make the child come down again alive and whole. Such almost are the jugglers' tricks of our publicists; after dismembering the social body, by a deception worthy of the fair, they recombine its parts, nobody knows how.

This error arises from their not having formed exact notions about the sovereign authority, and from their taking as parts of this authority what are only emanations from it. Thus, for example, the acts of declaring war and making peace have been regarded as acts of sovereignty, which is not the case, since neither of them is a law, but only an application of the law, a particular act which determines the case of the law, as will be clearly seen when the idea attached to the word *law* is fixed.

By following out the other divisions in the same way, it would be found that, whenever the sovereignty appears divided, we are mistaken in our supposition; and that the rights which are taken as parts of that sovereignty are all subordinate to it, and always suppose supreme wills of which these rights are merely executive.

It would be impossible to describe the great obscurity in which this want of precision has involved the conclusions of writers on the subject of political right when they have endeavored to decide upon the respective rights of kings and peoples on the principles that they had established. Every one can see, in chapters III and IV of the first book of Grotius, how that learned man and his translator Barbeyrac become entangled and embarrassed in their sophisms, for fear of saying too much or not saying enough according to their views, and so offending the interests that they had to conciliate. Grotius, having taken refuge in France through discontent with his own country, and wishing to pay court to Louis XIII, to whom his book is dedicated, spares no pains to despoil the people of all their rights, and, in the most artful manner, bestow them on kings. This also would clearly have been the inclination of Barbeyrac, who dedicated his translation to the king of England, George I. But unfortunately the expulsion of James II, which he calls an abdication, forced him to be reserved and to equivocate and evade, in order not to make William appear a usurper. If these two writers had adopted true principles, all difficulties would have been removed, and they would have been always consistent; but they would have spoken the truth with regret, and would have paid court only to the people. Truth, however, does not lead to fortune, and the people confer neither embassies, nor professorships, nor pensions.

Whether the General Will Can Err

It follows from what precedes that the general will is always right and always tends to the public advantage; but it does not follow that the resolutions of the people have always the same rectitude. Men always desire their own good, but do not always discern it; the people are never corrupted, though often deceived, and it is only then that they seem to will what is evil.

There is often a great deal of difference between the will of all and the general will; the latter regards only the common interest, while the former has regard to private interests, and is merely a sum of particular wills; but take away from these same wills the pluses and minuses which cancel one another, and the general will remains as the sum of the differences.

If the people came to a resolution when adequately informed and without any communication among the citizens, the general will would always result from the great number of slight differences, and the resolution would always be good. But when factions, partial associations, are formed to the detriment of the whole society, the will of each of these associations becomes general with reference to its members, and particular with reference to the State; it may then be said that there are no longer as many voters as there are men, but only as many voters as there are associations. The differences become less numerous and yield a less general result. Lastly, when one of these associations becomes so great that it predominates over all the rest, you no longer have as the result a sum of small differences, but a single difference; there is then no longer a general will, and the opinion which prevails is only a particular opinion.

It is important, then, in order to have a clear declaration of the general will, that there should be no partial association in the State, and that every citizen should express only his own opinion. Such was the unique and sublime institution of the great Lycurgus. But if there are partial associations, it is necessary to multiply their number and prevent inequality, as Solon, Numa, and Servius did. These are the only proper precautions for ensuring that the general will may always be enlightened, and that the people may not be deceived.

The Limits of the Sovereign Power

If the State or city is nothing but a moral person, the life of which consists in the union of its members, and if the most important of its cares is that of self-preservation, it needs a universal and compulsive force to move and dispose every part in the manner most expedient for the whole. As nature gives every man an absolute power over all his limbs, the social pact gives the body politic an absolute power over all its members; and it is this same power which, when directed by the general will, bears, as I said, the name of sovereignty.

But besides the public person, we have to consider the private persons who compose it, and whose life and liberty are naturally independent of it. The question, then, is to distinguish clearly between the respective rights of the citizens and of the sovereign, as well as between the duties which the former have to fulfill in their capacity as subjects and the natural rights which they ought to enjoy in their character as men.

It is admitted that whatever part of his power, property, and liberty each one alienates by the social compact is only that part of the whole of which the use is important to the community; but we must also admit that the sovereign alone is judge of what is important.

All the services that a citizen can render to the State he owes to it as soon as the sovereign demands them; but the sovereign, on its part, cannot impose on its subjects any burden which is useless to the community; it cannot even wish to do so, for, by the law of reason, just as by the law of nature, nothing is done without a cause.

The engagements which bind us to the social body are obligatory only because they are mutual; and their nature is such that in fulfilling them we cannot work for others without also working for ourselves. Why is the general will always right, and why do all invariably desire the prosperity of each, unless it is because there is no one but appropriates to himself this word *each* and thinks of himself in voting on behalf of all? This proves that equality of rights and the notion of justice that it produces are derived from the preference which each gives to himself, and consequently from man's nature; that the general will, to be truly such, should be so in its object as well as in its essence; that it ought to proceed from all in order to be applicable to all; and that it loses its natural rectitude when it tends to some individual and determinate object, because in that case, judging of what is unknown to us, we have no true principle of equity to guide us.

Indeed, so soon as a particular fact or right is in question with regard to a point which has not been regulated by an anterior general convention, the matter becomes contentious; it is a process in which the private persons interested are one of the parties and the public the other, but in which I perceive neither the law which must be followed, nor the judge who should decide. It would be ridiculous in such a case to wish to refer the matter for an express decision of the general will, which can be nothing but the decision of one of the parties, and which, consequently, is for the other party only a will that is foreign, partial, and inclined on such an occasion to injustice as well as liable to error. Therefore, just as a particular will cannot represent the general will, the general will in turn changes its nature when it has a particular end, and cannot, as general, decide about either a person or a fact. When the people of Athens, for instance, elected or deposed their chiefs, decreed honors to one, imposed penalties on another, and by multitudes of particular decrees exercised indiscriminately all the functions of government, the people no longer had any general will properly so called; they no longer acted as a sovereign power, but as magistrates. This will appear contrary to common ideas, but I must be allowed time to expound my own.

From this we must understand that what generalizes the will is not so much the number of voices as the common interest which unites them; for, under this system, each necessarily submits to the conditions which he imposes on others—an admirable union of interest and justice, which gives to the deliberations of the community a spirit of equity that seems to disappear in the discussion of any private affair, for want of a common interest to unite and identify the ruling principle of the judge with that of the party.

By whatever path we return to our principle we always arrive at the same conclusion, viz., that the social compact establishes among the citizens such an equality that they all pledge themselves under the same conditions and ought all to enjoy the same rights. Thus, by the nature of the compact, every act of sovereignty, that is, every authentic act of the general will, binds or favors equally all the citizens; so that the sovereign knows only the body of the nation, and distinguishes none of those that compose it.

What, then, is an act of sovereignty properly so called? It is not an agreement between a superior and an inferior, but an agreement of the body with each of its members; a lawful agreement, because it has the social contract as its foundation; equitable, because it is common to all; useful, because it can have no other object than the general welfare; and stable, because it has the public force and the supreme power as a guarantee. So long as the subjects submit only to such conventions, they obey no one, but simply their own will; and to ask how far the respective rights of the sovereign and citizens extend is to ask up to what point the latter can make engagements among themselves, each with all and all with each.

Thus we see that the sovereign power, wholly absolute, wholly sacred, and wholly inviolable as it is, does not, and cannot, pass the limits of general conventions, and that every man can fully dispose of what is left to him of his property and liberty by these conventions; so that the sovereign never has a right to burden one subject more than another, because then the matter becomes particular and his power is no longer competent.

These distinctions once admitted, so untrue is it that in the social contract there is on the part of individuals any real renunciation, that their situation, as a result of this contract, is in reality preferable to what it was before, and that, instead of an alienation, they have only made an advantageous exchange of an uncertain and precarious mode of existence for a better and more assured one, of natural independence for liberty, of the power to injure others for their own safety, and of their strength, which others might overcome, for a right which the social union renders inviolable. Their lives, also, which they have devoted to the State, are continually protected by it; and in exposing their lives for its defense, what do they do but restore what they have received from it? What do they do but what they would do more frequently and with more risk in the state of nature, when, engaging in inevitable struggles, they would defend at the peril of their lives their means of preservation? All have to fight for their country in case of need, it is true; but then no one ever has to fight for himself. Do we not gain, moreover, by incurring, for what insures our safety, a part of the risks that we should have to incur for ourselves individually, as soon as we were deprived of it? . . .

The Law

By the social compact we have given existence and life to the body politic; the question now is to endow it with movement and will by legislation. For the original act by which this body is formed and consolidated determines nothing in addition as to what it must do for its own preservation.

What is right and comfortable to order is such by the nature of things, and independently of human conventions. All justice comes from God, He alone is the source of it; but could we receive it direct from so lofty a source, we should need neither government nor laws. Without doubt there is a universal justice emanating from reason alone; but this justice, in order to be admitted among us, should be reciprocal. Regarding things from a human standpoint, the laws of justice are inoperative among men for want of a natural sanction; they only bring good to the wicked and evil to the just when the latter observe them with every one, and no one observes them in return. Conventions and laws, then, are necessary to couple rights with duties and apply justice to its object. In the state of nature, where everything is in common, I owe nothing to those to whom I have promised nothing; I recognize as belonging to others only what is useless to me. This is not the case in the civil state, in which all rights are determined by law.

But then, finally, what is a law? So long as men are content to attach to this word only metaphysical ideas, they will continue to argue without being understood; and when they have stated what a law of nature is, they will know no better what a law of the State is.

I have already said that there is no general will with reference to a particular object. In fact, this particular object is either in the State or outside of it. If it is outside the State, a will which is foreign to it is not general in relation to it; and if it is within the State, it forms part of it; then there is formed between the whole and its part a relation which makes of it two separate beings, of which the part is one, and the whole, less this same part, is the other. But the whole less one part is not the whole, and so long as the relation subsists, there is no longer any whole, but two unequal parts; whence it follows that the will of the one is no longer general in relation to the other.

But when the whole people decree concerning the whole people, they consider themselves alone; and if a relation is then constituted, it is between the whole object under one point of view and the whole object under another point of view, without any division at all. Then the matter respecting which they decree is general like the will that decrees. It is this act that I call a law.

When I say that the object of the laws is always general, I mean that the law considers subjects collectively, and actions as abstract, never a man as an individual nor a particular action. Thus the law may indeed decree that there shall be privileges, but cannot confer them on any person by name; the law can create several classes of citizens, and even assign the qualifications which shall entitle them to rank in these classes, but it cannot nominate such and such persons to be admitted to them; it can establish a royal government and a hereditary succession, but cannot elect a king or appoint a royal family; in a word, no function which has reference to an individual object appertains to the legislative power.

From this standpoint we see immediately that it is no longer necessary to ask whose office it is to make laws, since they are acts of the general will; nor whether the prince is above the laws, since he is a member of the State; nor whether the law can be unjust, since no one is unjust to himself; nor how we are free and yet subject to the laws, since the laws are only registers of our wills.

We see, further, that since the law combines the universality of the will with the universality of the object, whatever any man prescribes on his own authority is not a law; and whatever the sovereign itself prescribes respecting a particular object is not a law, but a decree, not an act of sovereignty, but of magistracy.

I therefore call any State a republic which is governed by laws, under whatever form of administration it may be; for then only does the public interest predominate and the commonwealth count for something. Every legitimate government is republican; . . .

Laws are properly only the conditions of civil associations. The people, being subjected to the laws, should be the authors of them; it concerns only the associates to determine the conditions of association.

Community as the Basis for Free Individual Action

G. W. F. Hegel

The moral agent in G. W. F. Hegel's ethical and political theories is formed within an ongoing set of social practices and finds personal fulfillment within that structure. Ethical life, or Sittlichkeit, *is a system of social practices engaged in by rationally deliberative and socially responsive agents, which gives rise to objective principles of right. Individuals use these norms to assess their own actions and emend their set of social practices. Hegel's political philosophy locates the preconditions of individual freedom in the proper functioning of this complex of social practices, objective norms, and rational self-conscious agents. Once the members of a rational society understand how this ethical complex forms and is formed by the legal, political, and civil structures of their society and by the actions of individuals within these structures, they express their personal freedom by acting in accord with the social structure and adjusting it to meet their changing needs.*

Many elements of modern communitarianism can be seen in this brief summary of Hegel's philosophy: the social construction of the self, a harmony of interests between individuals and their community, a practical and historically developed ethics, a reliance on rational deliberation to counteract mere conformity and the ossification of social norms, and a conviction that individual liberty can only be realized within a rational ethical community.

The excerpts from Hegel's Phenomenology of Spirit *translated here first describe how one rationally self-conscious individual must interact with another to raise his or her subjective reason to a universal, transpersonal level. Only then will individuals be able to act freely, since the spiritual essence, or substance, of their common ethical life is the means by which they can escape mere conformity to customs as well as their own subjective prejudices. Hegel then explains why the concept of a solitary individual acting in isolated deliberation is unrealistic. The concept of an individual acting in unreflective conformity with custom, however, is not unrealistic; it has been a recipe for personal happiness in the past. In Hegel's view this happiness is no longer available to modern people, because the development of rational self-consciousness prevents mere conformity: a free people must recognize and critically evaluate their own customs and change them. But merely self-interested action, "the way of the world," is simply not humanly possible. In the last paragraph Hegel describes rational ethical life as a union of customary social practices and the activity of rational, principled practitioners. Hegel's text is printed in the left column and the translator's annotations appear in the right column.*

From G. W. F. Hegel, excerpts from *The Phenomenology of Spirit,* translated and annotated by Kenneth R. Westphal with permission from: *Gesammelte Werke* vol. 9 (Hamburg: Meiner, 1980), pp. 193.22–193.30, 194.1–195.36, 213.30–213.34, 238.28–239.14. © 1993 Kenneth R. Westphal. Printed by permission of the translator.

Text	Annotations

Text

[Rational self-consciousness] goes out of its self-sufficiency over into its freedom. At first this active reason is conscious of itself only as an individual, and as such must demand and bring forth its actuality in another; but therefore, since its consciousness raises itself to universality, it becomes *universal* reason, and is conscious of itself as reason, as already recognized in and for itself, and it unifies all self-consciousness in its pure consciousness. It is the simple spiritual essence, which, since it at the same time comes to consciousness, is the *real substance* . . .[1]

If we take up this goal in its reality, the *concept* that has already become for *us*, namely, the recognized self-consciousness that has the certainty of itself, and even its truth, in the other free self-consciousness,[2] or if we extract this still inner spirit as if it were the substance that is already extended to its existence,[3] then *the realm of ethical life* unlocks itself in this concept. For ethical life is nothing other than the absolute spiritual *unity* of the essence of individuals in their self-sufficient *actuality*; it is a self-consciousness which is universal in itself, which is so actual to itself in another consciousness that this other consciousness has complete self-sufficiency, or is a thing for consciousness,[4] through which consciousness is aware of its *unity* with the other consciousness, and first achieves self-consciousness in this unity with this objective being. This ethical *substance* in the *abstraction of universality* is just the *known* law; but it is just as much immediately actual *self-consciousness*, or *custom*. Conversely, the *single* consciousness is only this extant one, since it is conscious within its own individuality of the universal consciousness as its own being, since its action and existence is the general custom.[5]

In the life of a people, the concept has in fact the actualization of self-conscious reason; in the self-sufficiency of the *other* it can behold the complete *unity* with that other; or, in the free *thinghood* of the other that I find before me, which is the negative of myself, I have *my*

Annotations

1. These excerpts come from Hegel's analysis of the grounds and nature of rational self-consciousness. Prior to this Hegel has argued that human reason is more than a natural phenomenon, and that theoretical reason depends on practical reason. Beginning here Hegel argues that human reason is a social, not merely an individual, phenomenon. On this basis he argues against the idea that human freedom is found in individual self-sufficiency. He describes a rational self-conscious individual who comes to recognize that reason is social, and so depends upon others, as "raising itself to universality" and as becoming "universal reason," since such an individual realizes that reason is a collective (i.e., "universal") property of a whole group of individuals. Since reason is a collective property of a group, and since it is fundamental to the members' individual and collective efforts, reason is the "substance" that sustains individuals and their communities.

2. Hegel speaks of "a self-consciousness" in the sense of a self-conscious agent. He refers only to two self-conscious agents because once he shows that human reason depends on the mutual interaction and recognition between two individuals, he has made his case in principle against atomistic individualism.

3. Hegel here anticipates what he intends to show about the "concept" of reason described in note 1. He discusses it here "as if it were" not merely an idea, but an idea exemplified by an extant community ("the substance that is already extended to its existence").

4. Hegel here speaks of a consciousness as a "thing" or as "being objective" to stress that an extant individual is identified as a conscious agent who exists independently of whoever makes that identification.

5. The focus of Hegel's analysis is custom. Customs are familiar, socially accepted, standard ways of doing things. They "exist" only insofar as members of groups continue to abide by them. The most basic and important customs can be abstracted from social practices and formulated

Text	*Annotations*

being for *myself* as an object, which is its complete reality.[6] . . . The many individuals are conscious of themselves as many self-sufficient beings because they sacrifice their individuality and because this universal substance is their soul and essence; just as, conversely, this universal is their *act* as individuals, or it is the work they have brought forth.

The *purely individual* act and drive of the individual concerns needs, which it has as a natural being, that is, as an *existing individuality.* That even these, its most common functions, are not for naught, but have actuality, occurs through the universal sustaining medium, through the *power* of the whole people. —But not only does the individual have the *form* of *subsistence* of its act in general in the universal substance, therein it also has *the content* of its act; what it does *is* the universal capability and custom of all. This content, insofar as it is perfectly individuated, is embraced in its actuality in the activity of all. The *work* of the individual for his needs is just as much the satisfaction of the needs of others as it is of his own, and he achieves the satisfaction of his own needs only through the work of others. —Just as the individual in his *individual* work already *unconsciously* completes the *universal* work, so again he also completes the universal work just as much as he completes his *conscious* object.[7] The whole becomes his work *as a whole,* for which he sacrifices himself; precisely thus does he receive himself back from it. —There is nothing here that is not mutual, nothing in which the self-sufficiency of the individual does not give itself its *positive* significance of being for itself by the very dissolution of its being-for-self, by the self-*negation* of its self-sufficiency.[8] This unity of being for another, or of making oneself into a thing, and of being for oneself[9]—this universal substance speaks its *universal language* in the customs and laws of its people; but this existing unchanging essence is nothing other than the expression of the singular individuality itself, which seems to be opposed to it; the laws pronounce what each individual *is* and *does;* the individual knows them not only as his *universal* objective

as universal laws. Such formulation does not end their role as customary practices, while it can underscore, for individuals, what their activities are and that they are customary.

6. Hegel means to indicate how we can recognize in others our own characteristics as distinct, self-conscious, active agents. (For the sense of "thinghood" in this sentence, see note 4 re: "thing.")

7. "Object" here in the sense of aim or objective.

8. Hegel contends that we achieve a genuine sense of ourselves as active individuals by rescinding our (untenable) claims to individual self-sufficiency.

9. Our "unity of being for another" involves our performing actions that are useful both to others and to ourselves. Insofar as we act in ways that are useful to ourselves, we express "being for oneself." Insofar as we act in ways that are useful to others, we are a "thing," something useful to others. Our acts display both of these aspects, as do the acts of those with whom we interact. In our mutual interactions we must respect each other's ends and avail ourselves of what others offer. (Hegel extends Kant's views that as social beings we must rely upon and "make use of" each other, and that what is morally reprehensible is treating others *merely* as means by refusing to take their interests into account and doing nothing for them in return.)

Text	*Annotations*

Text

thinghood,[10] but just as much he knows himself in them, or he knows them as *individuated* in his own individuality and in each of his fellow citizens. Hence each has, in the universal spirit, only the certainty of himself, of finding nothing other than himself in the objective actuality; each is as certain of the other as he is of himself. —I behold in everyone that they are for themselves only this self-sufficient essence, just as I am; in them I behold the free unity with the other in such a way that this unity exists through me, just as much as through the others themselves. I behold the others as myself, and myself as them.

Therefore reason is in truth actualized in a free people; reason is the present living spirit in which the individual not only finds his *vocation,* that is, his universal and individual being, articulated and present as thinghood,[11] but also finds that he is this being, and that he has achieved his vocation. Hence the wisest among the ancients declared, *that wisdom and virtue consist in living in accordance with the customs of one's people.*

But self-consciousness has departed from the happiness of having achieved its vocation and of living in it; or, it has not yet achieved it, for both can equally well be said. This self-consciousness is initially only *immediately* and *in principle* spirit.

Reason *must depart from this happiness;* for the life of a free people is only *in itself* or *immediately* the *real ethical life* . . .[12]

The individuality of the way of the world[13] may indeed believe that it acts only *for itself* or *for its own advantage.* It is better than it believes; its act is at the same time *in itself* a *universal* act. If it acts only for its own advantage, then it just does not know what it does, and when it assures us that all people act only to their own advantage, then it merely maintains that no one is conscious of what action is.

The spiritual *essence* has already been designated as *ethical substance;* but spirit is *the ethical actuality.* It is the *self* of actual consciousness, to whom spirit, or rather who contra-

Annotations

10. That is, the individual knows the laws not merely as extant, objectively given universal principles.

11. That is, one finds that one's vocation exists objectively.

12. The higher form of spirit which contrasts with this deficient, "immediate" form involves explicit consciousness of the essence of the community. A merely customary community is not rationally adequate or acceptable, Hegel believes.

13. That is, the individual who pursues only his or her own worldly aims.

Text	*Annotations*

distinguishes itself from spirit as an objective actual *world,* but which as such has lost all significance for the self of something foreign, just as the self has lost all significance of something separated from the world, whether as a dependent or an independent being for itself.[14] *Substance* and the universal, self-identical, enduring essence is the unperverted and undissolved *ground* and *point of departure* for everyone's action, and it is their *purpose* and *aim* as the conscious *in itself* of all self-consciousness. —As such this substance is the universal *work* that is produced through the *act* of each and all as their unity and equality, for it is the *being for self,* the self, the act. Spirit, as *substance,* is unwavering upright *self-identity*; but as *being for self* spirit is the dissolved, the self-sacrificing benevolent essence, in which each completes his own work, dividing the universal being, and taking for himself his part from it. This dissolution and individuation of the essence is indeed the *moment* of the act and self of all; it is the movement and the soul of substance, and the effected universal essence. Precisely because substance is the being that this is dissolved in the self, it is not the dead essence, but is *actual* and *alive.*

14. Hegel's point, which is clearer in the remainder, is that human beings are fundamentally social practitioners; there are no individuals or individual actions apart from social practices. Likewise there are no social practices apart from a group of people who engage in them, who recognize their performance by others, and who modify them to meet new needs and insights. As a set of practices, customs form a social world in which individuals live ("ethical substance"); as a set of activities, customs exist only through the actions of individuals ("being for self"). Individuals who consciously engage in customary activities find their social world familiar, not foreign, precisely because their social world and their own activities within it are formed and informed by the same customs and principles. This "spiritual essence" exists (it is a "being") as a real, on-going community, an "ethical actuality."

Effects of Individualism Combated

Alexis de Tocqueville

Alexis de Tocqueville was a young French nobleman set adrift by the collapse of the old aristocratic order during the French Revolution. The ensuing chaos in French society led him to study the American experiment in democracy. From 1835 to 1840 he published a brilliant analysis of American democratic institutions and described the customs and peculiarities of the American people. One of his central interests was to discover how the Americans constructed a replacement for the old aristocratic order that had provided European people with the power, stability, and security of a community life. A social order created by community attachments, Tocqueville believed, was necessary for the well-being of any society. American society seemed to be successful, so Tocqueville sought to discover through what social and political arrangements Americans secured the functions of a communal life despite the absence of an aristocratic order. In this selection, Tocqueville first describes the evils that equality produces. Each citizen is thrown back on his or her own resources, resulting in an isolation and powerlessness that Tocqueville calls individualism. For this, only political freedom can provide an effective remedy. Tocqueville then describes how free institutions in America require neighbors to administer their local communities and how, in the process, they form the bonds of mutuality and affection typical of community associations. This principle of association is not limited to politics but is a deep and pervasive feature of American life. Tocqueville then argues that the principle of association is cultivated by the many independent and locally controlled newspapers. Finally, Tocqueville distinguishes American individualism, rightly understood, from mere selfishness.

Chapter I
Why Democratic Nations Show a More Ardent and Enduring Love of Equality Than of Liberty

The first and most intense passion that is produced by equality of condition is, I need hardly say, the love of that equality. My readers will therefore not be surprised that I speak of this feeling before all others.

Everybody has remarked that in our time, and especially in France, this passion for equality is every day gaining ground in the human heart. It has been said a hundred times that our contemporaries are far more ardently and tenaciously attached to equality than to freedom; but as I do not find that the causes of the fact have been sufficiently analyzed, I shall endeavor to point them out.

It is possible to imagine an extreme point at which freedom and equality would meet and blend. Let us suppose that all the people take a part in the government, and that each one of them has an equal right to take a part in it. As no one is different from his fellows, none can exercise a tyrannical power; men will be perfectly free because they are all entirely equal; and they will all be perfectly equal because they are entirely free. To this ideal state democratic nations tend. This is the only complete form that equality can assume upon earth; but there are a thousand others which, without being equally perfect, are not less cherished by those nations.

The principle of equality may be established in civil society without prevailing in the political world. There may be equal rights of indulging in the same pleasures, of entering

From Alexis de Tocqueville, *Democracy in America*, Henry Reeve, Esq., trans. (Toronto: Alfred Knopf, Inc., 1945), vol. II, book 2, pgs. 94–99, 102–114, 121–124.

the same professions, of frequenting the same places; in a word, of living in the same manner and seeking wealth by the same means, although all men do not take an equal share in the government. A kind of equality may even be established in the political world though there should be no political freedom there. A man may be the equal of all his countrymen save one, who is the master of all without distinction and who selects equally from among them all the agents of his power. Several other combinations might be easily imagined by which very great equality would be united to institutions more or less free or even to institutions wholly without freedom.

Although men cannot become absolutely equal unless they are entirely free, and consequently equality, pushed to its furthest extent, may be confounded with freedom, yet there is good reason for distinguishing the one from the other. The taste which men have for liberty and that which they feel for equality are, in fact, two different things; and I am not afraid to add that among democratic nations they are two unequal things.

Upon close inspection it will be seen that there is in every age some peculiar and preponderant fact with which all others are connected; this fact almost always gives birth to some pregnant idea or some ruling passion, which attracts to itself and bears away in its course all the feelings and opinions of the time; it is like a great stream towards which each of the neighboring rivulets seems to flow.

Freedom has appeared in the world at different times and under various forms; it has not been exclusively bound to any social condition, and it is not confined to democracies. Freedom cannot, therefore, form the distinguishing characteristic of democratic ages. The peculiar and preponderant fact that marks those ages as its own is the equality of condition; the ruling passion of men in those periods is the love of this equality. Do not ask what singular charm the men of democratic ages find in being equal, or what special reasons they may have for clinging so tenaciously to equality rather than to the other advantages that society holds out to them: equality is the distinguishing characteristic of the age they live in; that of itself is enough to explain that they prefer it to all the rest.

But independently of this reason there are several others which will at all times habitually lead men to prefer equality to freedom.

If a people could ever succeed in destroying, or even in diminishing, the equality that prevails in its own body, they could do so only by long and laborious efforts. Their social condition must be modified, their laws abolished, their opinions superseded, their habits changed, their manners corrupted. But political liberty is more easily lost; to neglect to hold it fast is to allow it to escape. Therefore not only do men cling to equality because it is dear to them; they also adhere to it because they think it will last forever.

That political freedom in its excesses may compromise the tranquillity, the property, the lives of individuals is obvious even to narrow and unthinking minds. On the contrary, none but attentive and clear-sighted men perceive the perils with which equality threatens us, and they commonly avoid pointing them out. They know that the calamities they apprehend are remote and flatter themselves that they will only fall upon future generations, for which the present generation takes but little thought. The evils that freedom sometimes brings with it are immediate; they are apparent to all, and all are more or less affected by them. The evils that extreme equality may produce are slowly disclosed; they creep gradually into the social frame; they are seen only at intervals; and at the moment at which they become most violent, habit already causes them to be no longer felt.

The advantages that freedom brings are shown only by the lapse of time, and it is always easy to mistake the cause in which they originate. The advantages of equality are immediate, and they may always be traced from their source.

Political liberty bestows exalted pleasures from time to time upon a certain number of citizens. Equality every day confers a number of small enjoyments on every man. The charms of equality are every instant felt and are within the reach of all; the noblest hearts are not insensible to them, and the most vulgar souls exult in them. The passion that equality creates must therefore be at once strong and general. Men cannot enjoy political liberty unpurchased by some sacrifices, and they never obtain it without great exertions. But the pleasures of equality are self-proffered; each of the petty incidents of life seems to occasion them, and in order to taste them, nothing is required but to live.

Democratic nations are at all times fond of equality, but there are certain epochs at which the passion they entertain for it swells to the height of fury. This occurs at the moment when the old social system, long menaced, is overthrown after a severe internal struggle, and the barriers of rank are at length thrown down. At such times men pounce upon equality as their booty, and they cling to it as to some precious treasure which they fear to lose. The passion for equality penetrates on every side into men's hearts, expands there, and fills them entirely. Tell them not that by this blind surrender of themselves to an exclusive passion they risk their dearest interests; they are deaf. Show them not freedom escaping from their grasp while they are looking another way; they are blind, or rather they can discern but one object to be desired in the universe.

What I have said is applicable to all democratic nations; what I am about to say concerns the French alone. Among most modern nations, and especially among all those of the continent of Europe, the taste and the idea of freedom began to exist and to be developed only at the time when social conditions were tending to equality and as a consequence of that very equality. Absolute kings were the most efficient levelers of ranks among their subjects. Among these nations equality preceded freedom; equality was therefore a fact of some standing when freedom was still a novelty; the one had already created customs, opinions, and laws belonging to it when the other, alone and for the first time, came into actual existence. Thus the latter was still only an affair of opinion and of taste while the former had already crept into the habits of the people, possessed itself of their manners, and given a particular turn to the smallest actions in their lives. Can it be wondered at that the men of our own time prefer the one to the other?

I think that democratic communities have a natural taste for freedom; left to themselves, they will seek it, cherish it, and view any privation of it with regret. But for equality their passion is ardent, insatiable, incessant, invincible; they call for equality in freedom; and if they cannot obtain that, they still call for equality in slavery. They will endure poverty, servitude, barbarism, but they will not endure aristocracy.

This is true at all times, and especially in our own day. All men and all powers seeking to cope with this irresistible passion will be overthrown and destroyed by it. In our age freedom cannot be established without it, and despotism itself cannot reign without its support.

Chapter II
Of Individualism in Democratic Countries

I have shown how it is that in ages of equality every man seeks for his opinions within himself; I am now to show how it is that in the same ages all his feelings are turned towards himself alone. *Individualism* is a novel expression, to which a novel idea has given birth. Our fathers were only acquainted with *égoïsme* (selfishness). Selfishness is a passionate and exaggerated love of self, which leads a man to connect everything with himself and to prefer himself to everything in the world. Individualism is a mature and calm feeling, which disposes each member of the community to sever himself from the mass of his fellows and to draw apart with his family and his friends, so that after he has thus formed a little circle of his own, he willingly leaves society at large to itself. Selfishness originates in blind instinct; individualism proceeds from erroneous judgment more than from depraved feelings; it originates as much in deficiencies of mind as in perversity of heart.

Selfishness blights the germ of all virtue; individualism, at first, only saps the virtues of public life; but in the long run it attacks and destroys all others and is at length absorbed in downright selfishness. Selfishness is a vice as old as the world, which does not belong to one form of society more than to another; individualism is of democratic origin, and it threatens to spread in the same ratio as the equality of condition.

Among aristocratic nations, as families remain for centuries in the same condition, often on the same spot, all generations become, as it were, contemporaneous. A man almost always knows his forefathers and respects them; he thinks he already sees his remote descendants and he loves them. He willingly imposes duties on himself towards the former and the latter, and he will frequently sacrifice his personal gratifications to those who went before and to those who will come after him. Aristocratic institutions, moreover, have the effect of closely binding every man to several of his fellow citizens. As the classes of an aristocratic people are strongly marked and permanent, each of them is regarded by its own members as a sort of lesser country, more tangible and more cherished than the country at large. As in aristocratic communities all the citizens occupy fixed positions, one above another, the result is that each of them always sees a man above himself whose patronage is necessary to him, and below himself another man whose co-operation he may claim. Men living in aristocratic ages are therefore almost always closely attached to something placed out of their own sphere, and they are often disposed to forget themselves. It is true that in these ages the notion of human fellowship is faint and that men seldom think of sacrificing themselves for mankind; but they often sacrifice themselves for other men. In democratic times, on the contrary, when the duties of each individual to the race are much more clear, devoted service to any one man becomes more rare; the bond of human affection is extended, but it is relaxed.

Among democratic nations new families are constantly springing up, others are constantly falling away, and all that remain change their condition; the woof of time is every instant broken and the track of generations effaced. Those who went before are soon forgotten; of those who will come after, no one has any idea: the interest of man is confined to those in close propinquity to himself. As each class gradually approaches others and mingles with them, its members become undifferentiated and lose

their class identity for each other. Aristocracy had made a chain of all the members of the community, from the peasant to the king; democracy breaks that chain and severs every link of it.

As social conditions become more equal, the number of persons increases who, although they are neither rich nor powerful enough to exercise any great influence over their fellows, have nevertheless acquired or retained sufficient education and fortune to satisfy their own wants. They owe nothing to any man, they expect nothing from any man; they acquire the habit of always considering themselves as standing alone, and they are apt to imagine that their whole destiny is in their own hands.

Thus not only does democracy make every man forget his ancestors, but it hides his descendants and separates his contemporaries from him; it throws him back forever upon himself alone and threatens in the end to confine him entirely within the solitude of his own heart. . . .

Chapter IV
That the Americans Combat the Effects of Individualism by Free Institutions

Despotism, which by its nature is suspicious, sees in the separation among men the surest guarantee of its continuance, and it usually makes every effort to keep them separate. No vice of the human heart is so acceptable to it as selfishness: a despot easily forgives his subjects for not loving him, provided they do not love one another. He does not ask them to assist him in governing the state; it is enough that they do not aspire to govern it themselves. He stigmatizes as turbulent and unruly spirits those who would combine their exertions to promote the prosperity of the community; and, perverting the natural meaning of words, he applauds as good citizens those who have no sympathy for any but themselves.

Thus the vices which despotism produces are precisely those which equality fosters.

These two things perniciously complete and assist each other. Equality places men side by side, unconnected by any common tie; despotism raises barriers to keep them asunder; the former predisposes them not to consider their fellow creatures, the latter makes general indifference a sort of public virtue.

Despotism, then, which is at all times dangerous, is more particularly to be feared in democratic ages. It is easy to see that in those same ages men stand most in need of freedom. When the members of a community are forced to attend to public affairs, they are necessarily drawn from the circle of their own interests and snatched at times from self-observation. As soon as a man begins to treat of public affairs in public, he begins to perceive that he is not so independent of his fellow men as he had at first imagined, and that in order to obtain their support he must often lend them his co-operation.

When the public govern, there is no man who does not feel the value of public goodwill or who does not endeavor to court it by drawing to himself the esteem and affection of those among whom he is to live. Many of the passions which congeal and keep asunder human hearts are then obliged to retire and hide below the surface. Pride must be dissembled; disdain dares not break out; selfishness fears its own self. Under a free government, as most public offices are elective, the men whose elevated minds or aspiring hopes are too closely circumscribed in private life constantly feel that they cannot do without the people who surround them. Men learn at such times to think of their fellow men from ambitious motives; and they frequently find it, in a manner, their interest to forget themselves.

I may here be met by an objection derived from electioneering intrigues, the meanness of candidates, and the calumnies of their opponents. These are occasions of enmity which occur the oftener the more frequent elections become. Such evils are doubtless great, but they are transient; whereas the benefits that attend them remain. The desire of being elected may lead some men for a time to violent hostility; but this same desire leads all men in the long run to support each other; and if it happens that an election accidentally severs two friends, the electoral system brings a multitude of citizens permanently together who would otherwise always have remained unknown to one another. Freedom produces private animosities, but despotism gives birth to general indifference.

The Americans have combated by free institutions the tendency of equality to keep men asunder, and they have subdued it. The legislators of America did not suppose that a general representation of the whole nation would suffice to ward off a disorder at once so natural to the frame of democratic society and so fatal; they also thought that it would be well to infuse political life into each portion of the territory in order to multiply to an infinite extent opportunities of acting in concert for all the members of the community and to make them constantly feel their mutual dependence. The plan was a wise one. The general affairs of a country engage the attention only of leading politicians, who assemble from time to time in the same places; and as they often lose sight of each other afterwards, no lasting ties are established between them. But if the object be to have the local affairs of a district conducted by the men who reside there, the same persons are always in contact, and they are, in a manner, forced to be acquainted and to adapt themselves to one another.

It is difficult to draw a man out of his own circle to interest him in the destiny of the state, because he does not clearly understand what influence the destiny of the state can have upon his own lot. But if it is proposed to make a road cross the end of his estate, he will see at a glance that there is a connection between this small public affair and his greatest private affairs; and he will discover, without its being shown to him, the close tie that unites private to general interest. Thus far more may be done by entrusting to the citizens the administration of minor affairs than by surrendering to them in the control of important ones, towards interesting them in the public welfare and convincing them that they constantly stand in need of one another in order to provide for it. A brilliant achievement may win for you the favor of a people at one stroke; but to earn the love and respect of the population that surrounds you, a long succession of little services rendered and of obscure good deeds, a constant habit of kindness, and an established reputation for disinterestedness will be required. Local freedom, then, which leads a great number of citizens to value the affection of their neighbors and of their kindred, perpetually brings men together and forces them to help one another in spite of the propensities that sever them.

In the United States the more opulent citizens take great care not to stand aloof from the people; on the contrary, they constantly keep on easy terms with the lower classes: they listen to them, they speak to them every day. They know that the rich in democracies always stand in need of the poor, and that in democratic times you attach a poor man to you more by your manner than by benefits conferred. The magnitude of such benefits, which sets off the difference of condition, causes a secret irritation to those who reap advantage from them, but the charm of simplicity of manners is almost irresistible; affability carries men away, and even want of polish is not always displeasing. This truth does not take root at once in the minds of the rich. They generally resist it as long as the democratic revolution lasts, and they do not acknowledge it immediately after that revolution is accomplished. They are very ready to do good to the people, but they still choose to keep them at arm's length; they think that is sufficient, but they are mistaken. They might spend fortunes thus without warming the hearts of the population around them; that population does not ask them for the sacrifice of their money, but of their pride.

It would seem as if every imagination in the United States were upon the stretch to invent means of increasing the wealth and satisfying the wants of the public. The best-informed inhabitants of each district constantly use their information to discover new truths that may augment the general prosperity; and if they have made any such discoveries, they eagerly surrender them to the mass of the people.

When the vices and weaknesses frequently exhibited by those who govern in America are closely examined, the prosperity of the people occasions, but improperly occasions, surprise. Elected magistrates do not make the American democracy flourish; it flourishes because the magistrates are elective.

It would be unjust to suppose that the patriotism and the zeal that every American displays for the welfare of his fellow citizens are wholly insincere. Although private interest directs the greater part of human actions in the United States as well as elsewhere, it does not regulate them all. I must say that I have often seen Americans make great and real sacrifices to the public welfare; and I have noticed a hundred instances in which they hardly ever failed to lend faithful support to one another. The free institutions which the inhabitants of the United States possess, and the political rights of which they make so much use, remind every citizen, and in a thousand ways, that he lives in society. They every instant impress upon his mind the notion that it is the duty as well as the interest of men to make themselves useful to their fellow creatures; and as he sees no particular ground of animosity to them, since he is never either their master or their slave, his heart readily leans to the side of kindness. Men attend to the interests of the public, first by necessity, afterwards by choice; what was intentional becomes an instinct, and by dint of working for the good of one's fellow citizens, the habit and the taste for serving them are at length acquired.

Many people in France consider equality of condition as one evil and political freedom as a second. When they are obliged to yield to the former, they strive at least to escape from the latter. But I contend that in order to combat the evils which equality may produce, there is only one effectual remedy: namely, political freedom.

Chapter V
Of the Use Which the Americans Make of Public Associations in Civil Life

---

I do not propose to speak of those political associations by the aid of which men endeavor to defend themselves against the despotic action of a majority or against the aggressions of regal power. That subject I have already treated. If each citizen did not learn, in proportion as he individually becomes more feeble and consequently more incapable of preserving his freedom single-handed, to combine with his fellow citizens for the purpose of defending it, it is clear that tyranny would unavoidably increase together with equality.

Only those associations that are formed in civil life without reference to political objects are here referred to. The political associations that exist in the United States are only a single feature in the midst of the immense assemblage of associations in that country. Americans of all ages, all conditions, and all dispositions constantly form associations. They have not only commercial and manufacturing companies, in which all take part, but associations of a thousand other kinds, religious, moral, serious, futile, general or restricted, enormous or diminutive. The Americans make associations to give entertainments, to found seminaries, to build inns, to construct churches, to diffuse books, to send missionaries to the antipodes; in this manner they found hospitals, prisons, and schools. If it is proposed to inculcate some truth or to foster some feeling by the encouragement of a great example, they form a society. Wherever at the head of some new undertaking you see the government in France, or a man of rank in England, in the United States you will be sure to find an association.

I met with several kinds of associations in America of which I confess I had no previous notion; and I have often admired the extreme skill with which the inhabitants of the United States succeed in proposing a common object for the exertions of a great many men and in inducing them voluntarily to pursue it.

I have since traveled over England, from which the Americans have taken some of their laws and many of their customs; and it seemed to me that the principle of association was by no means so constantly or adroitly used in that country. The English often perform great things singly, whereas the Americans form associations for the smallest undertakings. It is evident that the former people consider association as a powerful means of action, but the latter seem to regard it as the only means they have of acting.

Thus the most democratic country on the face of the earth is that in which men have, in our time, carried to the highest perfection the art of pursuing in common the object of their common desires and have applied this new science to the greatest number of purposes. Is this the result of accident, or is there in reality any necessary connection between the principle of association and that of equality?

Aristocratic communities always contain, among a multitude of persons who by themselves are powerless, a small number of powerful and wealthy citizens, each of whom can achieve great undertakings single-handed. In aristocratic societies men do not need to combine in order to act, because they are strongly held together. Every wealthy and powerful citizen constitutes the head of a permanent and compulsory association, composed of all those who are dependent upon him or whom he makes subservient to the execution of his designs.

Among democratic nations, on the contrary, all the citizens are independent and feeble; they can do hardly anything by themselves, and none of them can oblige his fellow men to lend him their assistance. They all, therefore, become powerless if they do not learn voluntarily to help one another. If men living in democratic countries had no right and no inclination to associate for political purposes, their independence would be in great jeopardy, but they might long preserve their wealth and their cultivation: whereas if they never acquired the habit of forming associations in ordinary life, civilization itself would be endangered. A people among whom individuals lost the power of achieving great things single-handed, without acquiring the means of producing them by united exertions, would soon relapse into barbarism.

Unhappily, the same social condition that renders associations so necessary to democratic nations renders their formation more difficult among those nations than among all others. When several members of an aristocracy agree to combine, they easily succeed in doing so; as each of them brings great strength to the partnership, the number of its members may be very limited; and when the members of an association are limited in number, they may easily become mutually acquainted, understand each other, and establish fixed regulations. The same opportunities do not occur among democratic nations, where the associated members must always be very numerous for their association to have any power.

I am aware that many of my countrymen are not in the least embarrassed by this difficulty. They contend that the more enfeebled and incompetent the citizens become, the more able and active the government ought to be rendered in order that society at large may execute what individuals can no longer accomplish. They believe this answers the whole difficulty, but I think they are mistaken.

A government might perform the part of some of the largest American companies, and several states, members of the Union, have already attempted it; but what political power could ever carry on the vast multitude of lesser undertakings which the American citizens perform every day, with the assistance of the principle of association? It is easy to foresee that the time is drawing near when man will be less and less able to produce, by himself alone, the commonest necessaries of life. The task of the governing power will therefore perpetually increase, and its very efforts will extend it every day. The more it stands in the place of associations, the more will individuals, losing the notion of combining together, require its assistance: these are causes and effects that unceasingly create each other. Will the administration of the country ultimately assume the management of all the manufactures which no single citizen is able to carry on? And if a time at length arrives when, in consequence of the extreme subdivision of landed property, the soil is split into an infinite number of parcels, so that it can be cultivated only by companies of tillers, will it be necessary that the head of the government should leave the helm of state to follow the plow? The morals and the intelligence of a democratic people would be as much endangered as its business and manufactures if the government ever wholly usurped the place of private companies.

Feelings and opinions are recruited, the heart is enlarged, and the human mind is developed only by the reciprocal influence of men upon one another. I have shown that these influences are almost null in democratic countries; they must therefore be artificially created, and this can only be accomplished by associations.

When the members of an aristocratic community adopt a new opinion or conceive a new sentiment, they give it a station, as it were, beside themselves, upon the lofty platform where they stand; and opinions or sentiments so conspicuous to the eyes of the multitude are easily introduced into the minds or hearts of all around. In democratic countries the governing power alone is naturally in a condition to act in this manner, but it is easy to see that its action is always inadequate, and often dangerous. A government can no more be competent to keep alive and to renew the circulation of opinions and feelings among a great people than to manage all the speculations of productive industry. No sooner does a government attempt to go beyond its political sphere and to enter upon this new track than it exercises, even unintentionally, an insupportable tyranny; for a government can only dictate strict rules, the opinions which it favors are rigidly enforced, and it is never easy to discriminate between its advice and its commands. Worse still will be the case if the government really believes itself interested in preventing all circulation of ideas; it will then stand motionless and oppressed by the heaviness of voluntary torpor. Governments, therefore, should not be the only active powers; associations ought, in democratic nations, to stand in lieu of those powerful private individuals whom the equality of conditions has swept away.

As soon as several of the inhabitants of the United States have taken up an opinion or a feeling which they wish to promote in the world, they look out for mutual assistance; and as soon as they have found one another out, they combine. From that moment they are no longer isolated men, but a power seen from afar, whose actions serve for an example and whose language is listened to. The first time I heard in the United States that a hundred thousand men had bound themselves publicly to abstain from spirituous liquors, it appeared to me more like a joke than a serious engagement, and I did not at once perceive why these temperate citizens could not content themselves with drinking water by their own firesides. I at last understood that these hundred thousand Americans, alarmed by the progress of drunkenness around them, had made up their minds to patronize temperance. They acted in just the same way as a man of high rank who should dress very plainly in order to inspire the humbler orders with a contempt of luxury. It is probable that if these hundred thousand men had lived in France, each of them would singly have memorialized the government to watch the public houses all over the kingdom.

Nothing, in my opinion, is more deserving of our attention than the intellectual and moral associations of America. The political and industrial associations of that country strike us forcibly; but the others elude our observation, or if we discover them, we understand them imperfectly because we have hardly ever seen anything of the kind. It must be acknowledged, however, that they are as necessary to the American people as the former, and perhaps more so. In democratic countries the science of association is the mother of science; the progress of all the rest depends upon the progress it has made.

Among the laws that rule human societies there is one which seems to be more precise and clear than all others. If men are to remain civilized or to become so, the art of associating together must grow and improve in the same ratio in which the equality of conditions is increased.

Chapter VI
Of the Relation Between Public Associations and the Newspapers

---

When men are no longer united among themselves by firm and lasting ties, it is impossible to obtain the co-operation of any great number of them unless you can persuade every man whose help you require that his private interest obliges him voluntarily to unite his exertions to the exertions of all the others. This can be habitually and conveniently effected only by means of a newspaper; nothing but a newspaper can drop the same thought into a thousand minds at the same moment. A newspaper is an adviser that does not require to be sought, but that comes of its own accord and talks to you briefly every day

of the common weal, without distracting you from your private affairs.

Newspapers therefore become more necessary in proportion as men become more equal and individualism more to be feared. To suppose that they only serve to protect freedom would be to diminish their importance: they maintain civilization. I shall not deny that in democratic countries newspapers frequently lead the citizens to launch together into very ill-digested schemes; but if there were no newspapers there would be no common activity. The evil which they produce is therefore much less than that which they cure.

The effect of a newspaper is not only to suggest the same purpose to a great number of persons, but to furnish means for executing in common the designs which they may have singly conceived. The principal citizens who inhabit an aristocratic country discern each other from afar; and if they wish to unite their forces, they move towards each other, drawing a multitude of men after them. In democratic countries, on the contrary, it frequently happens that a great number of men who wish or who want to combine cannot accomplish it because as they are very insignificant and lost amid the crowd, they cannot see and do not know where to find one another. A newspaper then takes up the notion or the feeling that had occurred simultaneously, but singly, to each of them. All are then immediately guided towards this beacon; and these wandering minds, which had long sought each other in darkness, at length meet and unite. The newspaper brought them together, and the newspaper is still necessary to keep them united.

In order that an association among a democratic people should have any power, it must be a numerous body. The persons of whom it is composed are therefore scattered over a wide extent, and each of them is detained in the place of his domicile by the narrowness of his income or by the small unremitting exertions by which he earns it. Means must then be found to converse every day without seeing one another, and to take steps in common without having met. Thus hardly any democratic association can do without newspapers.

Consequently, there is a necessary connection between public associations and newspapers: newspapers make associations, and associations make newspapers; and if it has been correctly advanced that associations will increase in number as the conditions of men become more equal, it is not less certain that the number of newspapers increases in proportion to that of associations. Thus it is in America that we find at the same time the greatest number of associations and of newspapers.

This connection between the number of newspapers and that of associations leads us to the discovery of a further connection between the state of the periodical press and the form of the administration in a country, and shows that the number of newspapers must diminish or increase among a democratic people in proportion as its administration is more or less centralized. For among democratic nations the exercise of local powers cannot be entrusted to the principal members of the community as in aristocracies. Those powers must be either abolished or placed in the hands of very large numbers of men, who then in fact constitute an association permanently established by law for the purpose of administering the affairs of a certain extent of territory; and they require a journal to bring to them every day, in the midst of their own minor concerns, some intelligence of the state of their public weal. The more numerous local powers are, the greater is the number of men in whom they are vested by law; and as this want is hourly felt, the more profusely do newspapers abound.

The extraordinary subdivision of administrative power has much more to do with the enormous number of American newspapers than the great political freedom of the country and the absolute liberty of the press. If all the inhabitants of the Union had the suffrage, but a suffrage which should extend only to the choice of their legislators in Congress, they would require but few newspapers, because they would have to act together only on very important, but very rare, occasions. But within the great national association lesser associations have been established by law in every county, every city, and indeed in every village, for the purposes of local administration. The laws of the country thus compel every American to co-operate every day of his life with some of his fellow citizens for a common purpose, and each one of them requires a news-

paper to inform him what all the others are doing.

I am of the opinion that a democratic people without any national representative assemblies but with a great number of small local powers would have in the end more newspapers than another people governed by a centralized administration and an elective legislature. What best explains to me the enormous circulation of the daily press in the United States is that among the Americans I find the utmost national freedom combined with local freedom of every kind.

There is a prevailing opinion in France and England that the circulation of newspapers would be indefinitely increased by removing the taxes which have been laid upon the press. This is a very exaggerated estimate of the effects of such a reform. Newspapers increase in numbers, not according to their cheapness, but according to the more or less frequent want which a great number of men may feel for intercommunication and combination.

In like manner I should attribute the increasing influence of the daily press to causes more general than those by which it is commonly explained. A newspaper can survive only on the condition of publishing sentiments or principles common to a large number of men. A newspaper, therefore, always represents an association that is composed of its habitual readers. This association may be more or less defined, more or less restricted, more or less numerous; but the fact that the newspaper keeps alive is a proof that at least the germ of such an association exists in the minds of its readers.

This leads me to a last reflection, with which I shall conclude this chapter. The more equal the conditions of men become and the less strong men individually are, the more easily they give way to the current of the multitude and the more difficult it is for them to adhere by themselves to an opinion which the multitude discard. A newspaper represents an association; it may be said to address each of its readers in the name of all the others and to exert its influence over them in proportion to their individual weakness. The power of the newspaper press must therefore increase as the social conditions of men become more equal. . . .

Chapter VIII
How the Americans Combat Individualism by the Principle of Self-Interest Rightly Understood

When the world was managed by a few rich and powerful individuals, these persons loved to entertain a lofty idea of the duties of man. They were fond of professing that it is praiseworthy to forget oneself and that good should be done without hope of reward, as it is by the Deity himself. Such were the standard opinions of that time in morals.

I doubt whether men were more virtuous in aristocratic ages than in others, but they were incessantly talking of the beauties of virtue, and its utility was only studied in secret. But since the imagination takes less lofty flights, and every man's thoughts are centered in himself, moralists are alarmed by this idea of self-sacrifice and they no longer venture to present it to the human mind. They therefore content themselves with inquiring whether the personal advantage of each member of the community does not consist in working for the good of all; and when they have hit upon some point on which private interest and public interest meet and amalgamate, they are eager to bring it into notice. Observations of this kind are gradually multiplied; what was only a single remark becomes a general principle, and it is held as a truth that man serves himself in serving his fellow creatures and that his private interest is to do good.

I have already shown, in several parts of this work, by what means the inhabitants of the United States almost always manage to combine their own advantage with that of their fellow citizens; my present purpose is to point out the general rule that enables them to do so. In the United States hardly anybody talks of the beauty of virtue, but they maintain that virtue is useful and prove it every day. The American moralists do not profess that men ought to sacrifice themselves for their fellow creatures *because* it is noble to make such sacrifices, but they boldly aver that such sacrifices are as necessary to him who imposes them upon himself as to him for whose sake they are made.

They have found out that, in their country and their age, man is brought home to himself by an irresistible force; and, losing all hope of stopping that force, they turn all their thoughts to the direction of it. They therefore do not deny that every man may follow his own interest, but they endeavor to prove that it is the interest of every man to be virtuous. I shall not here enter into the reasons they allege, which would divert me from my subject; suffice it to say that they have convinced their fellow countrymen.

Montaigne said long ago: "Were I not to follow the straight road for its straightness, I should follow it for having found by experience that in the end it is commonly the happiest and most useful track." The doctrine of interest rightly understood is not then new, but among the Americans of our time it finds universal acceptance; it has become popular there; you may trace it at the bottom of all their actions, you will remark it in all they say. It is as often asserted by the poor man as by the rich. In Europe the principle of interest is much grosser than it is in America, but it is also less common and especially it is less avowed; among us, men still constantly feign great abnegation which they no longer feel.

The Americans, on the other hand, are fond of explaining almost all the actions of their lives by the principle of self-interest rightly understood; they show with complacency how an enlightened regard for themselves constantly prompts them to assist one another and inclines them willingly to sacrifice a portion of their time and property to the welfare of the state. In this respect I think they frequently fail to do themselves justice; for in the United States as well as elsewhere people are sometimes seen to give way to those disinterested and spontaneous impulses that are natural to man; but the Americans seldom admit that they yield to emotions of this kind; they are more anxious to do honor to their philosophy than to themselves.

I might here pause without attempting to pass a judgment on what I have described. The extreme difficulty of the subject would be my excuse, but I shall not avail myself of it;

and I had rather that my readers, clearly perceiving my object, would refuse to follow me than that I should leave them in suspense.

The principle of self-interest rightly understood is not a lofty one, but it is clear and sure. It does not aim at mighty objects, but it attains without excessive exertion all those at which it aims. As it lies within the reach of all capacities, everyone can without difficulty learn and retain it. By its admirable conformity to human weaknesses it easily obtains great dominion; nor is that dominion precarious, since the principle checks one personal interest by another, and uses, to direct the passions, the very same instrument that excites them.

The principle of self-interest rightly understood produces no great acts of self-sacrifice, but it suggests daily small acts of self-denial. By itself it cannot suffice to make a man virtuous; but it disciplines a number of persons in habits of regularity, temperance, moderation, foresight, self-command; and if it does not lead men straight to virtue by the will, it gradually draws them in that direction by their habits. If the principle of interest rightly understood were to sway the whole moral world, extraordinary virtues would doubtless be more rare; but I think that gross depravity would then also be less common. The principle of interest rightly understood perhaps prevents men from rising far above the level of mankind, but a great number of other men, who were falling far below it, are caught and restrained by it. Observe some few individuals, they are lowered by it; survey mankind, they are raised.

I am not afraid to say that the principle of self-interest rightly understood appears to me the best suited of all philosophical theories to the wants of the men of our time, and that I regard it as their chief remaining security against themselves. Towards it, therefore, the minds of the moralists of our age should turn;

even should they judge it to be incomplete, it must nevertheless be adopted as necessary.

I do not think, on the whole, that there is more selfishness among us than in America; the only difference is that there it is enlightened, here it is not. Each American knows when to sacrifice some of his private interests to save the rest; we want to save everything, and often we lose it all. Everybody I see about me seems bent on teaching his contemporaries, by precept and example, that what is useful is never wrong. Will nobody undertake to make them understand how what is right may be useful?

No power on earth can prevent the increasing equality of conditions from inclining the human mind to seek out what is useful or from leading every member of the community to be wrapped up in himself. It must therefore be expected that personal interest will become more than ever the principal if not the sole spring of men's actions; but it remains to be seen how each man will understand his personal interest. If the members of a community, as they become more equal, become more ignorant and coarse, it is difficult to foresee to what pitch of stupid excesses their selfishness may lead them; and no one can foretell into what disgrace and wretchedness they would plunge themselves lest they should have to sacrifice something of their own well-being to the prosperity of their fellow creatures.

I do not think that the system of self-interest as it is professed in America is in all its parts self-evident, but it contains a great number of truths so evident that men, if they are only educated, cannot fail to see them. Educate, then, at any rate, for the age of implicit self-sacrifice and instinctive virtues is already flitting far away from us, and the time is fast approaching when freedom, public peace, and social order itself will not be able to exist without education.

2

Individualism and the Socially Embedded Self

The Modern Identity

Charles Taylor

Charles Taylor's criticisms of liberal individualism over the last two decades have helped propel the issue of community into current political discourse. He argues that the institutions of liberal industrial societies have been strained to the breaking point by unameliorated capitalist development. People are caught in meaningless jobs, are humiliated by subordination, and are driven to acquire more and more commodities; they have very little control over their culture's priorities. This leads them, Taylor warns, to feel anomie and alienation, to experience a loss of self. By failing to satisfy its citizens' need to direct and realize their own personal fulfillment, the institutions, practices, and structures of liberal states are in danger of losing their legitimacy; they are undergoing a "legitimation crisis." He believes that much of this problem can be traced to the individualism and pursuit of individual rights embodied in liberalism. An overgrowth of this form of liberty shapes our modern identity. While endorsing both personal freedom and individual self-development, Taylor argues that they should be viewed as part of a system of social attachments in families, neighborhoods, and communities. In this selection Taylor analyzes the legitimation crisis for liberal industrial states in terms of how people see themselves, the modern identity. First he traces the development of the modern identity from its formulation in the seventeenth century to its current phase: its evolution in terms of how we understand human nature, what constitutes rationality, and how citizens can be effective in society. Now our modern identity is sustained by two features of society: our status as citizens with equal rights and our status as producers in the economy. Taylor considers these features of the modern identity a natural basis for a rights-based culture. He then shows the internal contradictions contained within the modern identity, so that, by undermining the family, citizenship, and community, it erodes the very conditions of freedom.

The Malaise of Modernity

Contemporary society suffers from a certain malaise of impending breakdown. This is not to say that we all worry about this all the time. On the contrary, we are often unbearably smug, particularly in this country. But from time to time, when some new dislocation looms or tension rises, the fear surfaces of a collapse in our political or legal order, betokening at best a dissolution of our polity, and perhaps even removing our safeguards against a condition of arbitrary violence and despotism of which each day's international news offers us vivid images from less fortunate parts of the globe.

What else is new? All societies at all times have suffered from such fears. In the case of all previously existing civilizations, not without reason, for they all ultimately did break down. What is special about our case is that we see the breakdown coming about in a particular way. We see it coming through hypertrophy, through our becoming too much what we have been. This kind of fear is perhaps definitive of the modern age: the fear that the very things which define our break with earlier "traditional" societies—our affirmation of freedom, equality, radical new beginnings, control over nature, democratic self-rule—will somehow be

From Charles Taylor, "Alternative Futures: Legitimacy, Identity, and Alienation in Late Twentieth Century Canada," In *Constitutionalism, Citizenship, and Society in Canada*, Alan Cairns and Cynthia Williams, eds. (Toronto: University of Toronto Press, 1985), pp. 183–205. Reprinted by permission of University of Toronto Press in cooperation with the Royal Commission on the Economic Union and Development Prospects for Canada: Vol. 33.

carried beyond feasible limits and will undo us. The hard-boiled optimist will perhaps see this fear as a relic of atavistic beliefs in divine nemesis as an answer to our hubris, but it is hard to conjure it away altogether in this fashion.

Various theories of modernity cast this fear of hypertrophy in different forms. According to some, modern society risks breakdown through the loss of meaning. What defines the modern break is the rejection of the sense, seemingly universal among pre-moderns, that human beings and their societies were set in a broader cosmic order which determined their paradigm purposes and defined what the good was for them. Our modern idea of the free, self-defining subject is of an agent who finds his paradigm purposes in himself and can legitimately have them defined for him by a larger order only if he has consented to this subordination. The social contract theories of the seventeenth century embed this new understanding of the subject.

One form that the fear of breakdown takes is the sense that the rejection of all such encompassing orders must also put an end to all horizons of meaning. The ideally free agent faces total emptiness, in which nothing can be recognized any more as of intrinsic worth. The ultimate viability of all horizons rested on the sense of being embedded in an order. For a time, there can be a purpose of human life in the *liberation* from this, but once the destructive task is completed, no positive purpose remains.

A threat of this kind seems to be preferred in the famous Nietzschean image of the death of God. And another form of this fear surfaces in the work of Max Weber, who was deeply influenced by Nietzsche. Modern political life needs ever new doses of charismatic leadership in order to stave off a kind of emptiness and imprisonment in the routine.

In this version of the fear of hypertrophy, modern freedom undermines itself by destroying meaning. But there are other versions of the hypertrophy fear in which the very excesses of modern freedom and equality lead directly to self-destruction. In one variant of these, the modern exaltation of individual freedom ends up eroding the loyalties and allegiances to the wider community which any

society needs to survive. This danger was first articulated in the period of the Restoration in France and was the starting point for the reflections of Tocqueville, who tried to determine how this consequence of modernity could be avoided, how indeed the Anglo-Saxon societies seemed at least provisionally to have avoided it. In a slightly different variant, influentially articulated by Burke, it is the modern aspiration to negate history and to create social structures from scratch, which has fateful and ineluctable self-destructive consequences.

According to another version again, it is not so much the hypertrophy of individual freedom but the insistence on political equality and mass participation which puts impossible demands on modern societies and leads to their downfall. The theorists of a revised, elite theory of democracy, who wrote in the wake of Schumpeter after World War II, entertained a view of this sort.[1] In the 1970s a new wave of theories arose whose purport was that modern democratic states were becoming "ungovernable," partly because of an overload of subjective demands, but also because the tasks of government in a contemporary technological-industrial society tend to escalate beyond its means.[2]

A rather different variant of the modern fear, which also stems from Weber, is the notion that capitalism, or modern industrial society, while depending on a certain ethic of austere self-discipline (the famous "Protestant ethic"), inevitably undermines this ethic by its very productive success, and fosters an outlook of hedonism and self-gratification which undermine the very success which gave rise to it. Daniel Bell has recently presented a view of this kind in his *Cultural Contradictions of Capitalism.*[3]

One of the most widely canvassed hypertrophy stories in our time is that propounded by the ecological movements—that modern society is in danger of destroying itself through its commitment to headlong growth. I will return to this critique in greater detail below.

The idea that modern society is bent on self-destruction through an excess of its own essential qualities is not necessarily pessimistic. Marxism presents a view of this kind about capitalism in which the outcome is for the best.

The breakdown allows for a higher, socialist organization of society in which the good qualities of modern civilization are at last integrally rescued and made compatible. But toward the end of the twentieth century it is hard for anyone, socialist or conservative, to look on breakdown with this kind of optimism. Almost no one can believe that a solution to the modern dilemma might be achieved just by the collapse of capitalism. And so the hypertrophy fear tends to haunt everyone, left and right.

Framing the fear of breakdown in terms of hypertrophy tends to suggest the idea that the most successful modern societies are those that have an admixture of the traditional, those that somehow avoid going too far down the road to modernity. There is a long tradition of comment on British democracy based on this theme—that the genius (or good luck) of British democracy lies simply in the welding of highly traditional elements, rooted in earlier centuries, with the modern aspirations to freedom, equality and democracy. The formula for survival in this view is modernity only in moderate doses.

Another very common notion which accompanies this is of the view of recent centuries as a march through modernity into the post-modern danger zone of hypertrophy. In this image, some societies are ahead of others and presage the possible future fate of these others. The United States today (in particular certain parts of it, such as California) is cast in this role. This view sees the formula for survival as having modernity occur as slowly as possible.

These two views—moderation or slowness as the key to survival—offer satisfaction and assurance to Canadians. We have a commonly established self-image of being more rooted in the past than American civilization, with part of our society steeped in the British tradition (stemming from the Loyalists who refused the American Revolution), and stemming from a French community cut off from the mother country before the Revolution. The very sense that we are "behind" the Americans can also be a source of reassurance and superiority when we think of the threatened rush of modernity into breakdown. These images provide the basis for a certain Canadian smugness which perhaps compensates for what we sometimes see as a certain unimaginative stodginess in the national character.

But perhaps this way of conceiving the danger in terms of "too much" or "too fast" is wrong. Or perhaps, to give it its due, it is close enough in certain respects to function as a tolerable first approximation, but fails to give real insight into the processes of modernity and the threats it can pose. This I believe to be the case. The straight hypertrophy story is too crude, because it understands the goods which have allegedly overgrown their limits—freedom, equality, technological control—from the outside only. Perhaps a finer-grained understanding of what they mean to moderns will put the issue in a quite different light. It will no longer just be a question of whether we have gained too much of them too fast; rather the difference between survival and breakdown may be seen to turn on our ability to realize these goods in an authentic form. Our agenda will then no longer be defined as limiting or slowing down the progress of modern values, but rather as finding a way to rescue them in their integrity, as against the distortions and perversions that have developed in modern history.

These two conceptions and their corresponding agendas—of limitation and rescue, respectively—belong to outlooks which one might describe as pessimistic and optimistic, and to some extent line up with policies which might be defined as conservative and reform, respectively.[4] I don't want to prejudge which of these approaches is right in this study, although I must admit that I belong to the second or "rescue" party. But I think that the issue cannot be properly joined until one abandons the merely external approach of most limitation theories and tries to define in a closer-grained fashion the understandings of the human good which have grown along with and underpinned the development of modern society.

This is what I intended to do first in this paper. My belief is that it is only against this background that we can fruitfully pose questions about the causes of (and potential cures for) breakdown, both in general and in the particular case of this country. So before considering the alternative futures which may lie before us in Canada, I want to attempt to define some relevant features of the spiritual climate of modern societies. Before embarking on this, I have a few preliminary remarks which will serve to define my question more clearly.

The danger of breakdown in modern societies can be understood in terms of another central Weberian concept, that of "legitimacy." This term is meant to designate the beliefs and attitudes that members have toward the society they make up. The society has legitimacy when members so understand and value it that they are willing to assume the disciplines and burdens which membership entails. Legitimacy declines when this willingness flags or fails. Using the term in this sense, we could say that the danger of breakdown arises for us in the form of a legitimation crisis.

Of course, there are other kinds of possible dangers which arise from hypertrophy of modern development. Certain unintended negative consequences of scale, for instance, can create severe strain, such as the sclerosis which might arise from large-scale bureaucratization, or the notorious pollution effects of certain kinds of economic growth, or the skewed economic priorities which some allege to be the inevitable outcome of uncontrolled free-enterprise capitalism. But severe as they may be, they couldn't by themselves bring about a breakdown in our political or legal order. Or rather they would do so only through their effect on the legitimacy of this order. Bureaucratic sclerosis is a threat to our political order, for instance, just because this order is self-professedly democratic. A process which makes it less and less possible for people to make effective decisions about their lives threatens to bring society into conflict with its central justifying principles, and this cannot but bring about a loss of legitimacy.

The focus on legitimacy is especially relevant for modern societies. This is not because all societies at all times haven't required legitimacy in this sense. But two things mark modern societies. The first is that an important part of the background out of which they arose was that legitimacy became a central philosophical problem. Underlying Weberian "legitimacy" is the seventeenth century use of the term not to describe people's *attitudes,* but as a term of objective evaluation of regimes.

Modern political theory is inaugurated in the seventeenth century around this central question of the conditions of legitimate rule.

The second reason why legitimacy is of particular importance in modern society is that the participation demands of this society are greater in two respects than previous ones.

First of all, modern industrial society is not only the fruit of an unprecedented degree of disciplined, dedicated, innovative productive activity; by an understandable reverse process, it comes to demand this kind of effort of its members. Firms operate in competition with each other, but so do all contemporary industrial societies. Any failure in that constellation of qualities which make for high productivity—which certainly includes a certain attitude toward work and certain patterns of investment—and the less competitive economy is threatened with relative de-industrialization and hence higher unemployment, slower growth, relative impoverishment, and all that goes with this. Contemporary societies cannot afford not to take production seriously—or rather, the costs of not doing so can be very high. Certainly some societies, like contemporary Britain, seem willing to pay these costs up to a point. But presumably even Britons would consider some level of relative impoverishment too high, and at that point would feel the full weight of competitive demand.

The second respect in which modern societies are more demanding is that, at least in the "First World" (Western societies plus Japan), they tend to be liberal democracies. This means that they are based on the principles of political participation, self-voted taxation burdens, the citizen army as the ultimate instrument of defense, and the like. As I argue below, this aspect of modern societies as self-governing is of central significance to the understanding of the good which is constitutive of modern society.

In these two respects, we can see why the modern problem of legitimacy has peculiar significance for modern society. If we define this in terms of the attitudes and beliefs of members which dispose them to assume or refuse to assume the disciplines and burdens of membership in a given society, we can understand how legitimacy increases in importance, the more weighty the disciplines and burdens that must be voluntarily assumed. For the ideal despotism, legitimacy carries a much lesser weight, at least until that point where oppression drives the subjects to revolt. But in contemporary industrial democracies, the everyday operations must call on an ever-present fund of positive identification.

This provides the background to the contemporary concern with legitimacy and to fears of a "legitimation crisis."[5] But how can we get an intellectual grip on this? One very simple way would be to see legitimacy as a function of satisfaction, defined in relatively tough-minded terms, e.g., those of economic living standards (in relation perhaps to expectations). In this view, a regime gains or loses legitimacy as it delivers or fails to deliver the goods. This would make our problem easier; and certainly no one can deny that economic satisfaction is one important factor in the survival and breakdown of political regimes. But it is obvious, too, that it is absurdly one-sided to consider this alone.

If we want to go deeper into the bases for legitimacy and its loss, we have to understand more about the conceptions of the good life, the notions of human fulfillment, of human excellence and its potential distortion, which have grown up along with modern society. We need that finer grained understanding noted above, an understanding of the notions which have framed the identity of our contemporaries.

When I speak of notions of the good which have grown up with modern society, I don't refer to some merely accidental correlation. Rather I mean the understandings of the good which have helped constitute this society and hence are essentially linked to its development.

These conceptions, which I gather together under the loose title of the modern identity, could only have developed within a society with structures, institutions and practices like ours. Take for example our widespread conception of ourselves as autonomous individuals, choosing our own values and modes of life. This self-interpretation, and hence idea, is not one that any one of us could have invented and sustained alone, in the midst, say, of a closed tribal society. It is one that is available for us because we live in a civilization where this conception has been formulated and defined. What is more, it is available to us because we live in a civilization in which this conception underlies many social practices.

For instance, we cast votes as individuals to reach social decisions. That is, we vote in isolation in a polling booth, and not in the sight of all in the ecclesia. We are expected to formulate our individual opinion and outlook, to arrive at them on our own, to take responsibility for them. Pollsters are constantly sampling for our individual opinions. Or again, we have a common practice of negotiation in which individuals or parties define their goals quite independently of the rest of society and then try to reach some agreed ground. Many of the ground rules that hold our institutions together are based on such contracts. We even have been induced to believe at various times that the most basic and ultimate framework, the political, was or ought to be established by contract. Or again, in our society the family is based on the freely chosen companionate marriage; you choose a partner according to your own affinities.

All these practices and institutions induce us to understand ourselves as individuals; more, they make it inevitable that we do so. I have *my* opinions, *my* values, *my* outlook, *my* affinities. We have developed in this direction to a degree unprecedented in history; some of our self-attributions would be shocking or even incomprehensible to our ancestors. What would a medieval or any but a few sophists among the ancients make of "my values"? The very word "value" belongs to our "subjectivist" civilization. None of us except a tiny number gifted with imaginative genius could have stepped out of that medieval or ancient outlook in our contemporary one. If what was incomprehensible to them seems self-evident to us, it is because we live in a civilization in which practices like the above are dominant.

The relation between practices and conceptions can be put in this way: the notion of myself as an individual is constitutive of these practices, is presupposed in them. A social practice is a rule or norm-governed activity. It is defined by certain norms of failure and success, of honesty and turpitude, of excellence or mediocrity, etc. A certain conception of the human person is presupposed in a practice if it is essential to understanding the norms which define it. But the norms defining modern citizen voting, or the companionate marriage, presuppose the autonomous individual. It is an *infringement* if someone else can oversee my vote, because I must be free of any intimidation and vote according to *my own* conscience. I am expected to marry someone *I* love; caving in to my extended family or to social expectation is a falling off, an acquiescence in the second best.

This relation of presupposition is directly relevant to legitimacy. Institutions are defined by certain norms and constituted by certain normative conceptions of man. It is these conceptions that they sustain. But the relationship of support also works the other way. It is these normative conceptions which give the institutions their legitimacy. Should people cease to believe in them the institutions would infallibly decay; they could no longer command the allegiance of those who participate in them. Institutions demand discipline, frequently sacrifice, always at least the homage of taking their norms seriously. When they lose legitimacy, they lose these.

The question for the "internal" perspective is this: on a proper understanding of the modern identity—the set of conceptions of man which has grown with modern society, constitutive of its institutions and practices—has the development of these structures, institutions and practices tended to their own undermining, either by shaking men's faith in their constitutive norms, or by making these practices and institutions appear as perversions of these norms? I think that in fact something of this kind has been and is now taking place, and that is why an exploration of the modern identity can help us to understand our contemporary legitimation crisis, and perhaps to arbitrate between the optimistic and pessimistic, the "rescue" and "limitation" perspectives adumbrated above.

Strains of the Modern Identity

I want to turn now to that family of conceptions of human beings, of freedom, and of human nature which emerge roughly in the

seventeenth century and which have been woven into our developing commercial and later industrial capitalist society. It is these concepts that I refer to collectively as the "modern identity." Two phases in its development continue to exert a strong influence in our time.

One of the key notions of the first phase was the new conceptions of freedom which emerged in the seventeenth century. This period saw a progressive rejection of world views in which humans were seen as forming part of some cosmic order, where their nature was to be understood by their relation to that order. Both the new conceptions of science and the new notion of autonomy pointed to a view of humans as beings who discover their purposes in themselves. "Nature" becomes internalized in the modern period. In this view, the free subject becomes someone who follows an internal purpose and who owes no a priori allegiance to a pre-existing order but gives it only to structures that were created by his/her own consent. Even the ancient conceptions of the freedom of the citizen, which were essentially defined as a certain relation to a whole—the polis or republic—go into eclipse, and we find atomist conceptions of freedom developing where persons are seen to enjoy "natural liberty" in a state of nature.

Along with this notion of freedom comes a new conception of what human nature demands. Traditional moral views grounded on nature, which descend from the ancients, offer what we might call a two-tiered view of the good life. This consists primarily in some higher activity distinct from the fulfillment of ordinary needs involved with the production and reproduction of life. Meeting these ordinary needs is of course unavoidable and good but is regarded simply as infrastructural to a distinct activity that gave life its higher significance. In one version this was defined as contemplation; in another influential version, the life of the citizen. In either version, lives which lacked the favoured activity and were entirely absorbed in meeting life needs were regarded as truncated and deprived. It followed that outside of very exceptional social contexts, the fullness of human life was only for the few.

To some extent Christianity worked against these aristocratic conceptions, but the Christian church too developed a notion of an exceptional vocation higher than that of the ordinary person, which was associated with celibacy. One of the central tenets of the Reformation was the rejection of this notion of the special vocation and the preaching of a vision of ordinary life as hallowed. A secularized version of this arises in the seventeenth century. The demands of nature, of the new internalized nature, just are the ordinary needs of life. There is no higher stratum of activity. Rather, what defines proper human activity is a certain manner of going about meeting these needs—in a sober, disciplined, clairvoyant, and rational way. This last term, "rationality," could be taken to sum up the properly human way of living. But it now, of course, changes its sense. It is defined less and less in terms of a vision of the true order of things and more and more in terms of instrumental reason. The rational pursuit of the needs of the life crucially includes seeking them in an effective manner.

The ethic which rejects a class distinction in purposes and activities is also anti-aristocratic in social thrust. The norm of rational pursuit of ordinary life needs is, in a sense, the bourgeois ethic. An example of the remarkable penetration of this ethos into our whole civilization is the development of the modern notion of the family. From the seventeenth century on, in the higher classes of Anglo-Saxon societies and spreading outward and downward from these, we find a new outlook in which the companionate marriage and the life of the nuclear family come more and more to be seen as one of the central fulfillments of human life. This has become so much a part of our contemporary world that we find it hard to imagine a time when it was not so. But it is relatively recent in human history. The modern need for privacy is part of this same development, as is the growing emphasis on sentiment. One of the ways of understanding modern consumer society is as an attempt to make available for the vast majority the conditions of self-enclosed family life as this ideal has developed in the past three centuries.[6] A second facet of this outlook has been the extraordinary development of forms of mass discipline—the regimenting of gesture and action to produce maximum effect—which begins in the eighteenth century in armies, schools, prisons, factories, and so on. This has been interestingly traced by Michel Faucault in his *Surveiller et Punir*.[7]

In connection with this last phenomenon, we can see a third leading notion developing in this period which I call "efficacy." The free individual meeting the demands of nature in the modern sense must aspire to a higher degree of control over himself and over nature. Exercising the control that enables one to effect one's purposes more fully and to a higher degree is a mark of rationality—i.e., one is pursuing one's life needs in a properly human way.

The modern identity can be sketchily characterized, I believe, in terms of these three notions—liberty, nature, and efficacy. They characterize what I call phase one. But there is another version of this identity which emerges in the late eighteenth century, partly in reaction to phase one. It is what we see in various forms in Rousseau, in Romanticism, and to some degree also in certain religious movements—arguably, for instance, in Methodism. Its secular variant can perhaps be identified as an alternative reading of the modern notion of life according to nature. In phase one, the rejection of aristocratic ethics takes place in favour of an ideal of the pursuit of ordinary purposes under rational control. The purposes themselves are not endowed with special significance. What is quintessentially human is the rational control. But for the new countertradition, the rejection of supposed higher activities means rather that our ordinary purposes are endowed with higher significance. To fulfill the true impulse of nature in us is not just to meet a biological need but also to satisfy a higher aspiration. It is, at the same time, a moral fulfillment. From Rousseau on, the true "voice of nature" is at the same time both the impulse of biological need and an aspiration to what is experienced as moral self-realization.

From this perspective the modern notion of life according to nature involves a *fusion* of the biological and the moral instead of their hierarchical ordering as with traditional moralities, or their setting in a relation of rational control as in the first form of the modern identity. This has been a tremendously influential idea in the last two centuries of modern culture, well beyond the epoch of Rousseau or the Romantics. Indeed, I would argue that it is central to the Marxist aspiration to a condition in which individuals would be creative (in the artistic sense) in their productive life. Closing the gap between creativity and production is another variant of this fused perspective.

This view has been the basis for many of the criticisms of modern industrial society, even as the first phase has provided much of the justification for it. For the fused perspective is naturally highly critical of the primacy accorded to instrumental reason which must presuppose that ends were given independently of reason and which tends to make us look at nature merely as a set of obstacles or instruments for our purposes. But however critical of the first phase, this second phase is recognizably a variant of the modern identity. It grows unquestionably out of the modern notion of the internalization of nature, and it develops its own conceptions of freedom as the following of autonomously generated purposes. However much they come in conflict, these two variants cannot wholly repudiate each other, and this fact is reflected in the complexity of their relations in modern culture.

This conception of life according to nature, in its two versions, has grown up with modern society. It has been embedded in the structures, practices, and institutions of this society—in our relations of production; in our application of technology to production on a massive scale; in our sexual relations and family forms; in our political institutions and practices. Some of these institutions and practices have been of crucial importance in sustaining this modern identity. This has generally been lost sight of because the modern identity itself (in phase one) has stressed individual autonomy to the point where the necessity of social mediation has been lost. The modern identity has too easily bred myths of social contract—and is still doing so today in a transposed way.[8]

But we can single out several features of modern society which have played a vital part in developing and sustaining our sense of ourselves as free agents. The first is equality. Clearly, the modern identity is incompatible with the status of serf or slave. However, the requirement is stronger than this. The identity of the free subject establishes a strong presumption in favour of equality. In contrast, hierarchical societies are justified on the old conception of a cosmic logos. Different groups are seen as expressing complementary principles. This has been the traditional justification of hierarchy everywhere—different classes and functions correspond to different links in the chain of being. Each is necessary for the other and for the whole, and the place of each relative to the others is thus natural, right, and according to the order of things. Once this view is swept aside, the basic justification of hierarchy disappears. All self-determining subjects are alike in this crucial respect. There is no further valid ground for hierarchy as an unquestionable, unchanging order of precedence.

Equality is thus one dimension of the free subject's relation to society. Another very obtrusive dimension is that one must be the subject of rights. As a free subject, one is owed respect for one's rights and has certain guaranteed freedoms. One must be able to choose and act, within limits, free from the arbitrary interference of others. The modern subject is an equal bearer of rights. This status is part of what sustains his identity.

Perhaps these two conditions express the basic minimum status of a modern subject in society without which identity must either founder or the predicament is experienced as intolerable. But there have been other important features of this status which are worth mentioning. One of the most important faculties of the modern subject is the ability to effect one's purposes. This is what I have called "efficacy." Subjects without efficacy, unable to alter the world around them to their ends, would either be incapable of sustaining a modern identity or would be deeply humiliated in their identity. To a considerable degree, each of us can have a sense of efficacy in our own individual action—getting the means to live, providing for the family, acquiring goods, going about our business, etc. The very fact that we command so much private space is important for our sense of efficacy. For example, the ability a car gives us to move around on our own notoriously gives many people the sense of power, of efficacy, of being able to do things and to get to places on their own, and also has affinities with a sense of sexual potency. But important as private efficacy is, it is not possible to make it the whole, to give no thought at all to one's efficacy as a member of society, affecting its direction or having a part in the global efficacy that society possesses relative to nature.

Thus, along with the sense of having equal rights, there are two other important features of our status in society which have played a role in sustaining the modern identity. The first is our status as citizens, in terms of which we collectively determine the course of social events. The modern West has taken up this ancient tradition—that only citizens are full persons capable of acting and making a name for themselves in human memory—and made this an integral part of our sense of efficacy. The fact that we govern ourselves is an important part of our dignity as free subjects.

The second dimension is that of production. As producers, in the broadest sense, we belong to a whole interconnected society of labour and technology which has immense efficacy in transforming nature, and produces more astonishing wonders every day. Insofar as we belong to this society, work in it, take part in it, contribute to it, we have a share in this efficacy. We can think of it as partly ours, as a confirmation of ourselves. This is an important part of our sense of what we are in an advanced industrial society. It is also an important source of malaise and of a creeping sense of unavoidable inferiority among Third World elites.

The modern subject, therefore, is far from being an independent, atomic agent. One may be so relative to the local community, but one cannot be so relative to the whole society. On the contrary, an individual is sustained, on one hand, by the culture which elaborates and maintains the vocabulary of his or her self-understanding and, on the other, by the society in which one has a status commensurate with free subjectivity—a status in which we have isolated four dimensions of the equal bearer of rights who is producer and citizen. All of this underpins one's identity as a free individual who could not long survive a state of nature.

The set of practices by which the society defines my status as an equal bearer of rights, an economic agent, and a citizen—practices such as the operation of the legal system, the political system of voting and elections, the practices of negotiation and collective bargaining—all have embedded in them a conception of the agent and his/her relation to society which reflects the modern identity and its related visions of the good. The growth of this identity can help to explain why these practices have developed in the direction they have—why, for instance, voting and collective adversary negotiation take a bigger and bigger place in our societies. But it may also help to explain why we experience a growing malaise today.

It is perhaps not hard to see how our contemporary society satisfies the modern identity. The first phase of the modern identity stressed three things: autonomy, fulfillment of our nature, and efficacy, the last being a confirmation of our control, our productive power, and hence our freedom from things. Modern consumer society satisfies these three demands, or appears to. It affords privacy, treats us as autonomous beings who are efficacious as producers and citizens, and seems aimed toward providing us a sense of fulfillment which we determine along with those with whom we have knit ties of intimacy. It also appears to satisfy some of the variants of natural fulfillment of the second version—particularly the Romantic-expressive ones—since much of our private fulfillment in our relationships and in our artistic and expressive life is drawn from expressive models. In a sense we are Romantics in our private existence—our love lives are drawn by a notion of Romantic mutual discovery. We look for fulfillments in our hobbies and in our recreation, while the economic, legal, and political structures in which we coexist are largely justified instrumentally.

But then this compromise between phases one and two which at times seems so stable at other times seems racked with tension. Now is one of those times. We can also understand some of the background for this. We have seen how phase two of our ideal of natural fulfillment can be turned into a powerful critique of the first version. So we immediately understand the strictures which are flung at our political, economic, and legal structures—that they are merely instrumental, that they deny community, that they are exploitative of humans and nature, and so on. In this we can see how closely interwoven both the affirmative and critical stances are to our contemporary society, how much they are from the same roots and draw on the same sources. But perhaps we can also hope to gain some insight into the dialectic between the two, how the balance tips now one way, now another.

What the efficacious industrial consumer society has going for it is, presumably, that it delivers the goods. But if we examine this society in the light of the modern identity, we can see that this achievement is not just a matter of meeting quantitative targets. Rather we see that in phase one efficacy is valued as the fruit and sign of rational control. Increasing production originally became a value in our civilization, against all the temptations to sloth and all the blandishments of traditional ethics, because in producing we came to see ourselves as not just meeting our needs but also as realizing our status as autonomous, rational agents. Continued accumulation bespoke a consistent, disciplined maintenance of the instrumental stance to things; it was a realization of our spiritual dimension. Far from being an obsession with things or an entrapment in them, as it might be stigmatized in a Platonic conception, it is an affirmation of our autonomy in that our purposes are not imposed on us by the supposed order of things. The instrumental stance toward nature is meant to be a spiritual declaration of independence from it.

From this we can understand the potential vulnerability of this kind of society and way of life. The ways and forms of its accumulation have to go on appearing as affirmations of freedom and efficacy. Should they be seen as degenerating into mere self-indulgence, then the society undergoes a crisis of confidence. This is a moral crisis but one which is also inescapably a political crisis. For what is impugned is the definition of the good actually embedded in our practices. Should we come to repudiate this, our allegiance to these practices and therefore our society itself are threatened. Thus it follows that our society has always

been vulnerable to a certain moral critique. It is in trouble if it stands self-convicted, in the eyes of its members, of pure materialism—that is, of aiming purely at material enrichment. This may not be evident because of certain commonplaces of sociological comment such as that which alleges we are more hedonistic in outlook than our ancestors.[9] There are some ways in which this is true, but it does not make any less important the underlying sense that our dignity consists in our capacity to dominate, and not to be dominated by, things. For this is rooted in the modern identity. If more people are willing to accept a "permissive" society today, it is because they see that such self-indulgence can be combined with the free self-direction whereby we determine our own purpose and fulfillment. In this they lean partly on certain post-Romantic notions of emotional fulfillment. Those who find this combination hard to accept are precisely those who are most worried and rendered most anxious by the permissive society. Even the revolutionaries who call for a total rejection of the work discipline of the "Protestant ethic" can do so because of a conception of freedom which is allegedly the fruit of such total abandonment. That this is not realistic should not blind us to the kind of hope it is—one still very much in line with modern identity.

Indeed, one could argue that the more a society is founded on the modern ideal of life according to nature in its first version, the more it should be vulnerable to doubts about its moral standing and the more these doubts will be unsettling. It is not surprising to find that this kind of worry is a very old one in the United States. Fred Somkin[10] has shown how the prosperity of the republic in the early nineteenth century raised soul searchings. On the one hand, it was just what one might expect—a proof of efficacy and, hence, of the spiritual excellence of America. On the other hand, it seemed to threaten vice, self-indulgence, a forgetfulness of republican virtue, and the demands of the spirit. As Somkin showed, it was essential for many Americans of the time to prove that prosperity was indeed a fruit of the spirit. The alternative was too unsettling to contemplate.

My claim is that we have not left behind the era when we could be shaken by this kind of doubt. It is not a relic of an earlier "puritan" era. In a transposed way, many of the features of the puritan era have been recreated in our contemporary variant of the modern identity, but only now the relevance of this has spread well beyond the United States and beyond the Anglo-Saxon world. Many societies have been made over so that their dominant practices, not only of economic and public life but also family life, reflect the modern identity. With this in mind, let us look at the features of contemporary society which tend to undermine our confidence in it as moderns.

The first of these is alienation at work. For a great many people, work is dull, monotonous, without meaning, and "soul-destroying," to use Schumacher's word.[11] Connected with this is the fact that, in work relations most individuals are far from the equal, autonomous subjects that they are at home or feel themselves to be as consumers. For the most part they stand very much as subordinates in command relations and have very little say about how they will work or in what conditions.

We enter here onto Marx's terrain. It is impossible to make a sensible critique of consumer society without invoking Marx. But there is one very important amendment which I want to make at the outset. I want to see the present formula of consumer society, with its mix of fulfillment and distortion, as a kind of historic compromise in which most of us have acquiesced. Orthodox Marxists, however, are committed to seeing it as an alienating (provided they want to use this word) formula imposed on the working masses by the ruling class through a mixture of force, mendacious persuasion, propaganda, control of information, divisive tactics, and so on. But this seems to me very wrong. The working class of early industrial society was certainly pitched into the proletarian role against its will, with terrible conditions of sweated labour and blighted townscape, and was held in place by force where it tried to resist. But in the one hundred fifty years since then, our societies have become mass democracies. Work conditions under capitalism have been profoundly modified, workers receive much greater remuneration; and have substantial control over conditions through trade unions and political power. It is difficult to argue that what re-

mains unmodified in capitalism remains so because of force and fraud when so much else has been changed, often against the better resistance of industrialists. Rather the compromise of affluent society must be seen to represent a tacit acquiescence—for the present anyway—in subordinate relations of labour on the part of the mass of workers. It consists in accepting alienated labour in return for consumer affluence. This compromise can seem to make sense in the lives of many people in part because this alienation can be represented as the necessary condition of affluence—by not demanding citizenship in the workplace the worker allows the provident engine of industry to run untrammeled and generate ever-growing prosperity. But the compromise can also be appealing because alienation is the obverse of noninvolvement, the condition of complete mobility. To become a citizen at work would require some commitment to the enterprise and the devotion of some of the worker's life energies to this community and its plans and decisions. Otherwise the participation becomes a mere sham or the manipulated instrument of active minorities. But this devotion is a price that the aspiring consumer-citizen may be unwilling to pay—a limitation on the self-contained life.

The development of the affluent society, in which the majority can preside over a self-contained life in adequate private space, has thus gone along with a tacit reluctance to challenge the regime of alienated, subordinate labour. This is the first distortion. The fact that it is connived in by the majority, rather than brutally imposed on them, does not make it any more healthy.

A second compromise that must be accepted in contemporary society is lack of control over priorities. The sense of the common interest that underlies this compromise is that the machine must run on. But the machine that we find ourselves with in our societies is a capitalist one—that is, it consists mainly of enterprises whose institutional goals are to grow through the accumulation and re-investment of profit. They have become immensely effective in some ways in the application of technology to this end. But they cannot easily tolerate interference which attempts to set priorities for the production process. A modern capitalist economy can take, indeed requires, much intervention to keep it going—fiscal and monetary controls, subsidies of all sorts. But basic to its operation is the principle that firms must be masters of their own investment, able to invest where they can accumulate the greatest profits, foster the greatest over-all growth, maintain market share most effectively, or some such objective. The condition of the machine running effectively is that no one tries to control its priorities too closely. Thus we get the culture that moral critics object to—the fixation on brute quantitative growth unalloyed by judgments of priority. The justification for this is an image of the good life in which the acquisition of more and more consumer goods—what the system is good at producing—is seen as a central purpose of life.

Once again, most of us acquiesced in this historic compromise for similar mixed reasons as we did to alienated labour. On the one hand the non-imposition of priorities seemed to be the condition of the machine's running continuously; on the other, the resultant mode of life satisfied us as modern subjects in certain ways. First, the disinvolvement, our collective silence on priorities, seemed the condition of our freedom severally to "hang loose," to build our own private spaces, and live our own self-contained lives. Secondly, the definition of the good life as continuing escalation in living standards has an inescapable appeal to unregenerated persons, which we all are. This Plato well knew. Appetite tends to run on to infinity unless controlled by reason. The consumer society appeals to the lowest in us. But this is only a half-truth. It is also the case that the consumer society comes to us dressed up in a form that meshes with some of the aspirations of the modern subject. Thus we are invited as consumers to acquire and furnish a private space as the condition of an autonomous, self-contained, unmediated existence. We need this space so that we and our family can grow and be close to nature (a garden, a house in the country). Much advertising plays on this aspiration to private space—the ads always show happy families filling those interiors, driving away in those cars, surrounding those barbecues, etc. Of course, what is not justified is the continued increase. Why

should the mobile private space we travel in become ever more rapid and high-powered? Why must labour-saving mechanization continue without stop, even up to electric toothbrushes and similar absurdities? This could never be justified intellectually, but somehow the implication is that more and more powerful accoutrements mean more of the fulfillment that they are meant to make possible. The commodities become "fetishized"—in a non-Marxist sense, endowed magically with the properties of the life they subserve, as though a faster car might actually make my family life more intense and harmonious.

There is a third reason why this compromise appeals to us that also aids in the fetishization of commodities. The runaway machine, doing prodigies of technological mastery of nature, satisfies our sense of collective efficacy. Members of this society can feel that participative efficacy as producers that I spoke of above. At the same time personal efficacy is a theme often played on fetishized commodities. That is what is appealing about high-powered cars and powerful engines generally. This in turn taps feelings of machismo and sexual potency. Advertisers are aware of this. Thus we acquiesce in the consumer goods standard of welfare. And we accept the suspension of our sense of priorities which then allows us to see as normal some truly absurd inversions, such as supersonic flight, until we break the thrall and look afresh and astonished at what we are doing.

These features of industrial society—the meaninglessness and subordination of work; the mindless lack of control of priorities; above all the fetishization of commodities—all represent a challenge to our image of ourselves as realized moderns determining our purposes out of ourselves, dominating and not being dominated by things. To the extent that we let these negative features impinge on our self-understanding, we cannot but feel a fading confidence, an unease, a suspicion that the continued sense of efficacy by which we sustain our self-image within the modern identity is a sham. If we see ourselves as the playthings of mindless impersonal forces, or worse, as the victims of a fascination with mere things (and this in the very practices which are supposed to sustain our identity and our conception of good), then we cannot but lose confidence in these practices. We are threatened with a kind of anomie in which we cease to believe in the norms governing our social life but have no alternative except to live by them. There is a crisis of allegiance to our society.

I believe this is part of what underlies our present malaise. In order to understand why it arises now, we have to see why these features have begun to press themselves on us in recent years. Our consumer society is in several ways the victim of its own success—this is the relative truth in the hypertrophy story—and these ways compound to put it in crisis.

First, the very prosperity of this society cannot but produce doubts and hesitations around its fetishization of commodities. When the society was still struggling to make decent housing and basic consumer durables widely available, the connection of all this effort and production with the goal of securing these goods for all was clear enough. But now that most have them, efforts to achieve refinements—the introduction of higher power, more speed, new models, frills, etc.—begin to look more and more disproportionate. It is harder to believe in all this as a serious social purpose.

Of course, a substantial minority has not yet entered the affluent society. Production for them would make sense. But the continuation of the consumer boom does not seem to be very effective in helping these "pockets of poverty." Wealth does not "trickle down" very adequately. This is partly because the continued boom goes with an upping of the ante—a whole range of new products which one has to get to be well-equipped at home, in the car, etc. Much of each year's growth is preempted by the already affluent who expect a rise in their standard of living. It is very hard to prise some off to redistribute to the poor. When growth slows down or stops, as we have seen in recent years, the resistance to redistribution increases. We have only to think of the negative attitude of nearly all Western electorates to government spending, and in particular of the widespread attack on the welfare state. Canada is in fact more moderate in this regard than some other Western democracies, such as Britain and the United States, but resistance to

the politics of redistribution has also had its impact here.

At the same time, the replacement of lower by higher technology can even make things worse for poorer people. It ups the cost of being poor, so to speak. One way is by making certain consumer durables essential. For example, if a society moves from the bicycle to the automobile, then cities are laid out accordingly and the proximity of housing to jobs is planned on the assumption that people have cars, so it becomes necessary to have a car in order to hold a job, at least a good job, and to get around safely on city streets. Another way is by raising the cost of housing. House prices and rents are far higher in Toronto than in less developed communities such as Sydney, Nova Scotia. Growth can thus make the lot of poor people worse.

The increasingly evident fetishistic character of the consumer standard and its steady rise do not seem able to alleviate suffering where it counts or to improve what is crying out for improvement. All of this contributes to a loss of faith in the consumer standard, in the value of an indefinite increase in consumer goods and services, and in indiscriminate growth. This may affect older people less, but it visibly emerges in skepticism, questioning, and rejection by younger people.

Among the things which may be cast into doubt in this crisis is the value of family life itself. This is particularly critical, because the version of the modern identity predominant in our society is one which aims toward a mobile subject who loosens the ties of larger communities and finds himself on his own in the nuclear family. But this gives a tremendously heightened significance to the nuclear family, which is now the main locus of strong, lasting, defining relations, and it has given family life and the emotions of family love a uniquely important place in the modern conception of natural fulfillment, beginning in the eighteenth century.

For this to be challenged is thus critical for the identity which has been dominant in our society. But it is under threat not only because it is associated with a (to some) discredited consumer way of life. It is also threatened by the very scope of the development of the modern identity. In effect, if the business of life is to find my authentic fulfillment as an individual, and my associations should be relativized to this end, in principle there seems to be no reason why this relativization should stop at the boundary of the family. If my development or even my discovery of self should be incompatible with a long-standing association, then it will come to be felt as a prison rather than a locus of identity. This places marriage under great strain, further intensified because the same aspiration to self-development and self-fulfillment leads women today to challenge the distribution of roles and emotional give-and-take of the traditional family.

Population concentration and mobility are other developments that are beginning to have social consequences which produce tension in our society. Beyond a certain threshold, the concentration of people in large cities begins to have negative consequences. Unless cities are well-designed with multiple centres, the ordinary business of daily life becomes more time-consuming and stressful, and relations with other people become more full of tension. In addition, large cities cost more per capita to run. As Hugh Stretton puts it, "They generate more travel, congestion and local pollution per head. They force wasteful rates of demolition and rebuilding on their inner parts. Intense competition for central and accessible locations makes it harder to solve problems of density, shares of space and—above all—land prices."[12] So concentration begins to raise the overhead costs of social existence.

Concentration and mobility do this in other ways as well. The bleeding of local communities for the megalopolis forces a write-off of the excess, unused stock of housing and public capital in declining communities. The decline of the extended family means that society must pick up the pieces for the old, the abandoned, the chronically sick, and so on. In all these ways, concentrated and mobile life virtually forces an expansion of the public sector. The prevailing doctrines about the efficiency of concentration and giant organizations ensure that the state will compound the error by over-bureaucratizing the public sector.

But the enlarged public sector, both as cost and as bureaucracy, creates great malaise. As a cost, it forces higher taxes. But these are resisted by citizens, as we have come more and

more to see ourselves as independent individuals. The link between high mobility—that is, the pattern of "hanging loose" from all partial communities—and the higher overheads of society is generally quite invisible to us. Ironically, it is just this pattern of hanging loose that makes us less capable of seeing the social costs of our way of life, and makes us look on the public sector as a barely necessary evil. So as we increase the need for public sector activity, we decrease our own readiness to assume the burden. This thoroughly irrational state of affairs leads to all kinds of tensions and eruptions of which the international surge of an aggressive "New Right"—advocating the impossible dream of a return to the negative state—is the most important consequence politically. What further justifies the revolt is the over-bureaucratization of the public sector. This not only makes it unnecessarily costly, but also less responsive to the public. Consequently, the process whereby we meet our needs through public mechanisms becomes even less transparent and this lack of transparency increases the alienation.

What is even worse is that the movement toward concentration and the break-up of partial communities is not entirely voluntary. Once the process goes a certain way, it acquires an élan which is sometimes hard to resist. One may want to stay in a smaller farming community, but may find it impossible to function there as the services move out and concentrate in larger centres, in response to earlier movements as well as general concentration. So more and more people follow the trend, and more services move—schools, suppliers, outlets, etc. And then more people move, and so on.

Thus three "successes," or hypertrophies, of the consumer society are bringing about increasing malaise: the very success of the growth of consumption tends to discredit the importance attached to material gains; the increasing stress on the goal of self-fulfillment tends to fragment the family, which was previously its privileged locus; and the increased concentration and mobility of our society alienates us from government. These strains also undermine that sense of our status within the larger society which is supportive of our identity. Unresponsive bureaucracies make us less sanguine, or frankly cynical, about citizenship; sometimes we even fear for our rights. The discredit of what I have termed the consumer standard—pursuing an indefinite increase in consumer goods and services—makes us feel less positive about the efficacy of the whole society in which we have a part as labourers.

But the hypertrophy of this sense of collective efficacy is itself a fourth cause of malaise. As our awareness of belonging to an organized, technological, productive society grew, so did the confidence that we could solve any problem, given the will and the concentration of resources. This sense of bullish confidence probably reached its high point in the postwar period during the Kennedy era in the United States, when intelligence, good will, and organizing science were set to tackle the age-old problems of poverty, inequality, and racial alienation through programs of the New Frontier. The sense of new creation was heightened by the symbolism of an attractive young man at the head of the enterprise. Since then, however, things have gone sour. We are made more and more aware that some problems, including the most grievous social ones like intractable poverty and racial division, resist even immense resources. They are more than problems; they are human dilemmas. The sense of our efficacy has taken a grievous blow.

In sum, by this combined effect we have been led partly to lose confidence in our definitions of the good life, partly to feel alienated from and even cynical about our governmental institutions, partly to feel uncertain and tense about our social relations and even about our family life, partly to feel unsupported by the larger society in our identity as modern subjects.

All of this is likely to make for strains, tensions, and mutual aggressiveness. As it happens, a bout of social conflict was probably coming our way after the halcyon decades of steady consumer growth in the earlier postwar period. This was partly because of the growth of the public sector and its consequent burden on the productive sector and on taxpayers. But it is also because we live in a society which has become more equal and "classless" in style and spirit, in which workers and the less well-off have acquired greater bargaining muscle through trade unions, in which the general standard of education has risen, and in which there is a prevailing belief that government can do anything, so that age-old poverty, or underdevelopment, or inequality, formerly seen as in the order of things, is now removable. Such a society will sooner or later make demands on government and the economy which by their very nature and number will be incompatible.

To face this, a society needs an even higher degree of cohesion, self-confidence, and mechanisms of effective self-management. Instead we confront this period with lower confidence, more inner tensions, and greater alienation from our institutions than before. The result has been a scramble for income and advantage in which powerful forces struggle to compete and maintain their position, but at the expense of the unorganized through inflation. We are being forced to return to more orderly consensus through the disastrous experience of inflation. But it is a slow and reluctant business and leaves many burning resentments and senses of grievance without vent, because we are being forced to decide about things that had previously been allowed to happen without planning, such as the distribution of income. We are being forced to take a greater hand in the collective direction of our economy. But agreement on this, hard enough at any time, is possible only with some sense of purpose. We would have found it much easier to agree on a wages policy in the 1950s. That, however, is exactly why we did not need one then. Because of our uncertain purpose and our faltering confidence in the overriding value of the society we are evolving through our economic efforts, the disciplines imposed by any incomes policy will often be felt as an imposition. And the angry reaction of one group, tearing through the limits, will stimulate others to do the same. High wage claims in one sector prompt similar claims in others. Taxpayers' revolts increase the bitterness of the poor. Inflation is the visible sign of our disarray and is itself an object of anxiety. It compounds our self-doubt.

To sum up the argument, the modern identity and the accompanying moral visions give the background to both the affirmative and critical stances to our society. They show them to be closely related. But they also help us understand the balance between the two. In fact the affirmative view does not just praise endless accumulation. It must also be seen as an affirmation of efficacy, of productive power, which in turn is a sign of autonomy and of our domination over things. Thus the affirmative view is vulnerable to whatever presses on us an understanding of the extent to which we are not in fact autonomous, are not dominating, but are enslaved to things. The word "fetish" is redolent of this. It connects with the earlier rejection of idolatry and the modern's sense of superiority over the primitive, of having won freedom from an obsession in things, from an immersion in them, and from a shaping of his/her life on their model.

Now in fact we live in a society whose practices embody a certain notion of identity and the human good. This notion must be ours or we cannot give it our allegiance; we are alienated from it. At the same time we rely to a great extent on these practices to maintain our sense of identity. If these practices which supposedly embody the modern identity can be shown to lead in fact to a failure to achieve it, as noted in the paragraph above, then our allegiance to them is shaken. Perhaps our faith in the conception of the modern identity is shaken as well. We turn to other models.

In the balance between affirmative and negative stances to our society, the affirmative relies largely on the first version of life according to nature, as this has become embedded in the political and economic, largely market-atomistic practices of our society. If we become convinced that we are dominated by mindless forces or enslaved to commodities which we fetishize, then we will withdraw allegiance from these practices and obviously from the first version, or at least this way of expressing the first version institutionally.

Does all this mean that the advanced, industrial-technological, capitalist, liberal society is on a course to self-destruction? Is some version of the hypertrophy story right after all?

Something like this might do as a first approximation. But if the above analysis is at all valid, this could turn out to be a dangerous oversimplification. The modern identity of the citizen producer who is a free and equal bearer of rights doesn't simply destroy itself when it is pushed beyond a certain point. A more accurate way of putting it would be to say that some sides of this identity threaten through hypertrophy to frustrate or undermine others, and hence endanger the whole. Part of the foregoing could be sketchily summarized by saying that our pursuit of efficacy as producers has come to threaten our efficacy as citizens. Another part could be explained by saying that freedom as mobility has begun to destroy the very conditions, in family and citizen community, of the identity of freedom.

Notes

This paper was completed in November 1984.

I would like to thank Alan Cairns, Don Molnar and Cynthia Williams for their suggestions during the preparation of this paper. An earlier version of the second section appeared as "Growth, Legitimacy and the Modern Identity," *Praxis International* 1, (July 1981): 111–25. This theme was also the subject of my Corry Lecture, delivered at Queen's University in January 1980.

1. Cf. his *Capitalism, Socialism and Democracy*, 3d ed. (New York: Harper and Row, 1950). Also Robert Dahl, *Preface to Democratic Theory* (Chicago: University of Chicago Press, 1956).

2. Cf. the interesting discussion in Clause Offe: "'Ungovernability': The Renaissance of Conservative Theories of Crisis," reprinted in C. Offe, *Contradictions of the Welfare State* (Cambridge, Mass.: MIT Press, 1984). Offe shows how much common ground there is between "overload" theories of the Left and the Right. An influential formulation of the former perspective was James O'Connor's *The Fiscal Crisis of the State* (New York: St. Martin's Press, 1973). For a recent discussion of the American scene from the latter perspective, see Samuel Huntington, *American Politics: The Promise of Disharmony* (Cambridge, Mass.: Harvard University Press, 1981).

3. Daniel Bell, *Cultural Contradictions of Capitalism* (New York: Basic, 1976), cf. especially chap. 1.

4. For an interesting contemporary theory aimed at the rescue of the goods implicit in modernity, see the recent work by J. Habermas, *Theorie des Kommunikativen Handelns (Theory of Communicative*

Action) (Boston: Beacon Press, 1983). The connection of this kind of theory with reform politics is evident in this case, in a form which is entirely freed from the illusions of original Marxism about socialism as the fruit of a breakdown of capitalism.

5. Cf. J. Habermas, *Legitimation Crisis* (Boston: Beacon Press, 1975).

6. Cf. L. Stone, *The Family, Sex and Marriage in England 1500–1800* (London: Weidenfeld and Nicolson, 1977).

7. Michel Faucault, *Surveiller et Punir* (Paris, 1976); English translation, *Discipline and Punish* (London: Allen Lane, 1977).

8. Cf. J. Rawls, *A Theory of Justice* (Boston: Harvard University Press, 1971); R. Nozick, *Anarchy, State and Utopia* (Boston: Basic, 1974). Rawls himself is by no means a prisoner of the atomist perspective.

9. Cf. Bell, *Cultural Contradictions of Capitalism.* I think Bell gives too much importance to the signs of a more positive valuation of hedonism in contemporary America. Or better, he puts this valuation in the wrong context. What happened in the 1960s and 1970s was not just a collapse of the old "Protestant ethic" into mere "permissiveness." To see things this way is to look at the whole development from the outside. But this utterly leaves out of account the moral passion and earnestness of this phase of youth culture across the Western world.

10. Fred Somkin, *Unquiet Eagle* (Ithaca: Cornell University Press, 1967).

11. E. Schumacher, *Small Is Beautiful* (New York: Harper and Row, 1973), p. 30.

12. H. Stretton, *Capitalism, Socialism and the Environment* (Cambridge: Cambridge University Press, 1976), p. 224.

Justice as Fairness

John Rawls

In his 1971 book A Theory of Justice, *John Rawls restructured liberal political theory to fit the world view of contemporary culture and institutions of American democracy. He presents an ingenious interpretation of contract theory. Using the fiction of a hypothetical "original position," Rawls shows how a group of rational individuals, who want to cultivate their own good and are capable of a sense of justice, would form a just society through their choice of governing principles. His theory has been so influential that it has simultaneously strengthened liberalism as a political philosophy and provoked much of the current communitarian criticism. In response to this criticism Rawls incorporated a more social and historical grounding for his principles. The selection reprinted here is taken from his original theory. Rawls begins by explaining his concept of "justice as fairness," then demonstrates how the participants in the original position would establish a society that is fair to all. The participants deliberate from behind a "veil of ignorance"; that is, they do not know what their social class would be, nor their talents, psychology, bodily form, tastes, or even their conception of the good. Since the participants do not know which role they would occupy in an actual society governed by the principles they adopt, presumably they would choose principles that would be fair to all, even the least-advantaged member. We can test the proposed principles, Rawls says, by a process of reflective deliberation. We can compare them with our own ethical judgments and make adjustments on both sides until they match. We have then reached reflective equilibrium, which justifies the process of selecting the principles. Last, Rawls states the two principles that he believes any rational individual would choose as the foundation of social justice.*

My aim is to present a conception of justice which generalizes and carries to a higher level of abstraction the familiar theory of the social contract as found, say, in Locke, Rousseau, and Kant.[1] In order to do this we are not to think of the original contract as one to enter a particular society or to set up a particular form of government. Rather, the guiding idea is that the principles of justice for the basic structure of society are the object of the original agreement. They are the principles that free and rational persons concerned to further their own interests would accept in an initial position of equality as defining the fundamental terms of their association. These principles are to regulate all further agreements; they specify the kinds of social cooperation that can be entered into and the forms of government that can be established. This way of regarding the principles of justice I shall call justice as fairness.

Thus we are to imagine that those who engage in social cooperation choose together, in one joint act, the principles which are to assign basic rights and duties and to determine the division of social benefits. Men are to decide in advance how they are to regulate their claims against one another and what is to be the foundation charter of their society. Just as each person must decide by rational reflection what constitutes his good, that is, the system of ends which it is rational for him to pursue, so a group of persons must decide once and for all what is to count among them as just and unjust. The choice which rational men would make in this hypothetical situation of equal liberty, assuming for the present that this choice problem has a solution, determines the principles of justice.

In justice as fairness the original position of equality corresponds to the state of nature in the traditional theory of the social contract. This original position is not, of course, thought of as an actual historical state of affairs, much less as a primitive condition of culture. It is understood as a purely hypothetical situation characterized so as to lead to a certain conception of justice.[2] Among the essential features of this situation is that no one knows his place in society, his class position or social status, nor does any one know his fortune in the distribution of natural assets and abilities, his intelligence, strength, and the like.

I shall even assume that the parties do not know their conceptions of the good or their special psychological propensities. The principles of justice are chosen behind a veil of ignorance. This ensures that no one is advantaged or disadvantaged in the choice of principles by the outcome of natural chance or the contingency of social circumstances. Since all are similarly situated and no one is able to design principles to favor his particular condition, the principles of justice are the result of a fair agreement or bargain. For given the circumstances of the original position, the symmetry of everyone's relations to each other, this initial situation is fair between individuals as moral persons, that is, as rational beings with their own ends and capable, I shall assume, of a sense of justice. The original position is, one might say, the appropriate initial status quo, and thus the fundamental agreements reached in it are fair. This explains the propriety of the name "justice as fairness": it conveys the idea that the principles of justice are agreed to in an initial situation that is fair. The name does not mean that the concepts of justice and fairness are the same, any more than the phrase "poetry as metaphor" means that the concepts of poetry and metaphor are the same.

Justice as fairness begins, as I have said, with one of the most general of all choices which persons might make together, namely, with the choice of the first principles of a conception of justice which is to regulate all subsequent criticism and reform of institutions. Then, having chosen a conception of justice, we can suppose that they are to choose a constitution and a legislature to enact laws, and so on, all in accordance with the principles of justice initially agreed upon. Our social situation is just if it is such that by this sequence of hypothetical agreements we would have contracted into the general system of rules which defines it. Moreover, assuming that the original position does determine a set of principles (that is, that a particular conception of justice would be chosen), it will then be true that whenever social institutions satisfy these principles those engaged in them can say to one another that they are cooperating on terms to which they would agree if they were free and equal persons whose relations with respect to one another were fair. They could all view their arrangements as meeting the stipulations which they would acknowledge in an initial situation that embodies widely accepted and reasonable constraints on the choice of principles. The general recognition of this fact would provide the basis for a public acceptance of the corresponding principles of justice. No society can, of course, be a scheme of cooperation which men enter voluntarily in a literal sense; each person finds himself placed at birth in some particular position in some particular society, and the nature of this position materially affects his life prospects. Yet a society satisfying the principles of justice as fairness comes as close as a society can to being a voluntary scheme, for it meets the principles which free and equal persons would assent to under circumstances that are fair. In this sense its members are autonomous and the obligations they recognize self-imposed.

One feature of justice as fairness is to think of the parties in the initial situation as rational and mutually disinterested. This does not mean that the parties are egoists, that is, individuals with only certain kinds of interests, say in wealth, prestige, and domination. But they are conceived as not taking an interest in one another's interests. They are to presume that even their spiritual aims may be opposed, in the way that the aims of those of different religions may be opposed. Moreover, the concept of rationality must be interpreted as far as possible in the narrow sense, standard in economic theory, of taking the most effective means to given ends. I shall modify this concept to some extent, . . . but one must try to avoid introducing into it any controversial ethical elements. The initial situation must be characterized by stipulations that are widely accepted.

In working out the conception of justice as fairness one main task clearly is to determine which principles of justice would be chosen in the original position. To do this we must describe this situation in some detail and formulate with care the problem of choice which it presents. . . . It may be observed, however, that once the principles of justice are thought of as arising from an original agreement in a situation of equality, it is an open question whether the principle of utility would be acknowledged. Offhand it hardly seems likely that persons who view themselves as equals, entitled to press their claims upon one another, would agree to a principle which may require lesser life prospects for some simply for the sake of a greater sum of advantages enjoyed by others. Since each desires to protect his interests, his capacity to advance his conception of the good, no one has a reason to acquiesce in an enduring loss for himself in order to bring about a greater net balance of satisfaction. In the absence of strong and lasting benevolent impulses, a rational man would not accept a basic structure merely because it maximized the algebraic sum of advantages irrespective of its permanent effects on his own basic rights and interests. Thus it seems that the principle of utility is incompatible with the conception of social cooperation among equals for mutual advantage. It appears to be inconsistent with the idea of reciprocity implicit in the notion of a well-ordered society. Or, at any rate, so I shall argue.

I shall maintain instead that the persons in the initial situation would choose two rather different principles: the first requires equality in the assignment of basic rights and duties, while the second holds that social and economic inequalities, for example inequalities of wealth and authority, are just only if they result in compensating benefits for everyone, and in particular for the least advantaged members of society. These principles rule out justifying institutions on the grounds that the hardships of some are offset by a greater good in the aggregate. It may be expedient but it is not just that some should have less in order that others may prosper. But there is no injustice in the greater benefits earned by a few provided that the situation of persons not so fortunate is thereby improved. The intuitive idea is that since everyone's well-being depends upon a scheme of cooperation without which no one could have a satisfactory life, the division of advantages should be such as to draw forth the willing cooperation of everyone taking part in it, including those less well situated. Yet this can be expected only if reasonable terms are proposed. The two principles mentioned seem to be a fair agreement on the basis of which those better endowed, or more fortunate in their social position, neither of which we can be said to deserve, could expect the willing cooperation of others when some workable scheme is a necessary condition of the welfare of all.[3] Once we decide to look for a conception of justice that nullifies the accidents of natural endowment and the contingencies of social circumstance as counters in quest for political and economic advantage, we are led to these principles. They express the result of leaving aside those aspects of the social world that seem arbitrary from a moral point of view.

The problem of the choice of principles, however, is extremely difficult. I do not expect the answer I shall suggest to be convincing to everyone. It is, therefore, worth noting from the outset that justice as fairness, like other contract views, consists of two parts: (1) an interpretation of the initial situation and of the problem of choice posed there, and (2) a set of principles which, it is argued, would be agreed to. One may accept the first part of the theory (or some variant thereof), but not the other, and conversely. The concept of the initial contractual situation may seem reasonable although the particular principles proposed are rejected. To be sure, I want to maintain that the most appropriate conception of this situation does lead to principles of justice contrary to utilitarianism and perfectionism, and therefore that the contract doctrine provides an alternative to these views. Still, one may dispute this contention even though one grants that the contractarian method is a useful way of studying ethical theories and of setting forth their underlying assumptions.

Justice as fairness is an example of what I have called a contract theory. Now there may be an objection to the term "contract" and related expressions, but I think it will serve reasonably well. Many words have misleading connotations which at first are likely to confuse. The terms "utility" and "utilitarianism" are surely no exception. They too have unfortunate suggestions which hostile critics have been willing to exploit; yet they are clear enough for those prepared to study utilitarian doctrine. The same should be true of the term "contract" applied to moral theories. As I have mentioned, to understand it one has to keep in mind that it implies a certain level of abstraction. In particular, the content of the relevant agreement is not to enter a given society or to adopt a given form of government, but to accept certain moral principles. Moreover, the undertakings referred to are purely hypothetical: a contract view holds that certain principles would be accepted in a well-defined initial situation.

The merit of the contract terminology is that it conveys the idea that principles of justice may be conceived as principles that would be chosen by rational persons, and that in this way conceptions of justice may be explained and justified. The theory of justice is a part, perhaps the most significant part, of the theory of rational choice. Furthermore, principles of justice deal with conflicting claims upon the advantages won by social cooperation; they apply to the relations among several persons or groups. The word "contract" suggests this plurality as well as the condition that the appropriate division of advantages must be in accordance with principles acceptable to all parties. The condition of publicity for principles of justice is also connoted by the contract phraseology. Thus, if these principles are the outcome of an agreement, citizens have a knowledge of the principles that others follow. It is characteristic of contract theories to stress the public nature of political principles. Finally there is the long tradition of the contract doctrine. Expressing the tie with this line of thought helps to define ideas and accords with natural piety. There are then several advantages in the use of the term "contract." With due precautions taken, it should not be misleading.

A final remark. Justice as fairness is not a complete contract theory. For it is clear that the contractarian idea can be extended to the choice of more or less an entire ethical system, that is, to a system including principles for all the virtues and not only for justice. Now for the most part I shall consider only principles of justice and others closely related to them; I make no attempt to discuss the virtues in a systematic way. Obviously if justice as fairness succeeds reasonably well, a next step would be to study the more general view suggested by the name "rightness as fairness." But even this wider theory fails to embrace all moral relationships, since it would seem to include only our relations with other persons and to leave out of account how we are to conduct ourselves toward animals and the rest of nature. I do not contend that the contract notion offers a way to approach these questions which are certainly of the first importance; and I shall have to put them aside. We must recognize the limited scope of justice as fairness and of the general type of view that it exemplifies. How far its conclusions must be revised once these other matters are understood cannot be decided in advance.

The Original Position and Justification

I have said that the original position is the appropriate initial status quo which insures that the fundamental agreements reached in it are fair. This fact yields the name "justice as fairness." It is clear, then, that I want to say that one conception of justice is more reasonable than another, or justifiable with respect to it, if rational persons in the initial situation would choose its principles over those of the other for the role of justice. Conceptions of justice are to be ranked by their acceptability to persons so circumstanced. Understood in this way the question of justification is settled by working out a problem of deliberation: we have to ascertain which principles it would be rational to adopt given the contractual situation. This connects the theory of justice with the theory of rational choice.

If this view of the problem of justification is to succeed, we must, of course, describe in some detail the nature of this choice problem. A problem of rational decision has a definite answer only if we know the beliefs and interests of the parties, their relations with respect to one another, the alternatives between which they are to choose, the procedure whereby they make up their minds, and so on. As the circumstances are presented in different ways, correspondingly different principles are accepted. The concept of the original position, as I shall refer to it, is that of the most philosophically favored interpretation of this initial choice situation for the purposes of a theory of justice.

But how are we to decide what is the most favored interpretation? I assume, for one thing, that there is a broad measure of agreement that principles of justice should be chosen under certain conditions. To justify a particular description of the initial situation one shows that it incorporates these commonly shared presumptions. One argues from widely accepted but weak premises to more specific conclusions. Each of the presumptions should by itself be natural and plausible; some of them may seem innocuous or even trivial. The aim of the contract approach is to establish that taken together they impose significant bounds on acceptable principles of justice. The ideal outcome would be that these conditions determine a unique set of principles; but I shall be satisfied if they suffice to rank the main traditional conceptions of social justice.

One should not be misled, then, by the somewhat unusual conditions which characterize the original position. The idea here is simply to make vivid to ourselves the restrictions that it seems reasonable to impose on arguments for principles of justice, and therefore on these principles themselves. Thus it seems reasonable and generally acceptable that no one should be advantaged or disadvantaged by natural fortune or social circumstances in the choice of principles. It also seems widely agreed that it should be impossible to tailor principles to the circumstances of one's own case. We should insure further that particular inclinations and aspirations, and persons' conceptions of their good do not affect the principles adopted. The aim is to rule out those principles that it would be rational to propose for acceptance, however little the chance of success, only if one knew certain things that are irrelevant from the standpoint of justice. For example, if a man knew that he was wealthy, he might find it rational to advance the principle that various taxes for welfare measures be counted unjust; if he knew that he was poor, he would most likely propose the contrary principle. To represent the desired restrictions one imagines a situation in which everyone is deprived of this sort of information. One excludes the knowledge of those contingencies which sets men at odds and allows them to be guided by their prejudices. In this manner the veil of ignorance is arrived at in a natural way. This concept should cause no difficulty if we keep in mind the constraints on arguments that it is meant to express. At any time we can enter the original position, so to speak, simply by following a certain procedure, namely, by arguing for principles of justice in accordance with these restrictions.

It seems reasonable to suppose that the parties in the original position are equal. That is, all have the same rights in the procedure for choosing principles; each can make proposals, submit reasons for their acceptance, and so on. Obviously the purpose of these conditions is to represent equality between human beings as moral persons, as creatures having a conception of their good and capable of a sense of justice. The basis of equality is taken to be similarity in these two respects. Systems of ends are not ranked in value; and each man is presumed to have the requisite ability to understand and to act upon whatever principles are adopted. Together with the veil of ignorance, these conditions define the principles of justice as those which rational persons concerned to advance their interests would consent to as equals when none are known to be advantaged or disadvantaged by social and natural contingencies.

There is, however, another side to justifying a particular description of the original position. This is to see if the principles which would be chosen match our considered convictions of justice or extend them in an acceptable way. We can note whether applying these principles would lead us to make the same judgments about the basic structure of society which we now make intuitively and in which we have the greatest confidence; or whether, in cases where our present judgments are in doubt and given with hesitation, these principles offer a resolution which we can affirm on reflection. There are questions which we feel sure must be answered in a certain way. For example, we are confident that religious intolerance and racial discrimination are unjust. We think that we have examined these things with care and have reached what we believe is an impartial judgment not likely to be distorted by an excessive attention to our own interests. These convictions are provisional fixed points which we presume any conception of justice must fit. But we have much less assurance as to what is the correct distribution of wealth and authority. Here we may be looking for a way to remove our doubts. We can check an interpretation of the initial situation, then, by the capacity of its principles to accommodate our firmest convictions and to provide guidance where guidance is needed.

In searching for the most favored description of this situation we work from both ends. We begin by describing it so that it represents generally shared and preferably weak conditions. We then see if these conditions are strong enough to yield a significant set of principles. If not, we look for further premises equally reasonable. But if so, and these principles match our considered convictions of justice, then so far well and good. But presumably there will be discrepancies. In this case we have a choice. We can either modify the account of the initial situation or we can revise our existing judgments, for even the judgments we take provisionally as fixed points are liable to revision. By going back and forth, sometimes altering the conditions of the contractual circumstances, at others withdrawing our judgments and conforming them to principle, I assume that eventually we shall find a description of the initial situation that both expresses reasonable conditions and yields principles which match our considered judgments duly pruned and adjusted. This state of affairs I refer to as reflective equilibrium.[4] It is an equilibrium because at last our principles and judgments coincide; and it is reflective since we know to what principles our judgments conform and the premises of their derivation. At the moment everything is in order. But this equilibrium is not necessarily stable. It is liable to be upset by further examination of the conditions which should be imposed on the contractual situation and by particular cases which may lead us to revise our judgments. Yet for the time being we have done what we can to render coherent and to justify our convictions of social justice. We have reached a conception of the original position.

I shall not, of course, actually work through this process. Still, we may think of the interpretation of the original position that I shall present as the result of such a hypothetical course of reflection. It represents the attempt to accommodate within one scheme both reasonable philosophical conditions on principles as well as our considered judgments of justice. In arriving at the favored interpretation of the initial situation there is no point at which an appeal is made to self-evidence in the traditional sense either of general conceptions or particular convictions. I do not claim for the principles of justice proposed that they are necessary truths or derivable from such truths. A conception of justice cannot be deduced from self-evident premises or conditions on principles; instead, its justification is a matter of the mutual support of many considerations, of everything fitting together into one coherent view.

A final comment. We shall want to say that certain principles of justice are justified because they would be agreed to in an initial situation of equality. I have emphasized that this original position is purely hypothetical. It is natural to ask why, if this agreement is never actually entered into, we should take any interest in these principles, moral or otherwise. The answer is that the conditions embodied in the description of the original position are ones that we do in fact accept. Or if we do not, then perhaps we can be persuaded to do so by philosophical reflection. Each aspect of the contractual situation can be given supporting grounds. Thus what we shall do is to collect together into one conception a number of conditions on principles that we are ready upon due consideration to recognize as reasonable. These constraints express what we are prepared to regard as limits on fair terms of social cooperation. One way to look at the idea of the original position, therefore, is to see it as an expository device which sums up the meaning of these conditions and helps us to extract their consequences. On the other hand, this conception is also an intuitive notion that suggests its own elaboration, so that led on by it we are drawn to define more clearly the standpoint from which we can best interpret moral relationships. We need a conception that enables us to envision our objective from afar: the intuitive notion of the original position is to do this for us. . . .

Two Principles of Justice

I shall now state in a provisional form the two principles of justice that I believe would be chosen in the original position. In this section I wish to make only the most general comments, and therefore the first formulation of these principles is tentative. . . .

The first statement of the two principles reads as follows.

First: each person is to have an equal right to the most extensive basic liberty compatible with a similar liberty for others.

Second: social and economic inequalities are to be arranged so that they are both (a) reasonably expected to be to everyone's advantage, and (b) attached to positions and offices open to all.

There are two ambiguous phrases in the second principle, namely "everyone's advantage" and "open to all." . . .

By way of general comment, these principles primarily apply, as I have said, to the basic structure of society. They are to govern the assignment of rights and duties and to regulate the distribution of social and economic advantages. As their formulation suggests, these principles presuppose that the social structure can be divided into two more or less distinct parts, the first principle applying to the one, the second to the other. They distinguish between those aspects of the social system that define and secure the equal liberties of citizenship and those that specify and establish social and economic inequalities. The basic liberties of citizens are, roughly speaking, political liberty (the right to vote and to be eligible for public office) together with freedom of speech and assembly; liberty of conscience and freedom of thought; freedom of the person along with the right to hold (personal) property; and freedom from arbitrary arrest and seizure as defined by the concept of the rule of law. These liberties are all required to be equal by the first principle, since citizens of a just society are to have the same basic rights.

The second principle applies, in the first approximation, to the distribution of income and wealth and to the design of organizations that make use of differences in authority and responsibility, or chains of command. While the distribution of wealth and income need not be equal, it must be to everyone's advantage, and at the same time, positions of authority and offices of command must be accessible to all. One applies the second principle by holding positions open, and then, subject to this constraint, arranges social and economic inequalities so that everyone benefits.

These principles are to be arranged in a serial order with the first principle prior to the second. This ordering means that a departure from the institutions of equal liberty required by the first principle cannot be justified by, or compensated for, by greater social and economic advantages. The distribution of wealth and income, and the hierarchies of authority, must be consistent with both the liberties of equal citizenship and equality of opportunity.

Notes

1. As the text suggests, I shall regard Locke's *Second Treatise of Government,* Rousseau's *The Social Contract,* and Kant's ethical works beginning with *The Foundations of the Metaphysics of Morals* as definitive of the contract tradition. For all of its greatness, Hobbes's *Leviathan* raises special problems. A general historical survey is provided by J. W. Gough, *The Social Contract,* 2nd ed. (Oxford, The Clarendon Press, 1957), and Otto Gierke, *Natural Law and the Theory of Society,* trans. with an introduction by Ernest Barker (Cambridge, The University Press, 1934). A presentation of the contract view as primarily an ethical theory is to be found in G. R. Grice, *The Grounds of Moral Judgment* (Cambridge, The University press, 1967).

2. Kant is clear that the original agreement is hypothetical. See *The Metaphysics of Morals,* pt. I *(Rechtslehre),* especially §§47, 52; and pt. II of the essay "Concerning the Common Saying: This May Be True in Theory but It Does Not Apply in Practice," in *Kant's Political Writings,* ed. Hans Reiss and trans. by H. B. Nisbet (Cambridge, The University Press, 1970), pp. 73–87. See Georges Vlachos, *La Pensée politique de Kant* (Paris, Presses Universitaires de France, 1962), pp. 326–335; and J. G. Murphy, *Kant: The Philosophy of Right* (London, Macmillan, 1970), pp. 109–112, 133–136, for a further discussion.

3. For the formulation of this intuitive idea I am indebted to Allan Gibbard.

4. The process of mutual adjustment of principles and considered judgments is not peculiar to moral philosophy. See Nelson Goodman, *Fact, Fiction, and Forecast* (Cambridge, Mass., Harvard University Press, 1955), pp. 65–68, for parallel remarks concerning the justification of the principles of deductive and inductive inference.

Justice and the Moral Subject

Michael Sandel

With the revitalization of liberalism following publication of John Rawls's A Theory of Justice *came a resurgence of criticism of the liberal program. Michael Sandel's attack on this theory was one of the most influential of the current communitarian critiques. Sandel examines Rawls's theory in detail, concluding that deontological liberalism is too narrow a view of the good society. Rawls's theory, Sandel charges, cannot support the liberal claim that justice is the primary virtue of a good society. His argument focuses on Rawls's claim that the self is prior to whatever values that self may have. This view of the moral subject, Sandel argues, ignores the fact that people are constituted by the social bonds within which they live, the ideals they follow, the social organizations that give structure to their lives, and the traditions that form their consciousness and habits. A plausible model of a good society, according to Sandel, must start with a fully constituted moral subject. In the selection reprinted here Sandel begins by examining Rawls's two contentions that subjects are mutually independent from each other and that they are not constituted by their values and goals (their ends), but possess them in that they can adopt them or drop them at will. If justice is to be the primary social virtue, a moral subject must have both traits, Sandel claims. He next examines the adequacy of these two claims in the light of the goals that real moral persons have, such as self-understanding and community commitment. Sandel finds that, because Rawls's theory rules out the possibility that the moral person is essentially constituted by family, culture, friendships, and locality, this asocial person could not have any realistic self-understanding. Last, Sandel examines Rawls's contention that each person chooses what values to adopt and what fundamental aims to accept. But, Sandel asks, what could be the basis for these choices, if a person has no prior conception of the good?*

The Self and Its Ends: The Subject of Possession

On the deontological ethic, "the self is prior to the ends which are affirmed by it" (560).[*] For Rawls, giving an account of this priority poses a special challenge, for his project rules out a self that achieves its priority by inhabiting a transcendent or noumenal realm. In Rawls' view, any account of self and ends must tell us not one thing but two things: how the self is distinguished from its ends, and also how the self is connected to its ends. Without the first,

[*]The page references appearing in parentheses refer to John Rawls's *A Theory of Justice* (Cambridge: Harvard University Press, 1971).

we are left with a radically situated subject; without the second, a radically disembodied subject.

Rawls' solution, implicit in the design of the original position, is to conceive the self as a subject of possession, for in possession the self is distanced from its ends without being detached altogether. The notion of the self as a subject of possession can be located in the assumption of mutual disinterest. This assumption looks on the surface like a psychological assumption—it says the parties take no interest in one another's interests—but given its place in the original position it works instead as an epistemological claim, as a claim about the forms of self-knowledge of which we are capable. This is why Rawls can coherently maintain that the assumption of mutual disinterest is "the main motivational condition of

From Michael Sandel, *Liberalism and the Limits of Justice* (Cambridge: Cambridge University Press, 1982), pp. 54–64, 152–154, 161–165. Reprinted with permission of Cambridge University Press. Some footnotes omitted.

the original position" (189), and yet "involves no particular theory of human motivations" (130).

We can now see how this is so. The assumption of mutual disinterest is not an assumption about what motivates people, but an assumption about the nature of subjects who possess motivations in general. It concerns the nature of the self (that is, how it is constituted, how it stands with respect to its situation generally), not the nature of the self's desires or aims. It concerns the *subject* of interests and ends, not the *content* of those interests and ends, whatever they may happen to be. As Kant argues that all experience must be the experience of some subject, Rawls' assumption of mutual disinterest holds that all interests must be the interests of some subject.

> Although the interests advanced by these plans are not assumed to be interests *in the self,* they are interests *of a self* that regards its conception of the good as worthy of recognition [emphasis added] (127).
>
> I make no restrictive assumptions about the parties' conceptions of the good except that they are rational long-term plans. While these plans determine the aims and interests *of a self,* the aims and interests are not presumed to be egoistic or selfish. Whether this is the case depends upon the kinds of ends which a person pursues. If wealth, position, and influence, and the accolades of social prestige are a person's final purposes, then surely his conception of the good is egoistic. His dominant interests are *in himself,* not merely, *as they must always be,* interests *of a self* [emphasis added] (129).

In the assumption of mutual disinterest, we find the key to Rawls' conception of the subject, the picture of the way we must be to be subjects for whom justice is primary. But the notion of the self as a subject of possession, taken alone, does not complete the picture. As the account of plurality suggests, not just any subject of possession will do, but only an antecedently individuated subject, the bounds of whose self are fixed prior to experience. To be a deontological self, I must be a subject whose identity is given independently of the things I have, independently, that is, of my interests and ends and my relations with others. Combined with the idea of possession, this notion

of individuation powerfully completes Rawls' theory of the person. We can appreciate its full consequences by contrasting two aspects of possession—two different ways an interest can be "of a self"—and seeing how the notion of antecedent individuation commits the deontological self to one of them.

In so far as I possess something, I am at once related to it and distanced from it. To say that I possess a certain trait or desire or ambition is to say that I am related to it in a certain way—it is *mine* rather than *yours*—and also that I am distanced from it in a certain way—that it is *mine* rather than *me.* The latter point means that if I lose a thing I possess, I am still the same "I" who had it; this is the sense, paradoxical at first but unavoidable on reflection, in which the notion of possession is a distancing notion. This distancing aspect is essential to the continuity of the self. It preserves for the self a certain dignity and integrity by saving it from transformation in the face of the slightest contingency. Preserving this distance, and the integrity it implies, typically requires a certain kind of self-knowledge. To preserve the distinction between what is *me* and what is (merely) *mine,* I must know, or be able to sort out when the occasion demands, something about who I am. Thus, Odysseus was able to survive his treacherous journey home by donning various disguises, and his ability to do so presupposed an understanding of who he was, to begin with, so to speak. Since his self-knowledge preceded his experience in this sense, he was able to return home the same person who had left, familiar to Penelope, untransfigured by his journey, unlike Agamemnon, who returned a stranger to his household and met a different fate.[1]

It is a consequence of the dual aspect of possession that it can fade or diminish in two different ways. I gradually lose possession of a thing not only as it is distanced from my person, but also as the distance between my self and the thing narrows and tends toward collapse. I lose possession of a desire or an ambition as my commitment to it fades, as my hold on it becomes more attenuated, but also, after a certain point, as my attachment to it grows, as it gradually becomes attached to me. As the desire or ambition becomes increasingly constitutive of my identity, it becomes more and more *me,* and less and less *mine.* Or as we might say in some cases, the less I possess it, and the more I am possessed *by* it. Imagine that a desire, held tentatively at first, gradually becomes more central to my overall aims, until finally it becomes an overriding consideration in all I think and do. As it grows from a desire into an obsession, I possess it less and it possesses me more, until finally it becomes indistinguishable from my identity.

A different sort of example: in so far as the American Declaration of Independence is correct, that man is endowed by his Creator with certain inalienable rights that among them are life, liberty, and the pursuit of happiness, its famous litany describes not what we *have* as free men but rather what we *are.* The endowment is less a possession than a *nature* of a certain kind; he who would abnegate his liberty or pursue a miserable existence would experience these endowments not as possessions but as constraints. In so far as these rights are truly inalienable, a man is no more entitled to do away with them in his own case than to take them from another. Suicide is on a par with murder, and selling oneself into slavery is morally equivalent to enslaving another.

As these images suggest, possession is bound up with human agency and a sense of self-command. Dispossession, from both points of view, can be understood as a kind of disempowering. When my possession of an object fades, whether because it slips from my grasp or looms so large before me that I am overwhelmed, disempowered in the face of it, my agency with respect to the object is diminished as well. Each challenge is associated with a different notion of agency, which implies, in turn, a different account of the relation of the self to its ends. We can think of the two dimensions of agency as different ways of repairing the drift toward dispossession, and distinguish them by the way they work to restore a sense of self-command.

The first kind of dispossession involves the distancing of the end from the self whose end it once was. It becomes increasingly unclear in what sense this is my end rather than yours, or somebody else's, or no one's at all. The self is disempowered because dissociated from those ends and desires which, woven gradually together into a coherent whole, provide a fixity of purpose, form a plan of life, and so account for the continuity of the self with its ends. Where the self is regarded as given prior to its ends, its bounds fixed once and for all such that they are impermeable, invulnerable to transformation by experience, such continuity is perpetually and inherently problematic; the only way it can be affirmed is for the self to reach beyond itself, to grasp as an object of its will the ends it would possess, and hold them, as it always must, external to itself.[*]

The second kind of dispossession disempowers in another way. Here, the problem is not to overcome the distance created by the drift of the end from the self, but rather to recover and preserve a space that increasingly threatens to collapse. Crowded by the claims and pressures of various possible purposes and ends, all impinging indiscriminately on my identity, I am unable to sort them out, unable to mark out the limits or the boundaries of my self, incapable of saying where my identity ends and the world of attributes, aims, and desires begins. I am disempowered in the sense of lacking any clear grip on who, in particular, I am. Too much is too essential to my identity. Where the ends are given prior to the self they constitute, the bounds of the subject are open, its identity infinitely accommodating and ultimately fluid. Unable to distinguish what is mine from what is me, I am in constant danger of drowning in a sea of circumstance.

We might understand human agency as the faculty by which the self comes by its ends. This acknowledges its close connection with the notion of possession without begging the question which dimension of possession is at stake, nor the question of the relative priority of self and ends. For if I am a being with ends, there are at least two ways I might "come by" them: one is by choice, the other by discovery,

[*]Compare Kant (1797: 62): "Therefore, the relation of having something external to oneself as one's own (property) consists of a purely de jure union of the Will of the subject with that object, independently of his relationship to it in space and time and in accordance with the concept of intelligible possession."

by "finding them out." The first sense of "coming by" we might call the voluntarist dimension of agency, the second sense the cognitive dimension. Each kind of agency can be seen as repairing a different kind of dispossession.

Where the self is disempowered because detached from its ends, dispossession is repaired by the faculty of agency in its voluntarist sense, in which the self is related to its ends as a willing subject to the objects of choice. The relevant agency involves the exercise of will, for it is the will that is able to transcend the space between the subject and its object without requiring that it be closed.

Where the self is disempowered because undifferentiated from its ends, dispossession is repaired by agency in its cognitive sense, in which the self is related to its ends as a knowing subject to the objects of understanding. Where the ends of the self are given in advance, the relevant agency is not voluntarist but cognitive, since the subject achieves self-command not by choosing that which is already given (this would be unintelligible) but by reflecting on itself and inquiring into its constituent nature, discerning its laws and imperatives, and acknowledging its purposes as its own. Where the faculty of will seeks to reverse the drifting apart of self and ends by restoring a certain continuity between them, reflexivity is a distancing faculty, and issues in a certain detachment. It succeeds by restoring the shrunken space between self and ends. In reflexivity, the self turns its lights inward upon itself, making the self its own object of inquiry and reflection. When I am able to reflect on my obsession, able to pick it out and make it an object of my reflection, I thereby establish a certain space between it and me, and so diminish its hold. It becomes more an attribute and less a constituent of my identity, and so dissolves from an obsession to a mere desire.

Where the subject is regarded as prior to its ends, self-knowledge is not a possibility in this sense, for the bounds it would define are taken as given in advance, unreflectively, by the principle of antecedent individuation. The bounds of the self are fixed and within them all is transparent. The relevant moral question is not "Who am I?" (for the answer to this question is given in advance) but rather "What

ends shall I choose?" and this is a question addressed to the will.

For the self whose identity is constituted in the light of ends already before it, agency consists less in summoning the will than in seeking self-understanding. The relevant question is not what ends to choose, for my problem is precisely that the answer to this question is already given, but rather who I am, how I am to discern in this clutter of possible ends what is me from what is mine. Here, the bounds of the self are not fixtures but possibilities, their contours no longer self-evident but at least partly unformed. Rendering them clear, and defining the bounds of my identity are one and the same. The self-command that is measured in the first case in terms of the scope and reach of my will is determined in the second by the depth and clarity of my self-awareness.

We can now see how the cluster of assumptions associated with the voluntarist notion of agency and the distancing aspect of possession fill out Rawls' theory of the person. The notion of a subject of possession, individuated in advance and given prior to its ends, seems just the conception required to redeem the deontological ethic without lapsing into transcendence. In this way, the self is distinguished from its ends—it stands beyond them, at a distance, with a certain priority—but is also related to its ends, as willing subject to the objects of choice.

The voluntarist notion of agency is thus a key ingredient in Rawls' conception, and plays a central role in the deontological ethic as a whole. "It is not our aims that primarily reveal our nature" (560), but rather our capacity to choose our aims that matters most, and this capacity finds expression in the principles of justice. "Thus a moral person is a subject with ends he has chosen, and his fundamental preference is for conditions that enable him to frame a mode of life that expresses his nature as a free and equal rational being as fully as circumstances permit" (561). This, finally, is why we cannot regard justice as just one value among others. "In order to realize our nature we have no alternative but to plan to preserve our sense of justice as governing our other aims" (574).

Individualism and the Claims of Community

In our reconstruction of the deontological subject we find at last the standard by which the descriptive premises of the original position may be assessed, the counterweight to our moral intuitions that provides Rawls' reflective equilibrium with a test at both ends. It is this conception of the subject, and no particular account of human motivations, that the assumption of mutual disinterest conveys.

We may recall that on Rawls' account, "the postulate of mutual disinterest in the original position is made to insure that the principles of justice do not depend upon strong assumptions" (129), and the point of avoiding strong assumptions is to make possible the derivation of principles that do not presuppose any particular conception of the good. "Liberty in adopting a conception of the good is limited only by principles that are deduced from a doctrine which imposes no prior constraints on these conceptions. Presuming mutual disinterest in the original position carries out this idea" (254). Strong or controversial assumptions would threaten to impose a particular conception of the good, and so bias the choice of principles in advance.

How strong or weak, then, *are* the assumptions that form Rawls' conception of the person? With what range of values and ends are they compatible? Are they weak and innocent enough to avoid ruling out any conceptions of the good in advance? We have already seen that the empiricist reading of the original position produces a litany of objections on this score; the circumstances of justice and especially the assumption of mutual disinterest are thought to introduce an individualistic bias, and to rule out or otherwise devalue such motives as benevolence, altruism, and communitarian sentiments. As one critic has written, the original position contains "a strong individualistic bias, which is further strengthened by the motivational assumptions of mutual disinterest and absence of envy. . . . The original position seems to presuppose not just a neutral theory of the good, but a liberal, individualistic conception according to which the best that can be wished for someone is the unimpeded pursuit of his own path, provided it does not interfere with the rights of others."[2]

But as Rawls rightly insists, his theory is not the "narrowly individualistic doctrine" that the empiricist objection supposes. "Once the point of the assumption of mutual disinterest is understood, the objection seems misplaced" (584). Notwithstanding its individualist dimension, justice as fairness does not defend private society as an ideal (522f), or presuppose selfish or egoistic motivations (129), or oppose communitarian values. "Although justice as fairness begins by taking the persons in the original position as individuals . . . this is no obstacle to explicating the higher-order moral sentiments that serve to bind a community of persons together" (192).

Rawls has emphasized in particular that the assumption of mutual disinterest does not bias the choice of principles in favor of individualistic values at the expense of communitarian ones. Those who suppose that it does overlook the special status of the original position, and mistakenly assume that the motives attributed to the parties are meant to apply generally to actual human beings or to persons in a well-ordered society. But neither is the case. The motives attributed to the parties in the original position neither reflect the actual motivations current in society nor determine directly the motives of persons in a well-ordered society.

Given the restricted scope of these assumptions, Rawls argues, "there seems to be no reason offhand why the ends of people in a well-ordered society should be predominantly individualistic."[3] Communitarian values, like any other values individuals might choose to pursue, would likely exist, and possibly even flourish in a society governed by the two principles of justice.

> There is no reason why a well-ordered society should encourage primarily individualistic values if this means ways of life that lead individuals to pursue their own way and to have no concern for the interest of others (although respecting their rights and liberties). Normally one would expect most people to belong to one or more associations and to have at least some collective ends in this sense. The basic liberties are not

intended to keep persons in isolation from one another, or to persuade them to live private lives, even though some no doubt will, but to secure the right of free movement between associations and smaller communities.[4]

On Rawls' conception of the person, my ends are benevolent or communitarian when they take as their object the good of another, or of a group of others with whom I may be associated, and indeed there is nothing in his view to rule out communitarian ends in this sense. All interests, values, and conceptions of the good are open to the Rawlsian self, so long as they can be cast as the interests of a subject individuated in advance and given prior to its ends, so long, that is, as they describe the objects I seek rather than the subject I am. Only the *bounds* of the self are fixed in advance.

But this suggests a deeper sense in which Rawls' conception is individualistic. We can locate this individualism and identify the conceptions of the good it excludes by recalling that the Rawlsian self is not only a subject of possession, but an antecedently individuated subject, standing always at a certain distance from the interests it has. One consequence of this distance is to put the self beyond the reach of experience, to make it invulnerable, to fix its identity once and for all. No commitment could grip me so deeply that I could not understand myself without it. No transformation of life purposes and plans could be so unsettling as to disrupt the contours of my identity. No project could be so essential that turning away from it would call into question the person I am. Given my independence from the values I have, I can always stand apart from them; my public identity as a moral person "is not affected by changes over time" in my conception of the good.[*]

But a self so thoroughly independent as this rules out any conception of the good (or of the bad) bound up with possession in the constitutive sense. It rules out the possibility of any attachment (or obsession) able to reach beyond our values and sentiments to engage our identity itself. It rules out the possibility of a public life in which, for good or ill, the identity as well as the interests of the participants could be at stake. And it rules out the possibility that common purposes and ends could inspire more or less expansive self-understandings and so define a community in the constitutive sense, a community describing the subject and not just the objects of shared aspirations. More generally, Rawls' account rules out the possibility of what we might call "intersubjective" or "intrasubjective" forms of self-understanding, ways of conceiving the subject that do not assume its bounds to be given in advance. Unlike Rawls' conception, intersubjective and intrasubjective conceptions do not assume that to speak of the self, from a moral point of view, is necessarily and unproblematically to speak of an antecedently individuated self.

Intersubjective conceptions allow that in certain moral circumstances, the relevant description of the self may embrace more than a single, individual human being, as when we attribute responsibility or affirm an obligation to a family or community or class or nation rather than to some particular human being. Such conceptions are presumably what Rawls has in mind when he rejects, "for reasons of clarity among others," what he calls "an undefined concept of community" and the notion that "society is an organic whole" (264), for these suggest the metaphysically troubling side of Kant which Rawls is anxious to replace.

Intrasubjective conceptions, on the other hand, allow that for certain purposes, the appropriate description of the moral subject may refer to a plurality of selves within a single, individual human being, as when we account for inner deliberation in terms of the pull of competing identities, or moments of introspection in terms of occluded self-knowledge, or when we absolve someone from responsibility for the heretical beliefs "he" held before his religious conversion. On intrasubjective conceptions, to speak of selves within a(n) (antecedently individuated empirical) self is not merely metaphorical but sometimes of genuine moral and practical import.

While Rawls does not reject such notions explicitly, he denies them by implication when he assumes that to every individual person there corresponds a single system of desires, and that utilitarianism fails as a social ethic in

---

[*]Rawls suggests at one point that my *private* identity as a moral person might not be similarly immune from constitutive attachments (1980: 545).[5]

mistakenly applying to society the principles of choice appropriate for one man. Since he takes for granted that every individual consists of one and only one system of desires, the problem of conflating desires does not arise in the individual case, and the principle of rational prudence can properly govern one's conduct toward oneself. "A person quite properly acts, at least when others are not affected, to achieve his own greatest good, to advance his rational ends as far as possible" (23). Whereas society consists of a plurality of subjects and so requires justice, in private morality, utilitarianism seems to suffice; where others are not involved, I am free to maximize my good without reference to the principle of right.[6] Here again Rawls departs from Kant, who emphasized the concept of "necessary duty to oneself," and applied the category of right to private as well as public morality.[7]

The assumptions of the original position thus stand opposed in advance to any conception of the good requiring a more or less expansive self-understanding, and in particular to the possibility of community in the constitutive sense. On Rawls' view, a sense of community describes a possible aim of antecedently individuated selves, not an ingredient or constituent of their identity as such. This guarantees its subordinate status. Since "the essential unity of the self is already provided by the concept of right" (563), community must find its virtue as one contender among others within the framework defined by justice, not as a rival account of the framework itself. The question then becomes whether individuals who happen to espouse communitarian aims can pursue them within a well-ordered society, antecedently defined by the principles of justice, not whether a well-ordered society is *itself* a community (in the constitutive sense). "There is, to be sure, one collective aim supported by state power for the whole well-ordered society, a just society wherein the common conception of justice is publicly recognized; but within this framework communitarian aims may be pursued, and quite possibly by the vast majority of persons."[8]

We can see now more clearly the relation between Rawls' theory of the person and his claim for the primacy of justice. As a person's values and ends are always attributes and never constituents of the self, so a sense of community is only an attribute and never a constituent of a well-ordered society. As the self is prior to the aims it affirms, so a well-ordered society, defined by justice, is prior to the aims—communitarian or otherwise—its members may profess. This is the sense, both moral and epistemological, in which justice is the first virtue of social institutions. . . .

For a subject to play a role in shaping the contours of its identity requires a certain faculty of reflection. Will alone is not enough. What is required is a certain capacity for self-knowledge, a capacity for what we have called agency in the cognitive sense. This can be seen by recalling the two accounts of agency and possession we considered in our initial reconstruction of Rawls' theory of the subject. The first account, corresponding to Rawls' conception, took the bounds of the self as given and related self to ends by agency in its voluntarist sense, as willing subject to objects of choice. This sort of agency depended on the faculty of will, for it is the will that allows the self to reach beyond itself, to transcend the bounds that are fixed in advance, to grasp the ends it would possess and hold them as it always must, external to itself.

The second account, by contrast, took the bounds of the self as open and conceived the identity of the subject as the product rather than the premise of its agency. The relevant agency here was not voluntarist but cognitive; the self came by its ends not by choice but by reflection, as knowing (or inquiring) subject to object of (self-)understanding. The problem here was not the distance of the self from its ends, but rather the fact that the self, being unbounded in advance, was awash with possible purposes and ends, all impinging indiscriminately on its identity, threatening always to engulf it. The challenge to the agent was to sort out the limits or the boundaries of the self, to distinguish the subject from its situation, and so to forge its identity.

For the subject whose identity is constituted in the light of ends already before it, agency consists less in summoning the will than in seeking self-understanding. Unlike the capacity for choice, which enables the self to reach beyond itself, the capacity for reflection enables the self to turn its lights inward upon itself, to inquire into its constituent nature, to survey its various attachments and acknowledge their respective claims, to sort out the bounds—now expansive, now constrained—between the self and the other, to arrive at a self-understanding less opaque if never perfectly transparent, a subjectivity less fluid if never finally fixed, and so gradually, throughout a lifetime, to participate in the constitution of its identity.

Now the capacity for reflection suggested by the cognitive account would seem precisely the feature Rawls' "wider subject of possession" requires if it is not to dissolve into a radically situated subject, for this capacity holds out the possibility of arriving at the bounds of the self without taking them to be given in advance. Indeed, once the presumed antecedent individuation of the subject is called into question, the predicament of the self would seem to approach the dispossession described on the *cognitive* account, in which the greater threat to agency is not the distance of the self from its purposes and ends but rather the surfeit of seemingly indispensable aims which only sober self-examination can hope to sort out.

But on Rawls' moral epistemology, the scope for reflection would appear seriously limited. Self-knowledge seems not to be a possibility in the relevant sense, for the bounds it would define are taken as given in advance, unreflectively, once and for all, by a principle of antecedent individuation. But once these bounds are seen to fall away, there is nothing to take their place. For a subject such as Rawls' the paradigmatic moral question is not "Who am I?", for the answer to this question is regarded as self-evident, but rather "What ends shall I choose?", and this is a question addressed to the will. Rawls' subject would thus appear epistemologically impoverished where the self is concerned, conceptually ill-equipped to engage in the sort of self-reflection capable of going beyond an attention to its preferences and desires to contemplate, and so to redescribe, the subject that contains them.

It seems clear at least that the question of community leads naturally to the question of reflection, and that in order to assess the role of reflection in Rawls' scheme, we need to examine in greater detail Rawls' theory of agency, his account of how the self arrives at its ends. We have seen that for Rawls the self comes by its ends by choosing them, or more elaborately, that the self is related to its ends as willing subject to objects of choice, and we have described this ability to choose as agency in the voluntarist sense. But what exactly goes on in this moment of choice, and what role, if any, does reflection play in arriving at it? . . .

Agency and the Role of Choice

As we have seen, Rawls' theory of the good is voluntaristic; our fundamental aims, values, and conceptions of the good are for us to choose, and in choosing them, we exercise our agency. As Rawls describes it, once the principles of rational (i.e. instrumental) choice run out, "*We must finally choose for ourselves* in the sense that the choice often rests on our direct self-knowledge not only of what things we want but also of how much we want them. . . . *It is clearly left to the* agent himself to decide what it is that he most wants" [emphasis added] (416). Since the principles of rational choice do not specify a single best plan of life, "a great deal remains to be *decided*. . . . We eventually reach a point where *we just have to decide* which plan we most prefer without further guidance from principle. . . . [W]e may narrow the scope of *purely preferential choice*, but we cannot eliminate it altogether. . . . *The person himself must make this decision*, taking into account the full range of his inclinations and desires, present and future" [emphasis added] (449, 551, 552, 557).

If it is clear that Rawls would describe my values and conceptions of the good as the products of choice or decision, it remains to be seen what exactly this choice consists in and how I come to make it. According to Rawls, we "choose for ourselves *in the sense that* the choice *often rests on* our direct self-knowledge" of what we want and how much we want it. But a choice that is a choice "in the sense that" it "often rests on" (is determined by?) my existing wants and desires is a choice only in a peculiar sense of the word. For assuming with Rawls that the wants and desires on which my choice "rests" are not themselves chosen but are the products of circumstance, ("We do not choose now what to desire now" (415)), such a "choice" would involve less a voluntary act than a factual accounting of what these wants and desires really are. And once I succeed in ascertaining, by "direct self-knowledge," this piece of psychological information, there would seem nothing left for me to *choose*. I would have still to match my wants and desires, thus ascertained, to the best available means of satisfying them, but this is a prudential question which involves no volition or exercise of will.

When Rawls writes that it is "left to the agent himself to *decide* what it is he most wants" (416), and that "we just have to *decide* which plans we most prefer" (551), the "decision" the agent must make amounts to nothing more than an estimate or psychic inventory of the wants and preferences he already has, not a choice of the values he would profess or the aims he would pursue. As with the collective "choice" or "agreement" in the original position, such a "decision" decides nothing except how accurately the agent has perceived something already *there,* in this case the shape and intensity of his pre-existing desires. But if this is so, then the voluntarist aspect of agency would seem to fade altogether.

To arrive at a plan of life or a conception of the good simply by heeding my existing wants and desires is to choose neither the plan nor the desires; it is simply to match the ends I already have with the best available means of satisfying them. Under such a description, my aims, values, and conceptions of the good are not the products of choice but the objects of a certain superficial introspection, just "inward" enough to survey uncritically the motives and desires with which the accidents of my circumstance have left me; I simply know them as I feel them and seek my way as best I can to their consummation.

It might be suggested that Rawls could escape the apparent collapse of this account of agency and choice in one of two ways. The first would be to introduce the idea that persons are capable of reflecting on their desires not only in the sense of assessing their inten-

sity but also in the sense of assessing their desirability; capable, that is, of forming second-order desires, desires whose objects are certain first-order desires.[9] I may thus want to have certain desires and not others, or regard certain sorts of desires as desirable and others less so. The fact that something was desired (and not unjust) would no longer be enough to make it good, for this would depend on the further question whether it was a desirable sort of desire or not. Once I ascertained what I (really) wanted as a matter of first-order desire, it would remain for me to assess the desirability of my desire and in this sense to affirm or reject it.

Indeed, Rawls seems vaguely to admit such a possibility when he writes that although "we do not choose now what to desire now," we can at least "choose now which desires we shall have at a later time. . . . We can certainly decide now to do something that we know will affect the desires we shall have in the future. . . . Thus we choose between future desires in the light of our existing desires" (415).

But even if a Rawlsian agent were capable of forming desires for certain other desires, his agency would not in any meaningful sense be restored. For he would have no grounds, apart from the mere fact of his second-order desire, on which to justify or defend the desirability of one sort of desire over another. He would still have only the psychological fact of his (now, second-order) preference to appeal to and only its relative intensity to assess. Neither the intrinsic worth of a desire nor its essential connection with the identity of the agent could provide a basis for affirming it, since on Rawls' account, the worth of a desire only appears in the light of a person's good, and the identity of the agent is barren of constituent traits so that no aim or desire can be essential to it. The affirmation or rejection of desires suggested by the formation of second-order desires would on Rawls' assumptions introduce no further element of reflection or volition, for such an assessment could only reflect a slightly more complicated estimate of the relative intensity of pre-existing desires, first- and second-order desires included. The resulting conception of the good could no more be said to be chosen than one arising from first-order desires alone.

A second possible attempt to restore the coherence of choice on Rawls' conception might be to imagine a case in which the various desires of the agent, properly weighed for their respective intensities, led to a tie, and where deliberation had already taken account of all relevant preferences such that no further preferences could be introduced to break the tie. In such a case, this account might continue, the agent would have no alternative but to plump, just arbitrarily, one way or the other, without relying on any preference or desire at all. It might be suggested that a "choice" thus independent from the influence of pre-existing wants and desires—a "radically free choice," as it is sometimes described— would allow for the voluntarist aspect of agency seemingly unavailable when the agent is bound to "choose" in conformity with his pre-existing wants and desires.

But Rawls rejects a wholly arbitrary form of agency that would escape the influence of pre-existing wants and desires altogether. "The notion of radical choice . . . finds no place in justice as fairness."[10] Unlike the principles of right, which express the autonomy of the agent and must be free from contingencies, conceptions of the good are understood to be heteronomous throughout. Where incompatible aims arise, Rawls speaks not of radically free or arbitrary choice, but instead of "purely preferential choice," suggesting the form of (non-)agency we first considered. In any case, the notion of a purely arbitrary "choice" governed by no considerations at all is hardly more plausible an account of voluntarist agency than a "choice" governed wholly by predetermined preferences and desires. Neither "purely preferential choice" nor "purely arbitrary choice" can redeem Rawls' notion of agency in the voluntarist sense; the first confuses choice with necessity, the second with caprice. Together they reflect the limited

scope for reflection on Rawls' account, and the implausible account of human agency that results.

Notes

1. I am indebted for this example to Allen Grossman.

2. Nagel, Thomas, 1973, "Rawls on Justice" in *Reading Rawls,* ed. N. Daniels, pp. 9–10, New York.

3. Rawls, John, 1975, "Fairness to Goodness," *Philosophical Review, 84,* p. 544.

4. Ibid, p. 550.

5. Rawls, John, 1980, "Kantian Constructivism in Moral Theory," *Journal of Philosophy, 77,* pp. 544–545.

6. In his discussion of deliberative rationality, Rawls stops just short of acknowledging an intrasubjective dimension and admitting the concept of right as a constraint on private moral choice: "One who rejects equally the claims of his future self and the interests of others is not only irresponsible with respect to them but in regard to his own person as well. He does not see himself as one enduring individual. Now looked at in this way, the principle of responsibility to self *resembles* a principle of right. . . . The person at one time, *so to speak,* must not be able to complain about actions of the person at another time" [emphasis added].

7. Kant, I. 1785, *Groundwork of the Metaphysics of Morals,* tr. H. J. Paton, 1956, New York, pp. 89–90, 96–97, 101, 105.

8 Rawls, 1975, p. 550.

9. Frankfurt, H., 1971, "Freedom of the Will and the Concept of a Person," *Journal of Philosophy, 68,* pp. 5–20.

10. Rawls, 1980, p. 568.

Communitarian Critics of Liberalism

Amy Gutmann

In this article Amy Gutmann responds to the current communitarian critique of liberalism and a politics of liberal rights. While her comments are sometimes addressed to the work of communitarians such as Alasdair MacIntyre, Charles Taylor, or Roberto Unger, her main argument is a point-by-point examination of Michael Sandel's critique of John Rawls's theory. Gutmann argues that Rawls does not need to be interpreted to make the strong claims that Sandel attributed to him. She presents textual evidence that Rawls did not assume that the moral subject is independent of all social and historical contingencies. The participants in the original position, Gutmann argues, can be interpreted as an expression of our deepest human aspirations, rather than as a contentless self-interest. She defends the liberal conception of individual rights from MacIntyre's contention that rights simply don't exist. Gutmann then shows how rights can be defended on the communitarians' own ground—as an established practice in our culture. In the next section she disparages the dualisms of individual versus community and egoist versus altruist as facile polemics. Her conclusion does not defend the positive value of liberalism; instead she makes the negative claim that the communitarian critique has failed to demonstrate liberalism's inadequacy. She admits that a positive case might be made for a communitarian politics that could be morally superior to liberalism, but so far no developed communitarian theory has been offered.

We are witnessing a revival of communitarian criticisms of liberal political theory. Like the critics of the 1960s, those of the 1980s fault liberalism for being mistakenly and irreparably individualistic. But the new wave of criticism is not a mere repetition of the old. Whereas the earlier critics were inspired by Marx, the recent critics are inspired by Aristotle and Hegel. The Aristotelian idea that justice is rooted in "a community whose primary bond is a shared understanding both of the good for man and the good of that community" explicitly informs Alasdair MacIntyre in his criticism of John Rawls and Robert Nozick for their neglect of desert;[1] and Charles Taylor in his attack on "atomistic" liberals who "try to defend . . . the priority of the individual and his rights over society."[2] The Hegelian conception of man as a historically conditioned being implicitly informs both Roberto Unger's and Michael Sandel's rejection of the liberal view of man as a free and rational being.[3]

The political implications of the new communitarian criticisms are correspondingly more conservative. Whereas the good society of the old critics was one of collective property ownership and equal political power, the good society of the new critics is one of settled traditions and established identities. For many of the old critics, the role of women within the family was symptomatic of their social and economic oppression; for Sandel, the family serves as a model of community and evidence of a good greater than justice.[4] For the old critics, patriotism was an irrational sentiment that stood in the way of world peace; for MacIntyre, the particularistic demands of patriotism are no less rational than the universalistic demands of justice.[5] The old critics were inclined to defend deviations from majoritarian morality in the name of nonrepression; the new critics are inclined to defend the efforts of local majorities to ban offensive activities in the name of preserving their com-

Amy Gutmann, "Communitarian Critics of Liberalism," *Philosophy and Public Affairs*, Vol. 14 (1985), pp. 308–322. Copyright © 1985 by Princeton University Press. Reprinted by permission of Princeton University Press.

munity's "way of life and the values that sustain it."[6]

The subject of the new and the old criticism also differs. The new critics recognize that Rawls's work has altered the premises and principles of contemporary liberal theory. Contemporary liberals do not assume that people are possessive individualists; the source of their individualism lies at a deeper, more metaphysical level. According to Sandel, the problem is that liberalism has faulty foundations: in order to achieve absolute priority for principles of justice, liberals must hold a set of implausible metaphysical views about the self. They cannot admit, for example, that our personal identities are partly defined by our communal attachments.[7] According to MacIntyre, the problem is that liberalism lacks any foundations at all. It cannot be rooted in the only kind of social life that provides a basis for moral judgments, one which "views man as having an essence which defines his true end."[8] Liberals are therefore bound either to claim a false certainty for their principles or to admit that morality is merely a matter of individual opinion, that is, is no morality at all.

The critics claim that many serious problems originate in the foundational faults of liberalism. Perhaps the most troubling for liberals is their alleged inability to defend the basic principle that "individual rights cannot be sacrificed for the sake of the general good."[9] Because Sandel and MacIntyre make the most detailed and, if true, devastating cases against believing in a liberal politics of rights, I shall focus for the rest of this review on their arguments.

The central argument of Sandel's book is that liberalism rests on a series of mistaken metaphysical and metaethical views: for example, that the claims of justice are absolute and universal; that we cannot know each other well enough to share common ends; and that we can define our personal identity independently of socially given ends. Because its foundations are necessarily flawed, Sandel suggests in a subsequent article that we should give up the "politics of rights" for a "politics of the common good."[10]

MacIntyre begins his book with an even more "disquieting suggestion": that our entire moral vocabulary, of rights and the common good, is in such "grave disorder" that "we have—very largely, if not entirely—lost our comprehension, both theoretical and practical, of morality."[11] To account for how "we" have unknowingly arrived at this unenviable social condition, MacIntyre takes us on an intriguing tour of moral history, from Homeric Greece to the present. By the end of the tour, we learn that the internal incoherence of liberalism forces us to choose "Nietzsche or Aristotle," a politics of the will to power or one of communally defined virtue.[12]

The Limits of Communitarian Criticism

Do the critiques succeed in undermining liberal politics? If the only foundations available to liberal politics are faulty, then perhaps one need not establish a positive case for communitarian politics to establish the claim that liberal politics is philosophically indefensible.[13] Although this is the logic of Sandel's claim concerning the limits of liberal justice, he gives no general argument to support his conclusion that liberal rights are indefensible.[14] He reaches this conclusion instead on the basis of an interpretation and criticism of Rawls's theory, which he reasonably assumes to be the best theory liberalism has yet to offer.

Sandel argues that despite Rawls's efforts to distance himself from Kantian metaphysics, he fails. Sandel attributes Rawls's failure to his acceptance of the "central claim" of deontology, "the *core conviction* Rawls seeks *above all* to defend. It is the claim that 'justice is the first virtue of social institutions.' "[15] As Rawls presents it, the "primacy of justice" describes a moral requirement applicable to institutions. Sandel interprets Rawls as also making a metaethical claim: that the foundations of justice must be independent of all social and historical contingencies without being transcendental.[16]

Why saddle Rawls's moral argument for the primacy of justice with this meaning? To be sure, Rawls himself argues that "embedded in the principles of justice . . . is an ideal of the person that provides an Archimedean point for judging the basic structure of society."[17] But to translate this passage into a claim that the grounds of justice can be noncontingent ignores most of what Rawls says to explain his Archimedean point, the nature of justification, and Kantian constructivism.[18] "Justice as fairness is not at the mercy, so to speak, of existing wants and interests. It sets up an Archimedean point . . . *without invoking a priori considerations.*"[19] By requiring us to abstract from our particular but not our shared interests, the original position with its "veil of ignorance" and "thin theory of the good" avoids reliance on both existing preferences and *a priori* considerations in reasoning about justice. The resulting principles of justice, then, clearly rely on certain contingent facts: that we share some interests (in primary goods such as income and self-respect), but not others (in a particular religion or form of family life); that we value the freedom to choose a good life or at least the freedom from having one imposed upon us by political authority. If we do not, then we will not accept the constraints of the original position.

Rawls's remarks on justification and Kantian constructivism make explicit the contingency of his principles of justice. The design of the original position must be revised if the resulting principles do not "accommodate our firmest convictions."[20] Justification is not a matter of deduction from certain premises, but rather "a matter of the mutual support of many considerations, of everything fitting together into one coherent view."[21] Since Rawls accords the view "that justice is the first virtue of social institutions" the status of a "common sense conviction,"[22] this view is part of what his theory must coherently combine. Rawls therefore does not, nor need he, claim more for justice as fairness than that "given our history and the traditions embedded in our public life, it is the most reasonable doctrine for us. We can find no better charter for our social world."[23]

Rawls could be wrong about our firmest convictions or what is most reasonable for us. But instead of trying to demonstrate this, Sandel argues that Rawls must show that the content and claims of justice are independent of all historical and social particularities.[24] If this

is what constitutes deontological metaphysics, then it is a metaphysics that Rawls explicitly and consistently denies.

What metaphysics must Rawlsian liberalism then embrace? Several commentators, along with Rawls himself, have argued that liberalism does not presuppose metaphysics.[25] The major aim of liberal justice is to find principles appropriate for a society in which people disagree fundamentally over many questions, including such metaphysical questions as the nature of personal identity. Liberal justice therefore does not provide us with a comprehensive morality; it regulates our social institutions, not our entire lives. It makes claims on us "not because it expresses our deepest self-understandings," but because it represents the fairest possible *modus vivendi* for a pluralistic society.[26]

The characterization of liberalism as nonmetaphysical can be misleading however. Although Rawlsian justice does not presuppose only *one* metaphysical view, it is not compatible with *all* such views. Sandel is correct in claiming that the Kantian conception of people as free and equal is incompatible with the metaphysical conception of the self as "radically situated" such that "the good of community . . . [is] so thoroughgoing as to reach beyond the motivations to the subject of motivations."[27] Sandel seems to mean that communally given ends can so totally constitute people's identities that they cannot appreciate the value of justice. Such an understanding of human identity would (according to constructivist standards of verification) undermine the two principles.[28] To be justified as the *political* ideals most consistent with the "public culture of a democratic society,"[29] Rawlsian principles therefore have to express some (though not all) of our deepest self-understandings. Rawls must admit this much metaphysics—that we are not radically situated selves—if justification is to depend not on "being true to an order antecedent to and given to us, but . . . [on] congruence with our deeper understanding of ourselves and our aspirations."[30]

If this, rather than Kantian dualism, is the metaphysics that liberal justice must admit, Sandel's critique collapses. Rawls need not (and he does not) claim that "justice is the first virtue of social institutions" in *all* societies to show that the priority of justice obtains *absolutely* in those societies in which people disagree about the good life and consider their freedom to choose a good life an important good.[31] Nor need Rawls assume that human identity is *ever* totally independent of ends and relations to others to conclude that justice must *always* command our moral allegiance unless love and benevolence make it unnecessary.[32] Deontological justice thus can recognize the conditional priority of justice without embracing "deontological metaethics" or collapsing into teleology. Sandel has failed therefore to show that the foundations of rights are mistaken.

Missing Foundations?

MacIntyre argues that the foundations are missing:

> The best reason for asserting so bluntly that there are no such rights is indeed of precisely the same type as the best reason which we possess for asserting that there are no witches. . . .: every attempt to give good reasons for believing there *are* such rights has failed.[33]

The analogy, properly drawn, does not support MacIntyre's position. The best reason that people can give for believing in witches is that the existence of witches explains (supposedly) observed physical phenomena. Belief in witches therefore directly competes with belief in physics, and loses out in the competition. The best reason for taking rights seriously is of a different order: believing in rights is one way of regulating and constraining our behavior toward one another in a desirable manner. This reason does not compete with physics; it does not require us to believe that rights "exist" in any sense that is incompatible with the "laws of nature" as established by modern science.[34]

MacIntyre offers another, more historical argument for giving up our belief in rights. "Why," he asks, "should we think about our modern uses of *good, right,* and *obligatory* in any different way from that in which we think

about late eighteenth-century Polynesian uses of taboo?"[35] Like the Polynesians who used *taboo* without any understanding of what it meant beyond "prohibited," we use *human right* without understanding its meaning beyond "moral trump." If the analogy holds, we cannot use the idea correctly because we have irretrievably lost the social context in which its proper use is possible.

But on a contextualist view, it is reasonable for *us* to believe in human rights: many of the most widely accepted practices of our society— equality of educational opportunity, careers open to talent, punishment conditional on intent—treat people as relatively autonomous moral agents. Insofar as we are committed to maintaining these practices, we are also committed to defending human rights.[36] This argument parallels MacIntyre's contextualist defense of Aristotelian virtue: that the established practices of heroic societies supported the Aristotelian idea that every human life has a socially determined *telos*. Each person had a "given role and status within a well-defined and highly determinate system of roles and statuses," which fully defined his identity: "a man who tried to withdraw himself from his given position . . . would be engaged in the enterprise of trying to make himself disappear."[37]

If moral beliefs depend upon supporting social practices for their validity, then we have more reason to believe in a liberal politics of rights than in an Aristotelian politics of the common good. In *our* society, it does not logically follow that: "I am someone's son or daughter, someone else's cousin or uncle; I am a citizen of this or that city, a member of this or that guild or profession; I belong to this clan, that tribe, this nation[,] *hence* what is good for me *has* to be THE good for one who inhabits these roles."[38] One reason it does not follow is that none of these roles carries with it only one socially given good. What follows from "what is good for me has to be the good for someone who was born female, into a first-generation American, working-class Italian, Catholic family"? Had Geraldine Ferraro asked, following Sandel, "Who am I?" instead of "What ends should I choose?" an answer would not have been any easier to come by.[39] The Aristotelian method of discovering the good by inquiring into social meaning of roles is of little help in a society in which most roles are not attached to a single good. Even if there is a single good attached to some social roles (as caring for the sick is to the role of a nurse, or searching for political wisdom to the function of political philosophers, let us suppose), we cannot accurately say that our roles determine our good without adding that we often choose our roles because of the good that is attached to them. The unencumbered self is, in this sense, the encumbrance of our modern social condition.

But the existence of supporting social practices is certainly not a sufficient condition, arguably not even a necessary one, for believing in liberal rights rather than Aristotelian virtue. The practices that support liberal rights may be unacceptable to us for reasons that carry more moral weight than the practices themselves; we may discover moral reasons (even within our current social understandings) for establishing new practices that support a politics of the common good. My point here is not that a politics of rights is the only, or the best, possible politics for our society, but that neither MacIntyre's nor Sandel's critique succeeds in undermining liberal rights because neither gives an accurate account of their foundations. MacIntyre mistakenly denies liberalism the possibility of foundations; Sandel ascribes to liberalism foundations it need not have.

The Tyranny of Dualisms

The critics' interpretive method is also mistaken. It invites us to see the moral universe in dualistic terms: either our identities are independent of our ends, leaving us totally free to choose our life plans, or they are constituted by community, leaving us totally encumbered by socially given ends; either justice takes absolute priority over the good or the good takes the place of justice; either justice must be independent of all historical and social particularities or virtue must depend completely on the particular social practices of each society; and so on. The critics thereby do

a disservice to not only liberal but communitarian values, since the same method that reduces liberalism to an extreme metaphysical vision also renders communitarian theories unacceptable. By interpreting Rawls's conception of community as describing "just a feeling," for example, Sandel invites us to interpret Aristotle's as describing a fully constituted identity. The same mode of interpretation that permits Sandel to criticize Rawls for betraying "incompatible commitments" by uneasily combining into one theory "intersubjective and individualistic images" would permit us to criticize Sandel for suggesting that community is "a mode of self-understanding *partly* constitutive" of our identity.[40] Neither Sandel's interpretation nor his critique is accurate.

MacIntyre's mode of interpreting modern philosophy similarly divides the moral world into a series of dualisms. The doomed project of modern philosophy, according to MacIntyre, has been to convert naturally egoistical men into altruists. "On the traditional Aristotelian view such problems do not arise. For what education in the virtues teaches me is that my good as a man is one and the same as the good of those others with whom I am bound up in human community."[41] But the real, and recognized, dilemma of modern liberalism, as we have seen, is not that people are naturally egoistical, but that they disagree about the nature of the good life. And such problems also arise on any (sophisticated) Aristotelian view, as MacIntyre himself recognizes in the context of distinguishing Aristotelianism from Burkean conservatism: "when a tradition is in good order it is always partially constituted by an argument about the goods the pursuit of which gives to that tradition its particular point and purpose."[42]

The dualistic vision thus tyrannizes over our common sense, which rightly rejects all "easy combinations"—the individualism MacIntyre attributes to Sartre and Goffman "according to which the self is detachable from its social and historical roles and statuses" such that it "can have no history,"[43] as well as the communitarian vision MacIntyre occasionally seems to share with Roberto Unger according to which the "conflict between the demands of individuality and sociability would disappear."[44] Because the critics misinterpret the metaphysics of liberalism, they also miss the appeal of liberal politics for reconciling rather than repressing most competing conceptions of the good life.

Beyond Metaphysics: Communitarian Politics

Even if liberalism has adequate metaphysical foundations and considerable moral appeal, communitarian politics might be morally better. But MacIntyre and Sandel say almost nothing in their books to defend communitarian politics directly. Sandel makes a brief positive case for its comparative advantage over liberalism in a subsequent article. "Where libertarian liberals defend the private economy and egalitarian liberals defend the welfare state," Sandel comments, "communitarians worry about the concentration of power in both the corporate economy and the bureaucratic state, and the erosion of those intermediate forms of community that have at times sustained a more vital public life." But these worries surely do not distinguish communitarians from most contemporary liberals, unless (as Sandel implies) communitarians therefore oppose, or refuse to defend, the market or the welfare state.[45] Sandel makes explicit only one policy difference: "communitarians would be more likely than liberals to allow a town to ban pornographic bookstores, on the grounds that pornography offends its way of life and the values that sustain it." His answer to the obvious liberal worry that such a policy opens the door to intolerance in the name of communal standards is that "intolerance flourishes most where forms of life are dislocated, roots unsettled, traditions undone." He urges us therefore "to revitalize those civic republican possibilities implicit in our tradition but fading in our time."[46]

What exactly does Sandel mean to imply by the sort of civic republicanism "implicit within our tradition"? Surely not the mainstream of our tradition that excluded women and minorities, and repressed most significant deviations from white, Protestant morality in the name of the common good. We have little reason to doubt that a liberal politics of rights is morally better than that kind of republicanism. But if Sandel is arguing that when members of a society have settled roots and established traditions, they will tolerate the speech, religion, sexual, and associational preferences of minorities, then history simply does not support his optimism. A great deal of intolerance has come from societies of selves so "confidently situated" that they were sure repression would serve a higher cause.[47] The common good of the Puritans of seventeenth-century Salem commanded them to hunt witches; the common good of the Moral Majority of the twentieth century commands them not to tolerate homosexuals. The enforcement of liberal rights, not the absence of settled community, stands between the Moral Majority and the contemporary equivalent of witch hunting.

The communitarian critics want us to live in Salem, but not to believe in witches. Or human rights. Perhaps the Moral Majority would cease to be a threat were the United States a communitarian society; benevolence and fraternity might take the place of justice. Almost anything is possible, but it does not make moral sense to leave liberal politics behind on the strengths of such speculations.[48]

Nor does it make theoretical sense to assume away the conflicts among competing ends—such as the conflict between communal standards of sexual morality and individual sexual preference—that give rise to the characteristic liberal concern for rights. In so doing, the critics avoid discussing how morally to resolve our conflicts and therefore fail to provide us with a political theory relevant to our world. They also may overlook the extent to which some of their own moral commitments presuppose the defense of liberal rights.

Constructive Potential

Even if the communitarian critics have not given good reasons for abandoning liberalism, they have challenged its defenders. One should welcome their work if for no other reason than this. But there is another reason. Communitarianism has the potential for helping us discover a politics that combines community with a commitment to basic liberal values.

The critics' failure to undermine liberalism suggests not that there are no communitarian values but that they are properly viewed as supplementing rather than supplanting basic liberal values. We can see the extent to which our moral vision already relies on communitarian values by imagining a society in which no one does more or less than respect everyone else's liberal rights. People do not form ties of love and friendship (or they do so only insofar as necessary to developing the kind of character that respects liberal rights). They do not join neighborhood associations, political parties, trade unions, civic groups, synagogues, or churches. This might be a perfectly liberal, arguably even a just society, but it is certainly not the best society to which we can aspire. The potential of communitarianism lies, I think, in indicating the ways in which we can strive to realize not only justice but community through the many social unions of which the liberal state is the super social union.

What might some of those ways be? Sandel suggests one possibility: states might "enact laws regulating plant closings, to protect their communities from the disruptive effects of capital mobility and sudden industrial change."[49] This policy is compatible with the priority Rawls gives to liberty and may even be dictated by the best interpretation of the difference principle. But the explicit concern for preventing the disruption of local communities is an important contribution of communitarianism to liberalism. We should also, as Sandel suggests, be "troubled by the tendency of liberal programs to displace politics from smaller forms of association to more comprehensive ones." But we should not therefore oppose all programs that limit—or support all those that expand—the jurisdiction of local governments. We may be able to discover ways in which local communities *and* democracy can be vitalized without violating individual rights. We can respect the right of free speech by opposing local efforts to ban pornographic bookstores, for example, but still respect the values of community and democratic participation by supporting local (democratic) efforts to regulate the location and manner in which pornographic bookstores display their wares. Attuned to the dangers of dualism, we can appreciate the way such a stand combines—uneasily—liberal and communitarian commitments.

Some ways of fostering communal values— I suspect some of the best ways—entail creating new political institutions rather than increasing the power of existing institutions or reviving old ones. By restoring "those intermediate forms of community that have at times sustained a more vital public life," we are unlikely to control "the concentration of power in both the corporate economy and the bureaucratic state" that rightly worries both communitarians and liberals.[50] If large corporations and bureaucracies are here to stay, we need to create new institutions to prevent them from imposing (in the name of either efficiency or expertise) their values on those of potentially more democratic communities. Realizing the relatively old idea of workplace democracy would require the creation of radically new economic institutions.[51] Recently mandated citizen review boards in areas such as health care, education, and community development have increased interest in democratic participation. Wholehearted political support of such reforms and others yet untried is probably necessary before we can effectively control bureaucratic power.[52] Although the political implications of the communitarian criticisms of liberalism are conservative, the constructive potential of communitarian values is not.

Had they developed the constructive potential of communitarian values, the critics might have moved further toward discovering both the limits of Rawlsian liberalism and a better charter for our social world. Instead, MacIntyre concludes that we should be "waiting not for a Godot, but for another—doubtless very different—St. Benedict."[53] The critics tend to look toward the future with nostalgia. We would be better off, by both Aristotelian and liberal democratic standards, if we tried to shape it according to our present moral understandings. At the end of his book, Sandel urges us to remember "the possibility that when politics goes well, we can know a good in common that we cannot know alone." But he has neglected the possibility that the only common good worth striving for is one that is not "an unsettling presence for justice."[54] Justice need not be the only virtue of social institutions for it to be better than anything we are capable of putting in its place. The worthy challenge posed by the communitarian critics therefore is not to replace liberal justice, but to improve it.

Notes

This review essay concentrates on the arguments presented in Michael Sandel, *Liberalism and the Limits of Justice* (New York: Cambridge University Press, 1982); Sandel, "Morality and the Liberal Ideal," *The New Republic*, May 7, 1984, pp. 15–17; Alasdair MacIntyre, *After Virtue* (Notre Dame: Notre Dame University Press, 1981); and MacIntyre, "Is Patriotism a Virtue?" *The Lindley Lecture* (University of Kansas: Department of Philosophy, March 26, 1984). Other works to which I refer are Benjamin Barber, *Strong Democracy: Participatory Politics for a New Age* (Berkeley: University of California Press, 1984); Charles Taylor, "Atomism," in Alkis Kontos, ed., *Powers, Possessions and Freedoms: Essays in Honor of C. B. Macpherson* (Toronto: University of Toronto Press, 1979), pp. 39–61, and "The Diversity of Goods," in *Utilitarianism and Beyond,* ed. Amartya Sen and Bernard Williams (New York: Cambridge University Press, 1982), pp. 129–44; Roberto Mangabeira Unger, *Knowledge and Politics* (New York: Free Press, 1975); and Michael Walzer, *Spheres of Justice* (New York: Basic Books, 1983).

1. MacIntyre, *After Virtue,* pp. 232–33.

2. "Atomism," p. 39.

3. *Knowledge and Politics,* pp. 85, 191–231; *Limits,* pp. 179–80.

4. Sandel, *Limits,* pp. 30–31, 33–34, 169.

5. "Is Patriotism a Virtue?" pp. 15–18 and passim.

6. Sandel, "Morality and the Liberal Ideal," p. 17.

7. *Limits,* pp. 64–65, 168–73.

8. *After Virtue,* p. 52.

9. Sandel, "Morality and the Liberal Ideal," p. 16.

10. Ibid., p. 17.

11. *After Virtue,* pp. 1–5.

12. Ibid., pp. 49, 103–13, 238–45.

13. I say "perhaps" because if defensibility is relative to our alternatives, then Sandel still would have to establish the positive case for communitarian politics before claiming that the faulty foundations of liberal politics render it indefensible.

14. The general argument that can be constructed from Sandel's work (using his conceptual framework) is, I think, the following: (1) To accept a politics based on rights entails believing that justice should have absolute priority over all our particular ends (our conception of the good); (2) To accept the priority of justice over our conception of the good entails believing that our identities can be established prior to the good (otherwise our conception of the good will enter into our conception of justice); (3) Since our identities are constituted by our conception of the good, justice cannot be prior. Therefore we cannot consistently believe in the politics of rights. But each of the steps in this argument are suspect: (1) We may accept the politics of rights not because justice is prior to the good, but because our search for the good requires society to protect our right to certain basic freedoms and welfare goods; (2) Justice may be prior to the good not because we are "antecedently individuated," but because giving priority to justice may be the fairest way of sharing the goods of citizenship with people who do not accept our conception of the good; (3) Our identities are probably not constituted, at least not exclusively, by our conception of the good. If they were, one could not intelligibly ask: "What kind of person do I want to become?" Yet the question reflects an important part (although not necessarily the whole) of our search for identity. If, however, we assume by definition that our identities are constituted by our good, then we must consider our sense of justice to be part of our identities. My commitment to treating other people as equals, and therefore to respecting their freedom of religion, is just as elemental a part of my identity (on this understanding) as my being Jewish, and therefore celebrating Passover with my family and friends.

15. *Limits,* p. 15. Emphasis added. See *A Theory of*

Justice (Cambridge, MA: Harvard University Press, 1971), pp. 3–4, 586.

16. *Limits*, pp. 16–17. Rawls must, in Sandel's words, "find a standpoint neither compromised by its implication in the world nor dissociated and so disqualified by detachment."

17. Rawls, *A Theory of Justice*, p. 584; see also pp. 260–62.

18. In interpreting Rawls, I rely (as does Sandel) on passages from both *A Theory of Justice* and "Kantian Constructivism in Moral Theory: The Dewey Lectures 1980," *The Journal of Philosophy* 77, no 9 (September 1980), pp. 515–72. Someone might reasonably argue that not until "The Dewey Lectures" does Rawls consistently and clearly defend the position on justification that I attribute to him. Had Sandel directed his criticism only against *A Theory of Justice*, his interpretation would have been more credible. But he still could not have sustained his central claim that Rawls's principles and liberalism more generally *must* rest on implausible metaethical grounds.

19. *A Theory of Justice*, p. 261. Emphasis added. See also "The Dewey Lectures," esp. pp. 564–67.

20. *A Theory of Justice*, p. 20. The reasoning is circular, but not viciously so, since we must also be prepared to revise our weaker judgments when principles match our considered convictions, until we reach "reflective equilibrium."

21. Ibid., pp. 21, 579.

22. Ibid., p. 586.

23. "The Dewey Lectures," p. 519. Cf. Sandel, *Limits*, p. 30.

24. *Limits*, p. 30. Sometimes Sandel comes close to making a more limited but potentially more plausible argument—that Rawls derives his principles of justice from the wrong set of historical and social particularities: from (for example) our identification with all free and rational beings rather than with particular communities. Such an argument, if successful, would establish different limits, and limits of only Rawlsian liberalism.

25. See Rawls, "The Independence of Moral Theory," *Proceedings and Addresses of the American Philosophical Association* 48 (1975), pp. 5–22.

26. Charles Larmore, "Review of *Liberalism and the Limits of Justice*," *The Journal of Philosophy* 81, no. 6 (June 1984): 338. See also Rawls, "The Dewey Lectures," p. 542.

27. Sandel, *Limits*, pp. 20–21, 149.

28. Rawls, "The Dewey Lectures," pp. 534–35, 564–67. See also *A Theory of Justice*, p. 260: "The theory of justice does, indeed, presuppose a theory of the good, but *within wide limits* this does not prejudge the choice of the sort of persons that men want to be." (Emphasis added.)

29. Rawls, "The Dewey Lectures," p. 518.

30. Ibid., p. 519.

31. Ibid., pp. 516–24. Cf. Sandel, *Limits*, pp. 28–40.

32. Rawls, *A Theory of Justice*, pp. 560–77. Cf. Sandel, *Limits*, pp. 47–65.

33. *After Virtue*, p. 67.

34. I am grateful to Thomas Scanlon for suggesting this reply.

35. *After Virtue*, p. 107.

36. We need not be committed to a thoroughly deontological moral apparatus. Sophisticated consequentialist theories justify these same practices and are consistent with believing in rights.

37. *After Virtue*, pp. 117, 119.

38. Ibid., pp. 204–5 (emphasis added). Sandel makes a very similar point in *Limits*, p. 179.

39. *Limits*, pp. 58–59.

40. Ibid., p. 150. When Sandel characterizes his own preferred "strong" view of community, it is one in which people conceive their identity "as defined *to some extent* by the community of which they are a part." (Emphases added.)

41. *After Virtue*, pp. 212–13.

42. Ibid., p. 206.

43. Ibid., p. 205. See also Sandel, *Limits*, pp. 40, 150. Cf. p. 180.

44. *Knowledge and Politics*, p. 220.

45. "Morality and the Liberal Ideal," p. 17.

46. Ibid.

47. Sandel may be correct in claiming that *more* intolerance has come—in the form of fascism—from societies of "atomized, dislocated, frustrated selves." But the truth of this claim does not establish the case for communitarian over liberal politics unless our only choice is to support a society of totally "atomized" or one of totally "settled" selves. This dualistic interpretation of our alternatives seems to lead Sandel to overlook the moral value of establishing some balance between individualism and community, and to underestimate the theoretical difficulty of determining where the proper balance lies.

48. Sandel might want to argue that societies like Salem were not "settled." Perfectly settled communities would not be repressive because every individual's identity would be fully constituted by the community or completely compatible with the community's understanding of the common good. This argument, however, is a truism: a perfectly settled society would not be repressive, because perfect settlement would leave no dissent to repress.

49. Ibid.

50. Ibid.

51. For a communitarian defense of economic democracy that is not based on a rejection of liberal values, see Michael Walzer, *Spheres of Justice,* pp. 161 and 291–303.

52. For a suggestive agenda of democratic re-forms, see Benjamin Barber, *Strong Democracy,* pp. 261–307. Although Barber attacks liberal theory as fundamentally flawed in the first nine chapters, the aim of his agenda for reform in the last chapter is "to reorient liberal democracy toward civic engagement and political community, not to raze it" (p. 308).

53. Ibid., p. 245. Roberto Unger similarly concludes *Knowledge and Politics* waiting for God to speak (p. 235).

54. Cf. Sandel, *Limits,* p. 183.

I am grateful to Robert Amdur, Michael Doyle, Steven Lukes, Susan Moller Okin, Judith Shklar, Dennis Thompson, Michael Walzer, Susan Wolf, and the Editors of *Philosophy & Public Affairs* for their helpful suggestions.

3

The Problems
of Pluralism

Complex Equality

Michael Walzer

Among the more important requirements of a theory of justice is that no one should be dominated by other individuals or by a group. Liberal theories of justice have guaranteed this freedom from domination by attributing to each individual inviolable rights to important private and social goods. Michael Walzer instead proposes a model of justice based on the shared understandings of a particular community and on how its members distribute the social goods they produce. Domination must be ruled out because it violates the group's social context, he argues, not because it violates a universal standard, like natural rights, as liberals have claimed. To accomplish his goal of a relative equality of power, Walzer segregates each social good into a separate sphere of influence. And each good—for example, land, wealth, personal possessions, time, reputation, kinship and love, knowledge, security, work and leisure, power, and honor—has its own meaning within a community. In Walzer's theory the community's members should regulate the creation and distribution of these goods, according to principles appropriate to each sphere. For example, the sphere of kinship and love's set of meanings is different from that of the sphere of power, and the meanings appropriate to the sphere of power differ from those in the sphere of knowledge or education. Each of these spheres should be regulated by principles appropriate to its meanings, Walzer argues, and should be autonomous. Domination occurs when a social good is not distributed according to the principles appropriate to that good but instead is given to members according to the principles of another good. For example, public office should not be distributed to a citizen on the basis of wealth or kinship. And a citizen with public office should not have an advantage in gaining access to medical care or business opportunities. This system of autonomously controlled communities, Walzer claims, rules out the possibility of domination and guarantees justice in a pluralistic society.

Pluralism

Distributive justice is a large idea. It draws the entire world of goods within the reach of philosophical reflection. Nothing can be omitted; no feature of our common life can escape scrutiny. Human society is a distributive community. That's not all it is, but it is importantly that: we come together to share, divide, and exchange. We also come together to make the things that are shared, divided, and exchanged; but that very making—work itself—is distributed among us in a division of labor. My place in the economy, my standing in the political order, my reputation among my fellows, my material holdings: all these come to me from other men and women. It can be said that I have what I have rightly or wrongly, justly or unjustly; but given the range of distributions and the number of participants, such judgments are never easy.

The idea of distributive justice has as much to do with being and doing as with having, as much to do with production as with consumption, as much to do with identity and status as with land, capital, or personal possessions. Different political arrangements enforce, and different ideologies justify, different distributions of membership, power, honor, ritual eminence, divine grace, kinship and love, knowledge, wealth, physical security, work and leisure, rewards and punishments, and a

From Michael Walzer, *Spheres of Justice* (New York: Basic Books, Inc., 1983), pp. 3–13, 17–20. Copyright © 1983 by Basic Books, Inc. Reprinted by permission of Basic Books, a division of HarperCollins Publishers. Some footnotes omitted.

host of goods more narrowly and materially conceived—food, shelter, clothing, transportation, medical care, commodities of every sort, and all the odd things (paintings, rare books, postage stamps) that human beings collect. And this multiplicity of goods is matched by a multiplicity of distributive procedures, agents, and criteria. There are such things as simple distributive systems—slave galleys, monasteries, insane asylums, kindergartens (though each of these, looked at closely, might show unexpected complexities); but no full-fledged human society has ever avoided the multiplicity. We must study it all, the goods and the distributions, in many different times and places.

There is, however, no single point of access to this world of distributive arrangements and ideologies. There has never been a universal medium of exchange. Since the decline of the barter economy, money has been the most common medium. But the old maxim according to which there are some things that money can't buy is not only normatively but also factually true. What should and should not be up for sale is something men and women always have to decide and have decided in many different ways. Throughout history, the market has been one of the most important mechanisms for the distribution of social goods; but it has never been, it nowhere is today, a complete distributive system.

Similarly, there has never been either a single decision point from which all distributions are controlled or a single set of agents making decisions. No state power has ever been so pervasive as to regulate all the patterns of sharing, dividing, and exchanging out of which a society takes shape. Things slip away from the state's grasp; new patterns are worked out—familial networks, black markets, bureaucratic alliances, clandestine political and religious organizations. State officials can tax, conscript, allocate, regulate, appoint, reward, punish, but they cannot capture the full range of goods or substitute themselves for every other agent of distribution. Nor can anyone else do that: there are market coups and cornerings, but there has never been a fully successful distributive conspiracy.

And finally, there has never been a single criterion, or a single set of interconnected criteria, for all distributions. Desert, qualification, birth and blood, friendship, need, free exchange, political loyalty, democratic decision: each has had its place, along with many others, uneasily coexisting, invoked by competing groups, confused with one another.

In the matter of distributive justice, history displays a great variety of arrangements and ideologies. But the first impulse of the philosopher is to resist the displays of history, the world of appearances, and to search for some underlying unity: a short list of basic goods, quickly abstracted to a single good; a single distributive criterion or an interconnected set; and the philosopher himself standing, symbolically at least, at a single decision point. I shall argue that to search for unity is to misunderstand the subject matter of distributive justice. Nevertheless, in some sense the philosophical impulse is unavoidable. Even if we choose pluralism, as I shall do, that choice still requires a coherent defense. There must be principles that justify the choice and set limits to it, for pluralism does not require us to endorse every proposed distributive criteria or to accept every would-be agent. Conceivably, there is a single principle and a single legitimate kind of pluralism. But this would still be a pluralism that encompassed a wide range of distributions. By contrast, the deepest assumption of most of the philosophers who have written about justice, from Plato onward, is that there is one, and only one, distributive system that philosophy can rightly encompass.

Today this system is commonly described as the one that ideally rational men and women would choose if they were forced to choose impartially, knowing nothing of their own situation, barred from making particularist claims, confronting an abstract set of goods.[1] If these constraints on knowing and claiming are suitably shaped, and if the goods are suitably defined, it is probably true that a singular conclusion can be produced. Rational men and women, constrained this way or that, will choose one, and only one, distributive system. But the force of that singular conclusion is not easy to measure. It is surely doubtful that those same men and women, if they were transformed into ordinary people, with a firm sense of their own identity, with their own goods in their hands, caught up in everyday troubles, would reiterate their hypothetical choice or even recognize it as their own. The problem is not, most importantly, with the particularism of interest, which philosophers have always assumed they could safely—that it, uncontroversially—set aside. Ordinary people can do that too, for the sake, say, of the public interest. The greater problem is with the particularism of history, culture, and membership. Even if they are committed to impartiality, the question most likely to arise in the minds of the members of a political community is not, What would rational individuals choose under universalizing conditions of such-and-such a sort? But rather, What could individuals like us choose, who are situated as we are, who share a culture and are determined to go on sharing it? And this is a question that is readily transformed into, What choices have we already made in the course of our common life? What understandings do we (really) share?

Justice is a human construction, and it is doubtful that it can be made in only one way. At any rate, I shall begin by doubting, and more than doubting, this standard philosophical assumption. The questions posed by the theory of distributive justice admit of a range of answers, and there is room within the range for cultural diversity and political choice. It's not only a matter of implementing some singular principle or set of principles in different historical settings. No one would deny that there is a range of morally permissible implementations. I want to argue for more than this: that the principles of justice are themselves pluralistic in form; that different social goods ought to be distributed for different reasons, in accordance with different procedures, by different agents; and that all these differences derive from different understandings of the social goods themselves—the inevitable product of historical and cultural particularism.

A Theory of Goods

Theories of distributive justice focus on a social process commonly described as if it had this form:

People distribute goods to (other) people.

Here, "distribute" means give, allocate, exchange, and so on, and the focus is on the individuals who stand at either end of these actions: not on producers and consumers, but on distributive agents and recipients of goods. We are as always interested in ourselves, but, in this case, in a special and limited version of ourselves, as people who give and take. What is our nature? What are our rights? What do we need, want, deserve? What are we entitled to? What would we accept under ideal conditions? Answers to these questions are turned into distributive principles, which are supposed to control the movement of goods. The goods, defined by abstraction, are taken to be movable in any direction.

But this is too simple an understanding of what actually happens, and it forces us too quickly to make large assertions about human nature and moral agency—assertions unlikely, ever, to command general agreement. I want to propose a more precise and complex description of the central process:

People conceive and create goods, which they then distribute among themselves.

Here, the conception and creation precede and control the distribution. Goods don't just appear in the hands of distributive agents who do with them as they like or give them out in accordance with some general principle.[2] Rather, goods with their meanings—because of their meanings—are the crucial medium of social relations; they come into people's minds before they come into their hands; distributions are patterned in accordance with shared conceptions of what the goods are and what they are for. Distributive agents are constrained by the goods they hold; one might almost say that goods distribute themselves among people.

Things are in the saddle
And ride mankind.[3]

But these are always particular things and particular groups of men and women. And, of course, we make the things—even the saddle. I don't want to deny the importance of human agency, only to shift our attention from distribution itself to conception and creation: the naming of the goods, and the giving of meaning, and the collective making. What we need to explain and limit the pluralism of distributive possibilities is a theory of goods. For our immediate purposes, that theory can be summed up in six propositions.

1. All the goods with which distributive justice is concerned are social goods. They are not and they cannot be idiosyncratically valued. I am not sure that there are any other kinds of goods; I mean to leave the question open. Some domestic objects are cherished for private and sentimental reasons, but only in cultures where sentiment regularly attaches to such objects. A beautiful sunset, the smell of new-mown hay, the excitement of an urban vista: these perhaps are privately valued goods, though they are also, and more obviously, the objects of cultural assessment. Even new inventions are not valued in accordance with the ideas of their inventors; they are subject to a wider process of conception and creation. God's goods, to be sure, are exempt from this rule—as in the first chapter of Genesis: "and God saw every thing that He had made, and, behold, it was very good" (1:31). That evaluation doesn't require the agreement of mankind (who might be doubtful), or of a majority of men and women, or of any group of men and women meeting under ideal conditions (though Adam and Eve in Eden would probably endorse it). But I can't think of any other exemptions. Goods in the world have shared meanings because conception and creation are social processes. For the same reason, goods have different meanings in different societies. The same "thing" is valued for different reasons, or it is valued here and disvalued there. John Stuart Mill once complained that "people like in crowds," but I know of no other way to like or to dislike social goods.[4] A solitary person could hardly understand the meaning of the goods or figure out the reasons for taking them as likable or dislikable. Once people like in crowds, it becomes possible for individuals to break away, pointing to latent or subversive meanings, aiming at alternative values—including the values, for example, of notoriety and eccentricity. An easy eccentricity has sometimes been one of the privileges of the aristocracy: it is a social good like any other.

2. Men and women take on concrete identities because of the way they conceive and create, and then possess and employ social goods. "The line between what is me and mine," wrote William James, "is very hard to draw."[5] Distributions can not be understood as the acts of men and women who do not yet have particular goods in their minds or in their hands. In fact, people already stand in a relation to a set of goods; they have a history of transactions, not only with one another but also with the moral and material world in which they live. Without such a history, which begins at birth, they wouldn't be men and women in any recognizable sense, and they wouldn't have the first notion of how to go about the business of giving, allocating, and exchanging goods.

3. There is no single set of primary or basic goods conceivable across all moral and material worlds—or, any such set would have to be conceived in terms so abstract that they would be of little use in thinking about particular distributions. Even the range of necessities, if we take into account moral as well as physical necessities, is very wide, and the rank orderings are very different. A single necessary good, and one that is always necessary—food, for example—carries different meanings in different places. Bread is the staff of life, the body of Christ, the symbol of the Sabbath, the means of hospitality, and so on. Conceivably, there is a limited sense in which the first of these is primary, so that if there were twenty people in the world and just enough bread to feed the twenty, the primacy of bread-as-staff-of-life would yield a sufficient distributive principle. But that is the only circumstance in which it would do so; and even there, we can't be sure. If the religious uses of bread were to conflict with its nutritional uses—if the gods demanded that bread be baked and burned rather than eaten—it is by no means clear which use would be primary. How, then, is bread to be incorporated into the universal list? The question is even harder to answer, the conventional answers less plausible, as we pass from necessities to opportunities, powers, reputations, and so on. These can be incorporated only if they are abstracted from every particular meaning—hence, for all practical purposes, rendered meaningless.

4. But it is the meaning of goods that de-

termines their movement. Distributive criteria and arrangements are intrinsic not to the good-in-itself but to the social good. If we understand what it is, what it means to those for whom it is a good, we understand how, by whom, and for what reasons it ought to be distributed. All distributions are just or unjust relative to the social meanings of the goods at stake. This is in obvious ways a principle of legitimation, but it is also a critical principle.* When medieval Christians, for example, condemned the sin of simony, they were claiming that the meaning of a particular social good, ecclesiastical office, excluded its sale and purchase. Given the Christian understanding of office, it followed—I am inclined to say, it necessarily followed—that office holders should be chosen for their knowledge and piety and not for their wealth. There are presumably things that money can buy, but not this thing. Similarly, the words *prostitution* and *bribery,* like *simony,* describe the sale and purchase of goods that, given certain understandings of their meaning, ought never to be sold or purchased.

5. Social meanings are historical in character; and so distributions, and just and unjust distributions, change over time. To be sure, certain key goods have what we might think of as characteristic normative structures, reiterated across the lines (but not all the lines) of time and space. It is because of this reiteration that the British philosopher Bernard Williams is able to argue that goods should always be dis-

---

*Aren't social meanings, as Marx said, nothing other than "the ideas of the ruling class," "the dominant material relationships grasped as ideas"?[6] I don't think that they are ever only that or simply that, though the members of the ruling class and the intellectuals they patronize may well be in a position to exploit and distort social meanings in their own interests. When they do that, however, they are likely to encounter resistance, rooted (intellectually) in those same meanings. A people's culture is always a joint, even if it isn't an entirely cooperative, production; and it is always a complex production. The common understanding of particular goods incorporates principles, procedures, conceptions of agency, that the rulers would not choose if they were choosing *right now*—and so provides the terms of social criticism. The appeal to what I shall call "internal" principles against the usurpations of powerful men and women is the ordinary form of critical discourse.

tributed for "relevant reasons"—where relevance seems to connect to essential rather than to social meanings.[7] The idea that offices, for example, should go to qualified candidates—though not the only idea that has been held about offices—is plainly visible in very different societies where simony and nepotism, under different names, have similarly been thought sinful or unjust. (But there has been a wide divergence of views about what sorts of position and place are properly called "offices.") Again, punishment has been widely understood as a negative good that ought to go to people who are judged to deserve it on the basis of a verdict, not of a political decision. (But what constitutes a verdict? Who is to deliver it? How, in short, is justice to be done to accused men and women? About these questions there has been significant disagreement.) These examples invite empirical investigation. There is no merely intuitive or speculative procedure for seizing upon relevant reasons.

6. When meanings are distinct, distibutions must be autonomous. Every social good or set of goods constitutes, as it were, a distributive sphere within which only certain criteria and arrangements are appropriate. Money is inappropriate in the sphere of ecclesiastical office; it is an intrusion from another sphere. And piety should make for no advantage in the marketplace, as the marketplace has commonly been understood. Whatever can rightly be sold ought to be sold to pious men and women and also to profane, heretical, and sinful men and women (else no one would do much business). The market is open to all comers; the church is not. In no society, of course, are social meanings entirely distinct. What happens in one distributive sphere affects what happens in the others; we can look, at most, for relative autonomy. But relative autonomy, like social meaning, is a critical principle—indeed . . . radical principle. It is radical even though it doesn't point to a single standard against which all distributions are to be measured. There is no single standard. But there are standards (roughly knowable even when they are also controversial) for every social good and every distributive sphere in every particular society; and these standards are often violated, the goods usurped,

the spheres invaded, by powerful men and women.

Dominance and Monopoly

In fact, the violations are systematic. Autonomy is a matter of social meaning and shared values, but it is more likely to make for occasional reformation and rebellion than for everyday enforcement. For all the complexity of their distributive arrangements, most societies are organized on what we think of as a social version of the gold standard: one good or one set of goods is dominant and determinative of value in all the spheres of distribution. And that good or set of goods is commonly monopolized, its value upheld by the strength and cohesion of its owners. I call a good dominant if the individuals who have it, because they have it, can command a wide range of other goods. It is monopolized whenever a single man or woman, a monarch in the world of value—or a group of men and women, oligarchs—successfully hold it against all rivals. Dominance describes a way of using social goods that isn't limited by their intrinsic meanings or that shapes those meanings in its own image. Monopoly describes a way of owning or controlling social goods in order to exploit their dominance. When goods are scarce and widely needed, like water in the desert, monopoly itself will make them dominant. Mostly, however, dominance is a more elaborate social creation, the work of many hands, mixing reality and symbol. Physical strength, familial reputation, religious or political office, landed wealth, capital, technical knowledge: each of these, in different historical periods, has been dominant; and each of them has been monopolized by some group of men and women. And then all good things come to those who have the one best thing. Possess that one, and the others come in train. Or, to change the metaphor, a dominant good is converted into another good, into many others, in accordance with what often appears to be a natural process but is in fact magical, a kind of social alchemy.

No social good ever entirely dominates the range of goods; no monopoly is ever perfect.

I mean to describe tendencies only, but crucial tendencies. For we can characterize whole societies in terms of the patterns of conversion that are established within them. Some characterizations are simple: in a capitalist society, capital is dominant and readily converted into prestige and power; in a technocracy, technical knowledge plays the same part. But it isn't difficult to imagine, or to find, more complex social arrangements. Indeed, capitalism and technocracy are more complex than their names imply, even if the names do convey real information about the most important forms of sharing, dividing, and exchanging. Monopolistic control of a dominant good makes a ruling class, whose members stand atop the distributive system—much as philosophers, claiming to have the wisdom they love, might like to do. But since dominance is always incomplete and monopoly imperfect, the rule of every ruling class is unstable. It is continually challenged by other groups in the name of alternative patterns of conversion.

Distribution is what social conflict is all about. Marx's heavy emphasis on productive processes should not conceal from us the simple truth that the struggle for control of the means of production is a distributive struggle. Land and capital are at stake, and these are goods that can be shared, divided, exchanged, and endlessly converted. But land and capital are not the only dominant goods; it is possible (it has historically been possible) to come to them by way of other goods—military or political power, religious office and charisma, and so on. History reveals no single dominant good and no naturally dominant good, but only different kinds of magic and competing bands of magicians.

The claim to monopolize a dominant good—when worked up for public purposes—constitutes an ideology. Its standard form is to connect legitimate possession with some set of personal qualities through the medium of a philosophical principle. So aristocracy, or the rule of the best, is the principle of those who lay claim to breeding and intelligence: they are commonly the monopolists of landed wealth and familial reputation. Divine supremacy is the principle of those who claim to know the word of God: they are the monopolists of grace and office. Meritocracy, or the career open to talents, is the principle of those who claim to be talented: they are most often the monopolists of education. Free exchange is the principle of those who are ready, or who tell us they are ready, to put their money at risk: they are the monopolists of movable wealth. These groups—and others, too, similarly marked off by their principles and possessions—compete with one another, struggling for supremacy. One group wins, and then a different one; or coalitions are worked out, and supremacy is uneasily shared. There is no final victory, nor should there be. But that is not to say that the claims of the different groups are necessarily wrong, or that the principles they invoke are of no value as distributive criteria; the principles are often exactly right within the limits of a particular sphere. Ideologies are readily corrupted, but their corruption is not the most interesting thing about them.

It is in the study of these struggles that I have sought the guiding thread of my own argument. The struggles have, I think, a paradigmatic form. Some group of men and women—class, caste, strata, estate, alliance, or social formation—comes to enjoy a monopoly or a near monopoly of some dominant good; or, a coalition of groups comes to enjoy, and so on. This dominant good is more or less systematically converted into all sorts of other things—opportunities, powers, and reputations. So wealth is seized by the strong, honor by the wellborn, office by the well educated. Perhaps the ideology that justifies the seizure is widely believed to be true. But resentment and resistance are (almost) as pervasive as belief. There are always some people, and after a time there are a great many, who think the seizure is not justice but usurpation. The ruling group does not possess, or does not uniquely possess, the qualities it claims; the conversion process violates the common understanding of the goods at stake. Social conflict is intermittent, or it is endemic; at some point, counterclaims are put forward. Though these are of many different sorts, three general sorts are especially important:

1. The claim that the dominant good, whatever it is, should be redistributed so that it can be equally or at least more widely shared: this amounts to saying that monopoly is unjust.
2. The claim that the way should be opened for the autonomous distribution of all social goods: this amounts to saying that dominance is unjust.
3. The claim that some new good, monopolized by some new group, should replace the currently dominant good: this amounts to saying that the existing pattern of dominance and monopoly is unjust. . . .

Tyranny and Complex Equality

I want to argue that we should focus on the reduction of dominance—not, or not primarily, on the break-up or the constraint of monopoly. We should consider what it might mean to narrow the range within which particular goods are convertible and to vindicate the autonomy of distributive spheres. But this line of argument, though it is not uncommon historically, has never fully emerged in philosophical writing. Philosophers have tended to criticize (or to justify) existing or emerging monopolies of wealth, power, and education. Or, they have criticized (or justified) particular conversions—of wealth into education or of office into wealth. And all this, most often, in the name of some radically simplified distributive system. The critique of dominance will suggest instead a way of reshaping and then living with the actual complexity of distributions.

Imagine now a society in which different social goods are monopolistically held—as they are in fact and always will be, barring continual state intervention—but in which no particular good is generally convertible. As I go along, I shall try to define the precise limits on convertibility, but for now the general description will suffice. This is a complex egalitarian society. Though there will be many small inequalities, inequality will not be multiplied through the conversion process. Nor will it be summed across different goods, because the autonomy of distributions will tend to produce a variety of local monopolies, held by different groups of men and women. I don't want to claim that complex equality would necessarily be more stable than simple equality, but I am inclined to think that it would open the way for more diffused and particularized forms of social conflict. And the resistance to convertibility would be maintained, in large degree, by ordinary men and women within their own spheres of competence and control, without large-scale state action.

This is, I think, an attractive picture, but I have not yet explained just why it is attractive. The argument for complex equality begins from our understanding—I mean, our actual, concrete, positive, and particular understanding—of the various social goods. And then it moves on to an account of the way we relate to one another through those goods. Simple equality is a simple distributive condition, so that if I have fourteen hats and you have fourteen hats, we are equal. And it is all to the good if hats are dominant, for then our equality is extended through all the spheres of social life. On the view that I shall take here, however, we simply have the same number of hats, and it is unlikely that hats will be dominant for long. Equality is a complex relation of persons, mediated by the goods we make, share, and divide among ourselves; it is not an identity of possessions. It requires then, a diversity of distributive criteria that mirrors the diversity of social goods.

The argument for complex equality has been beautifully put by Pascal in one of his *Pensées*.

> The nature of tyranny is to desire power over the whole world and outside its own sphere.
>
> There are different companies—the strong, the handsome, the intelligent, the devout—and each man reigns in his own, not elsewhere. But sometimes they meet, and the strong and the handsome fight for mastery—foolishly, for their mastery is of different kinds. They misunderstand one another, and make the mistake of each aiming at universal dominion. Nothing can win this, not even strength, for it is powerless in the kingdom of the wise. . . .
>
> *Tyranny.* The following statements, therefore, are false and tyrannical: "Because I am handsome, so I should command respect." "I am strong, therefore men should love me. . . ." "I am . . . et cetera."
>
> Tyranny is the wish to obtain by one means what can only be had by another. We owe different duties to different qualities: love is the proper response to charm, fear to strength, and belief to learning.[8]

Marx made a similar argument in his early manuscripts; perhaps he had this *pensée* in mind:

> Let us assume man to be man, and his relation to the world to be a human one. Then love can only be exchanged for love, trust for trust, etc. If you wish to enjoy art you must be an artistically cultivated person; if you wish to influence other people, you must be a person who really has a stimulating and encouraging effect upon others. . . . If you love without evoking love in return, i.e., if you are not able, by the manifestation of yourself as a loving person, to make yourself a beloved person—then your love is impotent and a misfortune.[9]

These are not easy arguments, and most of my book is simply an exposition of their meaning. But here I shall attempt something more simple and schematic: a translation of the arguments into the terms I have already been using.

The first claim of Pascal and Marx is that personal qualities and social goods have their own spheres of operation, where they work their effects freely, spontaneously, and legitimately. There are ready or natural conversions that follow from, and are intuitively plausible because of, the social meaning of particular goods. The appeal is to our ordinary understanding and, at the same time, against our common acquiescence in illegitimate conversion patterns. Or, it is an appeal from our acquiescence to our resentment. There is something wrong, Pascal suggests, with the conversion of strength into belief. In political terms, Pascal means that no ruler can rightly command my opinions merely because of the power he wields. Nor can he, Marx adds, rightly claim to influence my actions: if a ruler wants to do that, he must be persuasive, helpful, encouraging, and so on. These arguments depend for their force on some shared understanding of knowledge, influence, and power. Social goods have social meanings, and we find our way to distributive justice through an interpretation of those meanings. We search for principles internal to each distributive sphere.

The second claim is that the disregard of these principles is tyranny. To convert one good into another, when there is no intrinsic connection between the two, is to invade the sphere where another company of men and women properly rules. Monopoly is not inappropriate within the spheres. There is nothing wrong, for example, with the grip that persuasive and helpful men and women (politicians) establish on political power. But the use of political power to gain access to other goods is a tyrannical use. Thus, an old description of tyranny is generalized: princes become tyrants, according to medieval writers, when they seize the property or invade the family of their subjects. In political life—but more widely, too—the dominance of goods makes for the domination of people.

The regime of complex equality is the opposite of tyranny. It establishes a set of relationships such that domination is impossible. In formal terms, complex equality means that no citizen's standing in one sphere or with regard to one social good can be undercut by his standing in some other sphere, with regard to some other good. Thus, citizen X may be chosen over citizen Y for political office, and then the two of them will be unequal in the sphere of politics. But they will not be unequal generally so long as X's office gives him no advantages over Y in any other sphere—superior medical care, access to better schools for his children, entrepreneurial opportunities, and so on. So long as office is not a dominant good, is not generally convertible, office holders will stand, or at least can stand, in a relation of equality to the men and women they govern.

But what if dominance were eliminated, the autonomy of the spheres established—and the same people were successful in one sphere after another, triumphant in every company, piling up goods without the need for illegitimate conversions? This would certainly make for an inegalitarian society, but it would also suggest in the strongest way that a society of equals was not a lively possibility. I doubt that any egalitarian argument could survive in the face of such evidence. Here is a person whom we have freely chosen (without reference to his family ties or personal wealth) as our political representative. He is also a bold and inventive entrepreneur. When he was younger, he studied science, scored amazingly high grades in every exam, and made important discoveries. In war, he is surpassingly brave and wins the highest honors. Himself compassionate and compelling, he is loved by all who know him. Are there such people? Maybe so, but I have my doubts. We tell stories like the one I have just told, but the stories are fictions, the conversion of power or money or academic talent into legendary fame. In any case, there aren't enough such people to constitute a ruling class and dominate the rest of us. Nor can they be successful in every distributive sphere, for there are some spheres to which the idea of success doesn't pertain. Nor are their children likely, under conditions of complex equality, to inherit their success. By and large, the most accomplished politicians, entrepreneurs, scientists, soldiers, and lovers will be different people; and so long as the goods they possess don't bring other goods in train, we have no reason to fear their accomplishments.

The critique of dominance and domination points toward an open-ended distributive principle. *No social good* x *should be distributed to men and women who possess some other good* y *merely because they possess* y *and without regard to the meaning of* x. This is a principle that has probably been reiterated, at one time or another, for every y that has ever been dominant. But it has not often been stated in general terms. Pascal and Marx have suggested the application of the principle against all possible y's, and I shall attempt to work out that application. I shall be looking, then, not at the members of Pascal's companies—the strong or the weak, the handsome or the plain—but at the goods they share and divide. The purpose of the principle is to focus our attention; it doesn't determine the shares or the division. The principle directs us to study the meaning of social goods, to examine the different distributive spheres from the inside.

Notes

1. See John Rawls, *A Theory of Justice* (Cambridge, Mass., 1971); Jürgen Habermas, *Legitimation Crisis*, trans. Thomas McCarthy (Boston, 1975), esp. p. 113; Bruce Ackerman, *Social Justice in the Liberal State* (New Haven, 1980).

2. Robert Nozick makes a similar argument in *Anarchy, State, and Utopia* (New York, 1974), pp. 149–50, but with radically individualistic conclusions that seem to me to miss the social character of production.

3. Ralph Waldo Emerson, "Ode," in *The Complete*

Essays and Other Writings, ed. Brooks Atkinson (New York, 1940), p. 770.

4. John Stuart Mill, *On Liberty,* in *The Philosophy of John Stuart Mill,* ed. Marshall Cohen (New York, 1961), p. 255. For an anthropological account of liking and not liking social goods, see Mary Douglas and Baron Isherwood, *The World of Goods* (New York, 1979).

5. William James, quoted in C. R. Snyder and Howard Fromkin, *Uniqueness: The Human Pursuit of Difference* (New York, 1980), p. 108.

6. Karl Marx, *The German Ideology,* ed. R. Pascal (New York, 1947), p. 89.

7. Bernard Williams, *Problems of the Self: Philosophical Papers, 1956–1972* (Cambridge, England, 1973), pp. 230–49 ("The Idea of Equality"). This essay is one of the starting points of my own thinking about distributive justice. See also the critique of Williams's argument (and of an earlier essay of my own) in Amy Gutmann, *Liberal Equality* (Cambridge, England, 1980), chap. 4.

8. Blaise Pascal, *The Pensées,* trans. J. M. Cohen (Harmondsworth, England, 1961), p. 96 (no. 244).

9. Karl Marx, *Economic and Philosophical Manuscripts,* in *Early Writings,* ed. T. B. Bottomore (London, 1963), pp. 193–94. It is interesting to note an earlier echo of Pascal's argument in Adam Smith's *Theory of Moral Sentiments* (Edinburgh, 1813), vol. I, pp. 378–79; but Smith seems to have believed that distributions in his own society actually conformed to this view of appropriateness—a mistake neither Pascal nor Marx ever made.

To Each His Own: An Exchange on Spheres of Justice

Ronald Dworkin and Michael Walzer

This selection is a debate between noted liberal Ronald Dworkin and Michael Walzer. It was initiated by Dworkin's review of Walzer's Spheres of Justice *in the* New York Review of Books *and includes Walzer's rebuttal and Dworkin's rejoinder. In his review Dworkin charged that the concept of complex equality is neither attainable nor coherent. First, he argues that the spheres Walzer describes are not self-contained; they overlap and their meanings are highly contested in public debates. Then, he challenges the relativism that would be unavoidable when separate systems of justice rule in each social sphere. When the members of a community debate the meaning of internal to a sphere, no common understanding governs the debate, and therefore even in Walzer's terms there is no possibility of justice. Dworkin charges Walzer with a radical relativism in morals. He argues that part of the social meaning of our common political life is that justice is our critic; it does not merely reflect our own set of social arrangements as this leads to a conception of justice that is internally incoherent. Walzer's defense rests on the fact that liberalism also experiences "hard cases" in which the application of principles produces no clear indication of a just solution, but this does not discredit liberalism. Instead of using universal principles that are applicable to every person and in every situation, his own theory recognizes that different norms apply in different areas of life, and further, that these norms must be generated within each sphere if they are to be appropriate in regulating the conduct within it. Dworkin responds by pointing out that a tradition can be interpreted and applied at different levels of abstraction and that consensus on its internal meaning is unlikely to emerge. Affirmative action and medical care distribution are used to illustrate points made in this debate.*

From *The New York Review of Books,* 14 April 1983, pp. 4–6, and 21 July 1983, pp. 65–68. Copyright © 1983 Nyrev, Inc. Reprinted with permission of The New York Review of Books.

In his new book, Michael Walzer proposes a pluralistic theory of social justice which aims at what he calls "complex" equality. He rejects the goals of "simple" egalitarians who want to make people as equal as possible in their *overall* situation. He thinks they ignore the fact that the conventions and shared understandings that make up a society do not treat all goods as subject to the same principles of distribution. Our conventions, he argues, assign different kinds of resources and opportunities to different "spheres" of justice, each of which is governed by its own distinct principle of fairness. These conventions provide what Walzer calls the "social meaning" of different goods; for us it is part of social meaning, he says, that medicine and other necessities of a decent life should be distributed according to need, punishment and honors according to what people deserve, higher education according to talent, jobs according to the needs of the employer, wealth according to skill and luck in the market, citizenship according to the needs and traditions of the community, and so forth.

The theory of complex equality consists in two ideas. Each kind of resource must be distributed in accordance with the principle appropriate to its sphere, and success in one sphere must not spill over to allow domination in another. We must not allow someone who achieves great wealth in the market, for example, to buy votes and so control politics. But if we keep the boundaries of the spheres intact, then we need no overall comparison of individuals across the spheres; we need not worry that some people have yachts and others not even a rowboat, or that some are more persuasive in politics than others, or that some win prizes and love while others lack both.

This is a relaxed and agreeable vision of social justice: it promises a society at peace with its own traditions, without the constant tensions, comparisons, jealousies, and regimentation of "simple" equality. Citizens live together in harmony, though no one has exactly the wealth or education or opportunities of anyone else, because each understands that he has received what justice requires within each sphere, and does not think that his self-respect or standing in the community depends on any overall comparison of his overall situation with that of others. Unfortunately Walzer offers no comprehensive description of what life in such a society would be like, of who would have what share of the different types of resources he discusses. (I shall try to show, later, why in fact he cannot do this.) Instead he offers anecdotal and historical examples of how different societies, including our own, have developed distinct principles for distribution in different spheres.

His aim in providing these examples is not only practical. He hopes to break the grip that the formal style has lately had on Anglo-American political philosophy. Such philosophers try to find some inclusive formula that can be used to measure social justice in any society, and that can therefore serve as a test rather than simply as an elaboration of our own conventional social arrangements. John Rawls argues, for example, that no inequality in what he calls "primary goods" is justified unless it improves the overall position of the worst-off class, and this formula takes no account of which of Walzer's spheres such goods are drawn from. Utilitarians insist, on the contrary, that whatever social arrangement will in fact produce the greatest long-term happiness of the greatest number is just, and this means that justice might conceivably recommend violating one of Walzer's spheres by selling political offices at auction, for example, even though our conventions condemn this. "Simple" egalitarians argue that justice lies in everyone's having the same resources overall which might mean abandoning prizes and badges of honor, and "libertarians" argue that it lies in allowing people to buy whatever others rightfully own and are willing to sell, whether this is corn or labor or sex.

Theories like these ignore the social meanings of the goods they try to distribute. So they will inevitably be arid, unhistorical, and above all abstract. We can test them only against our private "intuitions" of what would be just in this or that circumstance, not by asking how they would strike most members of our own community, and we can argue them only through highly artificial examples tailored to bring out some stark contrast between isolated abstract principles. Such theories seem more at home with mathematics than with politics.

Walzer shows us how different, and how much more concrete, political analysis can be. His historical examples are often fascinating, and this, along with his clear prose, makes his book a pleasure to read. The examples are nicely judged to illustrate the characteristic features of each of his spheres of justice, and the persistence yet diversity of certain themes in the social meanings people give to their experience. The Greeks provided free public drama because they saw this as a social need, but they made the most rudimentary provision for the poor; the Middle Ages offered welfare for the soul but not for the body. Earlier communities provided everyone with holidays that guaranteed a public life; we have switched to vacations whose social meaning is rather private variety and choice. Some of Walzer's examples have a different function: they illustrate the dangers of failing to protect the boundaries between spheres. George Pullman, who invented Pullman cars, built a town around his factory and tried to own his employees' lives as he owned the machines at which they worked. He tried to use his success in the market to dominate the different spheres of politics and citizenship, and this explains why society and the courts checked his ambitions. Walzer's range is admirable: we are encouraged to consider the meritocracies of China under the dynasties, a cooperative garbage collecting firm in San Francisco, the *Kula* practice of gift exchange among the Trobriand Islanders, and education among the Aztecs.

Nevertheless his central argument fails. The ideal of complex equality he defines is not attainable, or even coherent, and the book contains very little that could be helpful in thinking about actual issues of justice. It tells us to look to social conventions to discover the appropriate principles of distribution for particular goods, but the very fact that we debate about what justice requires, in particular cases, shows that we have no conventions of the necessary sort. In the U.S. we sponsor medical research through taxes, and after long political struggles we offer Medicare to the old and Medicaid to the poor, though the latter remains very controversial. Walzer thinks these programs demonstrate that our community

assigns medical care to a particular sphere, the sphere of needs that the state must satisfy. But the brutal fact is that we do not provide anything like the same medical care for the poor as the middle classes can provide for themselves, and surely this also counts in deciding what the "social meaning" of medicine is in our society. Even those who agree that some medical care must be provided to everyone disagree about limits. Is it part of the social meaning of medicine that elective surgery must be free? That people "need" heart transplants?

Our political arguments almost never begin in some shared understanding of the pertinent principles of distribution. Every important issue is a contest between competing models. Nor do we accept that everything we find valuable must be wholly subject to a single logic of distribution: if we recognize spheres of justice we also recognize the need for interaction between them. The most important way in which wealth influences politics, for example, is by buying not votes but television time. Of course, those who favor restricting campaign expenses say that money should not buy office. But their opponents reply that such restrictions would violate rights of property as well as free speech, so the issue belongs to no settled sphere of justice, but is rather the subject of bargaining and compromise endlessly debated.

Walzer's response to these plain facts about political argument shows how feeble his positive theory of justice really is:

> A given society is just if its substantive life is lived in a certain way—that is, in a way faithful to the shared understandings of the members. (When people disagree about the meaning of social goods, when understandings are controversial, then justice requires that the society be faithful to the disagreements, providing institutional channels for their expression, adjudicative mechanisms, and alternative distributions.)

This passage confirms Walzer's deep relativism about justice. He says, for example, that a caste system is just in a society whose traditions accept it, and that it would be unjust, in such a society, to distribute goods and other resources equally. But his remarks about what justice requires in a society whose members disagree about justice are simply mysterious. Does "alternative distributions" mean medical care for the poor in some cities but not in others? How can a society that must make up its mind whether to permit political action committees to finance election campaigns really be "faithful" to disagreement about the social meaning of elections and political speech? What would "being faithful" mean?

If justice is only a matter of following shared understandings, then how can the parties be debating about justice when there is no shared understanding? In that situation no solution can *possibly* be just, on Walzer's relativistic account, and politics can be only a selfish struggle. What can it mean even to say that people disagree about social meanings? The fact of the disagreement shows that there is no shared social meaning to disagree about. Walzer has simply not thought through the consequences of his relativism for a society like ours, in which questions of justice are endlessly contested and debated.

Why does Walzer not recognize that his theory must be irrelevant in such a society? He does discuss a number of contemporary political issues in some detail, and these discussions suggest an explanation. He takes no position of his own about some of the issues he describes, and when he does express his own opinion he sometimes provides no argument at all for it. But when he does argue for his own views, by trying to show how these follow from the general scheme of complex equality, he reveals that he is actually relying on a hidden and mystical premise that plays no part in his formal statements of that scheme, but that helps to explain why he thinks that it can give practical advice for people in our circumstances.

What is this premise? He tacitly assumes that there are only a limited number of spheres of justice whose essential principles have been established in advance and must therefore remain the same for all societies. He also assumes that though any particular community is free to choose whether to assign some type of resource to one or another of these fixed spheres, by developing the appropriate conventions, it must do so on an all-or-

nothing basis. It cannot construct new patterns of distribution that have elements drawn from different spheres. So if a community recognizes medicine as something people need, or establishes political offices, or develops institutions of specialized higher education, or recognizes some group of people as citizens, it is thereby committed to every feature of the spheres of social welfare or merit or education or citizenship as Walzer understands these. A caste system is not in itself unjust, but if it develops an official bureaucracy of civil servants it may not restrict offices within that bureaucracy to higher castes, because the concept of bureaucracy belongs, according to Walzer, to its own sphere, the sphere of merit. A capitalist society, he argues, may, with perfect justice, assign medical care wholly to the market. Or (perhaps) it may assign only a fixed, minimum level of care to the sphere of need. But "so long as communal funds are spent . . . to finance research, build hospitals, and pay the fees of doctors in private practice, the services that these expenditures underwrite must be equally available to all citizens," and there is then "no reason to respect the doctor's market freedom."

Once the hidden assumption—that a community must accept a preestablished sphere on an all-or-nothing basis—is exposed, the fallacy in these arguments becomes clear. We cannot just rule out, in advance, the possibility that though justice requires the state to intervene in the market for medicine in order to ensure that the poor have some care, it does not require that the poor be provided the same medical care the rich are able to buy. Walzer takes the contrary view that justice demands a full national health service. We may find this attractive but we need an argument for it, and simply constructing an ideal sphere, and calling it the sphere of need, provides no argument. The point is a crucial one, because it might be that any genuine argument for a national health service would contradict Walzer's relativism. It might show that a rich society that leaves medical care entirely to the market would not be a just society, as he thinks, but would in fact be even more unjust than a society, like ours, that provides some but not enough free medical care.

Walzer relies even more heavily on the idea of fixed, preordained spheres in his discussion of university admission programs that give some preference to minority applicants. "In our culture," he says, " . . . careers are supposed to be open to talents," and "just as we could not adopt a system of preventive detention without violating the rights of innocent people, even if we weighed fairly the costs and benefits of the system as a whole, so we can't adopt a quota system without violating the rights of candidates." He knows, of course, that many people "in our culture" do not think that the affirmative action programs Walzer has in mind violate the rights of candidates. They reject the analogy to punishing the innocent. They deny that there is some canonical set of qualities, fixed in advance, such that people are entitled to be admitted to medical schools on the basis of these qualities alone, no matter what special needs a society might have for doctors or what larger needs might also be served through professional education. Walzer, on the contrary, believes that a certain conception of talent is automatically assigned to certain university places or professional offices, no matter how thoroughly the community is divided about this. So he says that any racial preference corrupts one of the spheres he has constructed—the sphere of "office"—in order to serve the sphere of welfare, and thinks he needs no better argument than that. He is bewitched by the music of his own Platonic spheres.

Criticism of Walzer's idea of complex equality must not end here, however, because his theory is not only unhelpful but finally incoherent. It ignores the "social meaning" of a tradition much more fundamental than the discrete traditions it asks us to respect. For it is part of our common political life, if anything is, that justice is our critic not our mirror, that any decision about the distribution of any good—wealth, welfare, honors, education, recognition, office—may be reopened no matter how firm the traditions that are then challenged, that we may always ask of some settled institutional scheme whether it is fair. Walzer's relativism is faithless to the single most important social practice we have: the practice of worrying about what justice really is.

So a theory that ties justice to conventions would not be acceptable even if it were available to us. Walzer sometimes seems to suggest that the only alternative is the "simple" equality he dismisses, which requires that everyone have exactly the same share of everything. But no one argues for that: no one suggests that punishments or Nobel prizes should be distributed by lot. Few egalitarians would even accept simple equality in income or wealth. Any defensible version of equality must be much more subtle; it must permit inequalities that can be traced to the choices people have made about what kind of work to do, what kinds of risks to take, what kind of life to lead.*

But we need to argue for any theory of justice of that kind, by finding and defending general, critical principles of the appropriate sort. So Walzer's book provides a wholly unintended defense of the style of philosophy he wants to banish. His failure confirms the instinct that drives philosophers to their formulas and artificial examples and personal intuitions. Perhaps we have gone too far in that direction. Mathematical preference functions, fictitious social contracts, and the other paraphernalia of modern political theory do sometimes blind us to the subtle distinctions Walzer teases out of history. Political philosophers who reflect on his historical studies—particularly his demonstration of how different societies have conceived very different resources as needs—will be more imaginative about the possibilities of social arrangements in our own society.

In the end, however, political theory can make no contribution to how we govern ourselves except by struggling, against all the impulses that drag us back into our own culture, toward generality and some reflective basis for deciding which of our traditional distinctions and discriminations are genuine and which spurious, which contribute to the flourishing of the ideals we want, after reflection, to embrace and which serve only to protect us from the personal costs of that demanding process. We cannot leave justice to convention and anecdote.

*In a recent issue of this review I described a version of equality more complex than simple equality in that way: "Why Liberals Should Believe in Equality," *The New York Review,* February 3.

* * *

To the Editors:

Ronald Dworkin's review of my *Spheres of Justice* [*NYR*, April 14] is also, and quite legitimately, a defense of his own approach to moral and political philosophy. It raises hard questions about how that enterprise ought to be carried on, but it provides, I'm afraid, easy answers. It avoids the difficulties of morality and politics. Indeed, that avoidance is, if I understand Dworkin correctly, the greatest advantage that he claims for his approach. I would like to argue (again) that the difficulties are unavoidable.

My own claim is that we cannot distribute goods to men and women until we understand what the goods mean, what parts they play, how they are created, and how they are valued, among those same men and women. Distributions flow out of and are relative to social meanings. But this argument fails, according to Dworkin, because social meanings are not in fact shared. They are "endlessly contested and debated." Our political arguments, he says, begin with disagreements about how this or that good functions in our social life and about what principles are appropriate to its distribution. Such disagreements can't be resolved unless we move outside our own traditions and understandings and appeal to "general" principles. We have to turn to an "inclusive formula that can be used to measure justice in *any* society" (my emphasis). I expect that Dworkin plans to propose such a formula, and I don't doubt that his proposal will be technically interesting and philosophically skillful (see his provisional statement, which is already very clever and very elaborate, in *Philosophy and Public Affairs,* Summer and Fall, 1981). But it probably won't surprise him if people find his formula contestable and if the debates go on "endlessly." The suggestion that someone is going to end the contest with a single knockdown argument is a piece of philosophical impetuosity.

What is the best way of carrying on the argument? Curiously, Dworkin has himself provided an excellent model in his account of how "hard cases" ought to be decided in a legal system like our own (*Taking Rights Seriously*

[Harvard University Press, 1977], pp. 81–130). Hard cases are contestable cases, and in an important sense the contest is endless: the judge's decision is merely one moment in an ongoing argument. But in principle, Dworkin insists, the judge can make the right decision. Exactly how he does this is not entirely clear; Dworkin's account is at once persuasive and ambiguous, and I shall pursue only one strand, which seems to me the most powerful strand, of his reasoning. The judge reaches the right decision not by appealing to principles external to the legal system, but by exploring the internal principles of the system itself—and of the legal and political culture in which it is embedded. He searches for "the political morality presupposed by the laws and institutions of the community" (p. 126). That is exactly the procedure that I too would recommend, and for all my "relativism," I share Dworkin's sense that in a particular case, in a particular culture, there is, in principle, a right decision. To be sure, Dworkin stipulates a miraculously intelligent judge, a stand-in for the author, who is named Hercules. But Hercules is not privy to some universal theory of justice; he is merely superhumanly learned in his own tradition, patient and skillful in studying its history, its underlying philosophy, and its institutional details. He teases out the deepest understanding of the "legal community."

I can think of no better way of discovering the appropriate distributive principles for medical care, political power, bureaucratic office, education, punishment, and so on. The moral world, of course, is more loosely structured than the legal world: there is no basic text like the constitution and no authoritative decisions (precedents), but there is a history; there are institutions and practices and underlying ideas. We must interpret these as best we can in order to get some grasp on the character of the goods we distribute to one another (they have no abstract or general character, or none that will help in determining who, among ourselves, should get how much of what). There will be different interpretations and, absent Hercules, no final and definitive interpretation. But that is not to say that we can't mark off better from worse arguments, deep and inclusive accounts of our social life from shallow and partisan accounts.

Dworkin seems to think that such a procedure will have no critical bite. But he recognizes readily enough that Hercules can be a legal critic, and he ought to recognize that I can be (I often am) a social critic. Social critics commonly don't, and certainly needn't, invent the principles they apply; they don't have to step outside the world they ordinarily inhabit. They appeal to internal principles, already known, comprehensible to, somehow remembered by, the people they hope to convince. Most often, as I have tried to show, they claim that such and such a good is not being distributed in accordance with its own meaning and the principles that flow from that meaning, but has been usurped and tyrannically controlled by men and women who hold some other good. They complain that religious communion is available only on terms set by the powerful, or that offices are bought and sold by the wealthy, or that punishment falls upon the poor rather than upon the guilty, or that the best commodities and services are reserved for members of the Party, and so on.

But this sort of complaint won't make for determinate criticism, according to Dworkin, unless one assumes (as he claims I do) that the different spheres of distribution, within which this or that principle is appropriate, are "fixed and preordained," established "on an all-or-nothing basis." I don't in fact make any such assumption; indeed, it is contrary to the method and intention of my book. Social goods and distributive spheres have first to be found through a process of empirical investigation, and then they have to be understood through a process of interpretation. They have the forms they take in a particular society; there are no preordained forms. It is entirely possible, on my view, that for some goods we will have complex rather than unitary distributive principles; and it is possible too that the boundaries we draw around a particular good, our understanding of what counts as a commodity, an office, or a punishment, will change over time.

"We cannot just rule out in advance," Dworkin writes, "the possibility that though justice requires the state to intervene in the market for medicine in order to ensure that the poor have some care, it does not require that the poor be provided the same medical care the rich are able to buy. Walzer takes the opposite view that justice demands a full national service." Not quite right: I don't rule out in advance, but consider and reject the possibility that Dworkin raises; and I argue that "justice demands" a more egalitarian distribution *in our society* because of what medical care means to us, the value we collectively assign to it, and the decision, already made, to provide it out of communal resources for some but not all the members of the community (*Spheres of Justice*, pp. 86–91). The argument is historical, sociological, contingent. Dworkin wants an entirely different kind of argument, so that one might say at the end, flatly, that a rich society that leaves medical care to the market "would not be a just society." I am in fact disinclined to say that *just like that*, for it may be the case that the wealth of some particular society ought to be spent on the cure of souls, not of bodies, or on defense, or drama, or education. I don't see how these priorities can be philosophically determined. But that is not to rule out radical criticism, for the actual distribution of salvation, security, and culture is likely to be distorted, has historically been distorted, by wealthy and powerful elites, and it is one of the tasks of moral philosophy (and of social theory too) to explain and condemn the distortions.

The case is the same with place and office. Here I criticize an argument that Dworkin made some years ago about the Bakke case (*NYR*, November 10, 1977), and he responds to my criticism, though without quite saying what is going on. "Walzer . . . believes that a certain conception of talent is automatically assigned to certain university places and professional offices, no matter how thoroughly the community is divided about this." Not quite right: I argue at considerable length (*Spheres of Justice*, Chapter 5) against the "automatic assignment" that meritocrats commonly make, and I try to account for the leeway that search and selection committees have and ought to have. But such committees don't have infinite leeway; powerholders are constrained in the way they give out offices by what offices are in the United States today. Dworkin thinks of offices, or at least of a very large number of offices, as a kind of currency, a social resource, to be distributed on essentially utilitarian grounds. But offices, like all other social goods, are not just things lying about to be used in any way we please; they are the products of a particular history; they have a special meaning in our culture—a meaning in this case hinted at though by no means fully revealed by, the revolutionary slogan about careers open to talents. I try to explore that meaning, inadequately, I suppose, since I am not Hercules. But without such an exploration, no distributive claim can ever be anything but arbitrary, no enforcement of a claim anything but tyrannical.

Let me come back to the problem of disagreement. Dworkin has some fun with the notion that people disagree about the meanings they share: if they disagree, he says, there are no shared meanings. In fact, two different kinds of disagreement are possible, which I have probably not sufficiently distinguished. First, people can disagree within a cultural tradition. They interpret meanings in somewhat different ways, or they take different positions on boundary disputes and on overlapping or entangled goods. This is the best way to understand current arguments about quotas and affirmative action. Dworkin's position on these questions has not figured in the actual debates; perhaps it is genuinely original, a philosophical feat. The standard arguments are very different from his, and they all pay tribute (there is honesty and hypocrisy on both sides) to the common understanding of office—which connects its distribution, though not very strictly, to talent and performance. This kind of disagreement displays rather than denies the existence of shared meanings.

Second, people disagree because they come out of radically different cultural traditions, as in many third world states today. I was thinking of cases of this second sort when I suggested that divided societies might have to provide "alternative distributions." Does this mean, Dworkin asks, "medical care for the poor in some cities, but not in others"? It might mean that, if the different cities were inhabited by people with, say, radically different understandings of medical care. If the populations were mixed, as they most often are, then it might be (morally) necessary to work out a political accommodation. Politics must sometimes substitute for justice, provid-

ing a neutral frame within which a common life slowly develops. (Even this is a critical idea, allowing us to deny the justice of imposed, rather than negotiated, distributions.)

Dworkin's deepest worry is that I am a relativist. (He is especially concerned about my views on the Indian caste system, of which he provides a very partial account: but that is an issue best left to another occasion.) I see his point, though most relativists would think me just as tiresomely judgmental as he is. Indeed, we share a desire to reach moral conclusions. We only disagree about the force or, better, the scope of our conclusions. I don't hope to make arguments that are conclusive for all human beings in all societies that exist or will exist or have ever existed. I don't subscribe to the idea—it seems to me distinctly odd—that the principles of justice appropriate to Americans must be appropriate as well to ancient Babylonians. Not that such an idea makes it impossibly hard to arrive at principles of justice; it makes it too easy, for the principles need not apply to anyone in particular. The hard task is to find principles latent in the lives of the people Dworkin and I live with, principles that they can recognize and adopt.

Michael Walzer

Princeton, New Jersey

Ronald Dworkin *replies*:

I appreciate Professor Walzer's thoughtful letter, but I do not think it meets my argument. I said that his theory, which makes justice depend on shared conventions, cannot be useful for us because our society is divided rather than united over which principles of distributional justice to apply to different types of resources. Many Americans disagree about how far medical care, for example, should be distributed in accordance with need rather than with ability to pay.

Walzer now replies that there are two kinds of disagreement about justice: disagreement within a cultural tradition when people "interpret" their own conventions and practices in somewhat different ways, and disagreement between very different traditions. He believes that our own political differences—about medicine and affirmative action, for example—are disputes of the first sort, and that his conventionalist account of justice permits him to take up critical positions in these debates, because it permits him to argue about what our traditions, properly understood and interpreted, *really* require.

It is unfortunate that Walzer did not develop this idea in his book, for he would then have told us what, in his view, could make one interpretation of a moral tradition better than another. Our record in providing medical care is a mixed one. The state sponsors some medical research, and we have some federal and state programs of free medical care for those most in need. But the rich have always been able to buy much better medical care for themselves. How shall we interpret this record? Shall we say that our traditions assign medicine to the market, with some inconsistent exceptions that should now be abandoned? Or that they assign medicine to the sphere of need, but with inconsistent backsliding in favor of wealth and privilege? Or that they express the more complex principle that justice requires leaving medicine to the market but insists on just the qualifications and exceptions that we have made? What could make one of these interpretations superior to the others?

Walzer says that he can think of no better account of the process he has in mind than my own description of the way judges decide hard cases at law. The ideal judge I imagine—Hercules—interprets the immense variety of past judicial decisions in his jurisdiction so as to find the scheme of principle that "underlies" them, and then decides new cases that come before him by applying that scheme. The set of principles he deploys as the best interpretation may not fit all the past decisions; it may show some of these to have been "mistakes" which should now be eliminated to achieve integrity in the law as a whole. Walzer suggests that we take my account of interpretation of past judicial decisions as a model for interpreting and reforming the moral culture of the community as a whole.

But this partial statement of my views about adjudication simply raises the same puzzle about interpretation in a new form. What does it mean to say that a particular principle—that medical care must be treated as a matter of need, for example—"underlies" the political

accommodations we have reached? How is that metaphor to be unpacked? Walzer seems unaware of how I myself answered that question. I said that a principle underlies a body of rules if it provides the best available *justification* for those rules, and I emphasized that this is not simply a mechanical test of counting how many past decisions "fit" the proposed principle. I said that if different schemes of interpretation each fit a great many rules but are inconsistent with others then Hercules must choose, as the "correct" interpretation, that which in his view comes closest to what abstract justice would require.

But of course this makes adjudication in hard cases turn on judgments of political morality that different judges will make differently. (Many critics reject my argument for that reason.) So Walzer cannot adopt my account of judicial interpretation without undermining his entire case. He would then have to say that the best interpretation of our arrangements about medicine, of those I just described, is the interpretation which is to be preferred on grounds of abstract justice. This would concede that he mainly wishes to deny, that justice is at bottom independent of the conventional arguments of any particular society. For if he continued to claim that justice is only a matter of what these conventions, properly interpreted, provide, his argument that one interpretation comes closer to abstract justice would be wholly circular and wholly ineffectual.[1]

So if Walzer is to protect his main position he cannot use my analysis after all. What other options does he have? I suggested one in my review. He might think that the various "spheres" of justice he describes are each preordained and distinct, so that an interpreter could ask whether our practices about medicine, taken together, are closer to those required by the pure, preordained sphere of need than they are to the pure, preordained sphere of market transactions, and then insist that they be reformed so as to be entirely like those of the sphere they most resemble. Of course these judgments of resemblance would be impressionistic—two interpreters might disagree—but the process does not seem to require any assumptions about nonconventional requirements of abstract justice. So Walzer could accept this story without abandoning his general position. That is why I suggested, in my review, that the idea of fixed, pre-ordained spheres is the "hidden" and "tacit" premise of his argument. I meant that I thought he was relying on that idea whether he understood this or not.

I am not surprised that he disowns the idea once it has been made explicit. But how else can he explain how one interpretation of our practices can be better than another when it is controversial which is better? Why is the argument defending the status quo in medical care—that the balance between market and need that politics has achieved itself provides the best interpretation of its moral traditions with respect to medicine—any worse than the argument for reform in either direction? If Walzer says that the compromise is a poorer interpretation because it is unprincipled, because it does not express a coherent and defensible vision of justice, then he is appealing to the idea of abstract justice he rejects; if he says it is illegitimate because it does not consistently enforce either the market or the need model then he is appealing to preordained spheres. Perhaps he can provide a different account of interpretation that will escape both these problems, but he has not yet indicated what this might be.

Walzer says that the remarks I quoted in my review, about what justice requires when "people disagree about the meanings of social goods," were intended to apply to disagreement of the second sort, between rival moral traditions. He says that in such cases politics must substitute for justice. This is the heart of our disagreement. The idea that the world is divided into distinct moral cultures, and that it should be the goal of politics to foster the value of "community" by respecting the differences, has for a long time been associated with political conservatism and moral relativism. It is once again fashionable in political theory, but its proponents have paid insufficient attention to their central concepts. Moral traditions are not clubs into which the peoples of the world are distributed so that everyone carries a membership card in one but only one. On the contrary, these traditions can be defined at different levels of abstraction, and people who belong to a common tradition

at one level of abstraction will divide at another, more concrete, level.

American liberals and members of the "Moral Majority," for example, belong at one level to a common moral tradition, because they share an idea that the state must act justly toward all, and share many opinions about what justice is. (So do two people from what Walzer calls radically different cultural traditions, like citizens of different "third world" countries.) But American liberals and members of the "Moral Majority" do not share a common moral tradition at another, more concrete, level because they disagree sharply about the role that justice permits or requires the state to play in the moral lives of its citizens. We can, if we wish, say that one side or the other better "understands" the more abstract principles about which they are agreed; that liberals have a better theory of what justice really requires. But this is not a neutral, anthropological judgment we can defend simply by studying the practices of American society. It is a moral judgment taking sides in the dispute, the kind of judgment that would make no sense if justice were simply a matter of convention. So the idea of a shared moral tradition cannot do the work Walzer wants; if society is divided on some issue, the tradition runs out where the dispute begins. If we accept his dictum, that politics must then replace justice, justice all but disappears for us. We are left with the politics of selfishness.

Walzer makes some harsh remarks about my own views about justice, though he does not say which of my views he has in mind. He says that my arguments provide only "easy" answers, that because they try to ground particular claims about particular societies in more general critical principles they can apply to no one in particular. He does not elaborate, and since he offers no examples I find it difficult to respond or even to see what he means. He mentions only my views about affirmative action, and what he calls my "elaborate" arguments about distributional justice, but he says these are both contentious and offers no reason to doubt my claim that anyone who does accept them is committed to particular positions in the practical debates of American politics.

He seems to assume that an argument can

have no practical bite if it begins in principles of some generality. The truth, as I have tried to show, is quite the contrary. Of course an argument of political morality cannot reach particular conclusions without taking into account relevant features of the community under discussion. Of course "we cannot distribute goods to men and women until we understand what these goods mean . . . among those same men and women." There is indeed no reason to expect that the concrete conclusions we reach about what justice requires for us will apply as well to the ancient Babylonians. Certainly an abstract theory of justice is useless politically if it cannot be advanced in practical politics. But the principles of justice we use to decide which features of a community are relevant to a just distribution of its goods and opportunities—and therefore which principles we should struggle to promote politically—must be principles we accept because they seem right rather than because they have been captured in some conventional practice. Otherwise political theory will be only a mirror, uselessly reflecting a community's consensus and division back upon itself.[2]

Notes

1. I do not mean myself to endorse the view that social justice depends on the best interpretation, even in the sense Hercules uses, of the past practices of the community. On the contrary the essential difference between the concepts of law and justice, I believe, is that while both invoke morality, justice is more radically independent of the past.
2. Walzer finds several of my summaries of his

views "not quite right." He says he provides an argument for a full national health service in our community, based on the fact that we have already decided to provide medical care "out of communal resources for some but not all members of the community." That is exactly the argument I said he made, and I can only repeat that this argument, without more, depends on ruling out the possibility that this qualified state intervention in the market for medical care is exactly what justice requires.

He is also dissatisfied with my summary of his argument about offices and merit. He does indeed say that search committees and others who fill offices must have some leeway, but he makes plain that this is leeway within "the range of permissible disagreement" which "has limits." He says that "we do know, at least in general terms, what qualities are relevant, for relevant qualities are inherent in the practice, abstracted from experience, of office holding." He thinks that color cannot be taken to be even within the range of qualities relevant for admission to medical school, in spite of the widespread view in America that we need more black doctors. He concludes that affirmative action programs of the sort he discusses violate the "rights" of white candidates, and goes so far as to suggest that my own contrary view is equivalent to sending innocent people to jail for the general good. How can this rigid view be "abstracted from experience," as part of some shared understanding, when our political debates include the view that these programs violate no rights because color *has* been made relevant, among other qualities, by our history and present needs? Once again, Walzer is relying on the assumption that his own controversial interpretation of our practices is the only permissible interpretation. But he has given no hint of what, within his general scheme, that claim could even mean.

The Concept of a Tradition

Alasdair MacIntyre

Alasdair MacIntyre is one of the major critics of liberalism in the current debate. He holds that a person is fully human only within a coherent tradition, since it is through a tradition that an individual gains self-understanding and it is through social practices that he or she is able to live a meaningful life. Morality is a function of this self-understanding and these social practices. By MacIntyre's account, modern liberal society is a collection of rudderless, often desperate people clutching at fragments of lost traditions with which to interpret their lives. The moral life of individuals and of society is in disarray. In this selection MacIntyre describes the life of a person as a narrative set in a particular cultural group and scripted by the stories and myths of a tradition. Through a tradition I cast myself as a character in the life of my community and adopt a life plan. I am not only the subject, or main character, of my own narrative, I am also a character in the narratives of other people. Morality originates in the accountability each of us has vis-a-vis others in these narratives. The good life consists of attaining the goods that are internal to the social practices in which I am a character, and the virtues are dispositions that both sustain these practices and my ability to act within them. Finally, MacIntyre explains that the good life can never be achieved by a person alone, but only as an integrated member of a community. This view of the moral life contrasts sharply with liberal morality and politics. The individualism, acquisitiveness, and adversarial relations found in liberal societies, MacIntyre argues, undermine the traditions through which people develop the social virtues necessary to their own well-being and the proper functioning of their community.

A central thesis then begins to emerge: man is in his actions and practice, as well as in his fictions, essentially a story-telling animal. He is not essentially, but becomes through his history, a teller of stories that aspire to truth. But the key question for men is not about their own authorship; I can only answer the question "What am I to do?" if I can answer the prior question "Of what story or stories do I find myself a part?" We enter human society, that is, with one or more imputed characters—roles into which we have been drafted—and we have to learn what they are in order to be able to understand how others respond to us and how our responses to them are apt to be construed. It is through hearing stories about wicked stepmothers, lost children, good but misguided kings, wolves that suckle twin boys, youngest sons who receive no inheritance but must make their own way in the world and eldest sons who waste their inheritance on riotous living and go into exile to live with the swine, that children learn or mislearn both what a child and what a parent is, what the cast of characters may be in the drama into which they have been born and what the ways of the world are. Deprive children of stories and you leave them unscripted, anxious stutterers in their actions as in their words. Hence there is no way to give us an understanding of any

From Alasdair MacIntyre, *After Virtue* (Notre Dame: University of Notre Dame Press, 1981), pp. 201–207. © 1984 by University of Notre Dame Press. Reprinted by permission of the publisher.

society, including our own, except through the stock of stories which constitute its initial dramatic resources. Mythology, in its original sense, is at the heart of things. Vico was right and so was Joyce. And so too of course is that moral tradition from heroic society to its medieval heirs according to which the telling of stories has a key part in educating us into the virtues. . . .

I would now like to make a . . . suggestion about another concept, that of personal identity. Derek Parfit and others have recently drawn our attention to the contrast between the criteria of strict identity, which is an all-or-nothing matter (*either* the Tichborne claimant *is* the last Tichborne heir; *either* all the properties of the last heir belong to the claimant *or* the claimant is not the heir—Leibniz's Law applies) and the psychological continuities of personality which are a matter of more or less. (Am I the same man at fifty as I was at forty in respect of memory, intellectual powers, critical responses? More or less.) But what is crucial to human beings as characters in enacted narratives is that, possessing only the resources of psychological continuity, we have to be able to respond to the imputation of strict identity. I am forever whatever I have been at any time for others—and I may at any time be called upon to answer for it—no matter how changed I may be now. There is no way of *founding* my identity—or lack of it—on the psychological continuity or discontinuity of the self. The self inhabits a character whose unity is given as the unity of a character. Once again there is a crucial disagreement with empiricist or analytical philosophers on the one hand and with existentialists on the other.

Empiricists, such as Locke or Hume, tried to give an account of personal identity solely in terms of psychological states or events. Analytical philosophers, in so many ways their heirs as well as their critics, have wrestled with the connection between those states and events and strict identity understood in terms of Leibniz's Law. Both have failed to see that a background has been omitted, the lack of which makes the problems insoluble. That background is provided by the concept of a story and of that kind of unity of character which a story requires. Just as a history is not a

sequence of actions, but the concept of an action is that of a moment in an actual or possible history abstracted for some purpose from that history, so the characters in a history are not a collection of persons, but the concept of a person is that of a character abstracted from a history.

What the narrative concept of selfhood requires is thus twofold. On the one hand, I am what I may justifiably be taken by others to be in the course of living out a story that runs from my birth to my death; I am the *subject* of a history that is my own and no one else's, that has its own peculiar meaning. When someone complains—as do some of those who attempt or commit suicide—that his or her life is meaningless, he or she is often and perhaps characteristically complaining that the narrative of their life has become unintelligible to them, that it lacks any point, any movement towards a climax or a *telos*. Hence the point of doing any one thing rather than another at crucial junctures in their lives seems to such a person to have been lost.

To be the subject of a narrative that runs from one's birth to one's death is, I remarked earlier, to be accountable for the actions and experiences which compose a narratable life. It is, that is, to be open to being asked to give a certain kind of account of what one did or what happened to one or what one witnessed at any earlier point in one's life the time at which the question is posed. Of course someone may have forgotten or suffered brain damage or simply not attended sufficiently at the relevant times to be able to give the relevant account. But to say of someone under some one description ("The prisoner of the Chateau d'If") that he is the same person as someone characterised quite differently ("The Count of Monte Cristo") is precisely to say that it makes sense to ask him to give an intelligible narrative account enabling us to understand how he could at different times and different places be one and the same person and yet be so differently characterised. Thus personal identity is just that identity presupposed by the unity of the character which the unity of a narrative requires. Without such unity there would not be subjects of whom stories could be told.

The other aspect of narrative selfhood is correlative: I am not only accountable, I am one who can always ask others for an account, who can put others to the question. I am part of their story, as they are part of mine. The narrative of any one life is part of an interlocking set of narratives. Moreover this asking for and giving of accounts itself plays an important part in constituting narratives. Asking you what you did and why, saying what I did and why, pondering the differences between your account of what I did and my account of what I did, and *vice versa,* these are essential constituents of all but the very simplest and barest of narratives. Thus without the accountability of the self those trains of events that constitute all but the simplest and barest of narratives could not occur; and without that same accountability narratives would lack that continuity required to make both them and the actions that constitute them intelligible.

It is important to notice that I am not arguing that the concepts of narrative or of intelligibility or of accountability are *more* fundamental than that of personal identity. The concepts of narrative, intelligibility and accountability presuppose the applicability of the concept of personal identity, just as it presupposes their applicability and just as indeed each of these three presupposes the applicability of the two others. The relationship is one of mutual presupposition. It does follow of course that all attempts to elucidate the notion of personal identity independently of and in isolation from the notions of narrative, intelligibility and accountability are bound to fail. As all such attempts have.

It is now possible to return to the question from which the enquiry into the nature of human action and identity started: In what does the unity of an individual life consist? The answer is that its unity is the unity of a narrative embodied in a single life. To ask "What is the good for me?" is to ask how best I might live out that unity and bring it to completion. To ask "What is the good for man?" is to ask what all answers to the former question must have in common. But now it is important to emphasise that it is the systematic asking of these two questions and the attempt to answer them in deed as well as in word which provide

the moral life with its unity. The unity of a human life is the unity of a narrative quest. Quests sometimes fail, are frustrated, abandoned or dissipated into distractions; and human lives may in all these ways also fail. But the only criteria for success or failure in a human life as a whole are the criteria of success or failure in a narrated or to-be-narrated quest. A quest for what?

Two key features of the medieval conception of a quest need to be recalled. The first is that without some at least partly determinate conception of the final *telos* there could not be any beginning to a quest. Some conception of the good for man is required. Whence is such a conception to be drawn? Precisely from those questions which led us to attempt to transcend that limited conception of the virtues which is available in and through practices. It is in looking for a conception of *the* good which will enable us to order other goods, for a conception of *the* good which will enable us to extend our understanding of the purpose and content of the virtues, for a conception of *the* good which will enable us to understand the place of integrity and constancy in life, that we initially define the kind of life which is a quest for the good. But secondly it is clear the medieval conception of a quest is not at all that of a search for something already adequately characterised, as miners search for gold or geologists for oil. It is in the course of the quest and only through encountering and coping with the various particular harms, dangers, temptations and distractions which provide any quest with its episodes and incidents that the goal of the quest is finally to be understood. A quest is always an education both as to the character of that which is sought and in self-knowledge.

The virtues therefore are to be understood as those dispositions which will not only sustain practices and enable us to achieve the goods internal to practices, but which will also sustain us in the relevant kind of quest for the good, by enabling us to overcome the harms, dangers, temptations and distractions which we encounter, and which will furnish us with increasing self-knowledge and increasing knowledge of the good. The catalogue of the virtues will therefore include the virtues required to sustain the kind of households and the kind of political communities in which men and women can seek for the good together and the virtues necessary for philosophical enquiry about the character of the good. We have then arrived at a provisional conclusion about the good life for man: the good life for man is the life spent in seeking for the good life for man, and the virtues necessary for the seeking are those which will enable us to understand what more and what else the good life for man is. We have also completed the second stage in our account of the virtues, by situating them in relation to the good life for man and not only in relation to practices. But our enquiry requires a third stage.

For I am never able to seek for the good or exercise the virtues only *qua* individual. This is partly because what it is to live the good life concretely varies from circumstance to circumstance even when it is one and the same conception of the good life and one and the same set of virtues which are being embodied in a human life. What the good life is for a fifth-century Athenian general will not be the same as what it was for a medieval nun or a seventeenth-century farmer. But it is not just that different individuals live in different social circumstances; it is also that we all approach our own circumstances as bearers of a particular social identity. I am someone's son or daughter, someone else's cousin or uncle; I am a citizen of this or that city, a member of this or that guild or profession; I belong to this clan, that tribe, this nation. Hence what is good for me has to be the good for one who inhabits these roles. As such, I inherit from the past of my family, my city, my tribe, my nation, a variety of debts, inheritances, rightful expectations and obligations. These constitute the given of my life, my moral starting point. This is in part what gives my life its own moral particularity.

This thought is likely to appear alien and even surprising from the standpoint of modern individualism. From the standpoint of individualism I am what I myself choose to be. I can always, if I wish to, put in question what are taken to be the merely contingent social features of my existence. I may biologically be my father's son; but I cannot be held responsi-

ble for what he did unless I choose implicitly or explicitly to assume such responsibility. I may legally be a citizen of a certain country; but I cannot be held responsible for what my country does or has done unless I choose implicitly or explicitly to assume such responsibility. Such individualism is expressed by those modern Americans who deny any responsibility for the effects of slavery upon black Americans, saying "I never owned any slaves." It is more subtly the standpoint of those other modern Americans who accept a nicely calculated responsibility for such effects measured precisely by the benefits they themselves as individuals have indirectly received from slavery. In both cases "being an American" is not in itself taken to be part of the moral identity of the individual. And of course there is nothing peculiar to modern Americans in this attitude: the Englishman who says, "*I* never did any wrong to Ireland; why bring up that old history as though it had something to do with *me*?" or the young German who believes that being born after 1945 means that what Nazis did to Jews has no moral relevance to his relationship to his Jewish contemporaries, exhibit the same attitude, that according to which the self is detachable from its social and historical roles and statuses. And the self so detached is of course a self very much at home in either Sartre's or Goffman's perspective, a self that can have no history. The contrast with the narrative view of the self is clear. For the story of my life is always embedded in the story of those communities from which I derive my identity. I am born with a past; and to try to cut myself off from that past, in the individualist mode, is to deform my present relationships. The possession of an historical identity and the possession of a social identity coincide. Notice that rebellion against my identity is always one possible mode of expressing it.

Notice also that the fact that the self has to find its moral identity in and through its membership in communities such as those of the family, the neighbourhood, the city and the tribe does not entail that the self has to accept the moral *limitations* of the particularity of those forms of community. Without those moral particularities to begin from there would never be anywhere to begin; but it is in moving forward from such particularity that the search for the good, for the universal, consists. Yet particularity can never be simply left behind or obliterated. The notion of escaping from it into a realm of entirely universal maxims which belong to man as such, whether in its eighteenth-century Kantian form or in the presentation of some modern analytical moral philosophies, is an illusion and an illusion with painful consequences. When men and women identify what are in fact their partial and particular causes too easily and too completely with the cause of some universal principle, they usually behave worse than they would otherwise do.

What I am, therefore, is in key part what I inherit, a specific past that is present to some degree in my present. I find myself part of a history and that is generally to say, whether I like it or not, whether I recognise it or not, one of the bearers of a tradition. It was important when I characterised the concept of a practice to notice that practices always have histories and that at any given moment what a practice is depends on a mode of understanding it which has been transmitted often through many generations. And thus, insofar as the virtues sustain the relationships required for practices, they have to sustain relationships to the past—and to the future—as well as in the present. But the traditions through which particular practices are transmitted and reshaped never exist in isolation for larger social traditions. What constitutes such traditions?

We are apt to be misled here by the ideological uses to which the concept of a tradition has been put by conservative political theorists. Characteristically such theorists have followed Burke in contrasting tradition with reason and the stability of tradition with conflict. Both contrasts obfuscate. For all reasoning takes place within the context of some traditional mode of thought, transcending through criticism and invention the limitations of what had hitherto been reasoned in that tradition; this is as true of modern physics as of medieval logic. Moreover when a tradition is in good order it is always partially constituted by an argument about the goods the pursuit of which gives to that tradition its particular point and purpose.

So when an institution—a university, say, or a farm, or a hospital—is the bearer of a tradition of practice or practices, its common life will be partly, but in a centrally important way, constituted by a continuous argument as to what a university is and ought to be or what good farming is or what good medicine is. Traditions, when vital, embody continuities of conflict. Indeed when a tradition becomes Burkean, it is always dying or dead.

The individualism of modernity could of course find no use for the notion of tradition within its own conceptual scheme except as an adversary notion; it therefore all too willingly abandoned it to the Burkeans, who, faithful to Burke's own allegiance, tried to combine adherence in politics to a conception of tradition which would vindicate the oligarchical revolution of property of 1688 and adherence in economics to the doctrine and institutions of the free market. The theoretical incoherence of this mismatch did not deprive it of ideological usefulness. But the outcome has been that modern conservatives are for the most part engaged in conserving only older rather than later versions of liberal individualism. Their own core doctrine is as liberal and as individualist as that of self-avowed liberals.

A living tradition then is an historically extended, socially embodied argument, and an argument precisely in part about the goods which constitute that tradition. Within a tradition the pursuit of goods extends through generations, sometimes through many generations. Hence the individual's search for his or her good is generally and characteristically conducted within a context defined by those traditions of which the individual's life is a part, and this is true both of those goods which are internal to practices and of the goods of a single life. Once again the narrative phenomenon of embedding is crucial: the history of a practice in our time is generally and characteristically embedded in and made intelligible in terms of the larger and longer history of the tradition through which the practice in its present form was conveyed to us; the history of each of our own lives is generally and characteristically embedded in and made intelligible in terms of the larger and longer histories of a number of traditions. I have to say "generally and characteristically" rather than "always," for traditions decay, disintegrate and disappear. What then sustains and strengthens traditions? What weakens and destroys them?

The answer in key part is: the exercise or the lack of exercise of the relevant virtues. The virtues find their point and purpose not only in sustaining those relationships necessary if the variety of goods internal to practices are to be achieved and not only in sustaining the form of an individual life in which that individual may seek out his or her good as the good of his or her whole life, but also in sustaining those traditions which provide both practices and individual lives with their necessary historical context. Lack of justice, lack of truthfulness, lack of courage, lack of the relevant intellectual virtues—these corrupt traditions, just as they do those institutions and practices which derive their life from the tradi-

tions of which they are the contemporary embodiments. To recognise this is of course also to recognise the existence of an additional virtue, one whose importance is perhaps most obvious when it is least present, the virtue of having an adequate sense of the traditions to which one belongs or which confront one. This virtue is not to be confused with any form of conservative antiquarianism; I am not praising those who choose the conventional conservative role of *laudator temporis acti*. It is rather the case that an adequate sense of tradition manifests itself in a grasp of those future possibilities which the past has made available to the present. Living traditions, just because they continue a not-yet-completed narrative, confront a future whose determinate and determinable character, so far as it possesses any, derives from the past.

Whose Traditions? Which Understandings?

Susan Moller Okin

In Justice, Gender, and the Family, *which contains this selection, Susan Okin charges that political philosophy has assumed that a citizen is a male head of a household. Freedom, justice, and equality have been sought for these citizens, but the special circumstances of women have been ignored. Women perform the labor that supports a household and raise the children. They receive no wages, must curtail their careers, and often bear the risks and burdens of single parenthood alone. On the other hand women occupy only a small portion of the elective offices, so they are impotent to secure their interests as free and equal citizens. Liberalism has failed to recognize the unequal distribution of family burdens and to acknowledge that women have a unique function in society. In this selection Okin examines the communitarian theories of Alasdair MacIntyre and Michael Walzer to see if "traditions" and "spheres" can help modern American women gain status, security, and rewards for constructing and maintaining families.*

She begins with the tradition of the Thomistic Middle Ages that MacIntyre has praised as the best example of a well-functioning tradition. Not surprisingly, she finds that this tradition was formed by and for men and cannot be expanded to accommodate women. For the typical American woman who is employed while she raises her children, there is no possibility of engaging in a conversation with any of the historical traditions that have MacIntyre's approval. Okin then turns to Walzer's Spheres of Justice. *But his reliance on shared understandings within a sphere to arbitrate moral questions leaves women prey to entrenched social practices, which rarely favor them. Walzer endorses caste systems and feudal societies. His criteria would also endorse gender hierarchy because it is formed by a single set of internal meanings based on male dominance.*

The past decade has witnessed the renewed appeal of traditional values and traditional culture. In particular, and in part in reaction to feminism, it has included an attempt to restore or recover the traditional family, perceived as a lost or dying institution. Some prominent examples include the Family Protection Act introduced into Congress in 1981, one of whose clauses would have prohibited the use of federal funds to question traditional sex roles, and the pope's 1988 statement that a woman's vocation is either motherhood or celibacy.[1]

Appealing to tradition and grieving for its loss has been evident in popular periodicals and rhetoric and more academic works. These range from a full-page advertisement for *Good Housekeeping* magazine in the *New York Times,* glorifying the "traditional" woman, and George Bush's stress in the 1988 presidential campaign on the family and its "traditional values," to popular academic books such as Christopher Lasch's *Haven in a Heartless World,* Robert Bellah's *Habits of the Heart,* Edward Shils's *Tradition,* and, . . . in Allan Bloom's *The Closing of the American Mind.*[2] Shils is particularly explicit about the connections between tradition and the patriarchal family.[3] At the extreme, "traditional" marriage has been invoked to argue against both the legal recognition of rape within marriage and the provision of shelters for battered wives.*

Contemporary with this general nostalgia for tradition has been the parallel movement in some theories of social justice toward reliance upon traditions, or "shared understandings." This has been closely linked with a sustained assault on liberal moral and political theories that attempt to invent or to formulate principles of justice from positions that the traditionalists regard as outside particular social contexts. Focusing their attacks primarily on the work of John Rawls, a number of these theorists, known as "communitar-

ians," have argued that attempts to disengage moral or political theories from the thinking of actual people living at specific times and in particular communities are doomed to failure or irrelevance.[6] In place of such theories, they aim to construct theories of justice by interpreting some combination of our traditions, the values latent or deeply rooted in our communities, or the meanings or understandings we share.

There is a ghostly element to the debate between liberals and communitarians, since the latter—including Alasdair MacIntyre, Michael Sandel, and Charles Taylor—have not yet come up with any kind of developed theory. Michael Walzer, who *has* developed a theory of justice, is only in part a communitarian, though he is similarly critical of Rawls's approach to justice. His reliance on "shared meanings" or "understandings" is in some respects akin to communitarian ideas and, as I shall argue in this chapter, shares some of their problems.[7] Whereas the implications of most communitarian arguments are reactionary and inegalitarian, however, Walzer interprets shared meanings or understandings in ways that lead to the defense of far more egalitarian conclusions. And whereas MacIntyre thinks that in contemporary times we have become incoherent, share no moral understandings, and need to rediscover philosophical traditions that have been lost, Walzer thinks that communities of ordinary people do have shared understandings, though they may be latent and need to be brought fully to consciousness. He sees this bringing forth of latent meanings as the task of the social critic.

As I shall argue here, both these ways of thinking have serious deficiencies. The appeal to "our traditions" and the "shared understandings" approach are both incapable of dealing with the problem of the effects of *social domination* on beliefs and understandings. They therefore prove to be useless or distorting ways of thinking when we include women as fully human subjects in our theorizing about justice or try to assess gender by the standards of justice. But a number of feminist theorists and scholars of moral development have come to look on communitarianism as an ally in their struggle against what they see as a masculinist abstraction and emphasis on jus-

*Opposing the enforcement of rape laws against husbands, Alaska Senator Paul Fischer said in 1985: "I don't know how you can have a sexual act and call it forcible rape in a marriage situation. . . . I still believe in the old traditional bond of marriage."[4] U.S. Senator Gordon Humphrey (N.H.) argued in 1980 against funding "so-called 'homes' for battered women," on the grounds that "the federal government should not fund missionaries who would war on the traditional family or on local values."[5]

tice, impartiality, and universality. They see such theories and conceptions of the self and its relation to context and community as more akin than theories of justice and rights to women's moral needs and concerns.[8] As the argument of this chapter shows, feminists need to be wary of such alliances. . . .

Whose Traditions?

. . . MacIntyre's eventual conclusion in *Whose Justice?* is that Thomas Aquinas's synthesis of Aristotle with Augustinian Christianity offers the best, the most defensible account of justice and practical rationality. Thomism is presented as a version of Aristotelianism that can be applied outside the context of the Greek city-state.[9] The works of Augustine and Aquinas have had immense influence on the development of the Christian tradition, not least on its attitudes toward women and their subordinate roles in church and society. But throughout his discussions of Augustine and Aquinas, aided by his use of falsely gender-neutral language, MacIntyre ignores the problems that are raised for a potential twentieth-century adherent to these traditions by what they have to say about the nature of women and about just relations between the sexes. In his praise for Aquinas's capacity to synthesize Aristotle's philosophy with Christian theology, he ignores the fact that on these issues, the synthesis compounds the sexism and the misogyny of both.

Theologians and political theorists have paid considerable attention to Augustine's and Aquinas's dispositions of women in recent years, but MacIntyre ignores their work.[10] Augustine's more complex and nuanced conclusions about women's place are well captured in Genevieve Lloyd's phrase "spiritual equality and natural subordination."[11] Perhaps in part because he regarded his mother as an ideal Christian, in part because of the influence of Plato, and in part because of his emphasis on the more egalitarian version of the creation myth,* Augustine believed that

*At Genesis 1:27, the Bible says: "And God created man in His own image, in the image of God He created him; male and female created He them."

men and women were equal in soul and in their capacity to share in the divine life: "not only men but also women might contemplate the eternal reasons of things."[12] However, he also said that, viewed alone, in her quality as man's "help-meet," woman is not, as man alone is, in the image of God; and he referred allegorically to man as higher reason and to woman as lower reason or sensuality. Because of her bodily difference from man and her association with carnality, passion, and therefore sin, as symbolized by Eve's role in the Fall, Augustine saw woman as properly and naturally subordinated to man. In the City of God, woman and man are equal, but in the City of Man woman is man's subject and properly restricted to the domestic sphere or, even better, to celibacy. That these are not mere archaic myths that can safely be ignored was confirmed in 1988, when Pope John Paul II reaffirmed these limitations on women, justifying them, as did Augustine, by the sin of Eve.[13]

In the works of Thomas Aquinas, in which MacIntyre sees the best account of justice and practical rationality to be found in any tradition, the Christian association of women with sin is synthesized with Aristotle's teleological biology. Aquinas places far more emphasis than Augustine on the City of Man—the world of politics and the family. Here his reliance on Aristotle is clear, most centrally in his notions that a woman is "a misbegotten male," intended only for the work of reproduction, defective in her reason, and therefore "naturally subject to man, because in man the discretion of reason predominates."[14] As Arlene Saxonhouse sums up his views:

> In Thomas' thought, the body and the soul are not separated, as they are in Augustine's. . . . Since the rational soul is proportionate to the body, the misbegotten body of the female has a soul that is proportionate to it and, therefore, inferior. Thomas concludes that she must be subordinate to the male for her own interest, since, as Aristotle had taught, the inferior must accept the rule of the superior. Like her children, woman benefits when she performs the role in marriage to which her lower capacities are suited.[15]

Apart from one brief mention of Aquinas's assumption that households were male-headed, MacIntyre simply ignores all this. He continually employs gender-netural language in his discussions of Augustine and Aquinas, just as in those about Homer and Aristotle. Moreover, he contrasts the inclusiveness of the thought of these Christian thinkers with the limitations and exclusions imposed by his historical context on Aristotle's conceptions of justice and practical rationality.[16]

It is by now obvious that many of "our" traditions, and certainly those evaluated most highly by MacIntyre, are so permeated by the patriarchal power structure within which they evolved as to require nothing less than radical and intensive challenge if they are to meet truly humanistic conceptions of the virtues. When MacIntyre begins to try to evaluate the rationality of traditions, he says: "The test for truth in the present, therefore, is always to summon up as many questions and as many objections of the greatest strength possible; what can be justifiably claimed as true is what has sufficiently withstood such dialectical questioning and framing of objections."[17] But he reaches his own conclusions about the superiority of the Thomistic synthesis without even subjecting it to what is one of the most crucial tests of it in his time—the challenge of whether this tradition can include women as full human beings.[18]

MacIntyre says that "the initial answer" to questions about practical rationality and justice (questions about "What ought I to do?"), in the light of the claims of the various traditions, "will depend upon who you are and how you understand yourself." Let us, then, imagine a young woman in the United States today taking up MacIntyre's invitation. Let us see whether she will find among his preferred traditions one in which her life will become intelligible and whether, by engaging in conversation with his traditions, she will be helped to become aware of her "incoherence" and to provide an account of it. Let us imagine, at first, that the woman is young, able-bodied, white, heterosexual, married, and that the income of her household is average. Raised in a fairly traditional family, she has nonetheless, like many of her peers, come to have expectations of leading a life that involves both motherhood and wage work. She is contented with her family and other personal relations, but frustrated by the boredom, dead-endedness, and low pay of her wage work,

which she stays with because its hours and demands are compatible with the responsibilities she perceives as hers as a wife and mother. She worries that taking up a more demanding though more interesting occupation might strain her marriage and shortchange her children. How will engaging in conversation with the Aristotelian-Christian traditions that MacIntyre prefers to liberalism help her?

To start with, these traditions have no comprehension of her need to be both family member and wage worker. Engaging in conversation with Aristotle will first tell her that her sex is "a deformity in nature," which exists only for the purpose of procreating the male sex, the original and true form of the human being. Engaging in conversation with MacIntyre on Aristotle's exclusion of women from all but domestic life will raise the possibility of Plato's solution: abolish the family. But this woman loves and cherishes her family life and does not relish the idea of living in communal barracks, mating when and with whom she is told to, and not knowing who her children are. And, even if she did, none of the other traditions that MacIntyre suggests she engage in conversation with would tolerate such an idea for an instant. For one thing, they regard sexual activity outside of lifelong marriage as a serious sin. Turning to Augustine, she may be comforted by his conviction that she is the spiritual equal to man, but his equally firm conviction that her physical sexuality makes her necessarily man's inferior is unlikely to help her provide an account of her "incoherence." It seems more likely to exacerbate it. Turning to Thomism—the tradition MacIntyre finds the best embodiment of rationality because of its ability to accommodate Augustinian insights with Aristotelian theorizing—she will encounter the problems of Aristotle and the problems of Augustinian Christianity compounded. For Aquinas synthesizes the Aristotelian view that women are a deformity in nature with the Christian view that women's sexuality is to blame for men's sinful lust. In this tradition, she will find serious consideration being given to questions such as whether women were included in the original Creation and whether, in order to be resurrected, they must be reborn as men. Aquinas is hardly likely to provide the calm coherence for this woman's life that MacIntyre finds in him. And the woman I have imagined presents the *easiest* female test of these traditions, being among the most advantaged of women. If she were poor, black, lesbian, old, disabled, a single parent, or some combination of these, she would surely be even less likely to find herself and her situation rendered more coherent by turning to MacIntyre's traditions.

MacIntyre says that traditions are also to be tested by whether they help persons to answer the real, difficult moral questions they may have to face. Our hypothetical woman's questions may include whether to have an abortion if she accidentally becomes pregnant just as she is completing many years of dedicated and joyful primary parenting and wants to become involved in a fulfilling job; whether to divorce her husband if he has an affair and neglects his family, even though she knows that she and the children are likely to be economically devastated as well as to be faced with the psychological and social stress of divorce; whether to run for office in order to contribute to the solution of political problems about which she has strong convictions, though she knows her children will have less of her time and attention than they are used to. How will MacIntyre's preferred traditions help her, given that with few exceptions the theories that constitute them are unwilling even to grant her the status of full humanity? She is unlikely to conclude from her attempt to engage in conversation with MacIntyre's traditions that she is incoherent, or to find her thinking about justice and practical rationality enhanced. She may indeed conclude, without looking much further into them, that there is something fundamentally incoherent about the traditions themselves and that she will have to look elsewhere for answers to questions about justice and rationality. . . .

Which Understandings?

In Walzer's recent works, he has argued that principles of justice should be based on the "shared understandings" of each culture.[19] He does not arrive at reactionary conclusions, such as those implied by MacIntyre's adherence to traditions. This is because he both seeks the answers to contemporary questions about justice not in past traditions but in currently shared understandings, and believes that the shared understandings of *our* culture are fundamentally egalitarian ones. This, however, should not blind us to the very real similarities in their methods of thinking about justice. . . . Walzer's *other* criterion for jutice— the "separate spheres" criterion, which requires that different social goods be distributed in different ways and independently of each other—is opposed to pervasive inequality and dominance. It has the potential to be a valuable tool for feminist criticism. As I shall argue here, however, the radical potential of the theory is blunted by its reliance on "shared understandings."

Like MacIntyre, Walzer is critical of philosophers who "leave the city . . . [to] fashion . . . an objective and universal standpoint."[20] He too rejects ways of thinking about justice that are not tied to a particular culture, that do not issue from the shared understandings or agreements of actual historical human beings with full knowledge of who they are and where they are situated in society. He argues, instead, for principles of justice in a way that is "radically particularist."[21] Beyond basic rights to life and liberty, he argues, men's and women's rights "do not follow from our common humanity; they follow from shared conceptions of social goods; they are local and particular in character." "Justice" he says, "is relative to social meanings. . . . A given society is just if its substantive life is lived . . . in a way faithful to the shared understandings of the members." And since "social meanings are historical in character," just and unjust distributions change over time.[22] If conclusions about justice are to have "force," Walzer claims, they must not be principles chosen in some hypothetical situation, in which we are deprived of knowledge of our individual characteristics and social situation. They must be arrived at in answer to the question: "What would individuals like us choose, who are situated as we are, who share a culture and are determined to go on sharing it? And this is a question that is readily transformed into, What choices have we already made in the course of our common life? What understandings do we (really) share?"[23]

The difficult issue is whether and how such a relativist criterion for the justice of social arrangements and distributions can have the critical potential Walzer claims for it. *Can* it apply, except where the basic equality of human beings is already assumed? At times, Walzer seems to doubt that it can. He says that if "a just or an egalitarian society . . . isn't already here—hidden, as it were, in our concepts and categories—we will never know it concretely or realize it in fact." The problems of Walzer's relativism are illuminated most clearly by what he says about justice in fundamentally hierarchical systems, such as feudal and caste societies. Such systems are, he says, "constituted by an extraordinary integration of meanings. Prestige, wealth, knowledge, office, occupation, food, clothing, even the social good of conversation: all are subject to the intellectual as well as to the physical discipline of hierarchy." The hierarchy in such systems is determined by a single value—in the case of the caste system, ritual purity, itself dominated by birth and blood—which dominates the distribution of all other social goods, so that "social meanings overlap and cohere," losing their autonomy. In such societies, Walzer acknowledges, where social meanings are integrated and hierarchical, "justice will come to the aid of inequality." Nevertheless, as he must, in light of his shared-understandings or social-meanings criterion for justice, he asserts unambiguously that such societies can meet "(internal) standards of justice."[24] By this criterion, indeed, there are no grounds for concluding that caste societies are any less just than societies that do not discriminate on the basis of inborn status or characteristics.

As Walzer acknowledges, he needs to defend his argument that moral philosophy is best approached through the interpretation of shared meanings against "the charge that it binds us irrevocably to the status quo—since we can only interpret what already exists—and so undercuts the very possibility of social criticism." "Don't the conditions of collective life," he asks, "—immediacy, closeness, emotional attachment, parochial vision—militate against a critical self-understanding?" Doesn't criticism require critical *distance*?"[25] In response, he relies on two connected counterarguments. First, he thinks of ideologies, in general, as competing and pluralistic. Groups with different ideologies will win out in turn: "There is no final victory, nor should there be." He adds: "Perhaps the ideology that justifies the seizure [of social goods] is widely believed to be true. But resentment and resistance are (almost) as pervasive as belief. There are always some people, and after a time there are a great many, who think the seizure is not justice but usurpation."[26] Thus the possibility of social change in general rests on the flourishing of dissent. Walzer's second, related line of defense is that "every ruling class is compelled to present itself as a universal class." First comes the work of the affirmers of the dominant culture: "priests and prophets; teachers and sages; storytellers, poets, historians, and writers generally."[27] But as soon as they do their work, the possibility of criticism exists, since they must represent the interests of the ruling group as the common interest of all. Thus their ideas must be presented as universal in form. Since this will set up standards that the rulers will not live up to, given their particular interests, the door is open to social criticism. The best social criticism, Walzer argues, will emerge from this built-in contradiction. It can be found, for example, in the writings and activism of the Italian communist leader Ignazio Silone, who became a revolutionary by "taking seriously the principles taught . . . by [his] own educators and teachers" and using them as a standard to test society, revealing the radical contradiction between its principles and its social practices and institutions.[28]

The weaknesses of both these lines of defense of a theory of justice built on the interpretation of shared meanings are readily exposed when we raise the issue of the justice or injustice of gender. The problem with the first counterargument—the reliance on dissent—is that the closer a social system is to a caste system, in which social meanings overlap, cohere, and are integrated and hierarchical, the less likely it will be that dissenting ideas appear or develop. The more thoroughgoing the dominance, and the more pervasive its ideology across the various spheres, the less chance there is that the whole prevailing system will be questioned or resisted. By arguing that such a system meets "(internal) standards of justice" if it is really accepted by its members, Walzer admits the paradox that the more likely a system is to be able to enshrine the ideology of the ruling group and hence to meet his "shared understandings" criterion for justice, the more *unjust* it will be by his other criterion, since dominance will be all-pervasive within it. The danger of his conception of justice, similar in this respect to the traditionalist conception of MacIntyre, is that what is just depends heavily upon what people are persuaded of.[29] It cannot cope with a situation of pervasive domination. Even if the social meanings in a fundamentally hierarchical society *were* shared, we should surely be wary of concluding, as Walzer clearly does, that the hierarchy is rendered just by that agreement or lack of dissent.[30]

When Walzer writes of caste societies, with their undifferentiated social meanings, he does so as if they were distant from anything that characterizes our culture. It is only on this assumption that he is able to perceive his two criteria for a just society as being not seriously in conflict in the contemporary context. But when we read his description of caste society, in which an inborn characteristic determines dominant or subordinate status in relation to social goods over a whole range of spheres, we can see that it bears strong resemblances to the gender system that our society still perpetuates to a large extent through the force of its economic and domestic structures and customs and the ideology inherited from its highly patriarchal past. There seem, in fact, to be only two significant differences between the hierarchies of caste and of gender: one is that women have not, of course, been physically segregated from men; the other is that whereas, according to Walzer, "political power seems always to have escaped the laws of caste,"[31] it has rarely escaped the laws of gender.

Like the caste hierarchy, the gender hierarchy is determined by a single value, with male sexuality taking the place of ritual purity. And, also like the caste hierarchy, that of gender ascribes roles, responsibilities, rights, and other social goods in accordance with an inborn characteristic that is imbued by society with tremendous significance. All the social goods listed in Walzer's description of a caste society have been, and many still are, differentially distributed between the sexes. In the cases of prestige, wealth, access to knowledge, office, and occupation, the disparities are fairly obvious. Better and greater amounts of food are often reserved for men in poorer classes and in some ethnic groups; women's clothing has been and still is designed either to constrain their movements or to appeal to men rather than for their own comfort and convenience; and women have been excluded from men's conversation in numerous social contexts, both formal and informal.[32] Although in some cases the disparities between the sexes in terms of social goods have begun to decline in recent years, in other important respects they have increased. . . .

As in caste societies, so too in patriarchy has ideology played a crucial part in perpetuating the legitimacy of hierarchy. Though Walzer says in the context of discussing caste societies that "we should not assume that men and women are ever entirely content with radical inequality,"[33] ideology helps us to comprehend the extent to which they often have been and are content. It is not difficult to see how this has operated in the case of gender. When the family is founded in law and custom on allegedly natural male dominance and female dependence and subordination, when religions inculcate the same hierarchy and enhance it with the mystical and sacred symbol of a male god, and when the educational system both excludes women from its higher ranks and establishes as truth and reason the same intellectual bulwarks of patriarchy, the opportunity for competing visions of sexual difference or questioning of gender is seriously limited. In fact, as feminist scholars have recently revealed, the ideology that is embodied in "malestream thought" is undoubtedly one of the most all-encompassing and pervasive ideologies in history.[34]

By now it should be clear that Walzer's second argument against those who question the critical force of his theory is also unsatisfactory. The affirmers of "our" culture, the priests and prophets, teachers and sages, and so on, have been almost uniformly male, and the culture and values they have affirmed have in a multitude of ways reflected the standpoint of men in gendered society. Like MacIntyre and the bearers of his traditions, they have defined a "human good" that not only excludes women but depends upon this exclusion. Thus it is by no means always the case that the ruling ideas are universal in form, so that, if taken literally, they have radical implications. Certainly, most of them were never intended to apply to women, any more than they were meant to apply to animals or plants. *Man* and *mankind,* those ostensibly generic words, have turned out to be far from generic when it comes to claiming rights and privileges.[35] Frequently, still, false gender neutrality serves the same purpose of disguising the exclusion of women, and even radical social critics have usually failed to question the hierarchy of gender.

Finally, social critics, to be effective, have to be articulate, and to be heard. But those to whom caste, class, race, or gender structures deny education are far less likely to acquire the tools needed to express themselves in ways that would be publicly recognized were they to interpret shared meanings literally and turn them into social criticism.[36] Even those who have the tools are likely to be made objects of derision when they make the case that those whom the dominant culture relegates to an inferior role should be treated as equal. This was certainly the case with most of those throughout history who dared suggest that accepted principles about rights and equality be extended to women. Abigail Adams, Mary Wollstonecraft, and John Stuart Mill, to name a few examples, were all ridiculed for such suggestions.

Contrary to Walzer's theory of shared understandings, in fact, oppressors and oppressed—when the voice of the latter can be heard at all—often disagree fundamentally. Oppressors often claim that they, aristocrats or Brahmins or men, are fully human in ways that serfs or untouchables or women are not, and that while the rulers institutionalize equal justice among themselves, it is both just and in the common interest for them to require the other categories of people to perform functions supportive of the fully human existence of those capable of it. But what if the serfs or untouchables or women somehow do become convinced (against all the odds) that they too are fully human and that whatever principles of justice apply among their oppressors should rightfully be applied to them too? With dis-

agreements this basic, rather than a meaningful debate being joined, there would seem to be two irreconcilable accounts of what is just. There would be no shared meanings on the most fundamental of questions.

Contemporary views about gender are a clear example of such disagreement; it is clear that there are *no shared understandings* on this subject in our society, even among women. The problem is rendered even more complex if there are fundamental disagreements not only between the oppressors and the oppressed but even within the ranks of the oppressed. As studies of feminism and antifeminism have shown, women are deeply divided on the subject of gender and sex roles, with antifeminist women not rejecting them as unjust but rather regarding the continued economic dependence of women and the dominance of the world outside the home by men as natural and inevitable, given women's special reproductive functions.[37] Feminists tend to attribute such attitudes at least in part to the influence of patriarchal ideology; clearly, religion is an important factor. Such an antifeminist posture becomes increasingly difficult to maintain once feminist reforms are instituted. For then, female proponents of it are faced with the problem of how to reverse political change while maintaining what they believe to be their proper, politically powerless role. Even among feminists, there has grown a rift between those who see the gender system itself as the problem and look forward to an androgynous society, and those who, celebrating women's unique nature and traditional roles, consider the problem to be not the *existence* of these roles but the *devaluation* of women's qualities and activities by a male-dominated culture.[38] Gynocentric feminism faces a similar problem to that faced by antifeminism: How *can* women's work, concerns, and perspectives come to be properly valued, unless women seek and attain power in the predominant, male realm?

These opposite poles of opinion about the very nature of sexual difference and its appropriate social repercussions seem to provide no shared intellectual structure in which to debate questions of distributions—if such debate can take place, as Walzer says it must, among "ordinary people, with a firm sense of their own identity."[39] Divisions between conservative and radical standpoints on such issues may be so deep that they provide little foundation from which the different parties, situated as they *actually* are, can come to any conclusions about what is just. Walzer's theory of justice provides no criterion for adjudicating between such widely disparate viewpoints, aside from an implausible appeal to some deeper, latent understandings that all supposedly hold, beneath their disagreements.

Unlike Walzer's shared meanings criterion, his "separate spheres" criterion for justice *can* successfully oppose pervasive inequality and domination, and has potential for feminist criticism. It leads Walzer to challenge, at least briefly, the entire social system of gender. Thus the paradox of his theory of justice is strikingly exemplified by the theory's feminist implications. Insofar as the reduction of male dominance requires a thoroughgoing feminism that undermines the very roots of our gendered institutions, it is in considerable tension with the relativist requirement that a just society be one that abides by its shared understandings. And insofar as the latter criterion is applied, the feminist implications of the theory lose their force, on account of deeply rooted attitudes about sex difference that have been inherited from our past and continue to pervade many aspects of our culture.

Notes

1. Family Protection Act, S. 1378, 97th Cong., 1st sess., 127 Congressional Record S6329 (1981); Pope John Paul II's Apostolic Letter, "On the Dignity of Women," as analyzed and quoted at length in the *New York Times* October 1, 1988, pp. A1 and 6.

2. *Good Housekeeping* advertisement, *New York Times,* October 6, 1988, p. D32; Christopher Lasch, *Haven in a Heartless World* (New York: Basic Books, 1977); Robert N. Bellah et al., *Habits of the Heart* (Berkeley: University of California Press, 1985), esp. chaps. 2 and 11; Edward Shils, *Tradition* (Chicago: University of Chicago Press, 1980); Allan Bloom, *The Closing of the American Mind* (New York: Simon & Schuster, 1987).

3. Shils, *Tradition.* See, for example, pp. 17, 173, 204.

4. *Daily News* (Juneau, Alaska), March 21, 1985. Quoted by Frances Olsen, "The Myth of State Intervention in the Family," *University of Michigan Journal of Law Reform 18,* no. 4 (1985): 840.

5. Quoted by Elizabeth Pleck, *Domestic Tyranny* (New York: Oxford University Press, 1987), p. 197.

6. Alasdair MacIntyre, *After Virtue* (Notre Dame: University of Notre Dame Press, 1981), and *Whose Justice? Which Rationality?* (Notre Dame: University of Notre Dame Press, 1988); Michael J. Sandel, *Liberalism and the Limits of Justice* (New York: Cambridge University Press, 1982); Charles Taylor, *Hegel and Modern Society* (Cambridge: Cambridge University Press, 1979), esp. pp. 111–69 and numerous papers, including those in *Philosophy and the Human Sciences* (Cambridge: Cambridge University Press, 1985), part 2, and, most recently, "Cross Purposes: The Liberal Communitarian Debate," in *Liberalism and the Moral Life,* ed. Nancy L. Rosenblum (Cambridge: Harvard University Press, 1989).

7. Michael Walzer, *Spheres of Justice: A Defense of Pluralism and Equality* (New York: Basic Books, 1983); *Interpretation and Social Criticism* (Cambridge: Harvard University Press, 1987), esp. chaps. 1 and 2, *The Company of Critics: Social Criticism and Political Commitment in the Twentieth Century* (New York: Basic Books, 1988).

8. See, for example, Annette C. Baier, "What Do Women Want in a Moral Theory?" *Nous* 19 (1985); Christina Hoff Sommers, "Filial Morality," in *Women and Moral Theory,* ed. Eva Kittay and Diana Meyers (Totowa, N.J.: Rowman and Littlefield, 1987). Similarities and differences between some communitarian and feminist views are summarized in the introduction to Seyla Benhabib and Drucilla Cornell, *Feminism As Critique* (Minneapolis: University of Minnesota Press, 1987), pp. 11–13. Other theorists who are, like Benhabib and Cornell, well aware of the problems of communitarianism for feminism include Marilyn Friedman, in "Feminism and Modern Friendship: Dislocating the Community," *Ethics* 99, no. 2 (1989); and Joan Tronto, in "'Women's Morality': Beyond Gender Difference to a Theory of Care," *Signs* 12, no. 4 (1987): 662.

9. MacIntyre, *Whose Justice?* p. 10. He says that it "escapes the limitations of the *polis.*"

10. For example, Kari Elizabeth Børreson, *Subordination and Equivalence: The Nature and Role of Women in Augustine and Thomas Aquinas* (Washington, D.C.: University Press of America, 1981; originally published Oslo: Universitetsforlaget, 1967); Maryanne Cline Horowitz, "The Image of God in Man—Is Woman Included?" *Harvard Theological Review* 72, no. 3–4 (July–October 1979); Genevieve Lloyd, *The Man of Reason: "Male" and "Female" in Western Philosophy* (Minneapolis: University of Minnesota Press, 1984), chap. 2; Martha Lee Osborne, *Woman in Western Thought* (New York: Random House, 1978), part 2; Saxonhouse, *Women in the History of Political Thought*, chap. 6.

11. Lloyd, *The Man of Reason*, p. 28.

12. Augustine, *Confessions*, 9.8; *De trinitate*, 12.7.12.

13. Pope John Paul II, "On the Dignity of Women," as quoted in the *New York Times*, October 1, 1988, pp. A1 and 6.

14. Aquinas, *Summa Theologica*, part 1, question 92, quoted from the translation in Osborne, *Women in Western Thought*, p. 69.

15. Arlene W. Saxonhouse, *Women in the History of Political Thought* (New York: Praeger, 1985), p. 147.

16. MacIntyre, *Whose Justice?* pp. 162–63, 181, 339. The middle passage reads, "As on Aristotle's view the law stands to the citizen in the best kind of *polis*, so on Aquinas' view the natural law stands to every human being in the *civitas Dei*." What he does not mention is that while the natural law, according to Aquinas, *applies* to every human being, it legitimizes the subjection of women to men.

17. Ibid., p. 358.

18. Another undeniable "test" the twentieth century presents Aquinas with, which MacIntyre also ignores, is the discovery of nuclear fission. The challenge here is whether the "just war" tradition can respond to the moral dilemmas of nuclear deterrence and the threat of human annihilation. See Susan Moller Okin, "Taking the Bishops Seriously," *World Politics* 36, no. 4 (1984).

19. Walzer's theory is most fully articulated in *Spheres of Justice*, the "shared understandings" theme of which is further developed in *Interpretation and Social Criticism* and *The Company of Critics*.

20. Walzer, *Spheres of Justice*, p. xiv; see also *Interpretation*, esp. pp. 11–16.

21. Walzer, *Spheres of Justice*, p. xiv.

22. Ibid., pp. xv, 312–13, 9.

23. Ibid., p. 5.

24. Ibid., pp. xiv, 27, 313, 315.

25. Walzer, *Interpretation*, pp. 3, 35–36.

26. Walzer, *Spheres of Justice*, p. 12.

27. Walzer, *Interpretation*, p. 40.

28. Ignazio Silone, *Bread and Wine*, quoted in Walzer, *The Company of Critics*, p. 104.

29. See Bernard Williams, "The Idea of Equality," in Peter Laslett and W. G. Runciman, *Philosophy, Politics and Society*, 2nd ser. (Oxford: Basil Blackwell, 1962), pp. 119–20, for a succinct discussion of social conditioning and the justification of hierarchical societies, critical of a position such as Walzer takes. See also Norman Daniels's review of *Spheres of Justice*, in *The Philosophical Review* 94, no. 1 (1985): 145–46.

30. See Ronald Dworkin's review of *Spheres of Justice*, in *New York Review of Books* (April 14, 1983): 4–5, and Walzer's response, July 21, 1983.

31. Walzer, *Spheres of Justice*, p. 27.

32. In a passage in which his gender-neutral language strains credibility, Walzer says that "in different historical periods," dominant goods such as "physical strength, familial reputation, religious or political office, landed wealth, capital, technical knowledge" have each been "monopolized by some group of men and women" (*Spheres of Justice*, p. 11). In fact, men have monopolized these goods to the exclusion of women (and still monopolize some of the most important ones) to at least as great an extent as any group of men and women have monopolized them to the exclusion of any other group.

33. Walzer, *Spheres of Justice*, p. 27.

34. This phrase was coined by Mary O'Brien in *The Politics of Reproduction* (London: Routledge & Kegan Paul, 1981).

35. One clear example of this has been raised by the issue of abortion. The rights basic to our political culture have been understood to include both the right to life and the right to control one's own body. Because liberal rights were framed as the rights of men, only relatively recently has the problem that arises when one (potential) person's life is inside another person's

body been confronted head-on. There is bitter opposition between those who assert that women, like men, have the right to control their own bodies and those who assert that, from the moment of conception, fetuses, like human beings, have the right to life. We have no currently "shared understandings" on abortion, partly because *both* basic liberal rights cannot be universalized to fetuses as well as to women.

36. It is worth noting that of the eleven social critics whom Walzer discusses in *The Company of Critics,* the great majority were born in the middle to upper ranks of their societies, almost all were well educated, and ten were male. The only woman among them, Simone de Beauvoir, was, as Walzer points out, able to be an insightful and effective critic of the situation of women partly because she herself to a large extent avoided it. This same fact, however, not only made her unable to value women's lives or characteristics or to criticize the world of men, but also rendered her ineffective in finding any solution to women's oppression except for those who, like her, could "escape" into the world of men (*The Company of Critics,* chap. 9, esp. pp. 155, 158–62). She suggests no way for women in general to fulfill themselves in what she regards as truly human ways.

37. For analyses of such attitudes, see Rebecca Klatch, *Women of the New Right* (Philadelphia: Temple University Press, 1987), esp. chap. 5; Kristin Luker, *Abortion and the Politics of Motherhood* (Berkeley: University of California Press, 1984), esp. chap. 8.

38. For a fair and lucid account of this division, see Iris Marion Young, "Humanism, Gynocentrism and Feminist Politics," *Hypatia: A Journal of Feminist Philosophy* 3, a special issue of *Women's Studies International Forum* 8, no. 3 (1985).

39. Walzer, *Spheres of Justice,* p. 5.

4

The Scope of Community

The Problem of Community

Robert Nisbet

Although community has taken many forms, at its core is a network of social relationships among people bound together by shared understandings, a sense of mutual obligation, emotional bonds, and common interests that encompass the whole of life. In this selection sociologist Robert Nisbet asks why the quest for community has become our dominant social tendency. He explains this spiritual longing as a search for the moral and psychological meaning that people once found in the networks of interpersonal relationships upon which they depended for their security, personal identity, and basic moral values. These small, intimate associations based on kinship, locality, and religious beliefs mediated between the individual and the economic and political order of the larger society. But, because the central state has great power and resources, it has gradually taken over the functions of small-scale groups and absorbing their power. Nisbet notes the proliferation of large-scale, bureaucratic institutions both public and private that now serve primary needs: corporations, medical establishments, charitable associations, educational institutions, social security for the old, orphaned, and disabled, welfare for the poor. Nowhere is this tendency as clear as in the status of the family. Deprived of its functions in serving its members' basic needs, the family has become a sentimental relic, he argues. So Nisbet interprets community in terms of its ability to wed the emotional and psychological bonds of personal relationships with the power of these associations to satisfy basic human needs, rather than in terms of shared understandings or traditions. Nisbet sees a form of totalitarianism in the increased power of the central state, driven by war to create a sense of cohesion and reinforced by an ethic of citizen sacrifice for the good of the nation. For Nisbet the multiplicity of small and overlapping communities, cooperatively controlled by their members, must regain their function in people's lives if personal freedom is to be preserved.

One

This is an age of economic interdependence and welfare States, but it is also an age of spiritual insecurity and preoccupation with moral certainty. Why is this? Why has the quest for community become the dominant social tendency of the twentieth century? What are the forces that have conspired, at the very peak of three centuries of economic and political advancement, to make the problem of community more urgent in the minds of men than it has been since the last days of the Roman Empire?

The answer is of course complex. Any effort to resolve the conflicting imperatives of an age into a simple set of institutional dislocations is both vapid and illusory. The conflicts of any age are compounded of immediate cultural frustrations and of timeless spiritual cravings. Attempts to reduce the latter to facile sociological and psychological categories are absurd and pathetic. Whatever else the brilliant literature of political disillusionment of our day has demonstrated, it has made clear the efforts to translate all spir-

From Robert Nisbet, *The Quest for Community* (1953) (San Francisco: The Institute for Contemporary Studies Press, 1990), pp. 41–65. Reprinted by permission of the Institute for Contemporary Studies, 243 Kearny Street, San Francisco, California 94108. Some footnotes omitted.

itual problems into secular terms are fraught with stultification as well as tyranny.

The problem before us is in one sense moral. It is moral in that it is closely connected with the values and ends that have traditionally guided and united men but that have in so many instances become remote and inaccessible. We do not have to read deeply in the philosophy and literature of today to sense the degree to which our age has come to seem a period of moral and spiritual chaos, of certainties abandoned, of creeds outworn, and of values devalued. The disenchantment of the world, foreseen by certain nineteenth-century conservatives as the end result of social and spiritual tendencies then becoming dominant, is very much with us. The humane skepticism of the early twentieth century has already been succeeded in many quarters by a new Pyrrhonism that strikes at the very roots of thought itself. Present disenchantment would be no misfortune were it set in an atmosphere of confident attack upon the old and search for the new. But it is not confident, only melancholy and guilty. Along with it are to be seen the drives to absolute skepticism and absolute certainty that are the invariable conditions of rigid despotism.

The problem is also intellectual. It cannot be separated from tendencies in Western thought that are as old as civilization itself, tendencies luminously revealed in the writings of Plato, Seneca, Augustine, and all their intellectual children. These are profound tendencies. We cannot avoid, any of us, seeing the world in ways determined by the very words we have inherited from other ages. Not a little of the terminology of alienation and community in our day comes directly from the writings of the philosophical and religious conservatives of other centuries. The problem constituted by the present quest for community is composed of elements as old as mankind, elements of faith and agonizing search which are vivid in all the great prophetic literatures. In large degree, the quest for community is timeless and universal.

Nevertheless, the shape and intensity of the quest for community varies from age to age. For generations, even centuries, it may lie mute, covered over and given gratification by the securities found in such institutions as family, village, class, or some other type of association. In other ages, ages of sudden change and dislocation, the quest for community becomes conscious and even clamant. It is this in our own age. To dismiss the present quest for community with vague references to the revival of tribalism, to man's still incomplete emancipation from conditions supposedly "primitive," is to employ substitutes for genuine analysis, substitutes drawn from the nineteenth century philosophy of unilinear progress. Moral imperatives, our own included, always hold a significant relation to *present* institutional conditions. They cannot be relegated to the past.

. . . The ominous preoccupation with community revealed by modern thought and mass behavior is a manifestation of certain profound dislocations in the primary associative areas of society, dislocations that have been created to a great extent by the structure of the Western political State. As it is treated here, the problem is social—social in that it pertains to the statuses and social memberships which men hold, or seek to hold. But the problem is also political—political in that it is a reflection of the present location and distribution of power in society.

The two aspects, the social and the political, are inseparable. For, the allegiances and memberships of men, even the least significant, cannot be isolated from the larger systems of authority that prevail in a society or in any of its large social structures. Whether the dominant system of power is primarily religious, economic, or political in the usual sense is of less importance sociologically than the *way* in which the power reveals itself in practical operation and determines the smaller contexts of culture and association. Here we have reference to the degree of centralization, the remoteness, the impersonality of power, and to the concrete ways in which it becomes involved in human life.

We must begin with the role of the social group in present-day Western society, for it is in the basic associations of men that the real consequences of political power reveal themselves. But the present treatment of the group cannot really be divorced from political considerations. . . .

Two

It has become commonplace, as we have seen, to refer to social disorganization and moral isolation in the present age. These terms are usually made to cover a diversity of conditions. But in a society as complex as ours it is unlikely that all aspects are undergoing a similar change. Thus it can scarcely be said that the State, as a distinguishable relationship among men, is today undergoing disorganization, for in most countries, including the United States, it is the political relationship that has been and is being enhanced above all other forms of connection among individuals. The contemporary State, with all its apparatus of bureaucracy, has become more powerful, more cohesive, and is endowed with more functions than at any time in its history.

Nor can the great impersonal relationships of the many private and semi-public organizations—educational, charitable, economic—be said to be experiencing any noticeable decline or disintegration. Large-scale labor organizations, political parties, welfare organizations, and corporate associations based upon property and exchange show a continued and even increasing prosperity, at least when measured in terms of institutional significance. It may be true that these organizations do not offer the degree of individual identification that makes for a deep sense of social cohesion, but disorganization is hardly the word for these immense and influential associations which govern the lives of tens of millions of people.

We must be no less wary of such terms as the "lost," "isolated," or "unattached" individual. However widespread the contemporary ideology of alienation may be, it would be blindness to miss the fact that it flourishes amid an extraordinary variety of custodial and redemptive agencies. Probably never in all history have so many organizations, public and private, made the individual the center of bureaucratic and institutionalized regard. Quite apart from the innumerable agencies of private welfare, the whole tendency of modern political development has been to enhance the role of the political State as a direct relationship among individuals, and to bring both its powers and its services ever more intimately into the lives of human beings.

Where, then, are the dislocations and the deprivations that have driven so many men, in this age of economic abundance and political welfare, to the quest for community, to narcotic relief from the sense of isolation and anxiety? They lie in the realm of the small, primary, personal relationships of society—the relationships that mediate directly between man and his larger world of economic, moral, and political and religious values. Our problem may be ultimately concerned with all of these values and their greater or lesser accessibility to man, but it is, I think, primarily social: social in the exact sense of pertaining to the small areas of membership and association in which these values are ordinarily made meaningful and directive to men.

Behind the growing sense of isolation in society, behind the whole quest for community which infuses so many theoretical and practical areas of contemporary life and thought, lies the growing realization that the traditional primary relationships of men have become functionally irrelevant to our State and economy and meaningless to the moral aspirations of individuals. We are forced to the conclusion that a great deal of the peculiar character of contemporary social action comes from the efforts of men to find in larger-scale organizations the values of status and security which were formerly gained in the primary associations of family, neighborhood, and church. This is the fact, I believe, that is as revealing of the source of many of our contemporary discontents as it is ominous when the related problems of political freedom and order are considered.

The problem, as I shall emphasize later in this chapter, is by no means restricted to the position of the traditional groups, nor is its solution in any way compatible with antiquarian revivals of groups and values no longer in accord with the requirements of the industrial and democratic age in which we live and to which we are unalterably committed. But the dislocation of the traditional groups must form our point of departure.

Historically, our problem must be seen in terms of the decline in functional and psychological significance of such groups as the family, the small local community, and the various other traditional relationships that have immemorially mediated between the individual and his society. These are the groups that have been morally decisive in the concrete lives of individuals. Other and more powerful forms of association have existed, but the major moral and psychological influences on the individual's life have emanated from the family and local community and the church. Within such groups have been engendered the primary types of identification: affection, friendship, prestige, recognition. And within them also have been engendered or intensified the principal incentives of work, love, prayer, and devotion to freedom and order.

This is the area of association from which the individual commonly gains his concept of the outer world and his sense of position in it. His concrete feelings of status and role, of protection and freedom, his differentiation between good and bad, between order and disorder and guilt and innocence, arise and are shaped largely by his relations within this realm of primary association. What was once called instinct or the social nature of man is but the product of this sphere of interpersonal relationships. It contains and cherishes not only the formal moral precept but what Whitehead has called "our vast system of inherited symbolism."

It can be seen that most contemporary themes of alienation have as their referents disruptions of attachment and states of mind which derive from this area of interpersonal relations. Feelings of moral estrangement, of the hostility of the world, the fear of freedom, of irrational aggressiveness, and of helplessness before the simplest of problems have to do commonly—as both the novelist and the psychiatrist testify—with the individual's sense of the inaccessibility of this area of relationship. In the child, or in the adult, the roots of a coherent, logical sense of the outer world are sunk deeply in the soil of close, meaningful interpersonal relations.

It is to this area of relations that the adjective "disorganized" is most often flung by contemporary social scientists and moralists, and it is unquestionably in this area that most contemporary sensations of cultural dissolution arise. Yet the term disorganization is not an appropriate one and tends to divert attention from the basic problem of the social group in our culture. It has done much to fix attention on those largely irrelevant manifestations of delinquent behavior which are fairly constant in all ages and have little to do with our real problem.

The conception of social disorganization arose with the conservatives in France, who applied it empirically enough to the destruction of the guilds, the aristocracy, and the monasteries. But to Bonald and Comte the most fundamental sense of the term was moral. The Revolution signified to them the destruction of a vast moral order, and in their eyes the common manifestations of individual delinquency became suddenly invested with a new significance, the significance of social disorganization, itself the product of the Revolution. The term disorganization has been a persistent one in social science, and there is even now a deplorable tendency to use such terms as disintegration and disorganization where there is no demonstrable breakdown of a structure and no clear norm from which to calculate supposed deviations of conduct. The family and the community have been treated as disintegrating entities with no clear insight into what relationships are actually disintegrating. A vast amount of attention has been given to such phenomena as marital unhappiness, prostitution, juvenile misbehavior, and the sexual life of the unmarried, on the curious assumption that these are "pathological" and derive clearly from the breakdown of the family.

But in any intelligible sense of the word it is not disorganization that is crucial to the problem of the family or of any other significant social group in our society. The most fundamental problem has to do with the *organized* associations of men. It has to do with the role of the primary social group in an economy and political order whose principal ends have come to be structured in such a way that the primary social relationships are increasingly functionless, almost irrelevant, with respect to these ends. What is involved most deeply in our problem is the diminishing capacity of organized, traditional relationships for holding a position of moral and psychological centrality in the individual's life.

Three

Interpersonal relationships doubtless exist as abundantly in our age as in any other. But it is becoming apparent that for more and more people such relationships are morally empty and psychologically baffling. It is not simply that old relationships have waned in psychological influence; it is that new forms of primary relationships show, with rare exceptions, little evidence of offering even as much psychological and moral meaning for the individual as do the old ones. For more and more individuals the primary social relationships have lost much of their historic function of mediation between man and the larger ends of our civilization.

But the decline of effective meaning is itself a part of a more fundamental change in the role of such groups as the family and local community. At bottom social organization is a pattern of institutional functions into which are woven numerous psychological threads of meaning, loyalty, and interdependence. The contemporary sense of alienation is most directly perhaps a problem in symbols and meanings, but it is also a problem in the institutional functions of the relationships that ordinarily communicate integration and purpose to individuals.

In any society the concrete loyalties and devotions of individuals tend to become directed toward the associations and patterns of leadership that in the long run have the greatest perceptible significance in the maintenance of life. It is never a crude relationship; intervening strata of ritual and other forms of crystallized meaning will exert a distinguishable influence on human thought. But, at bottom, there is a close and vital connection between the effectiveness of the symbols that provide meaning in the individual's life and the institutional value of the social structures that are the immediate source of the symbols. The immediacy of the integrative meaning of the basic values contained in and communicated by the kinship or religious group will vary with the greater or less institutional value of the group to the individual *and to the other institutions in society*.

In earlier times, and even today in diminishing localities, there was an intimate relation between the local, kinship, and religious groups within which individuals consciously lived and the major economic, charitable, and protective functions which are indispensable to human existence. There was an intimate conjunction of larger institutional goals and the social groups small enough to infuse the individual's life with a sense of membership in society and the meaning of the basic moral values. For the overwhelming majority of people, until quite recently the structure of economic and political life rested upon, and even presupposed, the existence of the small social and local groups within which the cravings for psychological security and identification could be satisfied.

Family, church, local community drew and held the allegiances of individuals in earlier times not because of any superior impulses to love and protect, or because of any greater natural harmony of intellectual and spiritual values, or even because of any superior internal organization, but because these groups possessed a virtually indispensable relation to the economic and political order. The social problems of birth and death, courtship and marriage, employment and unemployment, infirmity and old age were met, however inadequately at times, through the associative means of these social groups. In consequence, a whole ideology, reflected in popular literature, custom, and morality, testified to the centrality of kinship and localism.

Our present crisis lies in the fact that whereas the small traditional associations, founded upon kinship, faith, or locality, are still expected to communicate to individuals the principal moral ends and psychological gratifications of society, they have manifestly become detached from positions of functional relevance to the larger economic and political decisions of our society. Family, local community, church, and the whole network of informal interpersonal relationships have ceased to play a determining role in our institutional systems of mutual aid, welfare, education, recreation, and economic production and distribution. Yet despite the loss of these manifest institutional functions, and the failure of most of these groups to develop any new institutional functions, we continue to expect them to perform adequately the implicit psychological or symbolic functions in the life of the individual.

Four

The general condition I am describing in Western society can be compared usefully with social changes taking place in many of the native cultures that have come under the impact of Western civilization. A large volume of anthropological work testifies to the incidence, in such areas as East Africa, India, China, and Burma, of processes of social dislocation and moral insecurity. A conflict of moral values is apparent. More particularly, it is a conflict, as J. S. Furnivall has said, "between the eastern system resting on religion, personal authority, and customary obligation, and the western system resting on reason, impersonal law, and individual rights."[1]

This conflict of principles and moral values is not an abstract thing, existing only in philosophical contemplation. It may indeed be a crisis of symbolism, of patterns of moral meaning, but more fundamentally it is a crisis of allegiances. It is a result, in very large part, of the increasing separation of traditional groups from the crucial ends and decisions in economic and political spheres. The wresting of economic significance from native clans, villages, and castes by new systems of industry, and the weakening of their effective social control through the establishment of new systems of administrative authority has had demonstrable moral effects. The revolutionary intellectual and moral ferment of the modern East is closely connected with the dislocation of traditional centers of authority and responsibility from the lives of the people.

The present position of caste in India is a striking case in point. During the past twenty-five or more centuries various efforts have been made by political and religious leaders to abolish or weaken this powerful association through techniques of force, political decree, or religious persuasion. Whether carried out by ancient religious prophets or by modern Christian missionaries, the majority of such efforts have been designed to change the religious or moral *meaning* of caste in the minds of its followers. But such efforts generally have been fruitless. Even attempts to convert the untouchables to Christianity, to wean them away from the caste system of which they have been so horribly the victims, have been for the most part without success. The conversion of many millions to the Muslim creed led only to the creation of new castes.

But at the present time in widening areas of India there is a conspicuous weakening of the whole caste system, among the prosperous as well as among the poverty-stricken. Why, after many centuries of tenacious persistence, has the massive system of caste suddenly begun to dissolve in many areas of India?

The answer comes from the fact of the increasing dislocation of caste *functions*—in law, charity, authority, education, and economic production. The creation of civil courts for adjudication of disputes traditionally handled by caste *panchayats*; the growing assumption by the State and by many private agencies of mutual-aid activities formerly resident in the caste or subcaste; the rising popularity of the idea that the proper structure of education is the formal school or university, organized in Western terms; and the intrusion of the new systems of constraint and function in the factory and trade union—all of these represent new and competing values, and they represent, more significantly, new systems of *function* and *allegiance*.

When the major institutional functions have disappeared from a local village government or from a subcaste, the conditions are laid for the decline of the individual's allegiance to the older forms of organization. Failing to find any institutional substance in the old unities of social life, he is prone to withdraw, consciously or unconsciously, his loyalty to them. They no longer represent the prime moral experiences of his life. He finds himself, mentally, looking in new directions.

Some of the most extreme instances of insecurity and conflict of values in native cultures have resulted not from the nakedly ruthless forces of economic exploitation but from most commendable (by Western standards) acts of humanitarian reform. Thus the introduction of so physically salutary a measure as an irrigation district or medical service may be attended by all the promised gains in abundance and health, but such innovations can also bring about the most complex disruptions of social relationships and allegiances. Why? Because such systems, by the very *humaneness* of their functions, assume values that no purely exploitative agency can, and having become values they more easily serve to alienate the native from his devotion to the meanings associated with obsolete functional structures. The new technology means the creation of new centers of administrative authority which not infrequently nullify the prestige of village or caste groups, leading in time to a growing conflict between the moral meaning of the old areas of authority and the values associated with the new.

The beginnings of the welfare State in India, for example, along with the creation of new private agencies of educational, charitable, and religious activity, have led inevitably to the preemption of functions formerly resident (in however meager or debased manner) in the kinship and caste groups. It is irrelevant, for present purposes, that many of these preemptions have been responsible for physical improvement in the life of the people. What must be emphasized here are the social and moral effects irrespective of intent—whether accomplished by predatory mining and factory interests or by the liberal humanitarian. What is crucial is the invasion of the area of traditional function by new and often more efficient functional agencies—in charity, law, education, and economics. The consequence is a profound crisis in meanings and loyalties.

It is no part of my intent to offer these observations in any spirit of lament for the old. It is an evident conclusion that for technical as well as moral reasons much of the old order is inadequate to the demand constituted by population density and other factors. It is important to insist, however, that the solution by new administrative measures of technical and material problems does not carry with it any automatic answer to the social and moral difficulties created by the invasion of ancient areas of function. For all their humanitarian sentiments, a large number of native reformers, as well as Western, have been singularly insensitive to the moral problems created in such countries as China and India by the advent of Western techniques. The displacement of

function must lead in the long run to the diminution of moral significance in the old; and this means the loss of accustomed centers of allegiance, belief, and incentive. Hence the widely observed spectacle of masses of "marginal" personalities in native cultures, of individuals adrift, encompassed by, but not belonging to, either the old or the new. New associations have arisen and continue to arise, but their functional value is still but dimly manifest for the greater number of people, and their moral and psychological appeal is correspondingly weak. Hence the profound appeal of what the great Indian philosopher Tagore called "the powerful anesthetic of nationalism." Hence also the appeal, among a significant minority of intellectuals, of communism, which makes central the ethos of organization and combines it with therapeutic properties of concerted action.

What is to be observed so vividly in many areas of the East is also, and has been, for some time, a notable characteristic of Western society. The process is less striking, less dramatic, for we are directly involved in it. But it is nonetheless a profoundly significant aspect of modern Western history and it arises from some of the same elements in Western culture which, when exported, have caused such dislocation and ferment in foreign areas. We too have suffered a decline in the institutional function of groups and associations upon which we have long depended for moral and psychological stability. We too are in a state that can, most optimistically, be called transition—of change from associative contexts that have become in so many places irrelevant and anachronistic to newer associative contexts that are still psychologically and morally dim to the perceptions of individuals. As a result of the sharp reduction in meaning formerly inherent in membership, the problems of status, adjustment, and moral direction have assumed tremendous importance in the East as well as the West.

Five

Nowhere is the concern with the problem of community in Western society more intense than with respect to the family.[2] The contemporary family, as countless books, articles, college courses, and marital clinics make plain, has become an obsessive problem. The family inspires a curious dualism of thought. We tend to regard it uneasily as a final manifestation of tribal society somehow inappropriate to a democratic, industrial age, but, at the same time, we have become ever more aware of its possibilities as an instrument of social reconstruction.

The intensity of theoretical interest in the family has curiously enough risen in direct proportion to the decline of the family's basic institutional importance to our culture. The present "problem" of the family is dramatized by the fact that its abstract importance to the moralist or psychologist has grown all the while that its tangible institutional significance to the layman and its functional importance to economy and State have diminished.

It is doubtless one more manifestation of the contemporary quest for security that students of the family increasingly see its main "function" to be that of conferring "adjustment" upon the individual, and, for the most part, they find no difficulty at all in supposing that this psychological function can be carried on by the family in what is otherwise a functional vacuum. Contemporary social psychology has become so single-mindedly aware of the psychological gratification provided by the group for individual needs of security and recognition that there is an increasing tendency to suppose that such a function is primary and can maintain itself autonomously, impervious to changes in *institutional* functions which normally give a group importance in culture. For many reasons the contemporary family is made to carry a conscious symbolic importance that is greater than ever, but it must do this with a structure much smaller in size and of manifestly diminishing relevance to the larger economic, religious, and political ends of contemporary society.

Historically the family's importance has come from the fact of intimate social cohesion united with institutional significance in society, not from its sex or blood relationships. In earlier ages, kinship was inextricably involved in the processes of getting a living, providing education, supporting the infirm, caring for the aged, and maintaining religious values. In vast rural areas, until quite recently, the family was the actual agency of economic production, distribution, and consumption. Even in towns and cities, the family long retained its close relation to these obviously crucial activities. Organized living was simply inconceivable, for the most part, outside of the context provided by kinship. Few individuals were either too young or too old to find a place of importance within the group, a fact which enhanced immeasurably the family's capacity for winning allegiance and providing symbolic integration for the individual.

The interpersonal and psychological aspects of kinship were never made to rest upon personal romance alone or even upon pure standards of individual rectitude. Doubtless, deviations from the moral code and disillusionment with romance were as common then as now. But they did not interfere with the cultural significance of the family simply because the family was far more than an interpersonal relationship based upon affection and moral probity. It was an indispensable institution.

But in ever enlarging areas of population in modern times, the economic, legal, educational, religious, and recreational functions of the family have declined or diminished. Politically, membership in the family is superfluous; economically, it is regarded by many as an outright hindrance to success. The family, as someone has put it, is now the accident of the worker rather than his essence. His competitive position may be more favorable without it. Our systems of law and education and all the manifold recreational activities of individuals engaged in their pursuit of happiness have come to rest upon, and to be directed to, the individual, not the family. On all sides we continue to celebrate from pulpit and rostrum the indispensability to economy and the State of the family. But, in plain fact, the family is indispensable to neither of these at the present time. The major processes of economy and political administration have become increasingly independent of the symbolism and integrative activities of kinship.

There is an optimistic apologetics that sees in this waning of the family's institutional importance only the beneficent hand of Progress. We are told by certain psychologists and sociologists that, with its loss of economic and legal functions, the family has been freed of all that is basically irrelevant to its "real" nature; that the true function of the family—the cultivation of affection, the shaping of personality, above all, the manufacture of "adjustment"—is now in a position to flourish illimitably, to the greater glory of man and society. In a highly popular statement, we are told that the family has progressed from institution to companionship.

But, as Ortega y Gasset has written, "people do not live together merely to be together. They live together to do something together." To suppose that the present family, or any other group, can perpetually vitalize itself through some indwelling affectional tie, in the absence of concrete, perceived functions, is like supposing that the comradely ties of mutual aid which grow up incidentally in a military unit will long outlast a condition in which war is plainly and irrevocably banished. Applied to the family, the argument suggests that affection and personality cultivation can somehow exist in a social vacuum, unsupported by the determining goals and ideals of economic and political society. But in hard fact no social group will long survive the disappearance of its chief reasons for being, and these reasons are not, primarily, biological but institutional. Unless new institutional functions are performed by a group—family, trade union, or church—its psychological influence will become minimal.

No amount of veneration for the psychological functions of a social group, for the capacity of the group to gratify cravings for security and recognition, will offset the fact that, however important these functions may be in any given individual's life, he does not join the group essentially for them. He joins the group if and when its larger institutional or intellectual functions have relevance both to his own life organization and to what he can see of the group's relation to the larger society. The individual may indeed derive vast psychic support and integration from the pure fact of group membership, but he will not long derive this when he becomes in some way aware of the gulf between the moral claims of a group and its actual institutional importance in the social order.

All of this has special relevance to the family, with its major function now generally reduced by psychologists to that of conferring adjustment upon individuals. Yet in any objective view the family is probably now less effective in this regard than it has ever been. It is plain that the family is no longer the main object of personal loyalty in ever larger sections of our population, and it is an overstrain on the imagination to suppose that it will regain a position of psychological importance through pamphlets, clinics, and high-school courses on courtship and marriage. How quaint now seems that whole literature on sexual adjustment in marriage with its implicit argument that sexual incompatibility is the basic cause of the reduced significance of marriage. Some of the solemn preoccupations with "family tensions" which now hold the field of clinical practice will one day no doubt seem equally quaint.

The current problem of the family, like the problem of any social group, cannot be reduced to simple sets of psychological complexes which exist universally in man's nature, or to an ignorance of sexual techniques, or to a lack of Christian morality. The family is a major problem in our culture simply because we are attempting to make it perform psychological and symbolic functions with a structure that has become fragile and an institutional importance that is almost totally unrelated to the economic and political realities of our society. Moreover, the growing impersonality and the accumulating demands of ever larger sections of our world of business and government tend to throw an extraordinary psychological strain upon the family. In this now small and fragile group we seek the security and affection denied everywhere else. It is hardly strange that timeless incompatibilities and emotional strains should, in the present age, assume an unwonted importance—their meaning has changed with respect to the larger context of men's lives. We thus find ourselves increasingly in the position of attempting to correct, through psychiatric or spiritual techniques, problems which, although assuredly emotional, derive basically from a set of historically given institutional circumstances.

Personal crises, underlying emotional dissatisfactions, individual deviations from strict rectitude—these have presumably been constant in all ages of history. Only our own age tends to blow up these tensions into reasons for a clinical approach to happiness. Such tensions appear more critical and painful, more intolerable to contemporary man, simply because the containing social structures of such tensions have become less vital to his existence. The social structures are expendable so far as the broad economic and political processes of our society are concerned and, consequently, they offer less support for particular emotional states. Not a few of the problems that give special concern to our present society—sex role, courtship and marriage, old age, the position of the child—do so because of the modified functional and psychological position of the family in our culture.

The widely publicized problems of the modern middle-class woman do not result, as certain Freudians have seemed to suggest, from a disharmony between her innate psychological character and the present values of feminism. Whatever may be the neurological nature of the female, as compared with that of the male, the special and distinctive problem of the woman in our culture arises from certain changes in social function and conceptualized role. What has been called women's emancipation from patriarchalism is, in a highly relevant sense, an emancipation from clear, socially approved function and role within the institutionalized family group. To put it in these terms does not lessen the intensity of the problem in many quarters, but it takes it out of the vague realm of supposed innate complexes and places it within the determinable context of historical changes in social position. It puts the psychological problems of women in exactly the same context in which lie contemporary problems of the role of the father and the child. The former problems may be more intense, more explicit, but they do not differ in kind from those besetting the existences of other members of the family.

The oftentimes absurd worship of the female, especially the mother, in contemporary American society, has frequently been interpreted by ardent feminists as a reflection of her recent rise to eminence after centuries of subordination to the male. But it reflects rather an unconscious overcompensation for the historical fact of her release from any clear and indispensable *social role* within the family. And this is a part of the historical change in the function to society of the whole family group.

The sharp discrepancy between the family's actual contributions to present political and economic order and the set of spiritual images inherited from the past intensifies the problem of definition of sex role. From this basic discrepancy proceed all the elaborate, and frequently self-defeating, techniques of the "rational" cultivation of the family tie, the stunting dosages of scientific mother—love for the child, and the staggering number of clinics, conferences, lectures, pamphlets, and books on the subject of relations between parent and child, between husband and wife. It is this riot of rational techniques that has led to the bland and unexamined assumption that the family is today a more "affectionate" organization than it was a century ago.

In our society most of the period of storm and stress that is adolescence has little to do with the biological changes the child is undergoing. It has almost everything to do with the problem of role in the family and the clarity of the family's relation to society. In all past ages, and in many contemporary societies today, the development of the child into manhood or womanhood is attended, if not by actual lengthy and intense ceremonial rites, by relatively clear communications of value and purpose. And these have been possible only when there have been concrete institutional functions to symbolize and hence communicate. Today adolescence is the period, we are justified in saying, when the appalling discrepancy between shadow and substance in contemporary kinship first becomes evident to the child. It is then, in a profound if largely unconscious way, that he becomes aware of the gulf between inherited authority patterns and the actual functional contribution of the family. For in any group it is only the latter that can give effective meaning to the former.

Far more tragic in our culture is the position in which more and more of the aged find themselves. To interpret the present problem of old age as the consequence of living in a "youth-dominated" society is somewhat deceptive. All periods of culture have been characterized by great rewards for the young military leader, statesman, merchant, and writer. The age of some of the most distinguished members in the long history of Parliament in England is a case in point, and we may suppose that the brilliant young Pitt would find it far more difficult today to lead the House of Representatives in supposedly youth-dominated America than he did Parliament in eighteenth-century England. Conversely there is no clear evidence to indicate that the proportion of the aged who are now prominent in business, professions, and government is any smaller than in earlier times.

Since Cicero's *De Senectute* there has probably never been a period in which men have not faced the onset of old age with the feeling that its consolations must be compensatorily set down in writing in order to lessen the pathos of their enforced separation from previous activities. Today it is not the separation from wonted activities that is so painfully manifested in thought and behavior but the widening sense of alienation from family and society, a sense of alienation that is reflected not only in the staggering increase of the so-called senile neuroses and psychoses but in the old-age political movements.

In many instances the root causes are plainly economic, but the contemporary incidence of economic problems of the aged must itself be seen in relation to changes in social structure. To leave out of present consideration those whose position is purely the result of financial strain, there is obviously a growing number of elderly people whose estrangement comes from the altered social status and psychological role in which they find themselves. It is not always that they find themselves physically outside of a family group. In the most pathetic manifestations of this problem it is that such people find themselves in but not of the group. The change in the structure of the family has led to a change in the significance of individual members, especially of the aged.

The fantastic romanticism that now surrounds courtship and marriage in our culture is drawn in part no doubt from larger contexts of romanticism in modern history and is efficiently supported by the discovery of modern retail business that the mass-advertised fact of romance is good for sales. But the lushness of such advertising obviously depends on a previously fertilized soil, and this soil may be seen in large part as the consequence of changes in the relation of the family to the other aspects of the social order. The diminution in the functional significance of the family has been attended by efforts to compensate in the affectional realm of intensified romance. Probably no other age in history has so completely identified (confused, some might say) marriage and romance as has our own. The claim that cultivation of affection is the one remaining serious function of the family is ironically supported by the stupefying amount of effort put into the calculated cultivation of romance, both direct and vicarious. Whether this has made contemporary marriage a more affectionate and devoted relationship is a controversy we need not enter here.

The social roles of adolescence, old age, and affection have been profoundly altered by changes in the functional positions of the members of the family. Such states are *perceived* differently, both by the individuals immediately concerned and by others around them. So are the recurrent "crises" of personal life—birth, marriage, and death—regarded differently as a consequence of changes in the structure and functions of the family. Except from the point of view of the biologist, death, for example, is not the same phenomenon from one society to another, from one age to another. Death also has its social role, and this role is inseparable from the organization of values and relationships within which the physical fact of death takes place. Death almost everywhere is ritualized, ritualized for the sake of the deceased, if we like, but far more importantly for the sake of those who are left behind. Such ritualization has immensely important psychological functions in the direction of emotional release for the individuals most closely related to the dead person and in the direction, too, of the whole social group. But these death rites are not disembodied acts of obeisance or succor; they are manifestations of group life and function. They are closely related, that is, to other aspects of the family which have no immediate connection with the fact of death.

In our society we find ourselves in-

creasingly baffled and psychologically un-
prepared for the incidence of death among
loved ones. It is not that grief is greater or that
the incomprehensibility of death is increased.
It is in considerable part perhaps because the
smaller structure of the family gives inevitably
a greater emotional value to each of the
members. But, more than this, it is the result, I
believe, of the decline in significance of the
traditional means of ritual *completion* of the
fact of death. Death leaves a kind of moral
suspense that is terminated psychologically
only with greater and greater difficulty. The
social *meaning* of death has changed with the
social *position* of death.

Six

The problems arising from the diminished institutional and psychological importance of
the family in our society also extend into wider
areas of social and economic behavior. We
find ourselves dealing increasingly with difficulties that seem to resolve themselves into
matters of human motivation and incentives.
An older economics and politics and educational theory took it for granted that all the
root impulses to buying and selling and saving,
to voting, and to learning lay, in prepotent
form, in the individual himself. The relation
between crucial economic motivations and the
social groups in which individuals actually
lived was seldom if ever heeded by the classical
economists.

The late Harvard economist, Joseph
Schumpeter, wrote tellingly on this point. "In
order to realize what all this means for the
efficiency of the capitalist engine of production we need only recall that the family and the
family home used to be the mainspring of the
typically bourgeois kind of profit motive.
Economists have not always given due weight
to this fact. When we look more closely at their
idea of the self-interest of entrepreneurs and
capitalists we cannot fail to discover that the
results it was supposed to produce are really
not at all what one would expect from the
rational self-interest of the detached individual or the childless couple who no longer
look at the world through the windows of a
family home. Consciously or unconsciously,
they analyzed the behavior of the man whose
motives are shaped by such a home and who
means to work and save primarily for wife and
children. As soon as these fade out from the
moral vision of the business man, we have a
different kind of *homo economicus* before us
who cares for different things and acts in different ways.

Much of the predictability of human response, which the classical economists made
the basis of their faith in the automatic workings of the free market, came not from fixed
instincts but from the vast conservatism and
stability of a society that remained deeply
rooted in kinship long after the advent of the
capitalist age. Had it not been for the profound incentives supplied by the family and,
equally important, the capacity of the extended family to supply a degree, however
minimal, of mutual aid in time of distress, it is
a fair guess that capitalism would have failed
before it was well underway. The extraordinary rate of capital accumulation in the
nineteenth century was dependent, to some
extent at least, on a low-wage structure that
was in turn dependent on the continuation of
the ethic of family aid, even when this involved
child labor in the factories.

The same point may be made with respect
to the relation of kinship symbolism and population increase. What Malthus and his followers regarded as embedded in the biological
nature of man, the almost limitless urge to
procreate, has turned out to be inseparable
from the cultural fact of kinship, with its inherited incentives and values. As long as the
family had institutional importance in society,
it tended to maintain moral and psychological
devotions which resulted in high birth rates—
rates that invited the alarm of a good many
sociologists. But with the decline in both the
functional and psychological importance of
kinship, and with the emergence of a culture
based increasingly on the abstract individual
rather than the family, there has resulted a
quite different birth rate and a quite different
set of population problems.

To be sure we are dealing here, in this
matter of motivations and incentives, not
merely with the effects of the changed significance of the family but with those of the
changed significance of other social cohesions

upon which our economy and political order depended for a long period of time. What has happened to the family has happened also to neighborhood and local community. As Robert S. Lynd has written: "Neighborhood and community ties are not only optional but generally growing less strong; and along with them is disappearing the important network of intimate, informal, social controls traditionally associated with living closely with others.[3] Within all of these lay not merely controls but the incentives that supplied the motive force for such pursuits as education and religion and recreation.

The point is that with the decline in the significance of kinship and locality, and the failure of new social relationships to assume influences of equivalent evocative intensity, profound change has occurred in the very psychological structure of society. And this is a change that has produced a great deal of the present problem of incentives in so many areas of our society. Most of our ideas and practices in the major institutional areas of society developed during an age when the residual psychological elements of social organization seemed imperishable. No less imperishable seemed the structure of personality itself. Educational goals and political objectives were fashioned accordingly, as were theories of economic behavior and population increase.

But we are learning that many of the motivations and incentives which an older generation of rationalists believed were inherent in the individual are actually supplied by social groups—social groups with both functional and moral relevance to the lives of individuals.

Modern planners thus frequently find themselves dealing, not simply with the upper stratum of decisions, which their forebears assumed would be the sole demand of a planned society, but with often baffling problems which reach down into the very recesses of human personality.

Seven

Basically, however, it is not the position of the family or of any other single group, old or new, that is crucial to the welfare of a social order. Associations may come and go under the impact of historical changes and cultural needs. There is no single type of family, any more than there is a single type of religion, that is essential to personal security and collective prosperity. It would be wrong to assume that the present problem of community in Western society arises inexorably from the modifications which have taken place in old groups, however cherished these may be. But irrespective of particular groups, there must be in any stable culture, in any civilization that prizes its integrity, functionally significant and psychologically meaningful groups and associations lying intermediate to the individual and the larger values and purposes of his society. For these are the small areas of association within which alone such values and purposes can take on clear meaning in personal life and become the vital roots of the large culture. It is, I believe, the problem of intermediate association that is fundamental at the present time.

Under the lulling influence of the idea of Progress we have generally assumed until recently that history automatically provides its own solution to the basic problems of organization in society. We have further assumed that man is ineradicably gregarious and that from this gregariousness must come ever new and relevant forms of intermediate association.

It is tempting to believe this as we survey the innumerable formal organizations of modern life, the proliferation of which has been one of the signal facts in American history, or as we observe the incredible number of personal contacts which take place daily in the congested areas of modern urban life.

But there is a profound difference between the casual, informal relationships which abound in such areas and the kind of social groups which create a sense of belonging, which supply incentive, and which confer upon the individual a sense of status. Moreover, from some highly suggestive evidence supplied by such sociologists as Warner, Lazarsfeld, and especially Mirra Komarovsky, we can justly doubt that all sections of modern populations are as rich in identifiable social groups and associations as we have heretofore taken for granted.

The common assumption that, as the older associations of kinship and neighborhood have become weakened, they are replaced by new voluntary associations filling the same role is not above sharp question. That traditional groups have weakened in significance is apparently true enough but, on the evidence, their place has not been taken to any appreciable extent by new forms of association. Despite the appeal of the older sociological stereotype of the urban dweller who belongs to various voluntary associations, all of which have progressively replaced the older social unities, the facts so far gathered suggest the contrary: that a rising number of individuals belong to no organized association at all, and that, in the large cities, the unaffiliated persons may even constitute a majority of the population.[4]

As for the psychological functions of the great formal associations in modern life—industrial corporations, governmental agencies, large-scale labor and charitable organizations—it is plain that not many of these answer adequately the contemporary quest for community. Such organizations, as Max Weber pointed out, are generally organized not around personal loyalties but around loyalty to an office or machine. The administration of charity, hospitalization, unemployment assistance, like the administration of the huge manufacturing corporation, may be more efficient and less given to material inequities, but the possible gains in technical efficacy do not minimize their underlying impersonality in the life of the individual.

Much of the contemporary sense of the impersonality of society comes from the rational impersonality of these great organizations. The widespread reaction against technology, the city, and political freedom, not to mention the nostalgia that pervades so many of the discussions of rural-urban differences, comes from the diminished functional relationship between existent social groups in industry or the community and the remote efficiency of the larger organizations created by modern planners. The derivative loss of meaning for the individual frequently becomes the moral background of vague and impotent reactions against technology and science, and of aggressive states of mind against the culture as a whole. In spatial terms the individual is obviously less isolated from his fellows in the large-scale housing project or in the factory than was his grandfather. What he has become isolated from is the sense of meaningful proximity to the major ends and purposes of his culture. With the relatively complete satisfaction of needs concerned with food, employment, and housing, a different order of needs begins to assert itself imperiously; and these have to do with spiritual belief and social status.

"The uneasiness, the malaise of our time," writes C. Wright Mills, "is due to this root fact: in our politics and economy, in family life and religion—in practically every sphere of our existence—the certainties of the eighteenth and nineteenth centuries have disintegrated or been destroyed and, at the same time, no new sanctions or justifications for the new routines we live, and must live, have taken hold. Among white-collar people, the malaise is deep-rooted; for the absence of any order of belief has left them morally defenseless as individuals and politically impotent as a group. Newly created in a harsh time of creation, white-collar man has no culture to lean upon except the contents of a mass society that has shaped him and seeks to manipulate him to its alien ends. For security's sake he must attach himself somewhere, but no communities or organizations seem to be thoroughly his."[5]

The quest for community will not be denied, for it springs from some of the powerful needs of human nature—needs for a clear sense of cultural purpose, membership, status, and continuity. Without these, no amount of mere material welfare will serve to arrest the developing sense of alienation in our society, and the mounting preoccupation with the imperatives of community. To appeal to technological progress is futile. For what we discover is that rising standards of living, together with increases in leisure, actually intensify the disquietude and frustration that arise when cherished and proffered goals are without available means of fulfillment. "Secular improvement that is taken for granted," wrote Joseph Schumpeter, "and coupled with individual insecurity that is acutely resented is of course the best recipe for breeding social unrest."[6]

The loss of old moral certainties and accustomed statuses is, however, only the setting of our problem. For, despite the enormous influence of nostalgia in human thinking, it is never the recovery of the institutionally old that is desired by most people. In any event, the quest for the past is as futile as is that of the future.

The real problem is not, then, the loss of old contexts but rather the failure of our present democratic and industrial scene to create new contexts of association and moral cohesion within which the smaller allegiances of men will assume both functional and psychological significance. It is almost as if the forces that weakened the old have remained to obstruct the new channels of association.

What is the source of this failure? The blame is usually laid to technology, science, and the city. These, it is said, have left a vacuum. But the attack on these elements of modern culture is ill-founded, for no one of these is either logically or psychologically essential to the problem at hand. Neither science, nor technology, nor the city is inherently incompatible with the existence of moral values and social relationships which will do for modern man what the extended family, the parish, and the village did for earlier man.

Here, our problem becomes inevitably historical. For the present position of the social group in political and industrial society cannot be understood apart from the certain historical tendencies concerned with the location of authority and function in society and with certain momentous conflicts of authority and function which have been fundamental in the development of the modern State.

Notes

1. *Colonial Policy and Practice* (Cambridge University Press, 1948), p. 3.

2. There is a kind of historical awareness implicit in this focusing upon the family, for the overwhelming majority of communal or sacred areas of society reflect the transfer, historically, of kinship symbols and nomenclature to nonkinship spheres. We see this in the histories of religion, guilds, village communities, and labor unions. Kinship has ever been the archetype of man's communal aspirations.

3. *Knowledge For What?* (Princeton University Press, 1939), p. 83.

4. This paragraph is a paraphrase of Mirra Komarovsky's penetrating study, "The Voluntary Associations of Urban Dwellers," *American Sociological Review* (December 1946).

5. *White Collar: The American Middle Classes* (New York, 1951), p. xvi.

6. Op. cit. p. 145.

The Great Community

John Dewey

A quarter century before Robert Nisbet's observations, John Dewey also noted the disintegration of family life and the shifting composition of local communities. American democracy had traditionally functioned at the level of local communities, but with their decline, Dewey saw a decline in the practice of democracy. Without abiding attachments the American public loses its sense of self; it fails to find its purpose or to establish coherent goals. Whereas Nisbet blamed this on the growth of the centralized state, Dewey thought that the restless spirit of the American people and their ceaseless migrations caused the disruption of local communities. He accurately foresaw that this would continue and increase. But community, for Dewey, was the foundation of democratic practice. In this selection he seeks to form a community at the national level where public opinion could function much as citizen control did in local communities and could direct government policies. In Dewey's theory, the essence of community life, and democracy itself, is the joint activity of free and equal citizens who form the values and set the policies of the groups to which they belong. The question Dewey asks is, What are the conditions under which the Great Society (modern America) can be transformed into the Great Community? In exploring this question he develops a theory of community as it would apply to a democratically constituted public. Since democratic governments respond to public opinion in setting policy, the formation of public opinion is crucial, but Dewey observes that America is lacking the concerned, well-informed public needed for the formation of effective public opinion at the national level. While he is aware of the danger to individual freedom if public opinion is manipulated by a powerful elite, Dewey believes that public opinion rightly expressed could form a national democratic community. To turn the Great Society into the Great Community, Dewey calls for a free social inquiry and its full communication to all citizens.

We have had occasion to refer in passing to the distinction between democracy as a social idea and political democracy as a system of government. The two are, of course, connected. The idea remains barren and empty save as it is incarnated in human relationships. Yet in discussion they must be distinguished. The idea of democracy is a wider and fuller idea than can be exemplified in the state even at its best. To be realized it must affect all modes of human association, the family, the school, industry, religion. And even as far as political arrangements are concerned, governmental institutions are but a mechanism for securing to an idea channels of effective operation. It will hardly do to say that criticisms of the political machinery leave the believer in the idea untouched. For, as far as they are justified—and no candid believer can deny that many of them are only too well grounded—they arouse him to bestir himself in order that the idea may find a more adequate machinery through which to work. What the faithful insist upon, however, is that the idea and its external organs and structures are not to be identified. We object to the common supposition of the foes of existing democratic government that the accusations against it touch the social and moral aspirations and ideas which underlie the political forms. The old saying that the cure

From John Dewey, "The Public and its Problems," in *John Dewey: The Later Works, 1925–53*, vol. 2, *1925–27*, Jo Ann Boydston, ed. (Carbondale: Southern Illinois University Press, 1984), pp. 325–336, 339–342, 345–350. Reprinted by permission of Southern Illinois University Press. Footnotes omitted.

for the ills of democracy is more democracy is not apt if it means that the evils may be remedied by introducing more machinery of the same kind as that which already exists, or by refining and perfecting that machinery. But the phrase may also indicate the need of returning to the idea itself, of clarifying and deepening our apprehension of it, and of employing our sense of its meaning to criticize and remake its political manifestations.

Confining ourselves, for the moment, to political democracy, we must, in any case, renew our protest against the assumption that the idea has itself produced the governmental practices which obtain in democratic states: General suffrage, elected representatives, majority rule, and so on. The idea has influenced the concrete political movement, but it has not caused it. The transition from family and dynastic government supported by the loyalties of tradition to popular government was the outcome primarily of technological discoveries and inventions working a change in the customs by which men had been bound together. It was not due to the doctrines of doctrinaires. The forms to which we are accustomed in democratic governments represent the cumulative effect of a multitude of events, unpremeditated as far as political effects were concerned and having unpredictable consequences. There is no sanctity in universal suffrage, frequent elections, majority rule, congressional and cabinet government. These things are devices evolved in the direction in which the current was moving, each wave of which involved at the time of its impulsion a minimum of departure from antecedent custom and law. The devices served a purpose; but the purpose was rather that of meeting existing needs which had become too intense to be ignored, than that of forwarding the democratic idea. In spite of all defects, they served ther own purpose well.

Looking back, with the aid which ex post facto experience can give, it would be hard for the wisest to devise schemes which, under the circumstances, would have met the needs better. In this retrospective glance, it is possible, however, to see how the doctrinal formulations which accompanied them were inadequate, one-sided and positively erroneous. In fact they were hardly more than political war-cries adopted to help in carrying on some immediate agitation or in justifying some particular practical polity struggling for recognition, even though they were asserted to be absolute truths of human nature or of morals. The doctrines served a particular local pragmatic need. But often their very adaptation to immediate circumstances unfitted them, pragmatically, to meet more enduring and more extensive needs. They lived to cumber the political ground, obstructing progress, all the more so because they were uttered and held not as hypotheses with which to direct social experimentation but as final truths, dogmas. No wonder they call urgently for revision and displacement.

Nevertheless the current has set steadily in one direction: toward democratic forms. That government exists to serve its community, and that this purpose cannot be achieved unless the community itself shares in selecting its governors and determining their policies, are a deposit of fact left, as far as we can see, permanently in the wake of doctrines and forms, however transitory the latter. They are not the whole of the democratic idea, but they express it in its political phase. Belief in this political aspect is not a mystic faith as if in some over-ruling providence that cares for children, drunkards and others unable to help themselves. It marks a well-attested conclusion from historic facts. We have every reason to think that whatever changes may take place in existing democratic machinery, they will be of a sort to make the interest of the public a more supreme guide and criterion of governmental activity, and to enable the public to form and manifest its purposes still more authoritatively. In this sense the cure for the ailments of democracy is more democracy. The prime difficulty, as we have seen, is that of discovering the means by which a scattered, mobile and manifold public may so recognize itself as to define and express its interests. This discovery is necessarily precedent to any fundamental change in the machinery. We are not concerned therefore to set forth counsels as to advisable improvements in the political forms of democracy. Many have been suggested. It is no derogation of their relative worth to say that consideration of these changes is not at present an affair of primary importance. The problem lies deeper; it is in the first instance an intellectual problem: the search for conditions under which the Great Society may become the Great Community. When these conditions are brought into being they will make their own forms. Until they have come about, it is somewhat futile to consider what political machinery will suit them.

In a search for the conditions under which the inchoate public now extant may function democratically, we may proceed from a statement of the nature of the democratic idea in its generic social sense. From the standpoint of the individual, it consists in having a responsible share according to capacity in forming and directing the activities of the groups to which one belongs and in participating according to need in the values which the groups sustain. From the standpoint of the groups, it demands liberation of the potentialities of members of a group in harmony with the interests and goods which are common. Since every individual is a member of many groups, this specification cannot be fulfilled except when different groups interact flexibly and fully in connection with other groups. A member of a robber band may express his powers in a way consonant with belonging to that group and be directed by the interest common to its members. But he does so only at the cost of repression of those of his potentialities which can be realized only through membership in other groups. The robber band cannot interact flexibly with other groups; it can act only through isolating itself. It must prevent the operation of all interests save those which circumscribe it in its separateness. But a good citizen finds his conduct as a member of a political group enriching and enriched by his participation in family life, industry, scientific and artistic associations. There is a free give-and-take: fullness of integrated personality is therefore possible of achievement, since the pulls and responses of different groups reenforce one another and their values accord.

Regarded as an idea, democracy is not an alternative to other principles of associated life. It is the idea of community life itself. It is an ideal in the only intelligible sense of an ideal: namely, the tendency and movement of some thing which exists carried to its final limit, viewed as completed, perfected. Since

things do not attain such fulfillment but are in actuality distracted and interfered with, democracy in this sense is not a fact and never will be. But neither in this sense is there or has there ever been anything which is a community in its full measure, a community unalloyed by alien elements. The idea or ideal of a community presents, however, actual phases of associated life as they are freed from restrictive and disturbing elements, and are contemplated as having attained their limit of development. Wherever there is conjoint activity whose consequences are appreciated as good by all singular persons who take part in it, and where the realization of the good is such as to effect an energetic desire and effort to sustain it in being just because it is a good shared by all, there is in so far a community. The clear consciousness of a communal life, in all its implications, constitutes the idea of democracy.

Only when we start from a community as a fact, grasp the fact in thought so as to clarify and enhance its constituent elements, can we reach an idea of democracy which is not utopian. The conceptions and shibboleths which are traditionally associated with the idea of democracy take on a veridical and directive meaning only when they are construed as marks and traits of an association which realizes the defining characteristics of a community. Fraternity, liberty and equality isolated from communal life are hopeless abstractions. Their separate assertion leads to mushy sentimentalism or else to extravagant and fanatical violence which in the end defeats its own aims. Equality then becomes a creed of mechanical identity which is false to facts and impossible of realization. Effort to attain it is divisive of the vital bonds which hold men together; as far as it puts forth issue, the outcome is a mediocrity in which good is common only in the sense of being average and vulgar. Liberty is then thought of as independence of social ties, and ends in dissolution and anarchy. It is more difficult to sever the idea of brotherhood from that of a community, and hence it is either practically ignored in the movements which identify democracy with Individualism, or else it is a sentimentally appended tag. In its just connection with communal experience, fraternity is another name for the consciously appreciated goods which accrue from an association in which all share, and which give direction to the conduct of each. Liberty is that secure release and fulfillment of personal potentialities which take place only in rich and manifold association with others: the power to be an individualized self making a distinctive contribution and enjoying in its own way the fuits of association. Equality denotes the unhampered share which each individual member of the community has in the consequences of associated action. It is equitable because it is measured only by need and capacity to utilize, not by extraneous factors which deprive one in order that another may take and have. A baby in the family is equal with others, not because of some antecedent and structural quality which is the same as that of others, but in so far as his needs for care and development are attended to without being sacrificed to the superior strength, possessions and matured abilities of others. Equality does not signify that kind of mathematical or physical equivalence in virtue of which any one element may be substituted for another. It denotes effective regard for whatever is distinctive and unique in each, irrespective of physical and psychological inequalities. It is not a natural possession but is a fruit of the community when its action is directed by its character as a community.

Associated or joint activity is a condition of the creation of a community. But association itself is physical and organic, while communal life is moral, that is emotionally, intellectually, consciously sustained. Human beings combine in behavior as directly and unconsciously as do atoms, stellar masses and cells; as directly and unknowingly as they divide and repel. They do so in virtue of their own structure, as man and woman unite, as the baby seeks the breast and the breast is there to supply its need. They do so from external circumstances, pressure from without, as atoms combine or separate in presence of an electric charge, or as sheep huddle together from the cold. Associated activity needs no explanation; things are made that way. But no amount of aggregated collective action of itself constitutes a community. For beings who observe and think, and whose ideas are absorbed by impulses and become sentiments and interests, "we" is as inevitable

as "I." But "we" and "our" exist only when the consequences of combined action are perceived and become an object of desire and effort, just as "I" and "mine" appear on the scene only when a distinctive share in mutual action is consciously asserted or claimed. Human associations may be ever so organic in origin and firm in operation, but they develop into societies in a human sense only as their consequences, being known, are esteemed and sought for. Even if "society" were as much an organism as some writers have held, it would not on that account be society. Interactions, transactions, occur *de facto* and the results of interdependence follow. But participation in activities and sharing in results are additive concerns. They demand *communication* as a prerequisite.

Combined activity happens among human beings; but when nothing else happens it passes as inevitably into some other mode of interconnected activity as does the interplay of iron and the oxygen of water. What takes place is wholly describable in terms of energy, or, as we say in the case of human interactions, of force. Only when there exist *signs* or *symbols* of activities and of their outcome can the flux be viewed as from without, be arrested for consideration and esteem, and be regulated. Lightning strikes and rives a tree or rock, and the resulting fragments take up and continue the process of interaction, and so on and on. But when phases of the process are represented by signs, a new medium is interposed. As symbols are related to one another, the important relations of a course of events are recorded and are preserved as meanings. Recollection and foresight are possible; the new medium facilitates calculation, planning, and a new kind of action which intervenes in what happens to direct its course in the interest of what is foreseen and desired.

Symbols in turn depend upon and promote communication. The results of conjoint experience are considered and transmitted. Events cannot be passed from one to another, but meanings may be shared by means of signs. Wants and impulses are then attached to common meanings. They are thereby transformed into desires and purposes, which, since they implicate a common or mutually understood meaning, present new ties, converting a conjoint activity into a community of interest and endeavor. Thus there is generated what, metaphorically, may be termed a general will and social consciousness: desire and choice on the part of individuals in behalf of activities that, by means of symbols, are communicable and shared by all concerned. A community thus presents an order of energies transmuted into one of meanings which are appreciated and mutually referred by each to every other on the part of those engaged in combined action. "Force" is not eliminated but is transformed in use and direction by ideas and sentiments made possible by means of symbols.

The work of conversion of the physical and organic phase of associated behavior into a community of action saturated and regulated by mutual interest in shared meanings, consequences which are translated into ideas and desired objects by means of symbols, does not occur all at once nor completely. At any given time, it sets a problem rather than marks a settled achievement. We are born organic beings associated with others, but we are not born members of a community. The young have to be brought within the traditions, outlook and interests which characterize a community by means of education: by unremitting instruction and by learning in connection with the phenomena of overt association. Everything which is distinctively human is learned, not native, even though it could not be learned without native structures which mark man off from other animals. To learn in a human way and to human effect is not just to acquire added skill through refinement of original capacities.

To learn to be human is to develop through the give-and-take of communication an effective sense of being an individually distinctive member of a community; one who understands and appreciates its beliefs, desires and methods, and who contributes to a further conversion of organic powers into human resources and values. But this translation is never finished. The old Adam, the unregenerate element in human nature, persists. It shows itself wherever the method obtains of attaining results by use of force instead of by the method of communication and enlightenment. It manifests itself more subtly, pervasively and effectually when knowledge

and the instrumentalities of skill which are the product of communal life are employed in the service of wants and impulses which have not themselves been modified by reference to a shared interest. To the doctrine of "natural" economy which held that commercial exchange would bring about such an interdependence that harmony would automatically result, Rousseau gave an adequate answer in advance. He pointed out that interdependence provides just the situation which makes it possible and worthwhile for the stronger and abler to exploit others for their own ends, to keep others in a state of subjection where they can be utilized as animated tools. The remedy he suggested, a return to a condition of independence based on isolation, was hardly seriously meant. But its desperateness is evidence of the urgency of the problem. Its negative character was equivalent to surrender of any hope of solution. By contrast it indicates the nature of the only possible solution: the perfecting of the means and ways of communication of meanings so that genuinely shared interest in the consequences of interdependent activities may inform desire and effort and thereby direct action.

This is the meaning of the statement that the problem is a moral one dependent upon intelligence and education. We have in our prior account sufficiently emphasized the role of technological and industrial factors in creating the Great Society. What was said may even have seemed to imply acceptance of the deterministic version of an economic interpretation of history and institutions. It is silly and futile to ignore and deny economic facts. They do not cease to operate because we refuse to note them, or because we smear them over with sentimental idealizations. As we have also noted, they generate as their result overt and external conditions of action and these are known with various degrees of adequacy. What actually happens in consequence of industrial forces is dependent upon the presence or absence of perception and communication of consequences, upon foresight and its effect upon desire and endeavor. Economic agencies produce one result when they are left to work themselves out on the merely physical level, or on that level modified only as the knowledge, skill and technique which the community has accumulated are transmitted to its members unequally and by chance. They have a different outcome in the degree in which knowledge of consequences is equitably distributed, and action is animated by an informed and lively sense of a shared interest. The doctrine of economic interpretation as usually stated ignores the transformation which meanings may effect; it passes over the new medium which communication may interpose between industry and its eventual consequences. It is obsessed by the illusion which vitiated the "natural economy": an illusion due to failure to note the difference made in action by perception and publication of its consequences, actual and possible. It thinks in terms of antecedents, not of the eventual; of origins, not fruits.

We have returned, through this apparent excursion, to the question in which our earlier discussion culminated: What are the conditions under which it is possible for the Great Society to approach more closely and vitally the status of a Great Community, and thus take form in genuinely democratic societies and state? What are the conditions under which we may reasonably picture the Public emerging from its eclipse?

The study will be an intellectual or hypothetical one. There will be no attempt to state how the required conditions might come into existence, nor to prophesy that they will occur. The object of the analysis will be to show that *unless* ascertained specifications are realized, the Community cannot be organized as a democratically effective Public. It is not claimed that the conditions which will be noted will suffice, but only that at least they are indispensable. In other words, we shall endeavor to frame a hypothesis regarding the democratic state to stand in contrast with the earlier doctrine which has been nullified by the course of events.

Two essential constituents in that older theory, as will be recalled, were the notions that each individual is of himself equipped with the intelligence needed, under the operation of self-interest, to engage in political affairs; and that general suffrage, frequent elections of officials and majority rule are sufficient to ensure the responsibility of elected rulers to the desires and interests of the public.

As we shall see, the second conception is logically bound up with the first and stands or falls with it. At the basis of the scheme lies what Lippmann has well called the idea of the "omnicompetent" individual: competent to frame policies, to judge their results; competent to know in all situations demanding political action what is for his own good, and competent to enforce his idea of good and the will to effect it against contrary forces. Subsequent history has proved that the assumption involved illusion. Had it not been for the misleading influence of a false psychology, the illusion might have been detected in advance. But current philosophy held that ideas and knowledge were functions of a mind or consciousness which originated in individuals by means of isolated contact with objects. But in fact, knowledge is a function of association and communication; it depends upon tradition, upon tools and methods socially transmitted, developed and sanctioned. Faculties of effectual observation, reflection and desire are habits acquired under the influence of the culture and institutions of society, not ready-made inherent powers. The fact that man acts from crudely intelligized emotion and from habit rather than from rational consideration, is now so familiar that it is not easy to appreciate that the other idea was taken seriously as the basis of economic and political philosophy. The measure of truth which it contains was derived from observation of a relatively small group of shrewd businessmen who regulated their enterprises by calculation and accounting, and of citizens of small and stable local communities who were so intimately acquainted with the persons and affairs of their locality that they could pass competent judgment upon the bearing of proposed measures upon their own concerns.

Habit is the mainspring of human action, and habits are formed for the most part under the influence of the customs of a group. The organic structure of man entails the formation of habit, for, whether we wish it or not, whether we are aware of it or not, every act effects a modification of attitude and set which directs future behavior. The dependence of habit-forming upon those habits of a group which constitute customs and institutions is a natural consequence of the helplessness of infancy. The social consequences of habit have been stated once for all by James: "Habit is the enormous fly-wheel of society, its most precious conservative influence. It alone is what keeps us within the bounds of ordinance, and saves the children of fortune from the uprisings of the poor. It alone prevents the hardest and most repulsive walks of life from being deserted by those brought up to tread therein. It keeps the fisherman and the deck-hand at sea through the winter; it holds the miner in his darkness, and nails the countryman to his log-cabin and his lonely farm through all the months of snow; it protects us from invasion by the natives of the desert and the frozen zone. It dooms us all to fight out the battle of life upon the lines of our nurture or our early choice, and to make the best of a pursuit that disagrees, because there is no other for which we are fitted and it is too late to begin again. It keeps different social strata from mixing."

The influence of habit is decisive because all distinctively human action has to be learned, and the very heart, blood and sinews of learning is creation of habitudes. Habits bind us to orderly and established ways of action because they generate ease, skill and interest in things to which we have grown used and because they instigate fear to walk in different ways, and because they leave us incapacitated for the trial of them. Habit does not preclude the use of thought, but it determines the channels within which it operates. Thinking is secreted in the interstices of habits. The sailor, miner, fisherman and farmer think, but their thoughts fall within the framework of accustomed occupations and relationships. We dream beyond the limits of use and wont, but only rarely does revery become a source of acts which break bounds; so rarely that we name those in whom it happens demonic geniuses and marvel at the spectacle. Thinking itself becomes habitual along certain lines; a specialized occupation. Scientific men, philosophers, literary persons, are not men and women who have so broken the bonds of habits that pure reason and emotion undefiled by use and wont speak through them. They are persons of a specialized infrequent habit. Hence the idea that men are moved by an intelligent and calculated regard for their own good is pure mythology. Even if the principle of self-love

actuated behavior, it would still be true that the *objects* in which men find their love manifested, the objects which they take as constituting their peculiar interests, are set by habits reflecting social customs.

These facts explain why the social doctrinaires of the new industrial movement had so little prescience of what was to follow in consequence of it. These facts explain why the more things changed, the more they were the same; they account, that is, for the fact that instead of the sweeping revolution which was expected to result from democratic political machinery, there was in the main but a transfer of vested power from one class to another. A few men, whether or not they were good judges of their own true interest and good, were competent judges of the conduct of business for pecuniary profit, and of how the new governmental machinery could be made to serve their ends. It would have taken a new race of human beings to escape, in the use made of political forms, from the influence of deeply engrained habits, of old institutions and customary social status, with their inwrought limitations of expectation, desire and demand. And such a race, unless of disembodied angelic constitution, would simply have taken up the task where human beings assumed it upon emergence from the condition of anthropoid apes. In spite of sudden and catastrophic revolutions, the essential continuity of history is doubly guaranteed. Not only are personal desire and belief functions of habit and custom, but the objective conditions which provide the resources and tools of action, together with its limitations, obstructions and traps, are precipitates of the past, perpetuating, willy-nilly, its hold and power. The creation of a *tabula rasa* in order to permit the creation of a new order is so impossible as to set at naught both the hope of buoyant revolutionaries and the timidity of scared conservatives. . . .

The prime condition of a democratically organized public is a kind of knowledge and insight which does not yet exist. In its absence, it would be the height of absurdity to try to tell what it would be like if it existed. But some of the conditions which must be fulfilled if it is to exist can be indicated. We can borrow that much from the spirit and method of science even if we are ignorant of it as a specialized apparatus. An obvious requirement is freedom of social inquiry and of distribution of its conclusions. The notion that men may be free in their thought even when they are not in its expression and dissemination has been sedulously propagated. It had its origin in the idea of a mind complete in itself, apart from action and from objects. Such a consciousness presents in fact the spectacle of mind deprived of its normal functioning, because it is baffled by the actualities in connection with which alone it is truly mind, and is driven back into secluded and impotent revery.

There can be no public without full publicity in respect to all consequences which concern it. Whatever obstructs and restricts publicity, limits and distorts public opinion and checks and distorts thinking on social affairs. Without freedom of expression, not even methods of social inquiry can be developed. For tools can be evolved and perfected only in operation; in application to observing, reporting and organizing actual subject-matter; and this application cannot occur save through free and systematic communication. The early history of physical knowledge, of Greek conceptions of natural phenomena, proves how inept become the conceptions of the best endowed minds when those ideas are elaborated apart from the closest contact with the events which they purport to state and explain. The ruling ideas and methods of the human sciences are in much the same condition today. They are also evolved on the basis of past gross observations, remote from constant use in regulation of the material of new observations.

The belief that thought and its communication are now free simply because legal restrictions which once obtained have been done away with is absurd. Its currency perpetuates the infantile state of social knowledge. For it blurs recognition of our central need to possess conceptions which are used as tools of directed inquiry and which are tested, rectified and caused to grow in actual use. No man and no mind was ever emancipated merely by being left alone. Removal of formal limitations is but a negative condition; positive freedom is not a state but an act which involves methods and instrumentalities for control of conditions. Experience shows that sometimes the sense of external oppression, as by censorship, acts as a challenge and arouses intellectual energy and excites courage. But a belief in intellectual freedom where it does not exist contributes only to complacency in virtual enslavement, to sloppiness, superficiality and recourse to sensations as a substitute for ideas: marked traits of our present estate with respect to social knowledge. On one hand, thinking deprived of its normal course takes refuge in academic specialism, comparable in its way to what is called scholasticism. On the other hand, the physical agencies of publicity which exist in such abundance are utilized in ways which constitute a large part of the present meaning of publicity: advertising, propaganda, invasion of private life, the "featuring" of passing incidents in a way which violates all the moving logic of continuity, and which leaves us with those isolated intrusions and shocks which are the essence of "sensations."

It would be a mistake to identify the conditions which limit free communication and circulation of facts and ideas, and which thereby arrest and pervert social thought or inquiry, merely with overt forces which are obstructive. It is true that those who have ability to manipulate social relations for their own advantage have to be reckoned with. They have an uncanny instinct for detecting whatever intellectual tendencies even remotely threaten to encroach upon their control. They have developed an extraordinary facility in enlisting upon their side the inertia, prejudices and emotional partisanship of the masses by use of a technique which impedes free inquiry and expression. We seem to be approaching a state of government by hired promoters of opinion called publicity agents. But the more serious enemy is deeply concealed in hidden entrenchments.

Emotional habituations and intellectual habitudes on the part of the mass of men create the conditions of which the exploiters of sentiment and opinion only take advantage. Men have got used to an experimental method in physical and technical matters. They are still afraid of it in human concerns. The fear is the more efficacious because like all deep-lying fears it is covered up and disguised by all kinds of rationalizations. One of its commonest forms is a truly religious idealization of, and reverence for, established institutions; for example in our own politics, the Constitution, the Supreme Court, private property, free contract and so on. The words "sacred" and "sanctity" come readily to our lips when such things come under discussion. They testify to the religious aureole which protects the institutions. If "holy" means that which is not to be approached nor touched, save with ceremonial precautions and by specially anointed officials, then such things are holy in contemporary political life. As supernatural matters have progressively been left high and dry upon a secluded beach, the actuality of religious taboos has more and more gathered about secular institutions, especially those connected with the nationalistic state. Psychiatrists have discovered that one of the commonest causes of mental disturbance is an underlying fear of which the subject is not aware, but which leads to withdrawal from reality and to unwillingness to think things through. There is a social pathology which works powerfully against effective inquiry into social institutions and conditions. It manifests itself in a thousand ways; in querulousness, in impotent drifting, in uneasy snatching at distractions, in idealization of the long established, in a facile optimism assumed as a cloak, in riotous glorification of things "as they are," in intimidation of all dissenters—ways which depress and dissipate thought all the more effectually because they operate with subtle and unconscious pervasiveness. . . .

It has been implied throughout that knowledge is communication as well as understanding. I well remember the saying of a man, uneducated from the standpoint of the schools, in speaking of certain matters: "Sometime they will be found out and not only found out, but they will be known." The schools may suppose that a thing is known when it is found out. My old friend was aware that a thing is fully known only when it is published, shared, socially accessible. Record and communication are indispensable to knowledge. Knowledge cooped up in a private consciousness is a myth,

and knowledge of social phenomena is peculiarly dependent upon dissemination, for only by distribution can such knowledge be either obtained or tested. A fact of community life which is not spread abroad so as to be a common possession is a contradiction in terms. Dissemination is something other than scattering at large. Seeds are sown, not by virtue of being thrown out at random, but by being so distributed as to take root and have a chance of growth. Communication of the results of social inquiry is the same thing as the formation of public opinion. This marks one of the first ideas framed in the growth of political democracy as it will be one of the last to be fulfilled. For public opinion is judgment which is formed and entertained by those who constitute the public and is about public affairs. Each of the two phases imposes for its realization conditions hard to meet.

Opinions and beliefs concerning the public presuppose effective and organized inquiry. Unless there are methods for detecting the energies which are at work and tracing them through an intricate network of interactions to their consequences, what passes as public opinion will be "opinion" in its derogatory sense rather than truly public, no matter how widespread the opinion is. The number who share error as to fact and who partake of a false belief measures power for harm. Opinion casually formed and formed under the direction of those who have something at stake in having a lie believed can be *public* opinion only in name. Calling it by this name, acceptance of the name as a kind of warrant, magnifies its capacity to lead action astray. The more who share it, the more injurious its influence. Public opinion, even if it happens to be correct, is intermittent when it is not the product of methods of investigation and reporting constantly at work. It appears only in crises. Hence its "rightness" concerns only an immediate emergency. Its lack of continuity makes it wrong from the standpoint of the course of events. It is as if a physician were able to deal for the moment with an emergency in disease but could not adapt his treatment of it to the underlying conditions which brought it about. He may then "cure" the disease—that is, cause its present alarming symptoms to subside—but he does not modify its causes; his treatment may even affect them for the worse. Only continuous inquiry, continuous in the sense of being connected as well as persistent, can provide the material of enduring opinion about public matters.

There is a sense in which "opinion" rather than knowledge, even under the most favorable circumstances, is the proper term to use—namely, in the sense of judgment, estimate. For in its strict sense, knowledge can refer only to what *has* happened and been done. What is still *to be* done involves a forecast of a future still contingent, and cannot escape the liability to error in judgment involved in all anticipation of probabilities. There may well be honest divergence as to policies to be pursued, even when plans spring from knowledge of the same facts. But genuinely public policy cannot be generated unless it be informed by knowledge, and this knowledge does not exist except when there is systematic, thorough, and well-equipped search and record.

Moreover, inquiry must be as nearly contemporaneous as possible; otherwise it is only of antiquarian interest. Knowledge of history is evidently necessary for connectedness of knowledge. But history which is not brought down close to the actual scene of events leaves a gap and exercises influence upon the formation of judgments about the public interest only by guesswork about intervening events. Here, only too conspicuously, is a limitation of the existing social sciences. Their material comes too late, too far after the event, to enter effectively into the formation of public opinion about the immediate public concern and what is to be done about it.

A glance at the situation shows that the physical and external means of collecting information in regard to what is happening in the world have far outrun the intellectual phase of inquiry and organization of its results. Telegraph, telephone, and now the radio, cheap and quick mails, the printing press, capable of swift reduplication of material at low cost, have attained a remarkable development. But when we ask what sort of material is recorded and how it is organized, when we ask about the intellectual form in which the material is presented, the tale to be told is very different. "News" signifies something which has just happened, and which is new just because it deviates from the old and regular. But its *meaning* depends upon relation to what it imports, to what its social consequences are. This import cannot be determined unless the new is placed in relation to the old, to what has happened and been integrated into the course of events. Without coordination and consecutiveness, events are not events, but mere occurrences, intrusions; an event implies that out of which a happening proceeds. Hence even if we discount the influence of private interests in procuring suppression, secrecy and misrepresentation, we have here an explanation of the triviality and "sensational" quality of so much of what passes as news. The catastrophic, namely, crime, accident, family rows, personal clashes and conflicts, are the most obvious forms of breaches of continuity; they supply the element of shock which is the strictest meaning of sensation; they are the *new* par excellence, even though only the date of the newspaper could inform us whether they happened last year or this, so completely are they isolated from their connections.

So accustomed are we to this method of collecting, recording and presenting social changes, that it may well sound ridiculous to say that a genuine social science would manifest its reality in the daily press, while learned books and articles supply and polish tools of inquiry. But the inquiry which alone can furnish knowledge as a precondition of public judgments must be contemporary and quotidian. Even if social sciences as a specialized apparatus of inquiry were more advanced than they are, they would be comparatively impotent in the office of directing opinion on matters of concern to the public as long as they are remote from application in the daily and unremitting assembly and interpretation of "news." On the other hand, the tools of social inquiry will be clumsy as long as they are forged in places and under conditions remote from contemporary events.

What has been said about the formation of ideas and judgments concerning the public apply as well to the distribution of the knowledge which makes it an effective possession of the members of the public. Any separation between the two sides of the problem is artificial. The discussion of propaganda and propagandism would alone, however, demand a volume, and could be written only by one much more experienced than the present writer. Propaganda can accordingly only be mentioned, with the remark that the present situation is one unprecedented in history. The political forms of democracy and quasi-democratic habits of thought on social matters have compelled a certain amount of public discussion and at least the simulation of general consultation in arriving at political decisions. Representative government must at least seem to be founded on public interests as they are revealed to public belief. The days are past when government can be carried on without any pretense of ascertaining the wishes of the governed. In theory, their assent must be secured. Under the older forms, there was no need to muddy the sources of opinion on political matters. No current of energy flowed from them. Today the judgments popularly formed on political matters are so important, in spite of all factors to the contrary, that there is an enormous premium upon all methods which affect their formation.

The smoothest road to control of political conduct is by control of opinion. As long as interests of pecuniary profit are powerful, and a public has not located and identified itself, those who have this interest will have an unresisted motive for tampering with the springs of political action in all that affects them. Just as in the conduct of industry and exchange generally the technological factor is obscured, deflected and defeated by "business," so specifically in the management of publicity. The gathering and sale of subject-matter having a public import is part of the existing pecuniary system. Just as industry conducted by engineers on a factual technological basis would be a very different thing from what it actually is, so the assembling and reporting of news would be a very different thing if the genuine interests of reporters were permitted to work freely.

One aspect of the matter concerns particularly the side of dissemination. It is often said, and with a great appearance of truth, that the freeing and perfecting of inquiry would not have any especial effect. For, it is argued, the mass of the reading public is not interested in learning and assimilating the results of accurate investigation. Unless these are read, they cannot seriously affect the thought and action of members of the public; they remain in secluded library alcoves, and are studied and understood only by a few intellectuals. The objection is well taken save as the potency of art is taken into account. A technical high-brow presentation would appeal only to those technically high-brow; it would not be news to the masses. Presentation is fundamentally important, and presentation is a question of art. A newspaper which was only a daily edition of a quarterly journal of sociology or political science would undoubtedly possess a limited circulation and a narrow influence. Even at that, however, the mere existence and accessibility of such material would have some regulative effect. But we can look much further than that. The material would have such an enormous and widespread human bearing that its bare existence would be an irresistible invitation to a presentation of it which would have a direct popular appeal. The freeing of the artist in literary presentation, in other words, is as much a precondition of the desirable creation of adequate opinion on public matters as is the freeing of social inquiry. Men's conscious life of opinion and judgment often proceeds on a superficial and trivial plane. But their lives reach a deeper level. The function of art has always been to break through the crust of conventionalized and routine consciousness. Common things, a flower, a gleam of moonlight, the song of a bird, not things rare and remote, are means with which the deeper levels of life are touched so that they spring up as desire and thought. This process is art. Poetry, the drama, the novel, are proofs that the problem of presentation is not insoluble. Artists have always been the real purveyors of news, for it is not the outward happening in itself which is new, but the kindling by it of emotion, perception and appreciation.

We have but touched lightly and in passing upon the conditions which must be fulfilled if the Great Society is to become a Great Community; a society in which the ever-expanding and intricately ramifying consequences of associated activities shall be known in the full sense of that word, so that an organized, articulate Public comes into being. The highest and most difficult kind of inquiry and a subtle, delicate, vivid and responsive art of communication must take possession of the physical machinery of transmission and circulation and breathe life into it. When the machine age has thus perfected its machinery it will be a means of life and not its despotic master.

Democracy will come into its own, for democracy is a name for a life of free and enriching communion. It had its seer in Walt Whitman. It will have its consummation when free social inquiry is indissolubly wedded to the art of full and moving communication.

The Great Law of Peace

John Mohawk

John Mohawk extends the relationships of mutual respect and care that characterize a human community to include all animals, plants, rivers, air, and the earth itself. In this selection he transcribes the philosophy of the Iroquois people that has been passed down through an oral tradition. The Iroquois Confederacy, occupying much of the eastern section of the United States and southern Canada, has been governed through a political philosophy called the Great Law of Peace. This philosophy, based on the spiritual union of all natural beings, states that no one may abuse any other member of this natural community—a universal description of justice. Mohawk describes this philosophy as the natural law of peace, to be applied not only among a local people or between nations, but also between humans and other members of the spiritual community on which we depend for continued life and prosperity. The native philosophy given in this selection is expressed in the form of a narrative. The first part is taken from an Address to the Western World by the Iroquois Confederacy of Six Nations at a United Nations Assembly in Geneva, Switzerland, in 1977. Mohawk gives a history of the rise of Western political consciousness and establishes the claim of the surviving Iroquois Nation to criticize this philosophy in the name of all native peoples. The Iroquois people lived in freedom and harmony with the land for countless centuries, he writes, and the basis of this success has been a spiritual form of political consciousness. The next section recounts the formation of this spiritual consciousness as a political philosophy called the Great Law of Peace. In its political application the leaders are the true servants of the people. By a complex set of rules, local men and women form a consensus on each issue and send their representatives to a council, whose deliberations are referred back and forth to their home communities before being passed on to the chief for action. Mohawk credits this direct democracy, together with a respect for the natural world, with the success and longevity of the Iroquois Confederacy. In the last section Mohawk describes how this spiritual form of political consciousness can be used in the modern world to reestablish a respectful, sustainable relationship with the earth and nonexploitative relationships among peoples.

A Basic Call to Consciousness, edited by Akwesasne Notes, Mohawk Nation via Rooseveltown, New York, 1986, "Thoughts of Peace: The Great Law," pp. 7–12, "The Haudenosaunee Address to the Western World," pp. 49–55, 74–78. Reprinted by permission of John Mohawk, Professor of American Studies at the University of Buffalo, Buffalo, New York.

Spiritualism the Highest Form of Political Consciousness

The Haudenosaunee Message to the Western World

The Haudenosaunee, or the Six Nations Iroquois Confederacy, has existed on this land since the beginning of human memory. Our culture is among the most ancient continuously existing cultures in the world. We still remember the earliest doings of human beings. We remember the original instructions of the Creators of Life on this place we call Etenoha—Mother Earth. We are the spiritual guardians of this place. We are the Ongwhehonwhe—the real people.

In the beginning, we were told that the human beings who walk about on the Earth have been provided with all the things necessary of life. We were instructed to carry a love for one another, and to show a great respect for all the beings of this Earth. We are shown that our life exists with the tree life, that our well-being depends on the well-being of the Vegetable Life, that we are close relatives of the four-legged beings. In our ways, spiritual consciousness is the highest form of politics.

Ours is a Way of Life. We believe that all living things are spiritual beings. Spirits can be expressed as energy form manifested in matter—grass matter. The spirit of the grass is that unseen force which produces the species of grass, and it is manifest to us in the form of real grass.

All things of the world are real, material things. The Creation is a true, material phenomenon, and the Creation manifests itself to us through reality. The spiritual universe, then, is manifest to Man as the Creation, the Creation which supports life. We believe that man is real, a part of the Creation, and that his duty is to support Life in conjunction with the other beings. That is why we call ourselves Ongwhehonwhe—Real People.

The original instructions direct that we who walk about on the Earth are to express a great respect, an affection, and a gratitude toward all the spirits which create and support Life. We give a greeting and thanksgiving to the many supporters of our own lives—the corn, beans, squash, the winds, the sun. When people cease to respect and express gratitude for these many things, then all life will be destroyed, and human life on this planet will come to an end.

Our roots are deep in the lands where we live. We have a great love for our country, for our birthplace is there. The soil is rich from the bones of thousands of our generations. Each of us were created in those lands, and it is our duty to take great care of them, because from these lands will spring the future generations of the Ongwhehonwhe. We walk about with a great respect, for the Earth is a very sacred place.

We are not a people who demand, or ask anything of the Creators of Life, but instead, we give greetings and thanksgiving that all the forces of Life are still at work. We deeply understand our relationship to all living things. To this day, the territories we still hold are filled with trees, animals, and the other gifts of the Creation. In these places we still receive our nourishment from our Mother Earth.

We have seen that not all people of the Earth show the same kind of respect for this world and its beings. The Indo-European people who have colonized our lands have shown very little respect for the things that create and support Life. We believe that these people ceased their respect for the world a long time ago. Many thousands of years ago, all the people of the world believed in the same Way of Life, that of harmony with the universe. All lived according to the Natural Ways.

Around ten thousand years ago, peoples who spoke Indo-European languages lived in the area which today we know as the Steppes of Russia. At that time, they were a Natural World people who lived off the land. They had developed agriculture, and it is said that they had begun the practice of animal domestication. It is not known that they were the first people in the world to practice animal domestication. The hunters and gatherers who roamed the area probably acquired animals from the agricultural people, and adopted an economy, based on the herding and breeding of animals.

Herding and breeding of animals signaled a basic alteration in the relationship of humans to other life forms. It set into motion one of the true revolutions in human history. Until herding, humans depended on Nature for the reproductive powers of the animal world. With the advent of herding, humans assumed the functions which had for all time been the functions of the spirits of the animals. Sometime after this happened, history records the first appearance of the social organization known as "patriarchy."

The area between the Tigris and Euphrates Rivers was the homeland, in ancient times, of various peoples, many of whom spoke Semitic languages. The Semitic people were among the first in the world to develop irrigation technology. This development led to the early development of towns, and eventually cities. The manipulation of the waters, another form of spirit life, represented another way in which humans developed a technology which reproduced a function of Nature.

Within these cultures, stratified hierarchal social organization crystallized. The ancient civilizations developed imperialism, partly because of the very nature of cities. Cities are obviously population concentrations. Most importantly though, they are places which must import the material needs of this concentration from the countryside. This means that the Natural World must be subjugated, extracted from, and exploited in the interest of the city. To give order to this process, the Semitic world developed early codes of law. They also developed the idea of monotheism to serve as a spiritual model for their material and political organization.

Much of the history of the ancient world recounts the struggles between the Indo-Europeans and the Semitic peoples. Over a period of several millenia, the two cultures clashed and blended. By the second millenia B.C., some Indo-Europeans, most specifically the Greeks, had adopted the practice of building cities, thus becoming involved in the process which they named "Civilization."

Both cultures developed technologies peculiar to civilizations. The Semitic people invented kilns which enabled the creation of pottery for trade, and storage of surpluses. These early kilns eventually evolved into ovens which could generate enough heat to smelt metals, notably copper, tin and bronze. The Indo-Europeans developed a way of smelting iron.

Rome fell heir to these two cultures, and became the place where the final meshing occurs. Rome is also the true birthplace of Christianity. The process that has become the culture of the West is historically and linguistically a Semetic/Indo-European culture, but has been commonly termed the Judeo-Christian tradition.

Christianity was an absolutely essential element in the early development of this kind of technology. Christianity advocated only one God. It was a religion which imposed itself exclusively of all other beliefs. The local people of the European forests were a people who believed in the spirits of the forests, waters, hills and the land; Christianity attacked those beliefs, and effectively de-spiritualized the European world. The Christian peoples, who possessed superior weaponry and a need for expansion, were able to militarily subjugate the tribal peoples of Europe.

The availability of iron led to the development of tools which could cut down the forest, the source of charcoal to make more tools. The newly cleared land was then turned by the newly developed iron plow, which was, for the first time, pulled by horses. With that technology fewer people would work much more land, and many other people were effectively displaced to become soldiers and landless peasants. The rise of the technology ushered in the Feudal Age and made possible, eventually, the rise of new cities and growing trade. It also spelled the beginning of the end of the European forest, although the process took a long time to complete.

The eventual rise of cities and the concurrent rise of the European state created the thrust of expansion and search for markets which led men, such as Columbus, to set sail across the Atlantic. The development of sailing vessels and navigation technologies made the European "discovery" of the Americas inevitable.

The Americas provided Europeans a vast new area for expansion and material exploitation. Initially, the Americas provided new material and even finished materials for the developing world economy which was based on Indo-European technologies. European civilization has a history of rising and falling as its technologies reach their material cultural limits. The finite Natural World has always provided a kind of built-in contradiction of Western expansion.

The Indo-Europeans attacked every aspect of North America with unparalleled zeal. The Native people were ruthlessly destroyed because they were an unassimilable element to the civilizations of the West. The forests provided materials for larger ships, the land was fresh and fertile for agricultural surpluses, and some areas provided sources of slave labor for the conquering invaders. By the time of the Industrial Revolution in the mid-Nineteenth Century, North America was already a leader in the area of the development of extractive technology.

The hardwood forests of the Northeast were not cleared for the purpose of providing farmlands. Those forests were destroyed to create charcoal for the forges of the iron smelters and blacksmiths. By the 1890's the West had turned to coal, a fossil fuel, to provide the energy necessary for the many new forms of machinery which had been developed. During the first half of the Twentieth Century, oil had replaced coal as a source of energy.

The Western culture has been horribly exploitative and destructive of the Natural World. Over 140 species of birds and animals were utterly destroyed since the European arrival in the Americas, largely because they were unusable in the eyes of the invaders. The forests were levelled, the waters polluted, the Native people subjected to genocide. The vast herds of herbivores were reduced to mere handfuls, the buffalo nearly became extinct. Western technology and the people who have employed it have been the most amazingly destructive forces in all of human history. No natural disaster has ever destroyed as much. Not even the Ice Ages counted as many victims.

But like the hardwood forests, the fossil fuels are also finite resources. As the second half of the Twentieth Century has progressed, the people of the West have begun looking to other forms of energy to motivate their technology. Their eyes have settled on atomic energy, a form of energy production which has by-products which are the most poisonous substances ever known to Man.

Today the species of Man is facing a question of the very survival of the species. The way of life known as Western Civilization is on a death path on which their own culture has no viable answers. When faced with the reality of their own destructiveness, they can only go forward into areas of more efficient destruction. The appearance of Plutonium on this planet is the clearest of signals that our species is in trouble. It is a signal which most Westerners have chosen to ignore.

The air is foul, the waters poisoned, the trees dying, the animals are disappearing. We think even the systems of weather are changing. Our ancient teaching warned us that if Man interfered with the Natural laws, these things would come to be. When the last of the Natural Way of Life is gone, all hope for human survival will be gone with it. And our Way of Life is fast disappearing, a victim of the destructive processes.

The other position papers of the Haudenosaunee have outlined our analysis of economic and legal oppression. But our essential message to the world is a basic call to consciousness. The destruction of the Native cultures and people is the same process which has destroyed and is destroying life on this planet. The technologies and social systems which have destroyed the animal and the plant life are also destroying the Native people. And the process is Western Civilization.

We know that there are many people in the world who can quickly grasp the intent of our message. But experience has taught us that there are few who are willing to seek out a method for moving toward any real change. But if there is to be a future for all beings on this planet, we must begin to seek the avenues of change.

The processes of colonialism and imperialism which have affected the Haudenosaunee are but a microcosm of the processes affecting the world. The system of reservations employed against our people is a microcosm of the system of exploitation used against the whole world. Since the time of Marco Polo, the West has been refining a process that mystified the peoples of the Earth.

The majority of the world does not find its

roots in Western culture or traditions. The majority of the world finds its roots in the Natural World, and it is the Natural World, and traditions of the Natural World, which must prevail if we are to develop truly free and egalitarian societies.

It is necessary, at this time, that we begin a process of critical analysis of the West's historical processes, to seek out the actual nature of the roots of the exploitative and oppressive conditions which are forced upon humanity. At the same time, as we gain understanding of those processes, we must reinterpret that history to the people of the world. It is the people of the West, ultimately, who are the most oppressed and exploited. They are burdened by the weight of centuries of racism, sexism, and ignorance which has rendered their people insensitive to the true nature of their lives.

We must all consciously and continuously challenge every model, every program, and every process that the West tries to force upon us. Paulo Friere wrote, in his book, the *Pedagogy of the Oppressed,* that it is the nature of the oppressed to imitate the oppressor, and by such actions try to gain relief from the oppressive condition. We must learn to resist that response to oppression.

The people who are living on this planet need to break with the narrow concept of human liberation, and begin to see liberation as something which needs to be extended to the whole of the Natural World. What is needed is the liberation of all the things that support Life—the air, the waters, the trees—all the things which support the sacred web of Life.

We feel that the Native peoples of the Western Hemisphere can continue to contribute to the survival potential of the human species. The majority of our peoples still live in accordance with the traditions which find their roots in the Mother Earth. But the Native peoples have need of a forum in which our voice can be heard. And we need alliances with the other peoples of the world to assist in our struggle to regain and maintain our ancestral lands and to protect the Way of Life we follow.

We know that this is a very difficult task. Many nation states may feel threatened by the position that the protection and liberation of Natural World peoples and cultures represents, a progressive direction which must be integrated into the political strategies of people who seek to uphold the dignity of Man. But that position is growing in strength, and it represents a necessary strategy in the evolution of progressive thought.

The traditional Native peoples hold the key to the reversal of the processes in Western Civilization which hold the promise of unimaginable future suffering and destruction. Spiritualism is the highest form of political consciousness. And we, the Native peoples of the Western Hemisphere, are among the world's surviving proprietors of that kind of consciousness. We are here to impart that message.

Since the beginning of human time, the Haudenosaunee have occupied the distinct territories that we call our homelands. That occupation has been both organized and continuous. We have long defined the borders of our country, have long maintained the exclusive use-right of the areas within those borders, and have used those territories as the economic and cultural definitions of our nation.

The Haudenosaunee are a distinct people, with our own laws and customs, territories, political organization and economy. In short, the Haudenosaunee, or Six Nations, fits in every way every definition of nationhood.

Ours is one of the most complex social/political structures still functioning in the world. The Haudenosaunee council is also one of the most ancient continuously functioning governments anywhere on this planet. Our society is one of the most complex anywhere. From our social and political institutions has come inspiration for some of the most vital institutions and political philosophies of the modern world.

The Haudenosaunee is governed by a constitution known among Europeans as the Constitution of the Six Nations and to the Haudenosaunee as the Gayanashakgowah, or the Great Law of Peace. It is the oldest functioning document in the world which has contained a recognition of the freedoms the Western democracies recently claim as their own: the freedom of speech, freedom of religion, and the rights of women to participate in government. The concept of separation of powers in government and of checks and balances of power within governments are traceable to our constitution. They are ideas learned by the colonists as the result of contact with North American Native people, specifically the Haudenosaunee.

The philosophies of the Socialist World, too, are to some extent traceable to European contact with the Haudenosaunee. Lewis Henry Morgan noted the economic structure of the Haudenosaunee, which he termed both primitive and communistic. Karl Marx used Morgan's observations for the development of a model for classless, post-capitalist society. The modern world has been greatly influenced by the fact of our existence.

It may seem strange, at this time, that we are here, asserting the obvious fact of our continuing existence. For countless centuries, the fact of our existence was unquestioned, and for all honest human beings, it remains unquestioned today. We have existed since time immemorial. We have always conducted our own affairs from our territories, under our own laws and customs. We have never, under those laws and customs, willingly or fairly surrendered either our territories or our freedoms. Never, in the history of the Haudenosaunee, have the People or the government sworn allegiance to a European sovereign. In that simple fact lies the roots of our oppression as a people, and the purpose of our journey here, before the world community. . . .

Thoughts of Peace: The Great Law

Haudenosaunee oral history relates that long before the Europeans arrived, Native peoples of the Northeast woodlands had reached a crisis. It is said that during this time a man or woman might be killed or injured for any slight offense by his or her enemies, and that blood feuds between clans and villages ravaged the people until no one was safe. It was during this time that a male child was born to a woman of the Wyandot people living on the north side of Lake Ontario near the Bay of Quinte. It would become the custom of the people of the Longhouse that this person's

name would never be spoken except during the recountings of this oral history in the oral fashion (some say during the Condolence ceremony) and at other times he is addressed simply as the Peacemaker.

The Peacemaker became one of the great political philosophers and organizers in human history. It is impossible in this short essay to discuss more than a brief outline of his ideas and accomplishments, but it should become obvious that his vision for humankind was indeed extraordinary.

He concluded early in life that the system of blood feuds as practiced by the people inhabiting the forest at the time needed to be abolished. His ideas were rejected by the Wyandot and other Huron peoples, and while a young man he journeyed to the land of the People of the Flint located on the southeast shore of Lake Ontario and extending to the areas called today the Mohawk Valley. The People of the Flint, or Ganienkehaka, are known to English-speaking peoples as the Mohawks.

Upon arrival in the Mohawk country, he began seeking out those individuals who had the reputation as being the fiercest and most fearsome destroyers of human beings. He sought them out one at a time—murderers and hunters of humans, even cannibals—and he brought to each one his message.

One by one he "straightened out their minds" as each grasped the principles that he set forth. Nine men of the Mohawks—the nine most feared men in all Mohawk country—grasped hold of his words and became his disciples.

The first principle that the Peacemaker set forth was indisputable to those who first heard his words. He said that it has come to pass that in this land human beings are seen to abuse one another. He pointed to the world in which people live and said tht people should consider that some force or some thing must have created this World—the Giver of Life—had not intended that human beings would abuse one another. Human beings whose minds are healthy always desire peace, and humans have minds which enable them to achieve peaceful resolutions to their conflicts.

From that initial explanation—that the Giver of Life (later addressed as the Great Creator) did not intend that human beings abuse one another—he proposed that human societies must form governments which will serve to prevent the abuse of human beings by other human beings, and which will ensure peace among nations and peoples. Government would be established for the purpose of abolishing war and robbery among brothers and to establish peace and quietness. He drew the Mohawks together under those principles and then went to the Oneidas, Onondagas, Cayugas and Senecas with the same teachings. What is unique about his work is that he not only set forth the argument that government is desirable but he also set forth the principle—that government is specifically organized to prevent the abuse of human beings by cultivating a spiritually healthy society and the establishment of peace.

Other political philosophers and organizers have come to the conclusion that governments can be formed for the purpose of establishing tranquility, but the Peacemaker went considerably further than that. He argued not for the establishment of law and order, but for the full establishment of peace. Peace was to be defined not as the simple absence of war or strife, but as the active striving of humans for the purpose of establishing universal justice. Peace was defined as the product of a society which strives to establish concepts which correlate to the English words Power, Reason and Righteousness.

"Righteousness" refers to something akin to the shared ideology of the people using their purest and most unselfish minds. It occurs when the people put their minds and emotions in harmony with the flow of the universe and the intentions of the Good Mind or the Great Creator. The principles of Righteousness demand that all thoughts of prejudice, privilege or superiority be swept away and that recognition be given to the reality that the creation is intended for the benefit of all equally—even the birds and animals, the trees and the insects, as well as the humans. The world does not belong to humans—it is the rightful property of the Great Creator. The gifts and benefits of the world, therefore, belong to all equally. The things which humans need to survive—food, clothing, shelter, protection—these are things to which all are entitled because they are gifts of the Great Creator.

Nothing belongs to human beings, not even their labor or their skills, for ambition and ability are also the gifts of the Great Creator. Therefore all people have a right to the things they need to survive—even those who do not or cannot work, and no person or people has a right to deprive others of the fruits of those gifts.

"Reason" is perceived to be the power of the human mind to make righteous decisions about complicated issues. The Peacemaker began his teachings based on the principle that human beings were given the gift of the power of Reason in order that they may settle their differences without the use of force. He proposed that in every instance humans should use every effort to council about, arbitrate and negotiate their differences, and that force should be resorted to only as a defense against the certain use of force. All men whose minds are healthy can desire peace, he taught, and there is an ability within all human beings, and especially in the young human beings, to grasp and hold strongly to the principles of Righteousness. The ability to grasp the principles of Righteousness is a spark within the individual which society must fan and nurture that it may grow. Reason is seen as the skill which humans must be encouraged to acquire in order that the objectives of justice may be attained and no one's rights abused.

Having established the concept of Righteousness and Reason, the Peacemaker went on to discuss the nature of "Power." The Power to enact a true Peace is the product of a unified people on the path of Righteousness and Reason—the ability to enact the principles of Peace through education, public opinion and political and when necessary, military unity. The "Power" that the Peacemaker spoke of was intended to enable the followers of the law to call upon warring or quarrelling parties to lay down their arms and to begin peaceful settlement of their disputes. Peace, as the Peacemaker understood it, flourished only in a garden amply fertilized with absolute and pure justice. It was the product of a spiritually conscious society using its abilities at reason which resulted in a healthy society. The Power to enact Peace (which required that people cease abusing one another) was conceived to be both spiritual and political.

But it was power in all those senses of the word—the power of persuasion and reason, the power of the inherent good will of humans, the power of a dedicated and united people, and when all else failed, the power of force.

The principles of law set forth by the Peacemaker sought to establish peaceful society by eliminating the causes of conflict between individuals and between peoples. It was a law which was conceived prior to the appearance of classes and it sought to anticipate and eliminate anything which took the appearance of group or class interest even in the form of clan or tribal interest, especially in the area of property. The law was also based to an impressive degree on a logic which looked to Nature for its rules. It is one of the few examples of a "Natural Law" which is available to modern man. It is a law which clearly precedes "royal" law, or "mercantile" law or "bourgeois" property—interest law.

The government which is established under the Great Law provides, in effect, that the leaders or "chiefs" are the servants of the people. Everyone in the Six Nations, wherever the law prevails, has direct participation in the workings of the government. Direct democracy, when it involves tens of thousands of people, is a very complex business, and there are many rules about how meetings are conducted, but the primary rule about the flow of power and authority is clearly that the power and authority of the people lies with the people and is transmitted by them through the "chiefs." The fact that all the people have direct participation in the decision of their government is the key factor for the success and longevity of the Haudenosaunee.

Internally, the law was to be the power by which the people were united ideologically and administratively under a dispute settlement process to which all had agreed to submit and to remove those customs of the past which had sparked conflict and fostered disunity. The path to unity was a difficult one indeed. The territory of the People of the Longhouse, had been composed of five distinct countries, each of which sometimes jealously guarded their hunting lands from intrusion by the others. The Peacemaker abolished the concept of separate territories. The law unified the peoples, saying that they were distinct from one another only because they spoke different languages, and that the territories were common to all and that each individual member of any of the nations had full rights of hunting and occupation of all the lands of all the nations of the People of the Longhouse.

In terms of the internal affairs of the People of the Longhouse, the first and most important principle was that under the law of the people of the nations were one people. Since the Haudenosaunee call themselves the People of the Longhouse, the Peacemaker's admonition was that under the law, the country of the Haudenosaunee was itself a Longhouse, with the sky as its roof and the earth as its floor.

The peoples were assigned to clans by the Peacemaker, and so strong was to be the feeling of unity and oneness between them that members of the clan of one nation were admonished not to marry members of the same clan of another nation, so closely were they now related. The law bound them together as blood relatives.

In one motion, he abolished exclusive national territories and the concept of national minorities. Any member of the Five Nations was to have full rights in the country of any of the Five Nations with only one restriction— that he or she did not have the right to hold high public office, though that right could be conferred upon them by the host nation if they so wished.

The idea that the nations were united as one meant that the nations who were members of the Confederacy had agreed to surrender a part of their sovereignty to the other nations of the Confederacy. The Confederacy Council was to be the forum under which foreign nations and peoples could approach the People of the Longhouse. Any decision concerning the disposition of Seneca lands must first pass through the Confederacy Council where the other nations, who also have rights in Seneca lands, can participate in the decision-making process.

The Peacemaker envisioned that the principles under which the Five Nations were governed could be extended far beyond the borders of the Haudenosaunee to all peoples of the world. The law of the Peacemaker provides that any nation or people may find protection under the Great Tree of Peace which symbolized the laws of the Confederacy. He expected that the principles of the Confederacy would be well received by many nations, and that the Haudenosaunee would venture forth with the offer of a union which would be designed to prevent hostilities and to lay the basis of peaceful coexistence. With that in mind, the Constitution of the Five Nations provides that any nation may seek its protection through becoming knowledgeable about the laws and agreeing to follow the principles set forth in it. Many native nations accepted that offer.

The Five Nations agreed among themselves that in the event of an attack, they would organize a military force to repel the invader and to carry on the war in the invader's country until the war was concluded. The opponent had an absolute right to a cessation of the hostilities at any time by simply calling for a truce. At that point, the process of negotiation went into action. The Constitution of the Five Nations prescribes that, in the event that another people are conquered, the Five Nations shall not impose upon them the Five Nation's religion, nor collect tribute from them, nor subject them to any form of injustice. The Five Nations would not seize their territory. What was demanded was that the offending nation of people put away their weapons of war and that they cease military aggression.

Any individual or group of individuals had the right according to the Constitution, to approach the Five Nations, learn the law, and agree to abide by it. When that happened they were to be offered the protection of the law and the People of the Longhouse.

The vision of the Peacemaker that all the peoples of the world would live in peace under the protection of a law that required that hostilities be outlawed and disputes offered a settlement process is yet today an exciting prospect. When the idea of a United Nations of the world was proposed toward the end of the World War II, researchers were dispatched to find models in history for such an organization. For all practical purposes, the only model they found concerned the Constitution of the Five Nations whose author had envisioned exactly that.

In a way, the Peacemaker was centuries ahead of his time. He set forth a system of government organization which was a marvelously complex enactment of the concept of participatory (as opposed to representative) democracy.

Under the rules of the law, councils of women appointed men who were to act more as conduits of the will of the people than as independent representatives of the people.

The society was founded on concepts of moral justice and not of statute law and the rules of the society were designed to insure that each member's rights were absolutely protected under the law. Women have not only rights but have power as a community of people composing half of the population. The powers of women have never been fully articulated by Western observers and interpreters of Haudenosaunee culture.

Peoples were recognized to have a right to exist unmolested as peoples in the articles of the Constitution. Individuals were recognized as having the full rights to protection under the laws of the Confederacy—even individuals who were not members of the host nation—so long as they observed the rules of nonaggression and they didn't try to create factionalism among the people. The principle was set forth (and machinery to enact it was created) which provided that all peoples have a right to occupy their lands peacefully and that no one may deny them that right. A society was socialized to the ideology that if an injustice occurs, it is their moral duty to defend the oppressed against their oppressors. The principle was set forth that no one has a right to deprive another of the fruits of his own labor, and that no one has a right to a greater share of the wealth of society than any one else. The Peacemaker believed that if absolute justice were established in the world, peace would naturally follow.

Some of those ideas have begun to take root in the form of United Nations statements and declarations made in recent years. The genius of the Peacemaker was that he not only set forth the principles, but he also designed the machinery by which those principles might be enforced. He seems to have operated on the assumption that universal justice is the product of a spiritually strong society, and many of the rules which he proposed are designed to create a strong society rather than a strong government. That is one of the ideas that have not been widely accepted in the Twentieth Century and certainly not in a context that the Peacemaker would have understood.

The Peacemaker set out to give some order to society and to create peace among peoples and nations. The rules that he set down were called by the Mohawks "the Great Goodness," and by the Senecas "the Great Law." The English called that body of teachings the Constitution of the Five Nations. It has never been written down in English despite allegations to the contrary by anthropologists. The versions which exist in English are highly inadequate efforts compared to the oral versions of the Great Law. This effort is no better—it does not compare in any way to the complexity, beauty and eloquence of the Law.

Some people who have read the history of the Haudenosaunee will be able to point to episodes in the 17th and 18th Centuries during which some of the principles of this law appear to have been ignored. It is true that over nearly two centuries of intermittent warfare—warfare caused by pressures created by the expanding interests of European imperial nations—there was a considerable amount of social change and stress. French imperialist missionaries introduced the idea—an entirely foreign idea—that a divine will might guide the fortunes of a people in government and in warfare. That kind of thinking was not to be found in the philosophies of the Peacemaker, but throughout history it has been an idea which has accompanied empire builders everywhere. Many ideas of European origin were adopted by different peoples of the Haudenosaunee at different times, ideas which were in conflict with the principles of the Great Law. In the almost two centuries since the beginning of the so-called "reservation" period, many more ideas which are in conflict with the principles of the Great Law have been imposed by the colonizers.

Most of what passes as "Iroquois History" was an effort by English and French historians to discredit the Haudenosaunee and to justify the destruction of the Confederacy and the theft of Confederacy lands. There were few instances in which officials of the Confederacy violated the laws of the Great Peace, although individuals in any society do violate its laws. Following the American Revolution, the United States and especially New York State did everything in their power to dissolve the Confederacy and to deal with the individual nations. Great Britain, Canada, Ontario and Quebec have done the same thing. Since the invasion of the Europeans, the Haudenosaunee have produced a number of patriots but few great philosophers. The outstanding Haudenosaunee philosopher and teacher of the post-contact period was also a Confederacy Chief. His name was Handsome Lake and he led a spiritual revitalization which produced an oral document called "The Good Word," a teaching on the same level of significance and power in Haudenosaunee culture as the Great Law. Combined, the two are a powerful teaching. Against incredible odds, the Confederacy has survived and has continued to this day. Its Chiefs continue to meet periodically at the capital at Onondaga, and they continue to carry the titles bestowed upon them by the Peacemaker long before written history began. The ideas of the Confederacy continue to live also, and little by little the world is being exposed to those ideas. As long as those ideas remain alive the possibility remains that the Peacemaker's vision of a world in peace and harmony may yet be realized.

Our Strategy for Survival

The invasion of the Western Hemisphere by European powers was preceded by centuries of social development which had resulted in societies in which the interests of the few had effectively become national policies, and the interests of the many were without voice in national affairs. In order that we might formulate a strategy for survival in the modern world, it has been necessary that we look at the forces and processes which threaten survival, and to begin to understand the real motivations behind those forces. With such an analysis in mind, we may then begin to create viable alternatives and strategies which will enable us to survive in a predictable future.

When history has been presented to us by colonizers, the focal elements have always been political histories. Alexander the Great's armies conquered most of the known ancient world, and when ancient history is studied, Alexander is studied. But are political histories the really correct focus? Did it make any difference, in the long run, that Alexander the Great, or Nebucadnezzar, or Akhnaton, or any figure in political history ever lived? Other than the effect that Julius Caesar's rise to power had on some individuals in the Roman aristocracy, would history have been any different if some other general had ever dared cross the Rubicon? Are political histories the correct focus of history in the search for that which has affected the lives of billions of the earth's population?

The really crucial developments in world history have been largely ignored by historians. The most profound changes which have taken place have been in the areas of technological change. Social history has largely been the recounting of the fortunes of the interest groups which were committed for one reason or another to some form of technological and/or cultural movement. When we are seeking the real cultural revolutions of history, do we not find that the rise of agriculture or animal husbandry or irrigation technology was a thousand times more significant in the history of humankind than were the adventures and political fortunes of the aristocracy and rulers of European countries?

It is important that we who are seeking ways of survival in the 20th Century begin by establishing new definitions and new fields of vision as we try to better understand the past. We need to look to history primarily because the past offers us a laboratory in which we can search to find that inherent process of Western Civilization that paralyzes whole societies and makes them unable to resist the process of colonization. We need to identify that process which so often leads people who are honestly seeking to resist and destroy colonization to unconsciously recreate the elements, of their own oppression. And, lastly we need to understand that within colonization are the exact elements of social organization which are leading the world today to a crisis which promises a foreseeable future of mass starvation, deprivation, and untold hopelessness.

The current crisis which the world is facing is not difficult for people to understand. In the Western Hemisphere, the United States with six percent of the world's population, uses 40 percent of the world's energy resources. The world's supply of fossil fuels is finite, and it is estimated that within 30 years, at the present rate of consumption, the peoples of the world will begin to run out of some of those sources of energy, especially petroleum and natural gas. As the planet begins to run short of cheap energy, it is predictable that the world market economy will suffer and the people of the world who are dependent on that economy will suffer likewise. When the reality of world population growth is placed beside the reality of the current relationship of energy resources and food production, it becomes obvious that worldwide famine is a real possibility.

The spectre of regional famine, or even worldwide famines, cannot be interpreted as the simple product of a world of scarce resources overwhelmed by the needs of expanding human populations. The situation is not that simple. In the United States, for example, a simple program of energy conservation—insulation of dwellings, office and industrial buildings would cut back energy consumption by more than 25% in 10 years, and even given growth predictions in terms of populations and economy, the U.S. could conceivably enjoy the current standard of living in the year 2000 while consuming less energy than was consumed in 1980.

The fact is that it is highly unlikely that the United States will adopt a program of energy conservation along lines which would drastically cut back consumption. The present U.S. political system is controlled by energy interests which are concerned with profit growth, and energy lobbyists are not interested in conservation. In fact, there is no sector of the U.S. economy which will move toward energy conservation as a national energy policy, even though such a policy might conceivably conserve wasted energy which could have gone toward production of food. The problems which we are facing today, as a species which inhabits a planet of limited resources, arise not simply out of physical limitations but from political realities. It is a hard fact of life that the misery which exists in the world will be manipulated in the interests of profit. Politics and economics are intricately linked in the West, and social considerations command inferior priorities in the world's capitals. Energy conservation is not likely to become a policy in the Western countries generally, and the acceptable alternative in the eyes of the multinational energy corporations is the plan to create much more energy through the production of nuclear power plants, especially fast breeder reactors. The predictable misery caused by increases in energy prices which push up food prices (and thus drive the poor from the food market place) will also provide the grist for the promotion drives of the multinationals. Nuclear reactors will be made to sound more necessary.

Technologies have political cousins. The same people who own the oil interests have enough clout in many governments to discourage serious and broadbased efforts at energy conservation. They have the ability to command governments to support energy development schemes which will leave them in control of the world's usable energy sources and also in control of the world's marketplace. The same people constitute a class of interest in the Western world which seeks to control every aspect of the economic life of all peoples. Practically every people in the West will be dependent on their technologies for energy and food production, and all who enter the marketplace which they control will be colonized.

The roots of a future world which promises misery, poverty, starvation and chaos lie in the processes which control and destroy the locally specific cultures of the peoples of the world. To the extent that peoples and areas of the world are dependent on the giant multinational corporations which control production, distribution and consumption patterns and to that extent only is the future a dark and ominous one. For this reason, the definition of colonialism needs to be expanded in the consciousness of the peoples of the planet Earth. Colonialism is a process by which indigenous cultures are subverted and ultimately destroyed in the interests of a worldwide market economy. The interests of the worldwide market economy, quite contrary to all of the teachings of the colonists, are exactly the in-

terests which promise to create a crisis for humanity in the decades to come.

The dialectical opposite of that process would be the rekindling on a planetary basis of locally based culture. Prior to the advent of colonialism, culture was defined as the way of life by which people survived within their own environment, and their own environment was defined as the area which they lived. Thus the process of survival involved the use of locally developed technologies which met the specific needs of the area. It was mentioned earlier that technologies have political cousins, and locally developed technologies have political cousins too. Decentralized technologies which meet the needs of the people which those technologies serve will necessarily give life to a different kind of political structure and it is safe to predict that the political structure which results will be anticolonial in nature.

Colonialism is at the heart of the impending world crisis. The development of liberation technologies, many of which already exist but have been largely ignored by the political movements, (even the anticolonial political movements), are a necessary part of the decolonization process. Liberation technologies are those technologies which can be implemented by a specific people in a specific locality and which free those people from dependency upon multinational corporations and the governments which multinational corporations control. Liberation technologies are those which meet people's needs within the parameters defined by the cultures which they themselves created (or create) and which have no dependency upon the world marketplace. Windmills can be a form of liberation technology, as can water wheels, solar collectors, biomass plants, woodlots, underground home construction—the list is very long.

Colonialism, as we know it, was the product of centuries of social, economic and political development in the West. For hundreds of years, what have been euphemistically called "folk cultures" have been under pressure from a variety of sources, including warlords, kings, popes, and large landowners who found it in their interest to exploit the labor and lands of the poor and the dispossessed. That process is still taking place today, although it has been refined to the point where the exploitation is in the hands of huge multinational corporations which continue to reap profits at the expense of the world's poor.

It is possible to make a strong argument that food shortages are almost entirely the product of colonial interests. Areas of land in the Third World, usually the most productive farming areas, today produce exclusively export crops while the indigenous peoples, and even the descendents of the colonizers, go hungry laboring in the coffee, banana and other plantations of the multinationals. Political movements which have sought to correct those wrongs have generally attempted to overthrow the state because they correctly saw the state as the tool of oppression and as the repository of excess wealth for the interests of the exploiters.

Most of the past "liberation movements" have not been successful in correcting the most horrendous wrongs of colonialism, however, because they assumed that the problem lies solely in the fact that private interests controlled the state for their own benefit. The error of most such movements lies in the fact that they sought to liberate the country from living human beings, much as history assumes that Julius Caesar was somehow significant to the history of the West. They failed to understand that it did not matter whether Del Monte grew sugar cane or a liberated government grew sugar cane, that the problem was that export crops do not meet the needs of indigenous peoples. Most liberation efforts, therefore, recreate in some form the dependency which they sought to replace. They do not attempt to develop even the concept of liberation technologies, and they do not understand the need to become independent of the world market economy because the world market economy is ultimately controlled by interests which seek power or profit and which do not respond to the needs of the world's peoples.

Given the impending world crisis in the areas of food and energy, a comprehensive strategy for survival will include a concept of liberation technologies which free peoples from dependency on economies which are controlled by external interests. Liberation technologies have political cousins, just as colonizing technologies have, and those political cousins need careful consideration. Liberation technologies are accompanied by liberation political structures and liberation theologies. Of these two entities, colonized peoples in the West would be well advised to place considerable energy into the creation of true liberation theologies as a very high priority.

Liberation theologies are belief systems which challenge the assumption, widely held in the West, that the earth is simply a commodity which can be exploited thoughtlessly by humans for the purpose of material acquisition within an ever-expanding economic framework. A liberation theology will develop in people a consciousness that all life on the earth is sacred and that the sacredness of life is the key to human freedom and survival. It will be obvious to many non-Western peoples that it is the renewable quality of earth's ecosystems which makes life possible for human beings on this planet, and that if anything is sacred, if anything determines both quality and future possibility of life for our species on this planet, it is the renewable quality of life.

The renewable quality—the sacredness of every living thing, that which connects human beings to the place which they inhabit—the quality is the single most liberating aspect of our environment. Life is renewable and all the things which support life are renewable, and they are renewed by a force greater than any government's, greater than any living or historical thing. A consciousness of the web that holds all things together, the spiritual element that connects us to reality and the manifestation of an eagle or a mountain snowfall—that consciousness was the first thing which was destroyed by the colonizers.

A strategy for survival must include a liberation theology—call it a philosophy or cosmology if you will, but we believe it to be a theology—or humankind will simply continue to view the earth as a commodity and will continue to seek more efficient ways to exploit that which they have not come to respect. If these processes continue unabated and unchanged at the foundation of the colonizer's ideology, our species will never be liberated from the undeniable reality that we do live on a planet of limited resources and that sooner or later we must exploit our environment beyond its ability to renew itself.

Our strategy for survival is to create and implement liberation technologies which are consistent with and complementary to a liberation theology which arises out of our culture and is the product of the Natural World. It happens that we, the Haudenosaunee, have fallen heir to a liberation political structure which may be the oldest continuously operating governmental system in the world. We know that our traditional technologies arose from our traditional worldview, and that our political structure was largely a product of the technological and worldview elements of our society.

The Haudenosaunee presented three papers to the Non-Governmental Organizations of the United Nations at Geneva, Switzerland in 1977. Those papers were intended to introduce the people of the Western World to our understanding of the history of the West and the prospects for the future. We have taken many steps since the presentation of those papers to begin the process by which we may provide for the future of our people. Many of our communities are struggling against colonialism in all of its forms. We have established food co-ops, survival schools, alternative technology projects, adult education programs, agricultural projects, crafts programs, and serious efforts at cultural revitalization are underway.

5

Citizenship in a Democratic Community

Contract and Birthright

Sheldon Wolin

The members of a democratic society are citizens, but there are radically different interpretations of the concept of "citizen." In this essay Sheldon Wolin explores the differences between citizenship as a freely contracted agreement and citizenship as a historically formed set of duties and privileges acquired through birth into a community. An inherited position in society is not freely chosen and disposed of; it is more like a birthright. Wolin describes the mixed blessings of our American birthright in a compilation of stories starting with the conflicts between the English religious refugees and the native nations of the Americas, through the Revolutionary War, the founding of the United States, the development of the Federalist Constitution, African slavery and the Civil War, the conquest of the West, and continuing to the present. This is our heritage, our identity; it provides us with a mixed bag of responsibilities and rights. Wolin contrasts this vision with Rawls's theory of self-interested individuals founding a state through a mutually advantageous contract. Rawls's citizens voluntarily form a society for their own prosperity; their rights and responsibilities are only those they have freely adopted. Wolin condemns this scenario as a misinterpretation of citizenship. When citizenship is considered a birthright, citizens accept the responsibilities of political life because these are their national heritage; they claim the power to actively direct the institutions affecting their lives; and they construct a participatory democracy in tune with the history of their nation.

Once when Jacob was boiling pottage, Esau came in from the field, and he was famished. And Esau said to Jacob, "Let me eat some of that red pottage, for I am famished!" . . . Jacob said, "First sell me your birthright." Esau said, "I am about to die; of what use is a birthright to me?" Jacob said, "Swear to me first." So he swore to him, and sold his birthright to Jacob. . . . Thus Esau despised his birthright [Gen. 25: 29–34].

The story of Esau recounts how a man sold his birthright. In ancient times a birthright usually fell to the eldest son. He succeeded his father and received the major portion of his father's legacy. A birthright was thus an inherited identity and implicitly an inherited obligation to use it, take care of it, pass it on, and improve it. An inherited identity is, by definition, unique: Esau was the inheritor of Isaac, and hence a descendant of Abraham, the founder of Israel. Esau was also the inheritor of the profound experiences of his father, Isaac, whom Abraham had been pre-

pared to sacrifice for his God; and Esau was the inheritor of his father's father, and so on, according to the genealogies so beloved in the Old Testament, back in time to Adam and Eve. Esau's was thus a collective identity, bound up with a people and extending over time.

This unique identity Esau had bartered to fill a need that could be satisfied by any number of different foods. The Old Testament nowhere suggests that Esau was even remotely in danger of starvation. He had bartered what was unique and irreplaceable for a material good for which there were a number of available substitutes.

Although Esau is depicted as a crude man, the Old Testament leaves no doubt that his decision was free and uncoerced, even though there had clearly been an element of cunning on Jacob's part. The power of the biblical narrative depends upon the juxtaposition between the free nature of the choice and the unfree nature of a birthright. One does not

From Sheldon Wolin, "Contract and Birthright," *Political Theory 14*, 2 (May 1986): 179–193. Reprinted by permission of Sage Publications, Inc.

choose to be the eldest son of a particular father: That is a matter of one's special history. Contrary to what Jean-Paul Sartre would claim, the idea of a birthright denies that we are "thrown into the world."

Birthright has its own distinctive mode of discourse. As its name suggests, birth/right relies strongly on the language of natality. It is a way of "conceiving" the person; and we shall see how the fate of Esau and his brother Jacob is prefigured in the womb of their mother. Birthright language conceives the person as preformed, as an incorporation of elements of family, cult, and community. It asserts that we come into the world preceded by an inheritance. This is why if Esau is to disencumber himself of his inheritance he has to enter into a mode of discourse contrary to that surrounding a birthright.

In contractual discourse the self is performed rather than preformed. It awaits constitution. So it makes itself by a series of bargains. It is a negotiated and negotiable self.

Accordingly, the Biblical narrator says that Esau "swore" and "sold," that is, Esau entered into a contract of exchange. But the contractual mode presumes precisely what the birthright mode rejects: that the exchanged objects are equal in value. It is not that it is impossible to reduce a birthright and a bowl of pottage to a common measure of value but, rather, that the nature of one is more deeply violated than the other by that operation. In other words, there is an intuitive sense that protests that a birthright is not the kind of thing that should be the object of a contract—in much the same way perhaps, that we feel that Faust committed an act of self-mutilation when he contracted with Mephistopheles to make over his soul in exchange for power.

The idea of a contract not only is familiar to us as a legal instrument by which most business transactions are negotiated, but it is one of the archetypal metaphors of political theory. It is associated with such masters of political thought as Hobbes, Locke, Rousseau, Paine, and Kant. It has represented a distinctive vision of society, and nowhere has it been more influential, in both theory and practice, than in the United States. It is a core notion in two of the most widely discussed

political theories of recent years, those of John Rawls and Robert Nozick.

Briefly put, contract theory conceives of political society as the creation of individuals who freely consent to accept the authority and rules of political society on the basis of certain stipulated conditions: such as each shall be free to do as he or she pleases as long as his or her actions do not interfere with the rights of others, or that an individual shall not be deprived of his or her property except by laws that have been passed by duly elected representatives, and so on. Now the contractual element is needed, according to the theory, because, all persons being free and equal by nature and society being by nature in need of coercive power to protect rights, preserve peace, and defend against external invasion, the freedom of individuals will have to be limited and regulated. Individuals will contract, therefore, to surrender some part of their rights in exchange for the protection of the law and the defense of society from foreign or domestic enemies.

For more than three centuries the contract way of understanding political life has been criticized for being unhistorical, but the criticism has usually taken the form of arguing that contractualism gives a false account of how societies have actually come into existence. To which the contract theorist has quite properly replied that he or she has been engaged not in historical description but in prescribing the principles of a rights-oriented society. Yet that reply does expose an assumption: namely, that it is possible to talk intelligibly about the most fundamental principles of a political society as though neither the society nor the individuals in it had a history. It stands, therefore, in sharp contrast to the conception of a birthright, which, although not strictly historical in its approach to collective identity, might be said to have a quality of historicality.

I want to suggest that the conception of a birthright provides a more powerful way of understanding our present political condition than does contract theory, and that contract theory is less a solution to the political problem of our times than an exacerbation of it. I began with the story of Esau because it bears on the birthright that each of us has. Like Esau's, our birthright is an inheritance. Like Esau's, it is inherited from our fathers. Like Esau's, it is a birthright that concerns a unique collective identity. Like Esau's, our birthright is not being extracted from us by force; it is being negotiated or contracted away. Finally, like Esau, we have made it possible to contract away our birthright by forgetting its true nature and thereby preparing the way for it being reduced to a negotiable commodity, with the result that its disappearance is not experienced as loss but as relief.

The birthright that we have made over to our Jacobs is our politicalness. By *politicalness* I mean our capacity for developing into beings who know and value what it means to participate in and be responsible for the care and improvement of our common and collective life. To be political is not identical with being "in" government or being associated with a political party. These are structured roles and typically they are highly bureaucratized. For these reasons they are opposed to the authentically political.

A political inheritance or birthright is not something we "acquire" like a sum of money or our father's house; nor is it something we grow into naturally without effort or forethought, like reaching the age of 18 and automatically being entitled to vote. It is something to which we are entitled, as Esau had been; but we have to make it consciously our own, mix it with our mental and physical labor, undertake risks on its behalf, and even make sacrifices. What the "it" is was suggested more than 2500 years ago, when Heraclitus implored his fellow citizens to "cling to the common": that is, search out the concerns that represent what our collectivity identity is about, and seek to use them, take care of them, improve and pass them on.

Politicalness comes to us as a birthright, as an inheritance, and hence it has a historical quality without being merely historical. A birthright is defined by the historical moments when collective identity is collectively established or reconstituted. For Americans, these moments include the seventeenth-century beginnings in New England; the revolutionary founding and the redefinition of it symbolized by the ratification of the Constitution; the Civil War, with its vision of a nationalized society and its inconclusive at-tempt to radicalize republicanism; and two world wars that have affixed collective identity to the dream of world hegemony and have reconstituted the moments represented by the New Deal and civil rights movement so as to make them functional elements.

Historical things "are"; they have spatial and temporal attributes that can be described. But as elements of a birthright, they have to be interpreted. Interpretation is not historical description but a theoretical activity concerned with reflection upon the meaning of past experience and of possible experiences. Because birthrights need interpretation, they are contestable; and because contestable, there is not absolute finality to the interpretation. Birthrights are transmitted, and because of that their meaning will have to be reconsidered amid different circumstances. We inherit from our fathers, but we are not our fathers. Thus, the Constitution is part of our inheritance. Its formation and contents can be described historically, but the interpretations of its origins and its contents have been highly contestable subjects and remain so. No interpretation enjoys undisputed hegemony.

One reason for the contestability of historical things, whether located in the more remote past or the more immediate present, is their ambiguousness. Human actors intervene to enact a law or promote a policy, but they are never able to circumscribe its consequences, many of which prove to be unwanted. Or the intervention itself embodies contradictory motives, such as when a law reflects the aims of those who hope to prevent the law from achieving the ends of its proponents and so attach a "rider" to it. Most, if not all, defining historical moments are full of ambiguities. Our Constitution, for example, proclaims liberties and inhibits democracy. Every war since the Mexican War has its ambiguities, although this is not to say that some wars are not less ambiguous than others: World War II, for example, was less ambiguous than World War I—and World War III may be totally unambiguous!

Our birthright is composed of these ambiguous historical moments, and so its political meaning is rarely obvious. If we are to deal with the ambiguities of our birthright, we need an interpretive mode of understanding that is able to reconnect past and present experience, and we need to think in different terms about what it means to be political. We cannot, for example, experience the past directly. We can, however, share in the symbols that embody the experience of the past. This calls for a citizen who can become an interpreting being, one who can interpret the present experience of the collectivity, reconnect it to past symbols, and carry it forward.

This conception of the citizen differs from that made familiar by contemporary liberal and conservative thinkers and their neovariants. The latter conception tends to be two-dimensional. The individual is usually pictured as responding to the world as if in a situation of choice, in which he or she will decide according to whether a choice will advance or reduce, protect or threaten the interests of the chooser. The temporal dimensions of choice are typically reduced to two: the present and the future. In this context recall President Reagan's famous query to the voters, "Ask yourself, are you better off now than four years ago?" Thus, the citizen was asked to think about the past as a thin slice of time, four years, to reduce its political meaning to economic terms, and then to assess it in personal rather than communal or collective terms. It was not a request for an interpretation of the meaning of four years of the Reagan regime, but a calculation of personal gains. It was a question that tacitly rejected as nonsensical the possibility that "I" could be better off but that "we" were not. It was Esau-talk.

The reason that the president could successfully address this appeal to the voters is that social contract thinking has become so ingrained as to seem to be a natural part of the social world. There are two crucial assumptions made by social contract theory that present a particularly sharp contrast to the notion of a birthright. One is that the contracting individuals are equal because they have no prior history, the other that the contract represents a "beginning" in which society starts afresh like the beginning of a new footrace.

Each of these assumptions is deeply antihistorical. Individuals could be considered equal (that is, uniform in some important respects) only if they had no autobiographies with different backgrounds and experiences, if they had no personal histories. Obvious as this may seem, the contract theorist had to deny it, at least for the moment prior to the act of consent, otherwise no one would agree even to equal terms if they knew that others would be carrying forward previous advantages and hence could perpetuate or even increase their advantages. So the contract theorist has to posit a memoryless person, without a birthright, and so equal to all the others.

In the seventeenth and eighteenth centuries the memoryless person was said to exist in a state of nature in which no social, political, or economic distinctions existed. In our own day the notion has been perpetuated most ingeniously by John Rawls in his conception of a "veil of ignorance." Rawls asks us to imagine an apolitical condition in which individuals who know nothing specific about their personal identities choose certain conditions that they would accept precisely because they do not know who they are or what advantages or disadvantages they enjoy. They are forced by the logic of this situation to choose conditions that will be fairest for all. The same lack of historicality surrounds the society that results from the Rawlsian contract. It begins with no past, no legacy of deeds or misdeeds, nothing to remember. The contract depends upon collective amnesia.

In suggesting that I do not mean to devalue the idea of equality but to claim that its present chimerical status, in which it seems impossible to achieve yet impossible to abandon, is due in no small measure to the spell cast by contract thinking. We tend to assume that equality represents a condition that we are trying to recapture, that once we were equal, as in the moment before the contract, and so the task is to eliminate barriers, such as segregation or sex discrimination. When this is done equality is restored, because equality has come to be identified with equal opportunity. But equal opportunity merely restarts the cycle of competition in the race, and races are designed to produce a single winner. Then it becomes obvious that social competition cannot be compared to a footrace between trained athletes; that the race for education, jobs, income, and status is rarely between equals, but between those with greater advantages and those with greater disadvantages. The end result is that the quest for equality becomes an exercise in guilt, which is typified in Rawls's solution. Rawls argues that inequalities can be advantageous if they spur economic activity that improves everyone's situation, which, by definition, would include that of "the least advantaged." But this is an argument for improving the lot of those who are unequal. It does not follow that in doing so inequality is reduced, much less eliminated.

In reality the issue may be a different one: What kind of a collectivity is it that approaches its central value of justice by making the lot of the disadvantaged the test? The answer is that necessarily such a society will have to commit itself mainly to developing the economy, because only in that way will the lot of the disadvantaged be improved. As a consequence, the elites will be formed in response to that need and the structure of society will be shaped toward economic ends. The answer presupposes a polity that is, in reality, a political economy rather than a democracy. I shall return to this point.

I want now to set over against the social contract conceptions of membership and collectivity the notion of inheritance as suggested by the Esau story. One reason Esau may have bargained away his history or inheritance was that, in addition to the material benefits—his father's flocks and land—a birthright brought with it some accumulated burdens. He would inherit his father's "name"; that is, a family history that would likely have included its share of debts and obligations, responsibilities, quarrels, feuds, and so on. To live in the world for any length of time is to know shame, guilt, dishonor, and compromise.

It is not irrelevant to the notion of inheritance as a burden that the Old Testament described Esau as a hunter, which signified someone who prefers to travel unencumbered and who is disinclined to settle down. His brother Jacob, in contrast, was characterized as "a quiet man, dwelling in tents" (Gen. 25:27). The Old Testament clearly aimed to depict opposing types. It notes that before their birth "the children struggled together within" their mother's womb (25: 22). Their mother, Rebekah, was told,

Two nations in your womb,
and two peoples, born of you
shall be divided;
the one shall be stronger than
the other,
the elder shall serve the younger [25: 23].

Even when they were being born, Jacob was said to have grabbed hold of Esau's heel (25: 26). In their encounters it was Jacob who always won by virtue of some strategem. Thus, as Isaac lay dying Jacob and Rebekah conspire to deceive him into believing that Jacob is Esau. As a result the dying father gives his precious "blessing" to the wrong son.

Our natural response is to say, "Foolish father!" But the truth is that all fathers are foolish and all birthrights are a mixture of good and evil, justice and injustice. When Esau learns that Jacob has also tricked him of his blessing, he demands that Isaac give him another. Isaac complies but, under the rules, he cannot retract the first and superior blessing given to Jacob. So he gives Esau another but inferior blessing with the predictable result that Esau is resentful and threatens to kill Jacob, who then flees. Thus, the birthright sows seeds of conflict and the effort to mitigate the effects creates further conflicts.

An inheritance, then, is a mixed blessing from foolish fathers. And, lest we forget the scheming Rebekah, from foolish mothers as well. The same is true of our birthright. The Founding Fathers left us a mixed blessing, a Constitution that showed how power might be organized without leading to arbitrary authority, but also a document that was silent about women and accepted the institution of slavery. What is true of the Constitution is also true of the legacy of later centuries of American history. There is unparalleled economic opportunity and social mobility, but there are numerous blots and stains: the treatment of the Indians, the aggression against Mexico, the cruel war between the states, the imperialist expansion of American power abroad, and, not least, the use of the atomic bomb.

When set over against this ambiguous legacy, the function of social contract thinking becomes clear: to relieve individuals and society of the burden of the past by erasing the ambiguities. This function assumes practical importance because contractualism is not solely an academic philosophy. It is part of American political mythology, of the collective beliefs that define our identity and help to shape our political attitudes and opinions.

Parenthetically, although myth is a feature of so-called "advanced societies"—which might for the present purposes be defined as societies in which science and rationality become identified and their promotion becomes an object of public policies—there is a difference between the status of myth in such societies and its status in premodern and primitive societies. In an advanced society the study of history tends to be demythologizing. As a consequence, myth and historical consciousness coexist uneasily. In premodern societies, especially primitive ones, the historical consciousness can be critical without being instinctively debunking.[1]

This point has a practical bearing. President Reagan is rightly described as a president who appeals to "traditional values" and to the "nation's past." However, if those appeals are governed by the dehistoricizing tendencies of contract theory, as I believe they are, his appeals are not to history even when they appear to make reference to it. Rather, history returns as myth, because the critical relation between myth and history has dropped out.

Returning now to the main theme, anthropologists tell us that myth is kept alive by rituals. Accordingly, we should expect our political rituals to perpetuate the myth of contractualism.

One of our firmest rituals is the inauguration of a president. In his second inauguration address the president gave expression to the myth and so preserved it:

> Four years ago I spoke to you of a new beginning, and we have accomplished that. But in another sense, our new beginning is a continuation of that created two centuries ago, when, for the first time in history, government, the people said, was not our master. It is our servant; its only power is that which we, the people, allow it to have.

The president's formulation repeats the mythic formula of contract that there is not only a political beginning but, in principle, there can be any number of new beginnings. The basic myth that ties the beginnings

together is that "the people" are the dominant actor in the mythic drama: Like an Old Testament god, the people spoke and said, "Let government be servant and its powers limited." Note, however, that the myth is also being used to delegitimate as well as legitimate. The president also spoke disparagingly of recent efforts to employ governmental power to correct perceived social ills and wrongs:

> That system [presumably the original Constitution] has never failed us. But for a time we failed the system. We asked things of government that government was not equipped to give. We yielded authority to the national government that properly belonged to states or to local governments or to the people themselves.

Thus, a new beginning can, like a form of ritual, absolve us of past wrongs and put us in a saving relationship to "the system," which, like some patient father-god, will welcome back the prodigals. By restoring the original contract we are washed clean and made innocent once more. Moreover, we are all, potentially, made equal again: Blacks, Chicanos, Puerto Ricans, Jews, northern WASPS, and Southern gentle-folk can each and all accept the sacrament:

> Let us resolve that we, the people, will build an American opportunity society in which all of us—white and black, rich and poor, young and old—will go forward together, arm in arm.

The sacrament of innocence is absolution from the foolishness of our fathers and mothers. It soothes us with the knowledge that we were not there when blacks were treated as a species of property; when Indians were massacred and deprived of their ancestral lands; when suffragettes were attacked and humiliated; when the early strikes of workers were broken by the combined force of government and business corporations; when the liberal government of F.D.R. refused to admit refugees from Hitler's Germany; or when the Bomb was dropped, not once, but twice. As the president remarked in the inaugural address, "We, the present-day Americans, are not given to looking backward. In this blessed land, there is always a better tomorrow."

Bitburg was a symbolic occasion when contract/amnesia was celebrated at the expense of birthright/memory as an American president and a German chancellor confused themselves and the world about the distinction between forgiveness and forgetfulness, victims and victimizers.

Against this "Sweet Oblivious Antidote," in Shakespeare's phrase, we might set the words of Richard Hooker, an English theologian of four centuries ago:

> Wherefore as any man's deed past is good as long as he himself continueth; so the act of a public society of men done five hundred years hence standeth as theirs who presently are of the same societies, because corporations are immortal; we were then alive in our predecessors, they in their successors do live still.[2]

Clearly by Hooker's understanding, and that of the birthright idea, we can never renounce our past without rendering the idea of a political community incoherent. The reason we cannot has to do with the power that is aggregated by a political community. A political community exercises power in the world and against it. When we accept our birthright, we accept what has been done in our name.

Interestingly, the president also made allusion to the idea of a birthright:

> We will not rest until every American enjoys the fullness of freedom, dignity, and opportunity as our birthright. It is our birthright as citizens of this great republic.

At the center of the president's conception of birthright is the fundamental notion of contract theory, the idea of freedom:

> By 1980 we knew it was time to renew our faith, to strive with all our strength toward the ultimate in individual freedom consistent with an orderly society.
>
> We believed then and now there are no limits to growth and human progress when men and women are free to follow their dreams. . . . The heart of our efforts is one idea vindicated by 25 straight months of economic growth: freedom and incentives unleash the drive and entrepreneurial genius that are the core of human progress.

Freedom is thus conceived in essentially economic and material terms: It is not Esau's birthright that is at stake for the president but Esau's contract with Jacob for disposal of his birthright. For the president nowhere in his speech suggested that our birthright includes our right to participate, our right to be free from politial surveillance, our concern to protect urban habitats and natural environments—in short what was omitted was our birthright as political beings. Perhaps the most striking example of the reduction of our birthright to a bowl of pottage occurred in the use the president made of Lincoln's Emancipation Proclamation for freeing the slaves:

> The time has come for a new American Emancipation, a great national drive to tear down economic barriers and liberate the spirit in the most depressed areas of the country.

The president's image of "the opportunity society" symbolizes a profound transformation in collectivity identity that has been accelerated during the years since World War II. We have virtually ceased to think of ourselves as a political people. Our politicalness is interjected only as a convenient contrast with the Soviet Union. Then suddenly we are a "democracy." Democracy is not invoked when the discussion is about enforcing desegregation statutes, intruding religion into the schools, or preventing discrimination excepting reverse discrimination.

The silence about politicalness and the cynicism about democracy are related. Politicalness is at odds with the conditions required by the form of polity that has come into being, but that form lacks legitimation and so the democratic principle of "we the people" is shamelessly exploited to provide it. The new polity can be christened "the political economy." The name stands for an order in which the limits of politics are set by the needs of a corporate-dominated economy and of a state organization that works in intimate collaboration with corporate leadership.

In the theory of the political economy society is absorbed into "the economy" and, instead of economic relationships being viewed as embedded in a complex of social and political relationships, they are treated as though they constituted a distinct system that is at once autonomous, or nearly so, as well as constitutive or defining of all other types of relationships. The primacy of economic relationships does not operate solely as an explanatory device but as a first principle of a comprehensive scheme of social hermeneutics. Economic relationships constitute an interpretive category of universal applicability. It is used to understand personal life and public life, to make judgments about them, and to define the nature of their problems. It supplies the categories of analysis and decision by which public policies are formulated, and it is applied to cultural domains such as education, the arts, and scientific research. It is, we might say, a conception striving for totalization.

To the political economy a genuinely democratic politics appears as destabilizing. This is because those who govern fear that democratic institutions, such as elections, free press, popular culture, and public education can become the means to mobilize the poor, the less well educated, working classes, and aggrieved ethnic groups and to use them to bring demands for a revision of social priorities and a redistribution of values. This would kindle inflationary pressures and divert social resources to nonproductive uses, such as health care, low cost housing, and toxic waste disposal. Accordingly, the ruling elites have to discourage the mobilization of poorer groups by asserting that a rational investment policy requires different priorities. So, for example, the Pentagon's spokesman refuses to trim the defense budget and openly asserts the priority of defense over so-called "social spending."

The depoliticalization of the poor and the working classes was most clearly demonstrated in the anti-inflation strategy adopted by the state. The rate of inflation was successfully lowered at the expense of employment, which is to say, at the expense primarily, although not solely, of the working classes and minorities. The significance of this choice goes beyond the important matters of jobs and standards of living to the vital question of whether an unemployed person has not been deprived in some crucial sense of membership. For if the economy is the crucial sector of a political economy, it means that employment is, so to speak, the mark of citizenship in the important sense of being involved in productive activity that is widely believed to be the most important activity in society and, ultimately, the

foundation of American power and security. Economic production, we might say, is to the political economy as political citizenship was to Aristotle: namely, the mark of whether one was "in" or "outside" the polity.

It is clear that in today's high-tech society there is a substantial number of persons, mostly minorities, who are superfluous: They are unemployed and have practically no foreseeable prospect of becoming employed, except perhaps temporarily, and many are trapped in a cycle of unemployment that comprehends two and sometimes three generations. In a rapidly changing economy that replaces the skills of human operatives by machines in accordance with the relentless pace of technological innovation, superfluous members are being created constantly. If by chance some are returned to the work force in a period of economic upturn, this does little to reduce their anxieties about the future. Everyone knows that business cycles return. The consequence is to produce noncitizens who will be most reluctant to take political risks of the kind required by politicalness.

Similarly, when in the name of "the economy" public spending on social program is cut, this means more than the loss of substantial economic benefits. It reduces the power of individuals. Health care, education, aid for dependent children, job training—each of these holds out hope to an individual that he or she can increase his or her power to cope with the world. When social programs are reduced, then restored somewhat, only to be reduced again, tremendous power is lodged in the hands of the state, or of those who operate it. The economy becomes a means of denying power to some and denaturalizing them, as it were, rendering them wary of political involvements.

Underlying these programs, which combine pacification with demoralization and depoliticization of the lower classes, is a fear of Esau. We should recall the "blessing" that Isaac finally gave to the frustrated and enraged Esau, who had been doubly cheated:

By your sword you shall live,
and you shall serve your brother;
but when you break loose

you shall break his yoke from
your neck [Gen. 27:40].

The advent of the political economy does
not signal the disappearance of the state, despite the frequent and well-subsidized rhetoric
extolling the free market and attacking government regulation. Under the regime of political economy the state is actually strengthened. The military has for over 3000 years
been a key element in political power and a
crucial one in the apparatus of the modern
state. The astronomical rise in defense
budgets and the revival of an interventionist
foreign policy signify an increase in the power
of the state. The same can be said of the increasing control over information being exercised by the state.

The basic reason the present administration is concerned to mystify the presence of
the state and to denigrate its value is obvious:
They want to discredit the state as an instrument of popular needs without substantially
weakening it. It should never be forgotten that
the state is not necessarily weakened by reducing social welfare programs; it is often
strengthened under the guise of introducing
more efficient management practices.

For those who care about creating a democratic political life, a strong state must be rejected because the idea of a "democratic" state
is a contradiction in terms. By its very nature,
the state must proceed mainly by bureaucratic
means; it must concentrate power at the
center; it must promote elitism or government
by the few; it must elevate the esoteric knowledge of experts over the experience of ordinary citizens; and it must prefer order and
stability to experiment and spontaneity. The
result of state-centeredness is a politics in
which at one extreme are the experts struggling to be scientific and rational while at
the other is a politics of mass irrationality,
of manipulated images, controlled information, single-issue fanaticism, and pervasive
fear.

A democratic vision means a genuine
alternative. It means the development of a
politics that cannot be coopted, which is precisely what has happened to the original
democratic dream of basing democracy upon
voting, elections, and popular political parties.

These forms, as we know from the experience
of this century, can be taken over by corporate
money and manipulated by the mass media.
Democracy needs a noncooptable politics, that
is, a politics that renders useless the forms of
power developed by the modern state and
business corporation. This means different
actors, different scales of power, and different
criteria of success.

First, democracy means participation; but
participation is not primarily about "taking
part," as in elections or office holding. It
means originating or initiating cooperative action with others. This form of action is taking
place throughout the society in response to felt
needs, from health care to schools, from utility
rates to housing for the poor, from nuclear
energy to nuclear weapons, from toxic waste
disposal to homesteading in urban areas. One
of the most important aspects to these developments is that political experience is being
made accessible, experience that compels individuals to deal with the complexity of interests and the conflicting claims that have
hitherto been reserved to politicians and bureaucrats. In this way the political has become
incorporated into the everyday lives of countless people.

Second, democracy means diffusion of
power rather than centering it. Power can only
be diffused if problems are defined in smaller
terms. Not all problems can be, and it is not
necessary to abolish the state. Yet the more
that is taken on by smaller groupings, the less
justification there is for central regulation and
control. But power also has to be generated
differently. Hitherto it has been primarily conceived in terms of federal dollars derived from
taxation. Although it would be important to
increase local control over fiscal resources,
money is not the only form of power. Each
person is potential power: He or she has skill,
energy, intelligence, and a capacity for shared
effort. This is not to deny the importance of
material resources; it is to suggest that democracy can evoke forms of power not available to
bureaucratic and centralized organizations.

A democratic political life would, I believe,
set terms that would make it difficult for the
corporate bureaucratic system to coopt its activities. It would generate a politics that could
not be handled by the categories that are es-

sential to state-centered, bureaucratic, and mass-electorate politics. It would nurture a political life that would be decentered rather than centralized, pluralistic rather than hierarchical, participatory rather than managerial, egalitarian rather than efficient. It offers, I believe, the best hope for deconstructing the political economy and retrieving our birthright.

Notes

1. See Sheldon Wolin, "Postmodern Politics and the Absence of Myth," *Social Research* 52 (Summer 1985), 217–239.
2. *Of the Laws of Ecclesiastical Polity,* Book 1, x, 8.

A Renewal of Civic Philosophy

William M. Sullivan

Citizenship in a democratic community is marked by interpersonal relationships of mutual care and respect and a dedication to the institutions and customs supporting their common life. The republican interpretation of citizenship honors "civic virtue," an attitude of public spiritedness in the pursuit of the common good. The civic republican tradition stretches from the writings of Plato and Aristotle to the founding of the American Republic. Its central theme, well stated by Aristotle, is a life of virtue, a concrete way of life encompassing all of its important elements: psychological, economic, political, and social. William Sullivan gives this notion of citizenship a distinctly modern interpretation in the following selection. Participation in civic life is a form of personal development, he writes, a process of enlarging personal horizons to include other generations and different kinds of people and of expanding the ability to respond with care in an interdependent life. In the civic tradition individual fulfillment is achieved not through the pursuit of self-interest but through a commitment to a common good. Sullivan argues that the civic republican life dedicated to the common good is superior to the liberal life dedicated to the pursuit of individual satisfactions. He explores how a civic life is possible in today's cultural environment. As in all theories of civic virtue from the time of Plato's Republic, *Sullivan relies on a system of education in the civic virtues to bring his vision of an American republic into being.*

I

The classical notion of citizenship from which so much modern social thought has drawn its strongest nourishment has been a singularly long-lived and, in purely pragmatic terms, amazingly successful ideal. Citizenship as a symbol has evolved a whole understanding of human nature, of the good life, of authority, of man's place in the world. And like all genuinely emblematic symbols, that of the citizen in the commonwealth has remained powerful in part because of its compactness. It has at times evoked stirring loyalties, harkening back to the idealized classic ages of Greece and Rome, yet enabling generations of medieval jurists, Renaissance humanists, American and French revolutionaries, Hegelians and Marxists to sum up their very diverse understandings of the ideal of a public life. Through these varied channels it continues to provide us with vital images.

Even on a cursory inspection the classical notion of citizenship strikingly sums up a vision of life that is also a moral ideal. The tradition of republican citizenship stretching from Plato and Aristotle to the makers of the American Revolution links power and authority within the state with the social, economic, psychological, and religious realms. By contrast, modern discussions of citizenship that operate under largely liberal assumptions are far more abstract. The mechanisms of governance, the delineation of the institutions of the state as compared to those of society, the contractual relationship of citizens to each other, the ideas of authority and legitimacy all appear to float in a kind of Cartesian ether. Setting classical and modern views side by side, the troubling sense that there have been large losses as well as gains creeps upon us unavoidably. The principal loss is identifiable immediately. It is a loss of any relationship among political, social, economic, and psychological theorizing and the concreteness of citizenship as a way of life.

The contemporary starting point for understanding the classical conception of the citizen must be the recovery of a sense of civic life as a form of personal self-development. The kind of self-development with which the theorists of the civic life have been concerned is in many ways the antithesis of contemporary connotations of the notion of self-development in a "culture of narcissism." Citizenship has traditionally been conceived of as a way of life that changes the person entering it. This process is essentially a collective experience. Indeed, the notion of *citizen* is unintelligible apart from that of *commonwealth*, and both terms derive their sense from the idea that we are by nature political beings. Self-fulfillment and even the working out of personal identity and a sense of orientation in the world depend upon a communal enterprise. This shared process is the civic life, and its root is involvement with others: other generations, other sorts of persons whose differences are significant because they contribute to the whole upon which our particular sense of self depends. Thus mutual interdependency is the foundational notion of citizenship. The basic psychological dynamic of the participants in this interdependent way of life is an imperative to respond and to care.

From the viewpoint of modern liberalism

such a civic vision seems a distinct overvaluing of the political. Whatever loss may be incurred in finding public life to be only an impersonal mechanism of profit and loss is, for the liberal, offset by the room thereby created for a rich private life free of state tyranny. Indeed, the notions of mutual dependency and care do sound more like private than public values, as liberal culture makes that division. But—putting aside Tocqueville's revelations of the coercive effects of public conformity which liberal capitalist society seems condemned to generate—it is clear that no liberal regime actually operates without large doses of civic spirit.

Still, the cultivation of a more than instrumental citizenship is seen as a private matter. And, cut off from collective scrutiny and discussion as they are, the responses of individuals and groups to their social setting have often become as hostile, defensive, and self-serving as one might fear. Awareness of the interdependency of citizens and groups is basic to the civic vision because it enlightens and challenges these disparate parties about their mutual relations. The citizen comes to know who he is by understanding the web of social relationships surrounding him. This realization is not only cognitive, it requires experience, finding one's way about and thus coming to know, in practice, who one is.

However, it is important to see that the civic tradition does not simply romanticize public participation. The dangers of misguided, fanatical, and irresponsible civic involvement have been well documented, and some of the most eloquent warnings of those dangers have come from the classical theorists of citizenship. The point, rather, is that the notion of involved concern within an interdependent community provides the image for a collective enterprise in self-transformation. The civic ideal is thus alluring and disquieting, at once delicately fragile and morally consuming in the responsibility it demands.

As the questioning of the liberal assumptions of contemporary public policies for managing interests becomes progressively more fundamental, the self-confidence of the governing groups in America continues to weaken. The much-decried turning away from politics by many is surely related to these developments. However, the tremendous rise of interest in psychological and religious movements, the apparent national obsession with healing wounds, real or imagined, in the self are first of all social events. They undoubtedly reveal something of what the current American crisis of values is about. Instrumentalist, liberal politics is being abandoned not only because it is seen as ineffective, it is also being deserted because it is seen as corrupting and empty of a genuine sense of orientation. That political activity ought to be rooted in moral conscience, that politics is in an important way related to the search for a meaningful life—these themes, which were powerfully reenunciated in the movements of the sixties, have not disappeared. Instead, they seem to have become at least partially embedded in much apparent privatism. Part of the meaning of the current American retreat to privatism is a continuing search for what counts in life, a hunger for orientation that neither the dynamics of capitalist growth nor the liberal vision of politics provides.

For this reason, the resources of the civic republican tradition are especially well suited to speak to our situation. Those who read the American spirit as so dominantly individualistic that private comfort and competitive achievement define a monochrome of national traits are both dangerously distorting our past and threatening our future, because they are closing off a sense of that living civic tradition which has been and continues to be vital to national life.

The language of civic republicanism addresses directly the craving of the human self for a life of inclusion in a community of mutual concern. The civic tradition addresses the public value of exploring and developing those qualities of life that go beyond competitive success and economic well-being. It does this not by abstracting from social inequalities and economic needs but by addressing them as human, moral, personal realities rather than simply as the technical and distant issues of liberal understanding. In the imagination of great speakers for this tradition, as recently Martin Luther King spoke for it, social and economic relations become translated into the moral and personal meaning they have for members of the polity. Poverty and unemploy-

ment cease to be unfortunate side-effects of capitalist economic growth, to be neglected benignly or tidied up managerially. They appear in their full reality as institutionalized denials of dignity and social participation, glaring failures of communal responsibility. As such these issues emerge as painful spurs to challenge and change the shares of power and the institutions of collective coordination. The logic of King's republican understanding of politics led him to broaden the civil rights struggle to challenge institutions that perpetuate poverty. Finally, just before his assassination, he was advocating a coalition that would join opposition to the Indochina war and the military-industrial priorities to a broad struggle for economic and social democracy.

The great power of the civic vision, as contrasted with the liberal view, lies in its fundamental philosophic commitments. These entail the realization that the personal quest for a worthwhile life is bound up with the reality of interdependency and so with power. Large-scale social processes cannot remain merely technical issues but must be understood as part of the texture of personal living, just as personal life is woven into the patterns of collective organization.

Thus the fundamental language and symbols of the American civic tradition link private and public, personal and collective sensibilities in synoptic form. American patriotism is not a nationalism based upon immemorial ties of blood and soil, but neither is it in practice simply a kind of commercial contract. As observers from Tocqueville on have reported, the underlying conception that animates patriotism in America is a moral, even a religious, one: the notion of civic covenant. Unlike the liberal idea of contract, which emphasizes mutual obligations within clearly defined limits, a civic covenant is a bond of fundamental trust founded upon common commitment to a moral understanding.

Covenant morality means that as citizens we make an unlimited promise to show care and concern to each other. It is the commitment to such a trust that is summed up in the mutual pledge of loyalty, which concludes the American Declaration of Independence. Within the civic perspective, the business of politics at its highest is to fulfill these convenantal promises within the changing flow of events. In practice, which is almost never politics at its highest, the civic understanding provides the sense of conscience and idealism against which the institutions and the conduct of our collective life have to be judged. Again, Martin Luther King's relentless campaign for justice was a prime example of the practical efficacy of the civic imperative to care for the common good.

But what could the common good be? As a liberal would see it, the institutions of our society, the government, corporations, even the cities in which people live and work are all variations on the model of a business enterprise. Political, even social, vitality and progress are measured according to economic criteria. The public good, seen that way, becomes the utilitarian sum of individual satisfactions. A common interest can be presumed to lie only in ensuring advantageous conditions of general exchange—what is called, more realistically, a "good business climate." Beyond that interest in mutually advantageous exchanges, the civic language of a common good sounds to the liberal somehow darkly mystical or at least unnecessarily grandiose. Justice, as John Rawls makes clear, can be at most a matter of regulating these exchanges so that no one benefits unfairly. Why press further in confusing language, when it is likely to "overload" the political system, to encourage malcontents to assuage private wants, illegitimately, through public policy or mass movements?

To take this position is to fail to understand that the conception of the common good, with its long history in the civic tradition, is part of a language that articulates a way of living. In any practical context, language functions as more than the purely descriptive vehicle which is the ideal of analytic science. A political philosophy is always more than a neutral description; it is also, and more importantly, a proposal and a vision. Political philosophies propose to evoke an experience of a kind of living. Indeed, it is the important peculiarity of liberal political theory that political language should be shorn of its evocative dimensions. That opinion is, seen in larger context, itself a proposal to think and experience life in a certain way. Now, all forms of life, especially those that have been consciously

cultivated for generations, are rich with highly charged, compact phrases and gestures which serve to evoke a whole scheme of meaning. In the civic tradition, *common good* is one of these phrases.

Thus it is not surprising that such an emblematic phrase would cause puzzlement when heard from within an alien scheme of meaning such as liberal utilitarianism. But if we grant to the civic tradition the possibility that its language points to a way of life which is meaningful in its own terms, then our imagination can rise to a new possibility. This new possibility is the idea of a civic life. To understand this requires at first, in Wittgenstein's phrase, coming "to feel our way around" in its characteristic language. Such an adventure may enable us to see the contemporary morass of liberal capitalist politics in a fresh way.

A virtue of the civic republican tradition is that its language provides an understanding of the social conditions upon which it depends. The chief of these conditions is an interpretation of psychic and moral development importantly different from the liberal account. The immediate merit of this alternative is that it offers an understanding of what liberal theory cannot provide: an explanation for the missing connections in its own interpretation of social life.

II

How, then, is a civic life possible? That is to ask, how can we conceive of individual fulfillment as realized through mutual commitment to a common good? The answer the civic tradition provides is clear: civic life is possible because human nature is naturally disposed to find its fulfillment in what is called a life of virtue. This statement immediately calls up for us—partly as a kind of prophylaxis against a suspected tyranny—the proud ideal of freedom, the "core symbol" of liberalism. Leaving aside the confusions and controversies that continue to rage about the notion of freedom, in particular its relation to the other great liberal value of equality, the civic conception of virtue becomes clearer when contrasted with liberal freedom.

In important respects, in fact, freedom is virtue's ambiguous child. For the republican tradition, civic virtue is the excellence of character proper to the citizen. It *is* freedom in a substantive sense, freedom understood as the capacity to attain one's good, where *goodness* describes full enjoyment of those capacities which characterize a flourishing human life. Since humans are by nature social beings, living well requires a shared life, and a shared life is possible only when the members of a community trust and respect one another. To participate in such a shared life is to show concern for and reciprocity to one's fellows, and to do so is simultaneously fulfilling for the individual. Thus the individual's true good must consist not in attaining a sum of satisfactions but in showing in himself, and sharing as a participant, an admirable and worthwhile form of life.

Modern liberalism isolates the act of free volition, the will as self-assertion, and emphasizes the individual struggling against constriction. The classical image of freedom as virtue, however, is quite different. It focuses upon the exhibition of form as the flowering of potential powers. From the Promethean standpoint of modern culture it is easy to mistake this ideal for mere static completion or passivity, but in fact it is neither static nor passive or, rather, the categories of civic language propose a way of seeing life that is different from the utilitarian. This language suggests that what makes life worth living is not simple pleasure but the peculiarly human satisfaction of feeling oneself to be a significant member of an ongoing way of life that appeals because of its deep resonances of beauty and meaning. (Curiously, modern advertising, that most ostensibly utilitarian of capitalist institutions, grasps this point profoundly, if narrowly. What else is most advertising but the rhetorical association of a commodity, such as a car or a cigarette, with a symbol of a commonly desired way of life or admired character ideal: the Beautiful People or, *de gustibus*, the Cowboy?)

The task of civic intelligence is to bring these inchoate appeals to clarity, to find and to weave a harmony among the various threads of significance embodied in family life, in the various skills and crafts, in religious and artistic traditions. In its most general formulation, the civic sense of virtue as freedom is captured in the idea of human dignity. Medieval natural-law theorists brought Christian theological commitments to bear on Greek and Roman notions of a common humanity in their statement that the fundamental natural end or purpose of political life is to provide dignity for all.

Notice that it is consistent in this context to speak of the political community as natural because it is a necessary condition for, indeed is an essential manifestation of, a dignified human life. This dignity is the most basic, general, even ontological aspect of the flourishing of human nature. Practically, it is the reality that Martin Luther King called the sense of "somebodyness." Dignity is thus the realization of freedom. It is the evidence of the full development of civic virtue.

The idea of "free institutions" (which bulks large in American political discourse), while a phrase much used in liberal thought, has its roots in the same civic conception of dignity and virtue. When Montesquieu and other early liberals looked for positive qualities in the republics of the ancient world, they saw above all free, as opposed to despotic, regimes. By this they meant that the structure and powers of the state derived from no force outside the citizens themselves. Neither occupying army nor dictator's mercenaries nor isolated elite maintained the practices of life, the laws, the defenses of those cities; rather, their strength came from the concerted spirit of their citizens.

It seemed to the early liberals living in an age of monarchy and the Old Regime amazing that the ancients could sustain, even for brief periods, the public spirit of Periclean Athens or Republican Rome, for it was evident from the descriptions and discussions of the classical theorists that maintenance of a self-governing polity required a generally high degree of identification, on the part of the citizen, of his own good with the well-being of the community. Given the liberal assumptions of the early modern theorists, they had little trouble accounting for the "corruption" and decline of ancient republics into despotic empires. Indeed, as self-seeking competition weakened the bonds of commonwealth, those thinkers were proposing the liberal order as a way to engineer correctly what they took as the natural human gravitation toward competitive egoism. What seemed astonishing, and really hardly credible at all, was the notion of civic spirit, of civic acts as such. Yet, the sheer weight of historical testimony forced them to accept its reality.

Holding to our intention to extend to the civic tradition a presumption of experiential validity, it is clear that citizenship is taken by republicanism as the natural fulfillment of human powers, not as an extreme feat of moral athleticism. However rare the truly excellent examples may be, citizenship remains the common vocation, and the proper object of moral education.

We may shed light on the matter by trying to describe a civic act, as opposed to a merely private one. In modern electoral politics, candidates frequently try to persuade citizens to cast their votes because their interests will be advanced by so doing. While the civic philosophers would agree with this reasoning, the "interests" to be advanced would be rather differently defined. Indeed, the premise of public discussion of policy even in a liberal regime is not only to enlighten all interested parties as to what they stand to gain or lose in the event that a certain course of action is taken. When that is all or the greatest part of public debate, little "policy" results; instead there is a watering-down of choices to please everyone. Where the issue is simply a proposal to choose one kind of private enrichment over another, the arts of bargaining and political compromise are not inappropriate, tempered by a concern for fairness, like John Rawls's theory of justice, as a kind of rational and self-interested choice. But what about political decisions about making war, or the kinds of economic growth which should be pursued, or about use and care for the natural environment? Because these political decisions so affect the kinds of life that will prevail, public debate is critical for developing a shared understanding of the consequences of policy choices, of hidden costs and benefits to the whole community. Indeed, it is the general discussion of interdependency that brings a "public" into being. Public discussion aims to bring before the whole civic community an understanding of the "externalities" of policy choices—to use the language of liberal economics—precisely in terms of what pursuing these options will mean for the situation of various groups.

Voting to endorse a policy or candidate, were the choices really clear (which is another extremely critical matter), is a public, a civic act, because it carries with it responsibility for changing or maintaining the social, and often the natural, environment shared by all. Thus, to reduce such an act to a simple reflex of self-interest is fundamentally to misconceive the actual interdependence of citizens in a commonwealth. It is to imagine that the polity is a self-balancing mechanism—a familiar enough misassumption. But it is also to fail to take seriously the complicated web of interactions that ties together the lives of even the most private citizens. It is here that the liberal penchant for modeling political questions on economic choices in a marketplace shows its most dangerous and morally irresponsible side. Against the liberal claim that free institutions, in Montesquieu's sense, can be sustained merely by concentration upon an expanding market system, civic republican insight and historical experience strongly suggest that such a course is folly, because it rests on a misconception of politics and, finally, on too narrow an understanding of the reality of social life.

The strange utopian side of liberalism shows up clearly here. Confronted with the overwhelming fact of social interdependence, the liberal retreat to the mechanism of market choice is cloaked as humility! After all, one hears the argument, actually to make public decisions about the kinds of communities we should have, the kinds of lives people ought to lead, is moral arrogance and presumption. Let the ideal market of choices mediate. Then if consenting adults wish to commit capitalist or communalist acts, that is their private matter. But notice: this "value-neutral" position assumes that all humanly relevant goods can somehow be exchanged through the market, and that the moral qualities of respect and fairness can be developed in private life alone. Highly questionable assumptions indeed: not even the early modern liberal philosophers held such sanguine views.

To the early liberals the utopian element of classical republican morality was not the fact of interdependence and mutual responsibility but the expectation and requirement that citizens act in an appropriately responsible way in practice. For them, the key problem in the civic vision was the idea that self-interested motives could actually be transformed through a public culture to the extent that genuinely civic acts became widely practiced. Now, our present situation differs from theirs in one critical respect. We cannot fall back on the optimistic hope that an improved social mechanics will produce a functional equivalent of civic virtue by harnessing private egoism. Indeed, the viability of any self-governing institution is threatened by the failure of those dreams. We need to look closely at the civic tradition because, if democracy is to survive, we have no other option.

So, again, what conditions make civic life possible? Classical political philosophy understood the life of civic or moral virtue to stand in opposition to the life of self-interest which they called economic, meaning that the latter aimed at private satisfaction. Since economic life is concerned with wants that are in principle limitless, the motivation in dealings with others is always the expectation of gain. This is the marketing orientation familiar from utilitarian theory. By contrast, moral virtue represents a higher integration of the powers of the self. This integration was conceived as at once the goal and the effect of participation in civic life. Virtue, the *arete* ("excellence") of the Greek theorists, describes the disposition of a person whose conduct is guided by a shared value or principle rather than by private needs and desires. This kind of excellence, moreover, is a personal ideal as well as a collective one, in that it describes a personality sufficiently integrated both to live up to commitments and to cooperate with others to achieve common values. In traditional language such an integration of the personality was described as *courage*, the ability to sum oneself up in word and action, and *temperance*, or self-control, an ordering of the person so that the higher values consciously affirmed

can predominate over merely private impulses and desires.

The civic life has intrinsic value, then, because it is necessary for human maturation. The teleological conception of human nature which the civic tradition long maintained places the achievement of mature personhood within a context of interdependence and mutual concern. The great modern ideal of the autonomous self who is also respectful of others, as reflected in contractarian liberalism, is in reality a kind of echo of civic virtue. For the modern theorists of obligation, only autonomy is isolated from sociability, just as the modern theorists' state of nature locates man outside social relations. Given their assumption of the primacy of analytical reason, this conclusion appeared quite natural and obvious to the liberal thinkers. Again we see the tight connection among an understanding of politics, a theory of human nature, and a conception of reason. By contrast with liberalism, classical teleological reason situates achievement of an integrated self capable of self-reflection, and so of responsible action, within a continuity of life which is both social and natural.

What enabled classical thinkers to argue that a prudential reasoning, based upon a cultivated moral sense, could in fact be trusted to promote the good of the community? It was their vision of autonomy as always developing in tension with care for others in a particular shared situation. The whole classical notion of a common *paideia*, or moral-civic cultivation, rested on the assertion that growth and transformation of the self toward responsible mutual concern is the realistic concern of public life. Aristotle argued, and the civic tradition since then has agreed, that the first and final concern of politics, like that of the family though in a more universal way, is mutual moral cultivation. It is a precarious and difficult undertaking, but, to Aristotle, not wholly utopian, because it is rooted in what was to him an obvious observation about human life.

> A natural impulse is thus one reason why men desire to live a social life even when there is no need of mutual succor; but they are also drawn together by a common interest in proportion as each attains a share in the good life through the

union of all in a form of political association. The good life is the chief end, both for the community as a whole and each of us individually. But men also come together, and form and maintain political associations, merely for the sake of life, for perhaps there is some element of the good even in the simplest act of living, so long as the evils of existence do not preponderate too heavily.[1]

The notion at the end, that even survival gets its significance from its implicit aim at fuller realization of human powers, is the characteristic of the teleological approach.

Notice that Aristotle's position does not totally reject the economic or marketing orientation toward mere "life," nor does it depict virtue as a mere external counterbalance to private needs. His is not a pure ethics of obligation, remorselessly struggling to control an implacable nature. On the contrary, the teleology of desire implicit in this passage from the *Politics* suggests that the life of virtue is good because of the qualitatively better fulfillment it opens for the individual. The meaning of good as the achievement of natural potential includes the idea that self-conscious reason is as genuine an expression of nature as sensual wants, even more so in the sense that sociable and reasonable desires awaken uniquely human powers. Thus, the natural impulse to a shared life is not generated by a surplus of energies arising from analytically more primitive sensual needs. Aristotle's theory is in this way very different from Abraham Maslow's "hierarchy of needs." The teleology of human life reconciles the disparate desires of appetite and reason, lust and love, by giving each its due in the full achievement of personhood.

But the achievement of maturity, or moral virtue, consists in a genuine transformation of motives, not simply their combination. And this takes place only through a certain kind of educative social interaction. Civic moral education is, then, natural in that it fulfills humanity's distinctive need to be at once self-reflective and yet interdependent members of a community. Classical philosophy saw this human ideal as a reflection of its conception of the cosmos as a teleologically ordered relationship among different kinds of beings; yet, the

peculiarly human form of life requires active artifice for its continuation. We must take care to nurture ourselves and our environment, including our progeny and each other. And that task is only possible through the development and maintenance of a full moral education, a *paideia* that includes political culture. That is a difficult and complex task. A civic culture is necessarily defined by its two poles: it is aiming at a universal sympathy, an ideal enunciated by the Stoics and given powerful expression in Christian natural-law teaching: yet, civic culture is grounded and rooted in the historical circumstances of its place of origin and the particular conditions of life in which it comes to grow.

III

The tension between particular circumstances and the *telos* of a universal community reflects in another form the root polarities of individual autonomy and mutual care. It also poses the formidable cognitive problem of how to conceive of the relationship of practical politics and political theory. For the classical tradition, as for the Middle Ages, the civic life was considered to draw its ultimate referents from the realm of *theoria*, or disinterested contemplation of the universal principles of nature or God. The "higher reaches of human nature" were achieved not outside human society but in the qualitatively higher realm of philosophical sagehood, the egoless mirroring of the cosmos. Theoretical knowledge in this ancient sense provided a feeling for man's ends and place in nature, and situated the shifting events of politics within a universal perspective that showed the finitude of political endeavor.

But *theory* did not possess its modern meaning of explaining how things work; it thus lacked any technical application. Instead, moral and political life were conceived of as requiring another sort of knowledge which could only be acquired through guided experience. This knowlege Aristotle called *phronesis*, or prudence. Prudential knowledge is always situated and guided by qualitative analogies rather than abstract principles. The working out of *paideia* so that particular viewpoints and loyalties are given their proper places and are integrated into a wider framework of loyalty is at once a universal ideal and a highly particular—and valuable—achievement.

Modern liberalism began with an effort to circumvent the precarious nature of traditional prudence with a science of social engineering. Today the problems of that effort at political science make reappropriation of the classical insights increasingly desirable and perhaps even necessary. Chief among these insights is the dependence of a republican political life upon a vital political culture that continues the prudential tradition. If it is not to die, tradition must be recast with each generation.

The chief effort of civic education is to combat corruption—that is, in the civic view, to forestall despotic rule by which some group within the polity would substitute its particular conception of good for that of the whole. A despotism of "economic" men, of special interests, is what the tradition feared most, but it also warned of the dangers of a rule of the best and wisest untempered by the need of such groups to share power and thus aid in the civic development of the less good and wise. Corruption, then, is domination, as the good of the polity is justice, but both are continually shifting balances within the particular circumstances of the society. The common good and its corruption are always discriminations in the situation, arrived at through discussion already founded in the sense of justice transmitted by the civic *paideia*.

Statesmanship must, then, by its very nature remain a prudential art. The living reality of the civic vision is the repeated effort to institutionalize a moral ideal. But the ideal is understood not through a deduction of abstract concepts but within the kind of interpretive circle that describes all moral life. Political prudence is an informed understanding of what contributes to the genuine growth of responsible common life. That reflection takes its root in the implicit sense of goodness and right which is shared and developed in civic life. The attempt to formulate and fix this

understanding, as in theories of social and economic progress or in Kohlberg's theory of moral development, runs the heavy risk of omitting or disparaging just those concrete loyalties which provide a standing place for reflection and criticism. As with the moral education of the individual, the liberal penchant for a universal scheme of "development" in the end misses the critical problem of our time: the economic and administrative processes that threaten to sever the bonds of involved understanding which make possible the development of a rooted and responsible sense of self.

It is therefore important to understand the relationship of prudential reasoning to the classic teleology of human life. For that tradition, the criterion of value is the full realization of a meaningful life as a member of a just community. There is a form of consequentialist reasoning in this position, in that acts are judged good or bad not according to their motivations or formal qualities alone but as they advance this full self-realization. However, self-realization is defined not by subjective needs but by the ontological notion that humanity is inherently social and linguistic and so tends toward a responsible shared life.

In the classical conception, the *telos*, or end, is the display of the full capabilities of humanity, and this immanent tendency is thought to structure the relations among the parts of the developing whole. Thus, while analytic reason is given a significant place, it is conceived of as essentially a reconstructive process. One can gain a detailed knowledge of a compound, by reducing it to its parts, only after first grasping its whole and overall tendency. In direct opposition to the purely analytic method, teleological reasoning declares that truly to know a thing is to see it not in its simplest terms but in its fullest development, which means within the widest set of its interconnections.

Thus, while the modern individualistic notion of the state of nature has regarded generation of social ties as an instrumental process, the classical view begins from the *telos* of social life. Outside a linguistic community of shared practices, there would be biological *Homo sapiens* as logical abstraction, but there could not be human beings. This is the meaning of the Greek and medieval dictum that the political community is ontologically *prior* to the individual. The polis is, literally, that which makes man, as human being, possible. It is therefore, as an association of justice and fellowship, the fullest expression of human nature.

The tradition of modern social thought reaching from Hegel through Marx, Durkheim, Dewey, Parsons, and others can be seen as a prolonged effort to refocus this teleological insight against the distorting efforts of the reductive social science initiated by Hobbes.[2] Aristotle referred to his way of coming to understand this human *telos* as induction, a process of gradual discernment of the common form derived from experience of many analogous cases. The tempestuous history of controversy over what is needed for induction to take place defines much of Western epistemology; however, Aristotle, like Plato, seems oddly confident that such a progress is quite natural. He does not seem to wonder in amazement that the "mind" can know "the world," but takes it as unproblematical that cognition is some sort of participation of human beings in the environment that sustains them.

Even more perplexing to moderns formed by centuries of epistemological debate is the ancients' evident assumption that there is a connection between a right cognitive grasp of the human *telos* and an individual's moral character, as well as his socially cultivated experience. That idea reappeared in Hegelian philosophy, whence it was disseminated through Marx and the American pragmatists. Yet, it has rarely been considered of importance in "rigorous" philosophy or the "scientific" study of society. An interpretive conception of social inquiry and philosophical understanding helps clear up the perplexity. It can also make sense of the ancient teaching about the superiority of the contemplative to the active life.

From the modern point of view, the weak point in the classical notion that a knowledge of human ends must undergird and guide prudential reasoning is that this putative knowledge of ends is asserted to be available only to the well-ordered character; that is, the argument is circular. There are no democratic procedures of verification, open to all disinterested outside observers, by which to test the "common-sense" claim that "man is an animal so constituted that he is truly himself only when he shares life in a polis." Political—and so, for classical thinkers, genuine—anthropological knowlege rests upon a claim to an already interpreted experience.

Political authority in classical political thought ultimately rests not on any objectively testable "science" but upon a claim to a kind of experience. This experience is one that transforms the person who is shaped by it, so that the original trust in authority is redeemed by a kind of self-justifying fulfillment of its claims. But that means that knowledge of human ends cannot be had outside the experience of coming to realize them. The great task of the true statesman, said Plato, is to communicate this process and its value to others who have not yet undergone it. Socrates was the incarnation of this communication for Plato, though in a wider sense the whole tradition of *paideia* must play this critical practical role.

The contemplative life, if we can take Socrates as its embodiment, is, then, a detachment from action in its self-serving sense, a purification from private wants so as to respond to the common good and, indeed, to the world wider than human concerns. The contemplative life thus transcends the interdependent life of the polis, but only to make the theorist empty of any purely private goal. There is much here to suggest instructive comparison between this central concern of classical philosophy and the spiritual traditions of the world religions. The ideal of contemplative detachment as the highest fulfillment set distinct limits to the claims and demands of politics while it introduced a higher norm of authority into politics.

For civic republicans, then, moral authority has been embodied in a common understanding of justice as a proportionate sharing in the common good. While liberal theorists have viewed justice as a contract of reciprocity motivated by equality in fear and need, the civic tradition has always maintained that justice finds its *telos* and so its orientation beyond itself in *philia*, or fellowship. Because men in fact pursue a multitude of goods and can make various claims as to what is their due,

principles of justice must remain general. At
the same time, however, the tradition maintains that all members of a differentiated community must be enabled by common agreement and concerted public effort to take full
part in the good life, that is, citizenship. It is
this concern for participation which has given
the civic tradition its recurrently radical edge.

Equality is a part of the complex value of
justice. Because the *telos* of justice is fellowship,
a polity must be so ordered that all citizens
share the grounds for uncoerced participation. Neither equality of result nor of opportunity per se, this "common sense" of justice for
centuries led civic republicans to identify political justice with a widespread distribution of
the necessities of life and rough equality of
wealth. Office and honor were to be awarded
on the basis of advancement of this vision of
the common good. Reciprocity is thus a part of
justice but ultimately has no meaning without
a conception of what the good polity should be
like, of what each citizen requires to share the
good life of virtue.

In the republican vision the ideal of justice
is characterized as proportional, not arithmetical—meaning that distribution of the possibilities for sharing the good life must seek to
treat all citizens with equal concern but must
recognize their different needs and contributions to the overall community. Civic virtue
sets as a kind of minimum standard of competence for political participation the ability to
observe the common rules and laws, to understand how these laws are arrived at and
changed by reference to the notion of the
common good. Moreover, discernment of the
general good is the guiding norm for discussions of justice. That this discernment always depends on shared understandings derived from a tradition of cultivated experience
requires that the civic community continually
struggle to articulate anew the concrete meaning of justice for the situation. Republican
thinkers long acknowledged that this was a
precarious and difficult task.

Republics were admitted to be fragile and
always liable to corruption into a dictatorship
of particular groups and activities over others.
Furthermore, civic life was known to be an
interdependent life in which the individual's
moral development and happiness depended

directly upon the virtue and wisdom of his
fellow citizens' lives and vice versa. Yet, by
being aware of the complexity and difficulty of
concretely realizing the ideal of the just polity
through imperfect institutions in unpredictable circumstances, the formulators of the republican tradition were also drawing limits to
what politics could claim to achieve; hence,
their high valuation of civic life did not preclude their openness to the ultimate loyalties
expressed in philosophy and religion. The
danger of despotism they saw as always
present: talk of tradition can be used to cloak
vicious oppression as well as to sustain virtue.
But since they held no vision of an ultimate
achievement of a totally just society, the major
republican thinkers did not see as either good
or realistic the mobilization of total societies in
the name of future utopias. Republican
statesmanship is always a matter of achieving a
complicated and delicate balance.

All this explains the high hopes of the pro-
genitors of liberalism. They sought, rather im-
moderately, at last to overcome the limitations
and fragility of the traditional civic culture.
The new project was in part a response to the
great difficulty early modern thinkers faced in
bringing the new forces of commerce, warfare, and centralized government within the
republican conception of moral order. The
actual relations of interdependence among
European men grew ever more complex and
indirect after the sixteenth century, gravely
weakening the self-confidence of the traditional understanding of the individual. It was
more and more difficult for a person to know
who he was in terms of his "calling," which was
interpreted by both Christian and civic
humanist vocabularies in terms of ideal social
interrelationships.

The enormous crisis of orientation and
meaning that swept Europe in the sixteenth
and seventeenth centuries testifies with ter-
rifying eloquence to a great depth of confusion about where the individual was in the
world and what made life worth living. Instead
of the older confidence of knowing oneself
through one's social relations, however
fraught with moral precariousness that may
have been, the new age was one in which the
individual came to see himself as inhabiting a
strange world. It consisted of private passions

and concern for self-image no longer bound to a coherent set of social relations, the *amour propre* of which Rousseau would later be the great theorist. J. G. A. Pocock captures the situation well:

> He could explain this realm, in the sense that he could identify the forces of change that were producing it . . . but he could not explain himself by locating himself as a real and rational being within it. The worlds of history and value therefore extruded one another, and what would later be described as the alienation of man from his history had begun to be felt; but, far from seeing himself as a mere product of historical forces, the civic and propertied individual was endowed with an ethic that clearly and massively depicted him as a citizen of classical virtue, but exacted the price of obliging him to regard all the changes transforming the world of government, commerce and war as corruption. . . . Hence the age's intense and nervous neoclassicism.[3]

The search for a new understanding of these problems—anomalies, from the traditional republican perspective—led enterprising thinkers into the complex developments of modern political theory and culture. That liberal utilitarian modes of thinking should have dominated these developments is not surprising.

The utility-language of liberalism, once armed with the model of the self-balancing political economy of growth, could separate the inner quest for meaning from the public questions of administrative order, military power, and commercial expansion. The unique liberal answer to the classical problem of the just polity was the premise of moral neutrality of wants plus free market exchange among equals. Individuals could look to their inner gyroscopes as best they might. They might find personal solace in the notion of vocation or of devotion to family, but also by pursuing personal, corporate, and national aggrandizement. The primacy of material motives, especially fear and greed, led to a politics in which justice was best ensured by governmental umpiring of the economic games.

Because of the primacy of growth over justice, of the material over the spiritual, the idea of historical progress has played a crucial role in liberal culture as the replacement for the civic language of the common good. To its credit, Marxism has emphasized the moral quality of interdependent fellowship as the *telos* of historical progress in a way that liberal capitalism has not; yet, Marxists and liberals alike have consistently talked of the achievement of a just society as being dependent upon growth of the society's capacity to fulfill economic wants. This conception has provided sanction for the brutalities of "primitive accumulation" in both its capitalist and socialist forms, a sacrifice of presently living persons, most often peasants, for the sake of future abundance—on balance, a delivery from want that has been bloody indeed.

The great liberating aspect of the civic tradition for our present circumstances is its freedom from thrall to the idea of progress. A civic politics begins with the demand for justice as the condition for genuine growth. The test and measure of that growth is the realization of fellowship, replacing the hostility and antagonisms of social groups with an interrelationship of equal dignity. But the path toward that realization, always a difficult one, is made extremely complicated by the tremendous complexity of modern industrial society. Here the mutual dependence of all groups is more intricately woven than in any previous society, yet, it is denied by the curious rhetoric of individualism—a situation that perpetuates a corporate dominance of American life the more pervasive because it is so denied. Our liberal conception of politics, however, makes the tracing out of these factual relationships of unequal participation seem unnecessary. Economic advancement, tempered by an eye cast toward playing fairly—in a word, progress—must work inscrutably toward a better tomorrow. That is the dream turned nightmare from which we are struggling to awake.

A recovery of democratic politics in America must start with reawakening a living sense of the social and historical relationships within which we stand. A recovery of citizenship would be at the same time a crucial reinvigoration of a sense of personal responsibility. The paradox of citizenship is that civic virtue entails conflict in a way that liberal civility does not, yet, the conflict inevitably triggered by any challenge to the threatening despotism, soft or hard, is in fact a sign of vitality in our republic.

There is a second kind of conflict which the

recovery of democratic citizenship entails. That is the painful struggle which must go on in the body politic and within ourselves as we become aware, at personal cost, of our general complicity in unjust social arrangements that provide advantages for some at the expense of dignity for others. The struggle for democratic politics is always a struggle for a more inclusive community, and that will require changing our sense of who we are both in public and in subtly private ways. In this sense the civic vision is a personal moral challenge as much as a critical perspective on the social status quo. Peace, as King reminded us, is not the absence of tension but the presence of justice.

The major contribution we can hope for from a cultural and intellectual reinvigoration of civic republicanism is that it will bring to the emerging movements for grassroots democracy the historical vision and wisdom of such a long and rich tradition. Chief among these insights is the understanding that citizenship is rooted in a moral tradition. The civic heritage shares the understanding that practical reasoning moves in a circle, growing by the efforts of citizens formed by the civic *paideia* to extend and realize the ideal of a more human and just commonwealth. This requires a creative, indeed, an experimental reinterpretation of the meaning of their primary commitments for the contemporary situation.

In America the civic tradition has numerous roots, many of them religious, as is appropriate in a diverse society and for a political vision focused on integrating diversity. Yet, the central symbols of the citizen and the commonwealth—the moral imperative to live according to the principles of justice and mutual support grounded in civil covenant—are held in common. It is the sharing of these ideals, rather than blood, soil, or economic growth, that holds out hope for a renewed struggle toward a just community that embodies the sense of dignity, of "somebodyness" in a nation worthy of the respect of all. And this too is appropriate, for the quality of political fellowship is determined by what is shared.

This, then, is the hope civic republican ideals hold out to us. The difficult task is to articulate successfully this possibility, to bring the resources of that tradition into the present national and international arenas so as to provide a new political vision for a confused and divided public. The lurking suspicion that undermines our confidence in any tradition is that our capitalist and bureaucratic modern society has, like a cancer, grown beyond the point at which its corruption could be healed by self-regeneration. The great intellectual challenge is to develop conceptual means to reinterpret the formidable problems that prevent realization of an authentic citizenship. And the first step in that direction must be to assess, with the present crisis in view, the resources the American civic experience has previously brought to its struggles. By those reflections it may become possible to tap a still-living civic energy with which to generate a new political and social vision for the American present.

Notes

1. *The Politics of Aristotle*, translated by Ernest Barker (New York: Oxford University Press, 1962), bk. III, ch. 5, p. 111. See also the useful discussion of contrasts between Aristotle's notion of a politics of virtue and the modern notion of obligation in Stephen G. Salkever's "Virtue, Obligation and Politics," *American Political Science Review* 68, 1 (March 1974): 78–92.

2. This is the position of Roberto M. Unger: see the discussion in his *Law in Modern Society: Toward a Criticism of Social Theory* (New York: Free Press, 1976), esp. pp. 1–46.

3. J. G. A. Pocock, *The Machiavellian Moment* (Princeton: Princeton University Press, 1975), p. 466.

Unitary Democracy

Jane J. Mansbridge

Political scientist Jane Mansbridge interprets citizenship as a form of friendship in a unitary democracy. Unitary democracy is a polity based on respect, equality, common interests, face-to-face interactions, and consensus decision making. Adversary democracy, on the other hand, is an association of strangers who have conflicting interests and who resolve their differences by majority vote with secret ballots. In the selection reprinted here Jane Mansbridge sets out the distinctive character of a unitary polity and assesses its advantages and disadvantages for a modern society, as she has observed them in her study of two small democracies. Her case studies are a political democracy in the small Vermont town of Selby and a workplace democracy in a crisis center, Helpline, Inc. She begins by developing a theory of unitary democracy in terms of common interests, consensus decision making, and face-to-face interaction. Assuming that in even the smallest, most cohesive group the members' interests will differ, she shows how a common interest can nevertheless be formed. Face-to-face contact is crucial in this process, since empathetic understanding of another person's standpoint allows parties to expand their own interests to include the interests of others and appreciate the interest of the group. Equal respect and equal status are necessary to accomplish such adjustments of interests. She also notes some of the drawbacks of a unitary democracy. Consensus formation can be marred either by a fear of conflict in face-of-face situations or by the imposition of conformity on deviant perspectives. Also, in a unitary democracy a deadlock favors the status quo.

The Basis in Friendship of Unitary Democracy

The strength of unitary democracy derives partly from its simplicity: it makes formal and extends to the level of a polity the social relations of friendship. The Greeks were aware of this connection. With the phrase, "Friendship [*philia*] appears to hold city-states together,"[1] Aristotle illuminates the bond between citizens in a unitary polity. Friendship has a meaning close to love. It is a relation with other human beings that almost everyone has enjoyed, and it is a good in every culture. Drawing from the experience of friendship, a democrat could easily believe that relations between citizens ought to be like relations between friends. Friends are equals. They choose to spend time together. They share common values. They expand in each other's company. So, too, in a democracy based on friendship, participants are equal in status; the costs of participation, of which some make so much, do not feel heavy. Citizens "fly to the assemblies" as if to meet their friends. They value the time they spend on their common affairs. They share a common good, and are able, as a consequence, to make their decisions unanimously. The characteristics of unitary democracy—equal respect, face-to-face contact, common interest, and consensus—are from this perspective nothing but the natural conditions that prevail among friends.

Any polity based on friendship must be a

democracy, for it is based on a fundamental equality among its members. Friends are always equals. In all cultures, friendship demands a rough equality of respect. Friends need not be equal in every quality that they value; indeed, in order for the union to be anything but narcissistic, each must bring to it qualities that the other does not have. Friends must be complementary, rather than the same. But for a friendship to be viable, the total respect that friends hold for each other must be roughly equal. Friendships do not form between individuals who recognize between them a distinct inferiority or superiority. Because friendship is, next to the family, the closest relation between human beings, it becomes a "natural" or "organic" basis for democracy, just as the family is the natural metaphor for legitimating a monarchy.

Unitary democracy is not only egalitarian, in this sense of equality of respect; it is also consensual. Adversary democrats, who tend to equate consensus with suppression, should think first of their own friendships. Friends make their decisions by consensus, reaching a decision by drawing together subtle preferences, intensities, and information. Among friends, everyone's pleasure is reduced if any one of the group cannot join them or goes along reluctantly. For each individual, the pleasure of the collective experience outweighs his or her individual preferences. Equally important, the friends make each other's pleasure their own. Because the group's unity has a value for each individual greater than the value of most differences in individual preferences, a group of friends will rarely, if ever, settle its decisions with a vote. Voting symbolizes, reinforces, and institutionalizes division. Voting produces a result that excludes the minority, whose interests the others have partly made their own, while a decision by consensus includes everyone, reinforcing the unity of the group.

Consensus can only work among friends because by and large they have common interests. Their private interests tend to coincide, they sometimes subordinate their private interests to the friendship they have formed together, and they often take up each other's interests as their own. For, as Aristotle observed, "Those who wish well to their

friends for their sake are most truly friends."[2]

The face-to-face interaction of friends helps to create and to maintain their common interests. Friends enjoy the drama of each other's existence and value the time they spend together rather than resenting it. They come to respect and to know one another by piecing together, over time, informal cues derived from their intimate contact. Without such contact, friendship usually withers. Thus, for a polity built on friendship face-to-face assemblies are a benefit as well as a cost. These four central features of friendship—equal status or respect, consensus, common interest, and face-to-face contact—recur in unitary democracies throughout history.

The Original Unitary Democracy

Unitary democracy almost certainly has a longer history than any other form of government. For more than 99 percent of our existence, we human beings lived in hunter-gatherer bands, which in all probability practiced unitary democracy.

We know relatively little about the hunter-gatherers of earlier times. What we do know derives from archaeological finds, from accounts of European travelers and explorers who recorded some characteristics of hunter-gatherer groups when they first encountered them, and from systematic studies of anthropologists on the handful of hunter-gatherer tribes that have survived into the twentieth century. But these three sources of evidence agree on one point: the remarkable degree of economic equality among hunter-gatherers. More recent evidence suggests a comparable degree of political equality. At least in the past few centuries, hunter-gatherers have habitually made their decisions as equals, by consensus, and in face-to-face meetings. It seems fairly safe to infer that hunter-gatherers always operated as unitary democracies.

The economic equality in hunter-gatherer bands supports this political equality. These bands, both now and probably back to their earliest origins, divide up any major catch after a hunt. Sharing eliminates the need for storage and permits greater mobility. As for gathering, two to four hours of collecting fruits and nuts usually provides amply for a family. In hard times, the custom of sharing a catch allows the whole band, excepting the very oldest and the very youngest members, to survive. When food becomes extremely scarce, the bands leave their oldest members behind and move on, and mothers smother their newborns. Those who stay with the band share the food. The hunter-gatherers have a similar pattern of equality in possessions. The constant mobility of a band makes possessions more a burden than an asset, and each adult can make housing, bedding, clothing, and even cooking and carrying utensils quickly from naturally available materials. A family therefore carries with it little more than a few ornaments, spare flints, skin blankets, and a bag.

At least in modern bands, equality in political status parallels this equality in food and possessions. Each adult male comes to the band's decision-making council as an equal. Some bands have no head at all; others select an older man to act as a peacemaker and arbitrator in the council, not to hold a higher rank or exercise any formal power. This fundamental equality in status does not necessarily imply equal influence on decisions. The opinions of an individual who combines skill in hunting and in warfare with the personal qualities of generosity, kindness, self-control, experience, and good judgment may well carry more weight than those of other men. But the influence of such a man does not derive from a position of formal authority, entails no obligation on the part of other members of the band, and is not accompanied by any marks or perquisites of higher status.

This kind of equality in political status is not new. The first Europeans in Tierra de Fuego, the Great Lakes region, and the Canadian plains reported, in the words of one, that the Indians they met would not "endure in the least those who seem desirous of assuming superiority over others." Even war parties chose only a temporary leader. No member of the war party was obliged to accept the leader's direction, and after the action, the war leader would sometimes participate in a formal ceremony divesting him of whatever unequal standing he had acquired.

There are two principal exceptions to this general pattern of equality among hunter-gatherers. First, women never attended councils or enjoyed political equality. Second, since age bespeaks experience in these societies, older males were apt to speak with more weight. But relations among families and among men of the same age were essentially equal. Even among men of different ages there was a kind of equality, for the young were not without experience and would inevitably acquire more.

This portrait of equality among the hunter-gatherers runs counter to the usual impression that primitive social organizations are hierarchical, and that equality is a modern preoccupation. Most people's picture of primitive social organization is not based on the hunter-gatherers, however, but on settled societies that engage in some form of agriculture. These societies, which have usually had some form of hierarchy, are in the long view of human history a relatively recent phenomenon.

European and American intruders also confused the picture when they forced hunter-gatherers to adopt some form of hierarchy. As recently as 1965, the federal government insisted that the Potawatami Indians in Topeka, Kansas, elect a formal leader before they could receive poverty funds. None of the Indians wanted to elect a leader, and none wanted to be one. According to the assistant director of the local Office of Economic Opportunity, "Some of them even commented, 'You'll never get an Indian to be a leader!'" The adult males of the tribe insisted on equality of status.

The hunter-gatherers also make their decisions face to face, sometimes shoulder to shoulder, wrist to wrist, and arm to waist. Some hunter-gatherers are "extremely dependent emotionally on the sense of belonging and companionship," a sense reinforced by their frequent touching. While their intimacy does not eliminate conflict between individuals and families, a hunter-gatherer band often works as if the interests of the members of a band are similar. Questions of when to move to a different camp or in what direction to hunt have one more or less correct answer, and discussions are expected to discover the course of action best for all. In such societies, even personal conflicts can be settled in a way that is "best." Hunter-gatherer bands reach consensus because their interests generally coincide, because the members of the band are emotionally and economically interdependent, and because a relatively static culture prescribes a common interpretation of events.

In short, decision making in a hunter-gatherer council is egalitarian, face to face, and consensual. It assumes that the band as a whole has a common interest. But only very small societies can make this assumption and can maintain this kind of decision making. With increasing membership, the probability of a group's achieving a common interest, and therefore genuine consensus, diminishes rapidly. The participants in a large polity may never meet, and if they do, they will usually know each other in only one role, often one that dramatizes conflicts of interest. Large-scale organization also requires a hierarchy of some sort, if only for communication. Finally, sheer numbers make impossible a face-to-face meeting of all members at once. For these and other reasons, unitary democracy has had no large-scale form.

When large-scale polities first developed, they retained the central ideal of common interest while scrapping the democratic paraphernalia of equal status, consensus, and face-to-face assembly. In chiefdoms, monarchies, and even empires, one individual often personified the whole, becoming a unifying force in the face of increasingly diverse interests. The authority structure in these unitary, but non-democratic, polities mirrored that of hunter-gatherer families rather than that of hunter-gatherer councils. Large-scale democracies had to await the full development of a theory of adversary democracy.

Athens: The Classic Balance

The Athens of the fifth and fourth centuries B.C. owes something of its eternal fascination to the balance it achieved between adversary and unitary democracy. On the adversary side, Athenians accepted as legitimate the separate interests of citizens. Aristotle argued that the city would not be a real polis if individual interests were identical, "all men saying 'Mine' and 'Not mine' at the same time and of the same object."[3] The Athenian assembly allowed its decisions to be made by a formal vote, with majority rule, and a formal vote is the crucial mark of the legitimacy of conflict. A vote signals both the passing of a belief that decisions have a correct solution and the introduction of a procedural substitute for common interest. In ancient Athens, political clubs further institutionalized the conflict of interests by managing lawsuits and elections for their members. In votes of ostracism, for instance, these clubs acted like political machines, supplying voters with ballots of potsherd marked in advance with one man's name.

Yet amidst the competing interests of individuals, the clash of rich and poor, and the organized competition of factions, Athenian citizens could still believe that the goal of their deliberations, when they met regularly face to face in the assembly, should be the common good. They could even acknowledge, without deserting the ideal, that some of their number used the rhetoric of the common good to further their own interests. The ideal remained *homonoia*—unanimity, being "of one mind." Although the assembly used majority rule, it may well have made most of its decisions by consensus.[4] Aristotle, again making friendship a model for the polity, noted that "unanimity [*homonoia*], which seems akin to friendship, is the principal aim of legislators. They will not tolerate faction at any cost."[5] He evidently believed that in a polity based on friendship *homonoia* was possible, and by *homonoia*, he meant congruence of interest on "matters of consequence" in which "it is possible for both or all parties to get what they want."

We . . . say that a city is unanimous [*homonoein*] when men have the same opinion about what is to their interest, and choose the same actions, and do what they have resolved in common.[6]

The belief that citizens could often be of one mind, having the same opinion about what is to their interest, allowed Athenian democrats to be less interested in equal power (which would help them protect their interests equally) than in maintaining the floor of equal respect that is necessary to friendship. The ancient Greeks had early recognized that equal respect, or a sense of equal worth, was the necessary basis of personal friendship. They codified this understanding in a common maxim: "Friendship is equality," and they saw equality as playing an active role in maintaining friendship, rather than being only a passive prerequisite:

> Equality, which knitteth friends to friends
> Cities to cities, allies unto allies,
> Man's law of nature is equality.[7]

Athenian democrats went further to make equal status the basis of the state. In one important sense, all Athenian citizens were of equal status, for each was a Greek and, moreover, Athenian born, rather than a barbarian. Greek democratic theory, therefore, derived equality among Athenian citizens from the underlying likeness of their common birth:

> The basis of this our government is equality of birth . . . [W]e and our citizens are brethren, the children all of one another, and we do not think it right to be one another's masters or servants, but the natural equality of birth compels us to seek for legal equality, and to recognize no superiority except in the reputation of virtue and wisdom.[8]

Assuming the possibility of a common good thus made it possible for Athenian democrats to concentrate on equal status rather than on equal power. Even writers as committed to democracy as Democritus took it for granted that those who could make the greatest contribution to the common good should have the greatest power.

The Adversary Revolution

By accepting some conflict as legitimate and by instituting the formal procedures of one-citizen/one-vote and majority rule, Athens became the first society to move away from unitary democracy while preserving the democratic ideal of involving all full citizens in a decision. Many other assemblies in ancient Greece, Rome, and medieval Europe also adopted the vote and a formal system of majority rule, but they probably, like the English Parliament, made most of their decisions by consensus. It was not until the advent of the large-scale nation-state and the market economy that the foundations were laid for a full-fledged system of adversary democracy.

The fourteenth, fifteenth, and sixteenth centuries in Europe saw a feudal, traditional, and theoretically immutable system of "just" prices, "discovered" laws, and personal ties transformed into a national, fluid, and permanently transitory system of shifting prices, positive law, and a mobile, self-interested citizenry. Nascent capitalism required the loosening of personal ties and the legitimation of self-interest. The new market economy demanded labor and capital free to move where opportunities developed, free to contract at rates that shifted with supply and demand, and free to move on again when the market required it. Personal loyalties, local ties, and complex networks of mutual obligation obstructed this process. The machine of the market, moreover, worked on the steam of self-interest. In the incoming capitalist system, each person, pursuing a course of individual aggrandizement, was to help allocate wages, prices, and capital investment efficiently—driving wages and prices down to their lowest limits and bringing in capital or labor wherever wages or prices still hovered above the optimum dictated by supply and demand.

The new economic order required a new political ethos, for which Thomas Hobbes obligingly provided a rationale. Hobbes's seventeenth-century England was fraught with conflict. Disbanded private armies roamed the highways. Unlanded peasants became begging vagabonds on the highways or squatted in camps outside city walls, tripling the cities' populations. Local ties could no longer restrain the highwaymen, and the cities' medieval corporate laws could not oblige the newcomers outside their walls. A contemporary of Hobbes described the capitalists and drifters of this new age as loners, acting on the precept that "nature sent man into the world, without all company, but to care for one." For these "masterless men," Hobbes developed a political theory based on self-interest alone. His human beings single-mindedly pursue "power after power that ceaseth only in death." But eventually, their own interests in avoiding the continuing threat to their lives in a "war of all against all" lead them to contract on equal terms with one another and to submit to a government.

It is a commonplace that Hobbes was the first theorist systematically to legitimate self-interest as the cornerstone of political life. This idea, and the atheism it was held to imply, so appalled most of his contemporaries that they made "Hobbism" grounds for expulsion from political or religious service. Nonetheless, the modern democratic institutions that developed in England at the same time that Hobbes was writing also implicitly recognized the centrality of conflict and self-interest. The traditional monarchy had managed to maintain at least the semblance of common interest even in a polity the size of seventeenth-century England. But as the monarchy lost its ability to impose its will on Parliament, Parliament became increasingly adversary in character. By 1646, Parliament had departed enough from its traditional informal practice of unanimity to begin making decisions more than half the time by majority vote. A year later, the Levellers were arguing that the poor needed an equal vote in order to defend their interests. Finally, in this era parties began to develop into ongoing organizations that represented a coherent group of interests with a specific ideology, and the word "party" began to lose its unsavory connotation of a faction opposed to the common good.

Over the generations, the idea gradually gained acceptance that a democracy should weigh and come to terms with conflicting selfish interests rather than trying to reconcile them or to make them subordinate to a larger common good. John Locke, in the treatise that would inspire the framers of the American Constitution, borrowed more from Hobbes in this respect than he dared admit. In spite of the crucial role he sometimes gives to common interest, Locke has men unite in political society chiefly in order to protect their property

against others, and he defends majority rule on the grounds that it is required by the "contrariety of interests, which unavoidably happen in all collections of men."[9]

By the next century, the framers of the American Constitution explicitly espoused a philosophy of adversary democracy built on self-interest. Although James Madison believed in the existence of a "public good" and a "true interest of [the] country," he had adopted enough of the adversary logic to conclude that no government could eliminate the "causes of faction"—self-love and self-interest combined with differing economic circumstances. The task he set the framers of the Constitution was not the abolition of self-interested behavior but the "regulation of the various and interfering interests" in a way that actually "involves the spirit of party and faction in the necessary and ordinary operations of the government."[10]

Modern political theorists have taken this line of development to its logical conclusion. In current adversary theory, there is no common good or public interest. Voters pursue their individual interests by making demands on the political system in proportion to the intensity of their feelings. Politicians, also pursuing their own interests, adopt policies that buy them votes, thus ensuring accountability. In order to stay in office, politicians act like entrepreneurs and brokers, looking for formulas that satisfy as many, and alienate as few, interests as possible. From the interchange between self-interested voters and self-interested brokers emerge decisions that come as close as possible to a balanced aggregation of individual interests.

At bottom, this theory of adversary democracy is remarkably similar to modern laissez-faire economics. Following a modified version of Adam Smith's *Wealth of Nations*, laissez-faire economists not only accept the "marketplace" vision of a society based on self-interest but make it an ideal. They believe either that the invisible hand of supply and demand will aggregate millions of selfish desires into the common good, or that, because no one can know the common good, the aggregation of selfish desires is the best substitute. Like these economists, many modern political scientists also believe either that equally weighted votes, majority rule, and electoral competition can in principle aggregate millions of selfish political desires into one common good, or that, because no one can know the common good, the aggregation of selfish political desires is the best substitute.

Because both adversary democracy and laissez-faire economics are founded on self-interest, there is no room in either system for arguments that the interests of some people are better than those of others. Each individual's interests are of equal value. Politically, therefore, each individual's interests should carry equal weight. Assuming further that each individual is the best analyst of his or her interests, the adversary system settles conflicts with the formula of one-citizen/one-equally-weighted-vote. The central egalitarian ideal in an adversary democracy becomes the equal protection of interests, guaranteed by the equal distribution of power through the vote. The implication of combining the goal of equal protection of interests with the assumption that individuals always protect their own interests better than they protect other people's interests is that only a fully equal distribution of power can guarantee equal protection.

The logic of equal value, equal weight, and equal power has pushed adversary democracies both into extending the vote to more and more members of the polity and into efforts to ensure that each vote carries equal weight. This same logic inevitably produces disillusionment, however, since even an equal vote cannot guarantee equal power.

The adversary system also has another, more serious, drawback. The mechanical aggregation of conflicting selfish desires is the very core of an adversary system. But this idea verges on moral bankruptcy. It accepts, and makes no attempt to change, the foundations of selfish desire. Because interests often conflict in the modern nation-state, a fundamentally adversary system of electoral representation based on competing interests, equally weighted votes, and majority rule is probably the least dangerous method of managing these conflicting interests. Yet safety and practicality do not make this kind of democracy morally satisfying. Adversary de-

mocracies at the national level are therefore under continual pressure from their citizens to pursue unitary goals that will tie the nation together by emphasizing common interests and political friendship. . . .

Common Interests

No group of people, however small, ever has completely identical interests. Such a state would require not only that one course of action meet the enlightened preferences of every participant, but also that in every conceivable policy choice that could come before them, the enlightened preferences of every participant be the same. This condition is virtually never met.

Many groups can have a common interest on a particular policy. That is, if all the participants knew what their enlightened preferences were, they might indeed find that these preferences led them all to support one policy over another. Yet the participants' interests would still not be identical. They would probably have different reasons for preferring the policy, be willing to incur different costs to gain their preference, and have different enlightened preferences about how the policy could best be implemented. These differences might well become significant as other, hardly separable issues came up for decision.

A perfect unitary democracy would, over time, require identical interests—common interests on every conceivable policy that could come before the group. Perfect unitary democracy will therefore never be found in the real world. Neither will perfect adversary democracy, which assumes conflicts of interest on all issues except the peaceful settlement of disputes. These two ideal types are simply useful end points for a spectrum on which we can array real polities. Because interests are in fact never absolutely identical, I will use the term "identical interests" only when speaking theoretically, to express the distance between an actual situation and that theoretical point. In describing real situations, I will refer to "common interests" in a particular policy or policies and to "similar interests" on a wide range of issues.

If we allow both individual and group altruism into the definition of interest, then individuals may come to have common interests for any of three reasons. First, and most obviously, their private interests and ideals can overlap either by coincidence or because they arise from similar circumstances. Second, empathy can lead individuals to make one another's good their own. Individual interests do not then overlap; instead, the separate individuals fuse, in a sense, into one. Third, several individuals may adopt as their own the good not of one another but of the whole polity. This process can have two forms. The public-spirited can adopt as their own the good of others in their group, not as specific individuals, but as a collectivity. Thus they may favor a policy that promotes the group's general welfare even when it provides them with no personal benefits and may involve them in considerable cost or inconvenience. A second way of making the good of the whole one's own is to adopt as one's own the goal or function of the collectivity itself. Carried to its logical conclusion, this approach could lead to decisions that were against the selfish interest of every member of the polity. Thus, if the function of an academic department were to advance knowledge, its members could in principle conclude that the best way to do this would be for them all to resign and give up their places to more competent teachers and scholars. Adopting the good of the whole is therefore in some situations clearly not quite the same thing as making the good of the other individuals in the polity one's own. Yet if two or more people make the good of the whole their own, and if they understand this good in the same way, they will have a common interest.

The degree to which there are common interests in a democracy determines many of its other features: the kind of equality it seeks, its decision rule, and the intimacy of its relations. A democracy of common interests will emphasize equality of status rather than equal protection of interests, consensus rather than majority rule, and face-to-face contact rather than the more impersonal mechanisms of referenda or electoral representation. . . .

The Decision Rule: Consensus Versus Majority Rule

The decision rule of consensus also baffles most people who think in adversary terms. Only a polity in which individuals have many of their interests in common can use a consensus rule on every issue without its resulting in impasse or in extreme social coercion. When individual interests are in irresolvable conflict, a consensus requirement guarantees either deadlock in favor of the status quo or social pressure on dissenters to go along. These are admittedly serious drawbacks, but in practice, moments of common interest occur far more frequently than adversary theorists assume. When a decision encompasses problems with a correct solution, or when participants in a decision can sympathize with one another or make the good of the whole their own, common interests are possible. Most tribes, committees, and intimates, all groups where these conditions hold, make their decisions by reaching a consensus on each issue. Globally, consensual democracy is still at least as common as majority-rule democracy. In non-Western societies, the local village council, the corporation, and even the national legislature will consciously and frequently make their decisions by consensus. Even in Western societies, consensual decision making is far more common than we usually realize, partly because it is often disguised behind formal majoritarian procedures. The assumption of common interests and the dynamic of face-to-face contact can lead not only friends but business organizations, committees of all sorts, academic departments, and even legislatures to make most of their decisions by consensus. For most human beings, the face-to-face, consensual decision among equals is the everyday experience, and majority rule the exception.

I will use the term "consensus" to describe a form of decision making in which, after discussion, one or more members of the assembly sum up prevailing sentiment, and if no objections are voiced, this becomes agreed-on policy. Although the formal logic of consensus may be technically the same as that of a "una-nimity rule," the two terms conjure up quite different processes. In a consensual process, as under a strict unanimity rule, the determined opposition of one member can usually prevent collective action, and if the group acts in spite of that opposition, the dissenter will not be obligated by the group decision. But the consensual process differs in form from a strict unanimity rule in that no vote is taken, and it differs in purpose from strict unanimity rule in that people usually adopt it when they expect to agree, not when they expect to differ.

This last distinction is vital. The informal, nonquantitative, consensual process is not designed to protect individual interests. If the members of a group can acknowledge that their interests conflict, they can then agree unanimously to make a bargain, giving one part of the group the goods it desires on the condition that the other part of the group gets other goods that it desires ("side payments"). But collectivities whose members have many common interests often develop norms that make it difficult even to suggest that individual interests might conflict. Groups that are accustomed to using consensus find it hard to recognize and to legitimate conflicts of interest by allowing bargains, distributing benefits proportionately, taking turns, or making decisions by majority rule. Just like couples who feel they must act on every issue as if they were one, consensual groups often find themselves unable to shift to adversary techniques when their members' interests begin to conflict. Such groups end up either reinforcing the status quo or, in an informal and unacknowledged manner, forcing the minority to go along.

The spectrum which stretches from the unitary to the adversary polity does not end with the latter. When interests conflict on a sufficiently large number of interests and along sufficiently consistent lines, even majority rule becomes unworkable, because the losers refuse to be bound by the result. At this point, no polity is possible. Yet collective decisions are still possible on specific issues as long as all parties agree. Thus, as we shall see, the unanimity requirement appears in different forms at both extremes of the spectrum running from trust to mistrust. What I will term

consensus, as distinct from a formal unanimity rule, appears only in a unitary democracy.

Level of Intimacy: Face-to-Face Contact Versus the Secret Ballot

There is no logical reason why individuals who meet face to face should not see most human relations in terms of conflict, make decisions by majority vote, or stress the equal protection of interests in the resolution of those decisions. Experience teaches us, however, that in practice face-to-face contact increases the perception of likeness, encourages decision making by consensus, and perhaps even enhances equality of status. It does this in a variety of ways. On the positive side, it seems to increase the actual congruence of interests by encouraging the empathy by which individual members make one another's interests their own. It also encourages the recognition of common interest by allowing subtleties of direct communication. On the negative side, it increases the possibility of conformity through intimidation, resulting in a false or managed consensus.

Rousseau believed that the groups of peasants he saw in Switzerland "regulating affairs of the State under an oak, and always acting wisely" were "among the happiest people in the world."[11] But whatever the effects of bringing the Swiss together under an oak, bringing the members of my two small democracies together in a meeting hall did not invariably make them the happiest people in the world. When citizens have a common interest, face-to-face contact—which allows debate, empathy, listening, learning, changing opinions, and a burst of solidarity when a decision is reached—can bring real joy. But in the face of conflict, emotions turn sour.

Even in representative systems, an aversion to conflict leads citizens to avoid discussing politics; in face-to-face assemblies, similar aversions have more profound effects. Some people do not attend meetings because they know in advance that they will get upset. If they do attend, they may still need the support of a faction before they can find courage enough to enter the fray. They may hold back what they have to say until they lose control and become too angry to listen. Fear of conflict leads those with influence in a meeting to suppress important issues rather than letting them surface and cause disruption. It leads them also to avoid the appearance of conflict by pressing for unanimity. If these techniques are successful, the consensual decision that results does not reflect a common interest. For these reasons, in both the town meeting and the democratic workplace, face-to-face decision making worked better in times of common interest than it did in times of irreconcilable conflict. When a polity has to handle many questions of conflicting interest, most people prefer a secret ballot and a method of combining preferences, like referenda or electoral representation, that puts some distance between them and their opponents.

Face-to-face meetings of all citizens are in any case impossible on a nationwide level, although meetings of smaller groups can still have a significant influence on national policy. All parliamentary systems, for instance, end up with face-to-face meetings of elected representatives. Although the incentives to finding a common interest are usually partially offset by the personality, professional socialization, and structural position of the representatives, face-to-face interaction in a legislature can take on the same character as in a direct town meeting or workers' assembly. Unitary or pseudo-unitary moments in a primarily adversary system often derive from these face-to-face pressures. If decisions in industry or government were decentralized to the level of workers' councils and neighborhood assemblies, and if these assemblies met face to face, as is to some degree the case in Yugoslavia, this too would affect what is now primarily an adversary system.

Notes

1. Although Aristotle (*Ethics,* 1155a22–23) distinguishes between justice and friendship (e.g., 1155a23), he does not seem to allocate the first to the political and the second to the purely personal realm. Kinds of friendship correspond to kinds of community, not only below the level of political community (1160a28) but also, it seems, at that level. Quantitative equality, for instance, characterizes the friendship (as well as the justice) appropriate to a democracy, while proportional equality characterizes the friendship (as well as the justice) appropriate to a monarchy and aristocracy (*Ethics* 1161a1off., and *Politics* 1317b1off.).

2. Aristotle, *Ethics,* 1156b9. See Adkins (1963, p. 37ff.) on this passage.

3. Aristotle, *Politics,* 1261b18–19.

4. It is unclear how often the Athenian assembly actually made decisions by consensus rather than by majority rule. It seems most likely that a formal majority rule was joined to a strong informal preference for unanimity.

5. Aristotle, *Ethics,* 1155a24ff. The equation of unanimity and friendship must have been a common maxim, or at least a commonly accepted concept, for Aristotle also writes: "Unanimity [*homonoia*] seems, then, to be political friendship [*philia*], as indeed it is *commonly held to be*" (*Ethics* 1167b2ff.; my emphasis).

Havelock contends that the central ideal of the Greek "liberals" was "natural amity . . . the basic identity of interest among human beings" (1957, p. 222; see also passim and pp. 222–247, 310–313, 379, 393, 402). This is in spite of the fact that some of these "liberals" (e.g., Callicles in Plato's *Gorgias* and Thrasymachus in *The Republic*) were more than familiar with the language of "interest" and "advantage."

6. Aristotle, *Ethics,* 1167a26–28.

7. Euripides' *Phoenician Maidens,* quoted in Sabine *A History of Political Thought* (New York: Henry Holt, 1950), p. 26.

8. Plato, *Menexenus,* 238e.

9. In regard to majority rule, Locke also argues that the majority has a "right" to conclude the rest because every individual implicitly agreed that the community should act as one body (II.8.96). John Locke, *Two Treatises of Government* [1689], Peter Laslett, ed. (New York: New American Library, 1965).

10. James Madison, "Ten Federalist," *The Federalist Papers* [1787] (New York: New American Library, 1961), p. 79.

11. Rousseau, *The Social Contract* [1762], G. D. H. Cole, trans. (New York: Dutton, 1950), p. 102.

Strong Democracy

Benjamin Barber

Benjamin Barber's conception of citizenship focuses on the quality of interaction among citizens of a democratic community. Before citizens can forge a common vision from their differing perspectives and settle on a plan of action, they must understand other people's needs and aspirations and be willing to accommodate them. A grass-roots participatory mode of self-government—a strong democracy in Barber's terminology—is the only form of political association that achieves this high quality of social interaction. Barber calls modern liberal democracies—that is, governmental systems that are more liberal than democratic—thin or weak democracy. In our current system citizens, who are often guided by their own self-interest, elect representatives by majority vote, and these representatives form public policy without the supervision of the citizenry. What is missing is a vision of the common good and citizen self-government. Barber begins his essay by presenting his alternative—strong democracy. A strong democracy relies on a democratic community that is constructed and controlled by an active citizenry, which educates its members in the art of citizenship and inspires a sense of civic responsibility. Involvement in the community is the means by which citizens transform their private interests into a conception of the common good. This is accomplished, Barber explains, primarily through talk, the kind of talking and listening that builds a common vision and consolidates a common purpose. Barber then proposes a decision-making process through which citizens are able to form a common will and act in concert. In the last section Barber reiterates the common theme of communitarian thinkers that human beings can find freedom and fulfillment only in community.

The future of democracy lies with strong democracy—with the revitalization of a form of community that is not collectivistic, a form of public reasoning that is not conformist, and a set of civic institutions that is compatible with modern society. Strong democracy is defined by politics in the participatory mode: literally, it is self-government by citizens rather than representative government in the name of citizens. Active citizens govern themselves directly here, not necessarily at every level and in every instance, but frequently enough and in particular when basic policies are being decided and when significant power is being deployed. Self-government is carried on through institutions designed to facilitate ongoing civic participation in agenda-setting, deliberation, legislation, and policy implementation (in the form of "common work"). Strong democracy does not place endless faith in the capacity of individuals to govern themselves, but it affirms with Machiavelli that the multitude will on the whole be as wise as or even wiser than princes and with Theodore Roosevelt that "the majority of the plain people will day in and day out make fewer mistakes in governing themselves than any smaller body of men will make in trying to govern them."

Considered as a response to the dilemmas of the political condition, strong democracy can be given the following formal definition: *strong democracy in the participatory mode resolves conflict in the absence of an independent ground through a participatory process of ongoing, proximate self-legislation and the creation of a political community capable of transforming dependent pri-*

From Benjamin Barber, *Strong Democracy* (Berkeley: University of California Press, 1994), pp. 150–155, 173–178, 198–202, 209–212, 213–217. Copyright © 1984 The Regents of the University of California. Reprinted by permission of the University of California Press. Some footnotes omitted.

vate individuals into free citizens and partial and private interests into public goods.

The crucial terms in this strong formulation of democracy are *activity, process, self-legislation, creation,* and *transformation.* Where weak democracy eliminates conflict . . . , represses it . . . , or tolerates it . . . , strong democracy *transforms conflict.* It turns dissensus into an occasion for mutualism and private interest into an epistemological tool of public thinking.

Participatory politics deals with public disputes and conflicts of interest by subjecting them to a neverending process of deliberation, decision, and action. Each step in the process is a flexible part of ongoing procedures that are embedded in concrete historical conditions and social and economic actualities. In place of the search for a prepolitical independent ground or for an immutable rational plan, strong democracy relies on participation in an evolving problem-solving community that creates public ends where there were none before by means of its own activity and of its own existence as a focal point of the quest for mutual solutions. In such communities, public ends are neither extrapolated from absolutes nor "discovered" in a preexisting "hidden consensus." They are literally forged through the act of public participation, created through common deliberation and common action and the effect that deliberation and action have on interests, which change shape and direction when subjected to these participatory processes.

Strong democracy, then, seems potentially capable of transcending the limitations of representation and the reliance on surreptitious independent grounds without giving up such defining democratic values as liberty, equality, and social justice. Indeed, these values take on richer and fuller meanings than they can ever have in the instrumentalist setting of liberal democracy. For the strong democratic solution to the political condition issues out of a self-sustaining dialectic of participatory civic activity and continuous community-building in which freedom and equality are nourished and given political being. Community grows out of participation and at the same time makes participation possible; civic activity educates

individuals how to think publicly as citizens even as citizenship informs civic activity with the required sense of publicness and justice. Politics becomes its own university, citizenship its own training ground, and participation its own tutor. Freedom is what comes out of this process, not what goes into it. Liberal and representative modes of democracy make politics an activity of specialists and experts whose only distinctive qualification, however, turns out to be simply that they engage in politics— that they encounter others in a setting that requires action and where they have to find a way to act in concert. Strong democracy is the politics of amateurs, where every man is compelled to encounter every other man without the intermediary of expertise.

This universality of participation—every citizen his own politician—is essential, because the "Other" is a construct that becomes real to an individual only when he encounters it directly in the political arena. He may confront it as an obstacle or approach it as an ally, but it is an inescapable reality in the way of and on the way to common decision and common action. *We* also remains an abstraction when individuals are represented either by politicians or as symbolic wholes. The term acquires a sense of concreteness and simple reality only when individuals redefine themselves as citizens and come together directly to resolve a conflict or achieve a purpose or implement a decision. Strong democracy creates the very citizens it depends upon *because* it depends upon them, because it permits the representation neither of *me* nor of *we,* because it mandates a permanent confrontation between the *me* as citizen and the "Other" as citizen, forcing *us* to think in common and act in common. The citizen is by definition a *we*-thinker, and to think of the *we* is always to transform how interests are perceived and goods defined.

This progression suggests how intimate the ties are that bind participation to community. Citizenship is not a mask to be assumed or shed at will. It lacks the self-conscious mutability of a modern social "role" as Goffman might construe it. In strong democratic politics, participation is a way of defining the self, just as citizenship is a way of living. The old liberal notion, shared even by radical democrats such as Tom Paine, was that a society is "composed of distinct, unconnected individuals [who are] continually meeting, crossing, uniting, opposing, and separating from each other, as accident, interest, and circumstances shall direct." Such a conception repeats the Hobbesian error of setting participation and civic activity apart from community. Yet participation without community, participation in the face of deracination, participation by victims or bondsmen or clients or subjects, participation that is uninformed by an evolving idea of a "public" and unconcerned with the nurturing of self-responsibility, participation that is fragmentary, part-time, half-hearted, or impetuous—these are all finally sham, and their failure proves nothing.

It has in fact become a habit of the shrewder defenders of representative democracy to chide participationists and communitarians with the argument that enlarged public participation in politics produces no great results. Once empowered, the masses do little more than push private interests, pursue selfish ambitions, and bargain for personal gain, the liberal critics assert. Such participation is the work of prudent beasts and is often less efficient than the ministrations of representatives who have a better sense of the public's appetites than does the public itself. But such a course in truth merely gives the people all the insignia and none of the tools of citizenship and then convicts them of incompetence. Social scientists and political elites have all too often indulged themselves in this form of hypocrisy. They throw referenda at the people without providing adequate information, full debate, or prudent insulation from money and media pressures and then pillory them for their lack of judgment. They overwhelm the people with the least tractable problems of mass society—busing, inflation, tax structures, nuclear safety, right-to-work legislation, industrial waste disposal, environmental protection (all of which the representative elites themselves have utterly failed to deal with)— and then carp at their uncertainty or indecisiveness or the simple-mindedness with which they muddle through to a decision. But what general would shove rifles into the hands of civilians, hurry them off to battle, and then call them cowards when they are overrun by the enemy?

Strong democracy is not government by "the people" or government by "the masses," because a people are not yet a citizenry and masses are only nominal freemen who do not in fact govern themselves. Nor is participation to be understood as random activity by maverick cattle caught up in the same stampede or as minnow-school movement by clones who wiggle in unison. As with so many central political terms, the idea of participation has an intrinsically normative dimension—a dimension that is circumscribed by citizenship. Masses make noise, citizens deliberate; masses behave, citizens act; masses collide and intersect, citizens engage, share, and contribute. At the moment when "masses" start deliberating, acting, sharing, and contributing, they cease to be masses and become citizens. Only then do they "participate."

Or, to come at it from the other direction, to be a citizen *is* to participate in a certain conscious fashion that presumes awareness of and engagement in activity with others. This consciousness alters attitudes and lends to participation that sense of the *we* I have associated with community. To participate *is* to create a community that governs itself, and to create a self-governing community *is* to participate. Indeed, from the perspective of strong democracy, the two terms *participation* and *community* are aspects of one single mode of social being: citizenship. Community without participation first breeds unreflected consensus and uniformity, then nourishes coercive conformity, and finally engenders unitary collectivism of a kind that stifles citizenship and the autonomy on which political activity depends. Participation without community breeds mindless enterprise and undirected, competitive interest-mongering. Community without participation merely rationalizes collectivism, giving it an aura of legitimacy. Participation without community merely rationalizes individualism, giving it the aura of democracy.

This is not to say that the dialectic between participation and community is easily institutionalized. Individual civic activity (participation) and the public association formed through civic activity (the community) call up two strikingly different worlds. The former is the world of autonomy, individualism, and agency; the latter is the world of sociability, community, and interaction. The world views of individualism and communalism remain at odds; and institutions that can facilitate the search for common ends without sabotaging the individuality of the searchers, and that can acknowledge pluralism and conflict as starting points of the political process without abdicating the quest for a world of common ends, may be much more difficult to come by than a pretty paragraph about the dialectical interplay between individual participation and community. Yet it is just this dialectical balance that strong democracy claims to strike. . . .

At the heart of strong democracy is talk. As we shall see, talk is not mere speech. It refers here to every human interaction that involves language or linguistic symbols. Talk has been at the root of the Western idea of politics since Aristotle identified *logos* as the peculiarly human and peculiarly social faculty that divided the human species from animals otherwise defined by similar needs and faculties. But as talk became a synonym for politics, its meanings became as multifarious as those of politics.

Modern democratic liberals certainly maintain the close identity of politics and talk, but they do so by reducing talk to the dimensions of their smallish politics and turning it into an instrument of symbolic exchange between avaricious but prudent beasts. "Descartes, Locke, and Newton took away the world," laments Yeats in his *Explorations*, "and gave us its excrement instead." Hobbes, Bentham, and Laswell take away talk and give us instead noise: animal expletives meant to signify bargaining positions in a world of base competition. The first ten books of *Leviathan* offer a scrupulously reductionist lexicography that gives to every term in the language of rhetoric an austere referent in the physics of psychology. Within three centuries, abetted by stimulus-response models of social behavior, by nominalist and behaviorist models of linguistics, and by logical-positivist models of social science, this lexicography has impoverished political talk, both as a medium of politics itself and as a tool for rendering political processes intelligible. Yet talk remains central to politics, which would ossify completely without its

creativity, its variety, its openness and flexibility, its inventiveness, its capacity for discovery, its subtlety and complexity, its eloquence, its potential for empathy and affective expression, and its deeply paradoxical (some would say dialectical) character that displays man's full nature as a purposive, interdependent, and active being.

Before embarking on a detailed discussion of the functions of talk in democracy, I want to make three general observations. First, strong democratic talk entails listening no less than speaking; second, it is affective as well as cognitive; and third, its intentionalism draws it out of the domain of pure reflection into the world of action.

In considering recent liberal theory and the idea of democracy as the politics of interest, one finds it easy enough to see how talk might be confused with speech and speech reduced to the articulation of interest by appropriate signs. Yet talk as communication obviously involves receiving as well as expressing, hearing as well as speaking, and empathizing as well as uttering. The liberal reduction of talk to speech has unfortunately inspired political institutions that foster the articulation of interests but that slight the difficult art of listening. It is far easier for representatives to speak for us than to listen for us (we do not send representatives to concerts or lectures), so that in a predominantly representative system the speaking function is enhanced while the listening function is diminished. The secret ballot allows the voter to express himself but not to be influenced by others or to have to account for his private choices in a public language.[1] The Anglo-American adversary system, expressed in legislative politics, in the judicial system, and even in the separation of powers into contending branches, also puts a premium on speaking and a penalty on listening. The aim in adversarial proceedings is to prevail—to score verbal points and to overcome one's interlocutors. In fact, speech in adversary systems is a form of aggression, simply one more variety of power. It is the war of all against all carried on by other means.

The participatory process of self-legislation that characterizes strong democracy attempts to balance adversary politics by nourishing the mutualistic art of listening. "I will listen" means to the strong democrat not that I will scan my adversary's position for weaknesses and potential trade-offs, nor even (as a minimalist might think) that I will tolerantly permit him to say whatever he chooses. It means, rather, "I will put myself in his place, I will try to understand, I will strain to hear what makes us alike, I will listen for a common rhetoric evocative of a common purpose or a common good."

Good listeners may turn out to be bad lawyers, but they make adept citizens and excellent neighbors. Liberal democrats tend to value speech, and are thus concerned with formal equality. Listeners, on the other hand, feel that an emphasis on speech enhances natural inequalities in individuals' abilities to speak with clarity, eloquence, logic, and rhetoric. Listening is a mutualistic art that by its very practice enhances equality. The empathetic listener becomes more like his interlocutor as the two bridge the differences between them by conversation and mutual understanding. Indeed, one measure of healthy political talk is the amount of *silence* it permits and encourages, for silence is the precious medium in which reflection is nurtured and empathy can grow. Without it, there is only the babble of raucous interests and insistent rights vying for the deaf ears of impatient adversaries. The very idea of rights—the right to speak, the right to get on the record, the right to be heard—precludes silence. The Quaker meeting carries a message for democrats, but they are often too busy articulating their interests to hear it.

A second major requirement of talk in strong democracy is that it encompass the affective as well as the cognitive mode. Philosophers and legal theorists have been particulary guilty of overrationalizing talk in their futile quest for a perfectly rational world mediated by perfectly rational forms of speech. Having abandoned Wittgenstein's later wariness about language and its limits, they are forever trying to domesticate unruly words with the discipline of logic, trying to imprison speech in reason, trying to get talk not merely to reveal but to define rationality. Bruce Ackerman's is only the most candid and explicit of the recent attempts to impose on language a set of "neutral constraints" that make speech

the parent of justice.[2] This verbal eugenics, in which justice is produced by the controlled breeding of words, threatens to displace entirely the idea of justice as the product of political judgment. Most philosophers would agree with Bertrand Russell that "real life" is "a long second-best, a perpetual compromise between the ideal and the possible," whereas the "world of pure reason knows no compromise, no practical limitations, no barrier to the creative activity embodying in splendid edifices the passionate aspirations after the perfect form." Thus the quest for philosophical justice becomes "an escape from the dreary exile of the actual world."[3] Talk disciplined by philosophy is not only fit to enter the world of pure reason, it is capable, as the common denominator between politics and philosophy, of taking politics with it. However, for the most part this brave experiment in otherworldliness has only impoverished politics without ever achieving the elevation of talk.

The philosophers are not really the primary culprits, however. They follow even as they lead, and if they have not always recognized, in Kolakowski's words, that "man as a cognitive being is only part of man as a whole," it is in part because the political liberals whom they wish to succor have persuaded them that man as a creature of interest is the whole man and that the rationalization of interest is the philosophical task that needs doing. The philosophers can hardly be blamed then for developing notions of rationality rooted in instrumental prudence and notions of justice legitimized by enlightened self-interest. How can speech be anything but cognitive under these circumstances?

Stripped of such artificial disciplines, however, talk appears as a mediator of affection and affiliation as well as of interest and identity, of patriotism as well as of individuality. It can build community as well as maintain rights and seek consensus as well as resolve conflict. It offers, along with meanings and significations, silences, rituals, symbols, myths, expressions and solicitations, and a hundred other quiet and noisy manifestations of our common humanity. Strong democracy seeks institutions that can give these things a voice— and an ear.

The third issue that liberal theorists have

underappreciated is the complicity of talk in action. With talk we can invent alternative futures, create mutual purposes, and construct competing visions of community. Its potentialities thrust talk into the realm of intentions and consequences and render it simultaneously more provisional and more concrete than philosophers are wont to recognize. Their failure of imagination stems in part from the passivity of thin democratic politics and in part from the impatience of speculative philosophy with contingency, which entails possibility as well as indeterminateness. But significant political effects and actions are possible only to the extent that politics is embedded in a world of fortune, uncertainty, and contingency.

Political talk is not talk *about* the world; it is talk that makes and remakes the world. The posture of the strong democrat is thus "pragmatic" in the sense of William James's definition of pragmatism as "the attitude of looking away from first things, principles, 'categories,' supposed necessities; and of looking toward last things, fruits, consequences, facts."[4] James's pragmatist "turns toward concreteness and adequacy, toward facts, toward action, and toward power. . . . [Pragmatism thus] means the open air and possibilities of nature, as against dogma, artificiality and the pretense of finality in truth." Strong democracy is pragmatism translated into politics in the participatory mode. Although James did not pursue the powerful political implications of his position, he was moved to write: "See already how democratic [pragmatism] is. Her manners are as various and flexible, her resources as rich and endless, and her conclusions as friendly as those of mother nature."[5] The active, future-oriented disposition of strong democratic talk embodies James's instinctive sense of pragmatism's political implications. Future action, not a priori principle, constitutes such talk's principal (but not principled) concern. . . .

Liberal representative democrats commonly assume that democracy means democratic *choice*. In an otherwise admirable little essay on the dilemmas of modern democracy, Stanley Hoffmann thus assures us that "politics is about choice."[6] And of all the institutions that we associate with democratic government in the West, none seems so central as voting, which many social scientists construe as choice epitomized. Talk to these thinkers is little more than a deliberative preliminary to the act of choosing. Representation, on the one hand, plays a dominant role for them because with representation votes can be counted, positions can be quantified, and power can be delegated. The deliberative process, on the other hand, lends itself neither to quantification nor delegation.

Those who identify democracy with decision-making through choice or voting capture the urgency of action without which politics becomes an abstract process that touches neither power nor reality. Yet to limit democracy to a selection among preferences and to think of efficient decision-making as its sole measure is to ignore all but the thinnest features of democracy. The reduction of democracy to voting implies that a ready-made agenda exists when none does and prompts the replication of private interests at higher levels where they are called *majorities* and *minorities* and where, as a consequence, they do even more damage. Majoritarianism is a tribute to the failure of democracy: to our inability to create a politics of mutualism that can overcome private interests. It is thus finally the democracy of desperation, an attempt to salvage decision-making from the anarchy of adversary politics. It is hardly surprising then that majoritarianism is often regarded as one of the great banes of democracy. In every age critics have had to do little more than link democracy to this threat in order to persuade the thinking and the wary that popular rule could only be a way station on the road to tyranny.

Conceiving of decision as majoritarian preference not only reduces public goods to weak aggregations of private interests and mutualism to the rambling willfulness of transient majorities, it also is unresponsive to intensity and commitment. Unable to recognize qualitative differences in voters' motivations, it precipitates one of representative democracy's classical dilemmas: that the weak and complacent majority can unthinkingly overrule an impassioned and obdurate minority and thereby destabilize the regime. Talk may seem inconsequential, but it measures intensity. Voting does not.

The briefest survey of the theoretical and the empirical literature suggests that thin democracy—which reduces decision-making to voting for elected representatives and relies on the institutions of majoritarianism and adversary politics (the single-member district, the two-party system, the convention system)—is anything but the generic of democratic decision-making. Brian Barry lists seven models of decision in his *Political Argument*: decision by combat, by bargaining, by discussion on merits, by voting, by chance, by contest, and by authoritative determination.[7] In recent years, students of comparative politics have introduced a provocative distinction between competitive (adversary) systems and "consociational" systems. The latter are defined by a "non-competitive 'cartelized' pluralist pattern" in which "amicable agreement" plays the leading role. The consociational model avoids the fractiousness of majority decision through a process of what we might call holistic bargaining, where agreements are limited to issues on which a genuine mutualism is possible. Another model is that of authoritative interpretation. Here a chairperson's "sense of the meeting" displaces actual votes and obviates the need for factions to form around adversary interests, or an executive rendering of the results of a complex balloting process imposes consensus upon diversity. . . .

Strong democracy offers an alternative model that incorporates certain of the virtues of liberal democracy's view of decision as choice in the face of necessity but promotes a richer, more mutualistic understanding of what it means to develop political judgment and to exercise political will. Indeed, strong democratic decision-making is predicated on will rather than choice and on judgment rather than preference. Strong democracy understands decision-making to be a facet of man as maker and as creator and consequently focuses on public willing. Liberal democrats, like the economists and analytic philosophers they have taken into their service, conceive the decision exclusively in terms of rational choice. Thus they render the critical democratic question as "What will we choose?" Strong democ-

racy poses the alternative question, "How do we will?" The challenge here is not how to make correct choices but how to make choices correctly, and this in turn is a question of judgment. Following Jean-Jacques Rousseau, strong democrats prefer the language of legitimate willing to the language of right choosing. To render a political judgment is not to exclaim "I prefer" or "I want" or "I choose such and such" but rather to say, "I will a world in which such and such is possible." To decide is thus to will into being a world that the community must experience in common: it is to create a common future, if only for selfish ends. In place of "I want Y," the strong democrat must say "Y will be good for us," a locution that is tested not by the incorrigibility of Y's philosophical origins but by the assent it finds in the community that must live with it.

It may now be evident that decision as willing belongs to the domain of power and action in a way that decision as choosing cannot. To will is to create a world or to bring about events in a world, and this act entails (and thus defines) power—the ability to create or modify reality. Our preferences are merely contemplative or speculative until we make them subjects of our wills and transform them into actions. In treating decision-making as an activity of the will, strong democrats honor the tradition of Rousseau and Kant, for whom the aim was not to choose common ends or to discover common interests but to will a common world by generating a common will. Legitimacy here is awarded not to the virtuous interest but to the general will, the will that incarnates a democratic community that is comprised in turn of the wills of autonomous citizens. The issue is not "I want" versus "you want" but "I want" versus "we will." More than a play of words is involved here, for conflicts of interest, while subject to bargaining, are finally intractable: my interest and your interest are separated forever by the particularity of me and you. The conflict of wills, on the other hand, is a contest over competing visions of a single possible future. However incompatible our wants, the world we will into existence can only be one world—a common arena in which our wants and interests will be satisfied or thwarted.

The fact that there can only be one world

(whereas there can be innumerable interests) makes the contest of wills far more difficult and far more consequential than the contest of interests; but by the same token, it is much more tractable. From the perspective of radical individualism, every interest may seem equally legitimate. Interests can all coexist in the world of reflective reason; one is as good as the next. But wills cannot all be equally legitimate in the same sense, because by willing one affects the world, and the world is finally one—our world—and can only be as legitimate as the process that willed it into being. With interests, we may ask: "Do you prefer A or B or C?" With wills, we must ask: "What sort of world do you will our common world to be?"

The second question may seem on the surface little more than a reformulation of the first. But it is a crucial reformulation because it subjects otherwise incommensurable interests to the test of something very much like the categorical imperative; that is to say, it builds the Kantian test of universalizability into the political process. As private persons we may prefer all sorts of things, but as citizens we must be ready to will into existence a world in which our preferences can be gratified, and that turns out to be a quite different matter. I may want a big, fast, lead fuel–powered automobile, but I may not be prepared to will into existence a world with polluted air, concrete landscapes, depleted energy resources, and gruesome highway death tolls; and so as a citizen I may act contrary to my private preferences. By definition, no felt private interest can ever fail the test of preference, but many fail the test of will, which universalizes by virtue of its effect on reality. This fact should remind us again that politics in the participatory mode is the art of public seeing and of political judgment—of envisioning a common world in which every member of the community can live. It is the realm of "we will" rather than of "I want," and every attempt to reduce its role to the adjudication of interests will not only demean it but will rob it of any possibility of genuine public seeing.

If public seeing requires public willing, and if public willing cannot be reduced to mere choosing, then it seems evident that voting is the weakest rather than the strongest expression of the spirit of democracy and that the

majority principle corrupts rather than nourishes political judgment. Rousseau suggested that the will of the majority (even the will of all) was not necessarily an expression of the general will. Particular interests can be counted and aggregated, but a will that is general entails a seeing that is common—which is something that numbers can neither measure nor certify.

Public seeing and political judgment are served, on the other hand, by political talk. Talk engenders empathy, nourishes affection, and engages imagination. From it are drawn the myriad visions that compete for the common will; in it are found the past abridged and the future dreamed. As in a marriage ceremony, where the couple's "I do" bespeaks a relationship already established and commitments already made, so in the process of decision under a strong democracy the "we will" certifies a vision already commonly imagined. Like the marriage vows, it is also a test of whether promises will be translated into actions and a vision of the future into present reality. Talk creates, but it creates conditionally: its visions are provisional and the shared consequences they promise are hypothetical. As in a simulation, the stakes are not yet real. The decision converts promise into reality and compels us to give irrevocable shape and life to what were initially only imaginings. It tests us by asking whether we can *will* that which until now we have only imagined, whether we are willing to mold the contours of a future still rich in possibility to the austere shape of our one dream. . . .

If common decision is the test of common talk, then common action is the test of common decision. Common work is a community doing together what it has envisioned and willed together. Thus might the citizens of an eighteenth-century Swiss village have decided to declare war on a harassing neighbor and then armed themselves and conducted that war, thereby implementing their vote with their muskets. Thus might the members of a union talk their way to a strike decision and then embark jointly upon common strike action. Thus might pioneers in a frontier community decide they need a new schoolhouse and then raise it together, sealing their decision with their own labor. Thus might an urban neighborhood take over an abandoned lot and convert it with the equity of their sweat into an urban farm.

In each of these cases common action exerts a powerful integrating influence on the doers even as they are achieving common goals. So great is the power of common military service to build a community spirit that some have traced the birth of modern nationalism to such experiences and the philosopher William James was moved to call for a "moral equivalent of war" that might inspire in a people at peace the fraternal passions associated with common defense. Georges Sorel was no great friend of democracy, but he did perceive in the General Strike not so much an efficient engine of economic improvement as a sanctified incubator from which might emerge a "new Socialist man."[8] The "language of movement" that Sorel discovered in the strike in fact characterizes every common action aimed at realizing a common good.

A community that will not affix to its decisions the seal of common implementation, whether it pleads the rights of privacy or mere incompetence, may quickly lose its grip on the decision process. Deference to "experts" and "professionals" in government begins with the executive branch, but it can spread to the legislative branch and leave citizens feeling like "amateurs" who can play no other role than client in the civic process. The failure of democracy at the level of common action ultimately jeopardizes democracy at the level of decision and talk.

In practical terms, wherever conditions facilitate common legislation, there is the possibility of common execution and implementation. In urban neighborhoods the possibilities are endless: common action could transform trash lots into pocket parks or urban farms; rehabilitate unused storefronts as community education and recreation centers; develop neighborhood teams skilled in carpentry, masonry, plumbing, and electricity to cooperate with tenants and owners in urban homesteading ("sweat equity") programs; organize block associations, "crime-watch" units, shool crossing guards; and so forth. The potential of course depends on the vitality of the neighborhood . . . , but such projects are not only feasible but already in place in a number of cities.

Smaller towns and rural areas could engage in still more ambitious public projects, on the model of the traditional barn-buildings and roof-raisings. In 1974, for example, the town of Thebes, Illinois, used a grant from the Department of Agriculture to rebuild a historic courthouse, using local labor from the ranks of the unemployed to complete the project. "Workfare" is a controversial idea that in practice has been widely abused, but it rests on a promising idea: that government clients can become contributing citizens by participating in common civic work for public ends.[9] In any case, common work ought to engage all citizens, the fully employed as well as the unemployed. It is not a substitute for private labor on behalf of private interests. Rather it complements private labor, diverting some "private" energy into social tasks while making citizenship mean more than the expression of preferences and the pulling of levers.

Whatever form they take—and they can be organized at the national level . . . as well as at the local level—programs of common work are valuable both to participants and to the communities they serve. They make communities more self-sufficient and thus more self-governing and build a genuine sense of community in the neighborhood. Such programs thereby lower the pressure on central government to monopolize the governing and administering functions. By addressing residents as citizens rather than as clients or wards, these programs also cultivate civic ideals of service and direct attention away from fractious private interests. They provide dignifying work for those who in the present economy are disqualified by age or race or training from succeeding in the private sector. And they confront every kind of dependency with the discipline of self-help and thus lay the foundation for self-government in individuals as well as communities. Finally, by completing the cycle of citizenship begun with common deliberation and common legislation, these projects provide a complete institutional framework for civic action and civic responsibility at the national level—where participation is harder but the stakes are much higher.

There is a growing resentment of government's efforts to redistribute income by fiat; those from whom the government takes may not deserve what they have, but neither do those to whom the government gives earn what they get—nor, indeed, are they allowed to earn it. Forced to give and forced to take, citizens of Western democracies are allowed neither to contribute nor to earn. They are treated as exploited or exploiters, to be coddled or scolded by an avuncular bureaucracy, but rarely as citizens responsible for their own destinies. They in turn disparage their government as a grasping Scrooge or as a foolish spendthrift, dissociating themselves from its pathologies—which, they prefer not to realize, only mirror their own. Common work earns for each a common share and helps to justify the redistribution by which a society assures that shares will be held justly and in common. It permits giving and legitimates taking; indeed, it shows that these are but the economic reflection of duties and rights, which are the two sides of citizenship, just as it forces citizens to see their own faces, for better or for worse, in the fragile mirror of their government.

The key to politics as its own epistemology is, then, the idea of public seeing and public doing. Action in common is the unique province of citizens. Democracy is neither government by the majority nor representative rule: it is citizen self-government. Without citizens there can be only elite/mass politics. "Create citizens," cried Rousseau, "and you will have everything you need."[10] Politics in the participatory mode relies in the final instance on a strong conception of the citizen. It makes citizenship not a condition of participation but one of participation's richest fruits.

If government is but the greatest of all reflections on human nature and if, in Rousseau's inversion of Madison's claim, a people can be "no other than the nature of its government," then there is no better way to elucidate the difference between strong democracy and liberal democracy than by comparing how they portray human nature.[11] . . . The liberal portrait of human nature . . . construes the human essence as radically individual and solitary, as hedonistic and prudential, and as social only to the extent required by the quest for preservation and liberty in an adversary world of scarcity.

This conception presented human behavior as necessarily self-seeking, albeit in a premoral way. People entered into social relations only in order to exploit them for their own individual ends. Because modern liberal democracy is an accretion of democracy on a liberal philosophical base, American democratic theory has from it beginnings been weighted down by radical individualism. This association has created tensions within liberal democracy that, because they are rooted in conflicting notions of the human essence, cannot easily be resolved by politics. Marx took note of these tensions in the aftermath of the French Revolution. Rather than resurrecting freedom, he remarked, it produced a profound cleavage between man conceived as an individual member of civil society pursuing his private aims in conflict with others and man conceived as a citizen cooperating in "illusory" universals—namely, the "political state."[12]

In the *Grundrisse,* Marx offered an alternative construction of human nature as socially determined, a construction that links Aristotle to the modern sociological conception. "The human being," Marx wrote, "is in the most liberal sense a *zoön politikon,* not merely a gregarious [*geselliges*] animal, but an animal that can individuate itself only in the midst of society."[13]

The social construction of man is not, however, simply the antithesis of the individual construction formed in social-contract theory. It is dialectical, for it perceives an ongoing interaction by which world and man together shape each other. Peter Berger and Thomas Luckmann capture the dialectic perfectly in this post-Marxist depiction of man's social nature: "Man is biologically predestined to construct and inhabit a world with others. This world becomes for him the dominant and definitive reality. Its limits are set by nature, but once constructed, this world acts back upon nature. In the dialectic between nature and the socially constructed world the human organism itself is transformed. In this same dialectic, man produces reality and thereby produces himself."[14]

Strong democratic theory posits the social nature of human beings in the world and the dialectical interdependence of man and his government. As a consequence, it places human self-realization through mutual transformation at the center of the democratic process. Like the social reality it refracts, human nature is compound; it is potentially both benign and malevolent, both cooperative and antagonistic. Certain qualities enjoin a "degree of circumspection and distrust," as Madison prudently notes in *The Federalist Papers*; others may "justify a certain portion of esteem and confidence."[15] But all these qualities may be transformed by legitimate and illegitimate social and political forces. For man is a developmental animal—a creature with a compound and evolving telos whose ultimate destiny depends on how he interacts with those who share the same destiny. Such creatures possess neither fixed natures nor absolute, independently grounded notions of reality and right. They seem rather to follow what Alexander Bickel has called the Whig model of political life. This model posits that human nature is "flexible, pragmatic, slow-moving, and highly political" and therefore that politics will be a process of "untidy accommodation."[16]

Political animals interact socially in ways that abstract morals and metaphysics cannot account for. Their virtue is of another order, although the theorists who have defended this claim have been called everything from realists to immoralists for their trouble. Yet Montaigne caught the very spirit of social man when he wrote, "the virtue assigned to the affairs of the world is a virtue with many bends, angles, and elbows, so as to join and adapt itself to human weakness; mixed and artificial, not straight, clean, constant or purely innocent."[17]

If the human essence is social, then men and women have to choose not between independence or dependence but between citizenship or slavery. Without citizens, Rousseau warns, there will be neither free natural men nor satisfied solitaries—there will be "nothing but debased slaves, from the rulers of the state downwards."

To a strong democrat, Rousseau's assertion at the opening of his *Social Contract* that man is born free yet is everywhere in chains does not mean that man is free by nature but society enchains him.[18] It means rather that natural freedom is an abstraction, whereas dependency is the concrete human reality, and that the aim of politics must therefore be not to rescue natural freedom from politics but to invent and pursue artificial freedom within and through politics. Strong democracy aims not to disenthrall men but to legitimate their dependency by means of citizenship and to establish their political freedom by means of the democratic community.

In *Emile,* Rousseau wrote: "We are born weak, we need strength; we are born totally unprovided, we need aid; we are born stupid, we need judgment. Everything we do not have at our birth and which we need when we are grown is given us by education."[19] The corresponding political assertion would be: "We are born insufficient, we need cooperation; we are born with potential natures, we require society to realize them; we are born unequal, we need politics to make us equal; we are born part slave, part free, we can secure full liberty only through democratic community."

Citizenship and community are two aspects of a single political reality: men can only overcome their insufficiency and legitimize their dependency by forging a common consciousness. The road to autonomy leads through not around commonality. As George Bernard Shaw wrote: "When a man is at last brought face to face with himself by a brave individualism, he finds himself face to face, not with an individual, but with a species, and knows that to save himself he must save the race. He can have no life except a share in the life of the community."[20]

Notes

1. In *On Representative Government,* John Stuart Mill argues against the secret ballot. He notes that "in any political election, even by universal suffrage, the voter is under an absolute moral obligation to consider the interest of the public, not his private advantage, and give his vote to the best of his judgment, exactly as he were bound to do if he were the sole voter, and the election depended on him alone." The secret ballot, in which the voter consults only his private interests

and is not required to justify his actions publicly, corrupts civic responsibility. For a thoughtful argument against the secret ballot, see Andreas Teuber, "The Democratic Case against the Secret Ballot" (work in progress).

2. Bruce Ackerman puts the idea of neutral dialogue at the center of his theory of justice in *Social Justice and the Liberal State* (New York: Basic Books, 1980). However, his scheme ends up as apolitical and abstract as the contractarian and utilitarian theories he means to challenge. For a critique of Ackerman emphasizing the nature of political language, see my "Unconstrained Conversations," in *Ethics* 93, 2 (January 1983).

3. Bertrand Russell, "The Study of Mathematics," *Mysticism and Logic* (New York: Doubleday/Anchor, 1957), pp. 57–58.

4. William James, *Pragmatism and the Meaning of Truth,* ed. A. J. Ayer (Cambridge, Mass.: Harvard University Press, 1978), p. 32.

5. Ibid., p. 44.

6. Stanley Hoffmann, "Some Notes on Democratic Theory and Practice," *The Tocqueville Review 2,* 1(Winter 1980): 69.

7. Brian Barry, *Political Argument* (London: Routledge and Kegan Paul, 1965), chap. 5.

8. Georges Sorel, *Reflections on Violence,* trans. T. E. Hulme and J. Roth (New York: Collier Books, 1961), pp. 127–28.

9. Punitive poorhouse and workhouse ideas borrowed from the nineteenth century have tainted what is potentially a good idea. In fact, a great many citizens are on welfare because they cannot work due to illness, disability, or parental responsibilities. And work assignments resting on makeshift or featherbedded projects are clearly not in the public interest. Nevertheless, offering work rather than welfare to those able to work obviously serves both individual dignity and public goods.

10. Jean-Jacques Rousseau, "A Discourse on Political Economy," in *Social Contract and Discourses* (London: Dent, 1913), p. 251.

11. Jean-Jacques Rousseau, *Confessions,* book 9. The full quotation reads: "I had come to see that everything was radically connected with politics, and that however one proceeded, no people would be other than the nature of its government."

12. In *On the Jewish Question,* Marx writes: Where the political state has attained to its full development, man leads . . . a double existence—celestial and terrestrial. He lives in the *political community,* where he regards himself as a *communal being,* and in *civil society* where he acts simply as a *private individual,* treats other men as means, degrades himself to the role of a mere means, and becomes the plaything of alien powers. . . . Man . . . in civil society, is a profane being. . . . In the state, on the contrary, where he is regarded as a species-being, man is the imaginary member of an imaginary sovereignty, divested of his real, individual life, and infused with an unreal universality. (In Robert C. Tucker, ed., *The Marx-Engels Reader* [New York: Norton, 1972], p. 32)

13. Karl Marx, *Grundrisse: Foundations of the Critique of Political Economy,* trans. M. Nicolaus (New York: Vintage Books, 1973), p. 84. In the better-known *Sixth Thesis on Feuerbach,* Marx and Engels wrote that "the human essence is no abstraction inherent in each single individual. In its reality it is the ensemble of social relations" (in Tucker, ed., *Reader, Theses on Feuerbach,* p. 109).

14. Peter L. Berger and Thomas Luckmann, *The Social Construction of Reality* (New York: Doubleday, 1966), p. 183. In his classic study *Community,* Robert MacIver makes the simple assertion: "Every individual is born into community and owes its life to community, . . . community is always there" ([London: Macmillan, 1917], p. 204).

15. James Madison et al., *Federalist Papers,* no. 55 (New York: Random House, 1937), p. 365.

16. Alexander Bickel, *The Morality of Consent* (New Haven: Yale University Press, 1975), p. 4.

17. Montaigne, "Of Vanity," in Donald M. Frame, ed., *The Complete Essays of Montaigne* (Stanford: Stanford University Press, 1965), p. 758.

18. Jean-Jacques Rousseau, *The Social Contract,* book 1, chap. 1.

19. Jean-Jacques Rousseau, *Emile, or Education,* trans. Allan Bloom (New York: Basic Books, 1979), p. 38.

20. George Bernard Shaw, "Commentary on Ibsen's *Little Eyolf,*" in Shaw, *The Quintessence of Ibsenism* (New York: Hill and Wang, 1957), p. 130.

Justifying Political Obligation

Carole Pateman

Carole Pateman has long been an advocate of participatory democracy. In this essay she examines what kind of relationship between citizens would generate political obligations. Pateman takes seriously the liberal claim that a citizen's obligation to the government results from a voluntary contract with all other citizens. She argues that such a contract would generate obligations only to other citizens. The authority claimed by liberal democratic governments cannot be derived from their own theory of the social contract, she writes; it is illegitimate. To demonstrate this thesis Pateman first examines how a person can assume an obligation. She observes that a free and equal person makes a commitment through an act of promising. If this is applied to the political sphere, then a citizen's obligation is to other citizens not to the government. How, Pateman asks, can this obligation be transferred to government officials? How do citizens give their consent to be governed? One proposal for bridging the gap between a contractual obligation among freely promising citizens and the claim of authority by government officials is the mechanism of voting. Pateman raises several objections to this, such as voters do not know what they are endorsing and most American citizens don't vote. Another suggestion for bridging the gap is the reciprocity argument: by accepting the benefits provided by the state a citizen acknowledges its authority. But then only citizens who have benefited by the existing social order would have political obligations. Pateman points out that political obedience is not a political obligation and is not justified in a society of free and equal individuals. She concludes that only a participatory democratic government could command allegiance through a social contract.

Political theorists today usually agree that political obligation poses a problem in the sense that it requires justification. Yet they are also almost unanimously agreed that there are no really serious or intractable difficulties in providing a justification for the authority of the liberal-democratic state or the political obligation of its citizens. Indeed, a few theorists have even gone so far as to claim that to suggest that political obligation requires a justification, to suggest that it genuinely does pose a general problem, is to show oneself as conceptually confused and in a state of philosophical disorder. I have taken issue with the latter claim elsewhere.[1] In this chapter I shall argue that not only is it a mistake to suppose that few problems exist in justifying political obligation in the liberal-democratic state, but that the justifications most frequently offered do not provide a solution to the problem. Political theorists typically appeal to voluntarist arguments that are, as I shall show, integrally bound up with the valued liberal principles of individual freedom and equality. These arguments cannot provide a justification of political obligation in the liberal-democratic state. Instead, they lead to the conclusion that it is only within a participatory or self-managing form of democracy that a justified political obligation can exist.

In discussing political obligation in the liberal-democratic state, theorists almost invariably rely on some form of voluntarism. Appeal is made to consent, contract, agreement, commitment or promises, or, more broadly, to the voluntary actions of individuals that, it is held, give rise to political obligation. That is to say, political theorists usually assume that political obligation is a form of self-assumed obligation, or a moral commitment

From Carole Pateman, *The Disorder of Women: Democracy, Feminism, and Political Theory*, ch. 3 (Stanford: Stanford University Press, 1989), pp. 58–70. Reprinted by permission of Carole Pateman.

freely entered into by individuals and freely taken upon themselves by their own actions. Underlying this assumption is a view of liberal democracy as a certain kind of society, with a specific kind of inhabitant, a view that has been nicely summed up by Rawls, who writes that liberal democracy comes "as close as a society can to being a voluntary scheme . . . its members are autonomous and the obligations they recognize self-imposed."[2] However, a striking feature of contemporary discussions of political obligation is that the question is rarely asked of exactly *why* voluntarism, or the ideas of consent, agreement and promising, are so important; why must obligations be self-assumed or self-imposed? An answer to this question is required if the magnitude of the problem of justifying political obligation in the liberal-democratic state is to be appreciated.

Political theories in which consent and the associated idea of the social contract were central and fundamental became prominent, as everyone knows, in the seventeenth and eighteenth centuries. Nor is this surprising. Political ideas and concepts, notwithstanding the way in which they are treated by so many political theorists, do not exist in a separate, timeless world of their own, but help to constitute specific forms of social life. Social contract and consent theories were formulated at a time of great socio-economic development and change, at a time when the capitalist market economy and the liberal constitutional state were beginning to emerge. As part of these developments, individuals and their relationships began to be seen in a new and revolutionary way. The contract theorists began their arguments from the premise that individuals are "born free and equal" or are "naturally" free and equal to each other. Such a conception was in complete contrast to the long-prevailing view that people were born in a God-created and "natural" hierarchy of inequality and subordination. Within this traditional perspective, although disputes could frequently arise about the scope of specific rulers' right of command, there was scarcely room for general doubts about political obedience; rulers and political obedience were part of God's way with the world. But once the idea gained currency that individuals were born free and equal or were "naturally" so

(and how were they freely to enter contracts and make equal exchanges in the market, and pursue their interests as they saw fit, if they were not?) then a very large question was also raised about political authority and political obedience.

The social contract theorists were very well aware of the problem that liberal individualism brought with it; namely, how and why any free and equal individual could legitimately be governed by anyone else at all. The full implications of this subversive query have not, even today, fully worked themselves out; consider, for example, the argument of the feminists that there is no good reason for the widely held belief that a free and equal individual woman should be subject to the authority of the man whom she marries. Moreover, the emergence of this basic question means that the security in which political authority and political obedience were wrapped for so long can never return. To avoid misunderstanding I should note here that I am not, like the philosophical anarchists, arguing that a completely unbridgeable gulf exists between political authority and individual autonomy, or between individual freedom and equality.[3] I am not claiming that an acceptable answer to this fundamental question of government is impossible and that political obligation is an irrelevant concept. Rather, I am arguing that political obligation can be justified—and that it always requires justification—but that the only acceptable justification has implications that most writers on the subject neglect to investigate.

Given the initial postulate of individual freedom and equality, there is only *one* rational and acceptable justification for political obligation and political authority. Individuals must themselves consent, contract, agree, choose or promise to enter such a relationship. Political authority must have its basis in individuals' own voluntary actions, or, to put this the other way round, they must freely assume their political obligation for themselves. With the development of liberal individualism the relationship between individual and government has to be transformed from one of mere *obedience*, however engendered, into one of *obligation*, into a relationship in which individuals are bound by their own free acts. But political obligation then becomes a general problem; it can never be taken for granted, and a very specific justification is always required. The frequency with which voluntarist justifications are encountered in discussions of political obligation illustrates how reluctant theorists are to give up the liberal heritage bequeathed by the contract theorists. It also illustrates the widely held assumption that political obligation in the liberal-democratic state can quite easily be justified in the appropriate manner. However, most theorists display an extremely ambiguous attitude to the voluntarist justification of political obligation, although the ambiguity is not usually acknowledged.

It is frequently argued that whether or not individuals have agreed, consented or promised, they do nevertheless have a justified political obligation in the liberal-democratic state. This claim both upholds the assumption that political obligation in a liberal democracy is unproblematic and avoids the notorious difficulties of specifying who performed these actions, when, and how. An especially memorable instance of this line of argument can be found in Tussman's *Obligation and the Body Politic*. He argues that the liberal-democratic state should be seen as a voluntary association in which membership is based on consent. But he also states that not all citizens consent; some (the majority?) are "child-bride citizens" who, like minors, are governed without their own consent. Yet these citizens too have a justified political obligation, although Tussman does not inform us as to its basis. It appears, then, that despite the apparent importance of consent, voluntarism is of only limited relevance to political life—and that political "obligation" does not seem to be the appropriate characterization of the relation between all citizens and the state.

In our everyday lives the paradigmatic way in which we assume an obligation is by making a promise. When an individual says "I promise . . . ," he or she has assumed an obligation and has committed himself or herself to perform (or refrain from) certain actions. Political theorists have often suggested that political obligation is like, or rests upon or is a special kind of, a promise. But this is to assume once more that the relationship between citizens

and the liberal-democratic state is indeed a form of self-assumed obligation. The comparison between political obligation and the social practice of promising is usually drawn in very general terms, and is rarely pursued. Yet it is precisely through a consideration of this comparison that the full extent of the problem of political obligation in the liberal-democratic state is revealed. In recent years moral philosophers have paid a good deal of attention to promising. I can mention here only some aspects of promising that are of particular importance for the present argument.[4]

Making promises is one of the most basic ways in which free and equal individuals can freely create their own social relationships. As part of their social and moral education, individuals learn how to take part in the social practice of promising and so develop as persons with certain kinds of capacities. These capacities include the ability to engage in the rational and reasoned deliberation required to decide whether, on this occasion, a promise ought to be made, and also the ability to look back and critically evaluate their own actions and relationships; sometimes a promise may justifiably be broken or altered or revised in some way. Now, if political obligation is like, or is a form of, promising there is an important question to be asked; namely, how can citizens assume their political, like their other, obligations for themselves; what form of political system would make this possible? In short, it must be asked what is the political counterpart of the social practice of promising.

In political life voting is the practice that enables individuals to engage in reasoned deliberation and decide for themselves how to order their political lives and environment. The result of a vote, like that of a promise, is a commitment or an obligation, although in the case of voting it will be a collective, not an individual, commitment. However, this abstract and conceptual connection between voting in general and political obligation does not tell us the specific form that voting must take if a political practice of self-assumed obligation is to exist. Political theorists frequently suggest that a liberal-democratic form of voting is required and I shall present some further objections to this suggestion later. At present it is sufficient to point out that, for the analogy with promising to hold, voting must enable individuals collectively to decide upon their political obligation for themselves. It is a direct or participatory democratic form of voting that allows them to do this. It is within a participatory form of democracy that individuals retain their political decision-making power as citizens. They exercise political authority over themselves in their private capacity as individuals (something which many people find an odd idea, so used are we to thinking of representatives exercising political authority over citizens), and they collectively commit themselves, or freely obligate themselves, to do whatever is necessary to implement their own decisions and to maintain their self-managed political association in being. It is also a participatory democratic form of voting that, like promising, enables citizens politically to exercise their capacity to reflect upon and evaluate their own actions and decisions and, if necessary, to change them. Thus, the liberal principle of individual freedom and equality and its corollary of self-assumed obligation lead towards and provide a justification for participatory, not liberal, democracy.

There are two further points that should be made here. The first, to which I shall return, is that political obligation, in a participatory democracy, is owed to fellow citizens and not to the state or its representatives. To whom else could it be owed? Second, it is important to emphasize that the question now being considered is *not* the question asked in recent discussions of political obligation. Theorists do not usually ask what are the political consequences of the ideal of self-assumed obligation—that would presuppose that there is a problem! Instead, following from their assumption that political obligation is justified in the liberal-democratic state, they (implicitly) ask: how is it that individuals voluntarily agree to their political obligation, or what are the voluntary actions that can reasonably be said to, or be inferred to, give rise to political obligation? Before looking at their answers to *this* question, I want to pause to say something about the relation of my argument, and recent discussions, to classic social contract theory, taking Locke's theory as my example.

The hypothesis of the contract is a way of showing how "in the beginning" free and equal individuals can rationally agree to live under political authority. However, the *liberal* social contract has two stages and the significance of each stage is very different.[5] It is the first part of the contract story that shows how the "dispersed" individuals form a new political community. This part of the social contract establishes an obligation between, and places authority in the hands of, the members of the community themselves. Thus the first stage of the contract, taken by itself, is related to the question about the comparison with promising. Locke treats the first part of the contract as necessary (a political community must be created) but as an unimportant preliminary. It is the second stage of the contract that is fundamental to liberal theory. The second stage embodies the assumption that it is necessary for the members of the new community to alienate their right to exercise political authority to a few representatives. The free agreement of the contract thus becomes an agreement that a few representatives shall decide upon the content of individuals' political obligation. Self-assumed obligation becomes an obligation to let others decide upon one's political obligation. The comparison with promising now begins to appear misplaced and, furthermore, political obligation is now owed to the state and its respresentatives, not by citizens to each other.

Locke could not complete his theory with the idea of the social contract. He had to meet the partriarchalists' objection that an agreement of the fathers could not bind sons, not if the latter were truly born free and equal. Locke had, therefore, to introduce the notion of consent into his theory.[6] The sons had, in their turn, voluntarily to consent or agree to the political arrangements made by their fathers. Locke had to answer the same problems as contemporary theorists: given a legitimate political system, how can individuals be said to consent to it? From what aspect of their actions can their political obligation be inferred?

In his discussion of consent, Locke remarks that no one doubts that express consent gives rise to political obligation and makes an individual the subject of government. The difficulty about consent arises "where he has made no Expressions of it at all." Locke solves this problem by his famous claim that the tacit consent of the members of the community can be inferred from their peaceful everyday interactions under the protection of government. But who gives express consent, and how? Locke's treatment of consent is hardly a model of clarity, but the most plausible answer to this question is that express consent is given by the individuals who inherit property, individuals who can also be called the politically relevant members of their society. Locke calls those who expressly consent "perfect members" of society and indicates that they, unlike individuals who merely consent tacitly, have no right of emigration.[7] It therefore seems that Locke is implying that a differential political obligation exists: those who expressly consent have a greater obligation than the rest.

In this hint of a differential political obligation, as in his other arguments, Locke closely foreshadows more recent discussions of political obligation. But there is also a very important difference between Locke's social contract theory and contemporary arguments. In the seventeenth century Locke could not merely take it for granted that the political obligation of citizens of the liberal state was justified. He argued, in his conjectural history of the state of nature, that the socio-economic developments of his day had rendered unacceptable the claims for the divine right of kings and for patriarchy. Only a liberal, constitutional, representative state could protect individuals' property—and the social contract story provides the necessary voluntarist justification for the authority of such a state. It must be emphasized that it is quite clear that Locke's contract is an answer to a *problem* of political authority and political obligation, whereas in the most recent revival of contract theory, as in other present-day discussions of political obligation, no such problem is admitted. Rawls, in *A Theory of Justice*, assumes that the liberal-democratic state exercises a justified political authority over its citizens. His "original position," and the choices of its "parties," is a device to show why "our" considered judgements about liberal democracy are rational and acceptable judgements. It shows us why we are right to regard the relationship of citizens and the state in the way that we do—as embodying a justified political obligation. Rawls's contract exhibits the rationality of the

state; unlike classic social contract theory it neither begins from the position, nor admits, that the authority of the state poses a problem. In other words, the liberal-democratic state is today entirely taken for granted as if it were a natural feature of the world. This marks a most significant shift from the classic contract theorists' view that the state is conventional.

That political obligation is no longer seen as a problem means that consent is now treated explicitly "as a constituent element of democratic ideology."[8] Criticisms of the ideological character of much liberal-democratic theory are now familiar and I shall not pursue this here, but it is worth commenting on one ideological assumption and its relationship to social contract theory.[9] It is widely assumed by liberal-democratic theorists that liberal-democratic voting works in practice as it is held to in theory and, in particular, that voting protects and furthers the interests of all citizens. Locke was able to make his inference about tacit consent because, during the contract, individuals exchange their "natural" freedom and equality for the civil freedom and legal equality of political subjects. The end of government is protection, and in their new status all citizens' "property," in both of Locke's senses of the term, is protected (or they would not enter the contract), no matter what substantive social inequalities divide them. Hence, all can be said to continue to give their consent. Since Locke's day, the status of political subject has been transformed and institutionalized as the formally equal political status of liberal-democratic citizenship, which includes civil liberties and the right to exercise the franchise. Voting, it is claimed, protects the interest of all citizens, no matter how substantively unequal they are; and so all can be said to consent.

It is therefore not surprising that the most popular recent argument about consent is that it can be said to be given through, or even equated with the existence of, the liberal-democratic electoral mechanism. I have already challenged the assumption that the general conceptual connection between voting and political obligation is given actual expression through liberal-democratic voting (although the general connection helps to explain why this may appear "obvious"). Even fairly cursory reflection on the empirical evidence about voting behaviour casts immediate doubt on the simple identification of consent with liberal-democratic voting. It is argued by Plamenatz, for example, that even electoral abstainers consent, and Gewirth states that the meaning of the electoral "method of consent" is that "one can participate if one chooses to do so" and, therefore, "the individual is obligated ... whether he personally utilizes his opportunity or not."[10] The close relationship of this argument to conclusions drawn about political apathy by empirical theorists of democracy is obvious; and so are its defects. What is ignored, of course, is who abstains and why they do so. The empirical evidence shows that electoral abstainers tend to be drawn disproportionately from lower socio-economic groups and from the female sex. The evidence also suggests that they abstain because voting does not seem worthwhile; that is, they do not believe that voting achieves what it is claimed to in liberal-democratic theory. As Verba and Nie have shown, political participation, including voting, "helps those who are already better off."[11] It hardly makes sense to insist that individuals are consenting when they refrain from an activity which helps reinforce their disadvantaged position.

Yet, it might be argued, those who vote can surely be said to consent. The question of the "meaning" of the vote is an extremely complex one and I can only briefly mention two of the major objections to this claim. The first objection concerns the votes of men and women. Political scientists often argue that men and women are doing something different when they vote; they argue that a female vote is "qualitatively different" from a male vote. Men, acting like good liberals, vote from self-interest; women vote for moral reasons, out of "a kind of bloodless love of the good."[12] But, if that is so, then can women's votes "mean" the same thing as men's votes, namely, consent? Either political theorists have to give up their male chauvinist prejudices or they have to construct a sex-differentiated argument about political obligation and voting.

The second objection centres on the requirements of a meaningful or genuine sense of "consent." When an individual makes a promise, he or she knows what they are committed to and can break or alter the obligation if this is necessary. An acceptable sense of "consent" also implies that those consenting can have reasonable knowledge of the consequences of their action, or can refuse or withdraw their consent. There are some familiar features of liberal-democratic elections that illustrate how difficult it is for this requirement to be met. I shall leave aside the problems consequent upon attempts by representatives and officials to "defactualize" the political world,[13] and from systematic lying on their part, and note, first, that parties and candidates are now "sold" to the electorate through commercial advertising techniques and that citizens are urged to vote on the basis of "images"; but in what sense can one consent to an image? Second, the crude equation of voting and consent ignores the arguments that liberal-democratic voting is no more than a ritual or, at least, contains large ritual elements. Certainly, many citizens see their vote as a "duty" associated with citizenship and, again, the important question is how far, if at all, this leaves room for anything that could reasonably be called freely and deliberately given "consent."

Some theorists of political obligation have now ceased to make any reference to "consent" at all. They offer a different form of voluntarist argument that, like Locke's doctrine of tacit consent, looks not to activities that are part of universal citizenship (which, of course, did not exist in Locke's day) but to everyday life. Such arguments typically appeal to individuals' acceptance of benefits from the state, or their participation in liberal-democratic institutions, as giving rise to obligations. This approach, like Locke's tacit consent, is neatly all-inclusive; indeed, it is a mere reinterpretation of "tacit consent." It is another way of inferring political obligation—yet apparently avoiding the difficulties associated with "consent." Locke's theory can be interpreted without reference to tacit consent and some commentators claim that this is the most appropriate reading.[14] Locke can be seen to argue that, having taken advantage of the social practice of inheritance, individuals (in fairness) have an obligation to play their part to keep the practice in being, or, having accepted the benefits of highways, they have an obligation to obey the government that builds and maintains them.

It is not clear that this approach does actually constitute an argument at all. It looks suspiciously like no more than an extended collection of conceptual truisms. The existence of an institution or practice necessarily implies that individuals are participating or cooperating within it; they "benefit" because all do their share ("recognize their obligation") to keep the institution going. However, the "benefits" cannot be independently specified apart from the participation, and the latter *is*, or constitutes, the practice itself. But even if this form of voluntarism is treated as a genuine argument, there are some basic objections to it.

It is not, for example, obvious how the obligations (if, indeed, there are such) consequent upon participation in the multiplicity of liberal-democratic institutions are related to *political* obligation. The equation of voting and consent does have the advantage that it focuses on a political activity. Moreover, because these arguments look to everyday life, they are immediately open to the challenge that, if they show anything, it is that a differential political obligation exists. I have not found any attempts in the relevant literature to specify what counts as a "benefit" but it seems clear that, taking liberal-democratic institutions in their entirety, some individuals "benefit" a good deal more than others and the outcome of participation is very different for some individuals and groups than for others. This applies even if one takes the fundamental "benefit" of liberal theory as an example; the protection of the property that individuals have in their persons. Empirical research shows that mortality rates differ between social classes;[15] that "the poor do not receive the same treatment at the hands of the agents of law-enforcement as the well-to-do or middle class. This differential treatment is systematic and complete";[16] and that women are not afforded the same protection as men from sexual and other assaults by men[17] (and it can be added that men are widely believed to own the property that women have in their persons). Why, then, should most political theorists assume that the obligation held to be consequent upon participation in institutions, or

acceptance of benefits, is an equal obligation for all citizens, whether rich or poor, working-class or middle-class, male or female?

Interestingly enough, Rawls concludes, on the basis of this form of voluntarist argument, that citizens are far from having an equal obligation—in fact, many citizens do not have a political *obligation* at all. It is only the "better-placed members of society," who also take an active part in political life, who have a political obligation. The rest of the population have merely a *natural duty* to obey, which, "requires no voluntary acts in order to apply."[18] While Rawls has drawn a logical conclusion from arguments about participation and "benefits," voluntarism and the ideal of social life as a "voluntary scheme" have now been thrown aside for the bulk of the population.

This highlights the dilemmas facing theorists who wish to retain voluntarism and to treat political obligation in the liberal-democratic state as unproblematic. An all-inclusive obligation can be inferred ("tacit consent"), but at the price of reducing the idea of self-assumed obligation to meaninglessness. Yet to admit that some individuals may have a lesser obligation than others, or that some have only a "natural duty" of obedience, is either to shake liberal-democratic theory to its foundations or to move well along the road to the abandonment of some basic liberal principles. And any attempt to give genuine content to the ideas of consent and self-assumed obligation immediately opens up all the critical questions about the liberal-democratic state that most contemporary theorists seem determined to avoid.

It is, perhaps, symptomatic of an unease about the present state of the argument about the relationship of the citizen to the liberal-democratic state that there is an increasing tendency for theorists to advance a rather startling argument. They argue that political obligation is owed primarily not to the state but to fellow citizens.[19] It must be added that they also assume that the state does have a justified claim on its citizens—but their own argument begins to cut the ground from under this assumption. The question cannot be avoided of why and on what grounds, if obligation is owed to fellow citizens, it must also be assumed that it is justifiably owed to the state.

It is not as surprising as it may appear at first sight that theorists have begun to argue in this way. The logic of the voluntarist arguments that look to everyday interactions of citizens, and to "benefits" and "participation," is that, if obligations are assumed in this way, they are owed to fellow members of institutions and fellow participants in social practices. I have already noted that this raises an important question about what counts as "political" obligation. If "political" obligation *is* owed to fellow citizens, then a sharp break must be made with liberal-democratic theory that insists that it is the state that is the locus of the political and the object of political obligation. The view of political obligation as owed to fellow citizens derives, as I have argued, from a perspective that takes seriously the idea of self-assumed obligation as a political ideal. This raises again the fundamental question of why, if self-assumed obligation is as important as 300 years of liberal argument assures us it is, we should not assume *all* of our obligations for ourselves and organize our political life on that basis.

Theorists of the liberal state have only one convincing answer to that question. They can argue that participatory democracy is not empirically feasible; the liberal-democratic state is the best that we can do. If that answer is given—and it is implicit in many discussions of political obligation—the consequences need to be spelled out. The answer implies that voluntarism is irrelevant to political life. Although we are capable of assuming obligations in our everyday life, the activity has no place outside the private sphere. It is, in short, to admit that the noble liberal ideal of individual freedom and equality and its corollaries of self-assumed obligation and the vision of social life as a "voluntary scheme" can only be very partially realized.

Furthermore, if political theorists dismiss the possibility of participatory or self-managing democracy, they should stop pretending that the liberal-democratic state rests on a voluntarist basis of genuine commitments. That is, they should stop pretending that the freely created relationship of political *obligation* is involved, because this

relationship is an integral part of a political ideal now admitted to be out of reach. Instead, they should argue directly that, given the empirical necessity of the liberal-democratic state and the advantages that it has over other existing forms of political system, there are good, but non-voluntarist, reasons for political *obedience*. Rawls's notion of a natural duty of political obedience, or a contemporary version of "my political station and its duties," may commend themselves for this purpose. And there are, of course, political theorists who present a utilitarian account of the relationship between citizens and the liberal-democratic state. The reason why I have ignored this obvious competitor to voluntarism in my argument should now be clear. No matter how economical an argument utilitarianism can provide, or how appropriate it may appear, utilitarian arguments, despite the manner in which they are so often presented, are arguments for obedience, not obligation. However, theorists are unlikely to argue only in terms of "obedience" instead of "obligation," for this would strip the liberal-democratic state of a major portion of its ideological mantle. It would be to recognize that central liberal ideas, if taken seriously, lead beyond the liberal-democratic state.

Notes

1. "Political Obligation and Conceptual Analysis," *Political Studies*, 21 (1973), pp. 199–218.

2. J. Rawls, *A Theory of Justice* (Oxford University Press, Oxford, 1972), p. 13.

3. A recent example of the philosophical anarchist argument can be found in P. Abbot, *The Shotgun behind the Door* (University of Georgia Press, Athens, GA, 1976). R. P. Wolff, *In Defense of Anarchism* (Harper & Row, New York, 1970) is equivocal about his philosophical anarchism. In the final section of the book he suggests that a solution to the problem of autonomy and authority can be found in institutions based on "voluntary compliance."

4. A detailed discussion of the social practice of promising and its relationship to political obligation and to contracts can be found in C. Pateman,

The Problem of Political Obligation: A Critical Analysis of Liberal Theory, 2nd ed. (Polity Press, Cambridge, 1985; University of California Press, Berkeley, CA, 1985).

5. Rousseau's social contract theory provides a brilliant critique of, and non-liberal alternative to, liberal contract theory. His critique is usually ignored by writers on political obligation.

6. For the distinction between the contract and consent, usually treated as synonymous, see G. J. Schochet, *Patriarchalism in Political Thought* (Basil Blackwell, Oxford, 1975), pp. 9, 262.

7. J. Locke, "Second Treatise of Government," in *Two Treatises of Government,* ed. P. Laslett, 2nd ed. (Cambridge University Press, Cambridge, 1967), 11, §116–22.

8. P. H. Partridge, *Consent and Consensus* (Macmillan, London, 1971), 23.

9. The continuing ideological importance of the legacy of liberal social contract theory is, rather curiously, overlooked by Marxist and neo-Marxist writers. C. B. Macpherson, in *The Political Theory of Possessive Individualism* (Oxford University Press, Oxford, 1962), ignores the contract in his interpretation of Hobbes and Locke, and argues that the liberal state was justified by the equal subordination of all individuals to the inevitable laws of the market. Similarly, J. Habermas, *Legitimation Crisis* (Heinemann, London, 1976), p. 22, argues that "the bourgeois constitutional state finds its justification in the legitimate relations of production." They thus neglect the directly *political* justification of the liberal state and the present ideological strength of the idea that all individuals have a common interest as citizens.

10. J. Plamenatz, *Man and Society* (Longmans, London, 1963), vol. 1, pp. 238–40; A. Gewirth, "Political Justice," in *Social Justice* ed. R. B. Brandt (Prentice Hall, Englewood Cliffs, NJ, 1962), p. 138.

11. S. Verba and N. H. Nie, *Participation in America* (Harper & Row, New York, 1972), p. 338.

12. R. E. Lane, *Political Life* (Free Press, New York, 1959), p. 212.

13. The term is H. Arendt's in "Lying in Politics," in *Crises of the Republic* (Penguin Books, Harmondsworth, Middlesex, 1973).

14. For a recent example of this interpretation, see A. J. Simmons, "Tacit Consent and Political Obligation," *Philosophy and Public Affairs,* 5 (1976), pp. 274–91.

15. See, for example, A. Antonovsky, "Class and the Chance for Life," in *Social Problems and Public Policy,* ed. L. Rainwater (Aldine, Chicago, IL, 1974).

16. W. J. Chambliss and R. B. Seidman, *Law, Order, and Power* (Addison-Wesley, Boston, MA, 1971), pp. 475.

17. See, for example, E. Pizzey, *Scream Quietly or the Neighbors Will Hear* (Penguin Books, Harmondsworth, Middlesex, 1974); B. Toner, *The Facts of Rape* (Arrow Books, London, 1977). See also the judgement of the Court of Appeal in *R. v. Holdsworth,* reported in *The Times,* 22 June 1977.

18. Rawls, *A Theory of Justice,* pp. 14, 116, 344.

19. See, for example, M. Walzer, *Obligations* (Simon & Schuster, New York, 1971); B. Zwiebach, *Civility and Disobedience* (Cambridge University Press, Cambridge, 1975); K. Johnson, "Political Obligation and the Voluntary Association Model of the State," *Ethics,* 86 (1975), pp. 17–29; R. K. Dagger, "What Is Political Obligation?," *American Political Science Review,* 71(1)(1977), pp. 86–94.

Democracy and Participation

Robert A. Dahl

In this selection Robert Dahl presents a hypothetical dialogue between contemporary exponents of participatory democracy and federalism. The character Jean-Jacques named for Rousseau, argues that full and meaningful citizenship in a democracy requires direct participation at all levels of government. James, named after James Madison, argues for a Federalist government by representatives chosen through elections, the system encoded in our Constitution. Dahl uses the term polyarchy, *rule by the many, to refer to a political order in which the vote is widely distributed among citizens who have the power to vote out of office the highest government officials. The United States is a polyarchy. Jean-Jacques and James first consider what self-government in a democracy means. Jean-Jacques insists on direct citizen direction of political life. James agrees that this would be ideal but charges that the problems of scale make this vision impractical. Not only are there too many people to allow direct participation, but it would be inefficient and take too much time from each citizen's other concerns. Jean-Jacques endorses a worldwide system of very small-scale communities that are entirely self-governing. But, James counters, such a system would be vulnerable to a predatory group. Communities must form alliances for protection. They agree on two points, however: (1) such alliances should be democratic, even if it might be necessary to use representatives, and (2) current polyarchal systems leave much to be desired in terms of citizen control.*

One consequence of transferring the idea of democracy from the city-state to the national state is that opportunities for citizens to participate fully in collective decisions are more limited than they would be, theoretically at least, in a much smaller system. For most people nowadays, these limits seem to be pretty much taken for granted. Yet the nature of the democratic idea, and its origins, prevent the hope from ever dying out that the limits can be transcended by creating new (or recreating ancient) democratic forms and institutions. Consequently a strong countercurrent favoring the ideal of a fully participatory democracy persists among advocates of democracy, who often hark back to the older democratic vision that was reflected in Rousseau's *Social Contract* and in images of the Greek democracy (as it existed not so much in historical reality as in the idealized polis).

Some of the central issues appear as Jean-Jacques and James renew their dialogue:

JAMES: I have often noticed, Jean-Jacques, that while you accept all the benefits of modern democracy, including the right to say whatever you please—a right you obviously cherish, since you exercise it so often—you nonetheless always seem to denigrate its institutions and achievements. I sometimes think that in democratic countries the breakdown of democracy is less likely to be brought about by its opponents than by its utopian advocates. With friends like you . . .

JEAN-JACQUES: . . . democracy doesn't need enemies. Definitely below the belt, James. That was unlike you and unworthy of you, good friend. You speak of democracy. If I'm critical it's because what you and others insist on calling "modern democracy" is not and cannot be very democratic. Why not give things their honest names and call modern democracy "oligarchy"?

JAMES: I'm sorry if I offended you, Jean-Jacques. I thought my remark perfectly exact.

From Robert Dahl, *Democracy and Its Critics* (New Haven: Yale University Press, 1989), pp. 225–231. Reprinted by permission of Yale University Press.

But I can see that you're loaded for bear today, so I'll take cover while you aim and fire. Please proceed.

JEAN-JACQUES: Thank you. Isn't it perfectly obvious why what you call "polyarchy" is a pitiful substitute for real democracy?

JAMES: Excuse me, but I have learned that the phrase "real democracy" usually means either unreal democracy or real oppression, and usually both. However, I await your enlightenment. I'll even ask the question you're fishing for: Why is polyarchy a pitiful substitute for real democracy?

JEAN-JACQUES: Because no government on the scale of a country can really be democratic. Democracy as it was classically understood meant above all direct citizen participation; either democracy was *participatory*, or it was a sham. As Rousseau argued, following the ancient tradition, if citizens are to be truly sovereign they must be able to gather together to rule in a sovereign assembly. To do so, the citizen body—and in those days the territory of the state as well—had to be small. As he pointed out, the greater the number of citizens the smaller must necessarily be the average share each has in ruling. In a large state that share is infinitesimally small. "The English people," he remarked, "thinks it is free. It greatly deceives itself. It is free only during the election of the members of Parliament. As soon as they are elected, it is a slave, it is nothing."[1] I know this is hard for people accustomed only to polyarchy to grasp, but an Athenian would have understood it immediately.

JAMES: I don't want to divert us from your argument by starting an interminable discussion of "what Rousseau really meant," which I'll happily leave to those who relish that sort of thing. So I'll ignore his perverse definition of democracy in the *Social Contract* where he stipulates that in a "democracy" the people must not only make the laws but administer them also. So "democracy" was impossible. "If there were a people of gods, it would govern itself democratically. Such a perfect government is not suited to men." On his definition, he's perfectly right. But what he called a republic we would call direct democracy or, even more to the point, assembly democracy. I'll also ignore the fact that he regarded repre-

sentation as totally unacceptable only in the *Social Contract*. In his previous work he had regarded it as a reasonable solution; he did so again in his later work. I suppose it was as obvious to him as it is to us that without representative governments Poland and Corsica, for example, could never be republics.[2]

JEAN-JACQUES: I agree that the argument can't be advanced by scholarly disquisitions on Rousseau. I didn't mention him in order to persuade you by citing a Great Name on my behalf, which we both agree proves nothing, though heaven knows it's a common form of argument in these matters. I mentioned him only because I happen to believe that he was perfectly correct about the consequences of size for political participation.

JAMES: It may surprise you, but so do I. I don't see how anyone can deny that the opportunity for every citizen to participate *directly* in collective decisions, except by voting, has to be inversely related to size. That's exactly why advocates of large-scale democracy so much admired representation. Representation is the obvious solution to an otherwise insoluble problem.

JEAN-JACQUES: But haven't you just conceded that representation doesn't solve the problem of participation? And haven't you also conceded by implication that the problem of participation simply can't be solved in a large system? Therefore it can be solved only on classical terms: by small-scale democracy.

JAMES: What you and most other advocates of assembly democracy don't seem to recognize is how swiftly your own argument turns against you. I've already agreed that, as the number of citizens grows larger, the opportunities for them to participate directly in decisions must necessarily decline. This is because, if nothing else has an upper limit, time does. Elementary arithmetic shows that if ten citizens were to meet for five hours—a long time for a meeting!—the maximum equal time each may be allowed for speaking, for parliamentary maneuvers, and for voting is thirty minutes. Small committees are the perfect example of participatory democracy, or at least they can be. Even so, as most of us know from experience, people who have other things to do would not look forward to attending many five-hour committee meetings a month. But you and Rousseau aren't talking about committees. You're talking about governing a *state*, for heaven's sake!

JEAN-JACQUES: Well, not only states. Other organizations and associations might also be democratically run.

JAMES: That is so, of course. But let's go back to the arithmetic of participation. Once you go beyond the size of a committee, the opportunities for all the members to participate necessarily decline rapidly and drastically. Look: If the length of the assembly meeting remains at five hours and the number of citizens goes up to no more than a hundred, then each member has three minutes. At three hundred members you approach the vanishing point of one minute. The number of citizens who were eligible to attend the assembly in classical Athens was twenty thousand, according to one common estimate; the best guesses of some scholars are two or three times that. With just twenty thousand, if time were allocated equally in a five-hour meeting each citizen would have less than one second in which to participate!

JEAN-JACQUES: Now, James, I can do arithmetic. I'm aware of calculations like these. But aren't they misleading? After all, not everyone wants to or has to participate by actually speaking. Among twenty thousand people there aren't twenty thousand different points of view on an issue, particularly if the citizens assemble after days, weeks, or months of discussions going on prior to the assembly. By the time of the meeting, probably only two or three alternatives will seem worth discussing seriously. So ten speakers, say, with about a half hour each to present their arguments, might well be plenty. Or let's say five speakers with a half hour each; that would leave time for brief questions and statements. Let's say five minutes for each intervention. That would allow thirty more people to participate.

JAMES: Bravo! Notice what you have just demonstrated. Thirty-five citizens actively participate in your assembly by speaking. What can the rest do? *They can listen, think, and vote.* So, in an assembly of twenty thousand, less than two-tenths of 1 percent actively par-

ticipate and more than 99.8 percent participate only by listening, thinking, and voting! A great privilege, your participatory democracy.

JEAN-JACQUES: I find these arithmetical calculations tedious. Depending on the numbers you start with, they come out as you wish. As they say about computers, garbage in, garbage out.

JAMES: Tedious these school exercises may be, but advocates of participatory democracy just don't want to face up to what they demonstrate. All I ask is that the True Believers in participatory democracy plug in their own numbers and then think hard about the results. If they do, they can't rationally escape the conclusion that a democratic system in which most members have full and equal opportunities to participate is possible only in *very* small groups. It's silly to debate precise numbers, but can I assume that you don't intend to restrict democratic government to political systems with less than a few hundred people? Let me be generous and suppose your upper limit is a thousand, perhaps even ten thousand. On that scale most citizens will be unable to participate in any given assembly by more than listening, thinking, and voting. *And that is what they could also do in a representative system.* What's the difference? A large meeting—say, a thousand or more people—is inherently a kind of "representative" system because a few speakers have to represent the voices of all those who can't speak. But without rules of fair representation, the selection of speakers—representatives—could be arbitrary, accidental, and unfair. Establish rules for selecting speakers and you're already close to a representative system. An obvious solution is to create a system in which any citizen may be selected to speak, and let all the citizens vote to choose the ones to speak on their behalf. Or let representatives be chosen by lot, if you prefer. Either way, you'll end up with a fairer system than your attempt to avoid representative government.

JEAN-JACQUES: There would still be one important difference between my solution and yours. In a representative system, the representatives would vote on the policies to be adopted. In an assembly with elected or randomly chosen speakers, the citizens would vote on the policies. So citizens would still exercise more direct control over decisions than under a representative government.

JAMES: I don't deny that. But I wonder if you don't have to reflect on why Rousseau believed "democracy," as he perversely defined it, was impossible: you really can't expect citizens to spend all their time, or even most of their time, in assemblies. The world's work has to be done. Periodic elections of representatives allow the world's work to be done. Are you assuming a pastoral society in which all the work of government might be accomplished by citizen assemblies meeting once a month or so?

JEAN-JACQUES: No, I'm not. Participatory democracy works in the kibbutzim of Israel, and the kibbutzim are highly efficient productive units, not just in agriculture but also in manufacturing and marketing.

JAMES: Are you assuming, then, that your participatory democracy would require a society composed exclusively of communes like the kibbutzim? And that people could freely choose whether they wanted to live and work on the communes? So far as I know, no such society has ever existed. Even in Israel 95 percent of the people don't live on the kibbutzim. In no country have purely voluntary communes ever attracted more than a tiny percentage of the population. The Chinese communes, we now know, were created by heavy coercion and did not survive when the people in the countryside were no longer compelled to join them.

JEAN-JACQUES: Human consciousness isn't forever fixed, you know. Anyway, the commune isn't the only model. Participation could occur in producer cooperatives, town governments, and so on.

JAMES: Town governments? Don't we need to distinguish between two radically different prescriptions for participatory democracy? In one—the one usually advanced by True Believers—it is a comprehensive solution: *All* governments are fully participatory. From our arithmetical exercises, it follows that governments could exist only in small and completely autonomous units. No units could be so

large as to make a highly participatory assembly government impossible. In my view that solution is absolutely utopian. In a more modest view of participatory democracy, on the other hand, only *some* units are governed as fully participatory democracies. Others, which are too large for assembly government, are governed by representative systems. If it is true that all the institutions of polyarchy are essential for the democratic process in the government of a large system, then the governments of these large systems would be polyarchies. Which of these two solutions do you have in mind?

JEAN-JACQUES: Though I don't expect it to arrive tomorrow morning, naturally I would prefer the first.

JAMES: I assumed you would. I really can't imagine how, starting with the world we now have, such a world would come about. I suppose a nuclear holocaust might do it, but I don't think you're proposing that particular means. Let's play God, though, and assume that a world with something like its present levels of population and technology will be inhabited only by people living in very small and politically autonomous units, each governed by a highly participatory assembly of all its citizens. Depending on the parameters we play with, there would be thousands or tens of thousands of these small participatory democracies.

JEAN-JACQUES: I distrust your playing God. I'd distrust you even more if you *were* God. But I suppose I have to let you have your fun. Go ahead and play God, if you insist.

JAMES: I appreciate your confidence. Now imagine that people in one of the independent units fall to quarreling with the people in another, or hankering after their goodies, or otherwise wanting to exercise greater control over them. In due time, one unit dominates another. Now that it has become larger than all its neighbors and has more resources, its people begin to exercise the rewards of empire. So they vanquish a few more tiny neighbors. Their little empire expands. Still, except for our little empire, none but tiny states cover the globe. What a dazzling prospect lies before this new and growing imperial power! All the other tiny states wait to be consumed like delicious tidbits. Let the Lobsterman weep ever so much for the poor oysters, but he will eat them all the same.

JEAN-JACQUES: As God, I suppose you can create what you wish. But your creation strikes me as artificial, unimaginative, or simply culture-bound. Why do you assume the inevitability of aggression and empire?

JAMES: I don't assume they're inevitable, just highly probable. Do you really think my scenario is improbable, Jean-Jacques? Then reflect on Athens. Reflect on Rome. Reflect on the history of mankind. Or do you want me, playing God, to restore us to Eden and banish evil from the world—this time, forever?

JEAN-JACQUES: No, but please return to earth. In your Jovian stratosphere the shortage of oxygen is making you lose your usual sense of realism. Don't you think that people in the independent self-governing units would resist? Of course they would. In fact, they would surely construct alliances to protect themselves from conquest or absorption by the empire.

JAMES: Exactly! And so they would take the first steps toward creating a larger system, a system too large for participatory democracy. Being democrats, reasoning from the logic of political equality they would create not only representative government but all the institutions of polyarchy.

JEAN-JACQUES: I hope not. Starting from a belief in the importance of full participation, reasoning from the logic of equality, and unburdened by the inertia of the institutions of a large national state, I believe they could find ways of transcending the participatory limits of polyarchy.

JAMES: I want you to explain how they might do that. But first I want you to see how far we have come. Unless you assume that the whole world might exist indefinitely in the form of very small and completely autonomous states (or if not states, then entirely voluntary associations), then you must believe that some associations too large for full participatory democracy are bound to exist. But, if so, then won't these associations need governments?

JEAN-JACQUES: Of course they will have to be governed.

JAMES: Then must you not make one of two choices? Either you will insist that these governments, even if not fully participatory, should satisfy the criteria of the democratic process so far as that may be possible, given their large scale. Or you will not insist that they be democratic, in which case presumably you must be prepared to accept their being governed nondemocratically. But everything in your political philosophy repels you from the second, whereas everything in your political philosophy must surely draw you toward the first. From your point of view, these large-scale governments cannot be perfectly democratic; but, if they must exist, better that they be as democratic as may be feasible than that they be nondemocratic. You will conclude that a second-best democracy is better than the best nondemocracy. So, if polyarchy is essential to the democratic process in these large-scale systems, you will advocate polyarchy. That's the final upshot of my argument. Perhaps we finally agree on that conclusion?

JEAN-JACQUES: Perhaps. But that isn't the end of the problem of participation. Even if I were to concede that large-scale systems are desirable and that polyarchy is necessary if the governments of large-scale systems are to be democratized, I do not have to conclude that the institutions of polyarchy are sufficient for democracy, even in large-scale systems.

JAMES: You're right, of course. So we agree on that, too.

JEAN-JACQUES: Yet I think we still disagree about the possibilities of participation. Even in large systems, opportunities for political participation could be immeasurably greater than the institutions of polyarchy now provide for. I'm certain that democracy hasn't reached its maximum feasible limits with polyarchy. Changes are surely possible that would go beyond polyarchy and produce a new level of democratization. We need to search for a new form of democracy that will expand opportunities for participation and democratic control not only in smaller units where the democratic process could be greatly strengthened but in the larger units as well.

JAMES: I approve of your ends. It is the means that elude me.

JEAN-JACQUES: Then we must both give thought to the problem. For surely we both must reject the complacent view that the democratic idea has finally reached its highest feasible level of attainment with the institutions of polyarchy in the nation-state.

JAMES: On that much we are fully agreed. Sometime we must explore both the limits and the possibilities of democracy under conditions we can reasonably expect to exist in the kind of world that we and our descendants are likely to inhabit.

Notes

1. Jean-Jacques Rousseau [1762]. *On the Social Contract, with Geneva Manuscript and Political Economy,* Roger D. Masters and Judith R. Masters, eds. (New York: St. Martin's Press, 1978), "On the Social Contract," Bk. 3, chap. 15, p. 102.

2. See especially Richard Fralin, *Rousseau and Representation* (New York: Columbia University Press, 1978).

6

Ethics and
the Law

The Tower of Babel

Michael Oakeshott

Social interactions in a community are guided by habitual patterns of support and defer-ence, traditional prohibitions and obligations, and a fund of stories that model acceptable conduct. For communitarians, such a locally generated and particular normative system is the core of ethics. In this essay Michael Oakeshott distinguishes this mode of moral life from one ruled by universal abstract principles and ideals, the mode favored by modern Western moral theories. The first mode flows from a person's unreflective habits and affec-tions and is used by most people most of the time if only because they must act or react immediately. We learn what to do morally, in the same way as we learn a language, by unconsciously acquiring the standards, values, and skills needed for living with others. Together these function as a tradition of moral conduct. The second form of moral life depends on a self-consciously reflective application of moral ideals and rules of conduct. Training in this form of moral life requires an intellectual grasp of moral ideals, self-consciously deliberative skills in adjudicating among conflicting ideals, an ability to assess the structure of a practical situation, and an ability to select the appropriate ideal and apply it correctly. In Oakeshott's theory every moral system is a mixture of these two forms of moral life. When the form based on habits and affections predominates, the morality of principles and ideals supports and corrects unreflective habitual conduct. But when the form based on moral ideals predominates, Oakeshott argues, it tends to undermine its com-panion form, leaving an incoherent and unstable moral system of rational principles and competing ideals. Oakeshott concludes that modern society has been brought to the brink of collapse, because our moral system is dominated by ideals and principles.

One

The project of finding a short cut to heaven is as old as the human race. It is represented in the mythology of many peoples, and it is rec-ognized always as an impious but not ignoble enterprise. The story of the Titans is, perhaps, the most complicated of the myths which por-tray this *folie de grandeur,* but the story of the Tower of Babel is the most profound. We may imagine the Titans drawing back after the first unsuccessful assault to hear one of their num-ber suggest that their programme was too ambitious, that perhaps they were trying to do too much and to do it too quickly. But the builders of the Tower, whose top was to reach to heaven, were permitted no such con-ference; their enterprise involved them in the babblings of men who speak, but do not speak the same language. Like all profound myths, this represents a project the fascination of which is not confined to the childhood of the race, but is one which the circumstances of human life constantly suggest and one which no failure can deprive of its attraction. It in-dicates also the consequences of such an enter-prise. I interpret it as follows.

The pursuit of perfection as the crow flies is an activity both impious and unavoidable in human life. It involves the penalties of impiety (the anger of the gods and social isolation), and its reward is not that of achievement but that of having made the attempt. It is an activ-ity, therefore, suitable for individuals, but not for societies. For an individual who is impelled to engage in it, the reward may exceed both

From Michael Oakeshott, *Rationalism in Politics and Other Essays* (Indianapolis: Liberty Press, 1991), pp. 465–487. Reprinted by permission of Dr. Shirley Letwin. Some footnotes omitted.

the penalty and the inevitable defeat. The penitent may hope, or even expect, to fall back, a wounded hero, into the arms of an understanding and forgiving society. And even the impenitent can be reconciled with himself in the powerful necessity of his impulse, though, like Prometheus, he must suffer for it. For a society, on the other hand, the penalty is a chaos of conflicting ideals, the disruption of a common life, and the reward is the renown which attaches to monumental folly. *A mesure que l'humanité se perfectionne l'homme se dégrade.* Or, to interpret the myth in a more light-hearted fashion: human life is a gamble; but while the individual must be allowed to bet according to his inclination (on the favourite or on an outsider), society should always back the field. Let us consider the matter in application to our own civilization.

The activity with which we are concerned is what is called moral activity, that is, activity which may be either good or bad. The moral life is human affection and behaviour determined, not by nature, but by art. It is conduct to which there is an alternative. This alternative need not be consciously before the mind; moral conduct does not necessarily involve the reflective choice of a particular action. Nor does it require that each occasion shall find a man without a disposition, or even without predetermination, to act in a certain way: a man's affections and conduct may be seen to spring from his character without thereby ceasing to be moral. The freedom without which moral conduct is impossible is freedom from a natural necessity which binds *all* men to act alike. This does not carry us very far. It identifies moral behaviour as the exercise of an acquired skill (though the skill need not have been self-consciously acquired), but it does not distinguish it from other kinds of art—from cookery or from carpentry. However, it carries us far enough for my purpose, which is to consider the *form* of the moral life, and in particular the form of the moral life of contemporary Western civilization.

In any manifestation of the moral life, form and content are, of course, inseparable. Nevertheless, neither can be said to determine the other; and in considering the form we shall be considering an abstraction which, in principle, is indifferent to any particular content, and indifferent also to any particular ethical theory. The practical question, What kinds of human enterprise should be designated right and wrong? and the philosophical question, What is the ultimate nature of moral criteria? are both outside what we are to consider. We are concerned only with the shape of the moral life. And our concern must be philosophical and historical, rather than practical, because neither a society nor an individual is normally given the opportunity of making an express choice of the form of a moral life.

The moral life of our society discloses a form neither simple nor homogeneous. Indeed, the form of our morality appears to be a mixture of two ideal extremes, a mixture the character of which derives from the predominance of one extreme over the other. I am not convinced of the necessary ideality of the extremes; it is perhaps possible that one, if not both, could exist as an actual form of the moral life. But even if this is doubtful, each can certainly exist with so little modification from the other that it is permissible to begin by regarding them as possible forms of morality. Let us consider the two forms which, either separately or in combination, compose the form of the moral life of the Western world.

Two

In the first of these forms, the moral life is *a habit of affection and behaviour;* not a habit of reflective *thought,* but a habit of *affection* and *conduct.* The current situations of a normal life are met, not by consciously applying to ourselves a rule of behaviour, nor by conduct recognized as the expression of a moral ideal, but by acting in accordance with a certain habit of behaviour. The moral life in this form does not spring from the consciousness of possible alternative ways of behaving and a choice, determined by an opinion, a rule or an ideal, from among these alternatives; conduct is as nearly as possible without reflection. And consequently, most of the current situations of life do not appear as occasions calling for judgment, or as problems requiring solutions;

there is no weighing up of alternatives or reflection on consequences, no uncertainty, no battle of scruples. There is, on the occasion, nothing more than the unreflective following of a tradition of conduct in which we have been brought up. And such moral habit will disclose itself as often in *not* doing, in the taste which dictates abstention from certain actions, as in performances. It should, of course, be understood that I am not here describing a form of the moral life which assumes the existence of a moral sense or of moral intuition, nor a form of the moral life presupposing a moral theory which attributes authority to conscience. Indeed, no specific theory of the source of authority is involved in this form of the moral life. Nor am I describing a merely primitive form of morality, that is, the morality of a society unaccustomed to reflective thought. I am describing the form which moral action takes (because it can take no other) in all the emergencies of life when time and opportunity for reflection are lacking, and I am supposing that what is true of the emergencies of life is true of most of the occasions when human conduct is free from natural necessity.

Every form of the moral life (because it is affection and behaviour determined by art) depends upon education. And the character of each form is reflected in the kind of education required to nurture and maintain it. From what sort of education will this first form of the moral life spring?

We acquire habits of conduct, not by constructing a way of living upon rules or precepts learned by heart and subsequently practised, but by living with people who habitually behave in a certain manner: we acquire habits of conduct in the same way as we acquire our native language. There is no point in a child's life at which he can be said to begin to learn the language which is habitually spoken in his hearing; and there is no point in his life at which he can be said to begin to learn habits of behaviour from the people constantly about him. No doubt, in both cases, what is learnt (or some of it) can be formulated in rules and precepts; but in neither case do we, in this kind of education, learn by learning rules and precepts. What we learn here is what may be learned without the formulation of its rules.

And not only may a command of language and behaviour be achieved without our becoming aware of the rules, but also, if we have acquired a knowledge of the rules, this sort of command of language and behaviour is impossible until we have forgotten them as rules and are no longer tempted to turn speech and action into the applications of rules to a situation. Further, the education by means of which we acquire habits of affection and behaviour is not only coeval with conscious life, but it is carried on, in practice and observation, without pause in every moment of our waking life, and perhaps even in our dreams; what is begun as imitation continues as selective conformity to a rich variety of customary behaviour. This sort of education is not compulsory; it is inevitable. And lastly (if education in general is making oneself at home in the natural and civilized worlds), this is not a separable part of education. One may set apart an hour in which to learn mathematics and devote another to the Catechism, but it is impossible to engage in any activity whatever without contributing to this kind of moral education, and it is impossible to enjoy this kind of moral education in an hour set aside for its study. There are, of course, many things which cannot be learned in this sort of education. We may learn in this manner to play a game, and we may learn to play it without breaking the rules, but we cannot acquire a knowledge of the rules themselves without formulating them or having them formulated for us. And further, without a knowledge of the rules we can never know for certain whether or not we are observing them, nor shall we be able to explain why the referee has blown his whistle. Or, to change the metaphor, from this sort of education can spring the ability never to write a false line of poetry, but it will give us neither the ability to scan nor a knowledge of the names of the various metric forms.

It is not difficult, then, to understand the sort of moral education by means of which habits of affection and behaviour may be acquired; it is the sort of education which gives the power to act appropriately and without hesitation, doubt or difficulty, but which does not give the ability to explain our actions in abstract terms, or defend them as emanations of moral principles. Moreover, this education must be considered to have failed in its purpose if it provides a range of behaviour insufficient to meet all situations without the necessity of calling upon reflection, or if it does not make the habit of behaviour sufficiently compelling to remove hesitation. But it must not be considered to have failed merely because it leaves us ignorant of moral rules and moral ideals. And a man may be said to have acquired most thoroughly what this kind of moral education can teach him when his moral dispositions are inseverably connected with his *amour-propre,* when the spring of his conduct is not an attachment to an ideal or a felt duty to obey a rule, but his self-esteem, and when to act wrongly is felt as diminution of his self-esteem.

Now, it will be observed that this is a form of morality which gives remarkable stability to the moral life from the point of view either of an individual or of a society; it is not in its nature to countenance large or sudden changes in the kinds of behaviour it desiderates. Parts of a moral life in this form may collapse, but since the habits of conduct which compose it are never recognized as a system, the collapse does not readily spread to the whole. And being without a perceived rigid framework distinct from the modes of behaviour themselves (a framework, for example, of abstract moral ideals), it is not subject to the kind of collapse which springs from the detection of some flaw or incoherence in a system of moral ideals. Intellectual error with regard to moral ideas or opinions does not compromise a moral life which is firmly based upon a habit of conduct. In short, the stability which belongs to this form of the moral life derives from its elasticity and its ability to suffer change without disruption. First, there is in it nothing that is absolutely fixed. Just as in a language there may be certain constructions which are simply bad grammar, but in all the important ranges of expression the language is malleable by the writer who uses it and he cannot go wrong unless he deserts its genius, so in this form of the moral life, the more thorough our education the more certain will be our taste and the more extensive our range or behaviour within the tradition. Custom is always adaptable and susceptible to the *nuance*

of the situation. This may appear a paradoxical assertion; custom, we have been taught, is blind. It is, however, an insidious piece of misobservation; custom is not blind, it is only "blind as a bat." And anyone who has studied a tradition of customary behaviour (or a tradition of any other sort) knows that both rigidity and instability are foreign to its character. And secondly, this form of the moral life is capable of change as well as of local variation. Indeed, no traditional way of behaviour, no traditional skill, ever remains fixed; its history is one of continuous change. It is true that the change it admits is neither great nor sudden; but then, revolutionary change is usually the product of the eventual overthrow of an aversion from change, and is characteristic of something that has few internal resources of change. And the appearance of changelessness in a morality of traditional behaviour is an illusion which springs from the erroneous belief that the only significant change is that which is either induced by self-conscious activity or is, at least, observed on the occasion. The sort of change which belongs to this form of the moral life is analogous to the change to which a living language is subject: nothing is more habitual or customary than our ways of speech, and nothing is more continuously invaded by change. Like prices in a free market, habits of moral conduct show no revolutionary changes because they are never at rest. But it should be observed, also, that because the internal movement characteristic of this form of the moral life does not spring from reflection upon moral principles, and represents only an unselfconscious exploitation of the genius of the tradition of moral conduct, it does not amount to moral self-criticism. And, consequently, a moral life of this kind, if it degenerates into superstition, or if crisis supervenes, has little power of recovery. Its defence is solely its resistance to the conditions productive of crisis.

One further point should, perhaps, be noticed: the place and character of the moral eccentric in this form of the moral life, when it is considered as the form of the moral life of a society. The moral eccentric is not, of course, excluded by this form of morality. (The want of moral sensibility, the hollowness of moral character, which seems often to inhere in peoples whose morality is predominantly one of custom, is improperly attributed to the customary form of their morality; its cause lies elsewhere.) We sometimes think that deviation from a customary morality must always take place under the direction of a formulated moral ideal. But this is not so. There is a freedom and inventiveness at the heart of every traditional way of life, and deviation may be an expression of that freedom, springing from a sensitiveness to the tradition itself and remaining faithful to the traditional form. Generally speaking, no doubt, the inspiration of deviation from moral habit is perfectionist, but it is not necessarily consciously perfectionist. It is not, in essence, rebellious, and may be likened to the sort of innovation introduced into a plastic art by the fortuitous appearance in an individual of a specially high degree of manual skill, or to the sort of change a great stylist may make in a language. Although in any particular instance deviation may lead the individual eccentric astray, and although it is not something that can profitably be imitated, moral eccentricity is of value to a society whose morality is one of habit of behaviour (regardless of the direction it may take) so long as it remains the activity of the individual and is not permitted to disrupt the communal life. In a morality of an habitual way of behaviour, then, the influence of the moral eccentric may be powerful but is necessarily oblique, and the attitude of society towards him is necessarily ambivalent. He is admired but not copied, reverenced but not followed, welcomed but ostracized.

Three

The second form of the moral life we are to consider may be regarded as in many respects the opposite of the first. In it activity is determined, not by a habit of behaviour, but by *the reflective application of a moral criterion*. It appears in two common varieties: as *the self-conscious pursuit of moral ideals,* and as *the reflective observance of moral rules.* But it is what these varieties have in common that is important, because it is this, and not what distinguishes

them from one another, which divides them from the first form of morality.

This is a form of the moral life in which a special value is attributed to self-consciousness, individual or social; not only is the rule or the ideal the product of reflective thought, but the application of the rule or the ideal to the situation is also a reflective activity. Normally the rule or the ideal is determined first and in the abstract; that is, the first task in constructing an art of behaviour in this form is to express moral aspirations in words—in a rule of life or in a system of abstract ideals. This task of verbal expression need not begin with a moral *de omnibus dubitandum;* but its aim is not only to set out the desirable ends of conduct, but also to set them out clearly and unambiguously and to reveal their relations to one another. Secondly, a man who would enjoy this form of the moral life must be certain of his ability to defend these formulated aspirations against criticism. For, having been brought into the open, they will henceforth be liable to attack. His third task will be to translate them into behaviour, to apply them to the current situations of life as they arise. In this form of the moral life, then, action will spring from a judgment concerning the rule or end to be applied and the determination to apply it. The situations of living should, ideally, appear as problems to be solved, for it is only in this form that they will receive the attention they call for. And there will be a resistance to the urgency of action; it will appear more important to have the right moral ideal, than to act. The application of a rule or an ideal to a situation can never be easy; both ideal and situation will usually require interpretation, and a rule of life (unless the life has been simplified by the drastic reduction of the variety of situations which are allowed to appear) will always be found wanting unless it is supplemented with an elaborate casuistry or hermeneutic. It is true that moral ideals and moral rules may become so familiar that they take on the character of an habitual or traditional way of *thinking* about behaviour. It is true also that long familiarity with our ideals may have enabled us to express them more concretely in a system of specific rights and duties, handy in application. And further, a moral ideal may find its expression in a type of human character—such as the character of the gentleman—and conduct become the imaginative application of the ideal character to the situation. But these qualifications carry us only part of the way: they may remove the necessity for ad hoc reflection on the rules and ideals themselves, but they leave us still with the problem of interpreting the situation and the task of translating the ideal, the right or the duty into behaviour. For the right or the duty is always to observe a rule or realize an end, and not to behave in a certain concrete manner. Indeed, it is not desired, in this form of the moral life, that tradition should carry us all the way; its distinctive virtue is to be subjecting behaviour to a continuous corrective analysis and criticism.

This form of the moral life, not less than the other, depends upon education, but upon an education of an appropriately different sort. In order to acquire the necessary knowledge of moral ideals or of a rule of life, we need something more than the observation and practice of behaviour itself. We require, first, an intellectual training in the detection and appreciation of the moral ideals themselves, a training in which the ideals are separated and detached from the necessarily imperfect expression they find in particular actions. We require, secondly, training in the art of the intellectual management of these ideals. And thirdly, we require training in the application of ideals to concrete situations, in the art of translation and in the art of selecting appropriate means for achieving the ends which our education has inculcated. Such an education may be made compulsory in a society, but if so it is only because it is not inevitable. It is true that, as Spinoza says,[1] a substitute for a perfectly trained moral judgment may be found in committing a rule of life to memory and following it implicitly. But, though this is as far as some pupils will get, it cannot be considered to be the aim of this moral education. If it is to achieve its purpose, this education must carry us far beyond the acquisition of a moral technique; and it must be considered to have failed in its purpose if it has not given both ability to determine behaviour by a self-conscious choice and an understanding of the ideal grounds of the choice made. Nobody can fully share this form of the moral life

who is not something of a philosopher and something of a self-analyst: its aim is moral behaviour springing from the communally cultivated reflective capacities of each individual.

Now, a moral life in which everyone who shares it knows at each moment exactly what he is doing and why, should be well protected against degeneration into superstition and should, moreover, give remarkable confidence to those who practise it. Nevertheless, it has its dangers, both from the point of view of an individual and from that of a society. The confidence which belongs to it is mainly a confidence in respect of the moral ideals themselves, or of the moral rule. The education in the ideals or in the rule must be expected to be the most successful part of this moral education; the art of applying the ideals is more difficult both to teach and to learn. And together with the certainty about how to *think* about moral ideals, must be expected to go a proportionate uncertainty about how to *act*. The constant analysis of behaviour tends to undermine, not only prejudice in moral habit, but moral habit itself, and moral reflection may come to inhibit moral sensibility.

Further, a morality which takes the form of the self-conscious pursuit of moral ideals is one which, at every moment, calls upon those who practise it to determine their behaviour by reference to a vision of perfection. This is not so much the case when the guide is a moral rule, because the rule is not represented as perfection and constitutes a mediation, a cushion, between the behaviour it demands on each occasion and the complete moral response to the situation. But when the guide of conduct is a moral ideal we are never suffered to escape from perfection. Constantly, indeed on all occasions, the society is called upon to seek virtue as the crow flies. It may even be said that the moral life, in this form, demands an hyperoptic moral vision and encourages intense moral emulation among those who enjoy it, the moral eccentric being recognized, not as a vicarious sufferer for the stability of a society, but as a leader and a guide. And the unhappy society, with an ear for every call, certain always about what it ought to *think* (though it will never for long be the same thing), in action shies and plunges like a distracted animal.

Again, a morality of ideals has little power of self-modification; its stability springs from its inelasticity and its imperviousness to change. It will, of course, respond to interpretation, but the limits of that response are close and severe. It has a great capacity to resist change, but when that resistance is broken down, what takes place is not change but revolution—rejection and replacement. Moreover, every moral ideal is potentially an obsession; the pursuit of moral ideals is an idolatry in which particular objects are recognized as "gods." This potentiality may be held in check by more profound reflection, by an intellectual grasp of the whole system which gives place and proportion to each moral ideal; but such a grasp is rarely achieved. Too often the excessive pursuit of one ideal leads to the exclusion of others, perhaps all others; in our eagerness to realize justice we come to forget charity, and a passion for righteousness has made many a man hard and merciless. There is, indeed, no ideal the pursuit of which will not lead to disillusion; *chagrin* waits at the end for all who take this path. Every admirable ideal has its opposite, no less admirable. Liberty or order, justice or charity, spontaneity or deliberateness, principle or circumstance, self or others, these are the kinds of dilemma with which this form of the moral life is always confronting us, making us see double by directing our attention always to abstract extremes, none of which is wholly desirable. It is a form of the moral life which puts upon those who share it, not only the task of translating moral ideals into appropriate forms of conduct, but also the distracting intellectual burden of removing the verbal conflict of ideals before moral behaviour is possible. These conflicting ideals are, of course, reconciled in all amiable characters (that is, when they no longer appear as ideals), but that is not enough; a verbal and theoretical reconciliation is required. In short, this is a form of the moral life which is dangerous in an individual and disastrous in a society. For an individual it is a gamble which may have its reward when undertaken within the limits of a society which is not itself engaged in the gamble; for a society it is mere folly.

Four

This brief characterization of what appear to be two forms of the moral life, while perhaps establishing their distinction or even their opposition, will have made us more doubtful about their capability of independent existence. Neither, taken alone, recommends itself convincingly as a likely form of the moral life, in an individual or in a society; the one is all habit, the other all reflection. And the more closely we examine them, the more certain we become that they are, not forms of the moral life at all, but ideal extremes. And when we turn to consider what sort of a form of the moral life they offer in combination, we may perhaps enjoy the not illusory confidence that we are approaching more nearly to concrete possibility, or even historical reality.

In a mixture in which the first of these extremes is dominant, the moral life may be expected to be immune from a confusion between behaviour and the pursuit of an ideal. Action will retain its primacy, and, whenever it is called for, will spring from habit of behaviour. Conduct itself will never become problematical, inhibited by the hesitations of ideal speculation or the felt necessity of bringing philosophic talent and the fruits of philosophic education to bear upon the situation. The confidence in action, which belongs to the well-nurtured customary moral life, will remain unshaken. And the coherence of the moral life will not wait upon the abstract unity which the reflective relation of values can give it. But, in addition, this mixed form of the moral life may be supposed to enjoy the advantages that spring from a reflective morality—the power to criticize, to reform and to explain itself, and the power to propagate itself beyond the range of the custom of a society. It will enjoy also the appropriate intellectual confidence in its moral standards and purposes. And it will enjoy all this without the danger of moral criticism usurping the place of a habit of moral behaviour, or of moral speculation bringing disintegration to moral life. The education in moral habit will be supplemented, but not weakened, by the education in moral ideology. And in a society which enjoyed this form of the moral life, both habit and ideology might be the common possession of all its members, or moral speculation might in fact be confined to the few, while the morality of the many remained one of the habit of behaviour. But, in any case, the internal resources of movement of this form of morality would be supplied by both its components: to the potential individual eccentricity which belongs to a traditional morality would be added the more consciously rebellious eccentricity which has its roots in the more precisely followed perfectionism of a morality of ideals. In short, this form of the moral life will offer to a society advantages similar to those of a religion which has taken to itself a theology (though not necessarily a popular theology) but without losing its character as a way of living.

On the other hand, a morality whose form is a mixture in which the second of our extremes is dominant will, I think, suffer from a permanent tension between its component parts. Taking charge, the morality of the self-conscious pursuit of ideals will have a disintegrating effect upon habit of behaviour. When action is called for, speculation or criticism will supervene. Behaviour itself will tend to become problematical, seeking its self-confidence in the coherence of an ideology. The pursuit of perfection will get in the way of a stable and flexible moral tradition, the naïve coherence of which will be prized less than the unity which springs from self-conscious analysis and synthesis. It will seem more important to have an intellectually defensible moral ideology than a ready habit of moral behaviour. And it will come to be assumed that a morality which is not easily transferable to another society, which lacks an obvious universality, is (for that reason) inadequate for the needs of the society of its origin. The society will wait upon its self-appointed moral teachers, pursuing the extremes they recommend and at a loss when they are silent. The distinguished and inspiring visiting preacher, who nevertheless is a stranger to the way we live, will displace the priest, the father of his parish. In a moral life constantly or periodically suffering the ravages of the armies of conflicting ideals, or (when these for the time have passed) falling into the hands of censors and inspectors, the cultivation of a habit of moral behaviour will have as little opportunity as the cultivation of the land when the farmer is confused and distracted by academic critics and political directors. Indeed, in such a mixture (where habit of behaviour is subordinate to the pursuit of ideals) each of the components is unavoidably playing a role foreign to its character; as in a literature in which criticism has usurped the place of poetry, or in a religious life in which the pursuit of theology offers itself as an alternative to the practice of piety.

These, however, must be counted incidental, though grave, imperfections in this mixture of extremes in the moral life; the radical defect of this form is the radical defect of its dominant extreme—its denial of the poetic character of all human activity. A prosaic tradition of thought has accustomed us to the assumption that moral activity, when analysed, will be found to consist in the translation of an idea of what ought to be into a practical reality, the transformation of an ideal into a concrete existence. And we are accustomed, even, to think of poetry in these terms; first, a "heart's desire" (an idea) and then its expression, its translation into words. Nevertheless, I think this view is mistaken; it is the superimposition upon art and moral activity generally of an inappropriate didactic form. A poem is not the translation into words of a state of mind. What the poet says and what he wants to say are not two things, the one succeeding and embodying the other, they are the same thing; he does not know what he wants to say until he has said it. And the "corrections" he may make to his first attempt are not efforts to make words correspond more closely to an already formulated idea or to images already fully formed in his mind, they are renewed efforts to formulate the idea, to conceive the image. Nothing exists in advance of the poem itself, except perhaps the poetic passion. And what is true of poetry is true also, I think, of all human moral activity. Moral ideals are not, in the first place, the products of reflective thought, the verbal expressions of unrealized ideas, which are then translated (with varying degrees of accuracy) into human behaviour; they are the products of human behaviour, of human practical activity, to which reflective thought gives subsequent, partial and abstract expression in words. What is good, or right, or what is considered to be reasonable behaviour may exist in advance of the situation, but only in the generalized form of the possibilities of behaviour determined by art and not by nature. That is to say, the capital of moral ideals upon which a morality of the pursuit of moral ideals goes into business has always been accumulated by a morality of habitual behaviour, and appears in the form of abstract ideas only because (for the purposes of subscription) it has been transformed by reflective thought into a currency of ideas.[2] This view of the matter does not, of course, deprive moral ideals of their power as critics of human habits, it does not denigrate the activity of reflective thought in giving this verbal expression to the principles of behaviour; there is no doubt whatever that a morality in which reflection has no part is defective. But it suggests that a morality of the pursuit of moral ideals, or a morality in which this is dominant, is not what it appears at first sight to be, is not something that can stand on its own feet. In such a morality, that which has power to rescue from superstition is given the task of generating human behaviour—a task which, in fact, it cannot perform. And it is only to be expected that a morality of this sort will be subject to sudden and ignominious collapse. In the life of an individual this collapse need not necessarily be fatal; in the life of a society it is likely to be irretrievable. For a society is a common way of life; and not only is it true that a society may perish of a disease which is not necessarily fatal even to those of its members who suffer from it, but it is also true that what is corrupting in the society may not be corrupting in its members.

Five

The reader, knowing as much as I about the form of the moral life of contemporary Christendom, will not need to be told where all this is leading. If what I have said is not wide of the mark, it may perhaps be agreed that the form of our morality is that of a mixture in which the morality of the self-conscious pursuit of moral ideals is dominant. The moral energy of our civilization has for many centuries been applied mainly (though not, of course, exclusively) to building a Tower of Babel; and in a world dizzy with moral ideals we know less about how to behave in public and in private than ever before. Like the fool, our eyes have been on the ends of the earth. Having lost the thread of Ariadne, we have put our confidence in a plan of the labyrinth, and have given our attention to interpreters of the plan. Lacking habits of moral behaviour, we have fallen back upon moral opinions as a substitute; but, as we all know, when we reflect upon what we are doing we too often conclude that it is wrong. Like lonely men who, to gain reassurance, exaggerate the talents of their few friends, we exaggerate the significance of our moral ideals to fill in the hollowness of our moral life. It is a pitiless wedding which we have celebrated with our shadowy ideal of conduct. No doubt our present moral distraction (which is now several centuries old) springs partly from doubts we have in respect of the ideals themselves; all the effort of analysis and criticism has not yet succeeded in establishing a single one of them unquestionably. But this is not the root of the matter. The truth is that a morality in this form, regardless of the quality of the ideals, breeds nothing but distraction and moral instability. Perhaps it is a partial appreciation of this which has led some societies to give an artificial stability to their moral ideals. A few of these ideals are selected, those few are turned into an authoritative canon which is then made a guide to legislation or even a ground for the violent persecution of eccentricity. A moral ideology is established and maintained because this appears the only means of winning the necessary moral stability for the society. But in fact it is no remedy; it merely covers up the corruption of consciousness, the moral distraction inherent in morality as the self-conscious pursuit of moral ideals. However, it serves to illustrate the truth that the one kind of society which must of necessity be the enemy of profitable moral eccentricity is the society whose moral organization springs from the pursuit of ideals; for the moral life of such a society is itself nothing better than an arbitrary selection of moral eccentricities.

Now, I am not contending that our morality is wholly enclosed in the form of the self-conscious pursuit of moral ideals. Indeed, my view is that this is an ideal extreme in moral form and not, by itself, a possible form of morality at all. I am suggesting that the form of our moral life is dominated by this extreme, and that our moral life consequently suffers the internal tension inherent in this form. Certainly we possess habits of moral behaviour, but too often our self-conscious pursuit of ideals hinders us from enjoying them. Self-consciousness is asked to be creative, and habit is given the role of critic; what should be subordinate has come to rule, and its rule is a misrule. Sometimes the tension appears on the surface, and on these occasions we are aware that something is wrong. A man who fails to practise what he preaches does not greatly disturb us; we know that preaching is in terms of moral ideals and that no man can practise them perfectly. This is merely the minor tension between ideal and achievement. But when a man preaches "social justice" (or indeed any other ideal whatsoever) and at the same time is obviously without a habit of ordinary decent behaviour (a habit that belongs to our morality but has fortunately never been idealized), the tension I speak of makes its appearance. And the fact that we are still able to recognize it is evidence that we are not wholly at the mercy of a morality of abstract ideals. Nevertheless, I do not think that anyone who has considered the matter will be disposed to deny that we are for the most part dominated by this morality. It is not our fault; we have been give little or no choice in the matter. It is, however, our misfortune. And it may be relevant, in conclusion, to consider briefly how it has come about.

On this subject, the history of European morals, I have nothing new to say; I can only direct attention to what is already well known. The form of contemporary western European morality has come to us from the distant past. It was determined in the first four centuries of the Christian era, that momentous period of our history when so much of our intellectual and emotional outlook began to emerge. It would, of course, be absurd to suggest that European morality sprang from some new

species of seed first sown in that period; what, if anything, was new at that time was the mixture of seed which was at the disposal of those generations, to be sown, cultivated and sown once more until its characteristic fruit became fixed. It was an age of moral change. In that Greco-Roman world the old habits of moral behaviour had lost their vitality. There were, no doubt, men who were good neighbors, faithful friends and pious citizens, whose confidence in the customs that determined their conduct was still unshaken; but, in general, the impetus of moral habit of behaviour seems to have been spent—illustrating, perhaps, the defect of a form of morality too securely insulated from the criticism of ideals. It was, in consequence, an age of intense moral self-consciousness, an age of moral reformers who, unavoidably, preached a morality of the pursuit of ideals and taught a variety of dogmatic moral ideologies. The intellectual energy of the time was directed towards the determination of an ideal, and the moral energy towards the translation of that ideal into practice. Moral self-consciousness itself became a virtue; genuine morality was identified with the "practice of philosophy." And it was thought that for the achievement of a good life it was necessary that a man should submit to an artificial moral training, a moral gymnastic, *ás,hsi.*; learning and discipline must be added to "nature." The age, of course, was able to distinguish between a man who attained to a merely intellectual appreciation of moral ideals and one who was successful in the enterprise of translating ideal into conduct, but it was common ground that the moral life was to be achieved only, as Philo said, "by reading, by meditation and by the calling to mind of noble ideals." In short, what the Greco-Roman world of this period had to offer was a morality in which the self-conscious pursuit of moral ideals was pre-eminent.

And our inheritance from that other great source of our moral inspiration, from early Christianity, was of a similar character: indeed it is not an inheritance which in this matter can be securely separated from that of the ancient world as a whole. In the earliest days, to be a Christian was to be a member of a community animated by a faith and sustained by a hope— faith in a person and hope for a coming event.

The morality of these communities was a custom of behaviour appropriate to the character of the faith and to the nature of the expectation. It was a way of living distinguished in its place and time by the absence from it of a formulated moral ideal; and it was a way of living departure from which alone involved the penalty of exclusion from the community. And further, it was a way of living which admitted, but did not demand, extremes of behaviour, counsels of perfection. The nearest thing to a moral ideal known to these communities was the ideal of charity; the nearest thing to a moral rule was the precept to love God and one's neighbour. It was a morality which found its characteristic verbal expression in the phrase, τοὺσ τρόπουσ, κυριου, the custom of the Lord. But over these earliest Christian communities, in the course of two centuries, there came a great change. The habit of moral behaviour was converted into the self-conscious pursuit of formulated moral ideals—a conversion parallel to the change from faith in a person to belief in a collection of abstract propositions, a creed. This change sprang from a variety of sources; from a change in the circumstances of the Christian's life, from the pressure of the alien intellectual world in which the Christian was set down, from the desire to "give a reason for the hope" that animated him, from the necessity of translating the Christian way of life into a form in which it could be appreciated by those who had never shared the original inspiration and who, having to learn their Christianity as a foreign language, needed a grammar. The urge to speculate, to abstract and to define, which overtook Christianity as a religion, infected also Christianity as a way of moral life. But, whatever was the impulse of the change, it appears that by the middle of the third century there existed a Christian morality in the familiar form of the self-conscious pursuit of moral ideals, and by the time of St. Ambrose the *form* of this morality had become indistinguishable from that of the morality of the surrounding world, a morality of virtues and vices and of the translation of ideals into actions. A Christian morality in the form of a way of life did not, of course, perish, and it has never completely disappeared. But from this time in the history of Christendom a Christian habit of moral behaviour (which had sprung from the circumstances of Christian life) was swamped by a Christian moral ideology, and the perception of the poetic character of human conduct was lost.

I do not wish to suggest that either the self-conscious morality of the Greco-Roman world at the beginning of our era, or the change which overtook Christian morality in the second and third centuries, was avoidable. The one was merely the filling of the vacuum left by the collapse of a traditional morality, and as for the other—perhaps, in order to convert the world, a morality must be reduced to the easily translatable prose of a moral ideal, must be defined and made intellectually coherent, even though the price is a loss of spontaneity and confidence and the approach of the danger of obsession. The fact, however, remains that the moral inheritance of western Europe, both from the classical culture of the ancient world and from Christianity, was not the gift of a morality of habitual behaviour, but of a moral ideology. It is true that, in the course of centuries, this moral form went some way towards being reconverted into a morality of habit of behaviour. Such a conversion is certainly possible when moral ideals become familiar and, finding expression in customs and institutions which exert a direct pressure upon conduct, cease to be mere ideals. And it is true, also, that the invading barbarians contributed a morality of custom rather than of idea. Nevertheless, modern European morality has never been able to divest itself of the form in which it first emerged. And having once committed the indiscretion of formulating itself in the abstract terms of moral ideals, it was only to be expected that its critics (who have never for long been silent) should seize upon these, and that in defending them against attack they should become rigid and exaggerated. Every significant attack upon Christian morality (that of Nietzsche, for example) has been mistaken for an attack upon the particular moral ideals of Christian life, whereas whatever force it possessed derived from the fact that the object of attack was a morality of ideals which had never succeeded in becoming a morality of habit of behaviour.

The history of European morals, then, is in

part the history of the maintenance and extension of a morality whose form has, from the beginning, been dominated by the pursuit of moral ideals. In so far as this is an unhappy form of morality, prone to obsession and at war with itself, it is a misfortune to be deplored; in so far as it cannot now readily be avoided, it is a misfortune to be made the best of. And if a morality of ideals is now all, or at least the best, of what we have, it might seem an injudicious moment to dwell upon its defects. But in order to make the best of an unavoidable situation, we need to know its defects as well as feel its necessity. And what at the present time stands between us and the opportunity (such as it is) of surmounting our misfortune is not our sense of the difficulty of doing so, but an erroneous inference we have drawn from our situation—the belief, which has slowly settled upon us, encouraged by almost all the intellectual tendencies of recent centuries, that it is no misfortune at all, but a situation to be welcomed. For the remarkable thing about contemporary European morality is not merely that its form is dominated by the self-conscious pursuit of ideals, but that this form is generally thought to be better and higher than any other. A morality of habit of behaviour is dismissed as primitive and obsolete; the pursuit of moral ideals (whatever discontent there may be with the ideals themselves) is identified with moral enlightenment. And further, it is prized (and has been particularly prized on this account since the seventeenth century) because it appears to hold out the possibility of that most sought-after consummation—a "scientific" morality. It is to be feared, however, that in both these appearances we are sadly deceived. The pursuit of moral ideals has proved itself (as might be expected) an untrustworthy form of morality, the spring neither of a practical nor of a "scientific" moral life.

The predicament of Western morals, as I read it, is first that our moral life has come to be dominated by the pursuit of ideals, a dominance ruinous to a settled habit of behaviour; and, secondly, that we have come to think of this dominance as a benefit for which we should be grateful or an achievement of which we should be proud. And the only purpose to be served by this investigation of our predicament is to disclose the corrupt consciousness, the self-deception which reconciles us to our misfortune.

Notes

"The Tower of Babel" was first published in *Cambridge Journal*, Volume II, 1948. It should not be confused with the paper of the same name which appeared in Oakeshott's *On History and Other Essays* (1983).

1. Benedict de Spinoza, *The Ethics*, Part V, Proposition X, R. H. M. Elwes, trans. (George Bell and Sons, 1883).

2. For example, Jên (consideration for others) in the Confucian morality was an abstraction from the filial piety and respect for elders which constituted the ancient Chinese habit of moral behaviour. The activity of the Sages, who (according to Chuang Tzu) *invented* goodness, duty and the rules and ideals of moral conduct, was one in which a concrete morality of habitual behaviour was sifted and refined; but, like too critical anthologists, they threw out the imperfect approximations of their material and what remained was not the reflection of a literature but merely a collection of masterpieces.

Group Egoism

Andrew Oldenquist

In this selection Andrew Oldenquist presents a moral theory of community life, a form of tribal morality that he calls "group egoism." He begins with a discussion of moral motivation, finding that two kinds of motivation have predominated in Western moral theory: rational self-interest and a commitment to impersonal duty. Oldenquist sets out to show that neither motivation can explain the social cohesion of a community. He argues that there is a third distinct kind of human motivation—group loyalty—that is the source of community attachments. Oldenquist calls people with this form of moral motivation "group egoists," because they expand the area covered by self-interest to include a specific group of related people. Oldenquist's justification of group egoism begins with a defense of egoism: As an egoist, I will favor myself over others independent of any merit or defects I might have. Then, he extends this partiality from "me" to "mine." Instead of acting to benefit "me," the group egoist acts to benefit "my" family, "my" neighborhood, "my" company, "my" country, "my" species. Again, the sole justification for this bias is that they are "mine." Tribal morality, Oldenquist argues, depends on this sense of possession. In a primitive tribe such loyalty motivates actions to benefit other members of the tribe and limits those obligations at the boundaries of the tribe. In a modern society, however, each person belongs to many different social groups, each claiming its members' loyalty. These loyalties may conflict with one another, thus forcing the moral agent to choose among them, or alternatively, leaving the person confused by and alienated from the moral demands of all groups. Liberal and utilitarian ethics, in Oldenquist's view, are group egoism writ large. They endorse the widest loyalty—species loyalty—as morally obligatory. This preference for loyalty to a larger over a smaller group, he argues, cannot be justified by size alone and neglects the powerful claims of the attachments in smaller groups.

Man cannot become attached to higher aims and submit to a rule if he sees nothing above him to which he belongs. To free him from all social pressure is to abandon him to himself and demoralize him. These are really the two characteristics of our moral situation. While the State becomes inflated and hypertrophied in order to obtain a firm enough grip upon individuals, but without succeeding, the latter, without mutual relationships, tumble over one another like so many liquid molecules, encountering no central energy to retain, fix and organize them.

To remedy this evil, the restitution to local groups of something of their old autonomy is periodically suggested. This is called decentralization. But the only really useful decentralization is one which would simultaneously produce a greater concentration of social energies.

Emile Durkheim[1]

Anglo-American social thought, from Hobbes and Locke to contemporary social scientists, considers just two foundations for the mutual restraint, cooperation, and commitment a society requires of its citizens if it is to be safe and satisfying: rational self-interest and impersonal social morality. I may be a good citizen because I think that is the best way to "look out for number one," or because I think it is my duty. The history of Western social thought, with the exception of German idealist philosophers and the Marxists, has primarily consisted in working out variations on these two themes.

The result has been a kind of "official theory" of human nature that attributes behavior to either selfishness or altruism and

From Andrew Oldenquist, "The Metaphysics of Self and Society" in *The Non-Suicidal Society* (Indianapolis: Indiana University Press, 1986), pp. 113–134. Reprinted by permission of the Indiana University Press.

admits no third alternative: something in our brains or souls flips one way, or flops the other way, like a switch. Believers in universal selfishness, including most American social scientists, think the switch is permanently glued in the selfish position; but they still find these two motives the only conceivable ones. Hence group loyalty and sense-of-community, the third ground of social life, is either ignored or else some pallid form of it is assimilated to self-interest.

However, the fundamental force that holds societies together has rarely if ever been either rational selfishness or the cold demands of duty. There has always been a "third way." We need to acquire a deeper understanding of this third way, which I have by turns been calling group egoism, group loyalty, and community. The egoist acts because doing so benefits himself, the group egoist acts because doing so benefits or protects what he has come to regard as *his,* for example, his family, his neighborhood, his company, his city, his country, or his species. When we shift from egoism to group egoism, the self expands beyond selfishness: There occurs an extension of the self that disposes us to care and sacrifice for something because it is ours. Defenders of duty and morality despise egoists for regarding only themselves, but they cannot despise group egoists on that ground.

The egoist Ayn Rand spoke of "grey, debilitating duty" and she thundered that morality is your enemy unless it serves your happiness. But people who come to regard their city as *their own* will be disposed to love and care for it. They will feel pride when it flourishes, shame when it declines or is disgraced, and indignation or anger when it is threatened. There is nothing cold and grey about this and they would not regard obligations derived from civic or national loyalty as "their enemy," however unselfish these obligations may be.

The group egoist has made the move from "I do it for *me*" to "I do it for *my so-and-so.*" When so-and-so is not just a personal possession, like a farm, but is a social unit such as my family, community, company, or labor union, I have a group loyalty. My norms are now social, which further removes them from selfishness: I can say not only that I work and care for the good of my community, I can say,

together with other people, that I work and care for the good of *our* community. Thus the shift from "me first" to "mine first" is of the last moment: It is what makes a tribe or society possible because it creates a group of people who can say "ours first." And this in turn creates a shared, non-instrumental good, a *common good.* When the object of my group loyalty is not only social but is a political unit, we can say that I possess the basis of good citizenship toward my community, my country, or possibly the world community.

Group egoism (group loyalty) is a third category of the normative: There is the realm of impartial morality, of rules, obligations, and thou-shalt-nots; there is rational selfishness which, never completely confident of itself, hopes and only half believes that being a nice guy pays best. Distinct from these, and sharing features with each, is group loyalty, the paradigm of which is tribal morality.

In American social thought group loyalties are either warned against or ignored, for reasons that concern our ultra-individualist heritage and, as well, the tragedies of twentieth century history. For are not loyalties *biases,* cases of putting your own kind first? Social scientists remind us, when they mention loyalties at all, of the death and wretchedness that tribalism in the name of racism and nationalism have brought upon the world.

But they are ambivalent because there is also a tradition of honoring the distinction between "community" and "society." People cannot have sense-of-community, presumably a good thing, without simultaneously accepting special obligations to the community *and* the idea of a boundary to it, in other words, accepting the idea of insiders and outsiders, of "us" and "them." Anglo-American social thinkers have never put the pieces together, nor could they do so, for they want a number of incompatible things: the values of community and local loyalty, an impartial global morality, and nearly limitless individual rights. Forced to choose between an alienating and chaotic radical individualism, and the tribalism and collectivism of an organic theory of society, most of them opt for the former.

Yet it is obvious that group loyalties, more than rational selfishness or moral rules, are what keep the social organism alive. When people work for the good of a community, city, school, church, company, or country, their willingness to invest time, effort, and money come largely from their perception of the thing as *theirs*. They are not pushed by duty or pulled by self-love. They are, instead, pulled out of themselves, caught up in the vision of the good of something larger than themselves, which is theirs, and of which they hope to be proud.

Pride and shame are impossible unless one has either self-love or loyalty. Someone who cares nothing about himself cannot be proud or ashamed of himself. Someone who is proud or ashamed of a neighborhood must connect it with himself, view it as *his own* neighborhood. I cannot be proud of an iceberg, nor ashamed of it, unless I have somehow come to think of it as *my* iceberg, perhaps because some clever fellow sold it to me. So, too, a person who is capable of neither pride nor shame regarding his community views it as he does an iceberg: Something that is just there, to be coped with, and not his own in that non-legal sense of possession which is necessary for group loyalty.

We cannot, however, forget the need alluded to earlier to attempt a deeper understanding of the self and society. . . . I [have] talked as though there were little or no need to ask what was meant by "selfishness" or "the self," and it may seem that philosophizing about these matters has little importance for crime, schools, and good citizenship. But it isn't so; how one understands "the self" has all the importance in the world for how one sets about trying to achieve the good society.

It is doubtful that animals are capable of selfishness; this is not because they are noble or altruistic but because the very idea of the self is too sophisticated a notion for them. Probably only human beings can be selfish because only we have the degree of rationality required for it. What I mean is the following. A lower animal that reacts immediately to avoid what is painful or frightening and get what is pleasant thinks of itself, if we imagine it thinking, without the dimension of time. A mouse, to its own consciousness, is a thin time-slice, even though we know it may live for months. As we say, it lives for the instant, and it will do what gratifies it even if doing so

causes its death a moment later. I shall call creatures that act in this way, and human beings when they emulate them, "pleasure/pain mechanisms." They do not act from self-interest or selfishness because the "self" is something that lives for weeks, or a month, or for years. They act instead for the sake of that thin time-slice, which is only a part of a self. To be conscious of oneself, in other words to know what one really is, is to be aware of a creature that endures through time, not one that exists only for a moment.

All kinds of animals do survive, of course, because evolution looked after tomorrow and next week: They do not—can not—think to the future, but their genetic program makes them find pleasure and pain in behavior which, more often than not, serves the self as a being that has a future. The caterpillar that eats and spins a cocoon acts in the interest of a being that includes the future moth—if we wished we could call this "behavioral selfishness" as a way of making a contrast with conscious selfishness. The caterpillar does not consciously act *from* self-interest; if it is conscious at all it is as a momentary time-slice and not as a being that endures through time.

There no doubt are degrees of this. A zebra or a bear, for all we know, has a tiny future it can worry about; but it is instinct, not thoughts of death by lions, that makes the zebra flee at a certain scent, and instinct, not thoughts of blizzards, that makes the bear seek a suitable place of hibernation. These animals, perhaps all of them except humans, and insofar as their behavior depends on felt reinforcements at all, are basically pleasure/pain mechanisms. It is doubtful any non-human can think of its own death, or its old age, or evaluate its life up to now.

Your idea of a self is complex. It is the idea that future states of a person, even after religious conversion or becoming senile, are still states of *you*, and that what hurts or pleases that person ten years from now hurts or pleases you. And self-interest, at its rational optimum, is the idea that those future pains and pleasures are as much yours as are present ones and, other things being equal, should count equally in your decisions of what to do. Of course, other things are never equal and it is always possible you will be dead in ten years, which is a rational ground for giving *some* edge to the present over the future. Nonetheless, we can understand ourselves in a way bears and caterpillars cannot, not as momentary time-slices but as time-worms: time-slices stacked in a long train extending from birth to death and comprising a single creature.

What the other animals cannot do at all we do imperfectly. "Imprudence" is a name we give to our imperfect rationality: We do not count future pains and pleasures as much as present or near ones, even though the future pains will hurt just as much as the present ones, and will hurt the same person. This is something everyone knows: If the likely bad effects of smoking won't show up for twenty years we behave almost as though the person likely to get sick in twenty years is someone else. Less commonly understood but equally plain is the reason why delayed criminal penalties are correlated with diminished deterrence: Criminals, just like cigarette smokers, imperfectly identify with their future selves, and heed less the punishment that does not come swiftly. It takes a degree of rationality no one possesses perfectly to see that the "you" of several years hence is just as much you as the "you" of this moment.

Sometimes people defend the idea that we always act from self-interest because they confuse the self with a pleasure/pain mechanism. Imagine a heroin addict who is reduced to committing night burglaries to support his habit and has lost his job, his wife and children whom he loves, and is watching his health deteriorate. Imagine also that he is intelligent, and now sits with his sleeve rolled up and the needle poised an inch above his vein. It is totally implausible to claim that the intelligent addict, when he goes ahead and takes his fix, believes what he is doing is best for him, on the whole and in the long run. "But he's addicted, and acts to get pleasure and avoid the pain of withdrawal, and thus acts selfishly." But of course he doesn't. The addict is destroying himself and knows it, and so he certainly isn't acting out of selfishness. He is acting as a pleasure/pain mechanism, as a bug acts, and at the same time acting contrary to self-interest. He is serving the good of a momentary time-slice, not the good of an enduring self.

This is what people who act imprudently from "weak will" are doing: In acting on the pleasures or discomforts of the moment they become pleasure/pain machines; they close their eyes to the rationality that understands future selves as identical with themselves. While weakness in the face of temptation can defeat self-interest, more interesting are people who lack, or have a very weak, concept of the self. A young person who jeopardizes his whole future as casually as he eats a hamburger is not a creature ruled by self-love, but in this kind of case it is not because of great temptation but because there does not exist, or does not yet exist or exist strongly enough, consciousness of a *person*, of an enduring being whose well-being he values.

So far I have suggested that humans, and perhaps only humans, can understand the self as a being who endures through time, changing greatly but remaining the person you care about in the special way you care about yourself. We also need to understand ourselves as distinct from other people. The first point involved acknowledging states of oneself that will exist in the *future;* now we must ask about self-identity and distinctness from others in the *present.* Both of these conceptions of the boundaries of the self vitally affect how we see ourselves in relation to society and how we are likely to behave. It is plain, for example, that a criminal who functions only as a pleasure/pain mechanism cannot usefully be reasoned with about his future.

I begin the discussion of this second aspect of the self with an analogy. Suppose you were offered a yacht, absolutely free, and told to choose from six side-by-side in the marina. It turns out that the eccentric millionaire offering this gift has provided six that are exactly alike, down to their colors and the details of their equipment. You might resort to whimsy: "Three is a nice number, so I pick yacht number three, counting from the left," but it is clear you can't place a higher *value* on one over the other if they are exactly alike. I mean any kind of value, not just dollar value. You cannot value one yacht over another unless you think there is some difference between them that makes a difference.

This tells us something about values: They appear at once to be subjective, a matter of judgment, and at the same time dependent on the real qualities of things. A good yacht must differ somehow from a bad one, and this is why the television commercial that said a certain brand of bread is "full of goodness" sounds slightly crazy. Do they pour in some wheat, yeast, the usual chemicals, and an ounce of goodness? The goodness isn't on a list of ingredients, as though someone might leave it out by mistake; this is what I meant by a "subjective" aspect. The goodness is instead a matter of a judgment we make *on the basis of its ingredients* (and their effects on us). The judgments we make about other people are similarly constrained: If a judge sentences Harry for ten years and Max for five, and they, their histories, and their crimes are perfectly similar, just like the yachts, we rightly accuse the judge of inconsistency.

The situation is strangely different when we come to how you value yourself (and here science fiction examples will help). Suppose someone could make six of "you," with the aid of a copying machine from the twenty-fifth century: You walk in one end of the machine and six of "you" walk out the other, identical in memories, thoughts, personalities, and bodily features; the six are then led off to six identical lab rooms. Now the problem, right off, is while there might be six of "you" *from an observer's point of view,* there certainly aren't, from *your* point of view: there are you and five copies. That is, no outside observer could justify special treatment for one of "you" over the others because, like the six yachts, you are all exactly alike. But from your own inner perspective you are completely distinct from the five replicas sitting in their five rooms (and thinking the thoughts you are thinking): You have two hands, not twelve, and if you pinch your hand you feel it but the replicas do not. If all six "clones" get toothaches and the scientist in charge says he will cure only one, it matters to you which he cures because you *feel* what happens to yourself and not what happens to them; but it cannot matter to an observer.

These "inner" and "outer" perspectives illustrate, respectively, nonsocial and social conceptions of the self. You can view yourself either way. The first conception allows a perfectly selfish individualism, the second is a perfectly social, collectivistic self. Your *nonsocial self* can put you (and, as we shall see, what is yours, such as your country) ahead of another person who may be exactly like you. It says, "I come first just because I am me," which sounds like a banality of nonsense, but is of the first importance for social thought: The possibility of this way of thinking is as essential for group loyalty as it is for egoism.

When you adopt the social perspective you appraise yourself as you do other people. You cannot favor yourself over another person just because "you are you," but must point to a difference between you. To your *social self* it can be relevant, in making a value judgment, that something causes pleasure, but not relevant that you yourself feel it. This public, social point of view is the basis of shared, social morality within a society, uniting the members under common rules.

Because, unlike robots, we are conscious, and unlike bugs we are rational, human beings are capable of operating from both points of view—from the egoist's all-important center of consciousness, and from the social conception of oneself as a being with qualities other people have too. The Golden Rule expresses the basis of social morality because part of what Christ meant was that we should think as social selves: He implied we should treat ourselves and other people by common principles. Normal persons feel the pull of each perspective and act from both at different times. . . .

The point of view of egoism can be philosophically puzzling. When I say, "I should keep the money because it will benefit *me*," I do not think of justifying features. It is enough that *I* will benefit. But what is this "I"? We have already seen that it is a thing that endures through time, despite changes, and cannot be understood by bears. Nevertheless, from the standpoint of egoism it doesn't matter what *kind* of thing the self is, it is simply "I," "me": I am a descriptionless point, a bare, featureless particular, a dimensionless kernel moving through time, and which lies behind all the features and properties I have. When I think as an egoist this qualityless kernel is the only thing that matters to me. This is why . . . a collection of egoists has no secure common basis for the adjudication of disputes or the allocation of benefits: There is no common thing they love in the way each loves himself. What basis there is depends on the perceived

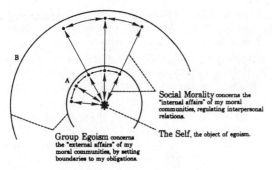

Figure 1. Group Egoism, Morality, and Self
Self and Society: My loyalties define the domains in which I acknowledge obligations, at the boundaries of my species, my city, etc., thereby creating the boundaries of moral communities. This is something only my non-social self can do. On the other hand, my social self sees itself as just one among many in its community, and bound by its rules.

usefulness of the society and its institutions to each individual. A society with this basis is necessarily an individualist one, its virtue is maximum liberty, its defects fragility and alienation.

Group loyalty is direct regard for the good of something distinct from oneself and it creates a moral community comprised of those who share this common good. Like selfishness it depends on prizing the self independently of its qualities. Think of family loyalty: It is obvious that I put my own family first because it is *mine* and not because I think that in some objective way it is better than other families. If I thought my family had royal blood or the best genes in the neighborhood, I might think it actually deserved special treatment; I would think my family was the best *kind* of family. But few of us think this way. We do not work and sacrifice for our families because they are rich, smart, beautiful, lovable, or utile, but because they are *ours,* with the full realization that, "objectively considered," there are other families with greater needs. I favor my family because of the relation it has to *me;* but this does not mean I think that *I* am especially rich, smart, beautiful, or useful. I need not think I have special qualities in order to be an egoist, and I need not think my family or nation has special qualities in order for me to be a group egoist.

This is why some people condemn tribal-

ism, patriotism, even community and family loyalty, as mere biases: "Why do you have stronger obligations to fight for so-and-so just because it is *your* so-and-so? It isn't any better just because it is yours." They are right, group loyalty is a bias. But . . . we shall see how social morality is itself founded on group loyalties.

When entomologists discuss social insects they save the term "eusocial" for species at the highest level of sociality, and recognize lesser degrees of sociality beneath that. I wish similarly to distinguish between fully developed and incomplete (or deteriorated) human societies. Whether a society is fully developed depends not only on whether it has a satisfactory social morality that is successfully passed on to the young, but also on whether its members have common objects of love and loyalty and a conception of a common good. The paradigm of a fully developed society is a traditional, undisturbed tribe, not because technology and modernity are necessarily antisocial, but because both their group loyalty and their intra-group rules usually are strong and plain to see. A completely individualistic society is a truncated society because it does not supplement rational egoism with group egoism. In this sense the whole radical individualist conception of society is presocial, from Thomas Hobbes through modern libertarians such as Ayn Rand and Robert Nozick.

Group loyalty poses dilemmas for modern man that traditional tribes did not have to face. Our families, neighborhoods, and to a lesser extent our cities, are pretty much alike, and not socially and geographically inaccesible to one another the way jungle tribes are. I cannot help but see that my family or neighborhood is just one among many and that whatever is good about mine is equally good about thousands of others. So we are threatened with having to wear these narrow loyalties on our sleeves, in vulnerable nakedness, for next door to my family is another one, "just as good" from an impartial point of view, next to my community another just as deserving.

The reason it is hard to be loyal to a "clone" is that when you are proud of something you want to show other people the features that you are proud of; if these features in no way distinguish it from a thousand others, pride and loyalty will appear foolish. America, Italy, and large cities such as New York and Moscow differ greatly, making it easy to find unique features by which to identify them and of which one can be proud. Traditional tribes usually have no problem of this sort, for they have their own languages, spirits, and rituals.

Now imagine that not you but your best friend Freda is duplicated: she walks into the twenty-fifth century machine and six of "her" emerge from the other end. You would want to know *which* of these six is your friend. First you might try to track her, that is, not let the original Freda out of your sight as she goes through the machine and afterwards. When you took your eye off her and lost the track, you would hunt for individuating scars or mannerisms, and when that failed, eventually you would cease to care who was which and your loyalty to your friend would die. What this shows is that love and loyalty, like self-love, is for a *particular* individual and not for just anything of the right kind. For example, if a mother fears the death of the child she loves, it will not do to tell her not to worry because we will get her another one just as good; it is *that* child she loves.

Switch the case to neighborhood loyalty and imagine that someone is out to show a visitor the neighborhood he is proud of. He would be humiliated if he became confused and couldn't tell his neighborhood streets and houses from adjoining ones. Such confusion is easy enough in many American suburbs. If you could "clone" a person—actually make six of him—his concept of self-identity and self-regard would be thrown into confusion; if you clone his community, his group egoism is thrown into confusion. Hence sense of possession and loyalty toward one's community depend on how it is individuated and marked off from other communities.

While an object of group loyalty need not have features that make it *better* than other communities, it needs features that individuate it and set it apart from others. It is very difficult, if not impossible, to be proud of something that is exactly like what everyone else has. In addition, if my sense of self-identity in part derives from my social affiliations, from the clans and tribes I call my own—

in other words, if my living quarters, community, job, and city partly define me, as I think they do, then seeing them duplicated promiscuously is damaging to my concept of self as well as to my loyalties. Self-identity depends partly on my territorial, institutional, and other *social* identities. Therefore clarity and coherence about my idea of a self depend on my ability to demarcate and reidentify my groups, territories, and social institutions.

Circling much of Moscow at the ends of the subway lines, like a great ring of Saturn, are hundreds of twelve- and sixteen-story white apartment buildings nearly exactly alike. It is an impossible shape for a neighborhood, people on opposite sides being separated by the mass of central Moscow. Is one's community a building, a street? If I pick up a pebble from the beach I can individuate it as "the pebble in *my* hand"—and from a strictly philosophical point of view that *would* do the trick. But I would feel foolish telling other people it was "*my* pebble" unless there were something distinctive about it, something that made it different from the millions of others on the beach.

What all this suggests is a fairly direct connection between the nature of the self and urban planning. The housing projects that sprang up in American cities beginning in the '50s were as monotonous as the Russian ones. To prize a dwelling or dwelling complex because it is *mine* (and hence want to be proud of it, and be less likely to vandalize it or let it go to ruin) is not to think it is better than its neighbors. But it does require features that individuate it publicly, features on which one can, so to speak, hang one's pride. Merely saying "my community is the one *I* live in" will not do, anymore than "my pebble is the one I hold in *my* hand." Group loyalties, however much they depend on a link with the conscious self, also depend on public criteria of identity.

We can summarize the difference between egoism and group egoism this way: The egoist puts himself ahead of others because, obviously, he *feels* what happens to himself and not what happens to others; so egoism confronts no problem of individuation: He knows that the tooth that hurts is *his* tooth. But when we turn from egoism to group egoism, what we prize cannot be individuated in this way. My family and neighborhood are mine but they are not me: I cannot distinguish my neighbor-hood from its "clone" as I can distinguish my toothache from my identical twin's toothache. My neighborhood is in the public realm of shared possessions; hence if I am loyal and proud of my neighborhood there must be something about its configuration, colors, cus-toms, or architecture that makes it different from what is not mine.

This is one reason why public art and deco-ration is so important; for original art, unlike an assembly line product, is unique. Group egoism dies if I cannot tell my workplace or neighborhood from others for the same rea-son that egoism would die if I could not distin-guish myself from other people. The in-dividuating function of self-consciousness in the latter instance must be taken over by such things as public art in the former. And the function of the unique in creating and strengthening group loyalty is greatly en-hanced if it is also grand. That is why great gorgeous skyscrapers, a giant modern sports stadium, a St. Louis arch are effective in creat-ing civic pride and morale, and thus in catalyz-ing cultural and educational bequests. People who do not think these things are worth the money often do not understand the complex basis of their appeal.

It is one of the merits of pride and loyalty that what creates them need not be scarce things or necessities, the possession of which by my community or city diminishes yours or subtracts from its fair share. Sense of commu-nity does not depend on mine being the best or better than someone else's. It depends on two different things, first, a basis for dis-tinguishing it from others, and second, *causes* of a sense of possession, of feeling that the community is *mine*.

It follows from these fairly abstract con-siderations that diversity is an essential part of any sound scheme of urban development, be-ginning with the smallest units of a society such as individual apartments, buildings, and parks. And insofar as a thing's history is more singular the older it is, history is the ally of community and therefore maintenance of the old an important cause of proprietary feelings toward one's community.

This goes against the grain of the dominant thinking in both the United States and the Soviet Union. We are now slightly more sensi-tive than the Soviets to the shortcomings of bulldozer mentality. We both crave monolithic solutions, in which we flex our national mus-cles and decide that what the whole nation or a whole city needs is so-and-so. Quantities of so-and-so's are then produced that are all alike—housing units, entire suburbs, trash re-ceptacles, park benches, shopping centers. We clone our environments, depriving ourselves of the effects of gradual accretions and mod-ifications made to what is old. Even a futurist and enemy of history such as Alvin Toffler sees this, thinking toward the end of *Future Shock* that we must fabricate traditions and rituals to serve in place of the past he gleefully sees being annihilated.[2] The irony is that a socialist such as Michael Harrington, who talks at length about alienation, argued that spank-ing new cities should be set down in the prairie. New cities in a prairie are a perfect formula for alienation.

Now we should step back and look at how these three motives—morality, rational selfish-ness, and group loyalty—might operate in citizens who are asked, say, to tax themselves for schools. It is difficult to know why people accept or reject school tax levies, so we can only speculate about the relative effectiveness of these motives. School levies recently have done poorly, forcing a few temporary system-wide closings and sharp cutbacks in school programs. Some people vote against school taxes to protest court-imposed integration plans, others because they are disgusted with what the schools offer with the funding they have, still others because they have children in Catholic or other private schools and are tired of paying twice. For the moment lay aside objections of this kind and suppose that an affluent suburban couple is asked to vote for a county-wide tax increase that will primarily benefit inner-city schools. Suppose further that this couple is rational; they will not believe *just anything* (this is one, obviously imperfect, way to predict how they will react to appeals).

Appeals to self-interest will simply be re-jected as sophistical. "Vote for the tax and it will benefit you," the pro-tax people say, and our suburban couple, being rational, answers, "Nonsense." For the inner-city slum is fifteen miles away, they never go there, and they have good police protection in the suburb. The argument is simply no good, as indeed are most public appeals to self-interest as reasons for paying higher taxes, allowing halfway houses and group homes into the neighborhood, allowing expressways to be built through your neighborhood, and so on. It usually is just not true that these things are in your interest, including long-term interest, and the irony is that public officials and pro-tax groups often think any other kind of appeal is "unrealistic." What rational self-interest dictates is that you should support adequate or even generous school financing in your district until the day the last of your own children graduates, and not one day longer. Rational selfishness does not even require that you actually *pay* the taxes, if you can get away with not paying, because the default of a single taxpayer does not appreciably affect the quality of the schools.

Appeals to ethics do not fare much better, even though arguments for schools taxes based on fairness often are good ones. The basic argument is that since our schooling was supported by the taxes of strangers when we were children, it is our turn now and only fair to support the schooling of the next generation, even if they are all strangers. This argument is not completely persuasive for people who have children in private schools, and therefore pay for two systems. But even if an argument is accepted, there is no assurance it will be followed by action. And if the suburban couple is told that it is their *duty* to help the schools in the black slum, or that they *owe* poor blacks because other white people mistreated black people in the past, the reaction most likely will be indignation. If people do not already feel a moral obligation to do something, or if they are not moved by it, the reaction to being told they are unethical usually is indignation.

The appeals most likely to succeed are to group loyalties, both civic loyalty and loyalty to humanity. They can be reminded that having a good school system is good for their city, and here I assume there already exists a strong sense of possession toward a central metropolis which, while not where they live, is where they work, visit, and do major shopping. If the school system is good, the city's citizens will be better, crime and welfare will decrease, and corporations will want to settle in it; in a word, the city will flourish more than otherwise and be a fitter object of pride.

The success of such appeals depends on the antecedent existence of a sense of civic loyalty. If our hypothetical couple has this sense to a strong degree they will sacrifice to make their city something of which they can be proud rather than ashamed. If instead they are alienated, they will not care and arguments will be fruitless. Loyalty cannot be the conclusion of an argument. Arguing with a person that he ought to be loyal to his city or his neighborhood is like arguing that he ought to love someone, even when we think, given his circumstances, that he *should* feel love or loyalty. He either does or he doesn't, and hence the issue is a causal one, one that has to do with the spiritual, institutional, and physical attributes of a community that cause loyalty in its citizens, or alternatively, cause citizens to be alienated. . . . One way to state the dilemma of modern man is that he belongs to too many tribes at once and becomes confused, and at the same time is tempted to retreat into himself and belong to nothing. Our ancient ancestors faced the problem of competing loyalties to a much lesser degree. Yet, the answer does not lie in eliminating group loyalties and replacing them with a single, global, impersonal loyalty. This probably could not be done and if it were we would be the more miserable for it. It would in any case not eliminate tribal morality but merely be a case of victorious tribal imperialism, one tribe—the global tribe—eliminating the multitude of loyalties we now have. Nor, on the level of our nation, is a single national loyalty that overpowers all others a rational goal; for when we take a hard look at the present state of American society it is clear that our social problems are not due nearly as much to the competition of loyalties as to their absence. In other words, they are due to alienation, loss of belonging, to not having affiliations about which one deeply cares. People whose primary interest is international and who are concerned with the dangerous competition between nations will see this differently. . . .

Competition between neighborhood loyalty and civic loyalty is a microcosm that is on all fours with competition between national and global loyalty. Suppose the city wants to put an expressway through my neighborhood. Is it better or more rational to support my city to the disadvantage of my neighborhood, or to support my neighborhood to the disadvantage of my city? Am I a traitor to my neighborhood if my loyalty is to some larger whole?

An obvious first move is to ask why they should conflict. Perhaps rational people will see that the conflict is unreal and that what is good for the city is good for the neighborhood, and vice versa. The mayor and the city development director argue that the new expressway will make everyone better off. True, some people will have to move and those who stay will see, instead of familiar houses and trees, a huge concrete expressway and they will hear the roar of trailer trucks all night long. But they will be able more easily to get to the airport, or wherever. The city as a whole will be more attractive to business and conventions, which will mean more jobs and prosperity for everyone. Even the people in the neighborhood, the city will say, will be better off "on the whole and in the long run."

The neighborhood organization offers counter-arguments. Everyone will be better off if the expressway does not go through their neighborhood but takes the more rational route through yours. Or they may argue that sacrificing first this, then another established neighborhood in the name of progress eventually diminishes the quality of life for everyone; and that what is good for the neighborhood is good for the city, "on the whole and in the long run." The city argues that what is good for the whole is good for the part and the neighborhood argues that what is good for the part is good for the whole. No other line is politically possible: Each argues that the rational interests of both parties are served by its position, because any other defense implies that someone must be sacrificed, which produces an irresolvable adversarial situation and resentment on the part of the loser.

Most of us realize it is just plain false that what is good for the whole is always good for the part. What is good for the world may not be good for America, what is good for America may not be good for General Motors or

New York, and what is good for New York may not be good for Greenwich Village. So, too, going the other way: What is good for Greenwich Village may not be good for New York, what is good for New York or General Motors may not be good for America, and what is good for American may not be good for the world. But then again, it may. There are, of course, many things we can do to benefit our cities or local communities that are noncompetitive and do not subtract from the good of our nation or neighborhoods—I have in mind such things as neighborhood clean-ups and local charity. But even here, if we look at objective needs we will discover other communities more deserving; after all, no matter how badly off your community might be, you can be sure that fifty dollars does more to reduce suffering in Calcutta or Chad than it does at home.

While it cannot be denied that the good of the whole often is incompatible with the good of a part, yet it still might be argued that our loyalties, *when they are rational and ethical,* will not conflict. For agreeing with what I have said so far does not settle the issue whether it is better, when there is conflict or competition, to support the larger unit such as mankind or America, or the smaller, such as one's city or neighborhood. This introduces us to the problems of the ethics of parts and wholes. In a clash between my city and my neighborhood, am I obliged to support *whichever side* is likely to produce the most good? And, we must ask, the most good *for whom?*

The circle model in Figure 2 generates vivid images of how loyalties, morality, and the self are related. If we are egoists, the way to understand the circle diagram is to think of the ripple pattern produced by a pebble dropped in water. Ripples are strongest near the central generating point, which we can think of as the self, and become weaker and more attenuated as they move out. Our first obligations are to ourselves, egoists conclude, then to what is most intimately ours, and then, with diminishing force, to wider groups with which we identify. Wide loyalties, represented by wide ripples, while in principle infinite, ultimately die out. Egoists would delight in pressing the analogy with the physics of ripples: There can be no more energy in a wide ripple than in a

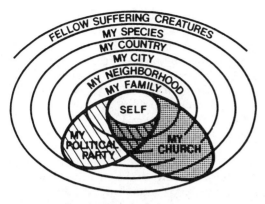

Figure 2. Nested and Overlapping Group Loyalties
The self is the "inward" logical limit on loyalty: When I shrink my commitments until I reach myself, I can pull in no further. Is there an "outer" limit, a widest loyalty, such as one's species or all living beings? There does not seem to be one that any arguments can prove, although there will be psychological limits that have biological and social causes.

narrow one, and if we think of these circles as enclosing people there will be less "energy"—benefit, concern, or love—for me to expend on each person in a big circle than in a small one.

Egoists think that whatever value I attach to my societies must be derived from the intimacy of its connections—social, legal, geographical—with the value I attach to *myself.* Sociobiologists offer a fairly exact parallel to the ripple model when they explain altruism by "kin selection," a postulated evolutionary mechanism . . . They explain altruism by the degree of genetic investment an organism has in those around it, this genetic investment diminishing with social and geographical distance. From the perspective of the dominant ethical traditions—Kantian, Christian, Marxist, Utilitarian—this is a pessimistic conception of human nature. The pessimism, at least from those traditional points of view, lies in the suggestion that we are naturally disposed to identify with smaller rather than larger tribes, and to have a weaker commitment to moral communities which are large and diverse. To put the matter starkly, are we by nature predisposed to value lives in inverse ratio to how far away they are? As a matter of

sociology and the history of nationalism and tribalism there is considerable truth in the pessimistic view.

Consider another way to interpret the circle diagram. Modern liberals and utilitarians see the circles as enclosing ever larger areas with ever larger needs. To them it is plain that our duty is to Humanity and that doing what benefits your neighborhood or country is wrong if it prevents a greater good for a larger whole. Hence, they say, the wider the loyalty, the greater its moral claim on us, and regional competition for resources or benefits is justified only when it is the more efficient way to maximize the good of everyone: The biggest circle is the only genuine one, the little ones inside have legitimacy only insofar as they serve the Good of the Whole. If you see that the new expressway will ruin your neighborhood, but also see that its benefit to the city is greater (however slightly) than the harm to your neighborhood, you must accept the expressway, for the simple reason that the total benefit is greater.

This position appears to present a dilemma for those who wish to take loyalties seriously. Should community leaders, mayors, or presidents always adopt the so-called impartial point of view regarding the allocation of effort and resources? They often will be disloyal to their constituencies if they do, and they will be judged unethical, from the viewpoint of the "general good," if they do not. The utilitarian asks, rhetorically, Does the mere fact that a university, community, or nation is *yours* add, even in the slightest degree, to what it deserves? Doesn't loyalty mean that you support policies because they benefit what is yours, even though from an impartial, ethical point of view these policies are not justified? On the other hand, if you are impartial, your community will not want you as their leader because you cannot be relied on to stand by them: You will be disloyal the minute you think the mayor has a better argument. So it looks as though you have to choose between doing what is right and being loyal; at least, this is how the utilitarian invites us to see things. Of course we all hope we can do what is best for everyone *and* remain loyal, but it takes someone with the mind of a Mary Poppins to think this is always possible.

There are a number of reasons why the utilitarian or "one world" attack on group loyalties is unconvincing. The first is that the utilitarians themselves simply assume that species loyalty is always the most demanding one. If it is claimed that it is the most demanding loyalty because it is the widest and the good and harm of everyone are at stake, the claim is incorrect. "Everyone" can be understood so as to exclude anyone, and while narrow understandings of "everyone" are common, wider conceptions of one's kind can be in terms of rational beings, beings capable of suffering, living beings—these are all alternative readings of "everyone." If family loyalty and patriotism are biases, in the sense of valuing a group more highly because it is one's own, so too is the claim that the greatest good is the happiness of the greatest number of human beings.

Utilitarians, who think making humanity the goal of morality is objective but having local loyalty is tribalism, confront a dilemma: If eliminating human suffering is more important than eliminating, say, animal suffering, either it is just a "bias" in favor of one's own species, or it is based on "justifying" features humans are supposed to have—commonly suggested are rationality, capacity for happiness, capacity for suffering, and a moral conscience.

However, any list of "objective" features presented to show that humans are more valuable than animals is bound to fail (even when we ignore the lack of moral proof of the features themselves), because of what we might call "the problem of imperfect specimens": It is inevitable that some senile or mentally retarded people will satisfy the list less well than chimpanzees or even the family dog. These "imperfect people" would lose their human rights. Perhaps we would have to conclude that they are more acceptable subjects for medical experiments than chimpanzees or dogs, if having human rights depends on having the objective features on the list.

Love of humanity has always been species loyalty, not an appraisal of worth based on "objective" criteria. In fact, the "ethics of love" is essentially tribal because the object of love is not an abstraction but a particular—one's lover, one's own family, community, nation, or species. Jesus asked us to love one another, period, without first checking whether someone who needs us satisfied philosophical criteria for full-blown personhood. When Mother Teresa visited war-ravaged Lebanon in 1982 she went first to a Beirut hospital for retarded children. She evacuated children who had no more potential for future happiness or for making scientific or artistic contributions to mankind than did the animals in the zoo. It was their being fellow human beings, not their rationality or the pleasure they would get or give, that counted with Mother Teresa, and it is for this kind of action that she was called a living saint.

Wide loyalties cannot be proven always to have greater moral authority than narrow ones. We are often urged to look beyond our community, city, or country in the name of impartiality, and treat what we had hitherto favored as our own as just one among many communities, cities, or countries. But this impartiality is never true impartiality, it is instead an invitation to give one's loyalty to a larger whole with which someone identifies; in other words, an invitation to join a larger tribe. If our first love is to some narrower group this forced shift may render our ethical concern and enthusiasm weak and pallid. Equal ethical concern for the whole of humanity is, for most of us, too diluted to be able to generate effective moral enthusiasm and too weak to outweigh narrow loyalties.

Sometimes people are unaware how tribal they are. An Ohio state legislator, after hearing me talk about these matters, announced he was a utilitarian; he did not seem to realize how attenuated his felt obligations and enthusiasm became beyond the boundaries of his district (and out of the range of his voters). Legislators are utilitarians regarding issues within their constituencies; they could not be utilitarians with regard to the whole world without their constituency being the world, and then Ohioans who want someone to represent *them* would find someone else. "Utility" is relative to a domain: To his Ohio constituents, the legislator who fairly serves their various interests is a perfect utilitarian, to people in Helsinki or Surabaya he is the perfect tribal moralist.

There is no hiding the evil to which unqualified tribal morality can lead, although it probably is not greater than the misery produced by the willingness to sacrifice anyone for the general good.

> While in the days of head hunting Nagas viewed every outsider with the suspicion and latent hostility appropriate to relations with a potential enemy, they treated their kinfolk and co-villagers of both sexes in a relaxed spirit of camaraderie and good will, and appeared in their company as a gay, humorous and well-mannered people. . . . The discrepancy is probably characteristic of most societies permanently threatened by hostile attacks and conditioned to an institutionalized hostility vis-a-vis the members of out-groups.
>
>   The Kalingas' attitude to homicide is similar to that of the Nagas. While the killing of a member of the in-group is looked upon with grave disapproval, . . . the killing of an outsider is regarded as morally neutral and in some cases even meritorious. . . . Here as among the Nagas we find that ideas of right and wrong conduct apply only to interaction with members of their own group, whereas the outsider is considered fair game. . . .[3]

Fürer-Haimendorf goes on to make the obvious point that this attitude to outsiders is not unique, the Spanish conquistadors having had a similar attitude toward new world Indians. Naga and Kalinga attitudes, we are told, hence do not betray an underdeveloped moral sense, but only "an intensive concentration of all sentiments of loyalty and moral obligation within comparatively narrow limits."[4] The problem with Nagas and Kalingas is not that they are loyal to their kind, but that they recognized no one else as belonging to their kind. They lacked multiple affiliations.

It is important to see that a person whose *only* loyalty is to humanity is a Naga writ large, another kind of one-tribe fanatic. These utilitarians may be even less tolerant than Nagas, given their intolerance of inside subgroups as well as outsiders. Nor is this position philosophically defensible: Utilitarians think a wider loyalty *must* carry greater weight just because it is wider; their slogan is "more is better." But the wider loyalty identifies one's kind under a different description than the narrower loyalty, and the obligation one feels depends on this description: I have extremely weak loyalty to the whole of living nature, relative to loyalty to my species, and weaker species loyalty than family loyalty or national loyalty. More is not always better; it is not always better because it is not always more of the same thing: My daughter and your daughter may both be human beings, but they are not both members of my family. One should not simply *assume* that patriotism, community loyalty, and family loyalty count for less simply because they count for fewer. Human beings also are few, as part of the wider world of living beings.

What this implies is the defensibility of the position that sometimes what benefits my family obligates me more than does a greater benefit to the whole of humanity; and also that a still greater benefit (or threat) to humanity might nevertheless obligate me on the side of humanity. It implies the acceptance of a world in which rational, moral people can have loyalties that are in limited competition with those of other people, for example, members of different families, communities, or nations. If this is so, the rational community leader is not always obliged to be a traitor: He need not accept the expressway that obliterates his neighborhood just because he sees that it is likely to produce a small, offsetting greater good for some larger whole. If he is honest with himself, he admits that his own neighborhood counts more for him than do other people's neighborhoods. This is simply the equivalent, in microcosm, of the patriot who says that his own country counts more for him than do other people's countries and the human being who says that his own species counts more for him than other species.

Notes

1. Durkheim, *Suicide,* John A. Spaulding and George Simpson, trans. (New York: The Free Press, 1951), p. 389.

2. Alvin Toffler, *Future Shock* (New York: Random House, 1970).

3. Fürer-Haimendorf, *Morals and Merit* (Chicago: The University of Chicago Press, 1967), pp. 112, 109.

4. Ibid., p. 110.

An Interactional Morality of Everyday Life

Norma Haan

Moral decision making for psychologist Norma Haan is the product of subtle personal interactions and negotiations, rather than the deliberations of a solitary moral agent who applies universal norms or who acts on self-interest expanded to include related others. She developed her theory while studying everyday morality as it is practiced by ordinary people in thir local communities. Through a series of experiments that subjected established friendship groups to an artificial crisis situation, she was able to document the members' moral reasoning as they struggled to reach a decision. She found that sensitivity to others and moral dialogue were the constant, distinctive features of her subjects' moral decision process. Haan's article begins with a transcript of some of these dialogues. She notes that the moral reasoning they use is at odds with traditional moral theories. Traditional theories describe morality as an intellectual enterprise in which moral agents learn to match a previously learned abstract principle to a current problem. Psychologist Lawrence Kohlberg claimed to find empirical evidence to support this cognitive theory of morality, and Haan presents her own theory as an alternative, empirically more accurate portrait of moral practice. In her theory morality is social and practical rather than solitary and cognitive. The main body of Haan's paper is a formulation of everyday morality in terms of moral dialogue. Parties to this dialogue negotiate claims, weigh facts, and adjust ther priorities during the course of their discussion. While Haan acknowledges a variety of moral motivations in her subjects, their predominant motivations when they engage in a moral dialogue are to strike a balance among their various interests and to secure a consensual agreement. Moral development in Haan's interactional morality is a process of learning how to negotiate in the complex and subtle exchanges of a moral dialogue. Haan ends her essay with a discussion of dialogues that do not reach a moral equilibrium or that reach a false balance.

Because social scientists' claims of value neutrality are no longer tenable . . . and because many moral ideas that social scientists inadvertently use can withstand neither public scrutiny nor professional debate, social science faces a crisis of legitimation. This difficulty might be alleviated if social scientists were to examine their moral bases, work to construct a theory based on wide consensus, and then come to use moral theory reflectively and openly.

My observations and analyses over some years of actual moral actions, coupled with certain new recognitions and rediscoveries in psychology, suggest to me that the construction of an empirically based, consensual theory of everyday morality may be possible. I describe such a formulation here as a working model.

Our Everyday Interest in Morality

People have intense interest in morality. In a way, morality is a vast and inescapable conspiracy in which we all participate. Clearly the morality of everyday life is not a capacity that resides exclusively in individuals; it is social interchange in itself. Lay morality seems to consist of shared understandings about the character that exchanges must have in order

From Norma Haan, "An Interactional Morality of Everyday Life," in *Social Science as Moral Inquiry,* Norma Haan, Robert N. Bellah, Paul Rabinow, and William Sullivan eds. (New York: Columbia University Press, 1983), pp. 218–224, 233–244. Reprinted by permission of the publisher. Some footnotes omitted.

to sustain and enrich individual and collective lives. So critical is morality for our well-being that invariably we all join in this compelling compact. As parents, we go to the greatest lengths to ensure our offspring's morality because we are certain that their commitment to morality will be elemental to their future welfare. Probably as a result of the great energy we all exert to induce the young to share our moral commitments and to retain our own, all people, even the most heinous criminals, work to maintain a sense of themselves as moral by whatever justification—accurate or distorted. Only for brief moments and in very limited ways do we admit our inevitable falls from grace. Interestingly, according to Plato's report, the Sophist Protagoras held the same view that "all men properly say they are righteous whether or not they really are. Or else if they do not lay claim to righteousness they must be insane."[1] (Our Freudian-informed insights tell us that those who wear guilt on their sleeves are engaged in some venture other than self-criticism.)

The view of the self as a moral entity starts early. The parents of a four-year-old boy, regarded by his teachers as a child of moral sensitivity, described how he defends his moral position when he hits his younger brother. He shouts *before* he is reprimanded, "It was an accident; it was an accident." When his brother was a baby, the father heard the then three-year-old boy chant sing-song fashion, "Crush the baby, kill the baby, crush the baby's head." When the father asked about the song, the boy removed himself from responsibility. He said it was "just a song" (the time-honored distinction we make between thought and action) and that "Indians sing it" (displacing responsibility onto those peoples who seem forever to exemplify savagery in the fantasies of American whites).

In addition, we have only to recall Adolph Eichmann's contention that he was a moral being—he merely performed his job when he gave orders to murder thousands of Jews. Thus, we all work to preserve our belief in ourselves as moral beings—ordinary criminals, the boy, and Eichmann, as well as social scientists.

I want to understand this powerful and compelling morality of practical life. Con-

sequently, in recent years my associates and I have been observing and listening to adolescents and young adults practice morality, recently extending our observations to preschoolers at play. Two examples of moral discourse among eighteen-year-olds will illustrate the interactive, dialogical aspects of the morality that I think must be reflected in the theory.

With the often direct wisdom of the untutored, a friendship group of eighteen-year-old university students confronted the question of governing themselves within an experience where they fully simulated being the sole survivors of a world disaster. First, they wished to avoid selecting a leader because, they said, everyone should be equal; they wanted leadership to be decided by simple rotation, and they would vote on particular decisions. When the specter of tie votes and, later, the rights of the minority came to their minds, concern and debate ensued. The following dialogue is only lightly edited for the sake of brevity, and I have added comments in brackets to draw attention to the implications of these young people's key considerations.

Phil: Then we'll just talk and talk and vote and vote. [Persistent attempts to understand each other might lead to consensus.]

Hilda: We'll need a coin, too. [Random draws are sometimes the only solution.]

Cissy: Everyone would have to listen and respect each other. [Without these properties of dialogue, moral solution is impossible.]

Betty: What if that doesn't happen?

Ray: The best we can hope for is mutual cooperation, but beyond that, we're just going to have to try. [No assurance of perfect compliance can be given beforehand.]

Charles: If we have *any* rule that we'll all accept—without having to evoke it—it is everyone has to accept the right of argument. Every person must be able to talk without their talk being oppressed or interrupted. [The core moral right lies in the procedure of making one's case known; for a right to be a moral right it must be accepted, not legislated.]

Ed: We'll have to have every individual evaluate everyone else's ideas.

Ray: But you can't force that on other people! When someone has an opinion just allow him to express it totally. [Again, a moral right must be accepted for itself; it cannot be enforced.]

Hilda: Is your rule that everyone has to cooperate?

Phil: It's not a rule, it's expected. It is an agreement—that's what we're doing—we're doing a mutual agreement. [A vision of how to achieve moral balances guides the group.]

Ray: It's a mutual agreement to listen to other people. We've all agreed on a mutual agreement.

Betty: There is still a problem: what if someone doesn't want to follow the other seven people? Are you going to force him? [How binding is the moral balance on all concerned?]

Charles: I think we all would realize we can't be loners. It's like a dance; I want to count the steps in fourths and the rest of you count in eighths, then I should realize that the dance won't work. [The social interdigitation of people cannot be questioned; acceptance of this fact makes human affairs work.]

Phil: We are supposed to have basic life supports in here [part of the simulation], so I don't think that a situation where we are *so* desperate that we can't get agreement is going to arise—or should arise. We're just going to have to work things out as they come up. [Considerations of survival do make procedures of achieving moral balances more delicate; however, the participants are not that desperate yet.]

Charles: But you can't ask someone to go against their principles. [The majority has responsibility to the dissident.]

Cissy: But maybe we'll change our minds if we listen, respect, and vote, or maybe he'd change his mind; we can listen and vote again. [Continual dialogue and exchanges of facts and opinions and expressions of need are the way to moral balances.]

Betty: I would still want to act on my principles.

Eve: But, Betty, jut try to convince us of them! If you believe something so *strongly,* you could change our minds. [Matters don't have to be left at A vs. B; recognition of our social interdigitation leads to A = B.]

Charles: Betty, you're twisting situations. We would probably find out we had the *same* morals if we really talk. [Dialogue uncovers our shared morality.]

Cissy: It's really hard; there are no clear answers for that, Betty. You just have to see what's going to happen. [There are no ultimate, perfect moral protections. We have to take risks.]

Betty: Would you take action against me if I opened the door [to the outer contamination] and the group didn't want me to?

Charles: You'd be acting violently by doing that. You'd not be respecting everybody else. If we forced you to stop, we'd just be saying there has to be fair representation. [Action must be based on the same standards as talk.]

Thus, this group of eighteen-year-olds regards its morality as a process which they

themselves keep in motion through the mutuality of their acceptances and fates and the commonality of their morals; their morality is not a given; instead, it is continually sought but not always securely or perfectly achieved.

An audio-recorded voice informs the group that a survivor of unknown condition is outside the group's cell; the group decides that everyone should voice an opinion, one at a time, about whether to let him in. The following statements are exemplary of the positions taken.

"That could be one of us. We may have the disease a little bit now for all we know. He is alive and we are alive, let him in." [The bonds of intersubjectivity hold.]

"If we leave the guy out there and then one of us gets sick, are we going to kick one of us out? We could set a precedent." [Our self-interest is synonymous with his.]

"To be human we have to sacrifice some things, and if we're selfish then we lose our values." [Our interest in being human is synonymous with his welfare.]

"We could help him get better. Also, he may not have a disease, so we have to take a chance." [Facts are important, but we don't know all the relevant ones, so to be human, risks have to be taken.]

"We already agreed to support everybody else, right? Just because he wasn't originally a part of our group doesn't mean we should reject him." [We made a universal agreement.]

"If more people join, we can come up with more ideas and better decisions." [Dialogue and balance are *the* forms of our morality.]

The group gives another argument for their socially bonded view of life when an audio voice "patches" them through to other cells and finally to a cell where a man wishes to commit suicide because of the desperate conditions.

Phil: I think his obligations come through the fact he's alive even if he doesn't know the people he's stuck with; he's obligated because he's in circumstances that overpower his right to kill himself.

Betty: What do you mean?

Phil: If he says he can kill himself, there's no reason why everybody else can't do the same and he wouldn't agree to that, so there's his obligation! He wouldn't want to start anything like death by chain reaction. [One's social bondedness holds even when facing death.]

Thus, they identify the value of life in interactional, secular terms, however some of them might consecrate life in their religious, spiritual beliefs.

Another such friendship group hotly argued with one another following a morally intense "game" experience that established an oppressive three-class society where socioeconomic mobility was not possible and where two members, Mike and Bob, had wielded total power. All other members had belonged to the lower or the middle class.

Bob: I have a question, Mike. What if you honestly thought you were the best leader—say you had a Ph.D. and your people were all illiterate. You knew you could satisfy their needs. Wouldn't you think you *should* take over? [Those with "superior" moral knowledge, he suggests, should lead.]

Mike: No. I'd explain to them, but if they didn't like my ideas that would be that. Maybe they'd ask me back later when things didn't work out for them. [His understanding of the social hazards of benevolent paternalism is not complete.]

Jane: But that isn't the real problem here. You leaders could have been open-minded and all that, but that still wouldn't necessarily mean we'd have an opportunity. We just couldn't get anywhere. [Kindness without participation is insufficient.]

Bob: Jane, you seemed to be thriving on being equal. What about when Mike and I said let's get back to the first, fair rules, but you guys wouldn't go for it. You're contradicting yourself. We gave you the opportunity for everything to be equal and fair, but you didn't go for it. [A logical contradiction, he thinks.]

Jane: But you were *giving* it to us! Besides, we weren't really going to be equal. You were still going to be in power, and what we wanted was a real voice. [Gifts without voice do not make a moral balance.]

Nancy: We wanted a chance to exercise our little power; we were getting organized to revolt against you, and then you said you wanted us to *forget* what you had done! That would mean we'd give up our organizing. [Their interests as active agents are at stake.]

Bob: Look, I was just asking to be treated normally. I had tried to be fair and think of good rules, so I was hurt when you wouldn't do it. [His intensions were good, so he should be forgiven, he thinks.]

Mike: Yeah, it was a matter of trust. I was really surprised that you didn't trust us. [It was the lower class's fault for not trusting!]

Ted: But you had screwed us already: it takes time to get over that. [Moral exchanges have a history.]

Janice: We *at least* had the right to be mad at you! I don't think you had the right to tell us to forgive you. It didn't mean we were going to do something bad to you. How could we promise *not* to be mad at you? [Morality is not just factual; our feelings are legitimate too. People are accountable over time for what they do.]

Thus, this group draws a precise distinction from its experience: having or being *given* the nominal conditions of justice is not morally sufficient; instead, people want a voice and opportunities to participate in the process of determining their own living conditions. Altruism from those who have power is inferior to the legitimate right of people to work for their own good. Thus, the society of prescribed just conditions is second best to the society of participation. . . .

A Morality of Interaction

The following is a brief description of the formulation of the everyday morality that I am testing.

The Moral Dialogue

Interaction is the invariant and distinctive feature of everyday moral consciousness, as it is regarded, experienced, and lived out in the minds of two people, within a single person who is initially of several minds, between people and society, and between societies. (Hereafter, I refer to all these combinations by the term "parties.") Moral claims, ideas, and facts are weighed and priorities set between parties until some balance is found, but the need for resolution never ceases—new considerations always arise. Thus, moral tensions are ubiquitous, and moral resolutions are constantly created, instead of occasionally reproduced.

Despite these obvious features, morality has not often been defined in interactional terms. Instead, it has been regarded as a quiescent capacity, resident in individual people, and activated only by the appearance of a moral problem. Then, it is thought, the person "looks up" a solution by matching the problem to a previously learned rule or principle (in the form of a nominal duty, consequence, or right). A person who has a properly developed moral character will choose the proper rule and behave accordingly to remove the problem. In this view, moral adequacy depends on the extent and accuracy with which the individual has learned the rules (of interest to psychologists, who tend to regard society's rules as immutable) and/or the comprehensive goodness of a particular set of rules (of interest to philosophers, who argue about which set of rules is best). The person who selects and acts on the most abstract and generalized rule, despite the peculiar needs of the parties and irregularities of the situation, is celebrated.

When social interaction is taken as the pivotal feature of morality, a different view of moral processes, decisions, guidelines, and individual capacities emerges. Some moral contretemps occurs between parties; then discussion must take place, whether literally or only in the mind of one person, because people do not tolerate moral disequilibrium for long. Relations must be reequilibrated, whether falsely or authentically. If they are not, the participants' commitments to each other begin to decay. Many inequities are never discussed in real life, but that does not prevent participants from angrily conducting imaginary dialogues within their own minds.

Moral dialogues literally and continuously occur as major or minor events throughout any given day and throughout the given lifetime of any person; these occurrences are not merely expository devices for the exegesis of theory. As minor events, dialogues often go unmarked. Dramatic and all but irresolvable episodes, like the ones philosophers concoct to confound one another or psychologists use to "test" subjects, are rare. People's expectancies of engaging in moral dialogue become so clear and strong as organized patterns of social thought and interchange (as was shown in the earlier examples of the eighteen-year-olds) that the social schema of moral dialogue can be regarded as the prime moral structure.

Dialogue is an exploration of mutual thought—a joint reflective inquiry into the facts and parameters of the moral issue at hand. Initially, parties make fumbling, awkward attempts to defend their views; but faced with antithesis, they back off in order to clarify the problem. Thus, statements of antithetical positions serve to identify the parameters of the issue. As its features are identified, elaborated, and finally simplified, the parties can begin fully to comprehend each other's views. For one person to understand another, attitudes of passivity, receptivity, and amity are required, and people must cast off their self-preoccupation. That people do cognize each other's moral positions is evidence of how important are moral motivations and how comprehensive the social embeddedness of humans. The dialogue persuades and corrects both parties despite their initial intentions. Typically, each party brings out cognitive-affective information. Sometimes people prefer and choose the best rational-cognitive argument (such is our commitment to logic and reality), but the objective circumstances do not always override the emotional importance of less rational views.

More often than not, each party's position is embedded in the other's position, and common grounds or compromises can be discovered. It is unreal to think that A and B are always completely opposed to each other or that a victory for A means a loss for B. The dialogue is as much to discover A's and B's similarities—parties have implicitly agreed to abate their narcissism by participating—as it is for them to press their differences. Only unthinking, overwrought partisanship defeats the dialogue's purpose. "Losing" is not necessarily devastating to participants in these dialogues, because "immorality" is a matter of what a person is doing, which can always be changed. "Immorality" in the dominant Platonic theories is a deficiency in moral capacity or character, a matter pertaining to who the person is, which cannot be readily changed.

The Moral Balance

Dialogical parties intend to strike a moral balance, that is, an agreement which equilibrates this particular contretemps because it wins both parties' endorsement. In the best circumstances, the achieved balance rests on the parties' creation of equity because they discover that they have common interest. But other balances are workable: compromises of advantages, wherein all receive smaller advantage than they initially wanted; compromises of disadvantages, wherein all suffer some disadvantages; or choice of the lesser of two evils. In real life, solutions are often rational, which is not always the same as their being logically impeccable. Given the complexity of human interchange and the unique needs of each person, we all expect to suffer occasional minor injustice, if it is not perpetuated and if it is the only nearly rational solution available. Various phrases express our understanding of moral balance, for example, "making it right with everybody," "evening things up," and "restoring the peace." Again, the highly organized meanings surrounding the idea of moral balance warrant the supposition that it is also a major moral structure.

The Moral Ground

The feature of dialogues that makes them moral is the question of grounding. However, from a psychological frame, motives for acting morally—"Why be moral?"—are not grounds. Instead, they are the empirical reasons *why* people pragmatically come to want to be moral, given our existence as social creatures who interact in ways that generate moral motivations. Thus, the questions "Why be moral?" can be expected to have empirical answers.

However, "What is moral?"—the key value or the grounds—must have a different kind of answer, a philosophic-logical one. People might universally endorse a definition of morality that guarantees that both one's own good and the good of others *should* be served as equitably as possible. (Such grounds have often been proposed.) Thus, I make a thin, ontological assumption about the desires and rationality of people: that equity-serving dialogues are the vehicle for people's rationally considered and socially experienced desires. Given an informed, unencumbered choice, surely all people would hope to present their morally relevant claims and have them considered than not. This wish is differentiated by practical experiences that inform us when we are very young that our moral claims can be validated only reciprocally, within the context of others' claims.

Various features of moral dialogues that promote accurate and full exchanges of views

come to be valued: all should be allowed to speak, none should dominate, and any can veto. These are not, however, grounds in themselves. Instead, they merely provide assurance that parties' interests will be heard and served, most of the time and over time.

Science relates to people's psychology in a fashion similar to the morality described here, and perhaps this explains why some people now turn to scientific techniques with cautious hope that the outlines of a "true" morality of everyday moral exchange may be discerned, one that can take the place of the "best" theories usually proposed. The structure of science and the structure of this morality provide ways for people to diminish their narcissistic interpretations of the world, rise above their self-containment and self-consideration, and meet the minds of others. Both structures attain these goals by following a set of procedural principles that are expected eventually to yield consensual outcomes. Both rest their cases on the procedure that gives all related evidence, whether provided by those high or low in status, even-handed acceptance and evaluation to ensure that the most penetrating, informed, and convincing resolution will have the greatest likelihood of being chosen. Both are expected and known frequently to yield recognizably imperfect solutions or superficially perfect solutions that are, nevertheless, forever liable to revision as new evidence is presented and new circumstances arise. Both are human triumphs—we bootstrap ourselves by assuming a third-person observer's attitude toward ourselves—we rebuild our raft plank by plank while we are at sea, Otto Neurath is supposed to have said. These are attempts to achieve objectivity; both science and morality undertake this task despite the difficulties of knowing more than the self. To get to know more than the self is done only by knowing others and the circumstances of their worlds. To know more than the self is the expected emancipatory outcome of both interactional morality and science.

Moral Motivations

The question of why people are willing to consider others' moral claims has some empirical answers, although clearly much more needs to be known. For instance, investigations of child abuse and juvenile delinquency indicate that children who are treated without consideration of their needs and whose wishes for equity-promoting dialogues are persistently thwarted become adults who treat others or their own children in the same way. The intense concern of juvenile delinquents for their peers is explained by the fact that they are more likely to have equity-promoting dialogue with them than with adults or society in general. However, the strongest empirical support for the force and pervasiveness of moral motivations is the complex justifications people construct to "prove" their moral purity. Freud's theory of the unconscious and the ego defenses is essentially centered on his observation that people cannot bear to think of themselves as immoral.

Although individual moral motivations are often posited, they are more often multiple and related; they can be classified as follows.

Motivation to Conserve One's Identity in Social Exchange.
Conservation of one's identity is a strong motivation, quite aside from moral considerations. However, one cannot be a person to oneself unless one is a person to others, and given the social requirements and enhancements of our rearing, an important part of personhood is our belief in the self as moral; thus, we are motivated to conserve our view of ourselves as moral.

Guilt Motivating Morality.
From the interactional view, guilt is a mismatch in identity—a matter of inconsistency—between the moral person one thinks one is and the immoral person one is afraid one has been. Guilt is not simply the anxiety of being caught; nor can it simply be the historic voice of the parent, given people's continuous construction of new meanings. Guilt surely must operate to produce moral consideration; however, extreme guilt usually produces excuses and unthinking distortions.

Motives Arising from Rational Considerations.
Rational reasons are motives enough in themselves. Various theorists have proposed that motivation arises from enlightened self-interest (Kurt Baier), from recognition that altruism makes sense in view of one's

future needs (Thomas Nagel), from self-interest traded off against others' self-interest (Rawls), or from guidance logically derived from one's extant imperative principles (Kohlberg).[2]

Motives as Intersubjective Accountability.
Piaget declared that children first avoid contradicting their own logic in the presence of others, an observation he used in support of his view that the social basis and requirements of logic make it a moral imperative in itself.[3] Swanson argues that people require one another to be what in fact they publicly allow themselves to seem to be.[4] I have argued that accuracy in intrasubjectively assessing and expressing one's own needs and accuracy in intersubjectively assessing others' needs and the situation are normatively expected because our social life ultimately depends on such accuracy to sustain, enhance, and make sense of our lives.[5] Thus, intersubjective honesty for Piaget, rectitude for Swanson, and accuracy for Haan all exemplify integrity among people, a matter of good faith.

The development of children's moral intersubjectivity literally depends on their experiencing others as accountable, that is, knowing "good faith" rather than betrayal. Tangible loss is only one reason why people cannot tolerate bad faith. Of equal anguish to people are foiled expectancies. They risk themselves on the possibility that others are credible and feel like fools if they are "taken in" or "set up." Entering a moral dialogue is risky because the self is then exposed, but it is the actualization of people's root knowledge that they have no alternative but isolation and alienation.

The Self and Other in Interactional Morality.
Given the social nature of human life, equity-promoting dialogue is what people normatively seek and commonly cherish; however, everyday solutions seldom maximize one person's claim, especially not at any given point in time. Thus, "losses" to the self as the price of commitment to others are inevitable, but they are countered by life-giving and -enhancing compensations that persuade most of us to continue to commit ourselves to others.

A morally adequate "taking all parties'

claims into account" requires that all parties be able to speak and desirous of speaking so that the import of their claims can be known and not overlooked or slighted. Thus, people's subjective self-interest and their third-person view of themselves as legitimate moral objects are as necessary to the moral dialogue as are their concerns for others as moral objects. That selves must guiltlessly receive their deserts in order to function givingly is an insight of modern psychology. If the self is not adequately considered by the self and if the self does not require the other to consider the self's claims, the stage is set for a morally corrupt, possibly masochistic relation. At some level of awareness and enactment, the self's anger and the others' guilt are entailed. Therefore, a thin, shaky line divides altruism and masochism. Solid moral balances are struck only when parties' claims are legitimately taken into account and negotiated. Balances cannot be benevolently achieved. Thus, we can see why the magnanimity of the welfare state morally violates rather than pleases its recipients; instead of impersonal gifts, people much prefer what is legitimately theirs.

Equity-promoting dialogue seems to be a variant of the ideal speech situation as it is envisioned by Habermas and by Rawls; however, there are important differences between the two. For Habermas the ideal speech situation is a means of discovering truth as consensus (not morality);[6] for Rawls it is a device to explicate the conditions he thinks are necessary in order for ideal moral contracts to be drawn.[7] However, I mean that equity-promoting dialogues literally occur and that people "believe" in equity (because of all the warrants and on the grounds I have proposed above), to the extent that they will support equity *against* their own desires! Equity is so critical in human interchange that people lie to themselves when they deprive others of it (for instance, by insincere dialogue) or when they themselves are deprived of equity and cannot bear to recognize their own powerlessness. Life without equity or hope of achieving equity is socially unbearable and without meaning.

In ideal circumstances, dialogues are likely to result in both parties taking the agreed-on action because their decisions are public and particular instead of private and general, as are decisions in the Platonic formulations. Because dialogical decisions are already a kind of action, preparation and consummation flow in sequence, and the usual disjunctures between private judgment and public act are less likely to occur. All eyes are on the resolutions. Moreover, the particular considerations of the situation and the parties involved are likely to match resolutions with the circumstances of the situation and the needs of the parties; thus, resolutions are less likely to be vacuous and grandiloquent or awkward to enact.

Development of Interactional Morality

Participation in moral exchanges begins when people are two or three years old. Recent studies of preschoolers' ideas about morality[8] and observations by my colleagues and I indicate that their morality is not physicalistic, as Piaget's early work suggested, and not oriented to propitiating power, as Kohlberg avers.[9] Nonetheless, as people grow older, they become more skilled in moral interchanges gradually, because understanding intersubjectivity is not an easy matter. The various concerns, intransigencies, priorities, and conditions of each party need to be considered, integrated, compromised, or discarded, and the possibilities for resolution are numerous and complex.

Capability of logical, philosophical reasoning is clearly not a precondition of higher development in the interactional system; instead, experiences in intersubjective exchanges, which occur in even the most "primitive" societies, are required. Who can say life among the Hopi Indians or the Sherpa of Nepal is morally inferior to life in New York City? In fact, moral experiences of sufficient social meaning to facilitate development may be few in number the more complex the living situation and society. Complexity tends to diffuse responsibilities and confuses knowledge of contingencies. Research concerning the responses of bystanders who have witnessed accidents and injuries indicates that people reared in cities are less likely to help victims than are those reared in small towns.[10]

Two critical differences between the interactional formulation and Kohlberg's

Platonic system are the latter's assertions that morality develops in stages and that the logical stages, described by Piaget, are necessary but insufficient preconditions of moral development. Setting aside the moral-political implications of this elite position that only those of higher logical stages can be morally "adequate," there are further countering empirical reasons for disagreeing. Children's experiences with morality are very different from their experiences with the invariance of the physical world (the experiences Piaget has shown are involved in the evolution of logical stages). A child's experience that gravity pulls is never contradicted, but people often morally contradict each other and themselves. Circumstances A and B, which seemingly differ in the smallest degree, can have vastly different implications. The small boy I described earlier knows that if his brother does not cry after being hit, the social results are different from those when his brother cries even a little bit.

Interactional morality does not evolve from the child's learning fixed moral categories and then progressively integrating and reintegrating these at different stages. Instead, moral development evolves from the considerably more situationally and intersubjectively responsive skill of coming to know how to engage in exchange, to know when, why, and how much to give in terms of the others' claims and needs and one's own, when all involved are deserving and all have a future together, invariably interacting and mutually needful and committed to each other. The invariant authority of the physical world probably has no counterpart in the everyday social world. More inventiveness, fluidity, and flexibility are required in moral dialogues and resolutions that can be embraced within stages, which, if not literally true, can be conceptually useful only if they represent invariant structures. Gradualism is the kind of learning involved in interactional morality.

Dialogues That Do Not Achieve Equilibration Among Parties

Full accounts of exceptional dialogues are not possible here, but three main kinds seem to exist: actual imbalances that are, nevertheless, legitimated—for instance, between parent and child; false balances that have a surface appearance of legitimation; and imbalances arising from exploited differences in social power like status or caste.

Several aspects of parent-child relations prevent full moral exchange and true equilibration. Unique to this dyad is the fact that children do not initially make a free, autonomous commitment to enter into the relationship with parents—they do not ask to be born—nor can they ordinarily terminate the relationship if it lacks moral equity. However, parents do (presumably) make a free, autonomous commitment to bear children. Entailed in that commitment are the parents' intentions "to rear" children—that is, to enhance children's development, power, and integration until they are "grown up" and, in less obvious ways, when they are adults. Children do not reciprocate moral concern equal to their parents', at least not until the parents are aged. In their own turn, the children will take disproportionate moral responsibility for their children. (As Rawls whimsically said, only the first generation of parents is deprived by this arrangement.) Another reason why these moral exchanges are imbalanced is that children are morally immature. Parents settle for less sensitive, less adequate resolutions, which attenuate their own good simply because children cannot grasp social nuances and lack power to enact commitments. In other words, equity is achieved, transcendentally and historically, by parents' awareness that they become morally indentured as they bear children and that their compensations are different in kind and come at a different time.

Thus, moral agreements achieved between parents and children are not literally equilibrated as are normative balances and are only eventually equilibrated by the transcendental meanings of parents' commitments in bearing and rearing children. Plainly, the actual imbalance is socially legitimated and socially required.

Legitimated imbalances can also occur between people of unequal personal resources; in fact, they *should* occur if long-term equity is to be sustained. Thus, we agree, for example, that special expenditures should be made to fix building entrances so that physically handicapped people can enter and participate in work and social life. At the same time, people of lesser power and resources violate the terms of the moral dialogue if they expect to receive in all ways or in ways not relevant to their handicaps.

False balances can arise from insincere, conscious freeloading or from unconscious folie à deux. However, moral theories that contain extensive provisions for the prevention of freeloading—a phobic response to sin—tend to make adversaries of discussants, no matter what their commonalities, and thereby close off opportunities for moral understanding to evolve. However, if a participant proves to be insincere on repeated appraisals, dialogue becomes futile. Sincere participants will protect themselves and their groups first by withdrawal but perhaps later by force, as they are entitled to do because they must be moral objects to themselves.

False balances based on the willingness of partners to accept inequitable relations—for instance, sadomasochistic pairs—seem to counter the grounds asserted here that all people want equity. The first easy explanation is to take the ontological stance that because all people basically want equity, parties would not knowingly or freely enter into a sadomasochistic relationship, and any happiness they report is false. In other words, the argument of neurotically diminished capacity could be advanced.

However, I argue that if the partners could be induced to reflect on their sadomasochistic choice, they would agree to the proposition that relations between master and slave are morally corrupt and would not recommend that relationship to their offspring or to future generations, although they might not choose to change their own ways. Their actual choices for themselves are not moral ones; neither party asks, "Should I (in a moral sense) enslave this masochist?" or "Should I enslave myself to this sadist?" Instead, strategic and instrumental considerations of safety, security, and gains dominate their choices. Their moral evaluations, if these could be secured without evoking guilt and arousing distortions, would be revealed by their recommendations for their offspring and future generations. Over the course of history, oppressed people have

hoped that their descendants would secure equity even when the cost of their gaining equity in their own lifetimes has been too high. What people actually choose is not synonymous with what they prefer. Sociohistoric necessities distort choice.

When a moral problem arises between two people or two societies of unequal power, no basis exists, within the interactional formulation, for discussants of greater power to dominate the dialogue. Merit, for instance, does not legitimate the use of power in dialogue; to use advantage extraneous to the issue is bad faith that disrupts dialogue or leads to unsatisfactory conclusions, outcomes that are evident when oppressed groups are dominated; they resort to underground strategies of sabotage and nonproductive pseudostupidity. However, if the oppressed's strategies become morally insensitive, they lose appeal to observers who might otherwise be moved to enter the dialogue to ensure society's moral equilibration.

Individual psychological statuses also lead to false moral consciousness. People can crystallize their basic approach to moral dialogue and negate moral information; they do not see the conflict, and, therefore, they are unperturbed. Stressful situations may cause some participants to accept or invent false balances that seem to protect their sense of self-consistency as moral beings. In other words, they choose compartmentalization instead of disintegration. Finally, deleterious life situations can positively favor participants' personal inclinations to accept false balances.

Notes

I wish to thank the many people who made comments on earlier drafts of this paper, but especially Eliane Aerts, Tom Andrae, Lynne English, Frederick Gordon, Richard Holway, Vicky Johnson, Andrew Phelps, Neil Thomasen, and Jerome Wakefield.
1. Eric Havelock, *The Liberal Temper in Greek Politics* (New Haven: Yale University Press, 1957), p. 169.
2. Kurt Baier, *The Moral Point of View* (Ithaca, N.Y.: Cornell University Press, 1958); Thomas

Nagel, *The Possibility of Altruism* (Oxford: Clarendon Press, 1970); John Rawls, *A Theory of Justice* (Cambridge: Belnap Press, 1971); and Lawrence Kohlberg, "From Is to Ought: How to Commit the Naturalistic Fallacy and Get Away With It in a Study of Moral Development" in Theodore Mischel, ed., *Cognitive Development and Epistemology* (New York: Academic Press, 1971).

3. Jean Piaget, *The Psychology of Intelligence* (London: Routledge & Kegan Paul, 1950).

4. Guy E. Swanson, "Self Process and Social Organization: An Interpretation of the Mechanisms of Coping and Defense," unpublished ms., 1968.

5. Norma Haan, *Coping and Defending: Processes of Self-Environment Organization* (New York: Academic Press, 1977).

6. Jürgen Habermas, *Communication and the Evolution of Society*, Thomas McCarthy, trans. (Boston: Beacon Press 1979).

7. Rawls, *The Theory of Justice*.

8. For example, see John Darley, Ellen Klosson, and Mark Zanna, "Intentions and Their Contexts in the Moral Judgments of Children and Adults," *Child Development* (1978), 49:66–74; at least twenty other reports suggest that young children's morality is more differentiated.

9. Jean Piaget, *The Moral Judgment of the Child* (1932; rpt., New York: Free Press, 1965); Kohlberg, "From Is to Ought."

10. Bibb Latané and John Darley, *The Unresponsive Bystander* (New York: Appleton-Century-Crofts, 1970).

Civility and Piety

Philip Selznick

In this selection Philip Selznick explores a theory of public virtue that integrates the habitual mores of a community with the self-reflective ethic of a diverse liberal democracy. He begins by describing the two foundations of a community's social order: civility and piety. Civility is the virtue of citizens; it is a respect for the views and values of others and a willingness to engage in dialogue to reach a common ground in the construction of a public life. Piety is an attitude of reverence and respect for those sources of a person's being that give life meaning, the attachments of the human community and the continuities between humanity and the other elements of the natural world. The demands of these two virtues often conflict, setting up a tension between the ethical systems based on them: critical morality based on civility and conventional morality based on piety. Each of these public virtues contributes to the growth of a well-functioning community, Selznick argues, but each also has destructive effects. A theory of public ethics must integrate these two systems in a way that preserves their distinctive benefits while controlling their more destructive effects. For this project Selznick relies on the philosophy of the American pragmatists. The pragmatic method submits the unconscious habits of traditional mores and passionate attachments to critical evaluation, using both local and universal principles. Conventional morality is then adjusted to meet these criticisms, producing a more adequate moral system. This process is well illustrated, Selznick believes, by the judicial process in common-law and constitutional adjudication. In the last two sections Selznick shows how the courts balance the claims of conventional morality with the wider perspective of critical morality in cases concerning victimless crimes, pornography, the right to privacy, and the right of communities to outlaw homosexual acts.

From Philip Selznick, *The Moral Commonwealth: Social Theory and the Promise of Community* (Berkeley: University of California Press, 1992), pp. 387–409. Copyright © 1992 The Regents of the University of California. Reprinted by permission of the University of California Press. Some footnotes omitted.

Two sources of moral integration compete for preeminence as foundations of community: civility and piety. Civility governs diversity, protects autonomy, and upholds toleration; piety expresses devotion and demands integration.[1] The norms of civility are impersonal, rational, and inclusive, whereas piety is personal, passionate, and particularist. The conflict between these very different aspirations generates troublesome issues of morality and community. Their reconciliation is a prime object of theory and policy. In this [essay] some strategies of reconciliation are explored, with special attention to problems of critical morality, tradition, religion, and ideology.

Modern thought is not comfortable with the idea of piety. The democratic and secular person is likely to associate it with sanctimonious devotion to ritual and uncritical subordination to religious authority. But piety has a broader and more attractive connotation, perhaps best expressed by George Santayana: "Piety, in its nobler and Roman sense, may be said to mean man's reverent attachment to the sources of his being and the steadying of his life by that attachment."[2] This "nobler" idea treats piety as an aspect of human nature, a reflection of the need for coherence and attachment. The distinctive virtues of piety are humility and loyalty.

John Dewey had a similar conception. He found "natural piety" in "human nature as a cooperating part of a larger whole."[3] Natural piety is an attitude of reverence and respect for human interdependence and for the continuities between humanity and nature. The root experience is a sense of connectedness or common mooring. Like Santayana, therefore, Dewey could think of piety as a pervasive human experience *and* as an enduring value.

Piety thus understood is not tied to any particular practice or belief. It does presume, however, something like a religious attitude. Such an attitude, as Dewey understood it, strives for "a working union of the ideal and the actual" at the same time that it takes into account human finitude and dependency.[4] To recognize an "enveloping world" beyond ourselves is to know that our achievements, however great, are not ours alone. "The essentially unreligious attitude," wrote Dewey, "attributes human achievement and purpose to man in isolation from the world of physical nature and his fellows." In truth, "our successes are dependent on the cooperation of nature."[5]

Thus piety is an attribute of the implicated self. Among its connotations are those of "faithfulness to the duties owed to parents and relatives, superiors, etc. . . . affectionate loyalty and respect, esp. to parents." These attachments have a claim to fidelity because they play a vital part in the formation of our selves. They are "sources of our being." In that sense, piety is ultimately an affirmation of self; a sign of psychological coherence; a foundation of self-respect.

In the life of piety, ideas are less important than feelings. But the feelings are not irrational:

> Piety is the spirit's acknowledgment of its incarnation. So, in filial and parental affection, which is piety in an elementary form, there is a moulding of will and emotion, a check to irresponsible initiative, in harmony with the facts of animal reproduction. . . . Piety is in a sense pathetic because it involves subordination to physical accident and acceptance of finitude. But it is also noble and eminently fruitful because . . . it meets fate with simple sincerity and labours in accordance with the conditions imposed. It exercises the eminently sane function of calling thought home. . . . For reason and happiness are like other flowers—they wither when plucked.[6]

In other (less poetic) words, piety exhibits a healthy strain toward particularity and rootedness.

And yet the objects of piety are not *wholly* concrete. Relationships are idealized; memories are filtered; history is touched up. Images of family, institution, locality, and nation resist abstraction; they are densely symbolic; but they typically contain at least a rudimentary basis for criticism and judgment. If the ideal aspect is suppressed—if there is no critical standpoint—piety becomes morally suspect.

Love of country is a classic form of piety. It is a virtue, and a highly effective one at that, capable of creating a potent union of self and place, self and history. Patriotism extends the reach of fellowship, enlarges the meaning of self-interest, and reinforces morality by securing it to a particular heritage. Like every other form of piety, however, it claims a core of unconditional devotion: "my child, my parent, right or wrong; my country right or wrong." The unconditional element in patriotism is necessary to its power; it is also a main source of moral failing. Therefore we are driven to invoke a higher patriotism, one that retains devotion but legitimates criticism.

Patriots must and do embrace, in some sense unconditionally, basic aspects of their community. But what aspects?

> The answer is: the nation conceived *as a project,* a project somehow or other brought to birth in the past and carried on so that a morally distinctive community was brought into being which embodied a claim to political autonomy. . . . What the patriot is committed to is a particular way of linking a past which has conferred a distinctive moral and political identity upon him or her with a future for the project which it is his or her . . . responsibility to bring into being. Only this allegiance is unconditional and allegiance to particular governments or forms of government or particular leaders will be entirely conditional upon their being devoted to furthering that project rather than frustrating or destroying it.[7]

Thus understood, patriotism is saved from idolatry, that is, from treating a limited, contingent reality as if it had an absolute claim to reverence and respect. In pledging allegiance to the nation "as a project" we identify ourselves with an idealized past, accept responsibility for failures as well as successes, and promise to care for the community's well-being. The commitment runs to *this* nation, not some other; therefore it remains particularized. As the meaning of patriotism is enlarged, however, critical distance is gained; a narrow parochialism is transcended.

Not only patriotism but every object of piety—friendship, kinship, parental love, institutional participation, religious faith—contemplates a relatively unconditional bond. In this respect each differs from more routine, more interchangeable, more transitory experiences and relationships. As an expression of devotion to particular persons, institutions, communities, and beliefs, piety is a foundation for *sacrifice.* Furthermore, piety avoids gestures of alienation, rejection, or separation. This strategy of acceptance or inclusion—and a corresponding willingness to subordinate one's own proximate interests to

another's, or to a higher good—is the benign face of piety.

But the same "unconditional" commitment—the same devotion to particularity—can be divisive, unjust, and destructive. Piety has corrupt forms that resist criticism, condemn apostasy, and create outcasts; that are self-righteous, intolerant, and unforgiving. This darker aspect of piety undercuts its moral worth. Therefore we need a complementary principle of order—the principle of civility.

Like "piety," "civility" has an old-fashioned ring, and it too has suffered a radical constriction of meaning. Today "civility" means little more than politeness or courtesy. In a broader and more ancient sense, however, civility is "behaviour befitting a citizen." It is "the virtue of the citizen, of the man who shares responsibility in his own self-government, either as governor or as one of the governed." To be civil is to be guided by the distinctive virtues of public life. These include, especially, moderation in pursuit of one's own interests, and concern for the common good. More particularly, civility signals the community's commitment to dialogue as the preferred means of social decision.

Thus civility presumes diversity, autonomy, and potential conflict. Whatever the context of public life—etiquette, justice, controversy—norms of civility are predicated on a regard for the integrity and independence of individuals and groups. Reconciliation is a keynote, and much attention is given to narrowing differences and encouraging communication. There is no question, however, of extinguishing interests or denying rights. In civility respect, not love, is the salient value.

Civility is not a morality of engagement, nor is it a call to passion or sacrifice. It is cool, not hot; detached, not involved. This is another way of saying that civility is a universalist ethic and as such must distance itself from the claims of particularism. . . . [A] universalist ethic progressively extends the reach of a moral community by enlarging the circle of belonging and fellowship.

This critical social function of civility is distorted and frustrated by the characteristic forms of piety, which build on primordial ties of origin and kinship. Nevertheless, civility and piety are by no means wholly antagonistic. Respect is not love, but it strains toward love as it gains substance and subtlety. Rudimentary respect is formal, external, and rule-centered—founded in fear of disruption and lack of cooperation. The corresponding civility can be chilly indeed, as some connotations of "being civil" suggest. An important change occurs when respect is informed by genuine appreciation for the values at stake in communication and good order. Freedom, dialogue, and diversity are then prized for their intrinsic worth, not merely suffered as burdens to be dealt with by the forms of civility. As sensitivity to values increases, the line between civility and piety blurs.

In truly civil communication, for example, something more is required than self-restraint and taking turns. An effort must be made really to listen, that is, to understand and appreciate what someone else is saying. As we do so we move from arm's-length "interaction" to more engaged "interaction." We discover and create shared meanings; the content or substance of the discussion becomes more important than its form. The outcome is often a *particular* community of discourse and a *unique* social bond. A foundation is laid for affection and commitment. In this way piety fleshes out the bare bones of civility.

Furthermore, civil speech takes into account human frailties and sensibilities. Contempt is the enemy of communication; patience and empathy are its allies. Hence we reject as uncivil personal abuse, intellectual intimidation, and indifference to offense. On especially sensitive issues—religion, nationality, race, for example—civil communication treads lightly, with special regard for the sources of personal identity. When it is thus open to the claims of piety, civility shows a human face.

Critical and Conventional Morality

A conspicuous feature of civility is the development of "critical" or "reflective" morality, based on reason and principle rather than passion and historicity. Piety, by contrast, is the realm of "conventional," "customary," or "positive" morality. The quality of community depends to a large extent on a proper mix of these ingredients.

By the conventional morality of a community is meant its historically given notions of right and wrong. Most of these beliefs are accepted unconsciously, as part of a world taken for granted, transmitted by socialization and reinforced by habit. Many are relatively superficial and easily changed. Others have deep psychological roots, and the prospect of change evokes strong emotional responses. These latter belong to what Freud called "superego morality." In either case, weak or strong, the beliefs and their associated practices may be justified and refined by reflection, but they are not founded on reflection.

Such a morality has characteristic failings. It is often *incoherent,* in that it sends contradictory messages as to what is morally right; *naive,* in concealing the uncertain and problematic nature of moral judgment; *unrealistic,* in not adapting to new circumstances, including changes in attitudes or practice; and excessively *parochial,* in too closely identifying morality with the interests of a particular group or community. These and other limitations of conventional morality create genuine problems of choice and interpretation, problems that must be faced, in one way or another, by any society. Hence moral reflection is a natural and recurrent response to the inherent complexity of social life.

We should not identify customary morality with everything that is "received" or even "traditional." A received culture—the culture handed down—can include beliefs and institutions that spring from and are sustained by reflection and criticism. When Americans speak of "our traditions," many have in mind the special forms of American democracy, such as freedom of speech, federalism, or four-year terms for presidents. Understood in this broad sense, "tradition" can and does include much that is based on rational design and abstract principle.

We lose purchase on reality, however, and evade important issues, if we do not acknowledge the special connection between tradition and customary morality. Not every practice is a tradition. A practice becomes a tradition *when it takes on symbolic meaning* as part of the unique ethos of a group, an institution, or a community. In the making of tradition the most important element is shared historical experience. This particularity is expressed in narrative and legend, in sacred texts, in the creation of heroes, in ritual, monuments, holidays, architecture, hymns, and flags. The most compelling traditions are suffused with and supported by expressive symbolism. The more effective the symbolism, the more unconditional the loyalty it calls forth. Piety, not civility, is the guiding ideal, and that is precisely what makes tradition problematic from the standpoint of critical morality.

There is a sense in which every morality is critical, if only because each upholds standard of right conduct. The differences lie in the sources of those standards and in the attitudes taken toward those sources. Customary morality does not look beyond historicity and convenience. Critical morality postulates that any received code of conduct is subject to criticism and reconstruction in the light of reflection and inquiry.

Nevertheless, critical morality cannot be a rootless figment of the moral imagination. It is not made up out of whole cloth, nor is it the product of concocted schemes or premises. Properly understood, critical morality is (1) informed by historical and comparative study of moral experience; (2) anchored in the ethos of a particular culture; (3) responsive to the demand for justification; (4) enriched by dialogue; and (5) refined by a reasoned elaboration of concepts and principles. This is to say that critical morality is governed by all the dimensions of reason . . . : experience, principle, prudence, dialogue, and order.

Thus understood, critical morality is continuous with customary morality. It requires assessment, evaluation, and an unending quest for principled justification, but there is no unbridgeable gap, no wall of separation. There is not even a prima facie case that any given product of reflection is necessarily superior to the adaptive outcomes of social life; if anything, the presumption goes the other way. Neither, however, is self-certifying. Custom must stand the test of reflection; reflection must yield to the verdict of experience.

The Moral Worth of Tradition

Critical morality must give due weight to the claims of tradition. This is so in part because the *pre*-judgments that form our minds are necessary starting points—and touchstones—for moral reflection.[8] We begin with, and come back to, the "intuitions" or "settled convictions" in which we have confidence.[9] This should not be understood as an individual experience. Rather, we take guidance from what a *representative* figure—the morally aware person—confidently believes is right or wrong. These historically determined premises are more than handy beginnings or rhetorical devices. They are indispensable for reflection because, in varying degrees, they are vehicles of congealed meaning and tacit understanding. Durkheim once said that "a society without prejudices would resemble an organism without reflexes."[10] He was not disparaging self-awareness but only reminding us that much social knowledge is tacit and subliminal.

My favorite example of the tacit knowledge in custom is Winston Churchill's explanation of why the chamber of the House of Commons is relatively small:

> [The chamber] should *not* be big enough to contain all its Members at once without overcrowding, and there should be no question of every Member having a separate seat reserved for him. The reason for this has long been a puzzle to uninterested outsiders, and has frequently excited the curiosity and even the criticism of new Members. Yet it is not so difficult to understand if you look at it from a practical point of view. If the House is big enough to contain all its Members, nine-tenths of its debates will be conducted in the depressing atmosphere of an almost empty or half-empty chamber. The essence of good House of Commons speaking is the conversational style, the facility for quick, informal interruptions and interchanges. Harangues from a rostrum would be a bad substitute. . . . But the conversational style requires a fairly small space, and there should be on great occasions a sense of crowd and urgency.[11]

"Logic," notes Churchill, "is a poor guide compared with custom."[12] His point is to show that custom has its reasons that logic may not know. The tacit knowledge of custom is often wiser than a scheme based on explicit theorizing, which may inadequately comprehend the subtle and multiple values at stake. Reflection, like tradition, has costs and weaknesses; it too is not self-justifying, nor does it necessarily improve the moral code it is criticizing. Reflection may be selective in its premises, mistaken in its logic, unsubtle in its characterization of a custom or idea. This is the truth behind Edmund Burke's rejection of speculative reason.

The fact that prejudgment can also be prejudicial in the modern sense of biased or bigoted, or be a reflex of ignorance, or short-sighted, underlines the need for criticism and reconstruction. But it does not cancel the claim of conventional morality to respectful and sympathetic examination. Critical morality, in other words, cannot be free-floating and self-contained. The attempt to judge without pre-conceptions, in a spirit of wholesale rejection, leads to sterility and irrelevance or to the arbitrary imposition of unworkable ideas.

It is an elementary lesson of social science that the human animal, if it is to grow and flourish, needs a framework of social support that must include moral guidance, symbolic expression, and a secure way of life. Hence we may say that, in principle, culture is a good thing. Within broad limits it does not matter what form a culture takes or what content it has. Any culture that is reasonably effective in forming personalities and transmitting a heritage is bound to contain elements out of which a more or less well-tempered moral order can be fashioned. This person-forming, life-enhancing work of culture is its main justification from the perspective of critical morality.

Because culture *is* a good thing, and because it is manifested in particularities of belief and practice, we reject ethnocentrism; we accept a prima facie obligation of cross-cultural respect and toleration. If such toleration is to be meaningful, however, it must extend to mores as well as to folkways. It is not enough to be tolerant of superficial variation, such as different ways of saying the same thing or exotic ways of eating dinner. We must also be tolerant of cultural premises (such as strong gender differences) and institutions (such as polygamy or theocracy) that we may consider wrong or offensive. We postulate the rough moral equivalence of many different ways of life, and this restrains a too easy application to

other cultures of a critical morality we have developed for our own use and mainly out of our own experience.

We should be careful to distinguish a generally positive attitude toward culture and tradition from the evaluation of specific institutions or practices. From the standpoint of critical morality no tradition is self-validating. Furthermore, *once we understand the role of tradition* in creating harmonious selves and societies, we can make that understanding a basis for assessment and revision of specific traditions. Although tradition in general has a presumption of moral worth, any given tradition may be impoverishing, destructive, divisive, even demonic. The same logic applies to family, friendship, and similar "good things." On the whole, abstractly considered, these are contexts within which virtue can flourish—but only if their positive potential is fulfilled and they are not, instead, crucibles of oppressive constraint, physical abuse, or emotional exploitation.

As a philosophy of the present, American pragmatism is properly associated with criticism of tradition and openness to new experience. It should not be forgotten, however, that William James, John Dewey, and George Herbert Mead thought of truth-finding as a social process. "Far from asserting that the individual could make knowledge in his or her own image, [James] was at pains to emphasize the power of socially possessed, traditional beliefs; he was, moreover, adamant about the obligation to integrate one's new experiences with the harvest of history."[13] In a characteristic phrase, James spoke of the "funded truths" gleaned from history, with which we are—and must be—in earnest dialogue.[14]

Moral reasoning and comparative study are indispensable, but what we learn is most pertinent and most compelling when it is applied reflexively, that is, to the understanding of our own moral identity. This self-engaged inquiry draws on intimate acquaintance with the nuances of conduct, the spirit as well as the letter of rules, the contexts of policy. Moralists speak in the accents of authenticity when, like Antigone, Jesus, and Martin Luther King, Jr., they find resources for criticism within a framework that is received, understood, and revered.

This argument echoes Hegel's critique of Kantian ethics. Hegel rejected the idea that morality is a matter of rational choice made in the light of abstract or formal presuppositions such as the categorical imperative. Rather, moral redemption occurs in and through a historically given moral order. The content and texture of morality, not the form, are all-important, and these are determined by an ongoing collective life. In this view, moral principles are derivative, not constitutive; secondary, not primary.

The Hegelian model does not deny—on the contrary, it proclaims—the need for critical morality to cure the limitations of conventional morality. The question is one of starting points. Hegel begins with the full concreteness of social practice and belief (*Sittlichkeit*) and from there moves to more general principles that purport to express the spiritual commitments or ethos of a people. These principles are often fiercely debated. Nevertheless, they are routinely appealed to as authoritative standpoints from which to criticize a given policy, practice, or belief. The elements of an ethos are not deductions from theoretical axioms. They are efforts to capture whatever internal coherence and latent message there may be in a moral order.

Hegel did not suppose that one ethos is as good as the next and that therefore only internal criticism is legitimate. He believed we could draw from the theory of community universal criteria of moral well-being, and he took the Athenian polis as a paradigm of moral achievement. But a morality is not worth much if it is not integral to a taken-for-granted world of cooperation and fellowship. Therefore critical morality must hold in tension the universal and the particular. It may reach for an ideal—Hebraic justice, Buddhist self-transcendence, Christian love, Greek civic participation—but the ideal must be grounded in and relevant to the historical experience of the community.

It could be argued that Hegel was addressing the *conditions* of morality rather than its *logic*, whereas Kant's main concern was the latter. But Hegel's critique goes to the heart of the Kantian view that distinctively moral conduct proceeds from a free and rational individual decision to embrace moral duty without regard to personal inclination or social consequence. For Hegel, morality springs, rather, from the continuities of individual and social life. To follow one's inclinations and assess social consequences, far from being alien to morality, is the best and most authentic way of being moral. This assumes, of course, that personal desires are at one with social norms and with the spirit underlying the norms, and that the consequences we care about have to do with *Bildung*, that is, the formation of character and culture.

A communitarian theory of morality has very practical significance for how we understand not only the *source* but also the *reach* of individual responsibility. Kantian doctrine is characteristically modern in tying moral responsibility to choice and intent. It is "free will" that defines to whom and for what we are responsible. In the more organic communitarian view, autonomous choice is only one criterion, and not always the most important. We are responsible for our *selves,* but the self as a biological and social formation is decisively affected by circumstances not chosen. Among these are memberships in family and community. A received identity has much to offer: inner coherence, security, self-esteem. Although people often detach themselves from their roots and try to send down new ones, the difficulties are great and the costs are high.

If unchosen belonging is a great advantage and is a critical part of self-hood, then the boundaries between individual and collective responsibility are indistinct. They cannot be neatly limited by the criteria of free choice and explicit intent. People who are nourished by a community and "accept" what they never dreamed of choosing cannot deny responsibility for their community's traditions and deeds. Contemporary Americans take pride in their political institutions and achievements; contemporary Germans are proud of their musical, literary, and scientific heritage. By the same token, however, Americans must take responsibility for the devastation of slavery, which extends to this generation and beyond; and Germans must take responsibility for the Nazi regime and the Holocaust. This does not settle what collective responsibility entails; there is an important difference between guilt and responsibility. But the principle cannot be dismissed as primitive or irrational or as simply a dangerous thought.

The great question is: Can critical morality be achieved in and through parochial achievements? Can people find their way to objective judgment while retaining and even deepening their special religious, national, or cultural identity? This has been a perennial challenge to moral sophistication. The appeal of a universal ethic—of civility—is forever countered by the persistent attraction of particular traditions and beliefs.

There is much to be gained, in strength and subtlety, from intimate acquaintance with a distinctive morality. The communicant experiences a tradition from within; draws self-confidence from a familiar idiom; learns from narrative and example; brings general principles to bear without rudely imposing an external ethic. The outcome is necessarily selective, as culture is selective. But if a people's uniqueness has something worthwhile to offer, its contribution will be most complete and most enduring if its agents are faithful to their origins. In an international assembly of scholars or judges or in an ecumenical gathering of religious leaders, we do not ask the participants to shed their distinctive identities. On the contrary, we hope to gain from their diversity.

From the standpoint of critical morality, however, parochial experience may not be taken as final or treated as an unqualified end in itself. A corollary commitment must be made to press the particular into the service of the general, that is, to draw from a special history a universal message. To do so is, inevitably, to create a basis for criticizing one's own heritage, not only from within but also in the light of other experiences and more comprehensive interests.

Two steps are necessary. The first, turning inward, examines the received culture to identify its moral premises. These serve as principles of criticism by means of which specific rules or practices can be assessed, revised, or rejected. Such principles, however, do not take us beyond culture-bound (though generalized) beliefs: for example, belief in the sanctity of heterosexual marriage or in the separation of church and state. The second step reaches for more universal judgments. We look to history and human nature for warranted conclusions about the conditions that make for personal and collective well-being.

The Enforcement of Morals

The interplay of critical and conventional morality is well displayed in common-law and constitutional adjudication. The judicial process—especially but not exclusively in appellate courts of the United States—may serve as a paradigm of the themes set out above. For the courts have a dual burden. They are responsible for a moral and legal heritage; they are also responsible for applying rules and doctrines to specific facts, which may mean doing justice in new or unforeseen circumstances. As they do so, they must articulate and reconstruct received law and custom; and they must bring to bear, inevitably if cautiously, a general understanding of social life, morality, and human nature. . . . Here we consider some special legal issues, bearing on obscenity and homosexual conduct, that have helped to make clear what it means to both invoke and criticize a customary morality.

Issues of "law and morals" sharply reveal both the tension and the continuity between customary and critical morality. In question is the propriety of enforcing conventional views regarding deviant sexual conduct, sexually explicit communication, gambling, blasphemy, birth control, abortion, vagrancy, and drug abuse. Laws prohibiting or controlling these and similar activities are usually justified by reference to a serious harm, but the alleged harm often turns out to be difficult to identify, highly controversial, or only distantly related to the offending act. Because the victim is often either the very person who commits the offense or someone quite willing to cooperate in it, such as a prostitute, these crimes are sometimes called "victimless crimes."

Those who oppose the use of law to coerce virtue draw on a principle made famous by John Stuart Mill: "The only purpose for which power can be rightfully exercised over any member of a civilized community, against his will, is to prevent harm to others. His own good, either physical or moral, is not sufficient warrant. He cannot rightfully be compelled to do or forbear because, in the opinion of others, to do so would be wise, or even right."[15]

Mill's position is countered by the view that the cohesion and integrity of a social order depend on the continued assertion of a common morality. The harm done by an offending pattern of conduct may be subtle and long-term; yet it may be of great significance to those who believe that their community's character and identity are at stake. And there may also be more immediate harm, in the form of environments perceived as degraded or of children exposed to destructive influences.

In the United States these matters raise constitutional issues of personal autonomy, abuse of power, and freedom of speech. A good example is the treatment of pornography. The courts have been torn between their commitment to freedom and their respect for what are taken to be widely shared and deeply held convictions about the limits of freedom.

During the first hundred and fifty years of the Republic, it was taken for granted that states and local communities could restrain "indecencies" of many kinds. The courts upheld broad legislative powers and wide official discretion. It seemed hardly necessary to define offenses that were distasteful to discuss and presumed to be self-evident to all right-thinking persons. In the late nineteenth century, however, American courts adopted the conception of obscenity formulated in an English case, *Regina v. Hicklin* (1868). The *Hicklin* test, as it came to be known, was whether "the matter charged" had a tendency "to deprave and corrupt those whose minds are open to such immoral influences, and into whose hands a publication of this sort may fall."[16] This broad standard said nothing about other merits "the matter" might have; made the susceptibilities of the most vulnerable elements of the population the criterion of what is harmful; and was read as allowing a publication to be banned on the basis of passages taken out of context rather than in consideration of the work as a whole. These criteria permitted local officials—and, through its postal laws, the federal government—to suppress distribution of literary works by James Joyce, D. H. Lawrence, Henry Miller, and William Faulkner, among many others.

The later history of obscenity law, as made by the Supreme Court, has been an effort to revise and limit this sweeping grant of discretion *while retaining the core of conventional morality and upholding the propriety of legal enforcement*. Although the Court has greatly liberalized the restrictions on what may be said and depicted, it has not repudiated the idea that pornography is an evil that the police power of local communities may suppress. This compromise has earned the Court the contempt of libertarians and the anger of conservative moralists. For our purposes, however, it may be seen as an effort to reconcile conventional and critical morality.

In a series of troublesome cases that began in 1957, the Supreme Court attempted, in the interests of competing values, to narrow the definition of what is legally obscene. The Court sought to protect works of "redeeming social importance" or, in a later, more restrictive formulation, works of "serious literary, artistic, political, or scientific value" and to fulfill the society's obligation to be open to diverse perspectives and new lifestyles. Pornographic appeal to "prurient interest"—lewd thoughts and longings—is obscene and not protected by the First Amendment. But even if a work is not meritorious it cannot be banned merely because it has a prurient element or aspect. The work must be "patently offensive" to the "average person" according to "contemporary community standards," which may change and vary from one community to another; and the legislation must be specific in stating what acts or depictions are prohibited.[17]

These restrictions show the rudiments of critical morality and, at the same time, a deference to conventional morality. That deference is not easy to justify on the part of an institution committed to rational argument. Some say it "undermines the whole idea of rationality in legislation, substituting a notion of tradition that is a mask for ignorance and intolerance."[18] But responsible criticism should not too quickly disparage the moral worth of tradition or dismiss the implicit truths it may contain. The judicial opinions have indeed been short on moral argument; they have not gone very far to clarify just why obscenity should be restrained. It does not follow, however, that the evil of obscenity is unreal or unimportant. The want of a good theory cautions legal restraint, but it is not a reason to abandon responsibility.

It is not difficult to construct a plausible argument defending the tradition that exploitation of prurient interest should be discouraged by law. Most important, perhaps, is the idea that public life is degraded by uninhibited displays of raw impulse and emotion, especially when the effect is to celebrate or make commonplace various forms of brutality, indifference to suffering, or extremes of self-debasement. The restraint of public executions, cockfighting, and other events that have the effect of stimulating such feelings reflects this concern. A special anxiety is the competence of parents to be effective in socializing their children if they cannot count on the community to uphold their efforts to encourage self-discipline and defer gratification. Still another anxiety is the fear that values of love and intimacy will suffer as the tie between sex and personal commitment is weakened. Most specific, and for many most compelling, at least in the United States, is the argument that pornography degrades women.

These ideas are worthy of respect because they resonate with much uncodified experience. Their logic has not been fully worked out, nor are they necessarily based on solid empirical evidence as to causes and effects. At bottom the obscenity decisions do not depend on scientific findings. Rather, the majority of the justices have deferred to conventional morality, insofar as it is expressed in local legislation, because they are persuaded it can have a rational, if unarticulated, basis and because they believe that, as a product of funded experience, it should be given the benefit of the doubt. This shifts the burden of proof to those who deny the claims of conventional morality. It means the tradition cannot be overturned by a showing of *any* benefit of pornography, for example, as therapy. There must be convincing argument that more fundamental values, such as legitimate freedoms of expression or the integrity of the arts, are in jeopardy.

In the obscenity cases the claims of conventional morality are offset by a clear constitutional commitment to freedom of speech. That commitment is a resource for testing and restraining majority will (including attitudes long held, deeply felt, and widely shared) in the light of accepted principle. Here the courts help to fashion a critical morality by reaffirming a tradition—the First Amendment and its history—that is legally enshrined but socially vulnerable.

The judicial task is more difficult when constitutional protection of personal autonomy is sought on grounds less firmly supported by the explicit text of the Constitution. For example, the rights of homosexuals and the practice of abortion raise special issues of constitutional interpretation. In these matters, more general conceptions of morality and community are brought to bear. The judges who defend a right to choose abortion (or homosexual conduct) invoke a broad right of "privacy," which in turn includes rights of self-definition and freedom of intimate association. The arguments counterpose very different approaches to community, tradition, and critical morality. (We deal with the prohibition of homosexual conduct in the following section, . . .)

The Hardwick Case

In 1986 the Supreme Court upheld as constitutional a Georgia statute that made sodomy a criminal offense punishable by imprisonment for one to twenty years.[19] The law was challenged by Michael Hardwick, whom the police found in his bedroom having sex with another man. (They had come to arrest him in connection with a different offense.) The local district attorney did not pursue the case, but Hardwick said the statute placed him in imminent danger of arrest. He claimed that under the federal Constitution private homosexual conduct by consenting adults could not be prohibited; and his argument was sustained by a court of appeals.

To invalidate the statute, the Supreme Court would have had to find that a fundamental right was violated. The Court's majority failed to find in the Constitution any right that would protect homosexual sodomy from legislative prohibition. As Chief Justice Warren E. Burger said, in a brief concurring opinion, "To hold that the act of homosexual sodomy is somehow protected as a fundamental right would be to cast aside millennia of moral teaching."[20]

In a vigorous dissent Justice Harry A. Blackmun argued that a customary morality is not self-justifying: "I cannot agree that either the length of time a majority has held its convictions or the passions with which it defends them can withdraw legislation from this Court's scrutiny." The real issue, he insisted, "is the fundamental interest all individuals have in controlling the nature of their intimate associations with others."[21]

The opinions reveal important differences in the way community and tradition are perceived. The majority opinion is communitarian in its own way. Those justices give great weight to customary morality as the foundation of community and as the preserver of its identity. In the theory to which they implicitly adhere, a genuine community is a community of observance, where customary rules and practices matter more than abstract principles. A corollary is that the sense of community is best expressed in localist terms. Moral autonomy should be granted at the local level, where social life is most fully experienced and appreciated. At that level, moreover, political majorities have a prima facie right to uphold conventional morality and thereby to determine the culture of the community.

This point of view should be distinguished from the argument that the enforcement of morals is justified by a general necessity to sustain a moral order. That in itself is no warrant for sustaining a *particular* moral code. But the real issue is: What is the moral claim of a community to uphold its view of what the moral order should be, and to do so by using the authority and coercion of government? This claim has special importance in the American federal system, which reserves to each of the fifty states broad powers of self-definition. In this case the Court decided that the issue of homosexual conduct should be left to the political process at the local level.

The dissenting justices have a very different view of community, tradition, and the rights of majorities. They find community and tradition in the American constitutional order.

The Constitution itself is a prime source of tradition—a tradition that allows for change and growth, criticism and reconstruction. It consists of *premises and values,* not of particular rules and practices. To identify such a tradition we must locate implicit principles and guiding purposes. A strategy of generalization is required. In this perspective the moral order is not constituted by particularities of belief, observance, or connectedness. Rather, the community is defined by more general ideals, such as democracy, equality, and the rule of law—in a word, by civility. The relevant moral community is the nation as defined by the Constitution. The claims of localism are to that extent diminished.

In their reading of American constitutional history, the minority justices find an evolving consensus on the importance of personal autonomy: "Our cases long have recognized that the Constitution embodies a promise that a certain sphere of individual liberty will be kept largely beyond the reach of government."[22] They find, *in the reasons behind* the Court's protection of basic family rights, such as whether or whom to marry and whether to have children, a vindication of personal rather than institutional values:

> We protect those rights not because they contribute, in some direct and material way, to the general public welfare, but because they form so central a part of an individual's life. . . . And we protect the family because it contributes so powerfully to the happiness of individuals, not because of a preference for stereotypical households. . . . The Court has recognized . . . that "the ability independently to define one's identity that is central to any concept of liberty" cannot be truly exercised in a vacuum; we all depend on the "emotional enrichment of close ties with others."
>
> Only the most willful blindness could obscure the fact that sexual intimacy is "a sensitive, key relationship of human existence, central to family life, community welfare, and the development of human personality." . . . The fact that individuals define themselves in a significant way through their intimate sexual relationships with others suggests, in a nation as diverse as ours, that there may be many "right" ways of conducting those relationships, and that much of the richness of a relationship will come from the freedom an individual has to *choose* the form and nature of these intensely personal bonds.[23]

Thus a central tenet of the moral order, as laid out in this judicial doctrine, is a shared belief in personal autonomy and privacy, especially in the realm of "intimate association." This belief, the justices hold, is an authoritative tradition because it is anchored in the Constitution and because it makes sense in the light of moral and psychological theory. If the Court is asked, What kind of a people are we? What is our culture? the ready answer is: We care about people as individuals and we believe they should be free to form their own identities.

An underlying assumption is that the alternative lifestyle—the intimate association in question—is reasonably viable, healthy, and unthreatening.[24] The minority opinion does not rule out prohibition of incest, prostitution, or polygamy. Despite some sweeping pronouncements in the dissenting opinion, it is not the case that every intimate association is defensible, nor does every one represent so fundamental an interest as to merit constitutional protection. In the logic of the minority view, however, the burden of proof lies elsewhere. Those who seek prohibition must justify their claim that the practice is undeserving of constitutional protection; only then would toleration or prohibition become a legitimate matter of public policy, to be decided by the political process.

Both arguments appeal to diversity, plurality, and toleration. The majority justices say the states may decide for themselves whether homosexual sodomy is a crime. The dissenters argue that diversity must be protected *within* each state, on the basis of individual preference rather than community sanction. In the majority view, whoever has the most votes may decide what traditions should be upheld. The dissenters, by contrast, want openness to change so that new political realities may emerge. If an alternative lifestyle is suppressed within a state, it will not have a reasonable chance to gain support for political change.

In its quest for latent principles in our legal culture and in its appeal to moral and psychological theory, the liberal minority of the Court clearly spoke for critical morality. The majority opinion, in its blunt appeal to history, made no contribution to reasoned elaboration of fundamental law. It does not follow, however, that the minority argument is wholly convincing. Exception may well be taken, for example, to the assertions quoted above that "we protect the family because it contributes so powerfully to the happiness of individuals" and that "much of the richness of a relationship will come from the freedom an individual has to *choose* the form and nature of these intensely personal bonds." A different understanding of family values and of what makes for rich personal relationships would convey a different message, even if it did not alter the legal conclusion.

Furthermore, the dissenting justices must rest, in part at least, on a finding of substantial support for the homosexual alternative or for toleration of it. A free society must present strong reasons for suppressing a minority. We therefore demand a showing of palpable harm: the liberty of thieves—no tiny minority—to pursue their occupation gets little sympathy. On questions of cultural identity, where specific harms are not shown, significant minorities should have a say in forming that identity. They should not be shut out by a mechanical and intractable majority. This principle is especially important when, as in the restraint of homosexual conduct and abortion, the political majority demands some major personal sacrifice.

But what if there is genuine consensus on, say, the wrongfulness of gambling, polygamy, suicide, or homosexual conduct? Does the individual's interest in freedom of choice overcome the community's interest in vindicating its beliefs—especially when a plausible case can be made for the merits of those beliefs? That some people gamble, others commit suicide, or have multiple spouses, or engage in homosexual acts does not in itself call a consensus into question. Under such circumstances the law is properly administered with compassion, and with an eye to the possibility that fundamental rights are abridged. It seems wrong, however, to withdraw from democratic decision every expression of cultural identity that interferes with personal autonomy.

To be sure, a political majority may or may not faithfully register a social consensus. Any widespread challenge to a custom or belief will affect the deference we show toward majority will. When the enforcement of morals is at

issue, it is important to know to what extent a
political outcome represents the views of the
community as a whole or is, instead, a device
for imposing the will of one part upon another. This does not mean the majority is
powerless to define the culture; it does mean
that its claim to do so must be scrutinized and
justified. Thus a prime focus of scrutiny is the
quality of consensus. As Ronald Dworkin
points out, "a conscientious legislator [or
judge, we might add] who is told a moral consensus exists must test the credentials of that
consensus."[25] Above all, we cannot accept as
moral a consensus marred by bigotry and contempt. There must be a threshold standard of
critical morality.

Notes

1. Compare this contrast with Durkheim's distinction between organic and mechanical solidarity. Organic solidarity generates rules of civility,
whereas mechanical solidarity is based on a
shared history and identity.

2. *The Life of Reason* (1933; reprint, New York:
Scribner's 1954), 258.

3. *A Common Faith* (New Haven: Yale University
Press, 1934), 25.

4. Ibid., 52.

5. Ibid., 25.

6. Santayana, *The Life of Reason* (1933), reprint
(New York: Schribner's 1954), 260f.

7. Alisdair MacIntyre, "Is Patriotism a Virtue?"
The Lindley Lecture (Lawrence: Kansas University Press, 1984), p. 13.

8. In modern thought this has been most strongly
emphasized by post-Kantian hermeneutic philosophers. For an influential contemporary treatment, see Hans-Georg Gadamer, *Truth and Method*
(New York: Crossroads Press, 1975), 239ff.

9. See John Rawls on "reflective equilibrium": *A
Theory of Justice* (Cambridge: Harvard University
Press, 1971), 20f., 48ff.

10. Emile Durkheim (1886), quoted in Robert N.
Bellah, ed., *Emile Durkheim on Morality and Society*
(Chicago: University of Chicago Press, 1973),
xxii.

11. Winston Churchill, *Closing the Ring* (Boston:
Houghton-Mifflin, 1951), 169.

12. Ibid.

13. Stanley Hollinger, "William James and the
Culture of Inquiry," *Michigan Quarterly Review* 20
(Summer 1981): 270.

14. William James, *Pragmatism: A New Name for
Some Old Ways of Thinking* (1907; reprint, New
York: Longmans, Green, 1948), 224, 233.

15. *On Liberty* (1859), in *Utilitarianism, On Liberty,
Considerations on Representative Government* (reprint, London: J. M. Dent, 1984), 78.

16. Regina V. Hicklin, L.R. 3Q.B. 360, 368
(1868).

17. Roth v. U.S., 354 U.S. 476 (1957); Stanley v.
Georgia, 394 U.S. 557 (1969); Miller v. Califor-
nia, 413 U.S. 15 (1973); Paris Adult Theatre I v.
Slaton, 413 U.S. 49 (1973).

18. David A. J. Richards, "Free Speech and
Obscenity Law: Toward a Moral Theory of the
First Amendment," *University of Pennsylvania Law
Review* 123 (November 1974): 90.

19. Bowers v. Hardwick, 478 U.S. 186 (1986).

20. Ibid., 197.

21. Ibid., 210.

22. Thornburgh v. American Coll. of Obst. &
Gyn., 476 U.S. 747, 772 (1986), cited in Justice
Blackmun's dissent.

23. Bowers v. Hardwick, 478 U.S. 186, 204f.
(1986).

24. It is instructive that the minority opinion
finds support in the Court's earlier recognition
that the state's interest in public education should
give way to a competing claim by the Amish community in Wisconsin that extended public schooling threatened its way of life. In that case the
Court said: "There can be no assumption that
today's majority is 'right' and the Amish and others like them are 'wrong.' A way of life that is odd
or even erratic but interferes with no rights or
interests of others is not to be condemned because it is different" (Wisconsin v. Yoder, 406
U.S. 205, 223 [1972]). The Court should have
said *"just* because it is different." There is an
assumption that the Amish way of life is a morally defensible alternative, to be respected and
tolerated, not merely endured. Furthermore, the
Amish case speaks to *local* diversity and community *control,* not to individual choice.

25. Ronald Dworkin, *Taking Rights Seriously*
(Cambridge: Harvard University Press, 1978),
254.

Preferences and Politics

Cass R. Sunstein

When a democratic government legislates for the good of its citizens without their support and against their expressed wishes, it is accused of "paternalism." In this article Cass Sunstein argues for a form of legal paternalism in which government regulation removes a coercion, thereby promoting citizens' freedom and welfare. He examines a recent trend in liberal theory that interprets citizens' interests as their "private preferences" and argues that a democratic and liberal government may sometimes override these preferences. He begins by exploring the difference between the citizens' interests (what would promote their welfare) and their existing preferences (their subjectively held beliefs and desires about what would promote their welfare). These preferences, he argues, are formed and change in response to a wide range of factors, such as existing laws, past conditioning, currently available information, and cultural mores. Sunstein presents examples to show that subjective preferences unduly influenced by such factors are not an expression of personal autonomy and may not serve that person's welfare. He concludes that these preferences do not have the moral standing of "interests" and that a democratic government is free to and may be obliged to override them. He then examines three kinds of subjective preferences that he believes should be overridden in the interests of personal liberty and welfare: those involving aspirations for a public good, those derived from unjust background conditions, and those involving addictive or myopic behavior. In all of these cases, Sunstein argues, a democratic government should be able to legislate to protect the quality of its citizens' lives without being hampered by the liberal commitment to neutrality among divergent conceptions of the good. In the last section he applies his views to some current problems in constitutional law, such as rights of access to the media, democratic control of the electoral process, hate speech, and pornography.

The drafting of the United States Constitution, it is often said, signaled a rejection of conceptions of politics founded on classical ideals in favor of a quite different modern view. The precise terms of the alleged shift are not altogether clear, but it is possible to identify the most prominent strands. The classical conception assumes a relatively homogeneous people and prizes active participation by the polity's citizenry. In the classical conception, the polity is self-consciously concerned with the character of the citizens; it seeks to inculcate in them and to profit from a commitment to the public good. Plato said that politics is the "art whose business it is to care for souls";[1] and under the classical conception, civic virtue, not private interest, is the wellspring of political behavior. Whether or not the state imposes a "comprehensive view"[2] on the nation, it relies relatively little on private rights to constrain government. The underlying vision of "republican" politics is one of frequent participation and deliberation in the service of decision, by the citizenry, about the sorts of values according to which the nation will operate.

In the modern account, by contrast, government is above all respectful of the divergent conceptions of the good held by its many constituents. People are taken as they are, not as they might be. Modern government has no concern with souls. Although electoral

From Cass R. Sunstein, "Preference and Politics," *Philosophy and Public Affairs, 20* (1991) no. 1, pp 3–34. Copyright © 1991 by Princeton University Press. Reprinted by permission of Princeton University Press. Some footnotes omitted.

processes are ensured, no special premium is placed on citizen participation. Self-interest, not virtue, is understood to be the usual motivating force of political behavior. Politics is typically, if not always, an effort to aggregate private interests. It is surrounded by checks, in the form of rights, protecting private liberty and private property from public intrusion.

In this system, the goal of the polity is quite modest: the creation of the basic ground rules under which people can satisfy their desires and go about their private affairs. Much of this is famously captured in *The Federalist* No. 10, in which Madison redescribed the so-called republican problem of the corruption of virtue as the so-called liberal problem of the control of factions, which, as Madison had it, were inevitable if freedom was to be preserved.

In fact, the conventional division between the American founders and their classical predecessors is far too crude. The founders attempted to create a deliberative democracy, one in which the institutions of representation, checks and balances, and federalism would ensure a deliberative process among political equals rather than an aggregation of interests. But respect for private preferences, rather than collective deliberation about public values or the good life, does seem to be a distinguishing feature of American constitutionalism. Indeed, the view that government should refuse to evaluate privately held beliefs about individual welfare, which are said to be irreducibly "subjective," links a wide range of views about both governmental structure and individual rights.

In this article I want to explore the question whether a contemporary democracy might not sometimes override the private preferences and beliefs of its citizens, not in spite of its salutary liberalism but because of it. It is one thing to affirm competing conceptions of the good; it is quite another to suggest that political outcomes must generally be justified by, or even should always respect, private preferences. A large part of my focus here is on the phenomenon of endogenous preferences. By this term I mean to indicate that preferences are not fixed and stable, but are instead adaptive to a wide range of factors—including the context in which the preference is expressed, the existing legal rules, past consump-

tion choices, and culture in general. The phenomenon of endogenous preferences casts doubt on the notion that a democratic government ought to respect private desires and beliefs in all or almost all contexts. It bears on a number of particular problems as well, including the rationale for and extent of the constitutional protection accorded to speech; proportional representation and checks and balances; and the reasons for and limits of governmental regulation of the arts, broadcasting, and the environment. I take up these issues at several points in this article.

The argument proceeds in several stages. In Section I, I set forth some fairly conventional ideas about welfare and autonomy, in conjunction with the endogeneity of desires, in order to argue against the idea that government ought never or rarely to override private preferences. In Section II, I contend that in three categories of cases, private preferences, as expressed in consumption choices, should be overridden. The first category involves what I call collective judgments, including considered beliefs, aspirations for social justice, and altruistic goals; the second involves preferences that have adapted to undue limitations in available opportunities or to unjust background conditions; the third points to intrapersonal collective action problems that, over a lifetime, impair personal welfare. In all of these cases, I suggest, a democracy should be free and is perhaps obliged to override private preferences. In Section III, I make some remarks about the relevance of these claims to several current issues of constitutional controversy. These include proportional representation in politics and governmental regulation of the speech "market," including rights of access to the media, democratic controls on the electoral process, hate speech, and pornography.

I. Against Subjective Welfarism

Should a constitutional democracy take preferences as the basis for political choice? In contemporary politics, law, and economics, the usual answer is affirmative. Modern economics, for example, is dominated by a conception of welfare based on the satisfaction of existing preferences, as measured by willingness to pay; in politics and law, something called "paternalism" is disfavored in both the public and private realms. But the idea that government ought to take preferences as the basis for political decisions is a quite modern one. This is not to say that the idea is without foundations. Partly a function of the perceived (though greatly overstated) difficulty of making interpersonal comparisons of utility, the idea is also a product of the epistemological difficulties of assessing preferences in terms of their true connection with individual welfare, and, perhaps most of all, the genuine political dangers of allowing government to engage in such inquiries.

The constellation of ideas that emerges from these considerations has been exceptionally influential. It embodies a conception of political justification that might be described as "subjective welfarism." On this view, the government, even or perhaps especially in a democracy, should attend exclusively to conceptions of welfare as subjectively held by its citizens. A wide range of prominent approaches to politics turn out to be versions of subjective welfarism. These include, for example, certain forms of utilitarianism; the view that some version of Paretian efficiency ought to be treated as the foundational norm for political life; opposition to paternalism in public and private life; approaches to politics modeled on bargaining theory (rational or otherwise); and conceptions of politics that see the democratic process as an effort to aggregate individual preferences.

It is important to understand that subjective welfarism, thus defined, may or may not be accompanied by a broader notion that ethical and moral questions should generally be treated in welfarist or subjectivist terms. It is as a political conception, rather than an ethical one, that subjective welfarism underlies a wide range of approaches to public life, including ideas about institutional arrangements and individual or collective rights. What I want to argue here is that subjective welfarism, even as a political conception, is unsupportable by reference to principles of autonomy or

welfare, the very ideas that are said to give rise to it.

The initial objection to the view that government should take preferences "as they are," or as the basis for political choice, is one of impossibility. Whether people have a preference for a commodity, a right, or anything else is in part a function of whether the government has allocated it to them in the first instance. There is no way to avoid the task of initially allocating an entitlement, and the decision to grant an entitlement to one person frequently makes that person value that entitlement more than if the right had been allocated to someone else. (It also makes other people value it less than they would otherwise.) Government must not only allocate rights to one person or another; it must also decide whether or not to make the right alienable through markets or otherwise. The initial allocation serves to reflect, to legitimate, and to reinforce social understandings about presumptive rights of ownership, and that allocation has an important causal connection to individual perceptions of the good or right in question.

For example, a decision to give employees a right to organize, farmers a right to be free from water pollution, or women a right not to be subjected to sexual harassment will have an impact on social attitudes toward labor organization, clean water, and sexual harassment. The allocation therefore has an effect on social attitudes toward the relevant rights and on their valuation by both current owners and would-be purchasers. And when preferences are a function of legal rules, the rules cannot be justified by reference to the preferences. Moreover, the initial assignment creates the basic "reference state" from which values and judgments of fairness are subsequently made, and those judgments affect preferences and private willingness to pay. Of course, a decision to make an entitlement alienable or inalienable (consider the right to vote or reproductive capacities) will have preference-shaping effects. Because of the preference-shaping effects of the rules of allocation, it is difficult to see how a government might even attempt to take preferences "as given" or as the basis for decisions in any global sense.

To some degree this concern might be put

to one side. Surely there is a difference between a government that concerns itself self-consciously and on an ongoing basis with private preferences and a government that sets up the basic rules of property, contract, and tort, and then lets things turn out however they may. If this distinction can be sustained, disagreements about the relationship between politics and preferences turn on competing notions of autonomy or freedom on the one hand and welfare on the other. Subjective welfarism is founded on the claim that an approach that treats preferences as sovereign is most likely to promote both individual freedom, rightly conceived, and individual or social welfare.

It will be useful to begin with welfare. Even if one accepted a purely welfarist view, one might think that the process of promoting welfare should take place not by satisfying current preferences but by promoting those preferences and satisfying them to such an extent as is consonant with the best or highest conception of human happiness. This view is connected with older (and some current) forms of utilitarianism; it also has roots in Aristotle. Here one does not take existing preferences as given, and one does not put all preferences on the same plane. A criterion of welfare remains the ultimate one, but the system is not focused solely on preference satisfaction, since it insists that welfare and preference satisfaction are entirely different things.

A central point here is that preferences are shifting and endogenous rather than exogenous, and as a result are a function of current information, consumption patterns, legal rules, and general social pressures. An effort to identify welfare with preference satisfaction would be easier to understand if preferences were rigidly fixed at some early age, or if learning were impossible; if this were so, democratic efforts to reflect on, change, or select preferences would breed only frustration. But because preferences are shifting and endogenous, and because the satisfaction of existing preferences might lead to unhappy or deprived lives, a democracy that treats all preferences as fixed will lose important opportunities for welfare gains.

With respect to welfare, then, the problem posed by the endogeneity of preferences is not the origin of desires but their malleability. At least if the relevant cases can be confidently identified in advance, and if collective action can be justified by reference to particular good reasons, the argument for democratic interference will be quite powerful. Respect for preferences that have resulted from unjust background conditions and that will lead to human deprivation or misery hardly appears the proper course for a liberal democracy.

For example, legal rules prohibiting or discouraging addictive behavior may have significant advantages in terms of welfare. Regulation of heroin or cigarettes (at least if the regulation can be made effective) might well increase aggregate social welfare, by decreasing harmful behavior, removing the secondary effects of those harms, and producing more healthful and satisfying lives. Similarly, governmental action relating to the environment, broadcasting, or culture—encouraging or requiring, for example, protection of beautiful areas, broadcasting about public issues, high-quality programs, or public support of artistic achievement—may in the end generate (or, better, prevent obstacles to the generation of) new preferences, providing increased satisfaction and in the end producing considerable welfare gains. The same may well be true of antidiscrimination measures, which affect the desires and attitudes of discriminators and victims alike. A system that takes existing private preferences as the basis for political choice will sacrifice important opportunities for social improvement on welfarist criteria. This point was a crucial one in the early stages of utilitarian thought; it has been lost more recently with the shift from older forms of welfarism to the idea of "revealed preferences."

Moreover, the satisfaction of private preferences, whatever their content and origins, does not respond to a persuasive conception of liberty or autonomy. The notion of autonomy should refer instead to decisions reached with a full and vivid awareness of available opportunities, with reference to all relevant information, and without illegitimate or excessive constraints on the process of preference formation. When these conditions are not met, decisions should be described as unfree or nonautonomous; for this reason it is most difficult to identify autonomy with preference satisfaction. If preferences are a product of available information, existing consumption patterns, social pressures, and governmental rules, it seems odd to suggest that individual freedom lies exclusively or by definition in preference satisfaction, or that current preferences should, on grounds of autonomy, be treated as the basis for settling political issues. It seems even odder to suggest that all preferences should be treated equally, independently of their basis and consequences, or of the reasons offered in their support.

For purposes of autonomy, then, governmental interference with existing desires may be justified because of problems in the origins of those desires. Welfare-based arguments that invoke endogeneity tend to emphasize the malleability of preferences after they are formed; arguments based on autonomy stress what happens before the preferences have been created, that is, the conditions that gave rise to them. Because of this difference, the two arguments will operate along different tracks; and in some cases autonomy-based arguments will lead to conclusions different from those that would emerge from arguments based on welfare. In many cases, however, considerations of autonomy will argue powerfully against taking preferences as the basis for social choice.

Consider, for example, a decision to purchase dangerous foods, consumer products, or cigarettes by someone unaware of the (serious) health risks; an employer's decision not to hire blacks because of a background of public and private segregation or racial hostility in his community; a person who disparages or has no interest in art and literature because the culture in which he has been reared centers mainly around television; a decision of a woman to adopt a traditional gender role because of the social stigma attached to refusing to do so; a decision not to purchase cars equipped with seat belts or not to wear a motorcycle helmet produced by the social pressures imposed by one's peer group; a lack of interest in environmental diversity resulting from limitation of one's personal experiences to industrialized urban areas; a decision not to employ blacks at a restaurant because of fear of violence from whites.

These examples are different from one an-

other. The source of the problem varies in each. But in all of them, the interest in liberty or autonomy does not call for governmental inaction, even if that were an intelligible category. Indeed, in many or perhaps all of these cases, regulation removes a kind of coercion.

One goal of a democracy, in short, is to ensure autonomy not merely in the satisfaction of preferences, but also, and more fundamentally, in the processes of preference formation. John Stuart Mill himself was emphatic on this point, going so far as to suggest that government itself should be evaluated in large measure by its effects on the character of the citizenry.[3] The view that freedom requires an opportunity to choose among alternatives finds a natural supplement in the view that people should not face unjustifiable constraints on the free development of their preferences and beliefs. It is not altogether clear what such a view would require—a point to which I will return. At the very least, however, it would see a failure of autonomy, and a reason for collective response, in beliefs and preferences based on insufficient information or opportunities.

Governmental action might also be justified on grounds of autonomy when the public seeks to implement, through democratic processes culminating in law, widely held social aspirations or collective desires. Individual consumption choices often diverge from collective considered judgments: people may seek, through law, to implement a democratic decision about what courses to pursue. If so, it is ordinarily no violation of autonomy to allow those considered judgments to be vindicated by governmental action. Collective aspirations or considered judgments, produced by a process of deliberation on which competing perspectives are brought to bear, reflect a conception of political freedom having deep roots in the American constitutional tradition. On this view, political autonomy can be found in collective self-determination, as citizens decide, not what they "want," but instead who they are, what their values are, and what those values require. What they "want" must be supported by reasons.

To summarize: On the thinnest version of the account offered thus far, the mere fact that preferences are what they are is at least sometimes and perhaps generally an insufficient justification for political action. Government decisions need not be and in some cases should not be justified by reference to preferences alone. More broadly, a democratic government should sometimes take private preferences as an object of regulation and control—an inevitable task in light of the need to define initial entitlements—and precisely in the interest of welfare and autonomy. Of course, there are serious risks of overreaching here, and there must be some constraints (usually denominated "rights") on this process. Checks laid down in advance are an indispensable part of constitutional government. Those checks will include, at a minimum, basic guarantees of political liberty and personal security, and such guarantees may not be comprised by processes of collective self-determination. I return to this point below.

II. Democratic Rejection of Revealed Preferences: A Catalogue

In this section I attempt to particularize the claims made thus far by cataloguing cases in which considerations of autonomy and welfare justify governmental action that subjective welfarism would condemn. In all of these cases, I claim that participants in a liberal government ought to be concerned with whether its citizens are experiencing satisfying lives and that the salutary liberal commitment to divergent conceptions of the good ought not to be taken to disable government from expressing that concern through law. The cases fall into three basic categories.

A. Collective Judgments and Aspirations

Citizens in a democratic polity might act to embody in law not the preferences that they hold as private consumers, but instead what might be described as collective judgments, including aspirations or considered reflections. Measures of this sort are a product of

deliberative processes on the part of citizens and representatives. In that process, people do not simply determine what they "want." The resulting measures cannot be understood as an attempt to aggregate or trade off private preferences.

1. Politics, Markets, and the Dependence of Preferences on Context. Frequently political choices cannot easily be understood as a process of aggregating prepolitical desires. Some people may, for example, support non-entertainment broadcasting on television, even though their own consumption patterns favor situation comedies; they may seek stringent laws protecting the environment or endangered species, even though they do not use the public parks or derive material benefits from protection of such species; they may approve of laws calling for social security and welfare even though they do not save or give to the poor; they may support antidiscrimination laws even though their own behavior is hardly race- or gender-neutral. The choices people make as political participants are different from those they make as consumers. Democracy thus calls for an intrusion on markets.

The widespread disjunction between political and consumption choices presents something of a puzzle. Indeed, it sometimes leads to the view that market ordering is undemocratic and that choices made through the political process are a preferable basis for social ordering.

A generalization of this sort is far too broad in light of the multiple breakdowns of the political process and the advantages of market ordering in many arenas. Respect for private markets is an important way of respecting divergent conceptions of the good and is thus properly associated with individual liberty. Respect for markets is also an engine of economic productivity, an important individual and collective goal. But it would be a mistake to suggest, as some do, that markets always reflect individual choice more reliably than politics; or that democratic choices differ from consumption outcomes only because of confusion, as voters fail to realize that they must ultimately bear the costs of the programs they favor; or that voting patterns merely reflect a willingness to seek certain goods so long as other people are footing the bill.

Undoubtedly, consumer behavior is sometimes a better or more realistic reflection of actual preferences than is political behavior. But in light of the fact that preferences depend on context, the very notion of a "better reflection" of "actual" preferences is a confusing one; there is no such thing as an "actual" (in the sense of unitary or acontextual) preference in these settings. Moreover, the difference might be explained by the fact that political behavior reflects a variety of influences that are distinctive to the context of politics, and that justify according additional weight to what emerges through the political setting.

These influences include four closely related phenomena. First, citizens may seek to implement individual and collective aspirations in political behavior but not in private consumption. As citizens, people may seek the aid of the law to bring about a social state that they consider to be in some sense higher than what emerges from market ordering. Second, people may, in their capacity as political actors, attempt to satisfy altruistic or other-regarding desires, which diverge from the self-interested preferences sometimes characteristic of markets. Third, political decisions might vindicate what might be called metapreferences or second-order preferences. People have wishes about their wishes, and sometimes they try to vindicate those second-order wishes, including considered judgments about what is best, through law. Fourth, people may precommit themselves, in democratic processes, to a course of action that they consider to be in the general interest. The adoption of a constitution is itself an example of a precommitment strategy.

Three qualifications are necessary here. First, some of these objections might be translated into the terms of subjective welfarism. Some preferences, after all, are most effectively expressed in democratic arenas, and that expression can be supported precisely on the grounds that they are subjectively held and connected to a certain form of individual and collective welfare. My broader point, however, is that political choices will reflect a kind of deliberation and reasoning, transforming values and perceptions of interests, that is often inadequately captured in the marketplace. It is this point that amounts to a rejection or at least a renovation of subjective welfarism as a political conception. It is here that democracy becomes something other than an aggregative mechanism, that politics is seen to be irreducible to bargaining, and that prepolitical "preferences" are not taken as the bedrock of political justification.

Second, to point to these various possibilities is not at all to deny that market or private behavior frequently reflects considered judgments, altruism, aspirations, or far more complex attitudes toward diverse goods than are captured in conventional accounts of preference structures. There are countless counterexamples to any such claim. All I mean to suggest is that divergences between market and political behavior will sometimes be attributable to phenomena of the sort I have described.

Third, a democratic system must be built on various safeguards to ensure that its decisions are in fact a reflection of deliberative processes of the sort described here. Often, of course, such processes are distorted by the fact that some groups are more organized than others, by disparities in wealth and influence, and by public and private coercion of various kinds. I am assuming here that these problems have been sufficiently overcome to allow for a favorable characterization of the process.

2. Explanations. Thus far I have suggested that people may seek, through law, to implement collective desires that diverge from market choices. Is it possible to come up with concrete explanations for the differences? There are a number of possibilities.

First, the collective character of politics, which permits a response to collective action problems, is critical here. People may not want to implement their considered judgments, or to be altruistic, unless there is assurance that others will be bound to do so as well. More simply, people may prefer not to contribute to a collective benefit if donations are made individually, with no guarantee that others will participate; but their most favored system, obtainable only or best through democratic forms, might be one in which they contribute if (but only if) there is assurance that others will do so as well. Perhaps people feel ashamed if others are contributing and they are not. Perhaps they feel victimized if they are contributing and others are not. In any case, the satisfaction of aspirations or altruistic goals will sometimes have the characteristics of the provision of public goods or the solution of a prisoner's dilemma.

Second, the collective character of politics might overcome the problem, discussed below, of preferences and beliefs that have adapted, at least to some extent, to an unjust status quo or to limits in available opportunities. Without the possibility of collective action, the status quo may seem intractable, and private behavior, and even desires, will adapt according-ly. But if people can act in concert, prefer-ences might take on a quite different form. Consider social movements involving the en-vironment, labor, and race and sex discrimina-tion. The collective action problem thus in-teracts with aspirations, altruistic desires, second-order preferences, and precommit-ment strategies. All of these are most likely to be enacted into law if an apparatus such as democratic rule is available to overcome col-lective action problems.

Third, social and cultural norms might in-cline people to express aspirational or altruis-tic goals more often in political behavior than in markets. Such norms may press people, in their capacity as citizens, in the direction of a concern for others or for the public interest.

Fourth, the deliberative aspects of politics, bringing additional information and per-spectives to bear, may affect preferences as expressed through governmental processes. A principal function of a democratic system is to ensure that through representative or partici-patory processes, new or submerged voices, or novel depictions of where interests lie and what they in fact are, are heard and un-derstood. If representatives or citizens are able to participate in a collective discussion of (for example) broadcasting or levels of risk in the workplace, they might well generate a far ful-ler and richer picture of diverse social goods, and of how they might be served, than can be provided through individual decisions as reg-istered in the market. It should hardly be sur-prising if preferences, values, and perceptions of both individual and collective welfare are changed as a result of that process.

Fifth, and finally, consumption decisions are a product of the criterion of private willingness to pay, which creates distortions of its own. Willingness to pay is a function of ability to pay, and it is an extremely crude proxy for utility or welfare. Political behavior removes this distortion—which is not to say that it does not introduce distortions of new kinds.

3. Qualifications. Arguments from collective desires are irresistible if the measure at issue is adopted unanimously. But more serious diffi-culties are produced if (as is usual) the law imposes on a minority what it regards as a burden rather than a benefit. Suppose, for example, that a majority wants to require high-quality television and to ban violent and dehumanizing shows, but that a significant minority wants to see the latter. (I put the First Amendment questions to one side.) It might be thought that those who perceive a need to bind themselves, or to express an aspiration, should not be permitted to do so if the conse-quence is to deprive others of an opportunity to satisfy their preferences.

The foreclosure of the preferences of the minority is unfortunate, but in general it is difficult to see what argument there might be for an across-the-board rule against collective action of this sort. If the majority is prohibited from vindicating its considered judgments through legislation, an important arena for democratic self-government will be eliminat-ed. The choice is between the considered judgments of the majority and the preferences (and perhaps judgments as well) of the minor-ity. On the other hand, the foreclosure of the minority should probably be permitted only when less restrictive alternatives, including private arrangements, are unavailable to serve the same end.

Of course, the argument for democratic outcomes embodying collective judgments is not always decisive. It is easy to imagine cases in which that argument is weak. Consider a law forbidding atheism or agnosticism, or barring the expression of unpatriotic political displays. And while I cannot provide in this space a full discussion of the contexts in which the case for democratic outcomes is overcome, it might be useful to describe, in a preliminary way, three categories of cases in which constraints on collective judgments seem especially appropriate.

First, if the particular choice foreclosed has some special character, and especially if it is a part of deliberative democracy itself, it is appropriately considered a right, and the majority has no authority to intervene. Political expression and participation are prime examples. The equal political rights of members of the minority, as citizens, should be respected even if a general aspiration, held by the majority, argues for selective exclusions. So, too, other rights fundamental to autonomy or welfare—consider consensual sexual activity—ought generally to be off-limits to government.

Second, some collective desires might be objectionable or a product of unjust background conditions. A collective judgment that racial intermarriage is intolerable could not plausibly be justified even if it is said to reflect a collective social aspiration. To explain why, it is of course necessary to offer an argument challenging that judgment and invoking principles of justice. Such an argument might itself involve notions of autonomy or welfare. However that may be, the example suggests that the collective judgment must not be objectionable on moral grounds.

Third, some collective desires might reflect a special weakness on the part of the majority: consider a curfew law, or perhaps prohibition. In such circumstances, a legal remedy might remove desirable incentives for private self-control, have unintended side effects resulting from the "bottling-up" of desires, or prove unnecessary in light of the existence of alternative remedies. When any one of these three concerns arises, the case for protection of collective judgments is implausible. But in many contexts, these concerns are absent, and democratic controls initiated on these grounds are justified.

B. Excessive Limitations in Opportunities or Unjust Background Conditions

Citizens in a democracy might override existing preferences in order to foster and promote diverse experiences, with a view to providing broad opportunities for the formation of preferences and beliefs and for distance on and critical scrutiny of current desires. This goal usually supports private ordering and freedom of contract as well. But it calls for collective safeguards when those forces push toward homogeneity and uniformity, as they often do in industrialized nations. Here the argument for governmental controls finds a perhaps ironic origin in Mill. Such controls are necessary to cultivate divergent conceptions of the good and to ensure a degree of reflection on those conceptions.

A system that took this goal seriously could start from a range of different foundations. It might find its roots in the principles that underlie a deliberative democracy itself. Here the notions of autonomy and welfare would be defined by reference to the idea of free and equal persons acting as citizens in setting up the terms of democratic life. That idea will impose constraints on the sorts of preferences and beliefs that a political system would be permitted to inculcate. Perhaps more controversially, the system could be regarded as embodying a mild form of liberal perfectionism. Such a system would see the inculcation of critical and disparate attitudes toward prevailing conceptions of the good as part of the framework of a liberal democracy. Liberal education is of course the principal locus of this concern, but the principles embodied in liberal education need not be confined to the school system. Still another foundation would be Aristotelian. Here the governing goal would be to ensure that individual capacities and capabilities are promoted and not thwarted by governmental arrangements. And this set of ideas, a different kind of perfectionism, is not so dramatically different from Mill's version of utilitarianism.

If government can properly respond to preferences that are based on limitations in available opportunities, it might well undertake aggressive initiatives with respect to the arts and broadcasting: subsidizing public broadcasting, ensuring a range of disparate programming, or calling for high-quality programming not sufficiently provided by the marketplace. Indeed, the need to provide diverse opportunities for preference formation suggests reasons to be quite skeptical of unrestricted markets in communication and broadcasting. There is a firm theoretical justification for governmental regulation here, including the much-criticized, and now largely abandoned, "fairness doctrine," which required broadcasters to cover controversial issues and to give equal time to competing views. In view of the inevitable effects of programming on character, beliefs, and even conduct, it is hardly clear that governmental "inaction" is always appropriate in a constitutional democracy. Indeed, the contrary seems true. I take up this issue in more detail below.

Market behavior is sometimes based on an effort to reduce cognitive dissonance by adjusting to undue limitations in current practices and opportunities. When this is so, respect for preferences seems unjustified on grounds of autonomy and under certain conditions welfare as well. Preferences might be regarded as nonautonomous insofar as they are reflexively adaptive to unjust background conditions, and collective responses to such preferences might yield welfare gains. The point has significant implications. For example, workers appear to underestimate the risks of hazardous activity partly in order to reduce the dissonance that would be produced by an accurate understanding of the dangers of the workplace. Democratic controls might produce gains in terms of both welfare and autonomy.

Similar ideas help account for principles of antidiscrimination. In general, the beliefs of both beneficiaries and victims of existing injustice are affected by dissonance-reducing strategies. The phenomenon of blaming the victim has distinct cognitive and motivational foundations: the strategy of blaming the victim, or assuming that an injury or an inequality was deserved or inevitable, permits nonvictims or members of advantaged groups to reduce dissonance by enabling them to maintain that the world is just—a pervasively, insistently, and sometimes irrationally held belief. The reduction of cognitive dissonance is a powerful motivational force, and it operates as a significant obstacle to the recognition of social injustice or irrationality.

Victims also participate in dissonance-reducing strategies, including the lowering of their own self-esteem to accommodate both the fact of victimization and the belief that the world is essentially just. Sometimes it is easier to assume that one's suffering is warranted than that it has been imposed cruelly or by chance. Consider here the astonishing fact that after a draft lottery, participants decided that the results of the purely random process, whether favorable or not, were deserved. The phenomenon of blaming the victim also reflects the "hindsight effect," through which people unjustifiably perceive events as having been more predictable than they in fact were, and therefore suggest that victims or disadvantaged groups should have been able to prevent the negative outcome. All of these phenomena make reliance on existing or revealed preferences highly problematic in certain contexts.

There is suggestive evidence to this effect in the psychological literature in this area. Some work here reveals that people who engage in cruel behavior begin to devalue the objects of their cruelty; observers tend to do the same. Such evidence bears on antidiscrimination law in general. Certain aspects of American labor and race discrimination law can be understood as a response to the basic problem of distorted beliefs and preferences. For example, the Supreme Court has emphatically rejected freedom-of-choice plans as a remedy for school segregation. Such plans would simply permit whites and blacks to send their children to whichever school they wished. The Court's rejection of such plans might well be puzzling to proponents of subjective welfarism, but the outcome becomes more reasonable if it is seen as based in part on the fact that, in this area, preferences and beliefs have conspicuously grown up around and adapted to the segregative status quo. Under these circumstances, freedom of choice is no solution at all; indeed, in view of the background and context the term seems an oxymoron.

In labor law as well, American law rejects freedom of contract and freedom of choice in order to protect collective bargaining. Some of this legislation must stand on a belief that private preferences have been adaptive to a status quo skewed against unionization. Special steps are therefore necessary in order to encourage collective bargaining, which also, of course, overcomes the prisoner's dilemma faced by individual workers, and therefore facilitates collective deliberation on the conditions of the workplace.

Poverty itself is perhaps the most severe obstacle to the free development of preferences and beliefs. Programs that attempt to respond to the deprivations faced by poor people—most obviously by eliminating poverty, but also through broad public education and regulatory efforts designed to make cultural resources generally available regardless of wealth—are fully justified in this light. They should hardly be seen as objectionable paternalism or as unsupportable redistribution. Indeed, antipoverty efforts are tightly linked with republican efforts to promote security and independence in the interest of creating the conditions for full and equal citizenship.

Sometimes, of course, preferences are only imperfectly adapted. At some level there is a perception of injury, but a fear of social sanctions or a belief that the cause is intractable prevents people from seeking redress. Here the collective character of politics, permitting the organization of numerous people, can be exceedingly helpful.

Standing by itself, the fact that preferences are shifting and endogenous is hardly a sufficient reason for the imposition of democratic controls. All preferences are to some degree dependent on existing law and current opportunities, and that fact cannot be a reason for governmental action without creating a license for tyranny. The argument for democratic controls in the face of endogenous preferences must rely on a belief that welfare or autonomy will thereby be promoted. Usually governmental interference should be avoided. But far too often, the salutary belief in respect for divergent conceptions of the good is transformed into an unwillingness to protect people from either unjust background conditions or a sheer lack of options.

The actual content of democratic controls here will of course be controversial, and it probably should begin and usually end with efforts to provide information and to increase opportunities. Thus, for example, governmentally required disclosure of risks in the workplace is a highly laudable strategy. In a few cases, however, these milder initiatives are inadequate, and other measures are necessary.

A moderately intrusive strategy could involve economic incentives, which might take the form of tax advantages or cash payments. For example, the government might give financial inducements to day-care centers as a way of relieving child-care burdens. Such a system might well be preferable to direct transfers of money to families, a policy that will predictably lead many more women to stay at home. In view of the sources and consequences of the differential distribution of child-care burdens, it is fully legitimate for the government to take steps in the direction of equalization. The most intrusive option, to be used rarely, is direct coercion, as in the case of governmentally mandated use of safety equipment.

The category of democratic responses to endogenous preferences of this sort overlaps with that of measures that attempt to protect collective aspirations. Frequently, aspirations form the basis for laws that attempt to influence processes of preference formation.

C. Intrapersonal Collective Action Problems

There is also a case for democratic controls on existing preferences when such preferences are a function of past acts of consumption and when such acts alter desires or beliefs in such a way as to cause long-term harm. In such cases, the two key facts are that preferences are endogenous to past consumption decisions and that the effect of those decisions on current preferences is pernicious. For government to act in this context, it is important that it be confident of its conclusions; in the face of uncertainty, freedom of choice is appropriate here. An absence of information on the part of the private actors is usually a necessary condition for collective controls.

Regulations of addictive substances, myopic behavior, and habits are familiar examples. In the case of an addiction, the problem is that the costs of nonconsumption increase dramatically over time as the benefits of consumption remain constant or fall sharply. The result is that the aggregate costs, over time or over a life, of consumption exceed the aggregate benefits, even though the initial consumption choice provides benefits that exceed costs. Individual behavior that is rational for each individual consumption choice ultimately leads people into severely inferior social states. In such cases, people, if fully informed, would in all likelihood not want to choose the good in the first place. Governmental action is a possible response.

Menahem Yaari offers the example of a group of traders attempting to induce alcoholism in an Indian tribe.[4] At the outset, alcoholic beverages are not extremely valuable to consumers. The consumers are willing to buy only for a low price, which the traders accept. But as a result of consumption, the value of the beverages to the consumers steadily increases to the point where they are willing to pay enormous sums to obtain them. Thus the traders are able "to manoeuvre the Indian into a position where rationality conflicts with Pareto-efficiency, i.e., into a position where to be efficient is to be irrational and to be rational is to be inefficient. . . . [T]he disadvantage, for an economic unit, of having endogenously changing tastes is that, even with perfect information and perfect foresight, the unit may find itself forced to follow an action which, by the unit's own standards, is Pareto-dominated."

Because of the effect over time of consumption on preferences, someone who is addicted to heroin is much worse off than he would have been had he never started, even though the original decision to consume was not irrational in terms of immediate costs and benefits. Statutes that regulate addictive substances respond to a social belief, grounded on this consideration, that the relevant preferences should not be formed in the first place.

We might describe this situation as involving an intrapersonal collective action problem, in which the costs and benefits, for a particular person, of engaging in an activity change dramatically over time. A central point here is that consumption patterns induce a significant change in preferences, and in a way that makes people worse off in the long run. In the case of addictions, there will also be interconnections between intrapersonal collective action problems and preferences and beliefs that are adaptive to unjust background conditions, at least as a general rule. (Yaari's own example, involving whites trading alcohol with native Americans, is a prime example.) The problem of drug addiction is hardly distributed evenly throughout the population, and the process of addiction is in large part a response to social institutions that severely limit and condition the range of options.

While addiction is the most obvious case, it is part of a far broader category. Consider, for example, myopic behavior, defined as a refusal, because the short-term costs exceed the short-term benefits, to engage in activity having long-term benefits that dwarf long-term costs. Another kind of intrapersonal collective action problem is produced by habits, in which people engage in behavior because of the subjectively high short-term costs of changing their behavior, regardless of the fact that the long-term benefits exceed the long-term costs. *Akrasia,* or weakness of the will, has a related structure, and some laws respond to its individual or collective forms.

For the most part, problems of this sort are best addressed at the individual level or through private associations, which minimize coercion; but social regulation is a possible response. Statutes that subsidize the arts or public broadcasting, or that discourage the formation of some habits and encourage the formation of others, are illustrations. There are similar arguments for compulsory recycling programs (the costs of participation in which decrease substantially over time, and often turn into benefits) and for democratic restrictions on smoking cigarettes.

The problem with collective controls in this context is that they are unlikely to be fine-tuned. They will often sweep up so many people and circumstances as to create serious risks of abuse. In some settings, however, citizens will be able to say with confidence that the effect of consumption on preferences will lead to severe welfare or autonomy losses. In such cases democratic controls are justified.

III. Examples

A. The Frontiers of Free Speech Law: The Fairness Doctrine, Campaign Speech, Hate Speech, and Pornography

The most important issues in the contemporary law of free expression have produced cleavages between groups and ideas that were previously closely allied. Thus the First Amendment has been invoked, with considerable vigor and passion, on behalf of cigarette companies seeking to advertise their products; corporations attempting to influence electoral outcomes; people engaged in racial hate speech; pornographers; and large networks objecting to a private right of access to broadcasting or to other efforts to promote quality and diversity in the media. The effort to invoke the First Amendment is increasingly resisted—often, ironically, on the theory that it runs counter to the goals of deliberative democracy and free expression itself—by individuals and groups formerly associated with an absolutist or near-absolutist position against governmental regulation of speech.

These debates raise exceedingly complex issues, and I can only touch on them briefly here. The complexities are increased by the fact that a system dedicated to freedom of expression ought to be highly sensitive to the idea that speech alters perferences and beliefs. It should also find that process to be one to which a democracy is generally quite receptive. As Justice Louis D. Brandeis wrote in what is probably the most distinguished judicial opinion in the entire history of free expression, "the fitting remedy for evil counsels is good ones. . . . If there be time to expose through discussion the falsehood and fallacies, to avert the evil by the processes of education, the remedy to be applied is more speech, not enforced silence."[5]

Justice Brandeis's statement notwithstanding, I want to suggest that attention to the endogenous character of preferences and to the considerations traced thus far provides some basis for receptivity to democratic controls in this context.

1. The Fairness Doctrine.
There is a growing consensus that the government should not concern itself with the airwaves and that total reliance on private markets and consumer preferences is the appropriate strategy for government. On this view, broadcasting should be treated like soap, cereal, or any other commodity. Indeed, there is a growing consensus that this result is ordained by the First Amendment. But if the claims made here are persuasive, the consensus is misguided.

The meaning of the First Amendment is a function of competing views about what sort of relation between government and markets will best promote democratic deliberation. Lawyers (and not a few nonlawyers) have an unfortunate habit of thinking that the meaning of the First Amendment precedes rather than postdates that inquiry.

The consequence of market-based strategies in broadcasting is a system in which most viewers see shows that rarely deal with serious problems; are frequently sensationalistic, prurient, dehumanizing, or banal; reflect and perpetuate a bland, watered-down version of the most conventional views about politics and morality; are influenced excessively by the concerns of advertisers; produce an accelerating "race to the bottom" in terms of the quality and quantity of attention that they require and encourage; and are often riddled with violence, sexism, and racism. It simply defies belief to suggest that such shows do not affect the preferences and even the character of the citizenry. Is it so clear that a constitutional democracy ought to consider itself unable to respond to this situation? Is it so clear that a First Amendment enacted in order to ensure democratic self-determination bars a democratic corrective here?

In my view, the considerations marshaled thus far suggest that citizens in a constitutional democracy ought to be conceded, and ought to exercise, the power to engage in a wide range of controls. If welfare and autonomy provide the governing criteria, large gains might be expected from such controls. All three of the categories I have described argue in favor of some form of regulation. Democratic controls would probably reflect collective desires, which deserve respect. They would respond to the fact that in spite of the large number of channels, the current regulatory regime diminishes genuine options, to the detriment of both welfare and autonomy; they would also counteract a kind of intrapersonal collective action problem faced by many of those habituated to the broadcasting status quo.

Such controls might permit the government to regulate advertising on television, certainly for children, but for others as well; to require broadcasters to pay attention to public affairs, as in, for example, an hour of compulsory programming per night; to ban gratuitous or prurient violence on television, especially when it is sexualized; to require, as a condition for licensing, a subsidy to public television; and to impose a broad fairness doctrine, in the form not only of an obligation of attention to important issues but also a chance to speak for divergent sides. The evident dangers notwithstanding, there would be a wide range of collective and external benefits from such controls, which would thus carry forward a strand of the liberal tradition that calls for governmental action in such cases.

At least in principle, rights of private access to the media for differing positions and associated kinds of controls ought to be considered congenial to the free speech guarantee. Surely this is so if that guarantee is understood as a protection of a deliberative process centered on public values rather than of a "marketplace." The First Amendment need not be seen as an obstacle to such efforts. If anything, the existing system might be thought to raise serious constitutional questions. A system in which access to the media, with its inevitable consequences for the shaping of preferences and beliefs, is made dependent on private willingness to pay raises genuine problems for free expression.

2. *Campaign Regulation.* It would not be difficult to argue that a variety of regulations on the electoral process are necessary both to promote a deliberative process among political equals and to ensure that the deliberative process is a genuine one. Properly conceived, such efforts would be highly congenial to the purposes of the free speech guarantee. Both restrictions on campaign contributions—to eliminate the distorting effects of wealth—and qualitative measures to reduce the "soundbite" phenomenon and to promote more in the way of reflective discussion hold considerable promise.

Currently, however, there is a large if ironic obstacle to such efforts: the First Amendment. The Supreme Court has generally been unreceptive to governmental efforts to regulate electoral campaigns.[6] In the key passage in *Buckley v. Valeo,* the Court said that "the concept that government may restrict the speech of some elements of our society in order to

enhance the relative voice of others is wholly foreign to the first amendment."[7] It is crucial to note here that the Court did not say that the effort to promote deliberation among political equals was insufficiently weighty or inadequately promoted by the legislation at hand. Instead the Court said, far more broadly, that the effort was constitutionally illegitimate.

Under the approach suggested here, campaign regulation would be treated more hospitably. In view of the effects of wealth on the formation of political beliefs, and the corrosive consequences of some forms of electioneering, democratic controls on the process might be welcomed. The First Amendment might be understood not as a guarantor of unrestricted speech "markets," and much less as a vehicle for the translation of economic inequalities into political ones, but instead as an effort to ensure a process of deliberation that would, under current conditions, be promoted rather than undermined through regulatory measures. This is so especially if citizens in a democratic polity support regulation of the electoral process in order to pursue their desire for a well-functioning deliberative process.

Of course, there are great risks here, and any regulatory efforts must be carefully monitored to ensure that they do not act as incumbent protection bills or as serious constraints on speech that should instead be encouraged. But the issue is far more complex, from the standpoint of the First Amendment itself, than existing law allows.

3. *Violent Pornography and Hate Speech.* Many Western democracies, including those firmly committed to freedom of speech, regulate speech that casts contempt on identifiable social groups (hate speech). Some such democracies also control sexually explicit speech, especially when it associates sex and violence. These controls have been justified on mixed grounds of human dignity, community morality, and sexual equality. In the United States, the precise status of such restrictions remains unclear. Probably the best account of current law is that hate speech is protected, as is most speech that associates sex and violence, even if that speech is not conceivably part of a serious exchange of ideas but instead qualifies as pornography.[8]

The cases of hate speech and pornography raise somewhat different problems. Hate speech is self-consciously directed toward an issue of public concern; it is conspicuously and intentionally political in nature. Violent pornography is of course political too, in the sense that it has political origins and consequences. But it cannot be thought to be a self-conscious contribution to democratic deliberation about public issues. In this way it differs from misogynist speech of a more straightforward sort, where the political content is explicit. In terms of its connection to the First Amendment, pornography should probably be thought to fall in the same category as commercial speech, libel of private persons, bribes, and conspiracies. The reason is that most pornography does not amount to an effort to contribute to deliberation on matters of public interest, even if that category is broadly conceived, as it should be. Expression that is not central to the free speech principle counts as speech, but it is entitled to a lesser degree of protection. It may be regulated, not on a whim, but on a basis of demonstration of harm that is weaker than that required for political speech.

Should the First Amendment be taken to disable government from regulating hate speech and pornography? The affirmative answer of current law may well be unsound. Both of these forms of speech have serious and corrosive effects on beliefs and desires. Both have the additional and unusual characteristic of denying victimized groups the right to participate in the community as free and equal persons. With respect to certain kinds of violent pornography, there are especially severe consequences in terms of how men and women perceive sexuality, how men perceive women, and how women perceive themselves. One need not believe that the regulation of violent pornography would eliminate sexual violence or even do a great deal to produce sexual equality in order to recognize that the pervasiveness of material that associates sex with violence has a variety of harmful social consequences.

The case for regulation of these forms of speech is strongest when the relevant speech is pervasive, when it causes tangible harm, and when it falls outside the category of speech that is guaranteed First Amendment protection unless there is a demonstration of unavoidable, imminent, and serious danger. The considerations marshaled here suggest that at least certain forms of violent pornography ought to be regulated, and that perhaps in certain restricted settings, hate speech may be an appropriate subject of democratic controls as well.

B. Proportional Representation

In recent years, there has been a revival of interest in systems of proportional or group representation, both for disadvantaged groups and perhaps generally as well. There is a solid constitutional pedigree for such systems, notwithstanding the constant and emphatic rejections, by the Supreme Court, of constitutionally based arguments for representation of members of racial minority groups. Despite the rigidity of the one person–one vote formula, with its majoritarian and individualistic overtones, group representation has always been a feature of American constitutionalism.

Moreover, the basic constitutional institutions of federalism, bicameralism, and checks and balances share some of the appeal of proportional representation, and owe their origins in part to notions of group representation. These institutions proliferate the points of access to government, increasing the ability of diverse groups to influence policy, multiplying perspectives in government, and improving deliberative capacities. In this respect, they ensure something in the way of group representation, at least when compared with unitary systems. Of course, both the separation of powers and bicameralism grew in part out of efforts to promote representation of diverse groups: bicameralism allowed representation of both the wealthy and the masses, while the notion of separation derived from (though it also repudiated) notions of mixed government, which was designed to ensure a measure of representation of groups defined in social and economic terms.

Proportional representation might be designed, as in its Western European forms, to ensure representation in the legislature of all those groups that are able to attain more than a minimal share of the vote. In another form, the system might be an effort to ensure that members of disadvantaged groups are given the power to exert influence on political outcomes. In America, the Voting Rights Act goes far in this direction for blacks.

There are serious problems with both of these efforts, and I do not mean to evaluate them in detail here. I do suggest that efforts to ensure proportional representation become much more acceptable if they are justified on grounds that do not take existing preferences as the basis for governmental decisions and if they emphasize the preference-shaping effects of discussion and disagreement in politics. The argument here is that deliberative processes will be improved, not undermined, if mechanisms are instituted to ensure that multiple groups have access to the process and are actually present when decisions are made. Proportional or group representation, precisely by having this effect, would ensure that diverse views are expressed on an ongoing basis in the representative process, where they might otherwise be excluded.

In this respect, proportional or group representation could be regarded as a kind of second-best solution for the real-world failures of Madisonian deliberation. And the primary purpose of access is not to allow each group to have its "piece of the action"—though that is not entirely irrelevant—but instead to ensure that the process of deliberation is not distorted by the mistaken appearance of a common set of interests on the part of all concerned. In this incarnation, proportional representation is designed to increase the likelihood that political outcomes will incorporate some understanding of all perspectives. That process should facilitate the healthy expression of collective values or aspirations and the scrutiny of preferences adaptive to unjust background conditions or limited opportunities.

For this reason, proportional representation may be the functional analogue of the institutions of checks and balances and federalism, recognizing the creative functions of disagreement and multiple perspectives for the governmental process. In this sense there is continuity between recent proposals for proportional representation and some of the

attractive features of the original constitutional regime. Indeed, Hamilton himself emphasized that in a system of checks and balances, the "jarring of parties . . . will promote deliberation."[9] If this is so, proportional representation is most understandable in a democracy that does not take existing preferences as the basis for social choice but instead sees the broadest form of deliberation, covering ends as well as means, as a central ingredient in democratic politics.

IV. Conclusion

A constitutional democracy should not be self-consciously concerned, in a general and comprehensive way, with the souls of its citizens. Under modern conditions, liberal constraints on the operation of the public sphere and a general respect for divergent conceptions of the good are indispensable. At the same time, it would be a grave mistake to characterize liberal democracy as a system that requires existing preferences to be taken as the basis for governmental decisions and that forbids citizens, operating through democratic channels, from enacting their considered judgments into law, or from counteracting, through the provision of opportunities and information, preferences and beliefs that have adjusted to an unjust status quo. Ironically, a system that forecloses these routes—and that claims to do so in the name of liberalism or democracy—will defeat many of the aspirations that gave both liberalism and democracy their original appeal, and that continue to fuel them in so many parts of the world.

Notes

1. *The Laws* 650b.

2. See John Rawls, "The Idea of an Overlapping Consensus," *Oxford Journal of Legal Studies* 7 (1987): 1–25.

3. See Mill, *Considerations on Representative Government,* ed. C. V. Shields (1861) (New York: Liberal Arts Press, 1958).

4. Menahem Yaari, "Endogenous Changes in Tastes: A Philosophical Discussion," in *Decision Theory and Social Ethics: Issues in Social Choice*, ed. Hans Gottinger and Werner Leinfellner (Boston: D. Reidel, 1978), pp. 59–98.

5. Whitney v. California, 274 U.S. 357, 377 (1927).

6. See Buckley v. Valeo, 424 U.S. 1 (1976), and First National Bank of Boston v. Bellotti, 435 U.S. 765 (1978).

7. 424 U.S. at pp. 48–49.

8. I collapse some complex issues here. See Miller v. California, 413 U.S. 15 (1973), and my "Pornography and the First Amendment," *Duke Law Journal* (September 1986): 589–627.

9. *The Federalist* No. 70.

Is Patriotism a Virtue?

Alasdair MacIntyre

In this essay Alasdair MacIntyre defends a morality of patriotism, sharply contrasting it with a morality of impartially applied principles, as used in liberalism. Patriotism, for MacIntyre, is not merely proprietary love of one's country; it is conditioned on and defined by a pride in its distinctive merits and a gratitude for benefits enjoyed as a member. MacIntyre finds that patiotism and liberal morality are incompatible moral systems, because patriotism at some point enjoins an uncritical acceptance of national goals or mores, whereas liberalism insists on submitting every aspect of national life to critical evaluation and possible rejection. In the next section MacIntyre shows how the morality of patriotism is developed through growing up within a particular family, learning a particular world view, sharing a cultural perspective with a particular group of people, and caring deeply about all of this. He argues that a person is brought into being as a moral agent through particular moral rules taught in a particular community with particular goods to share. A person who is detached from that community loses hold of genuine standards of judgment. MacIntyre defends patriotic acts of dissent from the policies of a current government when it is corrupt, but he acknowledges that there is a permanent moral danger in patriotic loyalty. Blind loyalty to a corrupt practice or unjustified program is always possible. While this is damaging to the case for a patriotic morality, MacIntyre charges that liberalism has its own Achilles' heel, presenting equal moral danger. A liberal morality based on mutual self-interest and a critical assessment of all aspects of communal life, he argues, tends toward the dissolution of social bonds and the destruction of the community that supports it. For MacIntyre the two moralities are incompatible, and the modern American attempt to fuse them leads to confusion and incoherence in our national life.

I

One of the central tasks of the moral philosopher is to articulate the convictions of the society in which he or she lives so that these convictions may become available for rational scrutiny. This task is all the more urgent when a variety of conflicting and incompatible beliefs are held within one and the same community, either by rival groups who differ on key moral questions or by one and the same set of individuals who find within themselves competing moral allegiances. In either of these types of case the first task of the moral philoso-

From Alasdair MacIntyre, *The Lindley Lecture* (Lawrence: Kansas University Press, 1984), pp. 3–20. First published by the Department of Philosophy, University of Kansas, as a Lindley Lecture, 1984. Reprinted by permission of the publisher and the author.

pher is to render explicit what is at issue in the various disagreements and it is a task of this kind that I have set myself in this lecture.

For it is quite clear that there are large disagreements about patriotism in our society. And although it would be a mistake to suppose that there are only two clear, simple and mutually opposed sets of beliefs about patriotism, it is at least plausible to suggest that the range of conflicting views can be placed on a spectrum with two poles. At one end is the view, taken for granted by almost everyone in the nineteenth century, a commonplace in the literary culture of the McGuffey readers, that "patriotism" names a virtue. At the other end is the contrasting view, expressed with sometimes shocking clarity in the nineteen sixties, that "patriotism" names a vice. It would be misleading for me to suggest that I am going to be able to offer good reasons for taking one of these views rather than the other. What I do hope to achieve is a clarification of the issues that divide them.

A necessary first step in the direction of any such clarification is to distinguish patriotism properly so-called from two other sets of attitudes that are all too easily assimilated to it. The first is that exhibited by those who are protagonists of their own nation's causes because and only because, so they assert, it is their nation which is *the* champion of some great moral ideal. In the Great War of 1914–18 Max Weber claimed that Imperial Germany should be supported because its was the cause of *Kultur,* while Emile Durkheim claimed with equal vehemence that France should be supported because its was the cause of *civilisation.* And here and now there are those American politicians who claim that the United States deserves our allegiance because it champions the goods of freedom against the evils of communism. What distinguishes their attitude from patriotism is twofold: first it is the ideal and not the nation which is the primary object of their regard; and secondly insofar as their regard for the ideal provides good reasons for allegiance to their country, it provides good reasons for anyone at all to uphold their country's cause, irrespective of their nationality or citizenship.

Patriotism by contrast is defined in terms of a kind of loyalty to a particular nation which

only those possessing that particular nationality can exhibit. Only Frenchmen can be patriotic about France, while anyone can make the cause of *civilisation* their own. But it would be all too easy in noticing this to fail to make a second equally important distinction. Patriotism is not to be confused with a mindless loyalty to one's own particular nation which has no regard at all for the characteristics of that particular nation. Patriotism does generally and characteristically involve a peculiar regard not just for one's own nation, but for the particular characteristics and merits and achievements of one's own nation. These latter are indeed valued *as* merits and achievements and their character as merits and achievements provides reasons supportive of the patriot's attitudes. But the patriot does not value in the same way precisely similar merits and achievements when they are the merits and achievements of some nation other than his or hers. For he or she—at least in the role of patriot—values them not just as merits and achievements, but as the merits and achievements of this particular nation.

To say this is to draw attention to the fact that patriotism is one of a class of loyalty-exhibiting virtues (that is, if it *is* a virtue at all), other members of which are marital fidelity, the love of one's own family and kin, friendship, and loyalty to such institutions as schools and cricket or baseball clubs. All these attitudes exhibit a peculiar action-generating regard for particular persons, institutions or groups, a regard founded upon a particular historical relationship of association between the person exhibiting the regard and the relevant person, institution or group. It is often, although not always, the case that associated with this regard will be a felt gratitude for the benefits which the individual takes him or herself to have received from the person, institution or group. But it would be one more mistake to suppose patriotism or other such attitudes of loyalty to be at their core or primarily responses of gratitude. For there are many persons, institutions and groups to which each of us have good reason to feel grateful without this kind of loyalty being involved. What patriotism and other such attitudes involve is not just gratitude, but a particular kind of gratitude; and what those who treat patriotism and other such loyalties as virtues are committed to believing is not that what they owe their nation or whomever or whatever it is is simply a requital for benefits received, based on some relationship of reciprocity of benefits.

So although one may as a patriot love one's country, or as a husband or wife exhibit marital fidelity, and cite as partially supporting reasons one's country's or one's spouse's merits and one's own gratitude to them for benefits received these can be no more than *partially* supporting reasons, just because what is valued is valued precisely as the merits of *my* country or spouse or as the benefits received by *me* from *my* country or spouse. The particularity of the relationship is essential and ineliminable, and in identifying it as such we have already specified one central problem. What *is* the relationship between patriotism as such, the regard for this particular nation, and the regard which the patriot has for the merits and achievements of his or her nation and for the benefits which he or she has received? The answer to this question must be delayed for it will turn out to depend upon the answer to an apparently even more fundamental question, one that can best be framed in terms of the thesis that, if patriotism is understood as I have understood it, then "patriotism" is not merely not the name of a virtue, but must be the name of a vice, since patriotism thus understood and morality are incompatible.

II

The presupposition of this thesis is an account of morality which has enjoyed high prestige in our culture. According to that account to judge from a moral standpoint is to judge impersonally. It is to judge as any rational person would judge, independently of his or her interests, affections and social position. And to act morally is to act in accordance with such impersonal judgments. Thus to think and to act morally involve the moral agent in abstracting him or herself from all social particularity and partiality. The potential conflict between morality so understood and patriotism is at once clear. For patriotism requires me to exhibit peculiar devotion to my nation and you to yours. It requires me to regard such contingent social facts as where I was born and what government ruled over that place at that time, who my parents were, who my great-great-grandparents were and so on, as deciding for me the question of what virtuous action is—at least insofar as it is the virtue of patriotism which is in question. Hence the moral standpoint and the patriotic standpoint are systematically incompatible.

Yet although this is so, it might be argued that the two standpoints need not be in conflict. For patriotism and all other such particular loyalties can be restricted in their scope so that their exercise is always within the confines imposed by morality. Patriotism need be regarded as nothing more than a perfectly proper devotion to one's own nation which must never be allowed to violate the constraints set by the impersonal moral standpoint. This is indeed the kind of patriotism professed by certain liberal moralists who are often indignant when it is suggested by their critics that they are not patriotic. To those critics however patriotism thus limited in its scope appears to be emasculated, and it does so because in some of the most important situations of actual social life either the patriotic standpoint comes into serious conflict with the standpoint of a genuinely impersonal morality or it amounts to no more than a set of practically empty slogans. What kinds of circumstances are these? They are at least twofold.

The first kind arises from scarcity of essential resources, often historically from the scarcity of land suitable for cultivation and pasture, and perhaps in our own time from that of fossil fuels. What your community requires as the material prerequisites for your survival as a distinctive community and your growth into a distinctive nation may be exclusive use of the same or some of the same natural resources as my community requires for its survival and growth into a distinctive nation. When such a conflict arises, the standpoint of impersonal morality requires an allocation of goods such that each individual person counts for one and no more than one, while the patriotic standpoint requires that I strive to further the interests of my community and you strive to further those of yours, and certainly where the survival of one community is at stake, and sometimes perhaps even when only large interests of one community are at stake, patriotism entails a willingness to go to war on one's community's behalf.

The second type of conflict-engendering circumstance arises from differences between communities about the right way for each to live. Not only competition for scarce natural resources, but incompatibilities arising from such conflict-engendering beliefs may lead to situations in which once again the liberal moral standpoint and the patriotic standpoint are radically at odds. The administration of the *pax Romana* from time to time required the Roman *imperium* to set its frontiers at the point at which they could be most easily secured, so that the burden of supporting the legions would be reconcilable with the administration of Roman law. And the British empire was no different in its time. But this required infringing upon the territory and the independence of barbarian border peoples. A variety of such peoples—Scottish Gaels, Iroquois Indians, Bedouin—have regarded raiding the territory of their traditional enemies living within the confines of such large empires as an essential constituent of the good life; whereas the settled urban or agricultural communities which provided the target for their depredations have regarded the subjugation of such peoples and their reeducation into peaceful pursuits as one of their central responsibilities. And on such issues once again the impersonal moral standpoint and that of patriotism cannot be reconciled.

For the impersonal moral standpoint, understood as the philosophical protagonists of modern liberalism have understood it, requires neutrality not only between rival and competing interests, but also between rival and competing sets of beliefs about the best way for human beings to live. Each individual is to be left free to pursue in his or her own way that way of life which he or she judges to be best; while morality by contrast consists of rules which, just because they are such that any rational person, independently of his or her interests or point of view on the best way for human beings to live, would assent to them, are equally binding on all persons. Hence in conflicts between nations or other communities over ways of life, the standpoint of morality will once again be that of an impersonal arbiter, adjudicating in ways that give equal weight to each individual person's needs, desires, beliefs about the good and the like, while the patriot is once again required to be partisan.

Notice that in speaking of the standpoint of liberal impersonal morality in the way in which I have done I have been describing a standpoint whose truth is both presupposed by the political actions and utterances of a great many people in our society and explicitly articulated and defended by most modern moral philosophers; and that it has at the level of moral philosophy a number of distinct versions—some with a Kantian flavour, some utilitarian, some contractarian. I do not mean to suggest that the disagreements between these positions are unimportant. Nonetheless the five central positions that I have ascribed to that standpoint appear in all these various philosophical guises: first, that morality is constituted by rules to which any rational person would under certain ideal conditions give assent; secondly, that those rules impose constraints upon and are neutral between rival and competing interests—morality itself is not the expression of any particular interest; thirdly, that those rules are also neutral between rival and competing sets of beliefs about what the best way for human beings to live is; fourthly, that the units which provide the subject-matter of morality as well as its agents are individual human beings and that in moral evaluations each individual is to count for one and nobody for more than one; and fifthly, that the standpoint of the moral agent constituted by allegiance to these rules is one and the same for all moral agents and as such is independent of all social particularity. What morality provides are standards by which all actual social structures may be brought to judgment from a standpoint independent of all of them. It is morality so understood allegiance to which is not only incompatible with treating patriotism as a virtue, but which requires that patriotism—at least in any substantial version—be treated as a vice.

But is this the only possible way to understand morality? As a matter of history, the answer is clearly "No." This understanding of morality invaded postRenascence Western culture at a particular point in time as the moral counterpart to political liberalism and social individualism and its polemical stances reflect its history of emergence from the conflicts which those movements engendered and themselves presuppose alternatives against which those polemical stances were and are directed. Let me therefore turn to considering one of those alternative accounts of morality, whose peculiar interest lies in the place that it has to assign to patriotism.

III

According to the liberal account of morality *where* and *from whom* I learn the principles and precepts of morality are and must be irrelevant both to the question of what the content of morality is and to that of the nature of my commitment to it, as irrelevant as *where* and *from whom* I learn the principles and precepts of mathematics are to the content of mathematics and the nature of my commitment to mathematical truths. By contrast on the alternative account of morality which I am going to sketch, the questions of *where* and *from whom* I learn my morality turn out to be crucial for both the content and the nature of moral commitment.

On this view it is an essential characteristic of the morality which each of us acquires that it is learned from, in and through the way of life of some particular community. Of course the moral rules elaborated in one particular historical community will often resemble and sometimes be identical with the rules to which allegiance is given in other particular communities, especially in communities with a shared history or which appeal to the same canonical texts. But there will characteristically be *some* distinctive features of the set of rules considered as a whole, and those distinctive features will often arise from the way in which members of that particular community responded to some earlier situation or series of situations in which particular features of difficult cases led to one or more rules being put in question and reformulated or understood

in some new way. Moreover the form of the rules of morality as taught and apprehended will be intimately connected with specific institutional arrangements. The moralities of different societies may agree in having a precept enjoining that a child should honor his or her parents, but what it is so to honor and indeed what a father is and what a mother is will vary greatly between different social orders. So that what I learn as a guide to my actions and as a standard for evaluating them is never morality as such, but always the highly specific morality of some highly specific social order.

To this the reply by the protagonists of modern liberal morality might well be: doubtless this is how a comprehension of the rules of morality is first acquired. But what allows such specific rules, framed in terms of particular social institutions, to be accounted moral rules at all is the fact they are nothing other than applications of universal and general moral rules and individuals acquire genuine morality only because and insofar as they progress from particularised socially specific applications of universal and general moral rules to comprehending them as universal and general. To learn to understand oneself as a moral agent just is to learn to free oneself from social particularity and to adopt a standpoint independent of any particular set of social institutions and the fact that everyone or almost everyone has to learn to do this by starting out from a standpoint deeply infected by social particularity and partiality goes no way towards providing an alternative account of morality. But to this reply a threefold rejoinder can be made.

First, it is not just that I first apprehended the rules of morality in some socially specific and particularised form. It is also and correlatively that the goods by reference to which and for the sake of which any set of rules must be justified are also going to be goods that are socially specific and particular. For central to those goods is the enjoyment of one particular kind of social life, lived out through a particular set of social relationships and thus what I enjoy is the good of *this* particular social life inhabited by me and I enjoy *it* as what *it* is. It may well be that it follows that I would enjoy and benefit equally from similar forms of social life in other communities; but this hypothetical truth in no way diminishes the importance of the contention that my goods are as a matter of fact found *here*, among *these* particular people, in *these* particular relationships. Goods are never encountered except as thus particularised. Hence the abstract general claim, that rules of a certain kind are justified by being productive of and constitutive of goods of a certain kind, is true only if these and these and these particular sets of rules incarnated in the practices of these and these and these particular communities are productive of or constitutive of these and these and these particular goods enjoyed at certain particular times and places by certain specifiable individuals.

It follows that *I* find *my* justification for allegiance to these rules of morality in *my* particular community; deprived of the life of that community, *I* would have no reason to be moral. But this is not all. To obey the rules of morality is characteristically and generally a hard task for human beings. Indeed were it not so, our need for morality would not be what it is. It is because we are continually liable to be blinded by immediate desire, to be distracted from our responsibilities, to lapse into backsliding and because even the best of us may at times encounter quite unusual temptations that it is important to morality that *I* can only be a moral agent because *we* are moral agents, that I need those around me to reinforce my moral strengths and assist in remedying my moral weaknesses. It is in general only within a community that individuals become capable of morality, are sustained in their morality and are constituted as moral agents by the way in which other people regard them and what is owed to and by them as well as by the way in which they regard themselves. In requiring much from me morally the other members of my community express a kind of respect for me that has nothing to do with expectations of benefit; and those of whom nothing or little is required in respect of morality are treated with a lack of respect which is, if repeated often enough, damaging to the moral capacities of those individuals. Of course, lonely moral heroism is sometimes required and sometimes achieved. But we must not treat this exceptional type of case as though it were typical. And once we recognize that typically moral agency and continuing moral capacity are engendered and sustained in essential ways by particular institutionalised social ties in particular social groups, it will be difficult to counterpose allegiance to a particular society and allegiance to morality in the way in which the protagonists of liberal morality do.

Indeed the case for treating patriotism as a virtue is now clear. *If* first of all it is the case that I can only apprehend the rules of morality in the version in which they are incarnated in some specific community; and *if* secondly it is the case that the justification of morality must be in terms of particular goods enjoyed within the life of particular communities; and *if* thirdly it is the case that I am characteristically brought into being and maintained as a moral agent only through the particular kinds of moral sustenance afforded by my community, *then* it is clear that deprived of this community, I am unlikely to flourish as a moral agent. Hence my allegiance to the community and what it requires of me—even to the point of requiring me to die to sustain its life—could not meaningfully be contrasted with or counterposed to what morality required of me. Detached from my community, I will be apt to lose my hold upon all genuine standards of judgment. Loyalty to that community, to the hierarchy of particular kinship, particular local community and particular natural community, is on this view a prerequisite for morality. So patriotism and those loyalties cognate to it are not just virtues but central virtues. Everything however turns on the truth or falsity of the claims advanced in the three preceding if-clauses. And the argument so far affords us no resources for delivering a verdict upon that truth or falsity. Nonetheless some progress has been achieved, and not only because the terms of the debate have become clearer. For it has also become clear that this dispute is not adequately characterised if it is understood simply as a disagreement between two rival accounts of morality, as if there were some independently identifiable phenomenon situated somehow or other in the social world waiting to be described more or less accurately by the contending parties. What we have here are two rival and incompatible moralities, each of which is viewed from within by its adherents as morality-as-such, each of which makes its exclusive claim to our allegiance. How are we to evaluate such claims?

One way to begin is to be learned from Aristotle. Since we posses no stock of clear and distinct first principles or any other such epistemological resource which would provide us with a neutral and independent standard for judging between them, we shall do well to proceed dialectically. And one useful dialectical strategy is to focus attention on those accusations which the adherents of each bring against the rival position which the adherents of that rival position treat as of central importance to rebut. For this will afford at least one indication of the issues about the importance of which both sides agree and about the characterisation of which their very recognition of disagreement suggests that there must also be some shared beliefs. In what areas do such issues arise?

IV

One such area is defined by a charge which it seems reasonable at least prima facie for the protagonists of patriotism to bring against morality. The morality for which patriotism is a virtue offers a form of rational justification for moral rules and precepts whose structure is clear and rationally defensible. The rules of morality are justifiable if and only if they are productive of and partially constitutive of a form of shared social life whose goods are directly enjoyed by those inhabiting the particular communities whose social life is of that kind. Hence *qua* member of this or that particular community I can appreciate the justification for what morality requires of me from within the social roles that I live out in my community. By contrast, it may be argued, liberal morality requires of me to assume an abstract and artificial—perhaps even an impossible—stance, that of a rational being as such, responding to the requirements of morality not *qua* parent or farmer or quarterback, but *qua* rational agent who has abstracted him or herself from all social

particularity, who has become not merely Adam Smith's impartial spectator, but a correspondingly impartial actor, and one who in his impartiality is doomed to rootlessness, to be a citizen of nowhere. How can I justify to myself performing this act of abstraction and detachment?

The liberal answer is clear: such abstraction and detachment is defensible, because it is a necessary condition of moral freedom, of emancipation from the bondage of the social, political and economic status quo. For unless I can stand back from every and any feature of that status quo, including the roles within it which I myself presently inhabit, I will be unable to view it critically and to decide for myself what stance it is rational and right for me to adopt towards it. This does not preclude that the outcome of such a critical evaluation may not be an endorsement of all or some of the existing social order; but even such an endorsement will only be free and rational if I have made it for myself in this way. (Making just such an endorsement of much of the economic status quo is the distinguishing mark of the contemporary conservative liberal, such as Milton Friedman, who is as much a liberal as the liberal liberal who finds much of the status quo wanting—such as J. K. Galbraith or Edward Kennedy—or the radical liberal.) Thus liberal morality does after all appeal to an overriding good, the good of this particular kind of emancipating freedom. And in the name of this good it is able not only to respond to the question about how the rules of morality are to be justified, but also to frame a plausible and potentially damaging objection to the morality of patriotism.

It is of the essence of the morality of liberalism that no limitations are or can be set upon the criticism of the social status quo. No institution, no practice, no loyalty can be immune from being put in question and perhaps rejected. Conversely the morality of patriotism is one which precisely because it is framed in terms of the membership of some particular social community with some particular social, political and economic structure, must exempt at least some fundamental structures of that community's life from criticism. Because patriotism has to be a loyalty that is in some respects unconditional, so in just those respects rational criticism is ruled out. But if so the adherents of the morality of patriotism have condemned themselves to a fundamentally irrational attitude—since to refuse to examine some of one's fundamental beliefs and attitudes is to insist on accepting them, whether they are rationally justifiable or not, which is irrational—and have imprisoned themselves within that irrationality. What answer can the adherents of the morality of patriotism make to this kind of accusation? The reply must be threefold.

When the liberal moralist claims that the patriot is bound to treat his or her nation's projects and practices in some measure uncritically, the claim is not only that at any one time certain of these projects and practices will be being treated uncritically; it is that some at least must be permanently exempted from criticism. The patriot is in no position to deny this; but what is crucial to the patriot's case is to identify clearly precisely what it is that is thus exempted. And at this point it becomes extremely important that in outlining the case for the morality of patriotism—as indeed in outlining the case for liberal morality—we should not be dealing with strawmen. Liberalism and patriotism are not positions invented by me or by other external commentators; they have their own distinctive spokesmen and their own distinctive voices. And although I hope that is has been clear throughout that I have only been trying to articulate what those voices would say, it is peculiarly important to the case for patriotic morality at this point that its actual historical protagonists be identified. So what I say next is an attempt to identify the common attitudes on this point of Charles Péguy and Charles de Gaulle, of Bismarck and of Adam von Trott. You will notice that in these pairs one member is someone who was at least for a time a member of his nation's political establishment, the other someone who was always in a radical way outside that establishment and hostile to it, but that even those who were for a time identified with the status quo of power, were also at times alienated from it. And this makes it clear that whatever is exempted from the patriot's criticism the status quo of power and government and the policies pursued by those exercising power and government never need be so ex-

empted. What then is exempted? The answer is: the nation conceived *as a project*, a project somehow or other brought to birth in the past and carried on so that a morally distinctive community was brought into being which embodied a claim to political autonomy in its various organized and institutionalised expressions. Thus one can be patriotic towards a nation whose political independence is yet to come—as Garibaldi was; or towards a nation which once was and perhaps might be again—like the Polish patriots of the 1860s. What the patriot is committed to is a particular way of linking a past which has conferred a distinctive moral and political identity upon him or her with a future for the project which is his or her nation which it is his or her responsibility to bring into being. Only this allegiance is unconditional and allegiance to particular governments or forms of government or particular leaders will be entirely conditional upon their being devoted to furthering that project rather than frustrating or destroying it. Hence there is nothing inconsistent in a patriot's being deeply opposed to his country's contemporary rulers, as Péguy was, or plotting their overthrow as Adam von Trott did.

Yet although this may go part of the way towards answering the charge of the liberal moralist that the patriot must in certain areas be completely uncritical and therefore irrationalist, it certainly does not go all the way. For everything that I have said on behalf of the morality of patriotism is compatible with it being the case that on occasion patriotism might require me to support and work for the success of some enterprise of my nation as crucial to its overall project, crucial perhaps to its survival, when the success of that enterprise would not be in the best interests of mankind, evaluated from an impartial and an impersonal standpoint. The case of Adam von Trott is very much to the point.

Adam von Trott was a German patriot who was executed after the unsuccessful assassination attempt against Hitler's life in 1944. Trott deliberately chose to work inside Germany with the minuscule, but highly placed, conservative opposition to the Nazis with the aim of replacing Hitler from within, rather than to work for an overthrow of Nazi Germany which would result in the destruction of the

Germany brought to birth in 1871. But to do this he had to appear to be identified with the cause of Nazi Germany and so strengthened not only his country's cause, as was his intention, but also as an unavoidable consequence the cause of the Nazis. This kind of example is a particularly telling one, because the claim that such and such a course of action is "to the best interests of mankind" is usually at best disputable, at worst cloudy rhetoric. But there are a very few causes in which so much was at stake—and that this is generally much clearer in retrospect than it was at the time does not alter that fact—that the phrase has clear application: the overthrow of Nazi Germany was one of them.

How ought the patriot then to respond? Perhaps in two ways. The first begins by reemphasising that from the fact that the particularist morality of the patriot is rooted in a particular community and inextricably bound up with the social life of that community, it does not follow that it cannot provide rational grounds for repudiating many features of that country's present organized social life. The conception of justice engendered by the notion of citizenship within a particular community may provide standards by which particular political institutions are found wanting: when Nazi anti-Semitism encountered the phenomena of German Jewish ex-soldiers who had won the Iron Cross, it had to repudiate German particularist standards of excellence (for the award of the Iron Cross symbolised a recognition of devotion to Germany). Moreover the conception of one's own nation having a special mission does not necessitate that this mission may not involve the extension of a justice originally at home only in the particular institutions of the homeland. And clearly particular governments or agencies of government may defect and may be understood to have defected from this mission so radically that the patriot may find that a point comes when he or she has to choose between the claims of the project which constitutes his or her nation and the claims of the morality that he or she has learnt as a member of the community whose life is informed by that project. Yes, the liberal critic of patriotism will respond, this indeed *may* happen; but it may not and it often will not. Patriotism turns out to be

a permanent source of moral danger. And this claim, I take it, cannot in fact be successfully rebutted.

A second possible, but very different type of answer on behalf of the patriot would run as follows. I argued earlier that the kind of regard for one's own country which would be compatible with a liberal morality of impersonality and impartiality would be too insubstantial, would be under too many constraints, to be regarded as a version of patriotism in the traditional sense. But it does not follow that some version of traditional patriotism may not be compatible with some other morality of universal moral law, which sets limits to and provides both sanction for and correction of the particularist morality of the patriot. Whether this is so or not is too large and too distinct a question to pursue in this present paper. But we ought to note that even if it is so—and all those who have been both patriots and Christians *or* patriots and believers in Thomistic natural law *or* patriots and believers in the Rights of Man have been committed to claiming that it is so—this would not diminish in any way the force of the liberal claim that patriotism is a morally dangerous phenomenon.

That the rational protagonist of the morality of patriotism is compelled, if my argument is correct, to concede this does not mean that there is not more to be said in the debate. And what needs to be said is that the liberal morality of impartiality and impersonality turns out also to be a morally dangerous phenomenon in an interestingly corresponding way. For suppose the bonds of patriotism to be dissolved: would liberal morality be able to provide anything adequately substantial in its place? What the morality of patriotism at its best provides is a clear account of and justification for the particular bonds and loyalties which form so much of the substance of the moral life. It does so by underlining the moral importance of the different members of a group acknowledging a shared history. Each one of us to some degree or other understands his or her life as an enacted narrative; and because of our relationships with others we have to understand ourselves as characters in the enacted narratives of other people's lives. Moreover the story of each of our lives is characteristically embedded in the story of one or more larger units. I understand the story of my life in such a way that it is part of the history of my family or of this farm or of this university or of this countryside; and I understand the story of the lives of other individuals around me as embedded in the same larger stories, so that I and they share a common stake in the outcome of that story and in what sort of story it both is and is to be: tragic, heroic, comic.

A central contention of the morality of patriotism is that I will obliterate and lose a central dimension of the moral life if I do not understand the enacted narrative of my own individual life as embedded in the history of my country. For if I do not so understand it I will not understand what I owe to others or what others owe to me, for what crimes of my nation I am bound to make reparation, for what benefits to my nation I am bound to feel gratitude. Understanding what is owed to and by me and understanding the history of the communities of which I am a part is on this view one and the same thing.

It is worth stressing that one consequence of this is that patriotism, in the sense in which I am understanding it in this paper, is only possible in certain types of national community under certain conditions. A national community, for example, which systematically disowned its own true history or substituted a largely fictitious history for it or a national community in which the bonds deriving from history were in no way the real bonds of the community (having been replaced for example by the bonds of reciprocal self-interest) would be one towards which patriotism would be—from any point of view—an irrational attitude. For precisely the same reasons that a family whose members all came to regard membership in that family as governed only by reciprocal self-interest would no longer be a family in the traditional sense, so a nation whose members took up a similar attitude would no longer be a nation and this would provide adequate grounds for holding that the project which constituted that nation had simply collapsed. Since all modern bureaucratic states tend towards reducing national communities to this condition, all such states tend towards a condition in which any genu-

ine morality of patriotism would have no place and what paraded itself as patriotism would be an unjustifiable simulacrum.

Why would this matter? In modern communities in which membership is understood only or primarily in terms of reciprocal self-interest, only two resources are generally available when destructive conflicts of interest threaten such reciprocity. One is the arbitrary imposition of some solution by force; the other is appeal to the neutral, impartial and impersonal standards of liberal morality. The importance of this resource is scarcely to be underrated; but how much of a resource is it? The problem is that some motivation has to be provided for allegiance to the standards of impartiality and impersonality which both has rational justification and can outweigh the considerations provided by interest. Since any large need for such allegiance arises precisely and only when and insofar as the possibility of appeals to reciprocity in interests has broken down, such reciprocity can no longer provide the relevant kind of motivation. And it is difficult to identify anything that can take its place. The appeal to moral agents *qua* rational beings to place their allegiance to impersonal rationality above that to their interests has, just because it is an appeal to rationality, to furnish an adequate reason for so doing. And this is a point at which liberal accounts of morality are notoriously vulnerable. This vulnerability becomes a manifest practical liability at one key point in the social order.

Every political community except in the most exceptional conditions requires standing armed forces for its minimal security. Of the members of these armed forces it must require both that they be prepared to sacrifice their own lives for the sake of the community's security and that their willingness to do so be not contingent upon their own individual evaluation of the rightness or wrongness of their country's cause on some specific issue, measured by some standard that is neutral and impartial relative to the interests of their own community and the interests of other communities. And, that is to say, good soldiers may not be liberals and must indeed embody in their actions a good deal at least of the morality of patriotism. So the political survival of any polity in which liberal morality had secured large-scale allegiance would depend upon there still being enough young men and women who rejected that liberal morality. And in this sense liberal morality tends towards the dissolution of social bonds.

Hence the charge that the morality of patriotism can successfully bring against liberal morality is the mirror-image of that which liberal morality can successfully urge against the morality of patriotism. For while the liberal moralist was able to conclude that patriotism is a permanent source of moral danger because of the way it places our ties to our nation beyond rational criticism, the moralist who defends patriotism is able to conclude that liberal morality is a permanent source of moral danger because of the way it renders our social and moral ties too open to dissolution by rational criticism. And each party is in fact in the right against the other.

V

The fundamental task which confronts any moral philosopher who finds this conclusion compelling is clear. It is to enquire whether, although the central claims made on behalf of these two rival modern moralities cannot both be true, we ought perhaps not to move towards the conclusion that both sets of claims are in fact false. And this is an enquiry in which substantial progress has already been made. But history in its impatience does not wait for moral philosophers to complete their tasks, let alone to convince their fellow-citizens. The polis ceased to be the key institution in Greek politics even while Aristotle was still restating its rationale and any contemporary philosopher who discusses the key conceptions that have informed modern political life since the eighteenth century is in danger of reliving Aristotle's fate, even if in a rather less impressive way. The owl of Minerva really does seem to fly at dusk.

Does this mean that my argument is therefore devoid of any immediate practical significance? That would be true only if the conclusion that a morality of liberal impersonality and a morality of patriotism must be deeply incompatible itself had no practical significance for our understanding of our everyday politics. But perhaps a systematic recognition of this incompatibility will enable us to diagnose one central flaw in the political life characteristic of modern Western states, or at least of all those modern Western states which look back for their legitimation to the American and the French revolutions. For polities so established have tended to contrast themselves with the older regimes that they displaced by asserting that, while all previous polities had expressed in their lives the partiality and one-sidedness of local customs, institutions and traditions, they have for the first time given expression in their constitutional and institutional forms to the impersonal and impartial rules of morality as such, common to all rational beings. So Robespierre proclaimed that it was an effect of the French Revolution that the cause of France and the cause of the Rights of Man were one and the same cause. And in the nineteenth century the United Stated produced its own version of this claim, one which at the level of rhetoric provided the content for many Fourth of July orations and at the level of education set the standards for the Americanisation of the late nineteenth century and early twentieth century immigrants, especially those from Europe.

Hegel employs a useful distinction which he marks by his use of the words *Sittlichkeit* and *Moralität*. *Sittlichkeit* is the customary morality of each particular society, pretending to be no more than this. *Moralität* reigns in the realm of rational universal, impersonal morality, of liberal morality, as I have defined it. What those immigrants were taught in effect was that they had left behind countries and cultures where *Sittlichkeit* and *Moralität* were certainly distinct and often opposed and arrived in a country and a culture whose *Sittlichkeit* just is *Moralität*. And thus for many Americans the cause of America, understood as the object of patriotic regard, and the cause of morality, understood as the liberal moralist understands it, came to be identified. The history of this identification could not be other than a history of confusion and incoherence, if the argument which I have constructed in this lecture is correct. For a morality of particularist ties and solidarities has been conflated with a morality of universal, impersonal and impartial principles in a way that can never be carried through without incoherence.

One test therefore of whether the argument that I have constructed has or has not empirical application and practical significance would be to discover whether it is or is not genuinely illuminating to write the political and social history of modern America as in key part the living out of a central conceptual confusion, a confusion perhaps required for the survival of a large-scale modern polity which has to exhibit itself as liberal in many institutional settings, but which also has to be able to engage the patriotic regard of enough of its citizens, if it is to continue functioning effectively. To determine whether that is or is not true would be to risk discovering that we inhabit a kind of polity whose moral order requires systematic incoherence in the form of public allegiance to mutually inconsistent sets of principles. But that is a task which—happily—lies beyond the scope of this lecture.

7

Women in the Family and in Public Life

Philosophers Against the Family

Christina Hoff Sommers

In this essay Christina Sommers defends the traditional conception of family responsibilities. She argues that we have duties to parents, children, mates, and siblings that are determined by the nature of the family. Although families and kinship systems have taken many forms, people have always acknowledged that family members owe one another special loyalty, support, and devotion. This traditional system of family morality, Sommers charges, is being undermined by contemporary moral philosophers. Current philosophical traditions insist that morality be universally applicable without regard to any relationships people might have with each other. The effect of this doctrine, she says, is to put the duty a family member owes another family member on a par with what would be owed to an unrelated individual. The demands of traditional family morality, then, seem to be beyond the call of duty. Sommers illustrates her point with quotes from some current philosophers on family ethics. She then considers the radical feminist attack on women who choose a traditional family commitment. Sommers believes that, rather than being dupes, prostitutes, and slaves as some radical feminists charge, women who choose to work mainly within a family have made an intelligent, responsible choice. On the abortion issue, Sommers raises the neglected issue of the maternal bond, arguing that its special responsibilities should be considered, along with other factors, by women when they choose an abortion. She ends her essay by discussing the effects of divorce on children and brings the weight of tradition to support her view that divorce should not be undertaken lightly.

Much of what commonly counts as personal morality is measured by how well we behave within family relationships. We live our moral lives as son or daughter to this mother and that father, as brother or sister to that sister or brother, as father or mother, grandfather, granddaughter to that boy or girl or that man or woman. These relationships and the moral duties defined by them were once popular topics of moral casuistry; but when we turn to the literature of recent moral philosophy, we find little discussion on what it means to be a good son or daughter, a good mother or father, a good husband or wife, a good brother or sister.

Modern ethical theory concentrates on more general topics. Perhaps the majority of us who do ethics accept some version of Kantianism or utilitarianism, and these mainstream doctrines are better designed for telling us about what we should do as persons in general than about our special duties as parents or children or siblings. We believe, perhaps, that these universal theories can fully account for the morality of special relations. In any case, modern ethics is singularly silent on the bread and butter issues of personal morality in daily life. But silence is only part of it. With the exception of marriage itself, the relationships in the family are biologically given. The contemporary philosopher is, on the whole, actively unsympathetic to the idea that we have *any* duties defined by relationships that we have not voluntarily entered into. We do not, after all, choose our parents or siblings, and even if we do choose to have children, this is not the same as choosing, say, our friends. Because the special relationships that constitute the family as a social arrangement are, in this sense, not voluntarily assumed, many moralists feel bound in principle to dismiss them altogether. The practical result is

From Christina Hoff Sommers, *Person to Person*, George Graham and Hugh LaFollette, eds. (Philadelphia: Temple University Press, 1989, pp. 82–105. Reprinted by permission of Temple University Press. Some footnotes omitted.

that philosophers are to be found among those who are contributing to an ongoing disintegration of the traditional family. In what follows I expose some of the philosophical roots of the current hostility to family morality. My own view that the ethical theses underlying this hostility are bad philosophy is made evident throughout the discussion.

The Moral Vantage

Social criticism is a heady pastime to which philosophers are professionally addicted. One approach is Aristotelian in method and temperament. It is antiradical, though it may be liberal, and it approaches the task of needed reform with a prima facie respect for the norms of established morality. It is conservationist and cautious in its recommendations for change. It is therefore not given to such proposals as abolishing the family or abolishing private property and, indeed, does not look kindly on such proposals from other philosophers. The antiradicals I am concerned about are not those who would be called Burkean. I call them liberal but this use of the term is somewhat perverse since, in my stipulative use, a liberal is a philosopher who advocates social reform but always in a conservative spirit. My liberals share with Aristotle the conviction that the traditional arrangements have great moral weight and that common opinion is a primary source of moral truth. A good modern example is Henry Sidgwick with his constant appeal to common sense. But philosophers like John Stuart Mill, William James, and Bertrand Russell can also be cited. On the other hand, since no radical can be called a liberal in my sense, many so-called liberals could be perversely excluded. Thus when John Rawls toys with the possibility of abolishing the family because kinship bias is a force inimical to equality of opportunity, he is no liberal.

The more exciting genre of social criticism is not liberal-Aristotelian but radical and Platonist in spirit. Its vantage is external or even supernal to the social institutions it has placed under moral scrutiny. Plato was as aware as anyone could be that what he called the cave was social reality. One reason for calling it a cave was to emphasize the need, as he saw it, for an external, objective perspective on established morality. Another point in so calling it was his conviction that common opinion was benighted, and that reform could not be accomplished except by a great deal of consciousness raising and enlightened social engineering. Plato's supernal vantage made it possible for him to look on social reality in somewhat the way the Army Corps of Engineers looks upon a river that needs to have its course changed and its waywardness tamed. In our own day much social criticism of a Marxist variety has taken this radical approach to social change. And of course much of contemporary feminist philosophy is radical.

Some philosophers are easily classifiable as radical or liberal. John Locke is clearly a liberal, Leon Trotsky is clearly a radical. I remarked a moment ago that there is a radical strain in Rawls. But it is a strain only: Rawls' attitude to social reality is not, finally, condescending. On the other hand, much contemporary social criticism is radical in temper. In particular, I suggest that the prevailing attitude toward the family is radical and not liberal. And the inability of mainstream ethical theory to come to grips with the special obligations that family members bear to one another contributes to the current disregard of the common-sense morality of the family cave. We find, indeed, that family obligations are criticized and discounted precisely because they do not fit the standard theories of obligation. If I am right, contemporary ethics is at a loss when it comes to dealing with parochial morality; but few have acknowledged this as a defect to be repaired. Instead the common reaction has been: If the family does not fit my model of autonomy, rights, or obligations, then so much the worse for the family.

To illustrate this, I cite without comment recent views on some aspects of family morality.

1. Michael Slote (1979) maintains that any child capable of supporting itself is "morally free to opt out of the family situation" (p. 320). To those who say that the child

should be expected to help needy parents for a year or two out of reciprocity or fair play, Slote responds: "The duty of fair play presumably exists only where past benefits are voluntarily accepted . . . and we can hardly suppose that a child has voluntarily accepted his role in family . . . life" (p. 230).

2. Virginia Held (1983) wants traditional family roles to be abolished, and she recommends that husbands and wives think of themselves as roommates of the same sex in assigning household and parental tasks. (She calls this the "Roommate Test.") To the objection that such a restructuring might injure family life, she replies that similar sorts of objections were made against factory workers when they demanded overtime.

3. The late Jane English (1979) defended the view that adult children are not morally indebted to their parents, and owe them no more than they owe to good friends. "After friendship ends, the duties of friendship end." A. John Simmons (1979, 162) and Jeffrey Blustein (1982, 182) also look with suspicion upon the idea that there is a debt of gratitude to the parents for what, in any case, they were duty-bound to do.

4. Where Slote argues for the older child's right to leave, Howard Cohen (1980, 66) argues for granting the right to young children who still need parental care. He proposes that every child be assigned a trusted adviser or agent. If the children want to leave their parents, their agent will be charged with finding alternative caretakers for them.

The philosophers I have cited are not atypical in their dismissive attitude to common-sense morality or in their readiness to replace the parochial norms of the family cave with practices that would better approximate the ideals of human rights and equality. A theory of rights and obligations that applies generally to moral agents is, in this way, applied to the family with the predictable results that the family system of special relations and noncontractual special obligations is judged to be grossly unfair to its members.

Feminism and the Family

I have said that the morality of the family has been relatively neglected. The glaring exception to this is of course the feminist movement. This movement is complex, but I am primarily confined to its moral philosophers, of whom the most influential is Simone de Beauvoir. For de Beauvoir, a social arrangement that does not allow all its participants the scope and liberty of a human subjectivity is to be condemned. De Beauvoir criticizes the family as an unacceptable arrangement since, for women, marriage and childbearing are essentially incompatible with their subjectivity and freedom:

> The tragedy of marriage is not that it fails to assure woman the promised happiness . . . but that it mutilates her: it dooms her to repetition and routine. . . . At twenty or thereabouts mistress of a home, bound permanently to a man, a child in her arms, she stands with her life virtually finished forever (1952, 534).

For de Beauvoir the tragedy goes deeper than marriage. The loss of subjectivity is unavoidable as long as human reproduction requires the woman's womb. De Beauvoir starkly describes the pregnant woman who ought to be a "free individual" as a "stockpile of colloids, an incubator of an egg" (p. 553). And as recently as 1977 she compared childbearing and nurturing to slavery (p. 2).

It would be a mistake to say that de Beauvoir's criticism of the family is outside the mainstream of Anglo-American philosophy. Her criterion of moral adequacy may be formulated in continental existentialist terms, but its central contention is generally accepted: Who would deny that an arrangement that systematically thwarts the freedom and autonomy of the individual is *eo ipso* defective? What is perhaps a bit odd to Anglo-American ears is that de Beauvoir makes so little appeal to ideals of fairness and equality. For her, it is the loss of autonomy that is decisive.

De Beauvoir is more pessimistic than most feminists she has influenced about the prospects for technological and social solutions. But implicit in her critique is the ideal of a society in which sexual differences are minimal or nonexistent. This ideal is shared by many contemporary feminist philosophers. The views of Richard Wasserstrom (1980), Ann Ferguson (1977), and Allison Jagger (1977; 1983; 1986) are representative.

Wasserstrom's approach to social criticism is Platonist in its use of a hypothetical good society. The ideal society is nonsexist and "assimilationist": "In the assimilationist society in respect to sex, persons would not be socialized so as to see or understand themselves or others as essentially or significantly who they were or what their lives would be like because they were either male or female" (1980, 26). Social reality is scrutinized for its approximation to this ideal, and criticism is directed against all existing norms. Take the custom of having sexually segregated bathrooms: Whether this is right or wrong "depends on what the good society would look like in respect to sexual differentiation." The key question in evaluating any law or arrangement in which sex difference figures is: "What would the good or just society make of [it]?" (p. 23).

Thus the supernal light shines on the cave revealing its moral defects. *There,* in the ideal society, gender in the choice of lover or spouse would be of no more significance than eye color. *There* the family would consist of adults but not necessarily of different sexes and not necessarily in pairs. *There* we find equality ensured by a kind of affirmative action which compensates for disabilities. If women are somewhat weaker than men, or if they are subject to lunar disabilities, then this must be compensated for. (Wasserstrom compares women to persons with congenital defects for whom the good society makes special arrangements.) Male-dominated sports such as wrestling and football will there be eliminated, and marriage as we know it will not exist.

Other feminist philosophers are equally confident about the need for sweeping change. Ann Ferguson (1977) wants a "radical reorganization of child rearing" (p. 51). She recommends communal living and a deemphasis on biological parenting. In the ideal society "love relationships would be based on the meshing together of androgynous human

beings" (p. 66). Carol Gould (1983) argues for androgyny and for abolishing legal marriage. She favors single parenting, co-parenting, and communal parenting. The only arrangement she emphatically opposes is the traditional one where the mother provides primary care for the children. Janice Raymond (1975, 61) is an assimilationist who objects to the ideal of androgyny, preferring instead to speak of a genderless ideal free of male or female stereotypes. Allison Jagger's ideal is described in a science-fiction story depicting a society in which "neither sex bears children, but both sexes, through hormone treatments, suckle them . . . thus [the author] envisions a society where every baby has three social 'mothers,' who may be male or female, and at least two of whom agree to breast-feed it" (1983, 41). To those of us who find this bizarre, Jagger replies that this shows the depth of our prejudice in favor of the natural family.

Though they differ in detail, these feminists hold to a common social ideal that is broadly assimilationist in character and inimical to the traditional family. Sometimes it seems as if the radical feminist simply takes the classical Marxist eschatology of the *Communist Manifesto* and substitutes "gender" for "class." Indeed, the feminist and the old-fashioned Marxist do have much in common. Both see their caves as politically divided into two warring factions: one oppressing, the other oppressed. Both see the need of raising the consciousness of the oppressed group to its predicament and to the possibility of removing its shackles. Both look forward to the day of a classless or genderless society. And both are zealots, paying little attention to the tragic personal costs to be paid for the revolution they wish to bring about. The feminists tell us little about that side of things. To begin with, how can the benighted myriads in the cave who do not wish to mesh together with other androgynous beings be reeducated? And how are children to be brought up in the genderless society? Plato took great pains to explain his methods. Would the new methods be as thoroughgoing? Unless these questions can be given plausible answers, the supernal attack on the family must always be irresponsible. The appeal to the just society justifies nothing until it can be shown that the radical proposals do not have monstrous consequences. That has not been shown. Indeed, given the perennially dubious state of the social sciences, it is precisely what *cannot* be shown.

Any social arrangement that falls short of the assimilationist ideal is labeled sexist. It should be noted that this characteristically feminist use of the term differs significantly from the popular or literal sense. Literally, and popularly, sexism connotes unfair discrimination. But in its extended philosophical use it connotes discrimination, period. Wasserstrom and many feminists trade on the popular pejorative connotations of sexism when they invite us to be antisexist. Most liberals are antisexist in the popular sense. But to be antisexist in the technical, radical philosophical sense is not merely to be opposed to discrimination against women; it is to be *for* what Wasserstrom calls the assimilationist ideal. The philosopher antisexist opposes any social policy that is nonandrogynous, objecting, for example, to legislation that allows for maternity leave. As Allison Jagger remarks: "We do not, after all, elevate 'prostate leave' into a special right of men" (1977, 102). From being liberally opposed to sexism, one may in this way insensibly be led to a radical critique of the family whose ideal is assimilationist and androgynous. For it is very clear that the realization of the androgynous ideal is incompatible with the survival of the family as we know it.

The neological extension of labels such as "sexism," "slavery," and "prostitution" is a feature of radical discourse. The liberal too will sometimes call for radical solutions to social problems. Some institutions are essentially unjust. To reform slavery or totalitarian systems of government is to eliminate them. The radical trades on these extreme practices in characterizing other practices—for example, characterizing low wages as "slave" wages and the worker who is paid them as a "slave" laborer. Taking these descriptions seriously may put one on the way to treating a system of a free labor market as a "slave system," which, in simple justice, must be overthrown and replaced by an alternative system of production.

Comparing mothers and wives to slaves is a common radical criticism of the family. Presumably most slaves do not want to be slaves.

In fact, the majority of wives and mothers want to be wives and mothers. Calling these women slaves is therefore a pejorative extension of the term. To be slaves in the literal sense these women would have to be too dispirited and oppressed or too corrupt even to want freedom from slavery. Yet that is how some feminist philosophers look upon women who opt for the traditional family. It does seem fanciful and not a little condescending to see them so, but let us suppose that it is in fact a correct and profound description of the plight of married women and mothers. Would it now follow that the term "slave" literally applies to them? Not quite yet. Before we could call these women slaves, we should have to have made a further assumption. Even timorous slaves too fearful of taking any step to freedom are under no illusion that they are not slaves. Yet it is a fact that most women and mothers do not *think* of themselves as slaves, so we must assume that the majority of women have been systematically deluded into thinking they are free. And that assumption, too, is often explicitly made. Here the radical feminist will typically explain that, existentially, women, being treated by men as sex objects, are especially prone to bad faith and false consciousness. Marxist feminists will see them as part of an unawakened and oppressed economic class. Clearly we cannot call on a deluded woman to cast off her bonds before we have made her *aware* of her bondage. So the first task of freeing the slave woman is dispelling the thrall of a false and deceptive consciousness. One must raise her consciousness to the reality of her situation. (Some feminists acknowledge that it may in fact be too late for many of the women who have fallen too far into the delusions of marriage and motherhood. But the educative process can save many from falling into the marriage and baby trap.)

In this sort of rhetorical climate nothing is what it seems. Prostitution is another term that has been subjected to a radical enlargement. Allison Jagger believes that a feminist interpretation of the term "prostitution" is badly needed and asks for a "philosophical theory of prostitution" (1986). Observing that the average woman dresses for men, marries a man for protection and so on, she says: "For contemporary radical feminists, prostitution is the archetypal relationship of women to men" (1986, 115).

Of course, the housewife Jagger has in mind might be offended at the suggestion that she herself is a prostitute, albeit less well paid and less aware of it than the professional street prostitute. To this the radical feminist reply is, to quote Jagger:

> Individuals' intentions do not necessarily indicate the true nature of what is going on. Both man and woman might be outraged at the description of their candlelit dinner as prostitution, but the radical feminist argues this outrage is due simply to the participants' failure or refusal to perceive the social context in which the dinner occurs (1986, 117).

Apparently, this failure or refusal to perceive affects most women. Thus we may even suppose that the majority of women who have been treated by a man to a candlelit dinner prefer it to other dining alternatives they have experienced. To say that these preferences are misguided is a hard and condescending doctrine. It would appear that most feminist philosophers are not overly impressed with Mill's principle that there can be no appeal from a majority verdict of those who have experienced two alternatives.

The dismissive feminist attitude to the widespread preferences of women takes its human toll. Most women, for example, prefer to have children, and few of those who have them regret having them. It is no more than sensible, from a utilitarian standpoint, to take note of the widespread preference and to take it seriously in planning one's own life. But a significant number of women discount this general verdict as benighted, taking more seriously the idea that the reported joys of motherhood are exaggerated and fleeting, if not altogether illusory. These women tell themselves and others that having babies is a trap to be avoided. But for many women childlessness has become a trap of its own, somewhat lonelier than the more conventional traps of marriage and babies. Some come to find their childlessness regrettable; this sort of regret is common to those who flout Mill's reasonable maxim by putting the verdict of ideology over the verdict of human experience.

It is a serious defect of American feminism that it concentrates its zeal on impugning femininity and feminine culture at the expense of the grass root fight against economic and social injustices to which women are subjected. As we have seen, the radical feminist attitude to the woman who enjoys her femininity is condescending or even contemptuous. Indeed, the contempt for femininity reminds one of misogynist biases in philosophers such as Kant, Rousseau, and Schopenhauer, who believed that femininity was charming but incompatible with full personhood and reasonableness. The feminists deny the charm, but they too accept the verdict that femininity is weakness. It goes without saying that an essential connection between femininity and powerlessness has not been established by *either* party.

By denigrating conventional feminine roles and holding to an assimilationist ideal in social policy, the feminist movement has lost its natural constituency. The actual concerns, beliefs, and aspirations of the majority of women are not taken seriously *except* as illustrations of bad faith, false consciousness, and successful brainwashing. What women actually want is discounted and reinterpreted as to what they have been led to *think* they want (a man, children). What most women *enjoy* (male gallantry, candlelit dinners, sexy clothes, makeup) is treated as an obscenity (prostitution).

As the British feminist Jennifer Radcliffe Richards says:

> Most women still dream about beauty, dress, weddings, dashing lovers, domesticity and babies . . . but if feminists seem (as they do) to want to eliminate nearly all of these things—beauty, sex conventions, families and all—for most people that simply means the removal of everything in life which is worth living for (1980, 341–42).

Radical feminism creates a false dichotomy between sexism and assimilation, as if there were nothing in between. This is to ignore completely the middle ground in which it could be recognized that a woman can be free of oppression and nevertheless feminine in the sense abhorred by many feminists. For women are simply not waiting to be freed from the particular chains the radical feminists are trying to sunder. The average woman enjoys her femininity. She wants a man, not a roommate. She wants fair economic opportunities, and she wants children and the time to care for them. These are the goals that women actually have, and they are not easily attainable. But they will never be furthered by an elitist radical movement that views the actual aspirations of women as the product of a false consciousness. There is room for a liberal feminism that would work for reforms that would give women equal opportunity in the workplace and in politics, but would leave untouched and unimpugned the basic institutions that women want and support: marriage and motherhood. Such a feminism is already in operation in some European countries. But it has been obstructed here in the United States by the ideologues who now hold the seat of power in the feminist movement (Hewlett, 1986).

In characterizing and criticizing American feminism, I have not taken into account the latest revisions and qualifications of a lively and variegated movement. There is a kind of feminism-of-the-week that one cannot hope to keep abreast of, short of giving up all other concerns. The best one can do for the present purposes is attend to central theses and arguments that bear on the feminist treatment of the family. Nevertheless, even for this limited purpose, it would be wrong to omit discussion of an important turn taken by feminism in the past few years. I have in mind the recent literature on the idea that there is a specific female ethic that is more concrete, less rule-oriented, more empathetic and caring, and more attentive to the demands of a particular context. The kind of feminism that accepts the idea that women differ from men in approaching ethical dilemmas and social problems from a care perspective is not oriented to androgyny as an ideal. Rather it seeks to develop this special female ethic and to give it greater practical scope.

The stress on context might lead one to think these feminists are more sympathetic to the family as the social arrangement that shapes the moral development of women and is the context for many of the moral dilemmas that women actually face. However, one sees as yet no attention being paid to the fact that feminism itself is a force working against the preservation of the family. Psychologists like Carol Gilligan and philosophers like Lawrence Blum concentrate their attention on the moral quality of the caring relationships, but these relationships are themselves not viewed in their concrete embeddedness in any formal social arrangement.

It should also be said that some feminists are moving away from the earlier hostility to motherhood (Trebilcot, 1984). Here, too, one sees the weakening of the assimilationist ideal in the acknowledgment of a primary gender role. However, childrearing is not primarily seen within the context of the family but as a special relationship between mother and daughter or—more awkwardly—between mother and son, a relationship that effectively excludes the male parent. And the often cultist celebration of motherhood remains largely hostile to traditional familial arrangements.

It is too early to say whether a new style of nonassimilationist feminism will lead to a mitigation of the assault on the family or even on femininity. In any case, the recognition of a female ethic of care and responsibility is hardly inconsistent with a social ethic that values the family as a vital, perhaps indispensable, institution. And the recognition that women have their own moral style may well be followed by a more accepting attitude to the kind of femininity that the more assimilationist feminists reject.

The Indirect Attack

Unlike the feminists, the philosophers do not directly criticize the family. In some cases, they do not even mention it; but each one holds a view that subverts, ignores, or denies the special moral relations that characterize the family and are responsible for its functioning. And if they are right, family morality is a vacuous subject.

Judith Thomson (1971) maintains that an abortion may be permissible even if the fetus is deemed a person from the moment of conception. For in that case being pregnant would be like having an adult surgically attached to one's body; and it is arguable that if we find ourselves attached to another person we have the right to free ourselves, even if this freedom is obtained at the price of the other person's death by, say, kidney failure. For the sake of this discussion I refer to the fetus as a prenatal child. I myself do not think the fetus is a person from the moment of conception. Nor does Thomson. But here we are interested in her argument for the proposition that abortion of a prenatal child/person should be permissible.

Now, many have been repelled by Thomson's comparing pregnancy to arbitrary attachment. Thomson herself is well aware that the comparison may seem bizarre. She says: "It may be said that what is important is not merely the fact that the fetus is a person, but that it is a person for whom the mother has a special kind of responsibility issuing from the fact that she is its mother" (p. 64).

To this Thomson replies that we do not have any such "special responsibility for a person unless we have assumed it, explicitly or implicitly." If the mother does not try to prevent pregnancy, does not obtain an abortion, but instead gives birth, and then takes the child home with her, then she has at least implicitly assumed responsibility for it.

One might object that although pregnancy is a state into which many women do not enter voluntarily, it is nevertheless a state in which one is *socially* expected to care for the prenatal child. Many pregnant women do feel such a responsibility to it, and they take measure to assure its survival and future health. But here one must be grateful to Professor Thomson for her clarity. A mother who has not deliberately sought pregnancy bears *no* special responsibility to her prenatal child. For she has neither implicitly nor explicitly taken on the responsibility of caring for it. Prenatally, the child's need is thus like the need of a sick man for the touch of Henry Fonda's cool hand on his brow (Thomson's analogy). Henry Fonda has the right to refuse to touch the sick man even if it were reasonably certain that his refusal means that man's death. So, too, the mother has the right to refuse the use of her body even if that means the death of the child in her womb. On the other hand, the postnatal act of taking the child home is at least implicitly an assumption of responsibility: By

choosing to take it with her, the mother is undertaking to care for the infant, and she no longer has a right to free herself of the burden of motherhood at the cost of the life of the child.

Note too that Thomson describes the relationship of the prenatal child-person to its mother as *biological*. This is consistent with giving no moral weight whatever to what might be called a sociological/normative relationship in which the child could be thought to have a right against its mother to prenatal care and protection. Here, too, Thomson is clear and uncompromising; there is no such right, either prenatally or postnatally, unless it be implicitly or voluntarily *conferred* on the child by the mother.

The assumption, then, is that there are no noncontractual obligations or special duties defined by the kinship of mother to child. As for social expectations, none are legitimate in the morally binding sense unless they have the backing of an implicit or explicit contract freely entered into. If that assumption is correct, sociological arrangements and norms have no moral force unless they are voluntarily accepted by the moral agent who is bound by them. I call this the volunteer theory of moral obligation. It is a thesis that is so widely accepted today that Thomson did not see the need to argue for it.

Michael Tooley's arguments in defense of infanticide provide another good example of how a contemporary philosopher sidetracks and ultimately subverts the special relations that bind the family. Tooley (1972) holds that being sentient confers the prima facie right not to be treated cruelly, and that possession of those characteristics that make one a person confers the *additional* right to life. Tooley then argues that infants lack these characteristics and so may be painlessly killed. In reaching this conclusion, Tooley's sole consideration is whether the infant intrinsically possesses the relevant "right-to-life-making characteristic" of personality. But this is to abstract from any right to care and protection that the infant's relation to its parents confers on it causally and institutionally. For Tooley, as for Thomson, the relations of family or motherhood are morally irrelevant. So it is perhaps not surprising that one finds nothing in the index under "family," "mother," or "father" in Tooley's book on abortion and infanticide.

Howard Cohen (1980, chaps. 5 and 6) is strictly concerned with the rights of persons irrespective of the special relations they may bear to others. Just as Thomson holds that the mother's right to the free unencumbered use of her body is not qualified by any special obligations to her child, so Cohen holds that the child's right to a no-fault divorce from its parents cannot be diminished because of the special relation it bears to them. Where Thomson is concerned with the overriding right of the mother, Cohen is concerned with the right of the child. But all three philosophers agree that the right of a child is not less strong than the right of any adult. Indeed, Thomson compares the unborn child to a fully grown adult; and Tooley holds that any person, be it child, adult, or sapient nonhuman, is equal in rights.

Our three philosophers are typical in holding that any moral requirement is either a general duty or else a specific obligation voluntarily assumed. Let us call a requirement a *duty* if it devolves on the moral agent whether or not it was voluntarily assumed. It is, for example, a duty to refrain from murder. And let us call a requirement an *obligation* only if it devolves on certain moral agents but not necessarily on all moral agents. One is, for example, morally obligated to keep one's promises. According to our three philosophers, all duties are general in the sense of being requirements on all moral agents. Any moral requirement that is *specific* to a given moral agent must be grounded in a voluntary commitment. Thus there is no room for any special requirement on a moral agent that has not been voluntarily assumed by that agent. In other words, there are no special duties. This is what I am calling the volunteer theory of obligation. According to the volunteerist thesis, all duties are general and only those who volunteer for them have any obligations.

This thesis underlies Cohen's view that the child can divorce its parents. For we do not need to consider whether the child has any special duties to the parents that could conflict with the exercise of its right to leave them. It underlies Thomson's view that the mother has no special responsibility to her unborn child and that any such responsibility that she may

later have is implicitly assumed by her voluntary act of taking it home with her. It underlies Tooley's psychobiological method for answering the moral question of infanticide by determining the rightmaking characteristics of personhood: All we need to know about the neonate is whether it possesses the psychological characteristics of personhood. If it does, then it has a right to life. If it does not, then it is not a person and so may be painlessly killed. We do *not* need to consider the question of whether the child has a special relation to anyone who may have a special responsibility to see to the child's survival.

What I am calling the volunteerist thesis is confidently held by many contemporary Anglo-American philosophers. It is easy to see that the thesis is contrary to what Sidgwick called common sense. For it means that there is no such thing as filial duty per se, no such thing as the special duty of mother to child, and generally no such thing as a morality of special family or kinship relations. And this is contrary to what most people think. For most people think we do owe special debts to our parents even though we have not voluntarily assumed our obligations to them. Most people think that what we owe to our own children does not have its origin in any voluntary undertaking, explicit or implicit, that we have made to them, or to society at large, to care for them. And, preanalytically, many people believe we owe special consideration to our siblings even at times when we may not *feel* very friendly to them. But if there are no special duties, then most of these prima facie requirements are misplaced and without moral force and should be looked upon as archaic survivals to be ignored in assessing our moral obligations.

One highly counterintuitive consequence of treating the mother–child relationship as morally irrelevant was pointed out to me by Fred Sommers. Given Thomson's reasoning, there will be circumstances in which the child will have the moral right to kill its mother. Suppose that in the seventh month of pregnancy the mother is found to be harboring a life-threatening virus that is held at bay by the special immunities of pregnancy. The virus loses its potency after six weeks so if the mother carries the child to full term, she will be safe. On the other hand, the longer the child remains in the womb, the greater is its risk of being damaged by the virus. Enter now one of the Cohen's child agents who demands the immediate removal of the child by Caesarean section. Medically and morally it is now the mother who is in the position of the dependent violinist. It is she who is making use of the child's body. By exact parity of Thomson's reasoning we should have no alternative but to detach the mother from the child even where this would mean her certain death. Thomson's view that the mother and father who have not committed themselves to the care of their unborn child have no more responsibility to it than the woman to the violinist has another, less exotic but equally unpalatable, consequence. In many cases the father will want an abortion, while the woman goes ahead and has the child. Legally we expect the father to help support the child. But morally, by Thomson's argument, that is totally unfair since only the mother has the special responsibility.

The idea that to be committed to an individual is to have voluntarily made an implicit or explicit commitment to that individual is generally fatal to family morality. For it looks upon the network of felt obligation and expectation that binds family members as a sociological phenomenon without presumptive moral force. The social critics who hold this view of family obligation are usually aware that promoting it in public policy must further the disintegration of the traditional family unit as an institution. But whether they deplore the disintegration or welcome it, they are in principle bound to abet it.

The Special Duties

I am suggesting that radical disrespect for the morality of the family cave is today rationalized in a strong philosophical thesis about moral rights and moral requirements, a thesis that excludes requirements that would have the status of special duties and their correlative rights against particular individuals. I think it is clear that the special duties cannot be put into the procrustean bed of voluntary undertakings implicitly assumed by the individuals who must discharge them. Thomson's confident assertion that the mother has no special obligation to the child-person she is carrying in her womb must be looked upon as a dogmatic expression of the rejection of special duties and, moreover, as a dogma that violates our basic intuitions about what counts as a moral obligation. It may be that so many philosophers have accepted this dogma because of an uncritical use of the model of promises as the paradigm for obligations. If all obligations are like the obligation to keep a promise, then indeed they could not be incumbent on anyone who did not undertake to perform in a specified way. But there is no reason to take promises as paradigmatic of obligation. Indeed, the moral force of the norm of promise keeping has itself to be grounded in a theory of obligations that moral philosophers have yet to work out (Sommers, 1986).

Once we reject the doctrine that a voluntary act by the person concerned is a necessary condition of special obligation, we are free to respect the common-sense views that attribute moral force to many obligations associated with kinship and other family relationships. We may then accept the family as an institution that defines many special duties but is nevertheless imperfect in many respects. And we still face the choice of how, as social philosophers, we are to deal with these imperfections. That is, we have the choice of being liberal or conservative in our attitude toward reform.

The Burkean conservative would change little or nothing, believing that the historical development of an institution has its own wisdom. This person is opposed to utopian social engineering, considering it to be altogether immoral in the profound sense of destroying the very foundations of the special duties. But the Burkean is also opposed to what Karl Popper called piecemeal social engineering, which seeks to remedy practices that are unjust without destroying the institution that harbors them. For such a person believes on empirical grounds that reform is always dangerous; that it usually has unforeseen consequences worse than the original injustices one is trying to eliminate. The conservative is thus very much like the environmental conservationists in their attitude toward an ecological system. Their general advice is extreme caution or hands off.

The liberal is more optimistic about the consequences of reform. Like the conservative, the liberal believes that the norms of any tradition or institution that is not essentially unjust have prima facie moral force. And that means we can rely on our common-sense beliefs that the system of expectations within the family is legitimate and should be respected. The liberal will acknowledge that a brother has the right to expect more help from his brother than from a stranger and not just because of what the one has done for the other lately. And the case is the same for all the traditional expectations that characterize the family members. On the other hand, there may be practices within the family that are systematically discriminatory and unfair to certain members. Unlike the conservative, the liberal is prepared to do some piecemeal social engineering to remove injustice in the family.

A better defense of the special duties would require much more space than I can give it here (Sommers, 1986). I believe it can be made far more plausible than the rival theory that rejects the special duties. My main objective has been to raise the strong suspicion that the volunteer theory of obligation is a dogma very probably wrong and misconceived, and certainly at odds with common opinion.

The space that remains is largely devoted to a survey of some of the social consequences of applying radical theory to family obligation. I have suggested that, insofar as moral philosophers have any influence on the course of social history, their influence has recently been in aid of institutional disintegration. Here now is some indication of how the principled philosophical disrespect for common sense in the area of family morality has weakened the family and how this affects the happiness of its members. Much of what I say now is fairly well known. But it is useful to say it in the context of an essay that is critical of the radical way of doing moral philosophy. For there are periods in history when the radical way has great influence. And it is worth seeing what happens when Plato succeeds in Syracuse.

The Broken Family

The most dramatic evidence of the progressive weakening of the family is to be found in the statistics on divorce. Almost all divorce is painful and most divorce affects children. Although a divorce does not end but merely disrupts the life of the child, the life it disrupts is uncontroversially the life of a person who can be directly wronged by the actions of a moral agent. One might therefore expect that philosophers who are carefully examining the morality of abortion would also be carefully examining the moral grounds for divorce. But here, too, the contemporary reluctance of philosophers to deal with the special casuistry of family relations is in evidence. For example, there are more articles on euthanasia or on recombinant DNA research than on divorce.

Each year there are a million and a quarter divorces in the United States affecting over a million children. In 90 percent of the cases the mother is granted custody, although legally that is no longer a matter of course. There is very persuasive evidence that children of divorced parents are seriously and adversely affected. Compared with children from intact families, they are more often referred to school psychologists, are more likely to have lower IQ and achievement test scores, are more likely to be arrested, and need more remedial classes (Weitzman, 1985). Moreover, these effects show little correlation to economic class. Children in the so-called latency period, between 6 and 12, are the most seriously affected. In one study of children in this age group, half the subjects showed evidence of a "consolidation into troubled and conflicted depressive behavior patterns" (p. 452). Their behavior pattern included "continuing depression and low self-esteem, combined with frequent school and peer difficulties" (Skolnick and Skolnick, 1929).

One major cause for the difference between children from broken and intact families is the effective loss of the father. In the *majority* of cases the child has not seen its father within the past year. Only one child in six has seen the father in the past week; only 16 percent have seen their fathers in the past month; 15 percent see them once a year. The remaining 52 percent have had no contact at all for the past year. Although 57 percent of college-educated fathers see their children at least once a month, their *weekly* contact was the same as for all other groups (one in six) (Weitzman, 1985, 259).

It would be hard to show that the dismissive attitude of most contemporary moral philosophers to the moral force of kinship ties and conventional family roles has been a serious factor in contributing to the growth in the divorce rate. But that is only because it is so hard in general to show how much bread is baked by the dissemination of philosophical ideas. It is surely fair to say that the emphasis on autonomy and equality, when combined with the philosophical denigration of family ties, has helped to make divorce both easy and respectable, thereby facilitating the rapid change from fault-based to no-fault divorce. If contemporary moralists have not caused the tide of family disintegration, they are avidly riding it. On the other side, it is not hard to show that there is very little in recent moral philosophy that could be cited as possibly contributing to *stemming* the tide.

There has in the past two decades been a celebrated resurgence of interest in applied or practical ethics. It would appear, however, that the new enthusiasm for getting down to normative cases does not extend to topics of personal morality defined by family relationships. So the children who are being victimized by the breakdown of the family have not benefited from it. Indeed we find far more concern about the effect of divorce on children from philosophers of a generation or two ago, when divorce was relatively rare, than we find today. Thus Bertrand Russell writes:

> Husband and wife, if they have any love for their children, will so regulate their conduct as to give their children the best chance of a happy and healthy development. This may involve, at times, very considerable self-repression. And it certainly requires that both should realize the superiority of the claims of children to the claims of their own romantic emotions (1929, 236).

And while Russell is not opposed to divorce, he believes that children place great constraints on it. "Parents who divorce each other,

except for grave cause, appear to me to be failing in their parental duty" (p. 238).

The discerning and sensitive observer of a generation ago did not need masses of statistics to alert him to the effects of divorce on children. And it did not then take a professional philosopher (citing statistics gathered by a professional sociologist) to see that acting to dissolve a family must be evaluated morally primarily in terms of what this action means for the children.

Writing in the *London Daily Express* in 1930, Rebecca West says:

> The divorce of married people with children is nearly always an unspeakable calamity. It is only just being understood . . . how much a child depends for its healthy growth on the presence in the home of both its parents. . . . The point is that if a child is deprived of either its father or its mother it feels that it has been cheated out of a right. . . . A child who suffers from this resentment suffers much more than grief; he is liable to an obscuring of his vision, to a warping of his character.

She describes the harmful effects of divorce on children as effects of "a radiating kind, likely to travel down and down through the generations, such as few would care to have on their consciences."

West's remarks contrast sharply with what one typically finds in contemporary college texts. In a book called *Living Issues in Ethics*, Nolan and Kirkpatrick (1983) are discussing unhappy parents and the moral questions they face in contemplating divorce. "We believe that staying together for the sake of the children is worse than the feelings and adjustment of separation and divorce" (p. 147).

Further on, the authors give what they feel to be a decisive reason for this policy: "Remaining together in an irreconcilable relationship violates the norm of interpersonal love."

One of the very few philosophers to discuss the question of divorce and its consequences for children is Jeffrey Blustein in *Parents and Children* (1982). He looks with equanimity on the priority of personal commitment to parental responsibility, pointing out that "the traditional view . . . that the central duties of husband and wife are the . . . duties of parenthood is giving way to a conception of marriage as essentially involving a serious commitment between two individuals as individuals" (p. 230).

He also tells us (without telling us how he knows it) that children are worse off if their parents are unhappily married than if their parents are divorced. "Indeed it could be argued that precisely on account of the children the parents' unhappy marriage should be dissolved" (p. 232). The suggestion that parents who are unhappy should get a divorce "for the sake of the children" is *very* contemporary.

Now, to my knowledge, no reliable study has yet been made comparing children of divorced parents to children from intact families when parents do not get on well together. So I do not know whether the claims of these authors are true. Moreover, any such study would be compromised by some arbitrary measures of parental incompatibility and one could probably place little reliance on them. It is therefore easy to see that contemporary philosophers are anxious to jump to conclusions that would not render implausible their interesting view that the overriding question in considering a divorce is the compatibility of the parents, and the marital ties should be dissolved when they threaten or thwart the personal fulfillment of one or both of the marital partners.

These philosophers set aside special duties, replacing them with an emphasis on friendship, compatibility, and interpersonal love among family members. This has a disintegrative effect. For if what one owes to members of one's family is largely to be understood in terms of feelings of personal commitment, definite limits are placed on what one owes. For as feelings change, so may one's commitments, and the structure of responsibility within the family is permanently unstable. The correct balance between responsibility and feeling is illustrated in these remarks by A. I. Melden: "The fact that, normally, there is love and affection that unites the members of the family . . . in no way undercuts the fact that there is a characteristic distribution of rights and obligations within the family circle" (1977, 67).

I have, in this final section, been illustrating the indifference of contemporary philosophers to the family by dwelling on their indifference to the children affected by divorce. I hope it is clear that nothing I have said is meant to convey that I am opposed to divorce. I am not. Neither Russell nor West nor any of the sane and compassionate liberal thinkers of the recent past opposed divorce. But they did not play fast and loose with family mores, they did not encourage divorce, and they pointed out that moralists who are doing their job must insist that the system of family obligations is only partially severed by a divorce that cuts the marital tie. Morally, as well as legally, the obligations to the children remain as they were. Legally, this is still recognized. But in a moral climate where the system of family obligation is given no more weight than can be justified in terms of popular theories of deontic volunteerism, the obligatory ties are too fragile to survive the personal estrangements that result from divorce. It is therefore to be expected that the parents (and especially the fathers) will be off and away doing their own thing. And the law is largely helpless. To deplore the plight of the children and their mothers and to call it morally wrong is easy enough. It is far harder to acknowledge the irresponsible part that philosophers have been playing in setting these mothers and their children adrift.

I have no social solutions to the tragedy of economic impoverishment and social deprivation that results from the weakening of family ties. I believe in the right of divorce and am not even opposed to no-fault divorce. I do not know how to get back to the good old days when moral philosophers had the good sense to acknowledge the moral weight of special ties and the courage to condemn those who failed in them—the days when, in consequence, the *climate* of moral approval and disapproval was quite different from what it is today. I do not know how to make fathers ashamed of their neglect and inadvertent cruelty. What I do know is that moral philosophers ought to be paying far more attention to the social consequences of their views than they are. It is as concrete as taking care that what one says will not adversely affect the students whom one is addressing. If what students learn from us encourages social disintegration, then we are responsible for the effects that this may have on their lives and the lives of their children. It is a grave responsibility, even graver than the responsibility we take in being for or against something like euthanasia or capital punishment, since most of our students will not face that question in a practical way in their own lives.

I believe then that the responsible moral philosopher is liberal or conservative but not radical. He respects human relationships and traditions and the social environment in which he lives as much as he respects the natural environment and its ecology. He respects the family. William James saw the rejection of radicalism as central to the pragmatist way of confronting moral questions and settling the "true order of human obligations."

> The casuistic scale is made for the philosopher already far better than he can ever make it for himself. An experiment of the most searching kind has proved that the laws and usages of the land are what yield the maximum of satisfaction. . . . The presumption in cases of conflict must always be in favor of the conventionally recognized good. The philosopher must be a conservative, and in the construction of this casuistic scale must put the things most in accordance with the customs of the community on top (1948, 80).

A moral philosophy that does not give proper weight to the customs and opinions of the community is presumptuous in its attitude and pernicious in its consequences. In an important sense it is not a moral philosophy at all. For it is humanly irrelevant.

References

Blum, Lawrence. 1980. *Friendship, Altruism, and Morality.* London: Routledge and Kegan Paul.

Blustein, Jeffrey. 1982. *Parents and Children: The Ethics of the Family.* New York: Oxford University Press.

Cohen, Howard. 1980. *Equal Rights for Children.* Totowa, N.J.: Rowman and Littlefield.

De Beauvoir, Simone. 1952. *The Second Sex.* H. M. Parshley, trans. New York: Random House.

———. 1977. "Talking to De Beauvoir." In *Spare Rib.*

English, Jane. 1979. "What Do Grown Children Owe Their Parents?" In Onora O'Neill and William Ruddick, eds. *Having Children,* pp. 351–56. New York: Oxford University Press.

Ferguson, Ann. 1977. "Androgyny as an Ideal for Human Development." In M. Vetterling-Braggin, F. Elliston, and J. English, eds. *Feminism and Philosophy,* pp. 45–69. Totowa, N.J.: Rowman and Littlefield.

Gilligan, Carol. 1982. *In a Different Voice: Psychological Theory and Women's Development.* Cambridge: Harvard University Press.

Gould, Carol. 1983. "Private Rights and Public Virtues: Woman, the Family and Democracy." In Carol Gould, ed. *Beyond Domination,* pp. 3–18, Totowa, N.J.: Rowman and Allanheld.

Grimshaw, Jean. 1986. *Philosophy and Feminist Thinking.* Minneapolis: University of Minnesota Press.

Held, Virginia. 1983. "The Obligations of Mothers and Fathers." In Joyce Trebilcot, ed. *Mothering: Essays in Feminist Theory,* pp. 7–20. Totowa, N.J.: Rowman and Allanheld.

Hewlett, Sylvia Ann. 1986. *A Lesser Life: The Myth of Woman's Liberation in America.* New York: Morrow.

Jagger, Allison. 1977. "On Sex Equality." In Jane English, ed. *Sex Equality,* Englewood Cliffs, N.J.: Prentice-Hall.

———. 1983. "Human Biology in Feminist Theory: Sexual Equality Reconsidered." In Goud, ed. *Beyond Domination.*

———. 1986. "Prostitution." In Marilyn Pearsell, ed. *Women and Values: Readings in Recent Feminist Philosophy,* pp. 108–21. Belmont, Calif.: Wadsworth.

James, William. 1948. "The Moral Philosopher and the Moral Life." In *Essays in Pragmatism,* New York: Hafner.

Kittay, Eva, and Diana Meyers, eds. 1987. *Women and Moral Theory.* Totowa, N.J.: Rowman and Littlefield.

Melden, A. I. 1977. *Rights and Persons.* Los Angeles: University of California Press.

Noddings, Nel. 1984. *Caring: A Feminine Approach to Ethics and Moral Education.* Berkeley: University of California Press.

Nolan, R., and F. Kirkpatrick, eds. 1983. *Living Issues in Ethics.* Belmont, Calif.: Wadsworth.

Raymond, Janice. 1975. "The Illusion of Androgyny." *Quest: A Feminist Quarterly*, 2.

Richards, Jennifer Radcliffe. 1980. *The Skeptical Feminist*. Harmondsworth: Penguin.

Russell, Bertrand. 1929. *Marriage and Morals*. New York: Liveright.

Simmons, A. John. 1979. *Moral Principles and Political Obligation*. Princeton: Princeton University Press.

Skolnick, A., and J. Skolnick, eds. 1929. *Family in Transition*. Boston: Little, Brown.

Slote, Michael. 1979. "Obedience and Illusions." In O'Neill and Ruddick, eds. *Having Children*.

Sommers, Christina Hoff. 1986. "Filial Morality." *Journal of Philosophy*, 8.

Thomson, Judith. 1971. "A Defense of Abortion." *Philosophy and Public Affairs*, 1.

Tooley, Michael. 1972. "Abortion and Infanticide." *Philosophy and Public Affairs*, 2.

Trebilcot, Joyce, ed. 1984. *Mothering: Essays in Feminist Theory*. Totowa, N.J.: Rowman and Allanheld.

Wasserstrom, Richard. 1980. *Philosophy and Social Issues*. Notre Dame, Ind.: University of Notre Dame Press.

Weitzman, Lenore. 1985. *The Divorce Revolution: The Unexpected Social and Economic Consequences for Women and Children in America*. New York: Free Press.

West, Rebecca. 1930. "Divorce." *London Daily Express*.

Antigone's Daughters

Jean Bethke Elshtain

In this essay Jean Bethke Elshtain criticizes feminist writers of the last several decades who have sought to win a place for women in the corporate and governmental power structures as equal partners with men. This stance, she argues, inflates the value of the social activities and goods that men produce in the public sphere, while it devalues those traditionally produced by women in the private sphere. Elshtain sees a danger in enhancing the power of the bureaucratic state and weakening the counterbalancing power of the private sphere. Public bureaucracies operate according to an instrumental rationality using technical rules to efficiently utilize human and material resources, and this ethic forms the traditional male identity. Women's historical social identity, on the other hand, has been bound up with their roles as wives, mothers, and grandmothers and has supported the values of caring friendship, neighborly generosity, and responsible community membership. Elshtain champions a view of public life that incorporates the characteristics of the traditional feminine world. She argues that this can only be done by embracing the ideals and values of the women's social world as powerful and positive alternatives to the dominant values of the bureaucratic state. She offers the vision of an ethical polity based on the personal, empathetic, and loving qualities of the maternal role. Elshtain illustrates her conception of feminine civic virtue with Sophocles' story of Antigone. Antigone defies the decree of King Creon and insists on burying her slain brother as is required by family honor. For Antigone, long-standing family tradition takes precedence over public law. Elshtain counsels modern women, as Antigone's daughters, to bring the values of family and community life into the public sphere.

From Jean Bethke Elshtain, "Antigone's Daughters," *Democracy 2*, no. 2 (1982): 46–59. Reprinted by permission of Jean Bethke Elshtain.

This essay advances a note of caution. It argues that feminists should approach the modern bureaucratic state from a standpoint of skepticism that keeps alive a critical distance between feminism and statism, between female self-identity and a social identity tied to the public–political world revolving around the structures, institutions, values, and ends of the state. The basis for my caution and skepticism is a sober recognition that any political order in our time which culminates in a state is an edifice that monopolizes and centralizes power and eliminates older, less universal forms of authority; that structures its activities and implements its policies through unaccountable hierarchies; that erodes local and particular patterns of ethnic, religious, and regional identities; that standardizes culture, ideas, and ideals; that links portions of the population to it through a variety of dependency relationships; that may find it necessary or convenient to override civil liberties and standards of decency for raison d'état or executive privilege; and that, from time to time, commits its people to wars they have had neither the opportunity to debate fully nor the right to challenge openly.

For feminists to discover in the state the new "Mr. Right," and to wed themselves thereby, for better or for worse, to a public identity inseparable from the exigencies of state power and policy would be a mistake. This is a serious charge. I shall defend and develop my argument by considering the ways in which certain important feminist thinkers, at times somewhat casually and carelessly, have presumed the superiority of a particular sort of public identity over a private one. I shall trace out the logic of these arguments, indicating what a fully public identity for women would require, including the final suppression of traditional female social worlds. Finally, I shall reclaim for women a social identity that locates them very much in and of the wider world but positions them against overweening state power and public identity defined in its terms. My aim is to define and to defend a female identity and a feminist perspective that enables contemporary women to see themselves as the daughters of Antigone. To recognize that women as a group experience their social worlds differently from men as a group complicates feminist thinking, deepens female self-awareness, and calls attention to the complexity and richness of our social experiences and relations.

The feminist protest of the past several decades has largely concentrated on the ways—official and unofficial, ideological and practical—in which women have been excluded from equal participation in public life and equal share in official power in government and business. Responding to constraints that curbed their participation as citizens and limited expression of their individual autonomy, the end of feminist protest was conceived as the full incorporation of women into the power, privileges, and responsibilities of the public arena. The stated aim of the largest feminist political organization, the National Organization for Women (NOW), founded in October 1966, is to gain "truly equal partnership with men." To this end, NOW's Bill of Rights contains a list of proposals and demands required to attain such equal partnership. These demands include the establishment of government sponsored twenty-four-hour child-care centers, abortion on demand, equal pay for equal work, aggressive recruitment of women for top positions in all political and business hierarchies, and so on. Each demand requires action by the federal government to promote women's interests and to achieve NOW's version of sex equality. The presumption behind these demands, as stated by Betty Friedan's *The Feminine Mystique*, is that contemporary woman suffers a particular assault against her identity by being housebound; the man, however, with other "able, ambitious" fellows, enters the success-driven ethos of the American public world and keeps "on growing."[1] Friedan contrasts, and devalues, the activities and identities of women in their "comfortable concentration camps" with the exciting, fulfilling, and presumably worthwhile world of the successful professional male.[2] In her more recent *The Second Stage*, Friedan remains innocent of any intractable tensions between simultaneous commitments to full intimacy and mobile success on market terms. She evades any serious questioning of her rosy, upbeat feminist project by transcending (her favorite word) every conflict that poses an apparent clash of interests, values, or purposes, or that seems to present obstacles to her vision of feminism's "second stage."[3]

Liberal feminists have not been alone in urging that private woman join public man. Susan Brownmiller, a radical feminist, presumes that all the central features of the current male-dominated power structure will remain intact indefinitely; therefore, women must come to control these structures fifty-fifty. Armies, for instance,

> must be fully integrated, as well as our national guard, our state troopers, our local sheriffs' offices, our district attorneys' offices, our state prosecuting attorneys' offices—in short the nation's entire lawful power structure (and I mean power in the physical sense) must be stripped of male dominance and control—if women are to cease being a colonized protectorate of men.[4]

Women should prepare themselves for combat and guard duty, for militarized citizenship with a feminist face.

Similarly, one fundamental presumption underlying more deterministic modes of Marxist feminism is the insistence that women will never be "liberated" to join hands with those men whose identities bear the teleologic seed of the future revolutionary order—the proletariat—until they are sprung from the ghetto of the home and wholly absorbed in the labor force, there to acquire an overriding public identity as a member of the class of exploited workers. The realm of intimacy is recast, crudely, as the world of reproduction, an analogue of the productive process.

These moves to transform women into public persons, with a public identity that either primarily or exclusively defines them and takes precedence in cases of conflict with private lives, were embraced or implicitly adopted by the most widely disseminated statements of feminist politics. As a feminist project this ideology required "the absorption of the private as completely as possible into the public."[5] Women, formerly the private beings, would be "uplifted" to the status of a preeminently public identity to be shared equally with men. Though this overstates the case for emphasis, it reflects accurately the main thrust of feminist thought and practice—particularly that of mainstream, liberal feminism—from

the late 1960s through the 1970s. What was conspicuously missing from the discussion was any recognition of the potential dangers inherent in calling upon the state as an instrument for sexual emancipation. Concentrating only upon the good purposes to be served, feminists did not bring into focus the possibilities for enhanced powers of state surveilance and control of all aspects of intimate social relations.

In practice, the demand for a shift in the social identities of women involves their full assimilation into a combined identification with the state and the terms of competitive civil society, terms which have permeated all aspects of public life due to the close entanglements between government and corporations. The modern state, however, is the locus of structured, "legitimate" public life. It is this state feminists look to to intervene, to legislate, to adjudicate, to police and to punish on their behalf.

This process emerges in stark relief in an *amicus curiae* brief filed by NOW with the Supreme Court that argues that the all-male draft violates the constitutional rights of women. The brief asserts that "compulsory universal military service is central to the concept of citizenship in a democracy" and that women suffer "devastating long term psychological and political repercussions" because of their exclusion from such service.[6] Eleanor Smeal, president of NOW, insists that barring women from the military and from combat duty is based "solely on archaic notions of women's role in society."[7] Whatever one's position on women and the draft, NOW's stance and the stated defense for it embodies the conviction that women's traditional identities are so many handicaps to be overcome by women's incorporation into male public roles.

What all feminist protests that inveigh against women's continued identification with the private sphere share is the conviction that women's traditional identities were wholly forced upon them—that all women have been the unwitting victims of deliberate exclusion from public life and forced imprisonment in private life. That is, women were not construed as agents and historic subjects who had, in their private identities as wives, mothers, and grandmothers, played vital and voluntary roles as neighbors, friends, social benefactors, and responsible community members. Though these latter roles are not necessarily gender related, historically they have been associated with women. Holding up the public world as the only sphere within which individuals made real choices, exercised authentic power or had efficacious control, the private world, in turn, automatically reflected a tradition of powerlessness, necessity, and irrationality. The darker realities of the public world, with the notable exception of its exclusion of women, went unexplored just as the noble and dignified aspects of women's private sphere were ignored.*

Feminists who celebrated "going public" could point to the long history of the forced exclusion of women from political life and participation—whether the franchise, public office, or education and employment—as evidence that women's private identities were heavy-handed impositions by those with superior power. They could also recall a tradition of political thought in which great male theorists located women outside of, and frequently at odds with, the values and demands of politics and the sphere of public action. In contrast, another strain of feminist thought, best called "difference feminism," questioned the move towards full assimilation of female identity with public male identity and argued that to see women's traditional roles and activities as *wholly* oppressive was itself oppressive to women, denying them historic subjectivity and moral agency.[8] They could point to a first-person literature in which women defined and appropriated a particular female identity, rooted in private activities and relations, as a source of individual strength and social authority. They suggested that feminists should challenge rather than accept the present public world. And, rather than chastizing Western political thinkers for their failure to incorporate women into their scheme of things, why not question that very scheme with its

devaluation of the traditional world and ways of women?

At this point it is important to take the measure of that public identity into which "liberated" women are to be inducted. Contemporary American public identity is a far cry indeed from Jefferson's noble republican farmer or Lincoln's morally engaged citizen, the "last best hope on earth." Instead we find a public life, political and economic, marked by bureaucratic rationalization and culminating in the state's monopoly of authority in most vital fields of human activity. This process of rationalization and centralization, in the words of Brian Fay,

> refers to the process by which growing areas of social life are subjected to decisions made in accordance with technical rules for the choice between alternative strategies given some set of goals or values. The characteristic features of these sorts of decisions are the quantification of the relevant data, the use of formal decision procedures, and the utilization of empirical laws; all of these are combined to form an attitude of abstraction from the traditional qualitative, and historically unique features of a situation in order to settle the question at hand "objectively." This sort of instrumental rationality is intimately connected with control over the various factors at hand, such that, by the manipulation of certain variables in accordance with some plan, some goal is best achieved.[9]

The aims are efficiency and control and powerful bureaucracies have been set up to implement these aims. Bureaucrats operate in conformity to certain impersonal, abstract, and rational standards: this is the price of entry into the predominant public identity available to anyone, male or female. It is the world Hegel called "civil society," in which individuals treat others as means to some end and carry out actions to attain self-interest in public.

For women to identify fully with the present public order is for them to participate (and there is pathos if not tragedy in this) in the suppression of an alternative identity described by Dorothy Smith, a feminist sociologist, as "the concrete, the particular, the bodily," an identity with which women have traditionally been defined and within which, for better *and* worse, they have located them-

---

*My argument should not be taken as a denial that women, historically, *have* suffered in specific ways. It is, however, a denial that this suffering has been so total that women are reduced to the status of objects—whether in the name of feminism or in the name of defenses of male supremacy.

selves as social and historic beings.[10] This world, once taken for granted and now problematic, exists in contrast to the abstracted "mode of ruling," the ways of acting of the powerful. Women's historic social identity, at odds with extreme versions of abstract individualism, public-oriented behavior aimed at good for others but not reducible to interest for self. The problem, as Jane Bennett points out in a recent study, is that women, as the "exemplars/defenders of civic virtue," were pressed to sacrifice individual goals altogether in order to preserve "a particular type of public good."[11]

Feminist protest that seeks the elimination of this sphere of the concrete, particular, smaller social world—viewing only the sacrifices forced upon women, not the good attained by women—is one response to identities grown problematic under the pressures of social rationalization and modernization. A second response, where growth is a measure of the anger and despair of its adherents, is the militant reaffirmation of a rigid feminine identity, one that aims to leave all the political stuff to men who are better equipped for the task—ironically, of course, such feminine women are actively promoting this passive end. Somewhat lost in the cross-fire between these hostile camps is a third alternative, which I shall call "social feminism," that opposes the rush toward a technocratic order and an overweening public identity and repudiates, as well, the standpoint of ardent feminine passivity.

The third way, a feminist *via media,* begins with a female subject located within a world that is particular, concrete, and social, and attempts to see it through her eyes. If one begins in this way, one cannot presume, with the feminists I discussed earlier, that this world is automatically one from which all women should seek, or need, to be wholly liberated. The French feminist writer, Julia Kristeva, observed in an interview: "Feminism can be but one of capitalism's more advanced needs to rationalize."[12] Those feminisms that embrace without serious qualification the governing consciousness and norms of social organization of the current public world serve in precisely this way.

To sketch my alternative requires that I begin from the standpoint of women within their everyday reality. Is it possible to embrace ideals and values from the social world of women, severed from male domination and female subordination? I am convinced this is possible only by not viewing women's traditional identities as devoid of vitality, as being tainted by relations of domination. What follows is my effort to reclaim for women, construed as social actors in the world, an identity that pits them against the imperious demands of public power and contractual relations, one that might serve as a locus for female thinking, acting, and being as transformed by social feminist imperatives. This locus is not some solid rock, not an ontological definition of female "being"; rather, it is a series of overlapping intimations of a subject in the process of defining herself both with and against the available identities, public and private, of her epoch.

The female subject I have in mind is an identity-in-becoming, but she is located historically and grounded in tradition; she belongs to a heritage at least as old as Antigone's conflict with Creon. This powerful myth and human drama pits a woman against the arrogant insistencies of statecraft. Recall the story: the *dramatis personae* that matter for my purposes are Creon, King of Thebes, and his nieces, Antigone and her sister, Ismenê, daughters of the doomed Oedipus. Creon issues an order in the higher interests of state that violates the sacred familial duty to bury and honor the dead. Antigone, outraged, defies Creon. She defines their conflict with clarity and passion.

Listen, Ismenê:
Creon buried our brother Eteoclês
With military honors, gave him a soldier's
    funeral,
And it was right that he should; but Polyneicês,
Who fought as bravely and died as miserably,—
They say that Creon has sworn
No one shall bury him, no one mourn for him
But his body must lie in the fields, a sweet
    treasure
For carrion birds to find as they search for food.
That is what they say, and our good Creon is
    coming here
To announce it publicly; and the penalty—
Stoning to death in the public square
        There it is,
And now you can prove what you are:
A true sister, or a traitor to your family.[13]

Ismenê, uncomprehending, asks Antigone what she is going to do, and Antigone responds: "Ismenê, I am going to bury him. Will you come?" Ismenê cries that the new law forbids it. Women, she cries, cannot fight with men nor against the law and she begs "the Dead/To forgive me." But Antigone, determined, replies: "It is the dead, not the living, who make the longest demands." Harshly, she orders Ismenê off with the words: "I shall be hating you soon, and the dead will too," for what is worse than death, or what is the worst of deaths, is "death without honor." Later, Antigone proclaims, "There is no guilt in reverence for the dead" and "there are honors due all the dead." This primordial family morality precedes and overrides the laws of the state. Creon must be defied, for there are matters, Antigone insists, that are so basic they transcend raison d'état, one's own self-interest, even one's own life.

Creon's offense is his demand that political necessity justifies trampling upon a basic human duty, an imperative that lies at the heart of any recognizably human social life. In her loyalty to her slain brother and to family honor, Antigone asserts that there are matters of such deep significance that they begin and end where the state's right does not and must not run, where politics cannot presume to dictate to the human soul. In "saving" the state, Creon not only runs roughshod over a centuries-old tradition, he presumes to override the familial order, the domain of women. In refusing to accept raison d'état as paramount, Antigone sets the course for her rebellion and pits the values of family and particular loyalties, ties, and traditions against the values of statecraft with its more abstract obligations. In her rebellion, Antigone is as courageous, honorable, and determined as Creon is insistent, demanding, and convinced of the necessity of his public decree.

Sophocles honors Antigone in her rebellion. He sees no need to portray a chastened Antigone, having confronted Creon but having failed to sway him, finally won over to the imperatives of raison d'état, yielding at last to Creon's fears of law-breakers and anarchy. Strangely, Antigone has not emerged as a feminist heroine. It is equally strange that a magisterial Greek thinker who would elimi-

nate altogether the standpoint of Antigone is sometimes honored by feminists for his "radical" rearrangements without apparent regard to gender. I refer to Plato of *The Republic,* a Plato dedicated to eradicating and devaluing private homes and particular intimate attachments (principally for his Guardian class). Such private loyalties and passions conflicted with single-minded devotion to the city. Plato cries: "Have we any greater evil for a city than what splits it and makes it many instead of one? Or a greater good than what binds it together and makes it one?"[14]

To see in Plato's abstract formulation for rationalized equality (for that minority of men and women who comprise his Guardian class) a move that is both radical and feminist is to accept public life and identity as, by definition, superior to private life and identity. Indeed, it is to concur in the wholesale elimination of the private social world to attain the higher good of a state without the points of potential friction and dissent private loyalties bring in their wake. This view accepts Plato's conviction that "private wives" are a potentially subversive element within the city. Plato cannot allow women their own social location, for that would be at odds with his aim for a unified city. Instead, he provides for women's participation under terms that deprivatize them and strip them of the single greatest source of female psychological and social power in fifth- and fourth-century Athens—their role in the household; their ties with their children. Effectively, he renders their sexual identities moot. In whose behalf is this dream of unity, and female public action, being dreamed?

The question of female identity and the state looks very different if one picks up the thread of woman's relationship to public power from the standpoint of an Antigone; if one adopts the sanctioned viewpoint of the handful of thinkers whose works comprise the canon of the Western political tradition; or if one tells the tale through the prism of unchecked realpolitik, from astride the horse of the warrior, or from the throne of the ruler. The female subject, excluded from legitimate statecraft unless she inherited a throne, is yet an active historic agent, a participant in social life who located the heart of her identity in a world bounded by the demands of necessity, sustaining the values of life-giving and preserving.

This sphere of the historic female subject generated its own imperatives, inspired its own songs, stories, and myths. It was and is, for many if not all, the crucible through which sustaining human relations and meaning are forged and remembered. It is easy to appreciate both the fears of traditionalists and the qualms of radicals at the suppression of this drama of the concrete and the particular in favor of some formal–legalistic, abstract "personhood," or to make way for the further intrusion of an increasingly technocratic public order. To wholly reconstruct female social identity by substituting of those identities available through the public order would be to lose the standpoint of Antigone, the woman who throws sand into the machinery of arrogant public power.

But how does one hold on to a social location for contemporary daughters of Antigone without simultaneously insisting that women accept traditional terms of political quiescence? The question answers itself: the standpoint of Antigone is of a woman who dares to challenge public power by giving voice to familial and social imperatives and duties. Hers is not the world of the *femme couverte*, the delicate lady, or the coy sex-kitten. Hers is a robust voice, a bold voice: woman as guardian of the prerogatives of the *oikos*, preserver of familial duty and honor, protector of children, if need be their fierce avenger. To recapture that voice and to reclaim that standpoint, and not just for women alone, it is necessary to locate the daughters of Antigone where, shakily and problematically, they continue to locate themselves: in the arena of the social world where human life is nurtured and protected from day to day. This is a world women have not altogether abandoned, though it is one both male-dominant society and some feminist protest have devalued as the sphere of "shitwork," "diaper talk," and "terminal social decay." This is a world that women, aware that they have traditions and values, can bring forward to put pressure on contemporary public policies and identities.

Through a social feminist awareness, women can explore, articulate, and reclaim this world. To reaffirm the standpoint of Antigone for our own time is to portray women as being able to resist the imperious demands and overweening claims of state power when these run roughshod over deeply rooted values. Women must learn to defend without defensiveness and embrace without sentimentality the perspective that flows from their experiences in their everyday material world, "an actual local and particular place in the world."[15] To define this world simply as the "private sphere" in contrast to "the public sphere" is to mislead. For contemporary Americans, "private" conjures up images of narrow exclusivity. The world of Antigone, however, is a *social* location that speaks of, and to, identities that are unique to a particular family, on the one hand; but, on another and perhaps even more basic level, it taps a deeply buried human identity, for we are first and foremost not political or economic man but family men and women. Family imagery goes deep and runs strong, and all of us, for better or worse, sporadically or consistently, have access to that imagery, for we all come from families even if we do not go on to create our own. The family is that arena that first humanizes us or, tragically, damages us. The family is our entry point into the wider social world. It is the basis of a concept of the social for, as Hegel recognized, "the family is a sort of training ground that provides an understanding of another-oriented and public-oriented action."[16]

What is striking about political theory in the Western tradition is the very thin notion of the social world so much of that theory describes. All aspects of social reality that go into making a person what he or she is fall outside the frame of formal, abstract analyses. In their rethinking of this tradition, many feminist thinkers, initially at least, locked their own formulations into an overly schematic public–private dichotomy, even if their intention was to challenge or to question it.[17] Those feminists who have moved in the direction of "social feminism" have, in their rethinking of received categories, become both more historical and more interpretive in their approach to social life. One important female thinker whose life and work form a striking contrast to the classical vision and to overly rigid feminist renderings of the public and private, particularly those who disdain anything that smacks of the traditionally "feminine," is Jane Addams. Addams embodies the standpoint of Antigone. A woman with a powerful public identity and following, who wielded enormous political power and influence, Addams's life work was neither grandly public nor narrowly private. Instead, she expressed the combined values of centuries of domestic tradition, and the dense and heady concoction of women's needs, and she brought these to bear on a political world that held human life very cheap indeed.

Addams recognized, in uncritical celebrations of heroic male action, a centuries-long trail of tears. What classical political theorists dismissed as ignoble—the sustenance of life itself—Addams claimed as truly heroic. Rather than repudiating human birth and the world surrounding it as a possible source of moral truth and political principle, Addams spoke from the standpoint of the "suffering mothers of the disinherited," of "women's haunting memories," which, she believed, "instinctively challenge war as the implacable enemy of their age-long undertaking."[18] At one point she wrote:

Certainly the women in every country who are under a profound imperative to preserve human life, have a right to regard this maternal impulse as important now as the compelling instinct evinced by primitive woman long ago, when they made the first crude beginnings of society by refusing to share the vagrant life of man because they insisted upon a fixed abode in which they might cherish their children. Undoubtedly women were then told that the interests of the tribe, the diminishing food supply, the honor of the chieftain, demanded that they leave their particular caves and go out in the wind and weather without regard to the survival of their children. But at the present moment the very names of the tribes and of the honors and the glories which they sought are forgotten, while the basic fact that the mothers held the lives of their children above all else, insisted upon staying where the children had a chance to live, and cultivate the earth for their food, laid the foundations of an ordered society.[19]

A feminist rethinking of Addams's category of the social, resituating it as an alternative to privatization and public self-interestedness, would allow us to break out of the rigidities into which current feminist discourse has fallen. Seeing human beings through the prism of a many-layered, complex social world suffused with diverse goods, meanings, and purposes opens up the possibility for posing a transformed vision of the human community against the arid plain of bureaucratic statism. This communitarian ideal involves a series of interrelated but autonomous social spheres. It incorporates a vision of human solidarity that does not require uniformity and of cooperation that permits dissent. The aim of all social activity would be to provide a frame within which members of a diverse social body could attain both individual and communal ends and purposes, without, however, presuming some final resolution of these ends and purposes; a social world featuring fully public activities at one end of a range of possibilities and intensely private activities at the other.

If this communal ideal is to be claimed as a worthy ideal for our time, a first requirement is a feminist framework that locates itself in the social world in such a way that our current public, political realities can be examined with a critical and reflective eye. One alternative feminist perspective, a variation on both "difference" and "social" feminism that helps us to do this is called "maternal thinking" by its author, Sara Ruddick.[20] According to Ruddick, mothers have had a particular way of thinking that has largely gone unnoticed—save by mothers themselves. That is, women in mothering capacities have developed intellectual abilities that wouldn't otherwise have been developed; made judgments they wouldn't otherwise have been called upon to make; and affirmed values they might not otherwise have affirmed. In other words, mothers engage in a discipline that has its own characteristic virtues and errors and that involves, like other disciplines, a conception of achievement. Most important for the purposes of feminist theory, these concepts and ends are dramatically at odds with the prevailing norms of our bureaucratic, and increasingly technological, public order.

Ruddick claims that one can describe maternal practices by a mother's interest in the preservation, the growth, and the social acceptability of her child. These values and goods may conflict, for preservation and growth may clash with the requirements for social acceptability. Interestingly, what counts as a failure within the frame of maternal thinking, excessive control that fails to give each unique child room to grow and develop, is the *modus operandi* of both public and private bureaucracies. Were maternal thinking to be taken as the base for feminist consciousness, a wedge for examining an increasingly over-controlled public world would open up immediately. For this notion of maternal thought to have a chance to flourish as it is brought to bear upon the larger world, it must be transformed in and through social feminist awareness.

To repeat: the core concepts of maternal achievement put it at odds with bureaucratic manipulation. Maternal achievement requires paying a special sort of attention to the concrete specificity of each child; it turns on a special kind of knowledge of this child, this situation, without the notion of seizure, appropriation, control, or judgment by impersonal standards. What maternal thinking could lead to, though this will always be problematic as long as mothers are socially subordinated, is the wider diffusion of what attentive love to all children is about and how it might become a wider social imperative.

Maternal thinking opens up for reflective criticism the paradoxical juxtapositions of female powerlessness and subordination, in the overall social and political sense, with the extraordinary psycho-social authority of mothers. Maternal thinking refuses to see women principally or simply as victims, for it recognizes that much good has emerged from maternal practices and could not if the world of the mother were totally destructive. Maternal thinking transformed by feminist consciousness, hence aware of the binds and constraints imposed on mothers, including the presumption that women will first nurture their sons and then turn them over for sacrifice should the gods of war demand human blood, offers us a mode of reflection that links women to the past yet offers up hope of a future. It makes contact with the strengths of our mothers and grandmothers; it helps us to see ourselves as Antigone's daughters, determined, should it be necessary, to chasten arrogant public power and resist the claims of political necessity. For such power, and such claims, have, in the past, been weapons used to trample upon the deepest yearnings and most basic hopes of the human spirit.

Maternal thinking reminds us that public policy has an impact on real human beings. As public policy becomes increasingly impersonal, calculating, and technocratic, maternal thinking insists that the reality of a single human child be kept before the mind's eye. Maternal thinking, like Antigone's protest, is a rejection of amoral statecraft and an affirmation of the dignity of the human person.

Notes

1. Betty Friedan, *The Feminine Mystique* (New York: Dell Books, 1974), p. 201.

2. Ibid., p. 325.

3. Betty Friedan, *The Second Stage* (New York: Summit Books, 1981).

4. Susan Brownmiller, *Against Our Will: Men, Women and Rape* (New York: Simon and Schuster, 1975), p. 388.

5. Robert Paul Wolff, "There's Nobody Here But Us Persons," in Carol Gould and Marx Wartofsky, eds., *Women and Philosophy* (New York: G.P. Putnam, 1976), pp. 140–41.

6. Linda Greenhouse, "Women Join Battle on All-Male Draft," *New York Times*, March 22. 1981, p. 19. We do have plenty of evidence on the devastating damage done men and women who served in a variety of capacities in Vietnam.

7. Ibid.

8. Examples of "difference feminism" include: Carol Gilligan, "In a Different Voice: Women's Conception of Self and Morality," *Harvard Educational Review* 47 (1977), pp. 481–517; some of the essays in the volumes *Women, Culture and Society,* ed. Michelle Rosaldo and Louise Lamphere (Stanford University Press, 1974); and *Discovering Reality: Feminist Perspectives on Epistemology, Metaphysics, Methodology and the Philosophy of Science* (Amsterdam: Dordrecht-Reidel, 1982).

9. Brian Fay, *Social Theory and Political Practice* (London: George Allen and Unwin, 1975), p. 44.

10. Dorothy E. Smith, "A Sociology for Women," in *The Prism of Sex: Essays in the Sociology of Knowledge,* ed. Julia A. Sterman and Evelyn Torton Beck (Madison, Wisconsin: University of Wisconsin Press, 1979), pp. 135–188.

11. Jane Bennett, "Feminism and Civic Virtue," unpublished paper (1981).

12. Julia Kristeva, "Women Can Never Be Defined," in Elaine Marks and Isabelle de Courtivron, eds., *New French Feminisms: An Anthology* (Amherst: University of Massachusetts Press, 1980), p. 141.

13. Sophocles, *The Oedipus Cycle,* "Antigone," trans. Dudley Fitts and Robert Fitzgerald (New York: Harvest Books, 1949), p. 186.

14. Plato, *The Republic,* trans. Allan Bloom (New York: Basic Books, 1968), Book V/460E–462D, p. 141.

15. Smith, "A Sociology for Women," p. 168.

16. Bennett, "Feminism and Civic Virtue."

17. I consider myself guilty on this score. See one of my earlier formulations on the public–private dilemma, "Moral Woman/Immoral Man: The Public/Private Distinction and Its Political Ramifications," *Politics and Society* 4 (1974), pp. 453–473. I try to restore a richness this initial foray dropped out in *Public Man, Private Woman: Women in Social and Political Thought* (Princeton: Princeton University Press, 1981).

18. Jane Addams, *The Long Road of Woman's Memory* (New York: MacMillan Co., 1916), p. 40.

19. Ibid., pp. 126–27.

20. Sara Ruddick, "Maternal Thinking," typescript. A shortened version has appeared in *Feminist Studies* (Summer 1980), but I draw upon the original full-length draft.

Feminist Theory and the Democratic Community

Carol C. Gould

In the past women experienced the social order from their unique position in the private sphere of family life and community relations. Feminist theorists are now using this experience to reformulate political theory to eliminate the injustices allowed by traditional democratic theory and to bring the virtues of the private sphere into the public domain. In this essay Carol Gould assesses feminist contributions to a reconstructed political philosophy that derives from two areas of women's experience: domination by men and their maternal relations of care. She first presents her reinterpretation of democratic theory. Personal liberty in Gould's theory requires freedom of self-development, which in turn depends on each individual's access to the conditions for exercising agency and effecting choices. Democracy, then, requires that each citizen have an equal right to participate in making decisions about common projects and activities. Gould believes that as citizens engage in these activities, they build relationships of reciprocal respect that constitute a democratic community. She then analyzes domination, distinguishing it from conditions of unequal power. Feminists have recast political theory in a way that would prevent one individual or group from dominating any other. In the second and larger half of her essay Gould assesses the care ethic of maternal experience to find aspects that can be transferred to the public domain. She recommends three features of the care model: concern for the individuality and differences of particular others, cooperative reciprocity that can form a vision of the common good, and concern for the vulnerable members of the community. However, Gould argues that the care ethic has serious limitations as a model for a democratic community. Among these limitations are that care is a nonreciprocal relationship, whereas the relationships between citizens are primarily reciprocal, that the affection between friends and intimates is not appropriate in citizen relations, and that the preferences for particular individuals necessary in personal relationships would translate into an unfair bias in public life.

From Carol C. Gould "Feminism and Democratic Community Revisited," in *NOMOS XXXV: Democratic Community,* John Chapman and Ian Shapiro, eds. (New York: New York University Press, 1993). © 1993 New York University. Reprinted by permission of New York University Press.

What contribution can feminist theory make to the conception of a democratic community? In recent years, feminists have drawn on women's experiences as the basis for a reconstructed political theory. They have sought to revise or replace the models of contract, or of the marketplace, or of formal justice with alternative models derived from the relations of care and mothering and from women's experiences of inequality and domination.[1] Some feminist theorists have also put in question what they regard as a prevailing Western model of rationality, sometimes characterized as logocentric, which they see as underlying the political conceptions. But there have been few attempts to articulate the connection between feminism and that important part of political philosophy that may be characterized as democratic theory.

Democracy and Democratic Community

To assess the feminist contributions to democratic theory, it will be helpful to operate with a basic normative conception of democracy to which these ideas can be shown to be relevant. It is no longer necessary, however, to hark back to the classical liberal theory of democracy to show how it ought to be transformed. Such a development has already taken place, in diverse but related ways, in the work of recent theorists like C. B. Macpherson, Carole Pateman, Jane Mansbridge, and Benjamin Barber.[2] In this context, I prefer to make use of the construction of the transformed theory of democracy that I develop in my book *Rethinking Democracy*,[3] particularly since it already reflects the contribution of feminist themes to some of the basic political norms. In fact, it was an early and ongoing concern with the critique of domination, with the idea of individual and gender difference in the critique of abstract universality, and with the nature of social relations—all of these partly defined in feminist terms, as well as in contexts of social theory more generally—that led to my conviction about the central importance of democratic theory in critical social philosophy.[4]

To put it briefly, the central constitutive idea of the conception of democracy that I develop is that of equal rights of participation in decision-making about common projects and common activities. This equal right is grounded in equal positive freedom, that is, an equal right to the conditions of self-development. Positive freedom goes beyond negative freedom, as freedom from constraint, in focusing on access to, or the availability of, means or conditions for exercising agency and effecting one's choices, and through this enabling the differentiated development of individuals. I argue that individuals have prima facie equal rights to the conditions of such self-development on the grounds of their equal agency as human beings, however differently each exercises it. This requires reciprocal recognition by each agent of the other's equal agency. One of the main conditions for self-development is common or joint activity in which people act together to achieve shared ends. Therefore, in contexts of common activity, the principle of equal positive freedom entails equal rights to participate in decision-making about common activity and its ends, since otherwise some would be deciding for others about the course of their agency and would be denying them the exercise of their freedom as self-development. But equal rights to participate in decision-making concerning the common activities is precisely the core of democracy. Further, since these contexts of common activities oriented to shared ends are characteristic not only of political institutions but also of economic and social ones more generally, it follows that democratic decision-making is required in these contexts as well.

As to the communal nature of democracy, we may say that democracy presupposes community in a minimal sense, namely, that agents in a democratic institution have a common interest in shared ends, in pursuit of which their cooperation is voluntary and not merely constrained by law or habit, or effected by coercion. That is, democratic community is constituted by the decisions of agents to engage in the determination of shared ends and free cooperation towards these ends. But I would like to maintain a distinction between a democratic community in this sense and the more organic and tradition- or culture-defined notions of community implied by Tonnies' concept of *Gemeinschaft* or by contemporary communitarian ideas. The issue of whether social relations of care or mutual concern or support are requirements of a democratic community needs further analysis and bears directly on the impact of feminism on the concept of democratic community.

Beyond Domination: Women's Experience and Democratic Community

A major area of women's experience that is clearly relevant to democratic community is domination. Unequal power is one thing and domination another. Though this may be a minor point of difference, there would seem to be a distinction between having less or greater power than another to effect one's ends and exercising power over another for one's ends. For example, we may say that a parent has more power than the child, but it does not follow by virtue of this alone that the parent stands in a relation of domination toward the child. Unequal power is a necessary but not a sufficient condition for domination.

A description of unequal power omits reference to the social relations of domination between men and women in personal contexts or through the functioning of institutions. Domination, as distinguished from coercion on the one hand and unequal power on the other, involves control or delimitation of the actions of another through control over the conditions of action, objective or subjective. Such domination is not necessarily fully conscious or deliberate, and may be implicit in the way certain social institutions or customs operate. Of course, many of the relations between men and women are not characterized by domination, but it remains a serious problem nonetheless, which tends to be slid over if described only in terms of inequalities of power.

The critique of domination presupposes a norm of equal freedom and a requirement of reciprocal recognition of equal agency. That is, individuals have equal rights to exercise their agency, in the development of their

capacities and the pursuit of long term projects. This entails a prima facie equal right to the conditions for such activity and requires recognition by others of these rights.[5] Though this much follows directly from the critique of domination, what may be less obvious is how this critique bears on the requirement for democracy. Equal agency, presupposed by the critique of domination, entails in general an equal right of self-determination of one's activity, within the constraints of respect for these equal rights of others. And where one's activity is common and shared, as it would be in a polity, or in economic or social institutions, it entails an equal right to participate in joint decision-making concerning this activity. But this is in effect the requirement for democracy. If, by contrast, others determine the range or direction of one's activity, or control the conditions necessary for carrying out that activity, whether this activity is individual or shared as in the institutional contexts of social, economic or political life, then this is, in one degree or another, a case of domination in the exercise of unequal power. It may in a certain sense seem obvious that the critique of domination, of which women's experience is a paradigmatic case, maps on to an institutional requirement for democracy, but the intrinsic relation between these concepts is not often articulated.

These implications for democracy of the norm of equal freedom implicit in the critique of domination also bear on the question of individual rights, that is, on the protection of individuals from interference with their liberties or from domination, either by other individuals or by the community as a whole, that is, negative liberties and rights. And it also suggests the need for certain positive rights. For if individuals are to be equally free, their basic freedom of choice needs to be protected by civil liberties and political rights from undue interference; and their power to effect their choices needs to be supported by positive rights to the conditions for their agency.

This view conflicts with the position recently taken by some feminists that rights-based theories of ethics and politics are misguided and ought to be replaced by theories based on caring and particular obligations. A care perspective, they argue, emerges from women's experience, in contrast to the rights and justice perspective held to be drawn from men's experience in the public sphere. Whatever the merits of this emphasis on care, which I will consider shortly, I would argue that some conception of equal rights is both implicit in the critique of domination and essential to the justification of democracy. In this way, preservation or further development of an approach that includes rights should not be abandoned by feminist theorists. Such an approach to rights may well need to be developed beyond traditional liberal conceptions.

Likewise, the principle of equal positive freedom, which is implied in the critique of domination, constitutes a principle of distributive justice, namely, that individuals have prima facie equal rights to the conditions necessary for their differentiated self-development. Thus, justice, which has been denigrated as the male gender-coded value in social and political theory, may itself be seen to have a source in the critique of domination that grows out of women's experience.

This interpretation supports not only a norm of equal rights but one of reciprocity as well. By reciprocity I mean a relation characterized by a shared understanding and free agreement that the actions of each individual with respect to the other(s) are equivalent. However, the form of reciprocity that I have in mind goes beyond what I have called instrumental reciprocity or what has been characterized by others as return for benefit done or as "tit for tat." This is the externalized form of a relation stripped of its richer aspects. Rather, the reciprocity that I believe grows out of the feminist critique of domination is an intentional relation of reciprocal recognition in which each recognizes the other as free and self-developing, hence as unique.[6]

This mode of reciprocity is most obviously applicable to face to face relations among individuals. But something like this may also be seen to be an essential feature of a democratic decision process in which each agent affords the other reciprocal recognition as a free and distinctive individual, and in which their differences are respected. Respect for differences may take two correlative forms: first, those individual differences that are irrelevant to the decision process—typically, in political

contexts, race, sex, religion, etc.—are respected by being treated as indifferent to it and therefore as not subject to discrimination; and second, those individual differences that *are* relevant to the decision process, that is, differences in judgments or beliefs, are respected by affording full freedom of such difference in the deliberative and decision procedure.[7]

The relation of reciprocity is most obviously characteristic of participatory democratic processes. But it applies to other modes of democratic deliberation and decision-making as well. In representative contexts, recognition of equal political rights and liberties—voting, eligibility for office, free speech, etc.—entails tacit, if not explicit, recognition by each citizen of the other's equal rights. However, I wish to distinguish this sort of reciprocity from that which is sometimes adduced of the care and mothering relation. This latter is a more problematic sense of reciprocity for politics, as I shall note later.

These reflections bear on the import of the feminist critique of domination for questions of individual freedom and rights. Some feminists, however, have criticized such an emphasis as implying an atomistic conception of individuals,[8] which in turn suggests an adversarial model of democracy. But this interpretation of freedom and equal rights seems to me mistaken. And it would be a further mistake to suggest that an emphasis on individual freedom and equal rights entails an atomistic conception of democracy. In fact, the slide from individual freedom and rights to atomic or abstract individualism may derive from a kind of dichotomous thinking that sees individuals and relations, or again justice and care, as mutually exclusive categories rather than as closely related aspects of a complex social reality. By contrast, I have argued that the basic entities that make up social life should be construed as individuals-in-relations or social individuals;[9] and that justice and care are complementary, rather than conflicting frameworks.[10] Moreover, emphasis on individual freedom and equal rights, when so understood, certainly does not entail an atomistic or adversarial conception of democracy, but in fact is entirely congruent with the concept of democratic community.

The concept of democratic community goes beyond the traditional and thinner notion of democracy as simply a matter of political representation and equal voting rights. This is most often understood as a mediation of individual differences or interests, that is, a fair method of adjudicating among them. Although it is compatible with a notion of a common interest, at least in an aggregative sense, and presupposes a minimal procedural common interest, liberal democratic theory stops short of a notion of community. By contrast, the very notion of equal rights of participation in shared decision-making concerning common activity connotes a common interest in the common activity, as well as in the process of decision-making concerning that activity. In effect, if unequal power and domination are to be replaced by a norm of equal freedom, or power, and shared authority, then relations among the individuals engaged in this process are just those relations that constitute a community, namely, reciprocal recognition and respect for individual difference and freely joined cooperation towards common ends. In this sense too, then, one consequence of thinking through the contribution of women's experience in the context of the critique of domination and of unequal power is a notion of democracy as involving community and not merely a mediation of differences.

Is Care an Adequate Model of Democratic Community?

The second major domain of women's experience that has increasingly been adduced as a normative model for ethics and politics is that of care, especially as it relates to the practice of mothering.[11] Care is held to encompass a range of characteristic dispositions, such as concern for the other not out of duty or obligation but out of feeling or sympathy; attention or attentiveness; sensitivity to the needs of others, and more strongly, taking the others' interests as equal to or more important than one's own; concern for the growth and enhancement of the other; and an orientation to the common interest of the family or of

those who are close or related to one. These feelings and dispositions are directed to particular others rather than universally, and so contrast with traditional notions of universal and impartial principles and obligations. Although some of the feminist literature associates these characteristics exclusively with a gender-defined experience of mothering, some feminists, including Mansbridge,[12] rightly see these features as not exclusively gender-related—and therefore I would say perhaps better characterized as related to parenting—although it is clear that the culturally dominant expression of these traits has heretofore been identified with the role and experience of women.

The presumption is that these experiences lend support to notions of community and hence to a richer conception of democracy. The question is how to interpret these dispositions of caring and attentiveness and the concern with the common interest of the family for the case of democracy. In one sense this seems obvious: These ways of expressing concern for others and for their needs that characterize the relation of care in intimate personal relations and in certain familial relations would seem to match the democratic community's requirement for relations of reciprocity and especially for reciprocal respect, though not all relations of care are reciprocal, as I shall discuss below. Further, the notion of a common interest seems to be easily extrapolated from the commonality of family feeling to a larger polity or community.

Indeed, the elements of what I have called democratic personality include just such features as a disposition to reciprocity, and receptivity or attentiveness to the views of others.[13] Further, a shared or common interest provides both the context for democratic decision-making and is also elaborated in the process of deliberation.[14] I think that the experience of caring and concern that is characteristically taken as women's facilitates an awareness of common interest that is fundamental to the possibility of a democratic community. In addition, I also believe that the typical concern for providing for the specific needs of others associated with mothering or parenting or with family relations more generally can usefully be imported into the larger democratic community in terms of a focus on meeting the differentiated needs of individuals and not simply protecting their negative liberties. Thus, care in this context translates into responsiveness to the particular needs and interests of individuals or groups instead of treating them all in the very same way. It also connotes a concern for providing the economic and social means for the development of individuals and not only refraining from impeding their choices. So far so good.

However, the notion of care as a model for democratic community has serious limitations. But to deal with them, I think it important to draw some distinctions in the concept of care that have been overlooked in the feminist discussion. In the recent literature, the idea of care seems to be drawn mainly from two sources or models, which are most often blended together. However, important differences exist between them, even though they are related. The first of these sources is mothering or parenting, in which care manifests itself largely as nurturance or concern for the vulnerable child and for its development. Care in this sense of nurturance is nonreciprocal, because in this relation, the parent takes care of the young child but, at this stage at least, the child is not in a position reciprocally to take care of the parent, even though they reciprocally care *about* each other and reciprocally adjust their responses to each other. The child is initially utterly dependent on the parent and the parent provides for, teaches, and has responsibility for the child. Of course, as Virginia Held points out, the mothering relation is aimed at raising an equal in the child so that the relation with the child becomes reciprocal with maturation;[15] and it is already reciprocal in that parent and child love each other. But *qua* mothering or parenting, the care is nonreciprocal. A somewhat related context of nonreciprocal relation is care for others who are vulnerable or dependent by virtue of their weakness, illness, or deprivation. Here, common models are nursing and welfare.

The nonreciprocal relation of care as nurturance may be characterized as a case of benign nonreciprocity by contrast with what we might call malignant nonreciprocity. The latter refers to nonreciprocal relations of domination or exploitation, in which one controls the actions of another and thus inhibits the

other's freedom or benefits at the other's expense.

The second main source for the feminist concept of care is that of love or intimate personal relation, which entails, ideally, a reciprocal or mutual concern of each for the other. Feminist theorists have most often interpreted this as involving mutuality, in a sense that connotes not only reciprocal recognition of the individuality of the other and respect for the other's needs, but beyond this, enhancement by each of the other, by altruistic actions. The distinction between the two models of care based on these two rather different sources—mothering and love—has largely been disregarded in the literature. But it remains a significant distinction between a nonreciprocal and a reciprocal relation.

Where care involves a reciprocal relation, as in the case of love or intimate personal connection, we need a further distinction between the strong case of mutuality, as a relation in which each individual consciously undertakes to enhance the other, and the more minimal model of care involved in social reciprocity or the reciprocity of respect. In this latter type of reciprocity, each recognizes the distinctive individuality of the other and has concern for the differences in the other's needs, and for their satisfaction. We have a relation of sympathy or understanding of the other but not yet the active engagement in enhancing the other that characterizes mutuality. A relation of reciprocal sympathy and understanding, or concern for the other, is clearly a feature of the relation of love or indeed of friendship. But it may also characterize a social relation among members of a community who are neither lovers nor friends. For example, among members of a tribal or ethnic or political community, there may be relations of such reciprocal sympathy, as a type of care.

In addition to the two sources for the conception of care, the maternal and the love relation, one should mention a third source for this concept in the feminist literature. This is the family as a model of common concern or a common good that relates all of the members to each other.* In addition to caring for each other, as in the case of love, on this model they are bound by a common interest in the well-

*By family here, I do not exclusively mean family by marriage or in terms of blood relations.

being of the family unit that is not identical with the care they have for each other as individuals. In such a case, we may speak of cooperative reciprocity as a relation among individuals engaged in activities towards common ends. It is easy to see how such a familial model could be interpreted for political community. The family metaphor is a commonplace in the history of political thought, though most often with a patriarchal interpretation, the King or the State as Father.

The limitations on the extension of the concept of care to the democratic community can be seen from this account of the various models of care. The maternal or parental model has obvious limitations in any extrapolation to political or institutional contexts of democratic communities. Even though it includes elements of reciprocity, parenting is more fundamentally a nonreciprocal relation. A democratic community, by contrast, is based on reciprocal relations among equals who share authority by virtue of their equal rights to participate in decision-making. This is not to say that the elements of personal care that characterize both parenting and care for the indigent or ill are irrelevant to democratic community. On the contrary, concern for specific needs and individual differences is one of the features that marks off democratic community from a society of abstract equality.

Another limitation of the maternal or parental model is the particularism and exclusivity that are characteristic of the caring concern for the child in the family. Though appropriate in that context, it can hardly provide a model for the democratic community, for there fairness requires equal rights and equal consideration of interests, independent of any particular feelings of care for given individuals. In fact, it is an acknowledged violation of democratic equality to act on the basis of favoritism, or of special interests, or to permit personal alliances to violate requirements of fairness. The same limitation holds for the model of love or intimate personal connection, as well as for the model of the family, which are characterized by particularism and exclusivity of care.

Yet it should be granted that the domain of politics, like those of the economy and social life, has its own modes of exclusivity and

particularism, some warranted and some not. For example, citizenship itself is an exclusionary category, at least as states are now constituted. And the criteria of membership in social institutions more generally is a live issue in contemporary political and social debate. Similarly, ethnicity connotes not only belonging but exclusion as well. Nonetheless, at the political/institutional level, membership or exclusion ought not to be on the basis of personal feelings that are relevant in the contexts of care. Similarly, universality and equality are norms for politics in the context of law and rights in ways that are inappropriate for the domain of personal relations.

The models of loving care and of the family in their extrapolation to political or other institutional contexts have the further problem that it would be misplaced or wrong to require in a democratic community that people act towards others out of feelings of love or even affection, or that they aim at the enhancement of particular others. Such mutuality is appropriate in interpersonal relations of love, family, or in the case of friendship, but cannot be expected or normatively required at an institutional level. It may be observed that the models of both mothering and intimate personal connection display the same problem as does the friendship model of democracy that has so often been drawn on,[16] namely, the problem of attempting to extrapolate what is appropriate for a two-person relation to institutional relations. More generally, I suggest that a norm like mutuality that is fully appropriate as an ethical desideratum in certain relations among individuals does not map onto the political level as an appropriate value, where instead we need to speak of the value of reciprocity, along with freedom, equality, and democracy. Further, the more complex norm of care cannot be simply taken over whole into political or institutional contexts of democracy. This does not rule out that certain personal relations and traits of character, as well as certain specifically ethical norms may themselves be conditions for the development of democratic community. Additionally, there may well be specific forms of family or personal relations, for example, shared childraising between parents, that are more conducive to democratic community than are other arrangements.

Despite these limitations, some features of these models of care can usefully be extrapolated to the larger context of democratic community. We may point to three relevant aspects: First, the concern for the specific individuality and differences of the other that is involved in social reciprocity or the reciprocity of respect. This type of reciprocity is, as we have seen, a prime feature of democratic community. It expresses a relation of care inasmuch as it involves a sympathetic understanding of the perspective of the other and the other's concrete individuality. In deliberation or decision-making in politics, or the workplace, social relations of this sort help to distinguish a democratic community from the merely procedural form of decisions by voting. However, reciprocal concern does not either presuppose or require that the individuals have any personal affection for each other. We are speaking of what we might call political feelings rather than personal sentiments or even moral feelings.

A second type of care that relates to democratic community, whether in politics, the economy, or social life more generally, is that involved in cooperative reciprocity. In this case, the concern that individuals have for each other is defined by their participation in a common activity oriented to shared ends, or to what they take to be a common good. The care in this case is therefore aimed at the achievement of this good that in turn requires their concern for each other's participation in this common activity and concern about their own responsibility for the joint undertaking.

The third type of political or social care is concern for the vulnerable that we have characterized as a benign form of nonreciprocity. In a democratic community, this concern expresses itself in support of and participation in those programs that provide for the welfare of the sick, the aged, the unemployed, and the otherwise dependent members of the community. Here, as in mothering, the aim of care is the elimination where possible of the conditions of dependence.

We have considered the contributions that the perspective of care makes to the concept of democratic community, and also the limitations of this perspective displayed in attempts to extrapolate it to the political/institutional level. However, other aspects of women's experience, in the contexts of mothering, love, and family life, must be recognized as negative and as potentially having a distorting effect on the concepts of care and democratic community. First, the ideal model of the caring mother, concerned with the good of the child, is not always realized in practice, for the relation is sometimes marked by domination or even abuse. Likewise, care in family relations between men and women is sometimes distorted by the subordination of the interests or the personality of one to the other. In consequence, women's experience may generate indifference to or even embarrassment over the exercise of effective power in social or political contexts, as if it were exclusively a male prerogative and therefore to be eschewed. This leads to a distortion of the idea of democratic community, where in fact the proper uses of power have an important place, and where effectiveness in reaching goals is as central as concern for others.

Another negative element in women's experience tends to be left out of discussion in some uncritical or romanticized accounts of care. There is a tendency to overlook the degree to which in our culture women are socialized to adopt the prevailing norms of competitive and possessive individualism, which may well describe contexts of the family and mothering, as well as work. Consumerism and self-seeking, antagonistic attitudes towards others including other women or families are not absent from women's contemporary experience. Where women act in these ways, whether at home or at work, it is not simply that they are emulating men, as it is frequently suggested, but these modes may be part of their own upbringing as well.

Further, it would be a mistake to focus the import of women's experience for democratic community exclusively on the domains of mothering, love, or family. This would make it appear that the context of work and of social engagement outside these personal relations is not a distinctive source of women's experience that is relevant to the concept of democratic community or indeed to the model of caring itself.

Beyond this, I suggest that the exclusive association of the model of care with women's experience overlooks the degree to which caring is also a deep feature of human experience generally. One is reminded of the early Heidegger's view that the Being of *Dasein* is care.[17] The term care obviously has wider connotations than the more limited notion of maternal concern. This has been noted by some feminists who distinguish different connotations of the term.[18] A further analysis of the concept, and the various concrete caring relations in the experience of men as well as of women, would lead to a more nuanced view of care, while recognizing the centrality of parenting and love.

In an earlier essay, I proposed that what was needed was what I called "political androgyny," that is, an importation into the public domain of politics, economics, and social life of the range of capacities, concerns and values deriving from women's historical experience, as a corrective for the predominance in public life of historically male concerns and values.[19] What is needed is a synthesis of these two, which would integrate considerations of care with those of justice, and of individuality with those of community. Here, I have tried to suggest some of these mediations. The gendering of these concepts, though historically important (as well as in most ways historically unfortunate) is incidental to their normative content. Nonetheless, only through an explicit study of women's experience that is the main source of the norm of care itself, can we realize the full depth of the concept and work out its relations to the concepts of justice, power, and democratic community.

One consequence of my analysis is that the conception of a democratic community cannot involve a reduction to a set of personal relations nor should it be understood in terms of a holistic or organic community imposed on a set of indifferent individuals. Instead, what I would propose is that democratic community is constituted by what I have called individuals-in-relations, who reciprocally recognize each other, share some ends, and take themselves to be members of the community. Further, in a democratic community, this same joint intentionality constitutes what comes to be represented as the common interest, but that is the beginning of another story.

Notes

1. Cf., for example, Virginia Held, "Non-contractual Society: A Feminist View," in M. Hanen and K. Nielsen, eds., *Science, Morality and Feminist Theory* (Calgary: University of Calgary Press, 1987); Sara Ruddick, *Maternal Thinking* (Boston: Beacon Press, 1989); and Iris M. Young, *Justice and the Politics of Difference* (Princeton: Princeton University Press, 1990).

2. C. B. Macpherson, *Democratic Theory: Essays in Retrieval* (Oxford: Oxford University Press, 1973); Carole Pateman, *Participation and Democratic Theory* (Cambridge: Cambridge University Press, 1970); Jane Mansbridge, *Beyond Adversary Democracy* (New York: Basic Books, 1980); Benjamin Barber, *Strong Democracy* (Berkeley: University of California Press, 1984).

3. Carol C. Gould, *Rethinking Democracy: Freedom and Social Cooperation in Politics, Economy, and Society* (Cambridge: Cambridge University Press, 1988).

4. Cf. Carol C. Gould, "The Woman Question: Philosophy of Liberation and the Liberation of Philosophy," in C. Gould and M. W. Wartofsky, eds., *Women and Philosophy: Toward a Theory of Liberation* (New York: G. P. Putnam's, 1976); and *Marx's Social Ontology: Individuality and Community in Marx's Theory of Social Reality* (Cambridge: The MIT Press, 1978).

5. Cf. C. Gould, *Rethinking Democracy*, chapter 1.

6. Carol C. Gould, "Beyond Causality in the Social Sciences: Reciprocity as a Model of Non-Exploitative Social Relations," in R. S. Cohen and M. W. Wartofsky, eds., *Epistemology, Methodology and the Social Sciences: Boston Studies in the Philosophy of Science*, vol. 71 (Boston and Dordrecht: D. Reidel, 1983), pp. 53–88; and *Rethinking Democracy*, pp. 71–80.

7. Cases in which there have been inequalities on the basis of, for example, race or sex, may require that these differences be taken into account to insure equality, that is, to insure that they are really indifferent. In a somewhat related way, differences in individual need may be relevant in decisions about individuals, since taking account

of individual differences in these contexts is required to assure equality of opportunity or equal access to the conditions of self-development.

8. See, for example, Carol Gilligan, "Moral Orientation and Moral Development," in E. F. Kittay and D. T. Meyers, eds., *Women and Moral Theory* (Totowa: Rowman and Littlefield, 1987), pp. 19–33.

9. C. Gould, *Rethinking Democracy,* chapter 2; and *Marx's Social Ontology,* chapter 1.

10. Cf. Carol C. Gould, "Philosophical Dichotomies and Feminist Thought: Towards a Critical Feminism," in H. Nagl, ed., *Feministische Philosophie,* Wiener Reihe, Band 4 (Vienna: R. Oldenbourg Verlag, 1990), pp. 184–190.

11. Cf., for example, Virginia Held, "Non-Contractual Society"; Sara Ruddick, *Maternal Thinking;* Carol Gilligan, *In a Different Voice* (Cambridge: Harvard University Press, 1982); Nel Noddings, *Caring: A Feminine Approach to Ethics and Moral Education* (Berkeley: University of California Press, 1984); and the essays in E. F. Kittay and D. T. Meyers, eds., *Women and Moral Theory.*

12. Jane Mansbridge, "Feminism and Democratic Community," in John W. Chapman and Ian Shapiro, eds., *NOMOS XXXV: Democratic Community* (New York: New York University Press, 1993).

13. C. Gould, *Rethinking Democracy,* chapter 10.

14. Cf. Carol C. Gould, "On the Conception of the Common Interest: Between Procedure and Substance," in M. Kelly, ed., *Hermeneutics and Critical Theory in Ethics and Politics* (Cambridge: The MIT Press, 1990), pp. 253–273.

15. V. Held, "Non-Contractual Society," p. 131.

16. Most recently by Jacques Derrida, "The Politics of Friendship," *Journal of Philosophy,* LXXXV, 12 (1988): 632–645.

17. Martin Heidegger, *Being and Time,* tr. by J. Macquarrie and E. Robinson (New York: Harper and Row, 1962), pp. 225–273.

18. Cf. Joan C. Tronto, "Women and Caring: What Can Feminists Learn About Morality from Caring?" in A. M. Jaggar and S. R. Bordo, eds., *Gender/Body/Knowledge* (New Brunswick: Rutgers University Press, 1984), pp. 172–187; and N. Noddings, *Caring.*

19. Carol C. Gould, "Private Rights and Public Virtues: Women, the Family and Democracy," in C. Gould, ed., *Beyond Domination: New Perspectives on Women and Philosophy* (Totowa: Rowman and Allanheld, 1984), 3–18.